On the Make

On the Make

THE RISE OF BILL CLINTON

Meredith L. Oakley

Regnery Publishing, Inc.
Washington, D.C.

Library of Congress Cataloging-in-Publication Data

Oakley, Meredith L., 1951–
On the make : the rise of Bill Clinton / Meredith L. Oakley.
p.   cm.
Includes bibliographical references (p.   ) and index.
ISBN 0-89526-493-5
1. Clinton, Bill, 1946–   .   2. Presidents—United States—
Biography.   I. Title.
E886.022   1994
973.929'092–dc20   94-10787
CIP

Published in the United States by
Regnery Publishing, Inc.
An Eagle Publishing Company
422 First St., SE, Suite 300
Washington, DC 20003

Distributed to the trade by
National Book Network
4720-A Boston Way
Lanham, MD 20706

Printed on acid-free paper.

Manufactured in the United States of America.

10 9 8 7 6 5 4 3 2 1

Books are available in quantity for promotional or premium use. Write to Director of Special Sales, Regnery Publishing, Inc., 422 First Street, SE, Suite 300, Washington, DC 20003, for information on discounts and terms or call (202) 546-5005.

To my parents, Tom and Pauline Oakley

Contents

Acknowledgements

AT ONE POINT in this yearlong project, a colleague inquired about the point of view from which I had approached my subject, leaving me momentarily at a loss for words, a most embarrassing and unusual predicament for a writer. The truthful answer, perhaps not the best but the one I gave, was that I was endeavoring to find the happy medium between the two roles I know best as a journalist: reporter and commentator.

It was not always easy to stand back from the story I was attempting to tell, because oftentimes I was a part of the story, albeit on the periphery as a member of the news media. If my efforts were successful, credit John R. Starr, my mentor and my friend, whose belief in my research, writing, and reporting abilities led him to assign me in 1979 to what became the Clinton beat, and whose careful, critical nurturing as I struggled to find my editorial voice in the mid-1980s gave me the confidence needed to undertake something as intimidating as a biography.

Bill Clinton did not cooperate with this endeavor, but he did not discernibly interfere with it. I appreciate very much those among his friends, advisers, and colleagues who agreed to speak with me, either on or off the record, and for the extra care taken by Thomas F. "Mack"

McLarty, III, the president's childhood chum and current chief of staff, to assure the accuracy of even the most minor details.

For their insightful contributions, my thanks must go specifically to Skip Rutherford, the greatest political animal of them all, and Joe Bell, lobbyist *extraordinaire*. Because they are too numerous to mention without a risk of some omission, let me collectively thank those current and former lobbyists and current and former members of the Arkansas General Assembly who spoke so candidly. I also wish to thank dozens of colleagues of the old *Arkansas Democrat* and the now-defunct *Arkansas Gazette*; of their successor, the *Arkansas Democrat-Gazette*; and at various newspapers and magazines around the world whose chronicles of the Clinton years contributed so much to this enterprise.

For assisting in the research of some of the more obscure or convoluted points, I am indebted to Andrew Everest, William Alan Pumphrey, Judy Crume, Kaye Williams Poole, Rex Spencer, Orval E. Faubus, and Jim Johnson.

Joe Sobran's humor and wise counsel kept the project on track at its most crucial stage, and his thoughtful and thought-provoking suggestions taught me much, for which any writer would be grateful. Patricia Bozell's keen eye and conscientious editing won my respect as surely as her warm and generous nature lifted my spirits.

Although my attic produced a small windfall of resource material on the Clinton years in Arkansas, my job would have been much more difficult without the resources of the *Arkansas Democrat-Gazette*, and for that I am grateful to Publisher Walter E. Hussman, Jr. Without the ability to work flexible hours at my day job, I could not have found the time for this project, and for that both Al Regnery and I are indebted to Paul Greenberg.

And, since book acknowledgments are like Oscars at the Academy Awards in that no one expects to be availed of a first opportunity to thank everyone, and once so fortunate, never expects to be presented with another, this section would be incomplete without a nod toward Hazel O'Dell, who predicted when I was only 13 that someday I would write a book.

Preface

DO YOU WANT TO SEE a political genius? Turn on the television and watch the evening news. Chances are you'll be looking at him.

Here in Arkansas, that happens all the time: Bill Clinton dominates the broadcast and print media, but then, that has been the case for most of the last eighteen years. Some folks actually thought we'd see less of him once he was in the White House, but no such luck. In between health care reform and NAFTA and summits there has been the revolving door of presidential appointments and Troopergate and the special counsel's investigation into the Whitewater Development Company.

About halfway through Clinton's first year as president, one of my colleagues at the *Arkansas Democrat-Gazette* went traipsing through the newsroom practically crowing: "Clinton didn't make the front page! Can you believe it? First time in more than seven months!"

It isn't just provincial pride that keeps Clinton at the top of the news in his home state. He manages to do that in other locales with almost the same frequency. He makes news even when he doesn't intend to, which admittedly isn't often. The television generation's first president is much better at generating publicity than any of his predecessors. America is fascinated by everything Bill and Hillary do.

Five, ten, even fifteen years ago, when most Americans would have greeted any reference to Clinton with "Bill who?" we Arkansans knew that barring some catastrophe, someday he would be president. It was his life's ambition and his life's work. Clinton is the consummate politician, a self-made politician only in that he decided in adolescence to become one and then singlemindedly pursued the politician's ultimate prize—the presidency. He received a great deal of help along the way from a carefully cultivated network of friends, compatriots, and admirers, but he is beholden to no one more than the woman who chose to accompany him on that exhilarating journey, Hillary Rodham Clinton.

To many who knew them in the 1970s, their pairing seemed unlikely. He was the boyishly attractive man about town, the charming rogue, ebullient, outgoing, and forever in pursuit of convivial company and good-looking women. She was the conscientious scholar, serious, quiet, independent, and rather plain. Friends insist that both Bill and Hillary could have married virtually anyone they wanted, and it seemed to some people incongruous that they wanted one another.

Not at all. Bill has always been attracted to strong, take-charge women. They have been a constant in his life, whereas the men to whom he looked for strength and guidance have come and gone. He never even knew his father, and his stepfather during his formative years was an ill-bred, drunken bully. His mother, Virginia Cassidy Blythe Clinton Dwire Kelley, worked hard, played hard, and loved her boys passionately. Hillary, reared in a traditional family guided by somewhat nontraditional mentors, grew up confident, self-sufficient, and determined to have the kind of success in life that would impress a demanding father and satisfy a mother whose own ambitions had been sublimated.

"Bill has always deferred to women to fight his battles," one childhood friend said, whereas Hillary, according to her mother, "just took charge, and [boys] let her."

They are balanced, with her strength offsetting his weakness, her steadiness bracing his impetuousness. Their brains (predominantly hers) and beauty (predominantly his) blend in almost perfect harmony.

Bill Clinton and Hillary Rodham were both exceptionally competitive, extraordinarily ambitious people drawn to one another at the stage in life where they had finished preparing for their life's works, and, according to those who know them well, rather than choose between love and life, they found a way to meld the two. Whether politics supplanted passion is debatable, something about which many disagree. After all these years, some say, they are still madly in love. No, suggest others, it's a comfortable relationship, fond and respectful. And still others say no again: it's a marriage of convenience held together by their love for their daughter, a mutual ambition, and a shared vision of attaining greatness for the two of them, a union to which they now are inextricably bound by duty.

Whether they are still "in love" or merely love what their partnership has produced is of little consequence; they have reached the pinnacle of power, a power shared in a manner that is unprecedented in American history. Hillary Rodham Clinton is no longer the woman behind the man, a role she loathed but tolerated for the greater good of the partnership; she is now the First Lady, a galling term foisted on her by tradition but one which she must accept because the wife of the president must be called something and the United States Constitution does not authorize co-presidents.

In assessing their lives, tracking their actions, and examining their motives, it is almost too easy to ascribe to her the love of power and to him the love of glory and call them evenly matched. Hillary loves the glory as much as he does when it comes under her own terms, as a result of her deeds and accomplishments, and Bill loves the power that is his ability to influence people's thoughts, deeds, and attitudes.

As one wag has observed, "Slick Willie" doesn't begin to describe Bill Clinton; it's like calling Hitler ornery. He loves to chase anything—an attractive woman, a recalcitrant legislator, a skeptical editorial writer, a cynical voter. As associates have noted, his enemies reap more rewards from him than his friends, who are expected to follow along and await his bidding. In Clinton, people see a man who believes passionately in himself, someone who seems to have the potential to do more than he is doing. This ability of Clinton to appear to be great without actually being so, is one of his most troubling traits. It was only after I had been writing about Clinton's political career for more than a decade that this insight came to me during a conversation I had with Clinton's former chief of staff, Betsey Wright. After a particularly grueling campaign season in Arkansas, we were sipping wine and reflecting on politicians we had known and I noted that Bill Clinton had not achieved the stature I had expected of him as governor of Arkansas.

"What really irritates me about Bill Clinton," I declared, "is that I *know* he could be so much better than he is."

"Yeah," Wright said with a knowing grin, "everybody thinks that."

That just about sums it up. Bill Clinton wants to be all things to all people, and he will do everything in his power to persuade those around him that he understands their wants and needs and will work his heart out to meet them. Perhaps he even means it at the time. But then that person or that group of people leaves and another with a new set of wants and needs takes its place, and irrespective of the previous encounter, Clinton will again say that he understands and will deliver, even if his promises to the second group contradict those he made to the first. Appease for the time being. Expediency's the thing. As long as you leave them smiling, you've done your job.

When Clinton promised Arkansans on a live television broadcast during his 1990 campaign that he would complete his term as governor if reelected, they believed it despite all the evidence to the contrary. That Clinton would break his promise was a given. He had been running for the presidency for most of his adult life, had become determined to run at the tender age of sixteen, and from the time he assumed the governorship, it was never a question of whether he would run for president but when.

During the many years I covered his political activities in Arkansas, first as reporter and chief of the *Arkansas Democrat*'s state Capitol bureau, and later as a political columnist, I documented numerous falsehoods, broken promises, and ruses, some of which never saw their way into print because of the personal nature of the exchanges. Fairly early in our professional relationship, I learned not to go "off the record" with Clinton; he had a clever way of saving his strongest and most colorful reactions to my criticism for those private exchanges, which he knew I was honor-bound not to publish.

I was never a Friend of Bill, but for the better part of his tenure in Arkansas politics, we maintained a cordial working relationship. There were occasional falling-outs, but the relationship survived in spite of them because, until he began running in earnest for the presidency, we needed one another. He had news to make. I had news to report. That was the heart of our relationship, and both of us knew it. This did not prevent us from communicating personally. When he telephoned just to pass the time of day, even if the hour were late, I knew he was doing so to keep the lines of communication open, or to reopen them after he and I had been angry with one another. It was an acceptable arrangement. Expediency, like opinion, is a two-way street.

Many biographers have viewed the Bill Clinton story from the perspectives of the 1992 presidential campaign and his first year in office. But this book is the first to show how Bill Clinton over the course of two decades in Arkansas politics acquired the skills he needed to become president.

On the Make

1

ROAD TO THE WHITE HOUSE

WHEN BILL AND HILLARY CLINTON AWOKE on the crisp November morning after the 1992 general election, Clinton would reveal later, they looked at one another and giggled like children.[1] The campaign had exhausted them, but they now hugged each other on the crumpled sheets, threw back their heads, and laughed in a burst of triumph.

When they descended the staircase of the Governor's Mansion a short time later to review the past evening's victory over morning coffee, they did so as president-elect and future First Lady of the United States, roles they had never doubted, even in their darkest hours, that they would attain. After all, Bill Clinton's mother had often said, "You can go as far as you want to go."[2] And he had found that Hillary Rodham, whom he once called "the major force in giving me the courage to try to live an active life in politics," was the perfect partner in that lifelong effort.[3]

It was Hillary Rodham Clinton who had kept her husband on the path to the presidency, the woman to whom he had turned at every bend in the road, the partner on whom he would continue to rely for emotional sustenance and political advice. There was nothing Hillary would not do, no role she would not play, to help Bill Clinton gain his

3

objective, overhaul his image, or salvage his career. Whatever was demanded—a stable family, a solid marriage, a new reason to justify his election—she provided. Over the years, Hillary Rodman Clinton changed her name, changed her image, went head-to-head with his opponents, and, when necessary, gritted her teeth and buttoned her lip whenever scandal erupted. The achievements of Bill Clinton's twelve years as governor of Arkansas, most notably the education reform movement in the early 1980s, are Hillary Clinton's as much as her husband's.

How history will remember the presidency of William Jefferson Clinton remains to be seen, but if history repeats itself, he will have about as much success escaping the appellation Slick Willie as Richard Milhous Nixon had with Tricky Dick. The disparaging nickname was born in Arkansas, where Clinton launched his political career twenty years ago with the White House as his focal point. He intended to supplant his idol John Fitzgerald Kennedy as the youngest chief executive in American history. Clinton might have done so had he been as prudent in his personal decisions as he was in his political ones. That is not to say that all his political choices had been good ones. He had stumbled several times on the path to the White House, despite the best efforts of Hillary and Betsey Wright and James Carville and an array of political consultants, and sometimes because of those efforts. At times Clinton's arrogance had overwhelmed his pragmatism, his self-absorption had undermined the greater public good. For while Bill Clinton has been a winner, a leader of near-messianic appeal, he has never mastered the art of winning.

Human frailties have played havoc with Clinton's public person. He cannot tolerate anyone's displeasure, particularly people of a certain standing in their community or their field, and he will attempt to ameliorate their disapproval whenever possible. Defeat is not in his lexicon. He does not like to lose. If he cannot win, he will compromise and declare victory. He likes to do as he pleases, and then explain his actions. He has been labeled a draft-dodger and a coward for his youthful dealings with the Selective Service System, and while his aim at the time was to avoid personal harm and keep to his political timetable, he could not, even then, resist defending his actions, in writing, to a virtual stranger whose respect he coveted. It is not, insists a former friend, that he wants to be loved, it is that he "enjoys the conquest, he enjoys bending people to his will."[4] When that is not possible, when charm and affability have been pushed to their limits, he erupts in anger, scattering papers and people in his wake, intimidating those who do not realize that confrontation deflates him. When Clinton loses, he quickly assumes the role of the injured party, going to great lengths to explain his good motives and the self-sacrifice and altruism with which he has invested his efforts, while all the time marveling that despite this he is so misunderstood.

To say that Clinton accomplished nothing as governor is incorrect, and yet outside the hard core of the Democrat party, Clinton fans are difficult to find in Arkansas. Even those who admit to having voted for him complain about his high taxes, broken promises, profligate spending, draft-dodging, womanizing, and blind ambition. They cannot commend his attempts at education reform without remembering how he deceived them in the process. They cannot acknowledge his efforts to expand rural and indigent health care without grumbling about his patronage of Dr. Joycelyn Elders, "the Condom Queen." They cannot recognize his economic and industrial development programs without grumbling about how he interfered on the side of management in union disputes, gave big tax breaks to out-of-state enterprises, and used the state's promotional budgets to fly across the nation and around the world, giving speeches and courting the rich, famous, and politically influential while the state government floundered. His critics believe he used and abused Arkansas in his climb to the top, and some of his fellow Democrats in the Arkansas legislature say that this abuse was greatest during his last year as governor, when his time was taken up preparing for the presidential race. Yet if his record was so disappointing and his performance so erratic, why was Bill Clinton elected governor of Arkansas five times?

In 1992, reporters poured into Little Rock from New York and Los Angeles, London and Tokyo, and all points in between with a wealth of questions about Bill Clinton. They wanted to know how he relaxed, whether he ever slept, who were his friends and his enemies; they explored his past and examined his campaign style, and on occasion they even looked into his record as governor. They were curious about his shoe size, his love of junk food, his allergies, and his temperament. They wanted the lowdown on his wife and his girlfriends. On some days, three out of five telephone calls placed to the state's political pundits were from out-of-state members of the press asking the age-old question: Who is this man? Yet, after preliminary, introductory inquiries about his life, his career, and his family, the question that was always asked was: Why, if he is so unpopular, do Arkansans keep reelecting him?

Some of the pundits developed an answer that became all too familiar. He had his detractors, they would concede, but when push came to shove, Bill Clinton was simply the best man for the job, and the voters recognized that. They realized he cared about them, understood their wants and needs, and strove to get them the best possible deal before an often petty, stubborn legislature, even when that meant compromises that diluted or destroyed new proposals. If Clinton failed to accomplish all he intended, well, he did the best he could, and that was probably better than most. No one gave the correct answer: He worked for it.

No one campaigns harder than Clinton. He is a candidate twenty-four hours a day—twenty or twenty-two, if you count only his waking hours—and whereas pushing paper, discussing policy, and dictating instructions to underlings can occupy him for short periods on any given day, it is incidental to the job of charming people and winning the next election. Clinton is always politicking. People are his food and polls are his drink, and if his instincts about them are not perfect, they are at least very, very good. Blessed with an incredible memory, he remembers faces and incidents even better than names, and he can retrieve numbers he finds useful, particularly election statistics, as quickly as a computer. He can then expound for hours. During his comeback efforts for governor in 1982, while making an all-day swing through several northwest Arkansas towns in the Third Congressional District, Clinton climbed into my car while I was covering his efforts for the day to ride the twenty miles from Ozark to Mulberry. He spent the entire trip reminiscing about his first campaign, the 1974 race against Representative John Paul Hammerschmidt. He did not discuss the issues but the votes he had received in the townships along the route this day's campaigning was taking him, recalling the percentages, and in many instances the actual vote count, garnered at each precinct. (I made a few notes afterward and checked the accuracy of his recollections. He was correct on all counts.)[5] Such discussions are common, and while they often bore the people around him, his enthusiasm never lags. He not only retains the results of his campaigns and those of others, he analyzes them and learns from them. He has lost only two races for elective office: the congressional campaign with which he began his political career in 1974 and his first reelection campaign as governor in 1980.

Actually, as a student, before entering politics, Clinton did lose a few minor-league elections. He was highly competitive from his earliest years and loved campaigning, but he could not tolerate opposition. Carolyn Yeldell Staley, a friend of more than thirty years, recalls that when she and the sixteen-year-old Clinton were pitted against one another in a runoff for junior class president at Hot Springs High School, he told her bluntly, "If you beat me, I will never forgive you."[6] He won, and they have remained close friends.

He experienced another defeat at Georgetown University in his junior year. Following two straight victories in bids for president of the freshman and sophomore classes, he was narrowly defeated by a savvy young man who persuaded classmates that he was not entrenched in politics whereas Clinton was the Old Guard.[7] Ever since, Clinton has always portrayed himself as the candidate for change.

School classmates remember Clinton as something of an over-achiever, driven to be the best, or at least to come in first, at whatever he undertook, and while he performed exceptionally well in most areas, he was usually a few points shy of being Number One. He graduated fourth in a high school class of 323. He was a National Merit Scholarship semifinalist. And he did better in contests that relied on his social attributes and social contacts than in those that challenged his intellect.

The reporters and pundits who have watched Bill Clinton for years marvel at Clinton's uncanny ability to make himself over into whatever image appeals to voters. "I have an idea that is the way he has spent his

8 *Meredith L. Oakley*

life—playing the role at the time," an old-time Arkansas politician once said.[8] Clinton could promise, as he did in three separate elections, not to raise taxes and then do so, and still manage to get reelected. He could face a statewide audience through the eye of a camera that recorded his every word and declare that he would not run for president if reelected, talk for months afterward about his "commitment" to the voters of Arkansas, and still claim that he had never made such a declaration. A gullible voting public could be momentarily dissuaded, as it was in his 1990 reelection campaign against Republican Sheffield Nelson, by reminders of his tax-and-spend record, and then be wooed back overnight by his hasty, half-baked claims that Republicans, not Democrats, were the true tax-and-spenders. Confronted with proof that he had manipulated the Selective Service System to avoid the draft, joined by the recent statements of people who were intimately involved in assisting him in this effort, he could claim that all knowledgeable sources were dead and that he had said all that needed to be said about the matter—and get away with it.

Former Governor Orval E. Faubus, a Democrat, who himself opposed Clinton in 1986, has often observed that no one, least of all Clinton, realizes how lucky Clinton has been in the caliber of opposition he has attracted throughout his career.[9] For various reasons, many of his opponents were unable or unwilling to use the ammunition available to them. For example, George Bush, a *bona fide* World War II hero, resisted all efforts in the 1992 campaign to take advantage of the draft evasion issue.

Moreover, until his presidential bid, Clinton didn't have to worry about a strong Republican party. Arkansas is practically a one-party state; more voters call themselves independents than Republicans. Only one in five Arkansans says he is a Republican although Arkansans in general are extremely conservative in fiscal and social matters. But they feel a kinship with politicians who get their foot in the door by whatever means, and they are extremely loyal at the ballot box, where only a handful of Republicans ever succeeds. Indeed, only four Republicans—two governors and two lieutenant governors—have been elected to statewide office in the twentieth century. It has been said of the state that it is so entrenched in Southern Democrat conservatism that its citizens would vote for a rabid skunk rather than a Republican, but this tradition is slowly changing. Since 1968, the state has voted Democratic only twice in presidential campaigns: it gave Jimmy Carter his second largest majority (66 percent) in 1976, and its native son, Bill Clinton, his only majority (53 percent) in the three-man race of 1992.

Arkansas is an amalgam, part deep South, part Midwest, part Southwest. Despite the quarter-million people who live in Little Rock, Arkansas is largely rural, provincial, and unapologetically political. Outside the northwest quadrant, where the well-to-do retirees from the North and East ensure a Republican stronghold, local political bosses still call the shots. In the eastern prairies and the Southern Delta, black preachers still deliver the Democratic vote in return for modest financial consideration, and fifth-generation politicians still control the placement of the ballot boxes and the paper ballots inside them in most of the seventy-five counties. There are enclaves of sophistication in a handful of small cities, but the typical Arkansan is a fifth-, sixth-, or seventh-generation native to the area, blue collar, high school educated but not much more, Southern Baptist, and a yellow-dog Democrat. While he cusses the national Democrats for being too liberal and votes Republican in presidential elections, he wants a Democrat in the statehouse, another in the courthouse, and the ear of the one man in the county who calls everyone by his first name and knows how to get a pothole or a speeding ticket fixed.

Arkansans enjoy an uncommon familiarity with their politicians: They may defer to the office in a face-to-face meeting, greeting the officeholder by his or her title, but as the conversation progresses, "Senator" or "Governor" gives way to "Dale" or "David" or "Bill." For many years, the powerful chairman of the Senate Foreign Affairs Committee was J. William Fulbright, but back home in Arkansas, he was always just plain Bill. It was an image he cultivated, as do other officeholders. Even Clinton wanted to be known as just plain Bill before he became president of the United States. Of course, Arkansans call their politicians by their first names even if they have never met, although chances are pretty good that they have. They expect to talk to their congressman or their senator when they call, and they're always a little ticked off if, when dropping in unannounced at the state Capitol, the governor is too busy to see them. (That may be a holdover from the twelve-year reign of Orval E. Faubus, who always welcomed drop-ins and never let a chance pass to shake a constituent's hand.) Most Arkansans will settle for a personal letter if an appointment cannot be arranged, or even a hasty handshake at the 'coon supper at Gillett, or the Mount Nebo chicken fry, or the Fourth of July picnic at Portia, or any other of the dozens of annual political events that no stump speaker worth his salt would miss if he wants to get or stay in office.

Not all politicians are officeholders, however; some are mere conduits to the powers that be—the local car dealer, the banker, the gentleman farmer, or the owner of the county's only newspaper, each of whom can expect a visit from the senator or governor whenever he's in the area. There are places one goes and people one sees if one is to get and keep a toehold in politics, and the smart money is on the neophyte who, once elected, doesn't forget where he came from and remembers to dance with the one who brung him.

That last admonition is a cardinal rule that Clinton temporarily forgot in his zeal to make his mark in politics. The nation's youngest governor, and before that the nation's youngest attorney general, his sights were aimed unblinkingly on Washington, his plan for getting there was in place, and he was right on schedule. A few years in the Governor's Mansion, a well-timed run for the presidency, and he would make history as the nation's youngest president. Attractive, energetic to the point of compulsion, and acutely savvy in political logistics and strategy, Clinton had already organized a dynamic network of friends, followers, and assorted contacts by the time he took his first oath of office in 1977.

Some of them had never set foot in Arkansas, but they saw in Clinton enough potential to shower him with campaign contributions and introductions from sources many pols never tap until they have made it to Congress. Through the years, some of his admirers have fallen away or been cast aside, but many have remained staunchly loyal to a man not generally known for returning the favor. "His enemies get more out of him than his friends," a longtime political colleague of Clinton once said. "The ones that claim to be his closest friends, the loyal people, they're the ones that he takes and takes and takes from and never gives. They don't ask anything, and hell, it wouldn't matter if they did, if it wasn't convenient for him."[10] Even castaways who concede that fidelity is not his long suit have remained quietly faithful; they may have outlived their usefulness, but they still believe in his capacity for greatness. This attitude dominates what has been called the Cult of Bill, many of whose members dedicated a large portion of their lives to building and enhancing his image as a presidential candidate. They were spurred to action on many occasions over the years when his personal foibles and administrative failures threatened to poke holes in the image.

A prime example was former Chief of Staff Betsey Wright's call to arms when former television reporter and nightclub singer Gennifer Flowers claimed during the New Hampshire primary that she had had a twelve-year affair with Clinton and produced audio tapes to prove it. Wright, whose sense of betrayal following her abrupt departure from the Clinton administration in the winter of 1989 led to a series of near-hysterical telephone calls to several of his closest male advisors, did not hesitate to abandon a prestigious Harvard fellowship in the spring of 1992 to help salvage his reputation. Her one-woman "bimbo patrol" crusade was so tireless, and so valuable, that it virtually forced the presidential campaign team in Little Rock to put her on the payroll despite serious misgivings about her emotional volatility. If Clinton was grateful, however, he did not demonstrate it by offering her a position in the administration, even after her assistance in defusing the "Troopergate" scandal in 1993.

One of the great ambiguities about Clinton is his sense of loyalty. While opinion is divided on this point, there is ample evidence that Clinton often remained steadfast when he should have feinted. For every political appointee he deserted, there were two or three whose tenure caused his administration many embarrassments. Thus a political contributor appointed to oversee state building contracts could be caught red-handed profiting from the contracts his agency awarded and be retained, and a woman who salvaged his political career could be muscled out.

"The first term I served with Bill Clinton as governor is when I came away with the feeling that loyalty was a one-way street, that if it was good for Bill Clinton, everything was chummy," said state Representative Pat Flanagin, a fellow Democrat from East Arkansas who met Clinton when he was attorney general. "But . . . if you need something in the other direction, don't count on it." He cited several examples, among them the case of a St. Francis County constituent who was Clinton's campaign coordinator through several elections, a fellow who stuck by Clinton during the dark months following his reelection defeat in 1980, and "went through thick and thin [with Clinton] when everybody else deserted him—put [Clinton] signs up in his yard when it was an embarrassing thing to do."[11] Years later, Flanagin recalled, when Clinton had the opportunity to repay the man's dedication with an appointment to the prestigious Arkansas Industrial Development Commission, a post the man coveted and had reason to believe he would receive, Clinton hemmed and hawed and dallied so long that, humiliated, the fellow took himself out of the running. According to Flanagin, Clinton's procrastination was for that very purpose because the person ultimately appointed was in a better position to help him politically.

If loyalty is a one-way street with Clinton, there are many politicians in Arkansas to whom proximity or public recognition by Bill Clinton is reward enough. "Sure, he used us," one habitual Clinton ally in the legislature has conceded. "But we used him, too."[12]

It was fortunate for Clinton that many of the professional politicians with whom he dealt were pragmatic by nature. Former Governor Faubus, for example, says he holds no grudge toward the young up-and-comer who before the 1978 governor's race secured Faubus's patronage by pledging to convince the legislature to take Faubus's sixty-four acre Madison County "retirement home" off his hands and turn the lush mountaintop property into a state park and museum. Once in office, Clinton reneged on the deal. Faubus says Clinton backed down when Faubus's old nemesis, the *Arkansas Gazette*, opposed the proposal.[13]

"I didn't say anything about it," Faubus remarked, "and I didn't complain, but that began to show a flaw in his makeup. Not that he's the only one that ever had such a flaw," Faubus hastened to add, "but I think it showed up rather plainly."

Faubus also displays no bitterness that the vestiges of his Madison County organization, which he "loaned" to Clinton for the 1978 campaign, stayed hitched when Faubus launched his own futile comeback effort against Clinton in 1986. "I couldn't get financed," Faubus said with a wry grin. "All those bigshots that used to help finance me were in his corner tight as they could be."

Faubus lost his old supporters because people love a winner, and Arkansas had never produced such a winner as they felt Clinton would prove to be. Despite the controversy and discord that marked his tenure as governor, he was a tenacious politician; the favorability ratings given him in the endless stream of polls that guided his every step were alternately among the highest and the lowest ever recorded, a pattern he might well repeat as president.

Given the familiarity with which Arkansans regard their public figures it's easy to distinguish between Clinton friends and Clinton foes. To the former, he remains Bill; to the latter, he is and likely ever shall be Slick Willie.

"Slick Willie" was coined by Jess L. Crosser of Calico Rock, Arkansas, a crusty septuagenarian who often berated the young governor in letters to the editor of the *Arkansas Democrat*, and it was popularized by the newspaper's managing editor, John R. Starr, who wrote an opinion column for the op-ed page. Starr loved nothing better than exposing waste and abuse in government, and an early example of profligacy in the first Clinton administration prompted him to create a dubious honor known as the Boondoggler of the Month Award.

The Great Energy Retreat of 1980 was convened by Paul Levy, whom Clinton had summoned from Massachusetts to oversee the newly created Arkansas Department of Energy. At a cost of about $2,000 in state funds, Levy treated 65 employees to a weekend at DeGray Lodge, about 85 miles southwest of Little Rock, and the *Democrat* duly reported the event. Afterward, Starr wrote a column in which he "half-facetiously [said] that the retreat should be nominated for a Boondoggle [sic] of the Month Award." Levy telephoned Starr early on the morning the sarcastic column appeared and asked Starr when he could pick up his award. "I am sure he did not intend to make me angry," Starr later recalled, "but he did. While his laugh was still ringing in my ears, I wrote a blistering column for the next day that took a lot of the humor out of his life."

Public reaction to the column was stunning. More than 50 calls came in that day, and dozens of letters followed, all applauding Starr's stance and denouncing Levy's arrogance. Soon afterward, at Clinton's behest, Levy presided over a weekend conference on energy conservation. Held at Little Rock's most expensive hotel, the conference cost a then-staggering $80,000. As a keepsake, the "delegates" each were given a goodie bag chock-full of Arkansas wine, foodstuffs, and assorted knick-knacks, most of them provided at no expense to the state. However, Levy's convention organizers had overlooked one important item in assembling the bags: corkscrews with which to decant the wine. Levy dispatched an underling to a local store to purchase fifty corkscrews at a cost of 75 cents apiece.

Tipped about the corkscrews, the *Democrat* discovered that almost $6,000 of the conference budget had been spent wining and dining the delegates. The public was outraged, but Starr was perversely delighted. He had one of the newspaper's editorial cartoonists design an award "to recognize wastrels in state and local government": a corkscrew placed upside down on a flat base. He dubbed the Boondoggler of the Month Award the Sweet William, and for the duration of Clinton's first term, Starr provided his readers with a list of boondoggling nominees on which they voted each month. Prompted by Crosser, Starr established a second award that he himself could bestow and christened it the Slick Willie.[14]

Over the years, many other disparaging terms have been used to describe both Bill and Hillary, among them HillBilly, Willie the Waffle, Hot Rodham (actually coined as a joke by Bill when asked by which name, Clinton or Rodham, their newborn daughter would be known) and, most recently, Billary, but none has had such universal appeal and staying power as Jess Crosser's Slick Willie.

As Clinton was completing his first hundred days in the White House, national pundits tried to figure out what his political principles were. In Arkansas, where their discoveries were old news, folks who still remembered the corkscrews just shrugged at the furor over a $200 haircut. What they saw in Washington looked very much like the Bill

Clinton they knew in Little Rock. Sure, they conceded, President Clinton's goals were "unfulfilled," he seemed to "lack direction," and his actions "often fall short of the sweeping promises his rhetoric seems to imply," but while he had taken "a series of damaging missteps," he had a point when he complained "that expectations have become too unrealistic." Wait and see, the analysts intoned. Just because he wants to do everything does not mean that everything will come quickly. "This omnivorous man," opined *The Economist*, "has been kept from sampling every policy dish on the table only because he has chosen two, deficit reduction and health care reform, whose size has slowed him down."

Yet if Clinton had not assembled a cabinet that looks like America, he had given America the first cabinet not dominated by white men; despite the dictates of his religion, he had reversed the national policy regarding abortion; he had tried, however clumsily, to extend the rights and privileges of American citizenship to homosexuals; if he had reneged on his pledge to welcome Haitian refugees, at least he had sent food to starving Bosnians; he might have backpedaled on his talk about cutting the federal deficit in half within four years, but that was because information not available to candidate Clinton was now in his possession; and if the activities of the health care reform task force were shrouded in secrecy and the medical community's input denied, still he had launched an unprecedented campaign to restructure the American system of health care.

According to one national poll, more Americans disapproved of the job Clinton had done during his first one hundred days in office than any president since such polling began in the 1950s. He had a ready excuse. "I do think I overextended myself, and we've got to focus on the big things," he said, allowing that he might have misjudged the ability of Congress's Republican minority to stymie his proposals. But just what kind of measure is one hundred days? "When people say to me, 'Well, what did you do in your first hundred days?' I say, 'What did the other guys do in their first hundred days?'" Besides, in case the pundits had not noticed, he reminded: "In the first three months of this administration we have fundamentally changed the direction taken by our national government."

Victory declared. End of debate.

2

AN AMERICAN MYTH

IT'S THE STUFF of which American myths are made: Bill Clinton, born "fatherless and impoverished in a dusty Arkansas town that offered little promise outside its name, Hope"; a wicked stepfather who cursed and abused and generally terrorized his family until that fateful day when fourteen-year-old Billy broke down the bedroom door, tore his fist-swinging stepfather away from his cowering mother, and threatened to whip the drunken bully's ass if he ever laid another hand on the woman; working his way through college and law school, winning academic kudos along the way for his brilliance and industry; returning home to be a country lawyer, marrying his college sweetheart, and entering politics to improve the lot of the poor, uneducated people of Arkansas.

A fighter, a survivor, a crusader: It was this image, not that of draft-dodger, womanizer, prevaricator, and opportunist, that was supposed to emerge in the 1992 presidential campaign, and for the most part, it did. The complete portrait of Bill Clinton was never presented to the American public by the reporters who covered him; presidential campaigns and the men and women who chronicle them move too superficially and too fast, and ever since the Gary Hart fiasco, all concerned have been fairly content to let the tabloids deal with the seamier side of history. By and large, the mainstream press was just as besotted with Clinton as was mainstream America, which had its own problems in 1992 and just wanted someone to fix them or to promise they would be fixed.

This self-styled New Democrat promised a fresh approach to old problems and a dynamic, progressive assault on emerging ones. Change did not intimidate him; he relished it, embraced it, symbolized it. He was, after all, the Man from Hope.

"Bill could have gone in several directions," his mother once observed. "I often wondered what he would choose. He loves to teach. For awhile, I probably thought he would be a teacher. And he has a good singing voice; he could have been a musician."[1] But on that bright, humid day in the summer of 1987, when Virginia talked about her son, she also conceded that "there is no doubt in my mind that if he runs [for the presidency] that he'll get the nomination and he'll win." No brag, as they say Down South, just fact.

Bill Clinton comes from what might politely be called people of modest means, working folks generally content to settle for three meals a day, a steady job, and church on Sunday but with ambitions for their offspring. He found his direction early, when his adolescent competitiveness and desire to succeed resulted in a hard-earned visit to Washington, D.C., and a handshake from a charismatic young president of the United States. Clinton had already become a politician; at that point he realized just how far politics could take him.

Clinton has been a professional politician for about 20 years, yet he has known only two defeats in bids for public office. In another time, he might never have been elected the first time, let alone survived the mistakes, foibles, and miscalculations with which his career is strewn but which in his time were used by him and his cadre of admirers and foot soldiers to keep him on a course to the presidency. There is little doubt that when he stood on the stage at Madison Square Garden in 1980, making his maiden speech before the Democractic National Convention, he and the Arkansans in that audience knew that he would someday return to become the convention's star attraction—

which, despite an ouster from office, a politically devastating speech at a subsequent convention, and one of the rockiest presidential campaigns in modern history, he did.

When Bill Clinton was born there in 1946, Hope, Arkansas, was an unpretentious farming town of eight thousand in rural Hempstead County. Hope was known for its annual Watermelon Festival, and most of its white inhabitants, about two-thirds of the population, made a fair living, aided by the area's fertile ground and the small industries that helped to win the war and survived the transition to peacetime manufacturing. During World War II, the Southwest Proving Grounds was established near Hope. After the war, the 53,000-acre facility was declared surplus and was parceled out to a variety of small industries.[2]

William Jefferson Blythe IV was born on August 19, 1946, a Monday, in Hope's Julia Chester Hospital. His mother, Virginia Dell Cassidy Blythe, was twenty-three and recently widowed.

"I was five months pregnant with Bill when his father was killed in an automobile accident," Virginia recalled later, although in fact her son arrived full-term three months later. "He had been overseas in the war for thirty-six months and hadn't been back long. I stayed in Hope with my mother when he went to Chicago to work and to buy a house. He was on his way to Hope to get me when the accident happened."[3]

Accounts of the accident given by Virginia and her son have varied through the years, but according to reports of the incident, William Jefferson Blythe III drowned in a rain-swollen ditch after his car veered off Missouri's Highway 60 near Sikeston. He had been driving his heavy Buick sedan too fast along the unfamiliar route when a tire blew. There was no evidence that he had been drinking, and witnesses speculated that the vehicle veered onto a slippery patch of gravel and rolled onto the shoulder, catapulting him through the windshield some twenty-five feet into a trench running alongside an alfalfa field. When the neatly clad body was located more than an hour later, the only sign of trauma was a small scratch on his forehead.[4]

Virginia and Bill Blythe, a twenty-seven-year-old traveling salesman from Sherman, Texas, met in 1943 when she was a student nurse in

Shreveport, Louisiana, and he an Army recruit. Bill, known to his family as W. J., brought a date to the emergency room of Tri-State Hospital for treatment—she had an acute attack of appendicitis.

"I thought that they were married, and so I called him by her last name, just to see if they were married," she told the *New York Times*. "He said, 'Excuse me, that isn't my name.' And so he asked me out."[5]

Virginia always insisted that it was love at first sight. Although he only had an eighth-grade education, Bill Blythe was by all accounts a charming, fun-loving sort who loved to drink and dance and make pretty women laugh. More than forty years later, the recollection of their first encounter still brought tears to Virginia's eyes. Theirs was a passionate, whirlwind courtship, during which, it must be inferred from Virginia's public statements, the groom shared few substantive intimacies with his young bride, among them his propensity for col-lecting marriage certificates.

Of all the controversies that befell Bill Clinton's presidency, the most bizarre was the saga of his natural father, born W. J. Blythe near Sherman, Texas, in 1918.[6]

W. J. was the sixth of nine children born to William Jefferson "Willie" Blythe and Lou Birchie Ayers Blythe. The Blythes were farmers, uneducated and poor but close-knit and hard working. They lived in a three-room, wood-frame house without electricity or run-ning water, and bartered for what they lacked the money to buy. Shortly after the Depression hit, Willie fell ill, and responsibility for family and farm fell to W. J., the eldest unmarried son.

At age fifteen, two years before his father lost a five-year battle with colon cancer, W. J. was forced to seek work at a local dairy to supplement the family's income. His sister, Vera Ramey, the youngest of the four Blythe daughters, later told the *Washington Post* that W. J. took his responsibilities seriously. "He would go to work in the afternoons after school at 2 or 2:30," she recalled in 1993, "and work till ten o'clock. Then he'd sleep till 3 A.M., when he would milk our cows, wash them down, [and] carry the milk to the dairy. Four hours of sleep a night was quite enough for him."

The Blythe family lost the farm and its forty acres of pasture land to foreclosure in 1936, a year after Willie's death. W. J. held a variety of jobs—dairy worker, garage mechanic—after his mother moved the family into a small apartment in downtown Sherman, until he eventually settled on a line of work that offered a little more adventure and a little more money: sales. By all accounts, W. J. was a natural-born salesman—friendly, good-humored, down-to-earth, and persuasive—and made a modest living traveling throughout the South and Midwest in a series of jobs, hawking auto parts and heavy equipment. Along the way, he acquired a string of wives.

The first one was Virginia Adela Gash, whom he married ten months after his father's death in 1935. According to Vera Ramey, Adela was pregnant when she and W. J. eloped to nearby Madill, Oklahoma, where they lied about their ages—both were seventeen—to obtain the marriage license. Ramey claimed that the child, a boy, was fathered not by W. J. but by another member of the Blythe family who was married at the time.

Tracked to her home in Apple Valley, California, by the *Washington Post* in 1993, Adele Blythe Ritzenthaler Coffelt said that she was not pregnant at the time but married W. J. because she wanted a home of her own, and he was in line for a job at the dairy that included company-owned living quarters.

The job and the apartment fell through, so W. J. and his bride moved in with his parents, sharing a bedroom with W. J.'s older brother, Earnest, and Earnest's wife, Ola Maye. That arrangement lasted only a few months; Adela went to Dallas to visit an aunt, and instead of coming to take her back home after a brief visit, W. J. sent his wife a package containing the clothing she had left behind. Adela stayed in Dallas, where she obtained a divorce in December 1936, but they continued to "keep company" whenever Adela visited Sherman. On one of those occasions, she said, W. J. fathered her son, Henry Leon Blythe. She stayed in Sherman for the birth, which occurred on January 17, 1938, then returned to California, where she had lived most recently. In 1939, she married Charles Ritzenthaler, who adopted Leon and was the only father he ever knew.

Neither Ritzenthaler nor his mother suspected a family tie to Bill Clinton, then a candidate for president of the United States, until a family member called Adela Coffelt's attention to a magazine article that identified Clinton's natural father as a former Sherman, Texas, salesman named William J. Blythe. In June 1992, Ritzenthaler tried without success to contact the Clinton campaign for information about his biological father. Not until June 1993, when the *Washington Post* broke the story of W. J.'s marriage to Adela Gash, their subsequent divorce, and Ritzenthaler's birth, did Bill Clinton acknowledge Ritzenthaler's existence.

Around the time that Adela remarried in 1939, she later said, W. J. married her sister, Faye, "to keep from having to marry a girl who was pregnant." That marriage broke up in 1940 or 1941, Adela said, and after that, she lost touch with W. J.'s activities.

No record of W. J.'s marriage to Faye Gash has surfaced, but there is evidence that he married Wanetta Ellen Alexander on May 3, 1941, in Kansas City, Missouri. By then, he had legally adopted his father's full name, William Jefferson Blythe, and was known to friends and acquaintances as Bill. Eight days after the wedding, Wanetta gave birth to a daughter, Sharron Lee Blythe, now Sharon Pettijohn. Wanetta told the *Arizona Republic* in 1993 that Blythe had fathered her daughter.

Blythe apparently was still married to Wanetta when he married Virginia Cassidy on September 3, 1943; Court records show that he and Wanetta did not divorce until March 1944. That being the case, the marriage of Virginia Cassidy and Bill Blythe, and their son's subsequent birth in 1946, was illegal under Arkansas law.

Virginia Kelley denied having had any knowledge of her late husband's previous marriage or any children born of those unions.

Virginia and Bill married after only two months of courtship, reportedly at her insistence, on September 3, 1943, at Texarkana, Arkansas. Shortly afterward, Blythe went off to war in Europe and Virginia returned home to Hope, where, by several accounts, she resumed her prenuptial revelries. Virginia was, according to several contemporaries, "a wild one" who wasted little effort keeping the home fires burning. She loved to get all dressed up and, shod in the clunky high heels of the day, go dancing and drinking until dawn. The couple was separated for almost three years—he was discharged on December 7, 1945, having attained the rank of technical sergeant third class—and had been reunited only a few months when Blythe died.

Virginia was with her parents, awaiting his return from Chicago, where he had secured a new sales job—he had been selling cars for a local dealership in the interim—and a house, when word reached her that her tall, good-looking husband was dead. He is buried in Hope.

Forced to abandon a much anticipated entry into big-city life, Virginia faced a different, rather bleak, future. She was more than welcome to remain at home with her loving parents, but she was high-spirited and ambitious, and there was the child to consider. There was nothing to do but return to her nursing studies.

"It was the hardest decision I think I've ever had to make in my life," she said, and she was often lonely.[7] Her son stayed with her parents while Virginia went to school. Visits with her son were infrequent, and each parting was painful. Virginia later recalled falling to her knees at the platform of the train station in New Orleans, choked and blinded by tears as her mother and her son waved goodbye after a brief visit. Although Bill could not understand why they were leaving his mother behind, and the anguish of parting made a keen impression on him, the trip to New Orleans would become the most vivid childhood memory of Bill Clinton's life, because he had never seen so much traffic and so many tall buildings. The hotel in which they stayed is said to be the first structure with more than two stories that he had ever seen.

Virginia's parents, Eldridge and Edith Grisham Cassidy, had moved to Hope from the undistinguished township of Bodcaw, twelve miles to the southwest. An ambitious woman who had studied nursing by correspondence course, Edith Cassidy wanted more opportunities for her family than life on a farm offered. Eldridge Cassidy, who often drank too much, held a variety of jobs, working as a sawmill watchman and delivering ice—anything to keep food on the table. Later he owned a small grocery store across from the Hope cemetery on North Hazel Street, selling staples, often on credit, to a predominantly poor, black clientele. Eventually his generosity would force him out of the grocery business.[8]

Cassidy pitied his poor customers and their hard-scrabble existence, for while he was not a wealthy man, he was leaps and bounds ahead of them and always would be. The difference between poor white trash and a colored man was that the colored man did not choose his lot, society chose it for him. It was a shame and a sin, but there it was, and white folks owed it to those less fortunate to lend a helping hand. The Cassidys took each day as it came, did well by their neighbors, and while there were few extras, they were not poor.

Though Clinton would later say otherwise, the Cassidys's two-story house at 117 South Hervey Street—"my log cabin," Clinton would quip—did not lack indoor plumbing during the four years he lived there.[9] He spent summer days running and jumping and climbing on a favorite tar-covered, wooden bridge with neighborhood children and racing his tricycle up and down the cracked sidewalks, the string of his ever-present cowboy hat dancing about his neck. Many evenings were spent chasing lightning bugs and languishing on the porch, poring over books and newspaper comic strips with his grandmother until the mosquitoes or the evening chill drove them inside.

His maternal grandparents were strong early influences on Billy Blythe. He was a precocious child, learning to read by the time he was three, and his grandparents encouraged his interest in books. His grandfather, whom Clinton calls "the kindest man I ever knew," often counseled the boy about the virtues of getting a good education so he could "make something of himself."[10]

Virginia was a doting mother, albeit absent for extended periods during her firstborn's formative years. She was not a pretty woman, but with her flashing blue eyes, ready grin, and throaty laugh, she cut a striking figure in her youth.

By most accounts, Virginia worked hard and played hard, with an affinity for nightclubs and the thoroughbred horse-racing track, the one form of gambling that was legal, but by no means the only form of gaming available, in nearby Hot Springs. In later years, her flightiness and raucous laughter coupled with her love of flashy and multiple pieces of jewelry and colorful ensembles gave her an Auntie Mame quality as surely as her jutting jaw, spidery false eyelashes, and quarter-moon grin gave her an uncanny resemblance to Bette Midler. In middle age, she said, she ceased dying the dramatic shock of silver hair that sprang naturally from her forehead; in later years, when the rest of her tresses began graying, she relied on hair dye to preserve the silver streak running through her jet black hair.

Virginia believed in living life to its fullest. When she was told of her breast cancer in August 1990, it seemed only to intensify her tremendous *joie de vivre*. "I've always been able to face anything in the world I've had to face," she often said.[11] The trappings of old age did not much interest her. Chelsea learned early that her grandmother was not "Grandma" but "Ginger."[12] Always heavily perfumed and liberally rouged, Virginia had no hair on her brow and so applied black pencil in sweeping arcs above expressive eyes offset by incredibly long false eyelashes. Those eyelashes were a running joke among Clinton's gubernatorial staff. Whenever she was on the premises, these yuppie aides would indicate her presence silently by waving their fingers in front of their eyes. Generally, they viewed her as eccentric and mildly embarrassing, but the local press found her charming. She rarely revealed anything of substance in interviews, but she was always good for a quote.

When Billy was four, Virginia, having completed her training as a nurse anesthetist at Charity Hospital in New Orleans, moved back to Hope and began working as a nurse for Dr. Jim McKenzie, who would remember her as "a lively gal . . . a good nurse. She had a good sense of humor."[13] It was McKenzie who set Billy's leg, broken in three places during a fall after neighborhood children badgered the reluctant youth into jumping rope and then pulled it tight to trip him. "He was wearing a pair of boots that he'd never take off," the doctor recalled. "They said he was clumsy." (It's also said that young Billy was told not to take piano lessons because he was "clumsy.") Billy was inconsolable as he lay in a heap, unable to stand, and the taunts of his playmates— "Billy's a sissy! Billy's a sissy!"[14]—only made him howl louder. The spill sent him to the hospital, where he was fitted with a cast stretching from ankle to mid-thigh, and he lay with his leg vertically suspended for several weeks, reading comic books and, having long since dried his tears, proudly holding court for a parade of awestruck young visitors.

Life was not all work for Virginia, who is remembered by old-timers as "something of a rounder."[15] During one of her frequent forays into Hot Springs nightlife, she met her second husband, Roger M. Clinton, alternately a Buick dealer, a parts manager, and a car salesman for the Buick dealership owned by his brother, Raymond, another strong influence in Bill Clinton's life. (While governor, Clinton frequently referred to Raymond G. Clinton as the most commanding male presence in his life, on several occasions referring to him as a father figure. Indeed, Raymond Clinton was the man who set in motion the events that allowed his stepnephew to avoid military service and the Vietnam War several years later.)

Roger also moonlighted as a bouncer at a local hot spot, and lifelong Hope residents have hinted that he pursued less savory forms of salesmanship on the side. They maintain that during his time in Hope, his modest automobile dealership was one of the few places around where one could quench a thirst with "3.2 beer"—the only alcohol one could buy in a city that had been dry since 1935—and that Virginia spent a great deal of time there.[16]

Virginia later claimed no memory of the circumstances of her first marriage to Roger M. Clinton, but the date was June 19, 1950, thirteen days after her twenty-seventh birthday.

Roger, thirteen years her senior, was a likeable, charming fellow when sober and a hulking, obnoxious brute when in the throes of bourbon-induced drunkenness. His weakness for the bottle was the cause of great pain and suffering in the Clinton household: When he drank, he often beat his wife and terrorized her young son. She claimed later that he was resentful of any activity she pursued on her own, even knitting.

"He is very jealous, continually calling to check on my where-abouts," she told the court during their divorce proceedings.[17] On one occasion, angered because Virginia insisted on visiting her gravely ill grandmother, he grabbed a loaded pistol and fired a shot into the wall of their modest house on East Thirteenth Street. It was one of many unsettling episodes that for many years mother and elder son hid from other family members and friends and about which Bill Clinton never spoke publicly until he was a candidate for president. When he did, the slant he placed on his relationship with his stepfather was far different from the type of relationship he described during divorce proceedings Virginia brought against Clinton in 1962.

Perhaps as a result of his tumultuous early years, Bill Clinton aggressively pursued friendships and tended to keep them. One of his playmates at "Miss Mary's kindergarten," as the locals referred to Miss Marie's School for Little Folk, the nursery school and kindergarten run by Marie A. Purkins, was Thomas F. "Mack" McLarty III, the son of one of the wealthiest men in town—another car dealer. Mack would later dabble in politics, find life in the foreground distasteful, and assume the role of lobbyist, confidant, and advisor to his more egocentric friend while using his own business and social acumen to amass a personal fortune in his family's automobile business and, later, as chief executive officer of Arkla, Inc., a lucrative natural gas utility. Eventually, McLarty would follow Bill Clinton to Washington, becoming White House chief of staff.

Bill entered public school at Brookwood Elementary, but in 1953, the Clintons headed north ninety miles to Hot Springs, population then about 29,000. Hot Springs was a decaying tourist town best known in that era for its illegal but wide-open gaming activity and raunchy nightclubs.

Before it came to share honors with the Watermelon Capital of the World as the hometown of a president—Bill would continue to call Hot Springs home until 1992, when it became more convenient, and more mellifluous, to be the product of a place called Hope—Hot Springs was best known for its naturally heated springs which made it a resort town in the early 1800s. The Spa City, as it is still known, became a year-round haven for wealthy Easterners who spent their nights at the local clubs and whorehouses, taking soothing baths and massages in the establishments along Bath House Row, and boating, fishing, golfing, and hiking through the mountainous pine forests overlooking the hillside bungalows, rooming houses, and residence hotels to which transients, aging hoods, and gangsters' widows retired. Until the late 1960s, in almost any bar in town, one could get a mixed drink regardless of the type of alcoholic beverage permit held, place a bet, play a punchboard or a pinball or slot machine, and gather vivid anecdotes, many of them firsthand accounts about Owney Madden, Al Capone, and any number of other colorful gangland bosses and capos who once gathered in the shadow of the Ouachita Mountains. Hot Springs was for many years neutral ground for the overseers and executors of organized crime, but its glory days had long since passed

when Republican Governor Winthrop Rockefeller launched his relentless and ultimately successful campaign to obliterate open gambling there.

For thirty years, until his death (of natural causes) at age seventy-
three in 1965, Owen Vincent "Owney" Madden was Hot Springs's
most notorious and most celebrated resident.[18] Head of New York's
notorious Gopher Gang and at one time part owner of Harlem's
Cotton Club, he "retired" to Hot Springs in 1935 after being ordered
out of New York City by Police Commissioner Lewis J. Valentine.[19]
At the time of Madden's forced retirement, the Spa City was a wide-
open town and remained as such until the mid–1960s, when Rockefeller ordered the state police to take axes to the roulette tables, the slot
machines, and assorted other accoutrements of the illegal gaming that
flourished there for decades.

The only discernible change between the Hot Springs of the 1930s
and the Hot Springs of the 1950s was the absence of big-name mobsters, most of whom were dead or wasting away in federal penitentiaries. The drinking, the gambling, and the whoring were unaffected
by their absence. Nightclubs like the Vapors Supper Club, the Southern Club, and the Pines were among the most popular watering holes,
and Bill Clinton's mother, Virginia, made the rounds whenever possible, occasionally dragging her son Billy on the night's merriment.

"Hot Springs now, as always, has only one reason for welcoming
killers, extortionists, kidnapers, and thieves: money," wrote Charles
Samuels in a special report for the November 1961 issue of *Cavalier*
magazine. "Bigshot goons like Al Capone, Frank Costello, Bugs
Moran, Bugsy Siegel, Charlie Lucky, Maxie 'Boo Boo' Hoff, and
others flung many bucks around Hot Springs. Though not gentlemen,
they tried to avoid killing one another while at the spa with their
women. They also refrained from moving in on local rackets. Instead,
they gambled wildly, played golf, and took the baths. In return, local
authorities tried to protect the mobsters from extradition by other
states and other annoyances."[20]

The Clintons enrolled Billy in St. John's Catholic School, where he
received good marks in everything except deportment.[21] (Bill talked
too much, and he was so eager to impress the nuns that he often blurted

out answers before other children could be recognized.) But Park Place Baptist Church, three blocks from their home, was Bill's primary place of worship, and neighbors remember seeing him walking solemnly and alone to and from Sunday school, which he rarely missed. The Clintons bought a house from Roger's brother Raymond at 1011 Park Avenue and acquired a shiny new Buick and a black-and-white television set before which Bill Clinton got his first taste of politics by watching the 1956 Democratic National Convention.[22] Virginia was more affluent than in the past, though she was on call twenty-four hours a day as a nurse anesthetist for Ouachita Memorial Hospital, a job she would hold until her abrupt departure in 1981 following her entanglement in several lawsuits involving the deaths of patients she had attended.

Roger Cassidy Clinton was born on July 25, 1956, about a month before Billy's tenth birthday, and was still a toddler when his father's drinking increased and his violent behavior intensified.[23] The tumult created by those drunken outbursts contributed to the close relationship between Bill and his half-brother, whom Billy often tended in his working mother's absence; certainly, the chronic disruptions fed Virginia's protective tendencies toward her sons. For instance, she always discouraged any interest either had in contact sports and encouraged their mutual interest in music because it kept them busy until Virginia could come home from work.

"The way I've had to work, my children had to mature early," Virginia once said.[24] But it was their homelife, not her profession as such, that most likely hastened that maturity, although her work often instigated her husband's outbursts.

"I have worked practically the whole time we have been married as an anesthetist, causing me to have to leave the house at different hours of the day and night," Virginia testified in her 1962 divorce proceedings against Roger. "He is very jealous, continually calling to check on my whereabouts, which is causing me considerable embarrassment with the people with whom I work."[25]

For the most part, Billy Clinton's friends were unaware of his tumultuous homelife. He is remembered as a regular kid, a little pudgy but with a ready grin beneath his unruly curls, Sunday-go-to-meeting manners, and dynamic energy. Relatives of William Blythe have said that Billy shared several of his father's traits, among them the desire to be liked by and the inclination to try to befriend everyone he met. Billy loved sports, particularly football, a pastime his mother discouraged and eventually forbade because, she declared, she had seen too many broken bones and bruised bodies, the result of competitive sports, in her work at the hospital.[26] A childhood friend, David Leopoulos, later told Clinton's biographer, Robert E. Levin, that within a week of his enrollment at Ramble Elementary in 1955, "most kids knew who he was and wanted to be around him."[27] As he grew older, he loved to take in Saturday matinees at the Malco Theater and slushy soft drinks at The Polar Bar. Many times he took Roger with him.

Clinton says he had "a normal childhood, but at times it was really tough." Virginia had long since grown accustomed to her husband's beatings, not all of them behind closed doors—on one occasion, while they were attending a dance, Roger had punched and kicked her in full view of other couples—but as her elder son grew older, taller, and more distressed by the increasing frequency of Roger's aggression toward his wife, she began to fear for Billy's safety. After a period of several months, during which Roger's outbursts landed him in police custody on at least two occasions, she became determined to end the marriage.[28]

Their divorce, finalized on May 15, 1962, was messy. She had to obtain a restraining order to get her husband out of the house on Park Avenue,[29] although he continued to hang around outside, perched drunkenly on the stoop, begging her to let him come home. In her deposition, Virginia recounted the years of verbal and physical abuse at the hands of a man she declared had repeatedly embarrassed and humiliated her, treating her with "studied neglect, unmerited reproach, and mental cruelty."[30] She said he refused to let her have many close friends and to associate with people outside her workplace.

Roger's drinking problem, she said, had been constant throughout their twelve-year marriage and had steadily worsened. She described several examples of his chronic abuse, which included slapping her around and, on at least one occasion, throwing her to the floor and beating her about the head with her own high-heeled shoe. She left him on that occasion and filed for divorce, but "because of our child's age"—young Roger was not quite three years old—"and the promises made . . . to quit drinking and to treat me with love and respect, I reconciled with him."[31]

"I am afraid of him when he is drinking," she said in a 1962 deposition. "He has continually tried to do bodily harm to myself and my son, Billy, whenever he attempts to attack me when he has been drinking."[32]

Bill Clinton did not speak of those harrowing times publicly until thirty years later, when he became a contender for the Democratic nomination for president. When he did, he painted a heroic portrait of his dealings with his bullying stepfather.

"One of the most difficult things for me was being fourteen years old and putting an end to the violence," he told *New York* magazine's Joe Klein in January 1992. "I just broke down the door of their room one night when they were having an encounter and told him that I was bigger than him now, and there would never be any more of this while I was there."[33]

The deposition prepared from his statements at his mother's divorce proceedings when he was fifteen presents a different picture.

He had witnessed his stepfather striking his mother on numerous occasions, Billy said, and on at least two occasions when he was twelve, he had summoned police to their home, resulting at least once in Roger's arrest.

"On one occasion in the last month," Billy testified, "I again had to call my mother's attorney because of [Roger's] conduct causing physical abuse to my mother and the police again had to be summoned to the house. He has threatened my mother on a number of occasions and because of his nagging [and] arguing with my mother, I can tell that she is very unhappy and it is impossible . . . for them to continue to live together. . . .

"The last occasion in which I went to my mother's aid, when he was abusing my mother, he threatened to mash my face in if I took her part."[34]

Nothing in his testimony indicates that young Billy was able, or even attempted, to stop Roger Clinton's beatings.

After the divorce was granted, Virginia got custody of the two children, a chandelier, and the 1960 Buick Le Sabre. Roger was ordered to sell the Park Avenue house, splitting the profits less expenses with Virginia, and to pay a minimum of $50 a month toward his only child's support but nothing toward Billy's upkeep.

Scarcely one month later, Virginia petitioned the Garland County Chancery Court in Billy's behalf to adopt his former stepfather's name.[35]

Roger never legally adopted Billy, but Billy had been known as William Jefferson Clinton throughout the marriage. He was deposed for the divorce hearing as William J. Clinton. In her petition, Virginia C. Clinton noted that Roger M. Clinton was the only father Billy had ever known and that he desired to take the name common to his mother and half-brother, Roger, then a month shy of his sixth birthday and due to enter elementary school that autumn. She further attested that "there are no pleasant associations connected with the name of Blythe, as [Billy] never knew his father and has always been known by his friends and in various organizations and school records as William Jefferson Clinton."

When reporters later would ask Bill Clinton why he would take the name of a stepfather who abused him, he would dismiss the matter by saying, simply, "The name doesn't matter, it's the man."[36]

An interesting discrepancy occurs in that petition, dated June 12, 1962: Billy is referred to throughout as William Jefferson Blythe III, and his father as William Jefferson Blythe II. As an adult, the future president said on numerous occasions that he was born William Jefferson Blythe IV. The public record is unreliable, because his father was given only the initials W.J. at birth and did not adopt his own father's name until years later. No official record identifying Virginia's first husband as anything except W.J. or William J. Blythe has been uncovered.

The divorce did not last. Roger and Virginia soon reconciled and remarried on August 6, 1962. Virginia later would say she felt sorry for him—he kept hanging around the house, casting pleading glances, mooning and crying for hours on end, and staying to fall asleep on the porch. "It was so sad," she recalled, "I couldn't stand it."[37] As it happened, very shortly after their second marriage, Roger was diagnosed with cancer. She stayed with him until his death in 1967, which she always counted as the second biggest tragedy in her life, the first being Bill Blythe's early death. Bill, then attending Georgetown University, finally made his peace with the only father he had ever known during Roger Clinton Sr.'s last six weeks of life.[38] In addition to young Roger, then ten, the elder Clinton left behind sons George and Roy Murphy, the product of a marriage that ended in 1948.

Despite the family's problems in the summer of 1962, many of Bill Clinton's friends saw no change in him. Outwardly, he was his same ebullient self, pursuing his interest in music—he played the tenor saxophone with some expertise—and filling his agenda with as many school and extracurricular activities as his schedule would allow, the Student Council, Key Club, Beta Club, DeMolay, various performance bands, regional high school festivals, solo competitions, and volunteer work at his mother's research hospital among them. With all this, he still found time to read an endless stream of books, particularly mysteries and biographies.

Bill turned sixteen that August, and with the coveted driver's license in his wallet, he often gathered a group for a cruise along Grand Avenue or to the top of nearby West Mountain, often leading the singing at the top of his lungs.[39] Group activities seemed to hold special appeal for Bill; friends say he rarely dated, preferring instead the company of many, against whom he would invariably emerge as the center of attention. None of his friends recalls begrudging him the spotlight, however, because he worked hard at including them in the fun. For example, he frequently would turn a solo performance— his favorite was an Elvis Presley imitation—into a sing-along. Nonetheless, he could be a ruthless card player, and although he was always willing to "lend money" to a losing Monopoly player, friends contend that a close game brought out the shark in him. He loved to win.[40]

Bill Clinton was also a talented musician in high school. He played tenor saxophone in the band, and later with a local trio—he was very adept at reading sheet music—and for a time he entertained romantic notions of becoming a professional musician, perhaps even a singer like his childhood hero, Elvis Presley, whose swaggering stance, lopsided grin, and affection for peanut butter and banana sandwiches the teenage Bill Clinton readily adopted. Something of a show-off, he never missed an opportunity to regale his friends and family with his own hearty rendition of "Hound Dog" or the softer, sweeter "Love Me Tender," a favorite of his mother, Virginia. As a youth, singing in the choir at Park Place Baptist Church in Hot Springs, he had a three-octave range. (Shortly after he won his first race for governor, he quipped that he "couldn't sing nine notes now.")[41]

He was a band major at Hot Springs High School and a first-chair All-State sax player, and he attended a band camp for several summers in northwest Akansas. Music, he once said, was a young man's way of "channeling [his] sensitivity," of creating something beautiful. "It taught me that it's just not enough to have the strong feelings. . . . It taught me that in order to bring them into expression, to do them justice, it takes a whole lot of work and discipline"[42]—discipline he was not willing to expend once he discovered the heady world of politics.

Bill played hard and, according to those around him, he worked hard, although he was not above taking shortcuts. Composer-musician Randy Goodrum, a high school chum, once recalled that he drew Clinton for a partner in a science fair project and, as usual, Clinton insisted on taking the lead. "He told me he'd take care of everything," Goodrum told biographer Robert E. Levin in 1992. "That was good, since I sure had no idea what we'd do. Finally the day before the fair, he came up with a curved, shiny piece of sheet metal and put a hot dog on it. Our project was a solar hot dog cooker. Great. I think we got the D we deserved."[43]

"When I was a kid," Clinton was quoted as saying in the 1992 campaign biography, The Comeback Kid, "I thought I was busier than anybody else I knew."[44] He had good reason to be. Despite their comfortable life, the Clintons could not afford to pay for the kind of education Bill hoped to pursue upon graduating from Hot Springs High School. As early as his sophomore year, he had set his sights on prestigious Georgetown University.

Edith Irons, his high school guidance counselor, has told the story many times, each time recalling more vividly how Billy Clinton, then fifteen, came to her early in his sophomore year seeking information about pursuing a career as a foreign diplomat. Without giving it much thought, she replied that Georgetown University had a fine foreign relations program, and she gave him both a Georgetown catalog and a promise to order catalogs from other universities that might fit the bill. At his insistence, she also ran down the steps he would need to follow to prepare for his college entrance exams. "Because of the great difficulty in getting accepted into Georgetown, I suggested he also apply to a couple of others," Irons remembers. That was the one piece of advice he ignored, but "this was typical of the confidence Bill had in himself," she said. "He had set his goal, investigated what needed to be done to accomplish it, did what was necessary, and never considered defeat."[45]

Except for the occasional fiasco, such as the solar hot dog cooker incident, Bill was a good student, particularly strong in mathematics and English, and teachers adored him. He could be a real cut-up in class, more amusing than annoying, and many classroom discussions turned into lively debates. Adults appreciated his insatiable curiosity and his serious efforts to exercise his logic and reason. Paul Root, who taught an advanced world history course in which Clinton was enrolled as a sophomore, would recollect that while all his students were very good that year, Clinton, with his probing mind and astute arguments, stood out. "The difference was Bill's depth of enjoyment of history. Even at that age, he was talking about working in the foreign service."[46]

He talked about foreign service, but at that juncture Bill was no more set on a career in diplomacy than he had been a year before when he toyed with the idea of becoming a musician. Essentially, he was exploring the possibilities, flexing his imagination, assessing one career path against other attractive options. His mother had always assured him that he could be whatever he chose to be; the challenge was to make the right choice. With Georgetown, the attraction was its exclusivity, its wide ranging curriculum, its location in Washington, and its distance from Hot Springs, Arkansas. In his midteens, Bill Clinton was an independent-minded individual with few chances to assert either independence or individuality. He could excel at music, get good grades, and enthrall his friends, but he needed more; he needed a larger world, a wider universe. He didn't want to be limited to the local state

teacher's college or the state university and end up with a predictable—and confined—career. Like Pip, he was primed with great
expectations.

The only incident that foreshadowed the future was a trip in the
summer of 1963, when his grades and enthusiastic recommendations
from his mentors brought him to the American Legion's Boys State
summer camp, which annually provides mock on-the-job training in
politics for a select group of high school juniors. For a week in June,
young men from across Arkansas, each of them considered to be the
leader of his class, lived in the sparse dormitory housing of North Little
Rock's Camp Robinson, an army basic training facility during the
First and Second World Wars. There they chose up sides for the
bipartisan elections that culminated in a day spent "running" state
government, actually taking over the offices of the state's seven constitutional officers, holding an abbreviated morning-long legislative session, and, on a slow news day, participating in actual interviews with
accommodating statehouse reporters.

In 1963, the publicity went to Mack McLarty, who in traditional
Arkansas style spent two virtually sleepless days and nights campaigning, and winning, the coveted title of governor of Boys State. Thus it
was Mack, thereafter dubbed "Guv," who stood alongside Governor
Orval E. Faubus in an army jeep in the traditional Boys State Review
parade on June 6. Bill had helped in the campaign, not because he did
not fancy the office, but because he was lobbying for what he saw as
the larger honor of becoming a delegate to Boys Nation, the national
equivalent of the American Legion state program wherein delegates
traveled to Washington, D.C., to watch national politics in action.

"The national press has tried to spin that I beat Clinton for governor," McLarty said in a 1993 interview. "I did not. What the basic deal
is, the governor's spot is the first top spot, and, of course, I was
fortunate enough to get elected to that . . . [but] Clinton had always
been running for Boys Nation."[47]

For a young man from tbe cramped, dirty, small town of Hot
Springs, the nation's capital was an awesome visual, aural, and intellectual experience. Clinton not only saw the houses of Congress but
dined in the Senate Dining Room with a newfound hero, Arkansas's

junior senator, J. William Fulbright, who in his eighteen years in Washington had acquired a statesman's stature largely due to his role as chairman of the Senate Foreign Relations Committee, which he headed from 1959 to 1975. Fulbright, a Rhodes Scholar, back-slid progressive, and born-again liberal, was to become one of the leading American doves during the Vietnam War. Bill listened carefully, enthralled, as the urbane, soft-spoken Fulbright patiently fielded questions and held forth on his political ideas.[48]

The meetings with members of Congress, the sightseeing, the affirmation at every turn that the delegates were watching history in the making, were heady stuff, but the crowning moment was the delegates' visit to the White House, when a gangly, raw-faced, crew-cut teenager briefly clasped hands with John F. Kennedy, the president of the United States. The moment was recorded for posterity, and future campaigns, in a photograph and on film.

At that pivotal moment, Bill Clinton, just a few weeks shy of his seventeenth birthday, had discovered the world beyond his backyard and his place in it. Kennedy was for him an icon, a vibrant, daring, and, relatively young politician whose wit and spunk had excited Bill Clinton ever since he watched Kennedy lose the vice presidential nomination to Tennessee's Estes Kefauver at the 1956 Democratic National Convention. Bill returned to Hot Springs not so much changed as consumed by the notion of making politics his life and the presidency his goal. His mother knew it, too; she saw it in his eyes: "He was just aglow."[49]

"I'd never seen him so excited about something," she told the *Arkansas Democrat*. "When he came back from Washington, holding this picture of himself with Jack Kennedy, and the expression on his face—I just knew that politics was the answer for him." She nurtured the dream, encouraging this ambition as she had virtually every goal he had ever set for himself, even when it meant sending him off to Georgetown University, and later to Oxford, England, leaving her for extended periods of time to cope with a precocious child and a very ill husband. Her pride in her firstborn, to whom she paid tribute every day of his life through an ever-expanding collection of awards and photographs and scrapbooks, sustained her. "I've always been proud of him," she invariably would reply to well-wishers on the occasion of each new accomplishment.

Through multiple marriages, separations, divorce, and even death, Virginia's strength was sustained by her consummate devotion to her sons, to whom she always referred as "the boys."

In 1969, Virginia married for a third time. Her new husband was George J. "Jeff" Dwire, a hairdresser two years her junior. Dwire died of a heart ailment complicated by diabetes in 1974, leaving behind two daughters from a prior marriage, among them Dianne Dwire Welch, whose life was fodder for the tabloids after the *National Enquirer* tracked her to Houston, Texas, and revealed her criminal record. (Armed robbery and drug trafficking were among her offenses, and she eventually did time in the Mountain View Maximum Security Prison at Gateville, Texas.) Welch would claim in the *Enquirer* interview that just days before the 1992 general election, the stepbrother with whom she had not spoken since 1975 sent two Democratic party henchmen to her $400-a-month apartment to warn her "to keep my mouth shut about who I really am" lest Bill Clinton's candidacy be undermined by another in a series of election-year scandals. Still later, she would claim to have been sequestered by them in a local motel until after the election so as not to create more unfavorable publicity for the Man from Hope.

If such a confrontation occurred—and it would not be out of character for Clinton's campaign organization, which spent as much time preventing brushfires as it did in putting them out—it was a mere loose end at that point. Clinton had more important matters on his mind, primarily his victory speech.

Virginia's fourth marriage, in January 1982, was to retired food broker Richard W. Kelley, with whom she found the joy and companionship only promised by her early union with Bill Blythe. Until Virginia's death in January 1994, Dick Kelley proved steadfast, reliable, and indulgent of her two passions: her sons and playing the ponies at $2 or $5 a bet.

"Everything is by comparison" was Virginia Blythe Clinton Dwire's enigmatic response to the *Hot Springs Sentinel Record*'s John Wallworth in 1974 when asked to summarize her personal philosophy.[50]

In retrospect, her meaning is clear: By comparison to most, she experienced numerous upheavals throughout her youth and middle age, yet all the pain and suffering and sacrifice was held in check by the pride she took in her offspring. Bill and Virginia's solid alliance was the constant in her life, and neither Bill's capricious political career nor Roger's prison sentence could shake her belief that her boys could and would be whatever they wanted to be. Whenever anyone commented on how proud she must be of her son's accomplishments, she would smile brightly and inquire, "Which one? I have two boys."

3

OFF AND RUNNING

WHILE BILL CLINTON'S INTRODUCTION to politics was by watching the 1956 political convention, it was a ninth-grade civics teacher, Mary Marty, who "quickened my interest in politics" by having her students debate the Kennedy-Nixon race of 1960, Clinton once told the *Arkansas Democrat*:[1]

"She and I were the only ones for Kennedy. Virtually everyone else was for Nixon. Garland County has always been strongly Republican. In fact, Jimmy Carter was the first Democrat to carry the county since Harry Truman."

But it wasn't until Bill Clinton's visit to Washington, D.C., in 1963 where he shook President Kennedy's hand that he decided that politics was to be his career. Virgil Spurlin, Clinton's high school music teacher, has suggested that politics won out over music because "I don't think the opportunities were as real for him in that field as they [were] in politics."[2]

When he headed back to Washington in 1964 to enroll in the School of Foreign Service at Georgetown University, Clinton endorsed liberal views. Camelot had dimmed, but in its place was the Great Society, the civil rights movement, and Medicare, an agenda that resonated with the young man from one of the poorest states in the South who, at his grandfather's knees, had learned about compassion for the less fortunate.

"When I went there in 1964," Clinton told the *Arkansas Democrat* in 1977, "it appeared that Lyndon Johnson was about to usher in the Great Society, and everyone was very optimistic. . . . I thought then that the great problems that politics would have to contend with would be foreign affairs. . . . I thought I could learn about the domestic problems just by being around Washington."[3]

He was, by all accounts, already greatly attuned to the dominant domestic problems of that time. Friends suggest that it was his Southern roots, and particularly his Arkansas heritage, that made Clinton sensitive to black America's struggle for equal rights, and they recall that he was quick to argue with anyone who seemed to be a bigot.

"Bill Clinton is the most unprejudiced person I have ever met," his college roommate Tom Campbell declares. "I have never heard him make a derogatory reference to a person's race, sex, or physical appearance. Any manifestation of bigotry distressed him."[4] He was not a saint, however. As any number of people who knew him later in life have attested, Clinton was not above letting his facial expressions do the talking whenever a particularly attractive female, particularly a busty blonde, caught his eye.

The launching in the summer of 1964 of the War on Poverty with passage of the Economic Opportunity Act held far more interest and meaning for Clinton than the passage of the Gulf of Tonkin Resolution, which authorized President Lyndon B. Johnson to take action in Vietnam after North Vietnamese boats allegedly attacked two U.S. destroyers.

Nonetheless, the notion of becoming a social worker or a civil rights lawyer had no appeal for the young collegian, who wanted not only to make a difference but to make a mark, which is the reason he chose Georgetown over the University of Arkansas.

"I knew that politically, it would be advantageous for me to stay here [in Arkansas] to go to school," he said years later, "but I felt that if I went away to school and exposed myself to the rest of the country and learned something about the rest of the world, then if I ever could get elected down here, I'd do a better job."[5]

Despite the tentative nature of Clinton's remembrance, there was little doubt in his mind at eighteen that he *would* be elected to public office someday and that he would work toward the presidency. Several of his Georgetown colleagues say that Clinton made no secret of his presidential ambitions, although Campbell contends that Clinton "did not think it a realistic possibility."[6]

Certainly, Clinton had been on campus only a few weeks when he launched his campaign for president of Georgetown's East Campus, a decision his roommate at the time, Tom Campbell, says Clinton had probably reached "before he left Hot Springs." Numerous alumni have recalled that their first meeting with the gregarious young Southerner began with an outstretched hand followed by the introductory: "Hi, I'm Bill Clinton, and I'm running for president of our class and I'd like your vote." They remember him as seemingly tireless, very outgoing, very hard working, and very political, which was not a very trendy thing to be at Georgetown in those days. He was, as one friend observed, "someone who was on the way to somewhere else and in a hurry to get there."[7]

The consummate social animal—unless engrossed in a good book, he becomes very restless when left alone and seeks out conversation, however mundane or inconsequential—Clinton made a point of meeting as many people as possible, and his insatiable curiosity about everyone he encountered served him well in striking up new and useful acquaintances.

One of the first people he sought out at Georgetown was Thomas Caplan, who had a reputation as a Kennedy familiar; he had spent time with the family at Hyannisport and had served an internship in the Kennedy White House. That first meeting, recounted by Caplan in *Clinton: Young Man in a Hurry*, occurred when Clinton knocked on Caplan's door and greeted him by saying, "Hello, I'm Bill Clinton. Will you help me run for president of the class?" Caplan recalls that he initially felt uneasy about Clinton and did not quite trust him, but in short order Clinton's affable nature and genuine interest in getting acquainted won him over.[8] They became friends, and Caplan was one of numerous near-instant allies who helped Clinton win that election. Campbell, with whom Clinton shared Room 225 in Loyola Hall, has said that even then, the Arkansan had a personality that "filled the room."[9] Christopher "Kit" Ashby, another dormitory mate who hailed from Texas, remarked that "from the very beginning, his most memorable and attractive characteristic was his friendliness. . . . He had an inner quality which I simply enjoyed being around."[10]

This "hail fellow well met" attitude—what one Arkansas politician has called "being real good at being real chummy"—has always been one of Clinton's biggest assets. Even people who have found themselves at odds with him do not deny that he is patently one of the most charming people with whom they have ever dealt. Former Governor Orval E. Faubus, no slouch at working a crowd, says Clinton is one of the best he has ever seen on the stump, patient, tolerant, and observant, taking care to get acquainted and to really listen when people speak.

"I used to say that Orval Faubus was the best politician this state has ever produced," Arkansas labor leader J. Bill Becker said. "Back in the 1957 days"—when Little Rock's Central High School had to be integrated with the aid of federal troops—"people would come down from Washington or outside the state, and on one or two occasions they would get a chance to meet with Faubus on something. And this is when he was one of the most hated guys in America. And they would come out of his office and say, 'Boy, he's really good, isn't he? He's a nice guy. He's right on a lot of issues, isn't he? I'm impressed!' But not anymore. He takes second place compared to Bill Clinton. Bill Clinton has that kind of charm and that kind of charisma and that kind of ability. . . . Yeah, he stands out in a crowd."[11]

"It's because of the charisma that Clinton has and desires to have, wanting to be liked, to be loved . . . that he develops a kind of rapport with legislators and with other people, and that serves him well with a lot of people, especially when he's trying to win votes on a particular issue," suggested Arkansas lawmaker Pat Flanagin, a fellow Democrat, whose basic distrust of Clinton began early in his first term as governor. "He has a talent for persuasion, for making you believe him, whether he's on the campaign trail, whether you're going into his office. . . . He's sitting there nodding, and you're thinking he's going to do everything you're asking him. . . . You'll notice that whenever you're getting this, it's always a setting where he's wanting something. Your vote in an election, your vote in committee, your vote on the House floor—your vote."[12]

Part of the charm, Flanagin said in all seriousness, is good eye contact. Others have noted it, too. One Arkansas pundit has noted that what set Clinton apart from many of his political challengers was his concentration on the person in front of him. When going through a receiving line, for instance, he will never be found shaking one hand while looking toward the next one. For the few moments a person stands before him, he is unwavering in his attention (throughout the years aides have tried—and failed —to keep him on schedule).

Mack McLarty, the president's chief of staff who has known Clinton since kindergarten, believes this ability "to connect with ordinary people" is one reason Clinton "broke out of the pack" in the 1992 Democratic primary.[13]

During his freshman campaign at Georgetown, Clinton so impressed classmate Helen Henry that she dropped her own bid for class president.

"He took the time to sit down with me and outline his platform," she told biographer Robert E. Levin. "By the end of our conversation, he had impressed me so much that I decided not to run. I simply had to admit that he was perfect for the job."[14]

She recalled him being "high-minded, yet practical."[15] As Campbell has noted, however, Clinton "was no country boy lost in the big city."[16] Unlike many of his competitors at Georgetown, however, Bill Clinton had a platform. Among other things, he wanted to tackle the university's parking problem and to get students who lived off-campus more involved in school activities. He distributed dozens of fliers, each one personally signed by the candidate, in which he gave assurances that "the feasibility of every plank has been carefully examined." His enthusiasm was so impressive and his allure so strong that, according to one classmate, "when you met Bill, you wanted to say to him, 'I want to vote for you. What office are you running for?' "[17]

If his constituents expected a leader, they were disappointed. Following his impressive victory, Clinton reminded students in the student-run *Georgetown Courier* that "the freshman year is not the time for crusading, but for building a strong unit for the future. You must know the rules before you can change them."[18] With these words, Clinton first expressed the carrot-on-a-stick approach to politics that would place and keep him in elective office: Promise but never completely deliver in the same time period; start a project in one term, execute it in another during which a new long-term project is launched; lay a foundation on which work can begin as a means of extending your stay for the purpose of finishing the job. This methodology would be employed in nearly every reelection campaign in which Clinton would be involved. He would always require more time to "get the job done."

Clinton kicked off his sophomore year at Georgetown with another campaign for the presidency of East Campus. This time he said he was ready to work for issues that were important to the student body. He won. His first order of business: driving down the high price of food on campus. "If the food service is to be a service to the students," he said, "its prices should be below or at least equal to competitive prices in the area. Some students just cannot afford the service the way it is now." Reportedly, his efforts paid off within a month.[19]

By all accounts, Clinton's expanding world did not reach beyond the realm of academia during his first few semesters at Georgetown, where he was pursuing a B.A. in international government studies. Although intellectual challenges abounded, and, with students from dozens of nations it was easy to hear first-hand the problems of the world, lower classmen were far more interested in the cost of campus meals than in debating the issues of the day, and rebellion consisted of drinking a few beers after the weekly basketball or polo game. Vietnam, as Campbell has noted, "was still very, very far away."[20]

So far away, apparently, that during his first semester, Clinton had no aversion to enrolling in the school's Air Reserve Officers Training Corps program. Campbell recalled their shared experience in uniform in a 1992 essay.

"We were Air Force ROTC cadets our first semester," Campbell wrote. "It was voluntary and carried no credit, but we enjoyed it. Bill could not march. I had gone to a Jesuit military high school and knew all about shining shoes, Irish pennants, gig lines, and marching. It was one of the few things I could do better than he, and it was fun to teach him to do an about-face. The Air Force cut the program from four to two years, and Bill and I turned in our uniforms. The Army unit was full."[21]

University life was everything Clinton had expected, both on and off campus. He pledged a service fraternity, Alpha Phi Omega, which ran elections and coordinated orientation activities on campus. For the first time in his life, he had a steady girlfriend, Denise Hyland, a tall, patrician, pearls-and-polish blonde from New Jersey. He was active in a variety of intramural clubs and activities. In the spirit of the true Southern politician, he worked hard and he played hard, and, thanks to a trick learned from a newfound mentor, his Western civilization professor, Carroll Quigley, did so on very little sleep.

The flamboyant and eccentric Quigley could be called a time freak; he believed that time could be used more efficiently if you slept sparingly at night and relied on a series of catnaps during the day. Clinton mastered the technique of falling to sleep quickly and snoozing for brief periods of time—as little as five minutes, but never more than twenty—and was fortunate that he could. He was not studious by nature, and although he made exceptional grades—he eventually won a Phi Beta Kappa key—he did so by routinely cramming for exams and relying on a photographic memory. He was, according to one of his Yale Law School colleagues, "the classic quick study,"[22] and judging by the lax study habits he displayed later at Georgetown, as well as at Oxford and Yale, he needed to be. Although family members supplemented his tuition, Clinton claims to have held a series of part-time jobs to make ends meet.

Quigley, Campbell says, "had a profound influence"[23] on Clinton. In his course on Development of Civilization, Quigley taught that "nothing was more critical to understanding our world . . . than the willingness of the European culture to make sacrifices today to secure a better future for the next generation, to prefer the future over the present," Campbell wrote.[24]

"Quigley was a fascinating lecturer and taught history with an emphasis on the larger issues and with little reference to dates. The technical limitations of getting water out of gold mines were an important factor in Western civilization, Professor Quigley said, because they forced the Romans to go further afield to capture hard currency. He discussed the methods of harnessing horses as a factor in history and the influence of the stirrup on the fall of the Roman Empire. A problem on his final examination was: 'Discuss the history of the Balkan Peninsula from the retreat of the Wurm glacier to the assassination of Franz Ferdinand in 1914.' "[25]

It was Quigley who first encouraged Clinton to do graduate work in England, and later he provided Clinton with one of several letters of recommendation required by the Rhodes Scholarship review committee.

Never one to sit placidly in the back of the class, Clinton availed himself of as many available intellectual and academic resources as his schedule would allow. Among them was a religion class for non-Catholics taught by the "stern but brilliant" dean of the School of Foreign Service, Father Joseph Sebes.[26] The course, entitled Comparative Cultures, exposed Clinton to a wide spectrum of religious beliefs, and gave him what he later called "a feel . . . for what I believe is the innate religious nature of human beings."[27]

"We went through all these cultures and all their religions," Clinton added, "and no matter how different they were, it was obvious they all had a hunger to find some meaning in their lives beyond the temporal things that consume most of us through most of our days. I really developed an immense appreciation for that."[28]

Unlike other members of his immediate family, Clinton has been a regular church-goer most of his life, even when it meant going alone, as he did as an eight-year-old boy in Hot Springs. At Georgetown, he often attended a nearby Presbyterian church with Kit Ashby—Ashby said there were no "good" Baptist churches nearby[29]—after which they would share their budding ideas about life, love, and the human condition over a submarine sandwich. Many times the discussion would center around the evolving civil rights movement, Ashby told Clinton's biographer in 1992. "He influenced me greatly in those discussions," said Ashby, who joked that he and Clinton were "about the only Southern Protestants at Georgetown that fall."[30]

"In those days," Ashby added, "I was still caught up in the arguments about states's rights versus federal rights that were so prevalent in Texas. He showed me that the place to start is with the individual, decide what is right for them, and then worry about how the legal system should fit."[31]

In the summer of 1966, before Clinton started his junior year at Georgetown, he volunteered for J. Frank Holt's campaign for governor of Arkansas. Orval E. Faubus had been governor of Arkansas for twelve years, but when he suddenly decided not to run for a seventh term, the Democratic party was left with virtually no one to succeed him. More alarming for the Democrats, who had occupied the statehouse since 1875, was that the man most likely to be governor was a Republican, Winthrop Rockefeller. This black-sheep grandson of the founder of Standard Oil (and brother of New York Governor Nelson Rockefeller) had wearied of his nonproductive lifestyle and playboy reputation and had sought refuge and a new beginning in Arkansas more than a decade earlier.

Rockefeller had run, unsuccessfully, against Faubus in 1964 but had held him to 56 percent of the vote, the narrowest victory of his career. Rockefeller's strong showing and the political infighting among the Democrats convinced Faubus that he would not be elected to a seventh term, and he opted out. The only likely Democrat successor to Faubus, longtime Lieutenant Governor Nathan Gordon, also had decided to retire from politics.

The two men who survived the Democratic primary for a runoff were Jim Johnson and Frank Holt, two Arkansas Supreme Court justices who resigned their $20,000-a-year positions, among the highest paid jobs in the state, to seek a governorship that paid, as politicos liked to say only half in jest, "$10,000 a year and all you can steal."

Holt, an amiable fellow whose diffidence made him better suited to judicial robes than politics was clearly outmatched by Johnson, who despite his arch-segregationist roots was one of the most effective stump speakers the state has ever produced. Johnson had run one campaign for governor, against Faubus in 1956, and he was confident enough to dismiss the affable Holt, all too aptly, as "a pleasant vegetable" and concentrate most of his energy on the "prissy sissy" from the East—Rockefeller.

Besides his obvious lackluster quality and his underestimation of Johnson's grass-roots campaign, Holt had another strike against him going into the governor's race: He was the machine candidate, practically hand-picked by the *de facto* head of the Faubus machine, financier Witt Stephens. For many years it was said that no one got elected in Arkansas without Stephens's blessing—he rarely contributed more than a pittance to any campaign but was highly effective at "persuading" others to give generously—and Holt counted on it. Home for the summer, Bill Clinton quickly enlisted in the Holt effort, distributing handbills, posting signs, and generally succumbing to what was for him high-stakes campaign fever.

Much to Clinton's chagrin, Holt lost the run-off to Johnson, but Clinton came out a winner: He had made some valuable contacts during the campaign, one of which paid off quickly, securing for him a part-time job on the staff of J. William Fulbright's Senate Foreign Relations Committee, which he held until June 1968.

Part of the Clinton myth is that Clinton was a "self-made" success because he got the Fulbright job without help. Not true. Clinton himself has said that he got the job, an assistant clerk's position better described as that of general flunky, "when I was nobody from nowhere. My family had no money, no political influence, nothing."[32] True as far as it goes, but Clinton had one thing going for him: a newfound friend in a position to do him a favor. Arkansas is no different from anywhere else: You don't need influence of your own so long as you know somebody who knows somebody. Clinton, as usual strapped for money, needed a reliable income, preferably from a source that would enhance his resumé. Jack Holt, Frank's nephew, whose acquaintance Clinton had made during the campaign, was pleased to recommend the eager young man to Lee Williams, Fulbright's administrative assistant.

The way both Williams and Clinton tell it, when Williams telephoned Clinton at his home in Hot Springs to offer him a job, he gave

Clinton a choice: a part-time job paying $3,500 a year or a full-time position paying $5,000.

"How about two part-time jobs?" Clinton asked.

"You're just the guy I'm looking for," Williams replied.

That was on a Friday evening. By Monday morning, Clinton had repacked the Buick, driven the 1,060 miles to Washington, D.C., and was able to report for work Monday morning.[33]

Back at school, Clinton made his third and final run for student elective office during his junior year, but despite what some observers considered a sophisticated campaign, complete with a telephone bank, lapel pins, and carefully hand-crafted signs, he suffered a stunning, unanticipated defeat at the hands of Terry Modglin, who had served as vice president during Clinton's sophomore stint as class president.

Modglin, whose demeanor was as nonpolitical as Clinton's was political, succeeded in painting Clinton as the establishment candidate, a label embraced by the student newspaper, the *Georgetown Hoya*, and himself as a pioneering agent of change. Modglin won by a 147-vote margin.

The defeat was enough to persuade Clinton to redirect his energy toward his grades, never a problem when he applied himself, and his work for Fulbright.

Clinton's last year at Georgetown was a full one, and he kept an exhaustive, and exhausting, scholastic, civic, social, and professional schedule that had been made more trying by the prolonged illness of his stepfather, Roger Clinton. Friends speak admiringly of the effort Bill made to end their estrangement. Roger, who Virginia said finally had put alcoholism behind him, had been battling cancer for several years. Reportedly, it was during a visit home, when Roger was too weak to care for himself, that Bill finally befriended him, even carrying him to and from the bathroom, and tucking him back into bed.[34] Roger's was a lingering death, and at one point, when he sought treatment at the Duke University hospital in Durham, North Carolina, Bill often drove more than 260 miles from the Georgetown campus to visit him. These were their best days together, possibly the only good ones in their relationship. "There was nothing else to fight over, nothing else to run from," Bill would tell an interviewer twenty-five years later. "It was a wonderful time in my life, and I think in his."[35]

During this time, Clinton became acquainted with James B. McDougal, who had joined Fulbright's staff in April 1968 as a field representative operating out of the senator's Little Rock office. McDougal, then twenty-seven, had an impressive set of Democratic party credentials.

An avid Young Democrat, McDougal had been elected to the Young Democrats State Committee at age seventeen, which had been followed by three two-year terms on the full party's state committee. In 1960, he had led the "youth campaign" for the reelection of Governor Orval E. Faubus, and had followed that in 1964 with a stint in the general election campaign of Lyndon B. Johnson and Hubert Humphrey. McDougal boasted of having managed the Kennedy-Johnson campaign in Arkansas, but that was not true. Dan D. Stephens, a longtime Faubus operative and former Northwest Arkansas prosecuting attorney, managed the Arkansas campaign, although McDougal did work in it.[36] For a five-month period in 1961, he had served as a research assistant for the Senate Permanent Investigations Subcommittee—the "Rackets Committee"—chaired by Arkansas's senior senator, John L. McClellan. He left that post to become an assistant bill clerk in the United States Senate.

McDougal was a minor legend among Arkansas Democrats because he had served as temporary chair of the controversial 1965 state convention of the Young Democrats at which Sam H. Boyce had been elected president over Sheffield Nelson. The assembly had broken into two factions, with each holding its own nominating convention, and McDougal had been involved in determining which of the two conventions was the legitimate one.

McDougal and Clinton, both of whom aspired to elective office, formed a cordial relationship during the Fulbright campaign that would blossom after Clinton entered politics. Eventually, both would attempt, unsuccessfully, to launch their political careers against Republican Representative John Paul Hammerschmidt—Clinton in 1974 and McDougal in 1982. McDougal, however, would prove more skillful at making money than at winning votes—he received about 34 percent of the general election vote against Hammerschmidt—and would concentrate most of his efforts on parlaying the modest return on his various business ventures into a real estate empire under the aegis of the Whitewater Development Company.

Through his work with the Senate Foreign Relations Committee, the Vietnam War, not yet an issue at Georgetown, began to be of great concern to Bill Clinton. He became well versed in Fulbright's pessimistic assessment of the Vietnam War because that was the atmosphere in which he moved. Nearly all of Clinton's friends and colleagues at Georgetown say that until his senior year at the university, the civil rights movement was uppermost in Clinton's thoughts and conversations. But, according to Clinton in his famous December 1969 letter to Colonel Eugene J. Holmes, the commander of the University of Arkansas ROTC program, the war in Vietnam had weighed heavily on his mind for quite some time. In the letter, Clinton admitted to having sought appointment to the Senate Foreign Relations Committee staff "for the opportunity of working every day against a war I opposed and despised with a depth of feeling I had reserved solely for racism in America before Vietnam."[37]

In that same letter, Clinton revealed that he "did not begin to consider" conscription as a separate issue until early 1968, apparently sometime before his graduation that June. "For a law seminar at Georgetown," he stated, "I wrote a paper on the legal arguments for and against allowing, within the Selective Service System, the classification of selective conscientious objection, for those opposed to participation in a particular war, not simply to 'participation in war in any form.'

"From my work I came to believe that the draft system itself is illegitimate. No government really rooted in limited, parliamentary democracy should have the power to make its citizens fight and kill and die in a war they may oppose, a war which even possibly may be wrong, a war which, in any case, does not involve immediately the peace and freedom of the nation."

Kit Ashby, who shared a house with Clinton and three other classmates during their senior year, would say later that their dinner conversations were "the most intellectually stimulating and exciting and educational part" of his Georgetown experience.[38] At the time, Ashby worked for Senator Henry M. "Scoop" Jackson, who was as supportive of America's involvement in Southeast Asia as Fulbright was against it, and Vietnam often supplanted idle dinner-time chatter. When they watched the evening news, they felt plugged into events in a way many of their peers did not.

This feeling was heightened midway through their last year at Georgetown. In January 1968, the Senate Foreign Relations Committee began investigating the Tonkin Gulf incident of August 1964 in which the U.S. Navy reported two armed encounters between North Vietnamese torpedo boats and American destroyers patrolling in the Gulf of Tonkin near Haiphong. The first incident had been real, an assault provoked by American commando raids along the coastline that resulted in the sinking of two North Vietnamese torpedo boats; the second had been bogus, a bad call later found to be the product of skittishness, erroneous radar readings, and misinterpretation of an intercepted North Vietnamese radio communique. Apprised almost immediately of the error, the Johnson administration nonetheless had used the second incident as the basis for launching America's first major air strike on the North Vietnamese capital of Hanoi.

Fulbright, who had been outraged by the two reported attacks and had hastened to support the Tonkin Resolution, a move tantamount to declaring war on North Vietnam, had come to doubt the veracity of the report of the second incident and to suspect that the Johnson administration had distorted intelligence information and withheld vital information from both the general public and Congress. As a member of the committee's staff, Clinton was involved in researching the Tonkin Gulf incidents. And as a draft-age male nearing the end of his undergraduate studies, Clinton's interest in the work of the committee was heightened by the questions raised by the Gulf of Tonkin inquiry. While he would continue to regard Johnson as "a great man," rather than concede the deviousness of the nation's commander-in-chief—even Fulbright publicly accused the Johnson administration of deceit—Clinton merely expressed disappointment that Johnson had let "the Vietnam War and his own paranoid aggression consume him."[39]

The committee inquiry unfolded during a particularly unsettling, often acrimonious period of U.S. foreign involvement. On January 23, the USS *Pueblo* and its eighty-three-man crew were seized by North Koreans in the Sea of Japan, and a number of senators were concerned that, as in the Gulf of Tonkin, the incident might have been provoked. A week later, the Viet Cong and the North Vietnamese launched the Tet offensive, attacking the South Vietnamese capital of Saigon and thirty provincial capitals, resulting in heavy military and civilian casualties, among them the reported massacre of three thousand villagers during the communists' brief occupation of Hue.

While the Gulf of Tonkin debate raged throughout the spring, the war spread across the borders of Laos, Cambodia, and Thailand. History records this period as the point at which American society was ripped apart by anger, fear, confusion, and distrust of its government, and even though the bombing of North Vietnam was curbed in March, when Johnson took himself out of the 1968 presidential race, the upheavals persisted.

Clinton was the only one among the five men who shared the house on Potomac Avenue who did not sign up for the armed forces during that period. He was determined to keep his student deferment, either by entering law school or pursuing postgraduate studies overseas. Quigley and several others whom he admired encouraged him to apply for a Rhodes Scholarship, and Fulbright agreed to recommend him for that honor.

"Bill was concerned about the Vietnam War and what it was doing to the country," Campbell wrote twenty-five years later. "His objection was not that the United States was immoral but that we were making a big mistake. He wondered how a great nation could admit that and change course. He thought America was wasting lives it could not spare. . . . To him, it was a problem of governing. Apart from his personal situation, he was trying to figure out how a government went about changing its mind."[40]

Campbell recalled that Clinton was particularly offended by the notion that a close friend, a graduate of MIT, had been drafted, only to be assigned to "cleaning pistols at an armory in Maryland."[41] This waste of talent was abhorrent to the resident expert on Vietnam, as Clinton apparently had pretensions of being, given the observation he made in a December 1969 letter to Holmes that "there was a time when not many people had more information about Vietnam at hand than I did."[42]

But despite the aura of sophistication that their peripheral proximity to movers and shakers fostered, Clinton and his house mates moved in rather conventional circles. Campbell attributes that to their desire to be "mainstream players" and, in Ashby and Clinton's case, a reluctance to embarrass their high-profile bosses.[43]

Despite his disillusionment with the Johnson administration and his growing distaste for the military's current mission, Clinton apparently took no part in actively protesting the war until after he was graduated in June 1968. Later, after he had secured the coveted Rhodes Scholarship, he was involved in moratorium activities in Washington, D.C., and England.

One of Virginia Kelley's favorite stories concerned their visit to the Georgetown campus for freshman orientation. Following a brief tour, a Jesuit priest sought to get better acquainted with the outgoing, clean-cut, young Southerner, asking him about his personal and educational background. Toward the end of the interview, Virginia said, the priest suddenly exclaimed: "What in the name of the Holy Father is a Southern Baptist who can't speak a foreign language doing in the mother of all Jesuit schools?"

"Don't you worry, Mother," Clinton reportedly assured her afterward. "They will know what I'm doing here when I've been here awhile."[44]

What he was doing, former classmates still marvel, was running for president of the United States, something he might not have been in a position to do if he'd gotten his ass shot off in Vietnam.

4

A PRIVATE WAR

POLITICAL NETWORKING PAID OFF again for Bill Clinton when he decided to apply for a Rhodes Scholarship. A professor had first suggested the possibility as a way to broaden his scholarship and expand his horizons—an opportunity to live and perform graduate study at historic Oxford University for two, possibly three years at no cost to him for tuition, room, and board.

Clinton had been active in politics and various intramural, religious, and civic activities both on and off campus—for awhile, he was a volunteer counselor at a student-run clinic for alcoholics, and although he was not an athlete, he chaired the Student Athletic Commission—and he was eager for more. The prospect of world travel was exciting for the young man from Arkansas, who had visited numerous college campuses in the past year to spur interest in an international conference of the Atlantic Community but had never left the United States. And he particularly wanted a Rhodes Scholarship because one of his idols, J. William Fulbright, had been a Rhodes Scholar in the 1920s. Perhaps the senator would give him a recommendation. The senator would and did.

Clinton's was one of thirty-two scholarships awarded that year to

Americans. Hot Springs was delighted with the success of its adopted son—it had been ten years since any student from the Spa City had been so rewarded—and Virginia added more newspaper clippings to her growing scrapbook. During spring break, Bill sat down for his first in-depth interview with Maurice Moore, a likeable, soft-spoken fellow but a seasoned investigative reporter whose work for the modest, Hot Springs-based Palmer News Bureau required that he pull double-duty as a feature writer. Years later, Moore, now deceased, would recall how impressed he had been by the shaggy-haired young man who spoke so earnestly about life's responsibilities and options on that April day in 1968. It was the duty of American college students to become politically aware and involved, Clinton told Moore, not merely with events at home but with those abroad.

"Students are gathered together in an atmosphere of learning, so they have a great advantage over rank-and-file people in our country," he said. "If we learn the facts, we can gain a healthy outlook on domestic and foreign affairs. I think more involvement is necessary."[1]

Clinton knew well enough what the rank-and-file was capable of. Scarcely three weeks before, he had seen portions of Washington in flames. He, his roommate Tom Campbell, and Carolyn Yeldell, who was spending part of her spring break in Washington, had stood atop Georgetown's Loyola Hall, the best vantage point at that end of campus, and watched the smoke swirl over the district during the riot that erupted following the April 4 assassination of the Luther King, Jr., in Memphis, Tennessee.[2]

Bill and Carolyn had come face-to-face with fury that day while walking through near-empty streets of downtown Washington to deliver foodstuffs and other supplies to a church whose basement was serving as a shelter for those left homeless by the fires. A red cross had been affixed to Clinton's beloved white Buick, and the two had heeded advice to don hats and scarves to disguise their race. It was somber but redeeming work on behalf of the Georgetown University Community Action Program's student relief effort. Then Bill suggested they take a closer look at the areas that had been burned and looted.

"We parked and walked a block or two through smoldering foundations and broken glass," Carolyn Yeldell Staley would recall twenty-four years later. "It was as if Bill wanted to get as close a look as he could at this terrible fragment of our nation's history."[3] They walked in silence mostly, numbed by the destruction, until Carolyn wished aloud that she had brought along a camera. Bill's head snapped around, and he glared, demanding to know why in the name of God she needed a camera to remember this stark scene.

Moments later they rounded a corner and spotted several young black men—at least four, possibly as many as six—walking down the middle of the street in their direction. "We calmly turned around, walked back to our car, and left," Staley said.[4]

After that, the group stayed close to the campus, "not certain," Campbell says, "what was coming next."[5] He and Staley remember the sadness which overtook the outgoing young Clinton that weekend as they watched the drama play out on television. Several times they caught him murmuring snatches of King's famous "I have a dream" speech.

That experience may have been on his mind several weeks later when Clinton was interviewed by Moore. With that and his growing awareness of the unrest spreading across the nation's campuses, and the growth of such radical groups as Students for a Democratic Society, Clinton eschewed militancy, but he was moved to explain the burgeoning activism of issues like Vietnam and civil rights and to defend it in terms an adult could understand.

"I have friends in Washington whom I suppose would be classified as hippies or members of the off-beat generation," said the clean-cut Clinton. "There has been, I think, in the hippie movement in this country a good deal of rather unhealthy negativism. There are many hippies I know who are highly ethical. They see a lot of contradictions in our society, and they can't find the answers. I have no quarrel with them. If they find self-expression in being hippies, then I think they have every right to act the way they feel. I don't think they are unhealthy for our society."[6]

But theirs was not his world, he made it clear. While he was undecided on his destination, his future course was to complete his studies at Oxford and either pursue a doctorate or enter law school. He had no plans to enter the foreign service: "I pursued studies in international affairs because I believe they are so vital to America's political life, and I am interested in domestic politics—electioneering, or some phase of it."[7]

King's death and the subsequent assassination of Robert F. Kennedy just four days before Clinton received his bachelor of arts degree in international studies "had a profound effect on Clinton," Tom Campbell would remember, teaching him that the self-sacrifice demanded to attain power and greatness could be as horrible as it was fulfilling.[8]

Altogether, 1968 was one of the most tumultuous years, as well as one of the most political ones, in modern American history. Powerful men were felled, both by bullets and by ballots, careers imploded, hippies gave way to Yippies. In Chicago, the Democratic National Convention, in one historian's words, "dissolved into near-chaos."

Back home after graduation, Clinton followed the presidential race. He was an avid supporter of Senator Eugene McCarthy of Minnesota and watched the 1968 Democratic convention from his mother's home. Clinton was active in state politics, supporting Senator Fulbright's reelection effort against Jim Johnson, who was also the state campaign coordinator of third-party candidate George Wallace. Clinton took no small amount of pleasure in serving occasionally as the senator's driver. The familiarity he enjoyed with his former boss was not appreciated by some of his co-workers in the campaign, however; in later years, they would recall him as a person "highly impressed with his own self-importance."

Clinton's old friend from Georgetown, Tom Campbell, later recalled that while on a visit to Arkansas that summer, he attended one of the election season's countless political rallies at which Clinton confronted Johnson in a receiving line. "You make me ashamed to be from Arkansas," Campbell heard Clinton tell Johnson. Ever the Southern gentleman, Johnson politely replied that if the young fellow really felt that way, he ought to put his thoughts into letter form and mail them to him. "It made an impression on Bill," Campbell would later recall, "and I think he learned something from a person he couldn't abide: How to handle criticism and to avoid confrontation."[9] If he ever did learn that lesson, he suffered from periodic bouts of amnesia, as his record in elective office would attest.

In October 1968, Clinton headed for England aboard the USS *United States*, where he began getting acquainted with the thirty-one other Oxford-bound collegians before the ship left its Manhattan berth. Tom Williamson was leaning over the railing, waving goodbye to his girlfriend at dockside, when Clinton walked over and introduced himself. "I was wary at first" of the young Southerner, said Williamson, who is black, "but he won me over."[10]

By all accounts, the young Arkansan was a charmer of the first order, kind, outgoing, and inquisitive about everyone with whom he came in contact. (One of his Oxford colleagues, Arkansas lawyer Cliff Jackson, said that Clinton claimed to have "invented networking before the term ever surfaced.")[11]

"I remember from the first moment we met how interested he was in talking with people and how much he enjoyed it," said Stephen Oxman. "He displayed an unusual ability to engage people from many different backgrounds in friendly, substantive conversation."[12]

"He was all big smiles and easy conversation," recalled James Crawford. "He was the glue to the party and the first one we got to know on the boat."[13]

Robert B. Reich later recalled spending the six-day voyage in his cabin, flat on his back between violent bouts of seasickness. "Bill knocked on my door twice a day to see how I was doing and bring me refreshments," he said.[14]

Clinton was conversant in a number of areas, notably music and politics, but he had neglected to do his homework in one regard. Darryl Gless, another student, remembered how awed Clinton was when, upon arriving at Southampton, one of the first people he noticed at dockside was a very proper Englishman whose natty attire included a bowler hat and an umbrella.

"Bill thought he was an entertainer in period costume," said Gless. "It was Edgar Williams, the warden of Rhodes House, who had come to meet us."[15]

Clinton threw himself into the Oxford experience like the seasoned politician he would become. He was twenty-two, a *bona fide* member of an elite, cosmopolitan class of postgraduate students brought together at one of the oldest universities in the world. He was enrolled in the oldest of Oxford's self-governing colleges, University College, commonly known as "Univ."

"Univ" is also noted as a bastion of leftist thinking. Two of its graduates, Clement Attlee and Harold Wilson, became Labour prime ministers. In Clinton's time, its most famous alumnus—some might say infamous, as he was "sent down" (expelled) in 1810 for collaborating on the tract entitled "The Necessity of Atheism"—was the poet Percy Bysshe Shelley, whose transgressions were eventually forgiven. Since the late nineteenth century, he has been memorialized on the grounds by a domed building housing a lifelike white marble statue. (Local guidebooks now boast of a new "most famous son" of Univ: Bill Clinton, president of the United States.)

In 1968, University College and its environs were literally a world and many ages removed from anything Clinton had known. A mixture of industry and academia and English market town, Oxford was vital yet comfortable. One could sit for hours nursing a pint of tepid bitter or a lager-and-lime at any of a number of thirteenth-century pubs dripping with romance and history. The numerous coffee houses, art galleries, museums, monuments, libraries, and assorted historic structures representing practically every style since the time of the Saxons provided the intellectually hungry Clinton with a veritable feast of culture. And should anyone require a drastic change of pace, London, which in 1968 was still swinging, was scarcely an hour away by motorcar. Hitch-hiking was standard practice, and if that failed, the railway station was within easy access.

"The first two weeks I was there I bet I walked fourteen hours a day," Clinton has said. "I visited all the colleges, went in all the churches, walked through all the parks."[16]

Unlike Georgetown, Oxford was a bubbling cauldron of student unrest. According to British journalist David Millward, Oxford at that time was "punctuated by demonstrations and skirmishes between students and the Bulldogs, bowler-hatted porters responsible for enforcing discipline. If the students were not trying to storm the Sheldonian, the symbol of the university establishment, many appear to have spent their time trying to smuggle lovers into college or enjoying the occasional illicit cannabis joint."[17]

Initially enrolled in multidisciplinary course work known as PPE— politics, philosophy, and economics—Clinton eventually "let his hair down both literally and metaphorically," a former classmate told the *Daily Telegraph* in 1992.[18] Americans at Oxford were far from the top of the collegiate social register. The Vietnam War made Americans *personae non grata* in many quarters. Growing their hair and beards was one way Americans tried to fit in. Clinton adapted. His style of dress also evolved from the decidedly preppie look of button-down shirts and sports jackets to mock-hippie—one friend recalls that he donned a pink poplin suit for a lecture by feminist Germaine Greer. His bedroom and study in a small row of converted almshouses known as Helens Court, located behind the college, became what has been described by the *Sunday Times* of London as "a modest salon for impromptu sherry parties, where the young expatriate would pour forth his views on Vietnam, race, and the Cold War."[19]

Clinton, recalled fellow Rhodes Scholar Alan Bersin, "ate, drank, breathed, and talked public policy."[20]

"It was a heady time," said Wilf Stevenson, another Oxonian who now heads the British Film Institute. "Students were looking inward to the antiquated world of Oxford and outward to the wider world of student revolution and the Vietnam War."[21]

Clinton showed a keen interest in nineteenth-century British diplomatic history, particularly the careers of Palmerston and Disraeli, and his instructors recall that he did well in the areas of Soviet and Eastern European affairs. While he did not distinguish himself, he was an articulate participant in class discussions. Zbigniew Pelczynski, a tutor at Pembroke College who taught him during his first two terms, said he used one of Clinton's essays as a model.

"He was a very good student, receptive and intelligent," Pelczynski told the *London Sunday Times*. "He was better in argument than on paper. His essay technique was not perhaps the best that I have seen, but he was obviously an avid reader."[22]

Clinton made frequent raids on the university's libraries—he claims to have read more than three hundred books during his first year—

checking out several demanding volumes each visit. Some were required reading, others were volitional. Clinton studied the works of
Locke, Hobbes, and Rousseau, and augmented his practical knowledge of American government with such works as *Presidential Leadership: The Political Relations of Congress and the Chief Executive* and *The
Structure of American Federalism.* He was also an avid reader of the works
of Dylan Thomas and American novels in general.[23]

Reportedly, one of his favorite books during that period was Lord
Blake's *Disraeli,* a favorite of Nixon! "I remember his [Clinton's] face
buried in that book," an unidentified friend told the *London Times.*
Another friend told the *Times* that Clinton was so obsessed by the
Vietnam War while at Oxford that he studied nineteenth-century
British diplomatic history for parallels. "It was his first real chance to
study that area," the friend said, "and he made full use of Oxford's
facilities. He was interested in looking through a historical prism to see
what happens when countries overstretch themselves."[24]

But despite all this reading, Clinton was known to be lackadaisical
about his studies, often skipping class lectures. According to Sir Edgar
Williams, the Rhodes House warden whose manner of dress had so
amused Clinton, this behavior was not unusual: "Many of the more
old-fashioned American Rhodes scholars tended to regard their time
here as their version of the 'Grand Tour.' They already had a degree
back home and were planning to go to Harvard or Yale Law School."[25]

Clinton was far more interested in holding court at his flat or his
favorite pub—"He was wordy, garrulous even, personable, outgoing,
[and] he knew how to enjoy himself," said another friend, Christopher
Laidlaw—and in making frequent weekend excursions to the countryside or to London.[26] Not all of Clinton's acquaintances, however,
succumbed to his charm, believing that it was superficial. "It was the
eyes that gave it away," Philip Hodson later told the *Sunday Times* of
London. "They moved on before he had finished talking to you."[27]

Like other young men, Clinton spent a great deal of time "chatting
up" female students who generally were not impressed by Rhodes
Scholars, particularly one who was, in the words of one female contemporary, "plumpish and ill-kempt—not a ladies's man."[28]

Classmate Michael Shea recalled that Clinton found it difficult to adjust to the dearth of women at the male-dominated university, whose colleges were not coeducational. "We talked a lot about women, and I remember Bill did better than most," Shea said. "He started dating and going out and having relationships."[29]

One of those relationships was with Sara Maitland, now an English feminist and novelist, who briefly shared an apartment with Clinton and several other students.

"A lot of Rhodes scholars had a hard time at Oxford because of a shortage of females," Maitland later said. "Bill liked female company and found the boys's world that was Oxford more difficult than men who had come from public [private] schools. We became such good friends; it wasn't just S-E-X."[30]

Maitland attributes her "politicization" to Clinton and his views on the Vietnam War.

"I remember sitting with him and his best friend, Frank [Aller], in a pub in Walton Street when they talked about napalming," she told the *Evening Standard* in 1993. "I started to cry, and Frank said, 'That's the only correct response,' and Bill said, 'No, it's not. If something makes you cry, you have to do something about it. That's the difference between politics and guilt.' "[31]

If Clinton did not actually adopt the philosophies of his more radical associates, he at least adopted their uniform: long hair, a scraggly beard, and granny glasses.

Mack McLarty recalls seeing his old friend during one of Clinton's occasional visits home. McLarty, by then married and "started [on] my adult life," said that Clinton "was still in the 'academic' mode" when he and an English girlfriend dropped by the Hot Springs Convention Center in hopes of catching McLarty during a break in an automobile sales meeting. McLarty had just entered the family business, a thriving Ford dealership.[32]

McLarty chuckles when he recalls the reaction Clinton's appearance elicited among the one hundred or so salesmen who filed by as McLarty in his suit and tie and Clinton in his best hippie attire sat talking.

Clinton "had that beard, and, you know, he was still in student mode, and of course all our salesmen were pretty much deer hunters and thought Faubus probably should be still governor and so forth . . . and here I'm visiting with this kind of disheveled-looking guy, and there's this [female] companion from England—I mean," McLarty broke into laughter, "it was not quite the reassuring image" that McLarty had hoped to project to his business associates. He said each salesmen who walked reacted visibly to McLarty's friendly attitude toward these anti-establishment types as though to say, "I'm not sure I want to be working for this guy. He looks like he's a little bit up in the clouds, over there talking to this Sputnik type."[33]

Afterward, McLarty's father, also present that day, observed of Clinton, "He's such a bright guy. I just hope he gets everything straightened up here," hastening for his son's benefit to add, "And I think he will."[34]

Clinton biographer Robert E. Levin has written that "by the standards of the counterculture of 1968," Clinton was "a pro-establishment moderate," and many of his Oxford colleagues concur. One who does not is Cliff Jackson, who was befriended by Clinton while attending nearby St. John's College on a Fulbright scholarship.

In an interview, Jackson, now a successful lawyer in Little Rock, recalled that their first encounter came when Clinton, upon learning that another Arkansan was on campus, dropped by Jackson's room. Subsequently, they were thrown together on numerous occasions; they dated two American girls who lived in the same house, and Jackson said that both men played basketball on one of the Oxford teams. Neither had ever formally played before—Clinton's mother had banned sports for Bill—and, as Jackson recalls, neither was very good at it, but they enjoyed the camaraderie of team sports and the frequent visits to other university campuses.[35]

Clinton also tried his hand at rugby, at which, as a second-row forward, he distinguished himself as a clumsy but fervent player who often tackled opponents who were not carrying the ball.

"He had an appetite for the game and he was an excellent member of the team, always enthusiastic, always good fun, so it didn't matter about his skills," said Chris McCooey, secretary-captain of the University College 2nd XV during the two years Clinton was at Oxford. McCooey also recalled that Clinton was "fairly unfit and not at all athletic—too lumpy for that."[36]

Jackson shared Clinton's interest in politics, which they often discussed while walking between their residences and the gymnasium. The fact that Clinton was a solid Democrat and Jackson a hard-core Republican made for some interesting discussions, although Jackson said that ideology played a minor part in the conversations. Clinton often picked Jackson's brain about various student leaders at Arkansas College, where Jackson had served as student body president. Jackson remembers that Clinton was keenly interested in who among Jackson's peers "might be an up-and-coming political star."[37] In this respect, Clinton's childhood chum, Mack McLarty, was discussed on several occasions. Jackson said he was somewhat amused by the line of questioning, which he viewed as assessing the competition to determine who at some future date might pose a threat to Clinton's political plans.

"He never mentioned [seeking] any particular political office," Jackson said, "but there was never any doubt in my mind that he would run for office and that he basically eyed the presidency."[38]

As well as Jackson could tell, the Georgetown graduate had no strong philosophical or political beliefs. "I never had any sense that he had an abiding, deeply entrenched conviction. On the contrary, my sense was that he did not." Jackson insists that others in their circle agreed. One of them, a Marshall Scholar whom he described as "a long-haired hippie type" who had been active in Students for a Democratic Society, used to reproach Clinton for paying only lip service to the antiwar movement.

The activists on campus, Jackson said, were disgusted that Clinton "professed to be antiwar, yet he would not stand up for his professed principles.[39] They wanted him to be more activist." It seemed the trendy thing to do, although Sir Edgar Williams later opined that "most student protests were rather secondhand imitations of what was happening on the Continent. Those who were student politicians in the U.S. weren't excited about what was happening here."[40]

Clinton either avoided or escaped association with the violent Revolutionary Socialist Students organization, which spearheaded many tumultuous protests in the late 1960s. In 1969, however, he did attend meetings of Group 68, a band of Americans backed by the pro-

Soviet British Peace Council and once described by Tariq Ali, a
biographer and former radical student leader, as the "soft wing" of the
hard-line antiwar coalition.[41]

Jackson, who played a key role in the effort to undermine Clinton's
presidential candidacy in 1992 by releasing information about Clinton's attempts to evade the draft, claims that no one was more surprised
than he that Clinton later became involved in organizing antiwar
demonstrations in London, because "that is *not* the Bill Clinton I
knew." Clinton, he said, was perceived as "a hypocrite, a fake, and a
phony, because he wouldn't stand up for his convictions," and he
"caught all kinds of flak from what we perceived as the extremist
element."[42]

Others do not share Jackson's assessment. They remember Clinton
as a young man of social conscience, sensitivity, and intellectual pro-
bity, one who believed his country and its constitution—to a point.

"He thought you should fight for your country," said a former
English girlfriend, Tamara Eccles-Williams, "but he didn't believe in
what was going on in Vietnam."[43]

According to another former girlfriend, Katherine Gieve, now a
lawyer in London, "Politics, as taught in Oxford then, was about ideas.
It was very distant from actual experience. But Bill was thinking about
people. He made a relationship between abstract ideas and the meaning of people's experiences. That was true for all of the Americans at
Oxford then. Because of the Vietnam War, demands were being made
by the state that were crucial to the way they lived their own ideas. . . .
My abiding impression of Bill is that he was a softie. He wasn't afraid of
expressing his feelings."[44]

To Tom Williamson he expressed his feelings about the civil rights
movement.

To Sara Maitland he expressed his feelings about feminism.

To Mandy Merck, a noted feminist and academic who says that he
was the first man to whom she admitted her homosexuality, he expressed his feelings about gay rights.

To Frank Aller he expressed his feelings about the Vietnam War.

Indeed, said Cliff Jackson, to whom he expressed his feelings about
politics in general, Clinton was so self-absorbed and bent on dominat-

ing conversations that others had difficulty getting a word in edgewise. "He was always holding forth," Jackson said, "not only expressing an opinion on the topic [of discussion] but to a large extent seeking to dominate the conversation."[45]

David Singer remembers Clinton as being "very politically ambitious and active. Nobody was ever in any doubt that he would do anything other than go for elected office, aiming to be president. Within forty-five minutes of meeting him I knew he would run for president."[46]

Jackson does not dispute that Clinton was ambitious, but he attributes it to "a consuming, burning desire to obtain power. I don't think that what he did with it was the objective. I think it was the obtaining of it."[47]

It was, perhaps, natural that as fellow Arkansans Clinton and Jackson would gravitate toward one another, but if they were ever friends in the literal sense, it appears to have been a transient bond born of proximity and circumstance. Certainly, Jackson was there for Clinton when he sought to postpone his date with the Selective Service System, just as Clinton was there for Jackson when he sought a White House fellowship. But during the eight or nine months they were acquainted at Oxford, and over the course of the subsequent weaning period in which they exchanged an occasional letter, Jackson came to look upon Clinton in the harshest of terms—a manipulator, a user, and an opportunist of the highest order.

If, for example, Clinton offended someone or someone was slow to warm to him, he would go out of his way to be charming or contrite or sympathetic toward that person, Jackson claimed.

"He's not trying to win [an adversary] over because he needs to be loved," Jackson opined, "but because he enjoys the conquest. He enjoys bending people to his will."[48]

In all their political discussions, Jackson said, "I had no perception that he had an agenda. I think it's power for the sake of power. He derives great pleasure out of the process of reaching for power . . . and of the exploitation and manipulation of people in attaining it. . . . It's an absolute drive to power that is unmatched in current politics."

Jackson's insights on Clinton are partially drawn from observing

Clinton's governance in Arkansas and his performance during the 1992 presidential campaign, but they are framed by several incidents during their student days at Oxford.

"One incident stands out very clearly in my mind," Jackson recalled. "It was one of those stereotypical cold, foggy English nights, and we were coming back from the gym. We were talking about politics. Bill recounted a story which he told to be true. He had heard a Fulbright staff member telling about a White House secretary walking into the Oval Office [at the height of the student protests against the Vietnam War] to find Lyndon [Johnson] and a certain attractive young woman who was one of the leaders in the antiwar movement engaged in sex on the Oval Office floor. She was on top [of President Johnson], and she had a peace symbol on a chain dangling between her breasts."

Jackson recalled the look of amusement on Clinton's face as the anecdote unfolded. "Sure, it's a funny little story, and we can all laugh," Jackson said, "but the impression I got was that Bill thought that it was so neat that Lyndon Johnson could get away with something like that. It was just his reaction to it that made it stand out in my mind. It was like—it's just the power, the idea that Lyndon had the audacity to do something like that right in the Oval Office at the height of the war. It was something above and beyond locker-room snickering. More like 'how slick, how neat that Lyndon could get away with this.' "

The story must have been a favorite of Clinton's. He mentioned it again, with a different twist, in a letter to Jackson written on Yale Law School stationery, dated Wednesday, November 17, 1970. "About the White House Fellowships," Clinton wrote in part. "The best story I know on them is that virtually the only non-conservative who ever got one was a quasi-radical woman who wound up in the White House sleeping with LBJ, who made her wear a peace symbol around her waist whenever they made love. You may go far, Cliff; I doubt you will ever go that far!" It was signed "Bill."[49]

Among other incidents that raised questions in Jackson's mind about Clinton's character pertained to his treatment of women with whom he was involved, including one to whom he was allegedly engaged while living with Hillary Rodham in Fayetteville, Arkansas. Like many young men in his situation, he pursued several relationships at

Oxford while keeping the home fires burning through love letters to a girl back home. His steady, Sharon Evans, a beauty queen who went on to become Miss Arkansas, was at that time professed to be the love of Clinton's life, the woman he wanted to marry and have babies with, yet his attitude was one of "she's there and I'm here, so I might as well have a good time," Jackson said.[50]

One of the women with whom he had a good time during his romance with Evans was Tamara Eccles-Williams, whom he affectionately called Mara. She remembers him as "very cuddly," fun-loving, and usually hard up for cash. "He never had much money," she told a reporter in 1992, "but he was a very easygoing and a very caring person."[51]

Their romance apparently was in full swing during Sharon Evans's visit to England in March 1969, because Eccles-Williams claims that her relationship with him did not end until he returned home at the end of his first year at Oxford.

During Evans's visit, Clinton attended his first English antiwar demonstration.

"We were down at Trafalgar Square for a Sunday afternoon," Evans recounted. "I said, 'Y'all, I want to go, I've never been to a demonstration.' So Bill said, 'Gosh, I'll go too.' "[52]

An estimated 12,000 demonstrators marched on the American Embassy, and violence erupted, as it had the month before. Apparently Clinton was a mere onlooker on that occasion; he would take no active role in antiwar protest until the autumn of 1969, after he received his second and final draft notice.

The notification came in April 1969, a month in which the death toll in Vietnam reached 33,641—exceeding the Korean War record. Any anxiety that milestone might have caused Clinton surely was exacerbated when he received a letter from Draft Board No. 26 in Hot Springs, Arkansas, ordering him to return to America for military service.

The definitive chapter in Jackson's relationship with Clinton has to do with the draft, which neither young man was anxious to face. "It was on April 22, a Tuesday," Jackson said, referring to the 1969 calendar on which he recorded both important events and trivia of the time. "He came to my room and said he had got his draft induction notice."[53]

Fortunately, the letter arrived late, and with the help of family back home, Clinton obtained a postponement until July 28. In the ensuing days, Jackson and Clinton talked at length about Clinton's predicament. Clinton had been classified I-A (available for military service) for more than a year. The II-S student deferment he had obtained upon entering Georgetown, and which his draft board had extended three times, had long since expired, and the United States government had stopped granting deferments to graduate students in late 1967.

Thanks to the intercessions of his uncle, Raymond Clinton, and the office of Senator J. William Fulbright, the Hot Springs draft board had consistently passed over Bill Clinton's file to facilitate his stay at Oxford, but on February 3, 1969, he had been summoned to London to report for his Armed Forces Physical Examination. He had passed it. Unless he could devise another gambit, and soon, he was boot-camp bound.

Among the "best and brightest," Jackson said, "any angle to avoid the draft was being looked at."[54] Clinton was no exception. Jackson said he had no problem with helping Clinton scheme to avoid induction because he was convinced that Clinton was opposed to the war, not the military.

"That was a very unpopular war," Jackson said. "I was not out protesting, but I was not supportive of it. Nobody with any sense was."

A young man presented with a draft notice in early 1969 had several options for avoiding induction or active duty: he could refuse induction, he could leave or remain outside the borders of the United States, he could obtain a postponement, or he could obtain a cancellation of the induction notice. The way the two Oxford men figured it, Clinton may have had several options, but there was only one real choice: He had to get the notice canceled.[55]

Local draft boards had limited authority to cancel or postpone a draft notice, but two people were empowered to cancel one for virtually any reason: the state Selective Service director and the national Selective Service director. Clinton had some good contacts within the Democratic party, and Jackson had some good ones within the GOP. Jackson was acquainted with Willard A. "Lefty" Hawkins, director of the Selective Service System in Arkansas. But better still, the executive director of the state Republican party, Van Rush, was a very close friend of Hawkins—and Jackson was going home in June to work for Rush as the state GOP's research director.

Clinton asked Jackson whether he thought he could be of some help. Jackson said he thought he could.[56]

5

MOBILIZING AGAINST
THE DRAFT

WHILE HUNDREDS OF YOUNG AMERICAN MEN avoided military service in Vietnam by extraordinary means—defecting to Canada or Sweden, maiming themselves, ruining their health with pills or diets, or other extreme measures—Clinton followed a more common route, albeit one open only to an elite few. Rather than joining the Reserves or the National Guard, he used every ounce of political pull he could muster to avoid any type of military affiliation.

As far back as 1978, when first confronted directly with the allegations of draft-dodging, Clinton denied not only that he had been active in the antiwar movement but that he had led protest demonstrations against American involvement in Vietnam.[1] Years later, he would claim never to have protested actively within the United States. He lied. He not only maneuvered to avoid military service, which included securing an ROTC deferment after having received and skirted an induction notice, but he was a volunteer for the Vietnam Moratorium Committee that organized the October and November 1969 activities in America and Europe.

Although he was questioning the war as early as 1964, by all accounts, he became actively involved in antiwar activity only following the Tet Offensive in January 1968.

Previous biographers have noted that Clinton was concerned about the war and had a difficult time applying himself to his studies at Oxford's University College because of it but that he did not actively engage in protest. They make these claims in the face of overwhelming evidence to the contrary, the most significant of which is the testimony, in a published book and in subsequent interviews, of Father Richard T. McSorley, director of the Center for Peace Studies at Georgetown University.

Clinton was often handled with kid gloves by the reporters who followed his 1992 campaign. When the first hints of controversy surfaced, members of the national media hesitated to hit Clinton with the hard questions. Among the numerous questions that reporters failed to ask about Clinton's experiences as a scholarship student in England were these: What was the extent of his involvement in the planning and execution of anti-American demonstrations in 1969; and how did he manage to finance an extended tour through Europe that took him to several Eastern Bloc countries and the Soviet Union during the 1969–70 Christmas holidays at Oxford University?

As a now infamous 1969 letter to the director of the Reserve Officers Training Corps at the University of Arkansas revealed, Clinton began speaking out against the war while an undergraduate at Georgetown and continued those activities while a student at University College at Oxford.

His first vital involvement in antiwar activity came shortly after graduation, when he became involved with a group of predominantly upper-class young activists who created the Vietnam Moratorium Committee. This group helped organize college students in scores of American cities and abroad to protest the war in October and November 1969.

According to David Mixner, a founder of the Vietnam Moratorium Committee who later would advise the Clinton presidential campaign on issues and policies pertaining to gay rights, he and Clinton were two of about forty "young leaders" who attended a weekend retreat in the summer of 1969 at swanky Martha's Vineyard "to explore ways that we could continue the important work started in the campaigns" of presidential hopefuls Robert F. Kennedy and Eugene McCarthy.[2] Mixner was the kind of activist Clinton could admire, if not emulate. At twenty-three, he had spent several months on crutches as a result of having been thrown through a plate-glass window by police during rioting at the 1968 Democratic National Convention in Chicago, and later had suffered a heart attack.[3]

Actually, the Martha's Vineyard group, and later the Vietnam Moratorium Committee, was top-heavy with supporters from the McCarthy campaign, including Mixner, the son of a Teamster whose specialty was rallying labor support. He had also organized caucuses in non-primary states in support of McCarthy. Two of the other co-founders of the Vietnam Moratorium Committee held key positions in the campaign: Sam Brown, a former divinity student whose father ran a chain of Midwestern shoe stores, was chief coordinator of the McCarthy campaign; and David Hawk, another former divinity student who was awaiting trial on a charge of resisting the draft, had worked for McCarthy in New Hampshire. The fourth co-founder was Marge Sklencar, the daughter of a research chemist who, while a student at Mundelein College in Chicago, had served as president of the campus chapter of Students for a Democratic Society. Among the group's advisors was the Reverend Joseph P. Duffey, chairman of Americans for Democratic Action, in whose congressional campaign Clinton would work the next year and who would become the Clinton administration's director of the U.S. Information Agency.

The VMC's *raison d'être* was to create a massive political movement to force the nation out of Vietnam. Most of its work had to do with undermining the American war effort in Southeast Asia through mass demonstrations, which encompassed everything from holding hands and singing to burning President Richard Nixon in effigy.

After their heady, heavy intellectual weekend, Mixner said, Clinton "volunteered his time and efforts" to organizing Vietnam Moratorium Committee-sponsored protests first in America and later in England.[4]

Sam Brown apparently was the prime force behind the creation of the Vietnam Moratorium Committee. He was the chief recruiter, the chief fundraiser, and, when its existence was announced in the summer of 1969, the chief spokesman. Clinton was an early volunteer in the organization's headquarters on Vermont Avenue, just four blocks from the White House.

The VMC had been formed with the idea of promoting nationwide work stoppages of short duration in protest of the war. The surprising success of the first such protest, aimed at college campuses and surrounding communities, on October 15, 1969, persuaded the committee's founders to undertake an even larger show of force, and they officially signed on with the more radical New Mobilization Committee to End the War in Vietnam.

"New Mobe" took up where the original Mobilization Committee to End the War in Vietnam had left off when its founder, noted pacifist and former Trotskyite A. J. Muste, died in 1967 shortly after having led a civilian "peace" mission to Hanoi. After leadership passed to former seminarian David Dellinger, the group became increasingly aggressive, leading stormy demonstrations in New York City in April 1967, the march on the Pentagon the following autumn, and the Chicago 1968 demonstrations. When the Vietnam Moratorium Committee and New Mobe announced their affiliation on October 21, 1969, Dellinger was unable to attend: He was standing trial as one of the "Chicago Seven" in Chicago on a charge of conspiring to start a riot at the Democratic National Convention.[5]

The Mobe was renamed and retooled after some members decided in early 1969 that the radical, often violent measures undertaken under Dellinger's leadership had alienated much of the public whose support it sought to attract.

New Mobe, according to Stewart Meacham, a former Presbyterian minister and Quaker who served on the executive committee, was "a broad coalition of individuals connected with some sixty organizations," among them the American Communist party, the Episcopal Peace Fellowship, the Socialist Workers' party, the National Council of Churches, the United Methodist Church, the New Democratic Coalition, and District 65 of the AFL-CIO Retail, Wholesale, and Department Store Workers's Union.[6]

According to Meacham, "the only two principles at work in the composition of the Mobe are, one, the principle of nonviolence, [and] two, the principle of nonexclusion, which we believe essential to a rich, free society."

New Mobe's organization of the November protests was well under way when affiliation with the VMC was announced at back-to-back news conferences at Washington's Ambassador Hotel. In a prepared statement, Brown unveiled the moratorium committee's contribution to the events of November 13 and 14: "educational" programs, organization of community referendums and resolutions calling for an immediate cease-fire and withdrawal of all troops from Vietnam, and symbolic activities like convening memorial services; wearing black arm bands, at which the names of American war casualties were read.[7]

On November 15, the two groups would join with the fledgling Student Mobilization Committee to End the War in Vietnam to lead the somber "March of Death" on Washington, which they hoped would be joined by several hundred thousand people, some of whose travel expenses would be supplemented by New Mobe and the VMC.

The Washington demonstrations, touted in the news media as a singular event, would be joined by similar activities planned for the same weekend in university towns and cities across America and Europe.

Bill Clinton claims to have been the coalition's man in London, although colleagues indicate that he was only a lieutenant in the effort. The major force behind the London protests of October and November was a twenty-five-year-old Pakistani named Tariq Ali, a graduate of Exeter College, Oxford, and part-time journalist who had been dubbed "the guru of protest."[8] Ali was one of the leaders of the so-called October 27th Ad Hoc Committee, the umbrella for numerous left-wing student groups, including the Vietnam Solidarity Committee, the Young Communist League, the International Marxist Group, the Radical Student Alliance, and the London May Day Manifesto Committee.

Some who knew Clinton during these tempestuous times say he was mainly terrified of being drafted, yet equally concerned about how his decision to evade military service would affect his political ambitions. Thus it was with great relief that he learned that in all probability he would be spared the draft. That relief had been a long time coming.

According to friends at Oxford, Clinton returned to Hot Springs, Arkansas, on July 3, 1969, having made no living arrangements for the second year of study under his Rhodes scholarship because he expected to be drafted.[9] But he underestimated the efforts of a great many people busy lobbying in his behalf.

When Cliff Jackson returned home in late May, one of his top priorities was to arrange a meeting between his friend Bill Clinton and Lefty Hawkins, the Republican appointee who headed the Selective Service System in Arkansas. Clinton, who was not scheduled to return until early July, had asked that his mother be included in the meeting, so Jackson had at least one telephone conversation with Virginia Dwire.[10]

"I had reservations about doing what I was doing," Jackson said years later. "I was pulling strings. . . . I thought at the time that he was more qualified to serve as an officer than as a draftee. It was preferential treatment [that was being sought], and it wasn't right, but we justified it because he was willing to serve his country as an officer."[11]

Among those he asked for help was Van Rush, his boss at the state Republican party headquarters. He told Rush that a couple of his friends "had a draft problem," and asked Rush to contact Hawkins about meeting with them to work it out. Rush agreed to do so.

Nothing had been resolved by the time Clinton reached home, and he was growing more agitated with each passing day. He had bought a year of grace to attend Oxford thanks to his uncle Raymond Clinton's involvement with the Naval League, an elite contingent of navy veterans from the Hot Springs area whose members included at least one member of the local draft board. And he had wangled a postponement of induction back in the spring when the first notice arrived at his Oxford residence after the reporting date—draft officials had sent it surface mail, which took an average of eleven days, rather than air mail. But now his second date with Uncle Sam, July 28, was fast approaching. As Jackson noted in a letter to a friend dated July 11, 1969, Clinton was "feverishly trying to find a way to avoid entering the Army as a drafted private."[12]

Clinton was I-A, healthy by United States army standards, and the only avenue open was the Army ROTC program at the University of Arkansas at Fayetteville. But even that was iffy, because the roster was full and enrollment for the fall semester had been closed.

Neither Clinton nor his mother ever publicly discussed the details of his maneuvering that summer, but Clinton kept Jackson apprised of much that was going on. According to Jackson, when mother and son met with Hawkins, Clinton agreed, in exchange for a canceled draft notice, to "serve his country in another capacity later on."[13] Then Clinton made the arduous journey to Fayetteville by car, about 250 miles each way, to meet with Colonel Eugene J. Holmes, who was in charge of the University of Arkansas Army ROTC program.

Clinton explained to Holmes that he intended to enroll in the University of Arkansas Law School and very much wanted to participate in the ROTC program, which was good for an additional four-year deferment but would require him to sign up for a six-year hitch in the army upon graduation.[14]

On August 7, because of the weight of his commitment to Holmes to enter the Army ROTC program at the start of the spring 1970 semester—Jackson says Clinton actually signed a letter of intent and gave a pledge to enter the university law school—Clinton's local draft board granted Hot Springs's esteemed Rhodes Scholar a new student deferment, I-D, the classification reserved for members of reserve components or students taking military training. It was stretching the rules—Clinton was not scheduled to begin his ROTC stint for another five or six months—but the draft board members had done that so many times before by passing over his "jacket" that once more did not seem to matter.

During the 1992 presidential campaign, Clinton would concede that sometime in the autumn of 1969—he did not give a date and since has declined to elaborate—he changed his mind about participating in ROTC and asked Draft Board 26 to change his status back to I-A. On October 30, the board complied. By then, Clinton was happily back at University College and neck-deep in anti-Vietnam protest activities.

Having no rooms of his own, Clinton initially slept on the floor of another Rhodes Scholar's apartment.[15] Presumably, he slept quite well, because despite claims during the 1992 presidential campaign that he voluntarily submitted himself to the draft, he could not have failed to know in October 1969 that his chances of induction were virtually nil.

There had been talk in Washington of contingency plans to withdraw troops from Vietnam since the spring, and in May President Richard M. Nixon had asked Congress to revise the existing draft laws drastically by imposing a lottery system wherein the youngest draftable group, nineteen-year-olds, would be the first selected. At the time able-bodied men between the ages of nineteen and twenty-six were subject to the draft.[16]

When Nixon unveiled his proposal, the *Wall Street Journal* pointed out that "many college men now join the Reserve Officer Training Corps programs largely to avoid the draft because they're eligible for induction until age 26" and that "some experts have feared a revision removing such long uncertainty might cause a major drop in ROTC enrollments."[17]

The debate in Congress was not conducted under a cloak of secrecy, and in general draft-age men kept abreast of the lottery issue. On June 8, Nixon and South Vietnamese President Nguyen Van Thieu announced the impending withdrawal of 25,000 American troops from South Vietnam.[18] By mid-June, Nixon was sending out strong signals that all American combat troops might be withdrawn before the end of 1970,[19] and optimism rose in July when well-placed leaks from the White House suggested that a continued lull in fighting could result in even greater troop withdrawals in the coming weeks.[20]

In September, Nixon announced that draft calls would be curtailed for the rest of the year.[21] Days before Clinton's I-A classification was officially restored, the president announced that draft-eligible students could finish the academic year before facing induction. Clinton notified officials at Fayetteville that he would not be entering their law school.

Strobe Talbott, a fellow Rhodes Scholar who also was active in the student antiwar movement, has said that Clinton broke his ROTC commitment because, over time, "he was troubled that while he would be earning an officer's commission and a law degree, some other, less privileged kid would have to go in his place to trade bullets with the Viet Cong."[22]

Colleagues say that around this time, Clinton started in earnest to grow a beard, traded his sports jackets for pullovers, switched his course of study from PPE to politics, and became engrossed in the activities of Group 68, one of the groups involved with Tariq Ali's organization. He was particularly interested in life under communism in Eastern Europe and the Soviet Union, but friends say this may have been due to the influence of Talbott, who was studying Russian language and literature, and another close friend, Jan Kopold, a Czechoslovakian refugee who had fled Prague during the Soviet invasion of his country in 1968.[23]

Apparently it was around this same time that Clinton first experimented with marijuana, a dalliance he would go to great lengths to avoid admitting during his years as governor of Arkansas. Only as a presidential candidate would he admit to having smoked pot while a student at Oxford. Even then, much to the delight of talk-show hosts and comedians, he would insist that "I didn't inhale."

Clinton eventually joined Talbott and Frank Aller in their apartment at 46 Leckford Road, a four-story brick Victorian house.[24] Several years later, it was the residence of Howard Marks, who in 1990 was convicted in the United States for operating a multimillion-dollar international drug cartel.[25]

The extent of Clinton's involvement in Group 68 is not clear, but Alan Bersin, a fellow Rhodes Scholar, told London's *Sunday Times* in 1992 that "the notion that Bill was a national organizer is not accurate. He took on the chore of contacting Americans in London. He was at the edge of it."[26]

Nonetheless, Clinton takes credit for having helped organize the demonstrations held outside the American Embassy in London's Grosvenor Square in mid-October and near Grosvenor Square over the course of a weekend in mid-November.[27] According to Tom Williamson, he and Clinton helped organize an "international student protest in London against the war in Vietnam" and served as unpaid marshals for the November 15 protest.[28]

"We were very much part of the peaceful demonstration, rationalist approach," Williamson told the *Sunday Times*.

The most extensive account of Bill Clinton's involvement in the Vietnam Moratorium is provided by Father Richard McSorley in his 1978 memoir, *Peace Eyes*. In it, Father McSorley recalled that the London Moratorium was held "to express their sorrow at America's misuse of power in Vietnam."[29]

> The next day I joined with about 500 other people for the interdenominational service. Most of them were young, and many of them were Americans. As I was waiting for the ceremony to begin, Bill Clinton of Georgetown, then studying as a Rhodes Scholar at Oxford, came up and welcomed me. He was one of the organizers, and asked me to open the service with a prayer. After my prayer we had hymns, peace songs led by two women with guitars, and the reading of poetry by a native white South American woman. The poems were very moving, especially one about napalm causing a horrible figure of a person who could not sit because his skin was just about gone and he had a crust speckled with pus. . . . I was glad to see a Georgetown student leading in the religious service for peace. After the service Bill introduced me to some of his friends. With them, we paraded over to the American Embassy carrying white crosses made of wood about one foot high. There we left the crosses as an indication of our desire to end the agony of Vietnam.[30]

Less than two weeks after the November protests, the lottery system became a reality. Numbers were allocated according to date of birth.

The newly established lottery had fanned out in Bill Clinton's favor: Assigned Number 311 in the drawing of December 1, he was among the estimated 20 percent of draft-age American men who would be spared involuntary military service; 195 was the highest number taken.

His good fortune after so many months of what he had called "mental torment" may have accounted for the degree of bluntness Clinton employed when on December 3 he penned a soul-searching missive to Colonel Holmes (see Appendix 1). Only five months before, he had sat across from Holmes at his house in Fayetteville, pouring out his desire to obtain an ROTC berth and become an officer in the service of his country. But now it was a moot point. He no longer needed an ROTC deferment.

Clinton did not understand the impact his soul-cleansing confessional would have on a career military man who had entered active service in 1940, had volunteered for the Luzon campaign, and had been captured by the Japanese at Bataan and held prisoner for three and a half years when he sat down to tie up a loose end.[31] His letter was a rambling effort to persuade the older veteran of his sincerity and good heart, intertwined with his thoughts about the illegitimacy of the draft, his opposition to the Vietnam War, and other modish stances. He ended by wishing Colonel Holmes a "Merry Christmas."

Christmas was not as merry as it might have been once Holmes had digested that letter. He felt used. Joining the ROTC program had seemed so important to the fresh-faced young scholar who had sought him out and engaged him in fervent conversation for two hours. And then there were the calls in the young man's behalf, calls from people too influential to be ignored. Holmes had secured that berth in good faith, and here was the ugly truth of it. It had all been a lie, a calculated, shoddy, fraudulent trick to avoid induction, to avoid service to his country.[32]

Holmes placed the letter in Clinton's file on the off chance that someday he would attempt once more to enter the ROTC program. Then his true motives, his true feelings about those who had marched in service to their country, would be there in black and white as proof of his unfitness.[33]

Within days of posting the guilt-purging letter to Holmes, Clinton took off on a forty-day tour of Scandinavia, the Soviet Union, and Eastern Europe. It is unclear how he managed this feat when, according to former girlfriends, he was always broke.

Proponents have suggested that he availed himself of travel stipends provided by the Rhodes program and saved money by staying at youth hostels; but that ignores the fact that travel to the Soviet Union was not only costly but had to be prepaid to Intourist, the government-owned and -administered tourist board. Detractors suggest that his expenses were paid by unidentified segments of the peace movement or, in the extreme, by the Soviet government, and that while in Moscow he actually crossed Soviet Central Asia to spend time in North Vietnam. This, according to Republicans only peripherally involved in the campaign, would go a long way toward explaining why the Bush administration took such a keen interest in Clinton's State Department jacket during the 1992 presidential campaign.

When Clinton disembarked from the train at Oslo, Norway, he met up with McSorley, and joined him in visiting several peace centers operated by so-called pacifist organizations that one Clinton critic has described as "so far to the left that even the main-line Communists had to apologize for some of their outrageous antics."[34] Father McSorley described this visit in his 1978 memoir, *Peace Eyes*. He recounted how he and Clinton spent a day visiting the Institute for Peace Studies at Oslo University and at least one nonuniversity peace center, talking with conscientious objectors and other antiwar activists about America's involvement in Vietnam.[35]

> A familiar face greeted me at the station at Oslo, Bill Clinton, a student from Georgetown University. He had been on the same train. When he learned I was going to visit the Institute for Peace Research at Oslo University he asked if could could come along. I was delighted.
>
> We were shown around the Institute by the Assistant Director. It is housed in a lovely old reconditioned mansion of Victorian design. Its program is designed to promote peace through research. We met three conscientious objectors working there. They objected to Norway's role in NATO. This was a new reason that we had not heard before.
>
> Together we visited Oslo University, lunched with a professor there and visited a peace center founded by two actors. Before Bill left he agreed that this was a good way to see a country.[36]

While at Oslo, Clinton visited a friend from Hot Springs, Jim Durham, who was studying at Oslo University. He spent Christmas with Richard Shullau in Helsinki, Finland, although he bedded down at a hostel.[37]

"We went round Helsinki for two days," Shullau recalled. "It was bitterly cold and Bill had a beard and a long coat. Afterwards he left to go to Moscow. He had no plans to meet anyone over there as far as I know."[38]

New Year's Eve found Clinton in Moscow, where through Intourist he had been booked for seven days at what arguably was the best accommodation in town, the prerevolutionary National Hotel overlooking Red Square. While there, he encountered a delegation of Americans who were negotiating with various Vietnamese, French, and Russian officials for an exchange of American prisoners of war in North Vietnam.

"Bill stayed around with us while this was going on," recalled Charlie Daniels, a civilian member of the delegation who was there as a private citizen to obtain information about servicemen missing in action. "He was not important to us, he just hung around, always hungry and broke."[39]

Following a week of sightseeing and visiting with friends at Moscow University, Clinton headed for Prague where he met the family of his roommate, Jan Kopold. According to the *Sunday Times* of London, the Kopold family were dissidents who had been imprisoned in the 1950s and had suffered further following the 1968 Soviet invasion.[40]

However much his consciousness had been raised by his tour of peace missions, his firsthand glimpse of life behind the Iron Curtain, and his late-night discussions about the renewed repression of the citizens of Prague, he returned to Oxford not discernibly enlightened about feminism. In late January, he invited Sara Maitland and Mandy Merck to a lecture on women in literature conducted by the radical feminist Germaine Greer.

"This was before *The Female Eunuch*," Maitland said. "I'd never heard of her and, as far as I know, the only thing Bill had heard was that she was more than six foot tall, had great legs, and was going to talk about sex. Her gist was that middle-class men were terrible at sex and intelligent women would only do it with lorry [truck] drivers."[41]

At the end of Greer's shockingly explicit presentation, there was a question-and-answer session in which no one was eager to speak until Clinton rose.

"In case you ever decide to give bourgeois men another chance," Maitland recalled him saying, "can I give you my phone number?"

"The answer," Maitland said, "was 'no.' "

Shortly thereafter, Maitland moved in with Clinton and Talbott, where, she said, "we lived in squalor. I don't think anyone scrubbed a floor for the entire two and a half years I was associated with the house."

Wayland Dennis, whose father owned the house on Leckford Road, remembers Clinton as "a thoroughly nice bloke, a well-mannered, well-behaved young American gentlemen."[42]

Maitland concurs.

"Six months after I met Bill, I went very batty and ended up in a psychiatric hospital," she told the *Evening Standard*. "It was the late sixties, a glamorous but difficult time to have a nervous breakdown. Bill was so consistently kind. He visited the hospital every day for weeks, even though it was impossible to get to. I was constantly complaining that the tea was undrinkable, so every visit he'd bring me one-ounce packs, exquisitely wrapped, and ever more exotic brands.

"Another time he arranged for me to go to the hairdressers, and because I was terrified of being trapped in the dryers, he planned, and paid, for my hair to be dried by hand. I can't imagine any other man thinking of that. It shows the very real way in which he is sensitive to the people around him."[43]

Mixner told Clinton's biographer, Robert E. Levin, that although he became acquainted with Clinton in 1969 during the organizational efforts of the Vietnam Moratorium Committee, they did not develop a friendship until 1970, when Mixner made a brief excursion to Europe that included a side trip to Oxford. The friendship "consisted of intense public conversations about public service, struggles about the draft, and our moral obligations to our country, our personal beliefs, where we would be in twenty years, and our ability to change the world for the better."[44]

"We all believed at that time," Mixner continued, "that the most noble direction we could take was to serve in elective or appointive

office. [Clinton] really deeply believed that government could feed
people, that we could end war, that poverty did not have to be a
permanent condition, that we could make our country great and
prosperous, and that our generation would be the one to do it.

"There was never any doubt in his mind that he would return to
Arkansas. He felt a deep, personal obligation to return to his home
state and to help the poor that he saw on a daily basis as a child."

Clinton was much too anxious to begin that adventure to languish
for another year in England and complete the degree program, however enjoyable his stay to date had been. Yale, to which he had received
a scholarship, would bring him additional credentials, new friends, and
another invaluable round of contacts that Oxford could not. He had
had the Oxford experience, it had been productive and even enlightening, and now that the draft was no longer a threat, it was time to
move on.

The value of that experience cannot be understated. It was at
Oxford that he and a growing cadre of associates from various walks of
life began what they refer to as "The Conversation."[45]

The Conversation apparently began as a typical collegiate exercise
in which a group of aspiring young intellectuals sat around hoisting or
toking a few while sharing their thoughts on the pitiful human condition and how best to remedy it. In the ensuing years, this ever-
expanding dialogue was concerned with the wheels of politics and all
its spokes: liberalism versus conservatism, civil rights issues, the economy, world trade, and America's place in the world.

It goes without saying that the participants in The Conversation,
people like Bill Clinton and Strobe Talbott and Robert B. Reich, were
among those who were going to save the world. What set them apart
was a sort of practical idealism, or social pragmatism. They were the
best and brightest, destined to become politicians and economists and
pundits and financiers and educators and gay-rights activists. Only the
faddish trappings of Flower Power appealed to them. In short, by
heritage, by upbringing, by class, and by conditioning, they were
hopelessly Establishment. They did not want to overthrow the system,
they wanted to change it. Over time, they came to believe as strongly
as he did that the man to change it was Bill Clinton.

Clinton saw himself at the core of this political and social change, and that as much as natural curiosity and inherent love of society fueled his networking.

Following Clinton's 1992 presidential victory, *The Guardian* cited yet another example of this "calculating charmer" who "networked his way to the White House."[46]

"I was a Fulbright Scholar at a NATO student conference in Georgetown," Rudi Loewe told the *Guardian's* Martin Walker. "I met Bill and he said, 'Since you're a Fulbright, would you like to meet with Senator Fulbright?' I replied, 'Well, I'm just a young German student and he is a great and powerful man who must be too busy.'

" 'Just say yes or no, lunch or breakfast,' Bill replied. I said, 'Yes, please,' and Bill made a phone call, and next morning we had breakfast with the chairman of the Senate Foreign Relations Committee, the leading critic of the Vietnam War.' "[47]

"That was the initial contact," Walker wrote. "Then came the letters, the phone calls, the visits, the building of an acquaintance into a solid friendship, and into a political asset. Loewe is now executive assistant to the head of Bavarian Television, and three years ago helped arrange Clinton's visit to Germany as a guest of the Bavarian government. When the Arkansas press criticised him for being out of state again, Clinton announced the fruits of his trip to Munich, a new Siemens factory in Little Rock, with 370 jobs.

"That story of networking—making friends who become useful contacts, using his connections to powerful patrons to widen his personal constituency—sums up this most relentless of campaigners, this purest of politicians."

The headline writer was dead on target when he entitled the *Guardian* story: "Clinton's America: Chief leads his tribe of friends to the ultimate prize they helped win." Few if any have ever peaceably assembled such a vast, dedicated, loyal, and effective network of allies, what Martin Walker so accurately called Clinton's personal think tank.

From the transcripts of a quarter-century of The Conversation would spring many campaign agendas, always with the same end.

"The Conversation . . . is a mixture of ruthlessness and ideals," Walker noted. "The first question has been how to elect a Democrat again. The answer was obvious: Never let the Republicans use their wedge issues on social questions, patriotism, and family values, and use economic wedge issues against them instead. Hence those ill-matched twins at the heart of Clinton's new Democratic party, Keynesian economics and the electric chair, more jobs and more cops.

"The second question has been how to reinvent government, how to make Lyndon Johnson's vision of a Great Society work without the bureaucracy and the entrenching of an underclass. Arkansas has been the test-tube. The priorities of education, jobs, and low taxes have been ruthless. Clinton rebuilt the Arkansas tax base with new industries that could take advantage of a low-skilled but also low-wage work force. So Arkansas is now the poultry capital of the world, raising more than a billion birds a year. The price is rivers that stink of what [George] Bush called 'coloform faecal bacteria,' and jobs whose only merit is a regular paycheck. And that provides the money which pays for the far longer-term investment in education."[48]

6

PARTNERS IN TIME

HILLARY RODHAM CLINTON once claimed that she was attracted to her future husband because "he wasn't afraid of me."[1] Maybe not, but the man whose career she would guide all the way to the top of the American political ladder admits to having been intimidated by her.

"I loved being with her," Clinton told Gail Sheehy in 1992, "but I had very ambivalent feelings about getting involved with her. . . . I could just look at her and tell she was interesting and deep."[2] She was so self-assured, so bright, so *capable* that he who had always had to be the best suspected that she was more than his match and that she would not be nearly so impressed with him as he was with her.

He was right about everything except her assessment of him. He was, in fact, exactly what she would have looked for had she been looking, which, at the time, she was not. Hillary Rodham had never intended to be the traditional wife, staying home and baking cookies and hosting teas. She was not romantic by nature; there was little of the schoolgirl about her. Her approach to life was focused, pragmatic, and aggressive. She had a pretty good idea of what she wanted to accomplish, and marriage and motherhood did not figure in her immediate plans.

Theirs was a fortuitious, even extraordinary pairing. He is the first to concede that without her determination, stability, and focus, he might never have realized his dream of becoming president. Cynics like to say that Bill Clinton and Hillary Rodham had one thing in common: They were both in love with Bill Clinton. That belies the compatibility of their mutual aspirations. He wanted political success. She wanted political power. Intelligent, talented, and committed—some would say driven—to change the face of American society, she was willing to redirect her own ambitions and efforts so that both might have what they sought. On her own, she could go far, but if the pace of history was any indication, the odds favored him going farther.

Hillary's upbringing was a far cry from Bill's humble beginnings. In Park Ridge, Illinois, there were no log bridges on which to climb, no sandy loam for growing vegetables or curb markets for buying and selling them, and no poor, ragged children, black or white, to pity. The Rodhams's home town was one of the most suburban suburbs in the United States. Like many of her peers, the round-faced, blonde-haired Hillary studied piano and dance. When not serving as referee for her younger brothers or playing at a nearby park at which she worked for several summers beginning at age thirteen—the Rodham children were not paid for their mandatory chores around the house—she loved to read. An ardent Girl Scout, she earned every badge available, relishing both the challenge and the competition while trying to curry favor with her devoted but strict father.

Hugh Rodham took great pride in his children's accomplishments but he always demanded more, scholastically, athletically, in virtually everything they elected or were required to do. He was a stern disciplinarian with little tolerance for less than the best, usually just a little more than his children had achieved, and he was not above spanking their bottoms when they misbehaved.

Hillary says she was "a quick learner [and] didn't run afoul of my parents very often."[3] The middle child, Hughie, usually met the challenge, too, although he was never the paragon that his sister was. He made his father proud by playing football at his alma mater, Penn State, from which Hugh, Jr., graduated in 1972, and by a subsequent stint with the Peace Corps in Colombia. The baby, Tony, has always been the family's unguided missile, drifting from job to job and task to task and leaving many challenges, among them pursuit of a college education, unmet. The straight-A report cards Hillary consistently brought home would elicit from her father the wry observation that she "must go to a pretty easy school,"[4] although "the boys," as the Rodham family always referred to Hugh, Jr., and Tony, grumbled that teachers expected a great deal of any brother of Hillary.

"Our parents didn't just pay attention to our grades," Tony told the *Washington Post* years later. "They cared about everything we did."[5] Once when Hillary's softball game was faltering, Hugh reportedly took the entire family to a nearby park, where he handed her a bat and spent hours pitching to her until she finally learned to control it.

If Hugh's standards were high, so were his wife Dorothy's. She had sublimated herself in the domestic role assigned most women of her generation, but she wanted more for her daughter. "Just because she was a girl didn't mean she should be limited," Dorothy Rodham once told a reporter. Dorothy was determined, she once said, "that no daughter of mine was going to go through the agony of being afraid to say what she had on her mind."[6]

In a 1992 interview with *Vanity Fair*, Dorothy Rodham recalled her daughter's first experience with assertiveness. Shortly after moving to Park Ridge, the four-year-old Hillary encountered the neighborhood bully, a feisty little girl named Suzy who loved nothing better than smacking Hillary around as a gaggle of admiring young boys shouted encouragement. "There's no room in this house for cowards," Dorothy recalled admonishing her daughter after yet another skirmish had sent the child rushing home in tears. "You're going to have to stand up to her. The next time she hits you, I want you to hit her back."

Hillary dutifully returned to the fray, but this time when Suzy approached with her cheering section in tow, Hillary threw the first punch. Moments later, she burst back into her house to tell her mother proudly, "I can play with the boys now!"[7]

Education figured heavily in the Rodham children's upbringing, although Hillary was the only true scholar among them. Hugh Rodham, Sr., had graduated from Pennsylvania State University, which he had entered on a football scholarship. Dorothy had only a high school education, but her hunger for and appreciation of knowledge—which she augmented in later years through extension courses—were instilled in Hillary at an early age. The Rodhams viewed a good education for their children as a duty to themselves as well as to society. Hillary did not disappoint.

While first lady of Arkansas, Hillary said that her parents "told me it was my obligation to go to school, that I had an obligation to use my mind. They told me that an education would enable me to have a lot more opportunities in life, that if I went to school and took it seriously and studied hard, not only would I learn things and become interested in the world around me, but I would open up all kinds of doors to myself so that, when I was older, I would have some control over my environment."

It was "education for education's sake," she added, "but also it was the idea that school was a real pathway to a better opportunity."

Hillary Rodham Clinton, like her husband, is at ease in virtually any echelon of society, but her friends lean more toward the intellectual, even cerebral types. She is not given to chit-chat or idleness. For Hillary, a half-hour workout on an exercise bicycle must be combined with something to read—a book, a court brief, a policy statement, something to break the monotony and to make the time productive.

People who know their backgrounds without knowing them would see the dichotomy in such a pairing, one that runs deeper than their disparate upbringings: Hillary grew up in a stable middle American household while Bill Clinton's youth was much more troubled.

Hillary is a lifelong Methodist who, when finally persuaded to marry, insisted that she and Bill Clinton recite their vows before a Methodist minister. Bill was reared Southern Baptist, and while his church attendance was fairly consistent during his youth, he did not become a regular church-goer until he became governor.

Bill's sense of humor, like his choice of language in informal settings, tends toward the lewd; despite his public sense of decorum, he enjoys telling and hearing off-color jokes, and the spontaneous quip comes to him as readily as the prepared one. Hillary is more inclined to react to humor than to instigate it, but when she does, her tendency is toward drollness. She handles solitude comfortably, often preferring it to uninspired company. He is almost compulsive in seeking people; many of those midnight telephone calls for which he is famous have no bearing on politics or business of any kind. Sometimes he has no more on his mind than contact with another human being, as evidenced by the time he telephoned a local reporter whose father had just died. Clinton moved through the entire conversation without ever offering his condolences or even indicating any specific reason for having called, but rather giving the bereaved journalist a summary of a book about politics he had been reading.

Hillary Diane Rodham was born at Edgewater Hospital on Chicago's north side on October 26, 1947, the first child and only daughter of Hugh Ellsworth Rodham and the former Dorothy Emma Howell. Hugh, a textile salesman following his wartime stint as a basic training instructor in the navy, wanted the quiet, stable environment suburbia promised for his family. He also wanted a good school district, and the one that served Park Ridge more than filled the bill. "That's what the motivation was for the ex-GIs after World War II . . . to try to find a good place to raise your kids and send them to school," Hillary would say later. Park Ridge was then, as now, a bastion of white-bread, Republican conservatism primarily populated by middle-class and upper-middle-class households in which the men worked and the women tended house and reared children. The Rodhams were not atypical.

Hugh Rodham was born in Scranton, Pennsylvania, to a family that emigrated from England when Hugh's father was four years old. One of three sons, Hugh would begin his career there after graduating from Pennsylvania State University. He was a fine enough athlete to win a football scholarship—he played end for three years with the Nittany Lions—and a popular enough fellow to have pledged Delta Upsilon fraternity before obtaining a B.S. degree in physical education in 1935.

By all accounts, the Rodhams were a proud, hard-working family with a strong ethic for making their own way, and making money was high on Hugh's agenda as the Great Depression dragged on. When he learned that there would be an indefinite wait to join the ranks of salesmen at the Scranton lace-making plant, he struck out on his own, moving first to New York and then to Chicago, where he latched onto a job selling curtains for the Columbia Lace Company. It was a fortuitous move, for there he met the pretty brunette with smiling eyes who, following World War II, became his wife.

Dorothy Howell, the daughter of a Welsh father and a Scottish, French, and Native American mother, was reared in Alhambra, California, just outside Pasadena. She met Hugh Rodham in 1937 when she went to the Columbia offices to apply for a job. They soon began keeping company, but in the best tradition of his English ancestors, Hugh did not move quickly to settle down. Their relationship withstood the separation of war, however, and through letters and photographs, their affection continued to flourish long distance. They finally married in 1942 and set up housekeeping in a one-bedroom apartment. Nine years and two children later—Hugh, Jr., was born in 1950—Rodham moved his family to a two-story, yellow brick, Georgian-style house at 235 North Wisner Road in affluent Park Ridge. Their youngest child, Tony, was born three years later. As in many suburbs of that era, doors were rarely locked, and the only gangs roaming the neighborhood were sidewalk skaters or bicyclists and ersatz cowboys and Indians. Hugh worked in the city, Dorothy kept house and chauffeured the children, and on weekends the mouthwatering scent of a barbecue wafted across the well-tended backyards.

As the children grew older, they were expected to pull their weight around the house.

"We were probably the only kids in the whole suburb who didn't have an allowance," Tony recalled. "We'd rake the leaves, cut the grass, pull weeds, shovel snow. All your friends would be going to a movie. After your errands, you'd walk in and say, 'Gee, Dad, I could use two or three dollars.' He'd flop another potato on your dinner plate and say, 'That's your reward.' "[8]

For Hugh, hard work was synonymous with success. He was close with his money, but not miserly. He dressed his wife and children well, and once he became successful—the money he had carefully set aside helped establish a drapery manufacturing business from which he retired at age sixty—he drove a Cadillac. But Hugh Rodham never forgot his roots. He maintained a summer home at Lake Winola in the Poconos, and every summer he and his family returned there for quiet recreation and visits with his childhood friends. It was this same sense of being rooted to a place and a people that later attracted Hillary to a gregarious young Arkansan who eschewed a potentially lucrative career with a high-powered metropolitan law firm in order to return to his rural moorings.

For all his gruffness, Hugh Rodham was a confirmed family man, and in later years, when he began suffering periodic bouts of ill health that led to triple bypass heart surgery while on a visit to Little Rock, this love of kin, coupled with his and Dorothy's desire to enjoy Chelsea's childhood, brought the Rodhams to Arkansas permanently in 1987. With the Clintons's help, they bought a condominium in an old, affluent neighborhood less than two miles from the Governor's Mansion, and took over most of the baby-sitting duties for their only grandchild.

Public appearances were few and far between, even during the presidential campaign, although Hugh relented after the 1992 election when the Clintons' strongest Hollywood boosters, Harry Thomason and his wife Linda Bloodworth-Thomason, persuaded him to do a cameo on their newest situation comedy, "Hearts Afire." Seated in a high-backed chair, a frail-looking Hugh Rodham had one line in which he paid tribute to the two women dearest to him. Upon overhearing a conversation in which a senatorial aide, played by actor John Ritter, observes that Hillary Clinton is a "fox," Rodham barks, "If you think she's a fox, you should see her mother!"

When Hugh died at age eighty-two on April 7, 1993, after a stroke three weeks previously, he was given a hero's farewell. A navy honor guard carried his flag-draped casket to and from funeral services held in both Little Rock and Scranton, and he was eulogized by his son-in-law, the president of the United States, the first Democrat for whom he had ever voted. He was interred beside his father in the family plot at Scranton's Washburn Street Cemetery.[9]

Friends say Hugh's death was deeply felt by his only daughter, who had maintained a sixteen-day vigil at his bedside. Hillary had prepared for this moment, and took comfort in her religious faith, and she fully intended to be with him and the rest of the family when the end came, but she was not. During that period, she had canceled a string of public appearances, including the opening session of her newly formed national task force on health care reform, but three days before Hugh died, she had returned to her White House duties.

Observers marveled at her composure upon returning to Arkansas to oversee funeral arrangements, and the calm demeanor she displayed throughout the services, but it was a painful undertaking. As Hugh, Jr., remarked during an interview several weeks before his father's death, "She was a daddy's girl, there's no doubt about it."[10]

Both Hillary and Bill came from segregated, predominantly Protestant communities, but whereas Bill had some passing contact with the black people who frequented his grandfather's grocery store, Hillary's was a white-bread existence. Her first real contact with people of different religious, social, and ethnic cultures came in high school, and she was fascinated by them. Sherry Heiden, a school chum, later told a biographer that Hillary "always liked to hang out with as many different groups of people as she could. She always had a really broad view of people. She was never a narrow person."[11] She was, however, sheltered by her Republican, upper-middle class environs.

Hillary's first glimpse of life beyond suburbia was sobering. Through the efforts of Don Jones, youth minister at the Methodist church she faithfully attended, Hillary and other young people made several visits to Chicago's inner city, meeting with poor and working-class Hispanics and blacks, some of them gang members, in one of the area's meanest neighborhoods. The members of Jones's youth group were tireless and impressionable do-gooders, seeking salvation through their good works, offering kindness and a helping hand to those less fortunate. While Bill Clinton was learning about the less fortunate through his grandfather's laments about racial injustice, Hillary was talking to young people who lived in some of America's most deprived areas.

"I don't think those kids had ever seen poverty before," Jones recalled. "Religion, going to church, tended to function there for most people to reinforce their rather traditional conservative values, and so when I came in and took that white, middle-class youth group into the inner city of Chicago, that was quite radical."[12]

When Bill Clinton was fifteen, his mother was dragging him into Hot Springs nightclubs. When Hillary Rodham was fifteen, she and

her youth group were following Don Jones to hear Martin Luther
King, Jr., speak to a group of ministers and laymen in Chicago.
Afterward the civil rights leader was introduced to and shook hands
with each of the young people, including Hillary.

"This may sound corny," Jones would say years later, "but the key to
understanding Hillary is her spiritual center. Unlike some people who
at a particular age land on a cause and become concerned, with Hillary
I think of a continuous textured development. Her social concern and
her political thought rest on a spiritual foundation."[13]

Jones, currently a professor of religion at New Jersey's Drew University, challenged his young charges to think, to discuss their principles, to examine them, and to learn about the secular world through
literature and art and politics and relating what they learned to Methodist theology. What the teenagers saw and experienced were the
topics of much discussion both at group gatherings and in one-on-one
conversations with Jones. Hillary, a frequent visitor to Jones's office,
"was an intellectual even then . . . openminded . . . just insatiable" for
knowledge, he told an interviewer, and he indulged her curiosity with
works from his own library.[14]

Family and friends remember Hillary as an introspective young
woman, but never self-absorbed, and not much interested in fashion as
a teenager, although the few published photographs of her high school
years reveal a neatly groomed, fashionably dressed young woman who
had taken care to remove her glasses before the shutter clicked. Dorothy Rodham now laughs when she recalls the frustration she felt over
her futile efforts to encourage Hillary to make the most of her physical
attributes.

"When she was fifteen or sixteen and the other kids started to use
makeup and fix their hair, she wasn't interested," Dorothy recalled.
"That used to annoy me a little bit. I used to think, 'Why can't she put
on a little makeup?' "[15] It was when she began attending Wellesley in
the mid–1960s that she stopped styling her hair and being self-
conscious about her glasses. She was apparently comfortable with this
stance until her husband's 1980 election defeat, when she was advised
that a more traditional approach to political wifedom would help
restore the couple to the good graces of the voters, so she began

wearing contact lenses, took a few makeup lessons, and overhauled a
decidedly matronly wardrobe.

Hillary's youthful disdain for powder and perfume annoyed some of
her peers, too; apparently Hillary did not need cosmetic embellish-
ment to captivate young men. Her biographer, Judith Warner, tells the
story of a vacation trip Hillary took with several high school chums. It
seems one of the girls who was "eager to meet boys struck out, while
Hillary, without even trying, ended up surrounded by a small circle of
followers. One night, after she'd sat out on the front porch with a new
male acquaintance and talked past midnight, she came in to bed and
found her friend seething with rage. It didn't do much for her sense of
female solidarity."[16] Neither did it shake her self-confidence. In those
days, Hillary gave little thought to how others saw her.

"I saw a lot of my friends who had been really lively and smart and
doing well in school beginning to worry that boys would think they
were too smart, or beginning to cut back on how well they did or the
courses they took, because that's not where their boyfriends were," she
later told the *Washington Post*, "and I can recall thinking, 'Gosh, why
are they doing that?' It didn't make sense to me."

Boys were attracted by Hillary's personality and the ease with which
she addressed them. Neither presumptuous nor flirtatious, she met
them as equals, and they accepted that, apparently never realizing how
much they acquiesced to do her bidding, whether undertaking a fund-
raising event to benefit the migrant workers who worked on the
nearby farms or organizing school assemblies for the 2,700-member
Maine Township High School-South. "Boys responded to Hillary,"
her mother would tell writer Gail Sheehy in 1992. "She just took
charge, and they let her."[17]

Like her future husband, Hillary favored group functions over formal dating, but she was just as happy studying as taking in a movie or
going ice-skating with her friends. She was a high achiever, juggling
extracurricular activities and schoolwork with ease, and when she
graduated in 1965 she was not only in the top 5 percent of her class, but
she was named most likely to succeed. Even then, friends say, she
thought about studying law—Hillary says she reached that decision
during her senior year at Wellesley—and while her agenda was not

clearly defined, through her activism on behalf of farm workers and her leadership in many school activities, she had discovered she had definite ideas, some of them unpopular, that she was capable of defending and promoting. According to a former classmate, "It wasn't a matter of her being a rebel in any sense. It was just that she was confident and had strong convictions and was able to follow through on them. She saw all sides of an issue, and she was able to integrate those and then make a judgment."[18]

It was more predictable behavior than sound reasoning that spurred Hillary to campaign door to door for Republican Barry Goldwater in 1964. She couldn't vote for four years and her only experience with politics had come a year before, when she sought and won the presidency of her high school junior class. But Hugh Rodham talked a great deal at the dinner table about big government and high taxes, and Goldwater was against both.

But Hillary's political evolution did not really begin until she went away to college and chose political science for her major. Although she had no personal aspirations toward elective office at that time, she once told a reporter that people had been urging her to run for public office "since I was in the eighth grade."[19] Her aim was to garner the kind of academic background that would best prepare her to study law.

Hillary has said she selected Wellesley College, progressive and exclusive, because a favorite teacher who had graduated from there convinced her of its scholastic and intellectual superiority. As her future husband had done the year before upon admission to Georgetown, Hillary stepped into a new world when she left suburban Chicago for suburban Boston.

Despite what has been described as her independent nature, Hillary's life had been nurtured, monitored, disciplined, and influenced by a conservative, traditional family. Wellesley, an expensive four-year liberal arts college for women, was a cauldron of progressive intellectualism. Admission standards were high, and the mostly privileged young women who strolled the five-hundred-acre campus were the elite, academically, socially, and economically. Hillary has said she found Wellesley "all very rich and fancy and very intimidating."[20]

And very stimulating. She was not so different from many other freshmen with whom she came into contact, altruistically hungry young white women to whom middle- and upper-class comforts were embarrassing in the tumultuous 1960s. Inevitably, some would become radicalized—the trend was most pronounced among well-to-do liberal-arts students at Eastern colleges and universities—in the process of "finding themselves." Others, like Hillary, who could not escape their privileged past, could at least adopt a progressive attitude toward the less fortunate, and dress and act appropriately. Thus Hillary abandoned stockings and hair ribbons and the Young Republicans for sandals and horn-rimmed glasses and Eugene McCarthy. In the words of her biographer, Judith Warner, "her academic career became a search for 'relevance.' "[21] The observation is simplistic. If Don Jones taught Hillary how to think above the mundane, Wellesley showed her what subjects to think about.

Jeff Shields, who dated Hillary while attending nearby Harvard, told Warner that during her freshman year, Hillary "tended to listen more than talk. But as time went by, she solidified her beliefs." Many of their dates, he said, were spent sitting with friends over a beer or a soft drink, "talking in an animated way about politics and government and social issues," among them civil rights, civil liberties, and the war in Southeast Asia.[22]

Outwardly, Hillary may have looked like thousands of other self-consciously "nonconformist" college students, but her intellectual outreach was only coincidentally trendy. At Wellesley, the ambiguity in her concern about social injustice began to break into its various parts, and she began to consider issues such as civil rights and feminism and economic opportunity more realistically. She had gone through her do-gooder stage while a teenager in Park Ridge. Jones had shown her a glimpse of Chicago's underside. And she had had occasional contact with the migrant workers on farms located outside the metropolitan area through a babysitting service that Jones organized.

At Wellesley, she continued her good works, teaching poor children to read and at one point serving as a sort of self-anointed mediator between the college's growing contingent of black students and the administration during a period of racial unrest. But Hillary also began to examine the causes behind the way "disadvantaged" people lived and to consider how those circumstances could be changed. She came to see herself as an advocate and determined to make that her life's work. Her senior thesis was a comparative study of community action programs for the poor, something her former political science professor, Alan Schechter, says "you don't choose to write about . . . unless you're concerned about poor people."[23]

"She had this idea of greater happiness through service," Schechter told *People.*

Hillary's interest in poor people, children, and women has remained a constant in her life.

"All during my growing up years," she once said, "I had a combined message of personal opportunity [and] public responsibility—that there were obligations that people who were as lucky as I was owed society."[24]

Mack McLarty, Bill Clinton's childhood playmate who now serves the president as chief of staff, likes to say that many of the opportunities life has afforded him are the result of sheer "serendipity." The same could be said of Hillary Rodham Clinton. Faced with the choice of Harvard or Yale at which to pursue her law degree, she chose Yale, where two years later, she would meet and eventually move in with a tall, glib, flirtatious Southerner whose focus was to her even clearer and more intense than her own.

"Bill's desire to be in public life was much more specific than my desire to do good," Hillary has conceded.[25]

The story of how she came to notice Bill Clinton has become part of the Billary legend. Walking through the Yale Student Union one day in 1971, over the roar of activity she heard a distinctly Southern accent declaring, "And not only that, but we grow the biggest watermelons in the world!"

"Who *is* that?" she asked a companion, nodding toward the bearded, bushy-haired fellow.

"Oh, that's Bill Clinton. He's from Arkansas, and that's all he ever talks about."

One evening, while studying in the Yale Law School library, her concentration was broken by a feeling that someone was looking at her. Looking up, she espied the usually boisterous Clinton staring at her while appearing to be in conversation with another student. He hastily looked away and she went back to her book. This routine was repeated several times until finally she got up and walked the considerable length of the library to where he sat.

"Look, if you're going to keep staring at me and I'm going to keep staring back," she reportedly said, "I think we ought to know each other's name. I'm Hillary Rodham.

"I was dumbstruck," Bill later would claim. "I couldn't think of my name."

It was a typically bold move on her part, if not a typically honest one, because Hillary already knew his name; and if the confrontation left Bill speechless, it was one of the few times in his life. Nonetheless, Robert Reich, a fellow Rhodes Scholar, takes credit for urging them toward their first date. Their initial wariness was understandable. Bill was quite a man about town: dashing, extroverted, charming, and bright, but less devoted to his studies than most because of his consuming interest in politics and his amazing ability to memorize many facts and figures quickly and to store them for use at will. His class attendance was sporadic. Hillary was congenial and well liked but not exactly the comely type usually seen at Clinton's side. She was very serious about her studies and very involved in social issues. She required less company than Clinton, who seemingly has never met a stranger in his life. Constant fellowship and playing the field simply were not her style.

They were, in some respects, opposites attracted. Bill has always been drawn to strong women, in whom he invariably arouses something akin to the maternal instinct. "Bill is just smart enough and just strong enough to enlist strong women in his cause rather than repel them," a longtime associate observed. "They see the potential and they're determined not to let him waste it."

Friends see the relationship in a different light.

"I think she has always been intrigued and attracted to [Bill's] intelligence, his moral commitments, his love of life, and his political life," Don Jones told The Associated Press shortly after the Clintons moved into the White House. "I think she shares all those things [although] love of life may be the least. I think he is more fun-loving than Hillary. She has less time for frivolous things."

"Hillary is not easily charmed," Harlon Dalton, a fellow Yalie, told the *Chicago Tribune*. "I don't believe she was charmed by Bill. She saw past the surface charm and [saw] someone who deeply wanted to make a difference and cared about the less fortunate."[26]

William T. Coleman III, the son of President Richard Nixon's transportation secretary who entered Yale in September 1970, made a similar observation in a 1992 essay. He was one of ten black students in a freshman class of 125, and he vividly recalled the day that "a tall, robust, friendly fellow with a Southern accent and a cherubic face unceremoniously violated the unspoken taboo by plopping himself down at the 'black table.' "[27]

Some at the table were taken aback by this brazen move, but Coleman said Clinton "was oblivious to the stares and engaged us in easy conversation. He was immensely curious about people. He had an ability, though in an unobtrusive manner, to get people to talk about themselves. He was fun and funny, on occasion even raucous. . . . He was serious, too, and would discuss social and moral issues with concern, depth, and insight. By simply being himself, Bill Clinton dissolved the unspoken taboo and became a regular and welcome member of the table."

Coleman, who within weeks of their meeting would move with Clinton and two other classmates into a beach house in Milford, Connecticut, about a twenty-minute drive from the Yale campus in New Haven, was particularly impressed by Clinton's views on racism, which he rejected "with a personal ardor that, frankly, I have found rare in people who are not themselves victims of racism."

"The unusually close ties that Bill established with the African-American community at the law school lasted well beyond graduation," Coleman wrote. "Bill maintained an especially close relationship with several of his African-American classmates. Seven or eight years after law school, the wedding at Martha's Vineyard of Lani Guinier, a close friend of mine and Bill's, provided an opportunity for what amounted to a reunion for fifteen or twenty of the African-American students who attended Yale Law School during the early

1970s. The only Caucasian members of our class to participate were Bill and Hillary Clinton and John Widerman."

Coleman says it was at Yale that "Bill established the wide web of relationships that enabled him to run for president without appearing to do so." Hillary, too, established many mutually beneficial relationships.

Like many other people born into privileged positions by virtue of race or wealth or caste, neither Bill nor Hillary was casual toward people with different ethnic backgrounds; both actively cultivated relationships with people who weren't WASPs. Clinton was more inclined to regard virtually everyone with whom he came into contact as "a close, personal friend"—Coleman has referred to his former roommate's Yale contacts as "the wide web of relationships that enabled him to run for president without appearing to do so."[28] Hillary's list of close associations was less expansive but by far better placed, and they tended to have a more direct and profound influence on her.

For instance, during her second semester at Yale, she joined forces with "the children's crusader," Marian Wright Edelman, whose activism on behalf of civil rights in the South a decade before Hillary greatly admired. Edelman, a leading advocate for children's rights and a well-known civil rights lawyer who in 1963 had become the first black woman to pass the Mississippi bar, had established the Washington Research Project in 1968 and was involved in it when she accepted a speaking engagement in the spring of 1970 at Yale, her alma mater. Hillary, who had spoken with her briefly at a previous League of Women Voters young leadership conference, was energized by Edelman's recollections about her work on behalf of voting rights for black Americans, a crusade that had put her in physical jeopardy, as well as in jail, on numerous occasions. Hillary took to heart Edelman's call to use her exceptional educational opportunities to serve the poor and afterward approached Edelman about working for the Washington Research Project.

Edelman was more than receptive to the proposal but had no money in her budget to pay the young woman. Hillary solved that problem as she would numerous others in her later public life: She obtained a grant of her own, one which paid law students a modest stipend for working in the field of civil rights law.

Among her assignments on behalf of the project was a research stint with a Senate subcommittee chaired by Walter Mondale in which she studied the conditions of workers in migrant labor camps and interviewed families to assess the impact this way of life had on their offspring. She brought some empathy to the task as a result of her high school volunteer work. In return, the assignment gave her a clearer notion of the career path she wanted to follow. With her sharp legal mind and her affinity for children's rights issues, she began to see an illustrious career as a children's advocate and took advantage of every opportunity to expand her knowledge in this area, from undertaking specialized courses to assisting instructors at the Yale Child Study Center. She was thrilled when one of her professors invited Anna Freud, the noted child psychoanalyst, to help teach a class in family law.

Hillary's relationship with Edelman was far and away the most worthwhile of her postgraduate studies and would be to Bill's and her mutual benefit in the ensuing years. By 1973, the year Hillary completed her law studies, the Washington Research Project had evolved into the Children's Defense Fund, a not-for-profit organization that lobbies on behalf of such issues as child care, youth employment, and prevention of teenage pregnancy. Hillary served a six-month stint as a CDF lawyer in Boston before joining the legal staff of the House Judiciary Committee.

She kept in close contact with Edelman and the CDF, however, joining the CDF board in 1978 and later serving six years as chairman. Edelman's early involvement in programs such as Head Start and the opportunities she extended to Hillary for firsthand experience in children's issues fueled the future first lady's growing interest in the prospects of helping disadvantaged children through educational and legal means.

It was through Edelman's influence that Hillary obtained a research position with the Carnegie Council on Children, a project of the Carnegie Corporation of New York. In that capacity, Hillary wrote several background papers on the legal rights of children and collaborated with Kenneth Keniston, who headed the council, on a chapter for his book, *All Our Children*, which dealt with children's rights to education and medical care. Although her basic philosophy was at odds with Keniston's belief that, ultimately, parents are the final authority over their children, it was another important learning experience in her chosen field.

During her years at Yale, Hillary also helped establish procedures for doctors at New Haven Hospital in dealing with child abuse cases, assisted in the development of children's programs for the fledgling Legal Services Organization, and served as a researcher for the New Haven Legal Assistance Association.

Penn Rhodeen, who at the time was a staff attorney at the New Haven Legal Assistance Association, recalled that Hillary made the first contact upon learning that he was involved in some particularly troublesome child custody cases.

"She heard about some of my battles with the welfare department and she called up and said she'd like to work with me," Rhodeen later told the *Chicago Tribune*. When he first met her, he said, "she had Gloria Steinem glasses, Gloria Steinem hair, a purple sheepskin jacket, and was driving a purple Gremlin. We hit it off well. She had a strong point of view about kids. I was very struck. When you're that young, you're not thinking about children typically. She had this wonderful passion. I don't quite know how she'd gotten so committed so fast."[29]

With no grant available, Hillary volunteered her time to the Legal Assistance Association, helping Rhodeen research his cases and discussing strategy.

"What I'm interested in . . . is called public service," Hillary told Arkansas author Shirley Abbott in a 1992 interview for *Glamour*. "I have a deep, abiding sense of obligation that makes it very hard for me to see the waste and the damage and the hurt that occur every day. I can't help wanting to do something about it."[30]

Bill, too, was interested in public service, although his definition differed somewhat from Hillary's. As his friends attest, he made it clear that after obtaining his law degree, he intended to return to Arkansas and begin his political career.

"While Yale was full of people who were interested in the political process," Coleman wrote, "I knew of no one else who at the age of twenty-four was prepared to define himself as a politician. For most of my classmates, such a statement would have been viewed as pretentious and egotistical. But the political aspect of Bill's personality was such a natural part of him that the statement was merely a description of who he was and what he planned to do. Just as you would describe one classmate as a future member of the law firm of Sullivan and Cromwell, you would describe Bill as a guy who was returning to Arkansas and was likely to run for governor or the United States Senate in several years."[31]

While Hillary's social agenda evolved, Bill immersed himself in political activity. The summer before entering Yale, he had worked for a citizens's lobby, Operation Pursestrings, which tried to halt the war in Vietnam primarily by promoting the bipartisan but ill-fated McGovern-Hatfield amendment to end funding for all combat activities in Southeast Asia by December 31, 1970, and to require withdrawal of all American forces by mid–1971. During that enterprise, he befriended Anthony Podesta, who persuaded him to get involved in the antiwar campaign of Joseph P. Duffey, who was running for the United States Senate from Connecticut.

Clinton organized Connecticut's Third Congressional District, a blue-collar region in which Yale was located where for many Italian was a first language, and he did so masterfully, setting up telephone banks and directing a number of student volunteers in door-to-door canvassing. Duffey lost the election to Lowell Weicker, but he carried the Third District.

There were other minor political involvements throughout his tenure at Yale, the most important of which proved to be George S. McGovern's 1972 campaign against Richard M. Nixon for the presidency. The McGovern campaign was for Bill what Marian Wright Edelman was for Hillary, a catalyst to the future. McGovern was acquainted with the young Arkansan through his work on behalf of the Senate Foreign Relations Committee and Operation Pursestrings, but once again Fulbright's patronage came into play. Fulbright was an early and avid McGovern supporter—he even directed the staff in his Little Rock office to help do the advance work for a visit McGovern made to that city in June 1972—and was pleased to recommend his former gofer for a position in the campaign. The assignment, coordinating McGovern's Texas campaign, was a substantial one and helped Clinton build upon his rudimentary network of potentially useful contacts in several states. And while little could have made it more attractive, Hillary's decision to go with him and work on behalf of McGovern registering Hispanic voters made this an opportunity he could not refuse.

7

LEARNING THE ROPES

JIM JOHNSON DOES NOT RECALL his first meeting with Bill
Clinton—at a political rally in the summer of 1968—but he does the
second one. The two were booked on the same flight to Miami for the
Democratic National Convention in July 1972, and Clinton, recogniz-
ing the longtime politician, struck up a conversation. After what he
thought was a most enlightening exchange, Johnson decided that this
young man was worth watching.

"Bill Clinton was on a mission down there in behalf of George
McGovern against his own people in Arkansas, and I met him on the
plane," Johnson recalls. "He was low-key, he wasn't pushy, he knew
how to play his role, and I have an idea that is the way he has spent his
life—playing the role at the time. . . . I didn't know the extent of his
role except that I found out he wasn't down there to help Wilbur."[1]

Congressman Wilbur D. Mills, then sixty-three and chairman of the
powerful House Ways and Means Committee, had been in the House
since 1937. In Arkansas, as in Washington, everybody who was anybody in politics, or wanted to be, knew "Mr. Chairman." Johnson had
been summoned to Miami by Mills to help in his small but resourceful
campaign for the Democratic presidential nomination, which had

109

begun in January with the announcement of a write-in campaign for the March 7 New Hampshire primary. Johnson was not alone: although Mills denied it at the time, roughly two dozen Arkansas operatives and dozens of supporters from other states had traveled to Miami at Mills's behest to round up delegate support.

That Johnson gave aid and comfort to the Mills effort initially surprised some who knew him well. An unabashed segregationist, Johnson appeared to have little in common with Mills.

"I just loved him," Johnson now says of the late congressman. "But I like a lot of people that I don't agree with their philosophy on a lot of things." The two were not philosophical opposites on all racial issues; for example, both were early opponents of busing students to achieve racial balance and supported a constitutional amendment to prohibit it. But Mills was something of a pragmatist and as a career politician tried to maintain a semblance of balance in his public stance, whereas Johnson was a hellfire and brimstone reactionary. Politics, moreover, was not their only bond: Mills was a distant relative of Johnson's wife, Virginia.

The Johnson relationship eventually cost Mills two of the twenty-seven Arkansas delegate votes pledged to his nomination. The defectors were Stephen Smith, a young state representative, and Dewey Stiles of the United Steelworkers Union, both of whom a few years later played prominent roles in Bill Clinton's gubernatorial administration.

Arkansas officialdom had done everything possible to assist Mills's effort. The state Democratic party had rejected the popular election of delegates in favor of selection by delegates to the state convention, ostensibly to ensure a broad representation of the electorate but primarily because Mills could expect more solid support from delegates handpicked at a state convention. It also had lowered the congressional filing fee, increased just two years before, from \$4,500 to \$2,500. In a special legislative session convened by Governor Dale Bumpers, who was elected in 1970, the General Assembly moved the state's primary election from late summer to May to accommodate a change in national Democratic party rules which made it impossible for Arkansas delegates to be certified if they were elected in late June. Mills was confident of getting the favorite-son vote from Arkansas on the first ballot, but he was counting on more than symbolism.

"I'm in the wings," Mills said. "If they have a deadlock and want me, I'll be there."

"Wilbur was trying to create an umbrella so that, if they could stop McGovern, all of the supporters of the other candidates running could get under his umbrella and give Wilbur the nomination as a compromise candidate—and actually, that effort was a lot more serious than the public was advised," Johnson recalled. "He wanted me there on the assumption that I could influence some [George] Wallace people, when they were beaten in the convention, to come over to the Mills camp."

During his years in Washington, Mills had forged connections "with people in every one of the presidential camps" that year, including those of Shirley Chisholm, Ed Muskie, Hubert Humphrey, and Scoop Jackson. Jackson, Johnson said, "had the labor support, but I was in Wilbur's apartment [at the Deauville Hotel] there in Miami [when] he got a confidential call from George Meany, who had been supporting Jackson but . . . was agreed to come with Wilbur" if McGovern could be stopped. Actually, although some labor organizations endorsed McGovern, for the first time in many years the AFL-CIO remained neutral in that campaign. Meany made no secret of the fact that he did not believe that McGovern was "good material" for the White House.

The general public seemed to agree. The incumbent president, Richard M. Nixon, led in the polls all the way and won overwhelmingly.

It did not help that a strong undercurrent running through the Democratic party wanted to stop McGovern's campaign for the nomination. Clinton has dismissed the notion that McGovern was rejected by voters because he was perceived as being too liberal. The problem, Clinton once told syndicated columnist and author David Broder, was that the American public saw the entire McGovern movement as "unstable [and] irrational."[2]

"The average person watching it on television in Arkansas, the kind of person who is the backbone of my support there, had the unsettling feeling that this campaign and this man did not have a core, a center, that was common to the great majority of the country," Clinton observed. "In Arkansas, there's probably a hard-core 30 percent that is always going to vote for the more conservative of the two candidates. But the election can still be won by a more progressive candidate if you can persuade people you've got a center core they can understand and relate to and trust."

Long before the Miami convention, which historian Gil Troy has noted "seemed overrun by long-haired kids in tie-dyed T-shirts,"[3] distrust for McGovern had begun at the worst possible level—among the rank-and-file in the state party structures. These voters had watched the South Dakota senator oversee a commission charged with revamping the Democrats's rules ostensibly to "democratize" the presidential nominating process, making it more accessible to blacks, women, and young people, but which they suspected would go a long way toward securing the 1972 nomination for McGovern.

Democrats had spent far too many conventions picking their candidates in smoke-filled rooms to trust that true populist reform was possible; and given the unusual number of states in which the delegate selection process was challenged that year, their suspicions were well founded. Some of the problems were the result of Democratic party "reforms" recommended by commissions headed by McGovern and Representative Donald M. Fraser of Minnesota; others were created when the local party blatantly disregarded the national rules changes as they pursued business as usual.

In Chicago, insurgent Democrats accused Mayor Richard J. Daley of improperly selecting fifty-nine Illinois delegates in closed-door meetings, a violation of new rules requiring proportional representation for women, young people, and minority groups.

In California, the winner-take-all primary splintered the already factionalized party organization when McGovern won by a plurality.

In Mississippi and in Florida, delegate selection had wound up in court. Altogether, a baker's dozen of state delegations was challenged before the Rules Committee, and more would follow on the convention floor.

Many Democratic party stalwarts felt completely disenfranchised by the process, so that by the end of the five-month nominating cycle the party was in disarray. It was not at all inconceivable that estranged partisans would turn to a compromise candidate at the convention in July, although Mills bluntly acknowledged that he would not have a chance at the nomination unless a deadlock occurred in Miami. Just to be on the safe side, he had filed as a candidate for reelection to his Second Congressional District seat following a meager fourth-place showing (4 percent) in New Hampshire.

McGovern, who had announced his candidacy in January 1971, was the voice of the antiwar movement, and the nucleus of his support was among young people, particularly those of draft age who later that year helped win the right for eighteen-year-olds to vote. With the advent of the Twenty-sixth Amendment, it was projected that half a million students would participate in the 1972 elections, and he embraced their causes—antiwar activism, civil rights, equal rights for women— although, in fact, only a small minority of these newly eligible voters would go to the polls that year. Out of step with mainstream Democrats, McGovern, at its onset, waged a youthful crusade which older partisans found highly suspicious, despite his strong showing in the early primaries.

One by one, his potential challengers, at least the serious ones, lost steam or failed to materialize. Ted Kennedy had been undone three years before by Chappaquiddick; Ed Muskie, who was already slipping in the polls when he topped the New Hampshire primary with 46 percent of the vote, lost too many other early primary votes and dropped out; George Wallace, although he would arrive in Miami still insisting he was a viable candidate, had been seriously wounded by a would-be assassin's bullet; and Hubert Humphrey had blown the important California primary. Of these, only Wallace's name would be placed in nomination. Before the roll call began, Mills would release one hundred non-Arkansas delegates from twenty-one states who were pledged to vote for him.

Mills, whose candidacy was never taken seriously outside Arkansas, assigned himself the role of sleeping giant under the premise, Johnson said, that someone "who had not been involved in the fight at all" was more likely to attract the support of the also-rans than someone with whom they had been bickering. Johnson insists that Mills "had set himself up as that compromise candidate [with] the inner power circles" of all the Democratic hopefuls save McGovern.[4]

"[T]his insurgent," Gil Troy pointed out in his 1991 study *See How They Ran*, "had to welcome traditional Democrats without alienating his 'army' of primary supporters. At the convention, any attempts McGovern's forces made to control the delegates or ally with party stalwarts were denounced as the 'old politics' of boss rule."[5]

Among the bosses shut out at the Miami convention was Chicago's Mayor Daley, whose early overtures to Muskie had given him some prominence among participants in the so-called "Stop McGovern" movement.

If there had been any doubt that maneuvering by the McGovern forces had alienated a good portion of the party structure, that doubt was dispelled during the Credentials Committee's week-long preconvention session, when a majority of the members voted to ignore California's winner-take-all primary and distribute 151 of McGovern's 271 delegates to other candidates in proportion to the total votes received in that state's primary.

Although this action had been precipitated and managed by a coalition of anti-McGovern forces, among them uncommitted delegates and supporters of Muskie, Jackson, Wallace, and Jackson, there was more to the committee's action than anti-McGovern sentiment. A week before, the Rules Committee had approved a reform charter that was even more liberal than the one promulgated by the McGovern-Fraser commissions. Among the proposed changes was abolition of winner-take-all primaries.

In keeping with the party's commitment to diversity and inclusion, the Credentials Committee also moved to oust the mayor of Chicago and fifty-eight other Illinois hand-picked delegates and seat a slate of challengers among whom McGovern was the clear-cut favorite.

Both actions—redistribution of the California vote and the ouster of the Illinois delegates—wound up before the United States Supreme Court, which returned the cases to the convention for resolution on the ground that judicial intervention in the political process was inappropriate.

Thus these matters were thrown before a fractious convention split into two camps, the McGovernites and everyone else, and the Mc-Governites won. McGovern had offered a compromise to the Daley bloc, proposing that both sets of delegates be seated with half-votes, but the offer was rejected. The Illinois replacements were upheld. The pivotal moment of the convention came soon afterward, when the seated delegates overwhelmingly rejected Convention Chairman Lawrence F. O'Brien's decision to distribute the California delegates proportionately.

"Wilbur [Mills] was there, and sitting on ready, and it came down to the vote under the new McGovern rules," Jim Johnson said, "but even playing by those rules, if the Daley group out of Illinois had been seated, we would have had enough votes in that convention to stop McGovern—all we wanted to do was stop them, bring it to a halt—and then the compromise would have come into being. And, in my view, Wilbur Mills would have been the first president of the United States from Arkansas had that happened."[6]

What happened instead was that less than twenty-four hours later, with the anti-McGovern coalition crumbling, both Muskie and Humphrey withdrew, giving McGovern a clear shot at the nomination.

"The thing about it [was that] all those people's philosophies were so close to each other," Johnson opined. "When you can't fall out over philosophy, then the campaign becomes personal—and you can't reconcile personal differences. You have to fight over personality, and they [the various factions] couldn't."

Johnson remains singularly unimpressed with the 1972 slate of Democrat might-have-beens, but he has never forgotten, or forgiven, the long-haired young man from Arkansas who did his part, however small, to quash another Arkansan's presidential dream.

"It caused me to watch him carefully from then on," Johnson said more than twenty years after the Miami convention. "I looked at him as a punk kid then, and I look at him as a punk kid now. . . . [But] he was clever enough to get around in the Mills camp to try to make it all right that he helped the other side. He's cunning."

Jim Johnson's son, Mark Johnson, who was serving an internship in Mills's Washington congressional office that summer, was at the airport to greet his father when the elder Johnson and Bill Clinton deplaned. Jim Johnson introduced them, "and I was just a little incredulous," Mark Johnson recalls. "Here was someone from Arkansas who was not supporting Mr. Mills. I mean, just from a standpoint of respect, you'd think he would be supporting a native son. . . . Years later, I asked Mr. Mills about that, and he said that Bill Clinton had sought his endorsement" to work in McGovern's behalf, and Mills had given his approval.

"I'm a realist," Mills said at the top of the convention, after a black Arkansas delegate, Henry Wilkins III, had broken with Mills's expressed wishes and voted to seat all of the California delegates favorable to McGovern because Wilkins was running for office in a predominantly black district and did not want to alienate his constituency. "A fellow has to take care of himself."[7]

To think it unusual that "a punk kid" from Hot Springs, Arkansas, would approach the powerful chairman of the House Ways and Means Committee for his blessings to work in an opponent's campaign is to ignore a cardinal rule of politics: Never burn bridges. Clinton realized that while Mills was a long shot for the nomination, he was likely to remain a powerful politician for years to come, and therefore someone whose friendship could prove valuable. As Clinton told a reporter in the summer of 1972, "It is important to keep a good, harmonious relationship" with other politicians if one is to be effective in politics.[8] He had, indeed, conferred with Mills before signing on with McGovern to track delegates, he told the *Arkansas Gazette*, and had received not only Mr. Chairman's blessings but his encouragement. His only interest in touching base with Mills's supporters, he said, was to obtain "a secondary commitment in case Mills releases the delegates" and lining up volunteers for the general-election phase of the McGovern campaign.

McGovern truly did have an excellent chance of winning the nomination for reasons other than his early entry. He may have been a Johnny-one-note candidate—next to the Nixon administration's Vietnam policy, the best attack against the incumbent was to criticize his support for workfare, a concept Clinton later would embrace as governor—but the note he sounded held great appeal for hundreds of thousands of young Americans who had just acquired the vote.

McGovern's supporters, that is, were just the people Clinton hoped to appeal to once he began his quest for public office—feminists, blacks, students, the underclass, each group with its own historical, economic, or social agenda, but united in its belief that the Vietnam War should be ended and the billions that American spent on the war go to domestic programs. McGovern may have been a star-crossed candidate, but he attracted and inspired some of the hardest-working, most dedicated young organizers of the era, many of whom would find the connections they made in the McGovern campaign useful when they matured and entered government and politics at all levels. Among these were former Colorado Senator Gary Hart, McGovern's 1992 campaign manager; Washington lobbyist Anne Wexler, who later married Joseph P. Duffey and whose Wexler Group now employs Betsey Wright, Clinton's former gubernatorial chief of staff and herself a McGovern campaign worker in 1972; and pollster Pat Caddell. "There are at least a million persons who would go out into the streets and work their heads off for McGovern," Clinton observed during the campaign.[9] One of the problems, however, was getting them to go to the polls in November. New voters stayed away in droves; history suggests that McGovern had a top-notch campaign organization, but the candidate was lacking.

From the day he signed onto the McGovern campaign in early 1972, Clinton availed himself of every opportunity to expand his growing list of contacts, so it is not surprising that once he stepped to the fore of campaign politics, much of his financial support came from other former McGovernites.

Clinton's 1976 resume, the one released to the news media when he announced for attorney general, describes his role in the McGovern campaign as that of state "co-coordinator" of Texas from August to November 1972—a period during which his resume also states that he was an instructor of constitutional law and criminal justice administration at the University of New Haven, "working with policemen in the largest law enforcement education program of its kind in the United States (February 1972 to June 1973)."

Even in the 1970s, Bill Clinton was not averse to assigning himself whatever title would enhance his standing before people of influence.

For example, in June 1972, in an interview with the *Arkansas Gazette*, he boasted that he had been a member of McGovern's national campaign staff for fifteen months—virtually from the moment that McGovern had announced his candidacy—and said he had been recruiting and organizing McGovernites in Connecticut while attending law school in New Haven.[10] Later that month, when McGovern made a stopover in Little Rock, Clinton's name appeared briefly in local newspaper accounts of the event as McGovern's "staff man for South Carolina and Arkansas."[11] By 1977, Clinton was billing himself as McGovern's campaign coordinator for the entire state of Texas in 1972, an unfortunate claim in face of Betsey Wright's assertion that her feminism "was crystallized" when the man sent by McGovern— apparently not Bill Clinton—to manage the Texas campaign harassed her unmercifully.

"[N]ot a day went by with this man, when I tried to talk to him about some of the political factors we had to consider, that he didn't ask me about my hormones or when was the last time I had been laid," she told David Broder for his 1980 book, *Changing of the Guard*.[12]

Wright, one of twelve children of a country doctor who for many years held the chairmanship of the Brewster County, Texas, Democratic Committee, was already neck-deep in politics when Bill Clinton and Hillary Rodham journeyed to Texas in the summer of 1972 to help with the McGovern campaign. As a five-year-old, Wright had placed the traditional Stetson hat atop President Harry S Truman's head during a whistle-stop in Alpine, Texas. She had begun working in campaigns at the county level at age fifteen, and by 1969, at age twenty-five, she had become the youngest president in the history of the Young Democrats of Texas. By late 1972, when she was wooed away from Common Cause to help organize the McGovern campaign, she had several statewide campaigns to her credit, including former Senator Ralph Yarborough's unsuccessful race against a fellow named Lloyd Bentsen, and Congresswoman Frances "Sissy" Farenthold's ill-fated bid for the Texas governorship. Among those who recruited her for the McGovern campaign, Wright later said, was a young Arkansan with Eastern airs named Bill Clinton.

Theirs relationship, as Wright once said, was to be an "almost symbiotic" one from which Clinton would derive more direct benefit than Wright.[13] The relationship is a complex one that periodically breaks down and reestablishes itself in times of crisis. Their friendship evolved as a result of Wright's rapport with his girlfriend, Hillary Rodham, who was part of the Wellesley network that became involved in a pilot project to register Hispanic voters, made possible by an act of Congress that granted a tax deduction for money donated for voter registration efforts.

"I knew Bill and Hillary were from Yale Law School, and as far as I was concerned, they were Easterners," Wright told the *Arkansas Gazette* in 1985. "I was impressed with how bright they were, [but] I was closer to Hillary than to Bill. I remember thinking that Hillary would make a wonderful lawyer and a wonderful political candidate wherever she ended up practicing law."[14]

That Wright would later abandon her prominent position as director of the National Women's Education Fund to help Clinton regain his political momentum after his 1980 defeat in the race for governor of Arkansas was more a testament to her affinity for Hillary than her loyalty to him. At some point in their relationship, most likely during that comeback campaign, when she became immersed in helping him reconstruct his shattered political fences, Wright became a dedicated, even fanatical, Clinton convert, what Justice Jim Johnson would call "a true believer," the kind of bull-headed loyalist who "digs in like a termite and works harder" than anyone else to accomplish a goal. Wright probably would not argue with that assessment. "I view campaigns as a means to an end," she once said.[15]

The McGovern campaign did much to strengthen the intellectual and philosophical bonds between Bill and Hillary, but their personal relationship still lacked direction, which may have accounted for Wright's subsequent observation that she "didn't even think at the time about their getting married."[16] That they slept together was not unusual in their generation, but they were not so besotted with one another that they minded sharing their living quarters with friends. Bill appreciated parties more than Hillary, but both of them enjoyed sitting with a roomful of friends discussing the current campaign or other political issues of the day. While some of their colleagues viewed their relationship as transitory, others insist that it was apparent that despite their personal indecision, Bill and Hillary would find a way to mesh their individual professional interests.

That breakthrough would be some time in coming, however. For one thing, Bill knew what he wanted to do once Yale was behind him, but Hillary did not. She was interested in some type of involvement with children's issues, but her goals were ill-defined and tentative. "Whereas his purpose was so fixed, she was undecided about what to do," author Taylor Branch, another colleague during the Texas campaign, told *U.S. News and World Report* in 1992.

Hillary also was uncertain about her lover's intentions, and her comments years later about that time indicate that the indecisiveness for which he would be often criticized as governor was a factor in the development of their relationship.

"When we both graduated from Yale," she would recall, "he came right home to Arkansas to teach in a law school, and I was very unsure about where I wanted to be. I certainly was not ready to move completely to Arkansas yet, because I just didn't know whether that would be a decision that Bill could stick to. I really didn't know what to expect."[17]

However single-minded his ambition, his friends and family say Bill Clinton was truly enamored of Hillary Rodham and perplexed about their relationship. While she has said she was attracted to him because he was not "afraid" of her, he was in awe of her. She was easily the most intelligent, thoughtful, capable woman with whom he had ever been involved.

"He was really concerned about whether she really would be happy in Arkansas or would even come," his mother recalled.[18]

Diane Blair, a Mills delegate from Arkansas who met Clinton at the Miami convention, later wrote about her "introduction" to Hillary Rodham; it was during a brief visit Clinton paid to her at the University of Arkansas at Fayetteville, where she was a political scientist, sometime before the November general election.

"Suddenly, halfway through lunch, he stopped me in mid-sentence to say that I was making him terribly lonely for the woman he loved, and he began telling me in glowing detail about Hillary," Blair wrote. "Since it was already clear to me that Bill would be returning to Arkansas and eventually getting into politics himself, I asked why he didn't marry this wonderful woman and bring her back to Arkansas with him. He would love to, he said, but Hillary was so uncommonly gifted and had so many attractive options of her own that he felt selfish about bringing her to what would be *his* state and *his* political future."[19]

(During their separations, Clinton often sought the sympathetic ears of strong, accomplished women, singing Hillary's praises and lamenting the obstacles in their path; after his marriage, in an apparent effort to establish rapport, he used similar approaches to evoke sympathy from other women. Upon entering public life, he occasionally professed to female reporters that he felt lonely and isolated by his office, although none of his known confidantes has admitted to offering more than a sympathetic ear.)

It never occurred to Clinton to stay in the East with Hillary and to subordinate his career to hers.

"I promised myself a long time ago," he told his mother at that juncture, "if the people of Arkansas will let me, I'll break my back to help my state. That's my life. And it's the way it has to be for me."[20]

"When you think that [he] graduated from Georgetown, Yale, he was a Rhodes Scholar—I mean, he could have gone anywhere, and he chose to come home," one longtime friend observed shortly after visiting Clinton in the White House. "He probably could have been a successful politician in many other states, so don't think [he returned to Arkansas] all for political reasons. I think that a lot of it was for personal reasons. . . . a lot of it was that people who have been here and lived in rural areas, small towns, small states where you know people, and people care about you, and it's a way of life to call people by their first name. I think Clinton liked that, and it contributed so much to his political style."[21]

When Bill returned to Yale for his final semester, he resumed his old habits. He studied little and attended few classes. To prepare for his finals, he borrowed the class notes of other students and disappeared for several days to commit the information to memory. "He was," classmate William T. Coleman has said, "the classic quick study."[22]

"He had an intellect that could absorb facts and analyze complicated information with computer-like precision," Coleman said. "When his natural tendency to be curious about everything was directed toward a specific subject, he could function with astonishing efficiency."

Following graduation, as Clinton was packing up his belongings in anticipation of his return to Hot Springs, where he hoped to borrow money with which to open a law office, one of his professors suggested that he apply for one of two vacancies at the University of Arkansas Law School. Upon inquiring, Clinton was told by the dean that at age twenty-six, he was too young to be considered for the job. Clinton's purported response: "I've been too young to do everything I've ever done."[23] He joined the faculty in August 1973.

Hillary, meanwhile, accepted the offer of a staff attorney's post with the Children's Defense Fund in Cambridge, Massachusetts. After about six months, she left to work for then-Representative Peter Rodino, Jr., Democrat of Newark, New Jersey, on the House Judiciary Committee. It was a plum assignment for a fledgling lawyer, because the committee was just then launching its investigation into the possible impeachment of President Nixon following the infamous Saturday Night Massacre. On October 23, 1973, Nixon had ordered Watergate Special Prosecutor Archibald Cox fired. Rather than comply, Nixon's attorney general, Elliot Richardson, and his deputy, William Ruckelshaus, had resigned.

A year before, late in the 1972 campaign, George McGovern had made a weak run at parlaying the break-in of the Democratic party headquarters the previous June into a campaign issue, but the public was not much interested. Now Watergate dominated the airwaves, newspaper headlines, and any political conversation.

John Doar, who had been an official in the civil rights division of the Kennedy Justice Department, was named director of the Rodino committee's special investigative staff, and given the scope of the impending inquiry, he went looking for able young lawyers to assist in the research. He had several possibilities in mind, among them Bill Clinton and Hillary Rodham, both of whom came highly recommended by his contacts at Yale. He had taken particular notice of both of them while judging a Barristers's Union mock trial for which the two had teamed the year before. Clinton takes credit for having recommended his future spouse for the job. So does Burke Marshall, one of her Yale professors and a former Justice Department colleague of Doar. It is possible that both recommended her; in any event, Doar has said he would have contacted her without a recommendation.

Bill, in his first semester of teaching at Fayetteville and preparing to test the political waters firsthand by embarking upon a campaign for Congress, rejected Doar's offer of performing "grunt work" on behalf of the investigative staff; Hillary, still undecided about her future, accepted. She began work in January 1974. Among her responsibilities was drafting the legal and parliamentary procedures that would be followed throughout the inquiry. One of her bosses in this endeavor was a young lawyer named Bernard Nussbaum, who would be tapped as chief counsel to the president in the Clinton White House.

The work was exhausting, Hillary later told the *Arkansas Democrat*, but "it was wonderfully exciting. We would work ten, fifteen, twenty hours a day or all night. It didn't matter."[24]

In her capacity as a researcher, she was one of a select few to hear the Nixon tapes, and although she and others had been hired with the admonition to remain neutral in the inquiry, Hillary was stunned not only by the substantive content of the tapes but by the tangential, desperate personality of the president of the United States that began to emerge.

"There was one [tape recording] we called the tape of tapes," she later recounted. "It was Nixon taping himself listening to the tapes, making up his defenses to what he heard on the tapes. . . . You could hear Nixon talk and then you'd hear very faintly the sound of a taped prior conversation with Nixon, [H.R.] Haldeman, and [John] Erlichman . . . and you'd hear [the president] say, 'What I meant when I said that was. . . .' It was surreal, unbelievable."[25]

Life was no less exhilarating for Bill. He was no longer merely plotting his course but had embarked upon it in, of all places, Fayetteville, Arkansas.

Fayetteville, home of the state's largest institution of higher learning, is widely seen by Arkansans as a bastion of intellectualism, academic progressiveness, and political liberalism in one of the few Republican parts of Arkansas.

But despite its apparent isolation, the University of Arkansas—or, as it is commonly known, "Fayetteville"—was a fruitful place for any would-be politician who wanted to make contacts.

"Most of our politicians—particularly those that are actually thinking at the time that they want to be politicians—recognize the contacts you make in a place like Fayetteville, the premier institution of higher learning in the state," said author John R. Starr, a longtime observer of Arkansas politics. "You get to know people from all over the state."[26]

It is understandable, therefore, that when Bill Clinton was given a choice between going into debt to open a modest law practice in Hot Springs and a $25,000-a-year salary as a professor at the university's law school, he quickly chose the latter. The contacts he made at Fayetteville, some of whom became lifelong friends, were crucial to his entry into politics, and they were almost immediately fruitful. He renewed his acquaintance with Diane Kincaid, a professor of political science, and her future husband, Jim Blair, general counsel to the Democrat party of Arkansas, both of whom he had met as delegates to the Miami convention. The university's administrator, Carl Whillock, a former aide to the late northwest Arkansas Congressman James W. Trimble, and his wife Margaret—whose brother, Rudy Moore, Jr., would sign on to run Clinton's 1978 campaign for governor—took the new professor under their wing, often inviting him to dinner and introducing him to their wide circle of politically involved friends.

"Clinton's consuming fascination with politics and with government was evident even in those days," recalls Whillock, who was one of the new friends to whom Clinton confided his desire to run for office. "If he had the urge, I said, he should do it. One evening in late autumn [1973], while we were all sitting on the floor around the fireplace, he said he thought he would do it. I climbed upstairs and got a card file with the names of people from throughout the congressional district who had helped Jim Trimble," who had been defeated for reelection in 1966 by John Paul Hammerschmidt.[27]

Since Trimble's unplanned retirement from politics, Whillock said,

a number of political hopefuls had sought his help to oppose Hammerschmidt, "but Bill was the first person whom I encouraged to run
and whom I helped."

Whillock advised Clinton to travel extensively throughout the congressional district, and to begin doing so as soon as possible, to meet
people who could help him. The clean-cut, conservative Whillock
accompanied him on his early rounds, introducing him to influential
Democrats, opening doors that otherwise might have been closed.

"Keep in mind that this was 1974, and bushy-headed and side-
burned young men were rare and not much admired out in the woods
of the Arkansas Ozarks," Whillock stated in a 1992 essay. "Yoked with
Ivy League and Oxford pedigrees, Clinton's appearance was apt to
provoke not only mistrust, but also dislike."

An anecdote Whillock tells about one of the doors he opened for
Clinton is particularly revealing. Whillock took Clinton to Mountain
Home, a city with slightly more than two thousand residents and the
county seat of predominantly Republican Baxter County. One of the
local pols to whom Whillock introduced him was Hugh Hackler, a
former state legislator and businessman who always was good for
rounding up a few thousand votes.

When they met in March 1974, Hackler already had committed to
another Democrat congressional candidate, state Senator Gene Rainwater, but Whillock persuaded him to give Clinton a hearing by
telling him that Clinton "was a bright young man who would someday be governor or United States senator and that in the years ahead
Hugh would want to support him."

Over coffee and soft drinks in a booth at the local drugstore,
Whillock broke the ice by asking Clinton where he was from.

"Hot Springs," Bill replied.

"I have a good friend in Hot Springs," Hackler said. "I doubt if you
know him. He has some drugstore there. Name is Gabe Crawford."

"Sure, I know Gabe Crawford. He and my dad are good friends. We
visit in his home all the time, and he and his family come over to our
house."

Whether Whillock had poor recall of the details of this meeting or
whether Clinton used the reference to his father as a gambit to

establish rapport is not clear, because his mother Virginia was at that time between husbands, but whatever the substance of Clinton's response, it worked. Whillock recalls that the conversation warmed at that point, and after about twenty minutes, Hackler said: "Carl, I'm going to call my friends in Fort Smith and tell them I want out of my commitment to support Senator Rainwater and that I'm going to support Bill."

"Because of conversations like this," Whillock said later, "I'm convinced that Bill could persuade two of every three voters to support him if he could have one-on-one conversations with them."

8

"BILL THINKS . . . BILL FEELS . . . BILL DOES

BILL CLINTON WAS ONLY SIX MONTHS out of Yale Law School when he launched his first campaign in 1974. It was a surprisingly well-financed endeavor even without the $10,000 loan his uncle Raymond Clinton co-signed for him. He had joined the faculty of the University of Arkansas Law School only three months before but persuaded the administration—not too difficult, given its liberal bent—to grant him unpaid leave and an erratic teaching schedule. (He managed this feat not once but twice, getting leave again in 1976 to run for attorney general after having told the university that he would not seek office for several years after his 1974 defeat. Clinton was on unpaid leave for most of the three years the law school carried him on the faculty roster.)

One of his first campaign recruits was a young man named Rudy Moore, Jr., a member of the Arkansas House of Representatives who had been advised by Fulbright to get acquainted with his former aide. Moore did that and more; he gave Clinton's congressional campaign an early boost with a few well-placed telephone calls and personal introductions to some of the district's most influential Democrats.

"Not long after his arrival in Fayetteville, Bill began talking about

127

running for office," Moore, who would serve as Clinton's chief of staff during his first term as governor, recalled in a 1992 essay. "Most of us recognized, from the first, his vast political potential. It was evident that he had running for office in mind when he moved to Fayetteville, and that it was only a matter of finding the right office."[1]

Moore said Clinton "never gave any thought to running for a local office or for the legislature; his goals were on a higher level." Clinton had begun scoping out the political terrain before he had completed his unpacking, and, as Moore noted, "it didn't take him long to settle on challenging for the seat of United States representative John Paul Hammerschmidt, a conservative Republican who, through assiduous service to constituents and a willingness to engage in mutual back-scratching with Democratic leaders, had, in only four terms, firmly entrenched himself."

Clinton's campaign attracted a number of volunteers from within the university community: some of the professors he had cultivated during visits while a law student at Georgetown, others he had met through the Fulbright and McGovern campaigns.

Clinton was especially popular with students, whose papers he routinely neglected to evaluate and whose grades he routinely forgot to post. He often brought their work along with him on the campaign trail, and occasionally, during a lapse in activity, he would even grade a few. In any event, any grounding his students received in constitutional law or criminal procedure was incidental, given his preoccupation with politics.

Former student and Arkansas state Senator Lu Hardin takes exception to the notion that Clinton was anything but "a very good teacher," although he concedes that his former criminal procedure professor was lackadaisical about grading papers, noting that grades for the spring 1974 semester were not posted until just before Labor Day.[2] Other former students claim that Clinton was usually ill-prepared for his classes. There were few formal lectures, and his classes often digressed into spirited discussions about political issues of the day. Clinton was not merely approachable; he sought to establish extracurricular relationships with his students, often playing half-court basketball or sharing a cup of coffee with them after class. A number of those students signed onto his campaign, and several went on to pursue political careers of their own.

These students and a handful of university colleagues constituted the first generation of Clintonites, a group one reporter described in September 1974 as "young—mostly women—former campus politicians, joiners, and gadflies who remind me of the volunteers who beat the bushes for Eugene McCarthy in 1968."[3]

The reporter, Michael Gaspeny, had been dispatched by a Fayetteville "underground" newspaper, *The Grapevine*, published off-campus as an alternative to the university's *Arkansas Traveler*, to get a handle on the young law professor. He provided a stark first glimpse of Clinton's appeal in his assessment of the Clintonites: "These are the kind of people who stand in the rain at high school football games to distribute campaign leaflets. The workers are influenced by the Dexedrine-like effects of campaigning white-line fever, an inversion that naturally seizes the members of a cult. The volunteers are extremely reluctant to talk about themselves. They constantly mutter the aspirant's name in hushed tones: 'Bill thinks . . . ,' 'Bill feels . . . ,' Bill does. . . .' "[4]

Arkansas's current state auditor, Julia Hughes Jones, recalls being introduced to the young congressional hopeful by her younger sister, an undergraduate at the University of Arkansas, on election night in 1974. "I remember thinking what a nice-looking kid"—here Jones burst into laughter—"because that's what he looked like, a gangly kid, and I could . . . see this magnetism line or something, you know, eye to eye, and I could tell that he was really a charmer because she was just, you know, she was really taken with him. . . . She was just totally fascinated with him. I mean, you could just tell that she just worshiped the ground the man walked on. But so did everybody else that was anywhere near him that night, all these kids, these students."[5]

Jones also observed that her sister and her friends at the university "were all just wounded" when he married Hillary Rodham a year later. "Everybody knew he took Hillary out, but there were so many others, too, that he was with all the time, and I think every one of them felt they had a shot." His appeal to young women, Jones conceded, was not unlike that of a rock star.

Building name recognition for a future statewide race had been Clinton's primary motive for entering the Third Congressional District race, although he figured that the Republican incumbent faced some degree of vulnerability as a result of the Watergate scandal. He had little interest in the legislative process, having closely observed the investment of time and tedium required to acquire power and influence on Capitol Hill. As one of his biographers noted, he was a young man in a hurry to make his mark in politics. One did not do that by way of Congress.

Today Bill Clinton claims that he ran for Congress only because "no one else would do it,"[6] but in truth, he was the second to file for what would be a four-man race for the Democratic nomination in the spring of 1974. The Republican incumbent, John Paul Hammerschmidt, had not yet made known his plans when, in mid-February 1974, David Stewart, a thirty-two-year-old lawyer whose work on behalf of Dale Bumpers in the 1970 gubernatorial campaign had netted him an appointment to the state Claims Commission, declared his candidacy. His was not necessarily a frivolous campaign—political patronage as recompense for campaign duty was how most ambitious young Democrats in Arkansas persuaded voters to let them try their hand at elective office—but it was uninspiring and decidedly underfinanced. Stewart placed third, ahead of James Scanlon, a small-town mayor and lawyer who served on the University of Arkansas faculty. Name recognition and the vote-splintering four-man field put W. E. "Gene" Rainwater, a popular state senator from Fort Smith, into the June runoff with Clinton, but it was no contest. He emerged from the runoff with an impressive 69 percent of the vote; whereas Clinton had entered the campaign fully expecting to lose, he now began to see an outside chance of victory come November.

Clinton's youth—he turned twenty-eight during the general election campaign—was an asset, a promise to special-interest groups of long and satisfying relationships to come, and he could boast of some firsthand knowledge of how Congress worked because of his stint as a gofer for Senator Fulbright. His affiliation with the George McGovern presidential campaign in 1972 was less appealing in conservative northwest Arkansas, but Clinton kept his long, unruly curls groomed,

he appeared comfortable in coat and tie, and his liberal leanings, which
he eagerly told reporters about in private, were kept carefully under
wraps by reporters, many of whom were only slightly older than he.
He was extremely accessible to the press, both on and off duty,
charming seasoned reporters as surely as he did a growing number of
potential voters—and friendships developed.

Thanks to the McGovern network, Clinton also forged early alliances with special-interest groups whose political influence reached
thousands of professional and blue-collar workers in the Third District, among them labor and teachers.

Though Clinton's relationship with organized labor would prove
thorny in later years, in 1974 labor was his greatest source of support.
Arkansas AFL-CIO President J. Bill Becker recalls meeting Clinton
during the 1972 presidential campaign when Clinton was a McGovern
organizer in Arkansas. Although the AFL-CIO remained neutral in
that campaign, Becker, who was then hosting a weekly radio program
on the 50,000-watt KAAY-AM, was referred to Clinton when he
went searching for someone to present "the McGovern side of the
story."

"He showed up at the studio with a long beard and overalls . . . I
think they were Big Smith overalls, which are union made, and it was
one of the easiest programs I ever did," Becker recalled. "I think I may
have asked him one question and he just talked for fifteen minutes—it
was a fifteen-minute program—about McGovern. That was my first
experience with Bill Clinton. I was very impressed with him."[7]

In the following months, during Clinton's occasional visits to his
home state during breaks in his law studies, the two men had several,
more informal meetings.

"He came out to my house a couple of times, had breakfast with the
family, and talked about the possibility of his running against Hammerschmidt in the Third Congressional District," Becker said. "And
we had a problem with that, although as I said, I was impressed with
him, because Gene Rainwater . . . was thinking about running for
Congress, and Gene Rainwater had a pro-labor record."

The labor leader told Clinton outright that Rainwater appeared to
have the inside track, but Clinton was not discouraged. He was full of

questions about issues before Congress in which the AFL–CIO had an interest.

"The AFL–CIO used to, and I still think does, produce a book on the last Congress," Becker said. "It runs 50–60 pages and has a paragraph or two about the issues and what the outcome was and what the status of it is, and in [Clinton's] asking about how to get familiar with the labor issues, I told him about that little booklet and gave him one, as I remember.

"And he must have studied," Becker said, laughing, "studied it hard. . . . He took the endorsement away from Rainwater because of the way he handled himself before the interviewing committee. He was so smart and so articulate and so knowledgeable about issues."

No one was more surprised than Rainwater when Clinton's candidacy garnered the support of organized labor in 1974. The Arkansas chapter of the AFL–CIO, virtually the only organized labor influence in the state, always endorsed the Democrats seeking state office, but Rainwater, a seasoned, albeit provincial, politician, had made a fatal error: He had not prepared for his interview with the AFL–CIO review committee.

Becker recollects that Rainwater "was pretty cool and secure that he was going to get the endorsement because of his voting record," but while the state senator was well versed in state labor matters, "he was not familiar with federal issues."

Becker, who would always follow the national organization's lead but who privately would come to distrust Clinton, appreciates the irony of the role he played in establishing what would become a love-hate relationship between Clinton and organized labor but which, at the onset of Clinton's political career, was paramount in giving him a foothold for the future.

"Clinton just captured the committee. . . . Our people just fell in love with the guy. He was so impressive with what he said, and he was right on so many issues. . . . He understood the issues and he could talk about the issues. Of course," Becker said, again laughing, "he had a head start, since I gave him that original book. He probably memorized it."

The committee representative of the Steelworkers Union, who had come to the interviews fully prepared to nominate Rainwater, was so taken with Clinton's responses that he made the motion to endorse the young law professor.

In a 1993 interview, Becker could not recall the issues of particular concern to the review committee in 1974—"labor issues are not discussed very much in [state] campaigns"—and he lamented that his organization did not keep a record of Clinton's or any other candidate's answers. "For the most part [we] still don't," he said, and, mumbling as though to himself, added: "We should. Might come in handy sometime, especially with guys like him."

Following his appearance before the AFL-CIO's review committee, the organization's laudatory statement described the Fayetteville newcomer as having "the brightest future of anyone who has been before this state convention in a long time." The endorsement was important because, although Arkansas was and remains a right-to-work state, the Third District was Arkansas's most industrialized region.

"That race was tremendously important to us," recalls Jim Clark, the longtime secretary-treasurer of the Arkansas AFL-CIO. "We worked overtime in the campaign, went into the Third District in carloads" to campaign for Clinton, to register voters, and, later, to drive them to the polls.[8] Union members also contributed the bulk of Clinton's campaign funds, although only about 16 percent was directly attributable to labor interests. "That's not enough to buy my vote," Clinton declared.[9]

Consumer groups fired their own salvo in an attempt to strengthen Clinton's candidacy. In a joint statement, Arkansas Consumer Research, Public Interest Citizen Action, and the Consumer Federation of America denounced as disgraceful Hammerschmidt's "incredibly consistent anti-consumer voting record" on behalf of oil companies and big business.[10] The United Mine Workers joined the assault, criticizing the incumbent at Clinton's behest for having voted against mine workers on nine separate issues, including benefits programs for those afflicted with black lung disease. (Among the cases Clinton inherited upon the death of his friend Jack Yates, a locally popular lawyer and former state senator Clinton had befriended, were a number of victims afflicted with the so-called coal miner's disease. It was

Yates who brought Hammerschmidt's voting record on these issues to Clinton's attention.)

The Clinton endorsement statement issued shortly before the Democratic primary by the Arkansas Education Association would prove somewhat embarrassing to education leaders in future years, noting as it did that the union's members "were particularly impressed by Clinton's consistent stand on issues affecting the quality of education in Arkansas,"[11] given his propensity for vacillating on education issues once he became governor.

The Young Democrats of Arkansas broke with tradition in sanctioning his candidacy: "(W)e feel that this race is of such importance that we should take an active part," read the statement issued by the YD's Executive Committee. "The Third Congressional District is the only major position in the state which is not held by a Democrat."[12]

The committee's unprecedented action had less to do with combatting the Republican party's iron grip on northwest Arkansas than with the fact that the earliest Clintonites controlled the committee. With considerable hyperbole, the Executive Committee declared that a Clinton victory would "restore to the people of the Third District proper, hard-working, and honest representation in Washington."

If ever there was an officeholder who epitomized proper, hard-working, and honest representation in Washington—and that perception was held inside and beyond the Third District—it was John Paul Hammerschmidt, whose unsullied career spanned twenty-six years, until his retirement in 1992.

At the time of the 1974 campaign, Hammerschmidt, who had amassed a fortune in the family lumber business, was one of the most popular politicians in Arkansas. A recognized civic leader in his hometown of Harrison, in Congress he had built a solid reputation for constituent services, responding to inquiries and complaints from outside his district when no one else would. Throughout his thirteen terms in office, only one opponent ever gave Hammerschmidt a run for his money—Bill Clinton, who in 1974 outspent every opponent, including Hammerschmidt, by $20,000, and campaigned sixteen to twenty hours a day for almost ten months.(When Jim McDougal, for example, attempted to unseat Hammerschmidt in 1982, he received only about 34 percent of the vote.)

Everyone had expected Hammerschmidt, who turned fifty-two that May, to seek a fifth term, although virtually into the eleventh hour he encouraged speculation that he would challenge Senator J. William Fulbright after polls suggested that Arkansas's governor, Dale Bumpers, could defeat Senator Fulbright's sixth-term aspirations. But Hammerschmidt refused to run for higher officer after Bumpers defeated Fulbright in the 1974 Democratic primary. Bumpers was elected and is now Arkansas's senior senator.

Although Clinton did not enter the race expecting to win, he opened several campaign offices throughout the Third Congressional District, which included twenty-one of the state's seventy-five counties stretching from the Missouri-Arkansas line in the northwest quadrant of the state down along the western border into south-central Arkansas and included his adopted home county of Garland and Hot Springs. He visited every county numerous times, often driving himself in his green 1970 Gremlin, and later a Chevrolet truck. By his own admission, he wore out three pairs of shoes.

No crowd was too small, no organization too far from his home base, for a Clinton appearance. Beauty pageants, civic clubs, parades, political groups, factory gates, county fairs—the young candidate dutifully made the circuit, honing his enthusiastic but inconsistent speaking style, perfecting his use of catch phrases and glittering generalities. Rarely the first to arrive—even then he found it impossible to keep a schedule—he usually was the last to depart, hanging around to chew the fat until the last straggler was all talked out. He rarely went immediately from one event to another, often pulling to the side of the road to shake hands with highway work crews or to press the flesh with the locals at a rural grocery store.

Hammerschmidt, an effective but reluctant campaigner did not make the traditional Fourth of July round of picnics and parades, as Clinton continued his exhaustive dawn-to-midnight pace, even doubling back for a second shot at the Springdale crowd following a side trip to a beauty pageant in nearby Gentry. Hammering his primary theme of strength and responsibility in Congress, he was a temporary

distraction for a small-town crowd anxious to dispense with the
speeches and the procession of contestants and candidates so the
fireworks could begin.

But he fared better at the Springdale rodeo. Wisely taking up a
position at the concession stand, he kept his exchanges friendly and
folksy. Moving later into the parking lot, where he greeted each
departing carload, he wrapped up the public part of the day encircled
by a handful of stragglers who vented their frustrations while he
listened and nodded and offered an occasional observation about the
need for effective representation in Washington. "They say you're just
a college professor," a participant decked out in cowboy gear declared,
"but I think you're one of us."[13]

With the exception of a few weekend excursions to his district,
Hammerschmidt, a decorated veteran of World War II and the ranking
minority member of the House Veterans Affairs Committee, spent
most of the summer in Washington, watchdogging constituent interests as the final act of the Watergate drama unfolded. The status of Fort
Chaffee, established as a World War II training center and kept alive for
years as a summer training facility for National Guard and Army
Reserve troops, was of particular concern. There was a move to close
the base and transfer the property to civilian control, which threatened
the jobs of 135 civilians and scores of veterans. Since a study of the
base-closing proposal had just been approved, a decision was months,
possibly years in coming. Hammerschmidt assured voters in his unassuming style that if they kept him in Washington, he would continue
to fight for Fort Chaffee every step of the way.

"If ever a seat appeared safe," wrote Robert Fisher of the *Arkansas
Democrat*, "it is Hammerschmidt's. Despite the fact that he is the state's
lone Republican officeholder in Washington"—in fact, he was the
first Arkansas Republican elected to Congress since Reconstruction—"despite Watergate and its manifold ramifications, and despite
the combined wrath of state Democrats, Hammerschmidt appears to
be so well entrenched that any effort to dislodge him has to be marked
as an exercise in futility."[14]

Hammerschmidt was seen as unbeatable because his private wealth
and the strength of the incumbency relieved him of worries about

raising campaign funds and because he represented the most conservative and only Republican region in the state. He had chalked up a 93
percent attendance record in Congress during the previous session and
spent at least every other weekend in the district, meeting constituents
and making public appearances. He relied very little on the press—
even his reelection announcement came in the form of a prepared
statement mailed from Washington—and emphasized case work with
both his district and Washington staffs. His supporters included numerous lifelong Democrats who approved of his conservative voting
record and appreciated being greeted warmly and called by name
whenever their paths crossed.

The only potential trouble spot for Hammerschmidt was Watergate.

The Watergate scandal, whose repercussions were being felt in
many elections across the nation, was not an issue Clinton wanted to
tackle head-on. Many of his supporters urged him to take broadside
hits at his Republican opponent using knowledge he had gleaned
from Hillary Rodham's involvement with the House Judiciary Committee while it was working on the impeachment of Richard M.
Nixon, but, at least initially, Clinton figured he could not afford to
do that in Republican northwest Arkansas. The wiser course was to
reproach Democrats as well as Republicans for letting the Nixon
administration "roll over Congress and kick it like a yard dog if it got
in the way."[15]

"Too many congressmen did not speak up," Clinton said before the
scandal came to a head, resulting in the unprecedented resignation of
an American president. "If they had, I believe we would not be faced
with the sad and dismal prospect of impeaching the president of the
United States." But no, he added, "the people of this country do not
perceive Watergate as completely a party problem. One man could not
have created all the trouble we have in the country today."[16]

Hammerschmidt, a longtime friend and ally of President Nixon,
was increasingly troubled by the Watergate inquiry. By August, he
admitted that he was giving strong consideration to voting for impeachment should it come to that.

The most damaging evidence the congressional inquiry unearthed
was that Nixon had withheld evidence from Congress and the special

prosecutor. "This puts a different light on the subject," Hammer-schmidt told reporters. "My mind is not made up. I'm still waiting. But this tends to help me make it up."[17] He lamented "the terrible display of cynicism, insensitivity, and many things I would deplore in govern-ment" which he had observed in the president and key aides, but what disturbed him most was the apparent abuse of power. That a president of the United States would sanction the use of government resources, such as the Internal Revenue Service, to obtain confidential tax infor-mation with which to "punish" Nixon's perceived enemies, was repre-hensible to Hammerschmidt.

Still, he was torn by indecision over which course Congress should follow. Reluctant to concede that a legally impeachable offense had been committed, he pondered the merits of a congressional censure and endorsed the language of a resolution that chastised the adminis-tration for "moral insensitivity" and "gross negligence."

He abjured the notion of a presidential resignation. "It might be nationally popular just because the people want this matter over with," he said, "but I don't think it's the right solution."[18] He insisted that Nixon was still capable of leading the country. Privately, Hammer-schmidt had his doubts even before the fateful afternoon of August 6, when, confronted with the damning transcript of a taped conversation between himself and Chief of Staff H.R. "Bob" Haldeman held just six days after the break-in at the Democratic National Committee headquarters at the Watergate Hotel, Nixon admitted to having dis-cussed replacing the FBI with the CIA in the investigation so that information about the break-in might be repressed in the name of national security.

When his conversation became public, Bill Clinton, campaigning in northwest Arkansas, called for the president's immediate resignation and criticized Hammerschmidt's reluctance to act. "This country has suffered long enough," Clinton said. "We need more people to say 'we need to do this' instead of saying 'I might do this.' "[19]

Following the Nixon resignation on August 9, Hammerschmidt issued a statement, insisting repeatedly that he had "only supported Nixon in areas beneficial to the Third District."

"Many times I disagreed with him, but in many instances a con-

gressman supports the executive branch because it supports programs
. . . that are needed to serve the people." He applauded the resignation
he had once opposed, saying it created "a better atmosphere" throughout the nation. He noted that the new president, Gerald R. Ford, was
"a good friend" with whom he enjoyed "a warm relationship" and "an
availability to his thinking far more than I did Nixon's."[20]

On the advice of Hillary Rodham, who had headed to Arkansas
after her job with the impeachment committee ended in August,
bringing what Diane Kincaid Blair said was a marked improvement
in "the professionalism and effectiveness of our ragtag volunteer
efforts,"[21] Clinton intensified his denunciation of corruption, arrogance, and abuse of power at the hands of Republicans. It played so
well before Democratic audiences, particularly following Nixon's
pardon by President Ford, that Clinton began narrowing the focus of
his criticism.

Hammerschmidt's seat was of such importance to the Democrats that
to draw attention to the race, Clinton was invited to give the keynote
address to the Democratic State Convention that September, unheard
of in a party that traditionally gave this honor to such elder statesmen as
Senators Fulbright and John L. McClellan, or Representative Wilbur
Mills. Clinton also was named temporary chair of the convention. (It
was at this gathering that Mack McLarty, Clinton's childhood chum,
moved to the fore of Democratic party politics. An avid, popular Young
Democrat leader, he was elected state party chairman with the backing
of Clinton and former Representative David Pryor, who would succeed
Bumpers in 1974. One of McLarty's first actions was to establish a
"Campaign Assistance Program" to help Democratic candidates in
"hotly contested races" in the general election by sponsoring hundreds
of radio advertisements asking Arkansans to vote the party line. Clinton's was the only hotly contested race, so most of the $2,500 spent on
the advertising was spent in the Third District.)

Caught up in the fever of partisan surroundings at the convention,
Clinton denounced Hammerschmidt as "one of the strongest supporters of, and apologists for, the abuse of presidential power and policies
that have wrecked the economy."[22] The Republicans, he declared,
were solely to blame for record consumer prices, record interest rates,

record budgets, record deficits, and the recession, and he praised Democrats for "protecting the American people from virtual dictatorship."

"We know that in every system of law, because men are frail and fall short of glory, justice must be tempered with mercy. But we want it remembered that, even for the favored few, mercy must be tempered with justice."

Clinton was the undisputed star of the show, but as much by design as by demonstration, because he was the only candidate present whose success in November was in doubt, since he was challenging the state's sole Republican incumbent.

Outside partisan arenas, Clinton generally stuck to what he called "the real issues" of the campaign while blasting Hammerschmidt's record and promoting a campaign agenda that relied heavily upon spiraling inflation, high consumer prices and interest rates, and the nagging energy shortage, all of which he said were the fault of the Republican White House.

He elicited enthusiastic applause each time he called for rolling back gasoline prices, which had escalated during the Arab oil embargo the previous year, and imposing an excess profits tax on large oil companies and multinational corporations. Hammerschmidt had voted against these proposals in the previous session of Congress, thus rejecting what Clinton called "a chance to vote for the working people, small businessmen, and family farms of Arkansas."[23]

(Congressman Hammerschmidt, however, had joined an effort to roll back propane prices. In July, Hammerschmidt issued a press release calling for an immediate revision of pricing regulations as a means of curbing "once-again exorbitant price levels."[24] As the release subtly pointed out to thousands of propane-dependent constituents, Hammerschmidt, as a member of Congress, had the ear of Federal Energy Office officials.)

A gasoline rollback, Clinton the populist emphasized at every turn, "is not only the right way to fight inflation, it's the best way." The nation's economic problems, he declared, "may require that you and I make a sacrifice, but it requires an even bigger sacrifice by those giant corporations that are making a killing from inflation . . . making a killing off our miseries."[25]

Indeed, Clinton hinted, Hammerschmidt had done his part to increase the miseries of his constituents with his votes in support of impounding funds for rural water systems, the Soviet wheat deal, and more taxes. The United States was wrong to allow grain sales to foreign countries at low interest rates without taking steps to curb escalating interest rates at home.

As election day drew closer, Clinton augmented such remarks with references to an eight-point plan he claimed would alleviate America's economic difficulties. His proposals, all short on specifics, included tax relief for low- and middle-income families coupled with establishment of a minimum corporate income tax; reduction of government waste; and cessation of "federal subsidy to big business, retail price maintenance, market domination by conglomerates, and federal regulation of transportation and other industries which obviously are inefficient."[26]

As a congressman, he said, inflation would be his main concern. It was, he emphasized, the principal issue on the minds of voters, and his plan for fighting it included reversing the Democratic policies of the Kennedy and Johnson administrations by putting an end to deficit spending. He proposed balancing the national budget by cutting foreign aid, especially to Middle East oil producers, and closing tax loopholes, such as the foreign investment tax credit enjoyed by corporations. He denounced unpopular wage and price controls—"They don't work"—but left himself what detractors called "wiggle room" by conceding that he might go along with such strictures if conditions worsened.

"It's very discouraging to me to have the present administration tell people on fixed incomes to tighten their belts and tell citizens in the middle-income group to pay more taxes," he lamented.

In the final weeks of the campaign, polls began to indicate a serious shift away from Hammerschmidt. Six days before the election, Opinion Survey and Research Corporation of Fayetteville went public with its findings, revealing that voters were moving from Hammerschmidt's column into the category of undecided. Projections gave Hammerschmidt 46 percent and Clinton 38 percent, marking a 5 percent gain for Clinton and a dramatic 19 percent drop-off for Hammerschmidt since the previous poll in mid-September. Clinton redoubled his efforts, running on little more than caffeine, junk food, and adrenalin.

"The campaign styles of the two candidates contrast dramatically. Clinton runs—literally, physically runs—from place to place as he strives to personally meet as many of the district's eligible voters as possible," observed reporter David Terrell. "Hammerschmidt's campaign is a low-key affair, geared to make his image as apolitical as possible."[27]

As, indeed, it was. Hammerschmidt had virtually ignored his young opponent until the last month of the campaign. Like most incumbents, he had expressed confidence throughout that his record would serve him well with voters. "I think people know me," he said. "I send out my voting record, and it is extensive."[28] He observed that his district was 85 percent Democrat, yet he had been returned to Washington three times. Just two years before, Arkansas had given Nixon 69.3 percent of the vote, and four years before that, George Wallace had carried the state. Third District support had been overwhelming in each case. Hammerschmidt was not concerned.

Generally, Hammerschmidt disregarded his young opponent's barbs and concentrated on Social Security and veterans' issues when addressing general audiences—veterans and retirees were among his strongest supporters—but the urbane, soft-spoken politician could not resist the occasional swipe, particularly as the summer drew to a close and advisors finally convinced him that Clinton's tireless campaigning and growing appeal posed a serious threat to his incumbency. Clinton espoused "a radical, left-wing philosophy" that he had managed to downplay, Hammerschmidt contended. "If he is able to hide his true philosophy, it might be the most effective thing he can do."[29]

When election time came around, Clinton in his first race carried fifteen of twenty-one counties and lost by a margin of 48.6 percent. It was Hammerschmidt's closest win since his first election to Congress in 1966, and Clinton was only slightly disappointed at the outcome, confident that name recognition would not be a problem next time.

While Clinton had not managed to overcome what he termed "the enormous, overwhelming power of incumbency," he had managed to escape the taint of liberalism despite Hammerschmidt's pointed references to his 1972 work on behalf of the McGovern campaign, and to avoid damage from the Hammerschmidt camp's muted attempts to impugn his patriotism, the best-known example being the circulation of the infamous tree-sitting story.

That story of the young Vietnam War protestor who climbed up a tree on the Fayetteville campus of the University of Arkansas has haunted Clinton since the 1974 campaign. Many Arkansans believe it to be true, and there are still a handful of people who claim to have been eyewitnesses to a shaggy-haired student named Bill Clinton's participation in the sit-in. It's a good story, and it is true except for the fact that Clinton was not the young man in question; he was not even in the country when the youth, Stephen R. Pollard, Jr., was arrested and charged with trespassing after a four-day, university-sanctioned student "occupation" of a large cypress tree in front of the University of Arkansas Student Union in April 1969.[30] (Pollard, who was not then a student, posted $28 bail and went back to the tree, where the protest was peaceably concluded on schedule. He was later fined $38 and given a ten-day suspended jail term.)

America's involvement in Vietnam was never really an issue in the 1974 campaign. Hammerschmidt knew too little about Clinton's stance, and Clinton was not about to open that door himself.

Though he lost, Clinton had built more than name recognition. His exhausting campaign, his dynamic persona, and his grasp of issues had caught the eye of special-interest groups and the public at large.

"He did quite well against Hammerschmidt, and our people thought he was the most wonderful guy and the guy who had a great political future," the AFL-CIO's Becker said. "He was just good. Impressed the hell out of people."[31]

In his 1975 officer's report, Becker wrote: "This was a period that another young politician, Bill Clinton, a University of Arkansas law professor, emerged to challenge Representative John Paul Hammerschmidt in the Third Congressional District. After leading the ticket in the Democratic preferential primary, Clinton received 69 percent of the vote in the runoff. However, he failed to unseat Hammer-schmidt by a narrow 3.6 percent margin . . . Bill Clinton will come back."

"Bill Clinton will come back," Becker said with a grin in 1993 as he closed the report from which he had been reciting. "How many times have we heard that?"

9

ON TRACK AT LAST

ONE LATE APRIL AFTERNOON in 1987, following his speech to a group of journalists and the subsequent formal question-and-answer session, Governor Bill Clinton sat down with a handful of reporters, grabbed an apple to munch, and "just visited" with them, expanding on a few of his previous comments. It was the type of encounter that Clinton occasionally enjoyed as attorney general and governor, whether his schedule permitted it or not. Then, as now, Clinton's style was not to converse but to hold forth. After about twenty-five or thirty minutes of Clinton's stream-of-consciousness monologue, his press secretary, Mike Gauldin, an easy-going fellow who could be extremely intrusive and firm when necessary, leaned toward Clinton and said with resolution: "Governor, you're about to violate rule number one of Clinton's rules of politics."

Actually, it was rule number seven, but it was the sort of cryptic attention-getter Gauldin needed to begin easing Clinton out the door.

Over the years, Clinton, singleminded in ambition but undisciplined by nature, has broken all of those rules numerous times. In a moment of whimsy he had, in fact, compiled a list of behavioral

guidelines which were occasionally invoked by his gubernatorial staff
to keep him on track.

BILL CLINTON'S RULES OF POLITICS

1. Most people are for change in general, but against it in particular.

2. Never tell anyone to go to hell unless you can make 'em go.

*3. Whenever someone tells you, "It's nothing personal," he's about to stick it
to you.*

*4. Whenever it is possible for a person to shift the heat from himself to the
governor, he'll do it.*

*5. Under enough pressure, most people—but not everybody—will stretch
the truth on you.*

*6. You're most vulnerable in politics when you think you're the least
vulnerable.*

7. When you start enjoying something, it's probably time to leave.

8. Never look past the next election; it might be your last.

9. There's no such thing as enough money.

10. Don't drink in public. You might act like yourself.

The only rule he consistently broke with greater frequency than
rule number seven was rule number eight. He couldn't help himself.
More than anything in life, he wanted to be president, and most of the
political moves he made, and many of the personal ones, were with
that objective in mind. So it was with the 1976 race for attorney
general.

Numerous admirers had been encouraging Clinton to make another run at Hammerschmidt's seat, but he was anxious to move on.
For a fellow with only one political campaign under his belt, he already
enjoyed fairly good name recognition in the most populous regions of
the state, northwest and central Arkansas, and good contacts within
the Democratic party. When he learned from Attorney General Jim
Guy Tucker in mid–1975 that Tucker was preparing to take a run at a
higher office, he decided to forgo another districtwide campaign and
seek statewide office.

In October, he and Hillary wed. Marriage wasn't a requirement for Arkansas politicians, but it was recommended, and however liberal Fayetteville might seem, the two felt they could not live together publicly without being married.

Hillary Rodham's job with the impeachment committee staff had ended when President Nixon resigned in August 1974, and she was delighted to join Bill Clinton in Fayetteville. She told friends she needed a break from the grueling pace she had followed for nine months, working eighteen- and sometimes twenty-hour days. During a visit the previous year, Clinton had introduced her to the dean of the law school, who had suggested she might join the faculty if and when she tired of Washington.

Fayetteville was at least a change of scenery for Hillary, for by all accounts she didn't slow down her pace. She jumped immediately into Bill's congressional campaign, taking charge of campaign head-quarters—her brother Hugh says the entire Rodham clan took an apartment in Fayetteville that summer to work in the campaign—and prepared to begin an assistant professorship at the law school.

Bill proved himself an excellent politician in respect to Hillary—selling Arkansas to her and selling her to his friends before she even arrived at Fayetteville. Her apprehensions—she freely admits to having worried greatly about being a stranger in a strange land—receded as Southern hospitality enveloped her, and she soon felt right at home.

Hillary loved practically everything about Fayetteville—the university community, her law school colleagues, the quaint Victorian houses, the clean air, and the harmonious, small-town feel that took the edge off the academic bustle—although some of the local attitudes were disconcerting. Friends recall that by Fayetteville standards, her fashion sense was more like that of the students than the faculty, and her Northern accent and somewhat exotic experience with the impeachment committee distinguished her from the other "pointy-headed liberals" on campus.

Some of her older male colleagues thought her forthrightness pushy and her self-confidence presumptuous. "She was highly intellectual, aggressive, blunt, very articulate, and fairly tough," Woody Bassett told one biographer. "A lot of people initially weren't sure how they felt about her, because she came on kind of strong."[1]

She was one of only a few women on the faculty at the law school and, as one of them, Diane Blair, later recalled, "Hillary's position as one of northwest Arkansas's few 'lady lawyers' . . . made her even more visible and controversial."[2]

"Both she and I had been raised and educated outside the South and were more accustomed to big-city anonymity than to small-town familiarity," Blair says. "Furthermore, we were both politically aware and active, anxious to advance the status of women, and eager to encourage more assertiveness and ambition in our students. We were equally dismayed by those who underestimated their abilities because they were from Arkansas and those who lowered their sights because they were female, and we considered it one of our chief professional duties to rout such inhibitions."

After passing the Arkansas bar exam, Bill supplemented his teaching schedule by practicing a bit of law—his first action was to file an *amicus* brief for his friend Steve Smith in a lawsuit involving a Republican challenge of election results—and soliciting advice from fellow Democrats about what his next campaign should be. Hillary plowed her extracurricular energies into establishing a legal clinic to train law students in the legal needs of indigent people and negotiating a contract with the Legal Services Corporation to obtain funds with which to operate Northwest Arkansas Legal Services, a legal aid bureau serving six of the region's counties.

Theirs was a comfortable, compatible relationship with only one discernible cloud: Where should it go from here? Both were activists after a fashion, Hillary on behalf of others, Bill on behalf of himself, and both viewed life in the public arena as the means to achieving their ambitions. But Bill was not likely to sublimate his ambitions for anyone, even the woman he loved; and even if it were realistic for the two to pursue separate political careers, Hillary had no constituency in Arkansas. Her conscientious attempts to alter her accent by dropping her G's and peppering her remarks with colloquial references to "y'all" could not attenuate her "foreignness." She would be hard pressed to win a local election, much less a greater one. If she stayed in Arkansas, she would have to find other, more productive outlets for her abilities, and that proved somewhat of a stumbing block to her relationship with Bill when he started to discuss marriage.

Hillary's oft-quoted explanation for committing her life to his ambition is that she followed her heart. Many Arkansans from whom she grudgingly won respect for her work on behalf of education in the 1980s are reluctant to accept that explanation. If her husband is the first to proclaim her intellectual superiority over his own, a large school of thought, both within and without Arkansas, believes he merely states the obvious.

An observation common to Arkansas legislators who were wooed and won to the 1983 education reform movement she conceived and spearheaded as the basis for her husband's political comeback was that the wrong Clinton was holding public office. Whereas he was manipulative, she was forthright. Whereas he pleaded and bargained and cajoled to reach his objectives, and did not hesitate to alter and redefine his objectives when defeat appeared inevitable, she explained and reasoned and never let accommodation give way to compromise. Clinton was angered when people disagreed with him; Hillary encouraged debate and seemed to give thoughtful consideration to all comers. Throughout their relationship, he has been her biggest fan, and she his staunchest defender.

Given her independence and capabilities, that she would hitch her horse to his wagon has puzzled some who have known them both for years. But not all.

"There have been more unbelievable love stories," says retired newsman John R. Starr, who maintained a warm personal relationship as well as a mutually satisfying professional one with Hillary for almost a decade before the Clintons moved to Washington. He believes love looms larger in Hillary's psyche than personal ambition, although there is ambition. He believes that she accepts that "the day's going to come when a woman can run for president, but it's not now, so that the best way for her to have influence in her lifetime is to help her man get elected president and then to have a lot of input into it."[3]

Starr was not persuaded by Hillary's insistence during the Gennifer Flowers controversy of 1992 that Hillary was not just "some little

woman . . . standing by her man," because, he says, "her standing by
him when this came up was critical to his salvation" in the presidential campaign.

Nevertheless, Starr is convinced that her explanation was not altogether self-serving or blind loyalty. However implausible it may sound,
Starr was not only one of Governor Clinton's harshest critics and one
of the first lady's most ardent supporters, he served both as advisor and
confidant on numerous occasions. With his intimate knowledge of both
Bill and Hillary, Starr feels sure that their relationship, having withstood one of the most emotionally jarring blows a marriage can
receive, is grounded in mutual respect, understanding, and emotional
fidelity.

Belief in Bill Clinton's reputation as a philanderer is widely held in
Arkansas, although Flowers was the first woman ever to claim extramarital involvement with him. As managing editor of the *Arkansas
Democrat* for most of Clinton's tenure as governor, Starr dispatched
many reporters to run down numerous claims of Clinton's alleged
sexual improprieties. But until Bill Clinton ran for president, none was
ever substantiated, so no one was more shocked than Starr when
Clinton admitted to at least one indiscretion.

"We were talking about the Gary Hart factor in politics," Starr
explained, "and I asked him something to the effect of 'Well, you
haven't ever done anything like that, have you?' You know, [I was]
expecting a negative answer, be it a lie or the truth. And he said 'Yes, I
have.' And I was somewhat taken aback, and I said, 'You mean, since
you've been married to Hillary?' and he said 'Yes. Do you want to
know about it?' " *It.* 'Do you want to know about *it?*' And I, to my
eternal regret, said 'No.' I just didn't want to know."[4]

As a consequence of that conversation and Clinton's abrupt decision
not to run for president in 1987, "when by all accounts it would have
been a much more propitious time for him to have run than run
against a sitting president," Starr said, "I made the conclusion that the
reason he dropped out was because he hadn't told Hillary about
whatever that was he was going to tell me if I had been willing to listen,
and that sometime between then and the time he announced for
president in 1991, he told Hillary. And I believe he told Hillary the

truth, the whole truth and nothing but the truth, because it would
have been really bad if he hadn't."

Given the credentials and contacts and opportunities Hillary
Rodham held in 1975, it is probable that love was the determining
factor when Hillary, three months shy of her twenty-eighth birthday,
returned to Fayetteville from a visit in Illinois and the East inclined to
accept the twenty-nine-year-old Clinton's marriage proposal. Any
remaining reluctance was dashed when he greeted her return with the
news that he had purchased a small brick and stonework house she
had admired. The wedding two months later, on October 11, 1975,
was a hastily assembled affair. Hillary bought her wedding gown, a
Victorian-style linen dress trimmed in lace, "off the rack" at a local
department store the night before. A small ceremony before their
immediate families was followed by a larger one before almost three
hundred friends and colleagues from Boston, New Haven, Washington, and Fayetteville. There was no question but that she would retain
her maiden name.

Hugh and Dorothy Rodham, along with sons Hughie and Tony,
accompanied the couple on their honeymoon to Acapulco. Upon
their return, Bill turned his attention to the 1976 campaign for
attorney general. As campaign manager Steve Smith has noted, it was
the shortest campaign in Clinton's career, "announced in March and
over in May, [when] he won a clear majority in the primary against
two opponents and faced no Republican opposition in the general
election."[5]

"The victory," Smith continued, "was clearly a result of Clinton's
superiority as a campaigner, combining the articulation of issues,
unbounded personal energy, an adequate media campaign, and a
strong traditional organization advantage."

The formal campaign was short, perhaps, but Clinton had used
the sixteen months between his November 1974 congressional defeat
and his March 17, 1976, announcement as a candidate for attorney
general to maintain and expand his political contacts throughout
Arkansas. He had become active in the Democratic party organization, chairing its affirmative action committee, a job that allowed
him to travel the state explaining delegate selection procedures for

the 1976 presidential convention to the party's county central committees and civic clubs. He also set up a satellite political base in the
state capital by arranging to teach a course in criminal justice and law
enforcement to police officers at the University of Arkansas at Little
Rock. His hair was still bushy, but he was now clean-shaven and
becoming better acquainted with suits and ties. He linked up with a
not-for-profit outfit known as the Arkansas Housing Development
Corporation, which specialized in providing home repairs and increased insulation to low-income households, and as chairman was
able to give personal assurances to poor Arkansans that he would do
all in his power to obtain these services for them. He even joined the
Fayetteville Jaycees.

Shortly before Christmas 1975, Clinton applied to the dean of the
law school for a leave of absence for the spring semester and became so
involved in his precampaign activities that he failed to check and see
whether leave had been granted.

In the weeks before the announcement, Clinton remained coy
with the media about his intentions, claiming he had not ruled out
another race against Congressman Hammerschmidt and impressing
upon reporters that under no circumstances would he run against the
incumbent attorney general, Jim Guy Tucker, who he knew had
already decided to run for the Second Congressional District seat
being vacated by the scandal-weary Wilbur D. Mills. The director
of Tucker's consumer protection division, a tentative, self-effacing
young lawyer with a wry, self-deprecating sense of humor named
Clarence Cash, was the only other rumored candidate for attorney
general, and while he had coordinated all three of Tucker's winning
campaigns—one for prosecuting attorney and two for attorney
general—Tucker reportedly had misgivings about Cash's ability to
attract a following.

Other than several speeches to partisan groups during which he
tried to explain the new delegate selection process for the upcoming
presidential primary, all of Clinton's public appearances during that
period focused on issues better identified with a person interested in
statewide office: crime, sentencing laws, consumer concerns.

On the morning of March 17, 1976, in a series of news conferences begun at Little Rock and repeated at Fort Smith, Texarkana, El Dorado, and Jonesboro—all the major media markets in Arkansas save for Memphis-West Memphis—Clinton announced his candidacy for attorney general on a populist platform whose major planks were consumer protection and criminal justice reform. He spoke in vague terms about increasing the effectiveness of existing laws in an effort to deter crime and "closely following decisions made by all state regulatory bodies so that when citizens's basic services are provided at a reasonable price, industries are allowed a fair and healthy rate of return," and "working closely with state officials" to help them administer recently enacted legislation. His only specific promise was to create an ombudsman's office to gather consumer complaints from citizens "about any of their dealings with their state government."[6]

"I believe that I can offer the background, experience, and interest in all the areas in which the attorney general's office must be interested," he said.

Clinton refused to answer questions about what changes he would make in the staff and administration of the attorney general's office, but to the dismay of other liberal Democrats, he endorsed the death penalty when the laws governing it are "narrowly drawn and fairly applied."

By the time Clarence Cash announced his candidacy at noon, nobody much cared. And the entry of longtime political operative George O. Jernigan, Jr., several days later went virtually unnoticed, although his political contacts and his status as secretary of state—he had been appointed by Governor David Pryor to complete the term upon the death of the elected secretary of state—did enable him to run an extremely distant second in the primary. The *Arkansas Democrat* had already given Clinton the first headlines and the coffee-shop edge. The pundits of the press quickly bestowed front-runner status upon the handsome, dynamic young law professor, and shortly afterward the opinion polls validated their call.

That is not to say that the press created Bill Clinton. He was more a made-for-the-media candidate than media-made. Second only to his personal commitment to make his name in politics was the part special-interest groups played in facilitating his early success by what they did and did not do in his behalf.

J. Bill Becker, the AFL-CIO's man in Arkansas, discounts that theory, possibly because his criticism of the Democrat front-runner for president was stifled by the national organization in 1992. He was compelled by the organization's own political structure to stand before a national AFL-CIO convention and sing Clinton's praises, albeit with the vague caveat that "over the years, our relationship with Governor Clinton has not been altogether smooth."[7] Nonetheless, Becker first glimpsed what he came to believe were Clinton's true colors early in the 1976 campaign, and "it pissed our people off something tremendous."

It occurred less than forty-eight hours after Clinton's official entry into the race when, in an interview with the CBS television affiliate in Fort Smith, Clinton expressed his "serious reservations" about a campaign to modify the state constitution's right-to-work amendment, which prohibits making payment of union dues a requirement of employment.[8] The Arkansas chapter of the AFL-CIO was leading a petition effort to place the changes on the November general election ballot.

Clinton defended his lack of support by saying that many of his friends in the labor movement "think it's the wrong time to bring it up" because of the ongoing recession. "We want to try to keep as many jobs and attract as many jobs as we can," he declared.[9]

His comments were a sharp and unexpected slap in the face of organized labor, which had endorsed him in 1974 and had, in Becker's words, carried on a two-year love affair with him in the interim in anticipation that he would seek office again.

"I think what happened in the race, like it's happened in Arkansas politics before, [is that] he ran such a hell of a race against Hammerschmidt that he began to get support from the establishment types," Becker said in 1993. "The people who opposed him in Hammerschmidt's race got on his little bandwagon when he ran for attorney general. A lot of people jumped on board because, like we said here [at the AFL-CIO], he's a comer."[10]

Most people love a winner, and labor is no different, Becker conceded. Clinton looked like a winner, and so while he may have received some support from individual unions, as an organization the AFL–CIO stayed out of it, neither publicly opposing nor endorsing his candidacy.

The steel workers, among Clinton's earliest supporters in the previous congressional campaign, were so incensed at Clinton's stance, Becker recalled with a chuckle, "that they went and got their damned furniture" from Clinton's Fort Smith campaign office to which they had lent it. There were other similar incidents, but they all occurred quietly.

Clinton was equally stung by labor's reaction, which had been telegraphed to him within hours of the interview's broadcast. Publicly, he said he still expected to get labor's support, and certainly he would ask for it.

In his defense, Clinton said that the argument over loss of jobs under closed-shop laws "is an argument that has to be answered. Both sides are entitled to be heard. I only commented on the timing of their petition drive and I don't think labor should be particularly disturbed until the debate begins." But debate, he hastened to add, should not begin at this point, because "we're not even sure it's going to be on the ballot."[11]

Privately, he was sick with worry. Not only had he spoken out against labor, but he had refused to sign the right-to-work petition. Rumors circulated that he had tried intentionally to divest himself of union support because he believed it a hindrance to his candidacy, but this was untrue.

"Bill Clinton came to our convention [in April 1976] seeking our support with tears in his eyes—literally, tears in his eyes, trying to explain his position," Becker said. "But our people were so unhappy with what he said that we stayed neutral in the race. . . . Not that it made a hell of a lot of difference. . . . He had the bandwagon effect going for him. . . . My guess is, looking at the competition, a lot of our people voted for him anyhow."[12]

The stupidity of Clinton's political *faux pas* still amazes Becker, who points out that the right-to-work issue "had no relevance in the attorney general's race at all. He had every reason in the world to avoid it, but he didn't."

While not garnering an endorsement, Clinton made his peace in his appearance before the AFL–CIO executive committee, and while Becker believes that "the relationship we had in the first campaign was the height of a good relationship," Clinton would receive the AFL–CIO's endorsement in every subsequent general election campaign.

Could labor's public opposition in Arkansas have hindered Bill Clinton's political ambitions? That, Becker insists, is a moot point. "But I think in any race, labor can be the margin of victory or margin of loss. I don't think we vote as a block, but when you get a Bill Clinton putting together labor people, and everyone's in agreement that this is our guy, you get a substantial vote, and a substantial vote in a close race can make a difference. I would say we can be the swing vote in any race, even today."

But this was not a close race. Even given general election opposition, labor in Arkansas, as elsewhere, does not vote Republican. And, most telling, nearly twenty years later, Becker had to struggle to remember the names of the other two Democrats in the race, although Cash went on to become a minor personality on statewide public television and Jernigan, at the time of the 1993 interview, was the state Democratic party chairman. Clinton was a comer. Labor was not going to interfere with a man with whom its leaders might be dealing for many years to come. Those dealings, Becker conceded, have been "a mixed bag."

A love–hate relationship?

"Call it anything you damn well please," Becker said, breaking into hearty laughter.

At one point, Clinton's desperate opponents tried to make an issue of his lack of legal experience. While Cash touted his experience as a deputy prosecuting attorney and an assistant attorney general, both under Tucker, Jernigan boasted that he was "the only candidate that has had any clients."[13] Not true, countered Clinton, who laid claim to having represented clients from fifteen of the state's seventy-five counties in matters ranging from property disputes and adoption proceedings to disability cases and criminal proceedings. He claimed his practice was limited only by a state law which restricted the activities of law school faculty members. That he was not licensed to practice before the United States Supreme Court was, he said, "a mere formality" with which he would comply before taking office.[14]

The editorially liberal *Arkansas Gazette* was the first to broach the matter of Clinton's wife's use of her maiden name. Asked whether he thought that would hurt his chances, Clinton replied, "I hope not."[15] He pointed out that during their five-year courtship, she "had quite a career for herself as a lawyer" that had resulted in her being "nationally recognized as an authority on children's legal rights." As a successful lawyer and advocate, he said, it was important that his wife maintain the recognition she had acquired as Hillary Rodham. If he was aware that some of Arkansas's good old boys were snickering about his claim that he would be able to get by on the attorney general's $6,000-a-year salary without practicing law on the side because his wife would supplement his income, he gave no indication of it. At that time, she was earning about $18,000 a year at the law school and expected to draw about $8,000 for her work on a government grant her legal services organization had received.

Hillary Rodham was supportive behind the scenes, but she had no discernible public presence in the campaign. The scant amount of coverage she received—and the first time her name appeared as a subject in a statewide newspaper—involved a speech she gave during the University of Arkansas's annual Women's Week activities in March about the legal rights of rape victims.

Again, Clinton proved himself a tireless campaigner, although the higher profile afforded by a statewide campaign made the stumping easier, because the money flowed into the campaign in larger lumps. Bankers and businessmen were his financial base, and their generosity was responsible for improvements made in his media strategy. Direct mail, outdoor advertising, and paid publicity on radio and newspaper were the major tools—he used television only minimally—but he extended his reach through the free publicity provided by local radio stations.

The routine, which Clinton adopted for every future statewide campaign, was to hit as many places where people congregate whenever visiting a small town, shake hands and distribute campaign brochures, and finish up with a surprise visit to the local radio station.

Few station managers and announcers turned down the opportunity to interrupt their regular programming with a brief "interview" with the candidate. To a lesser extent, he used the same tactic with many local weekly newspapers, most of whose editors were pleased to give him prominent front-page play, as they did to any visiting politico. But Clinton believed he could reach the most people with the local radio station, and he probably used it more than any previous candidate.

Even back then in 1976, the Clinton campaign benefited from the budding expertise of Patrick Caddell, presidential hopeful Jimmy Carter's favorite pollster. Caddell and Clinton had become acquainted during the 1972 presidential campaign, when Caddell, then only twenty-two, was conducting surveys for the McGovern organization, and had expanded their acquaintanceship in 1974, when Caddell was polling for the National Committee for an Effective Government, a nonpartisan organization that backed liberal candidates, primarily Democrats, in campaigns for the United States House of Representatives. The committee had contributed heavily to Clinton's bid against Hammerschmidt, even bankrolling a public opinion survey that Caddell designed and Clinton volunteers executed. His polling helped Clinton considerably in the race for attorney general.

Campaign literature stressed Clinton's educational qualifications, his memberships in the Jaycees and the Baptist Church, and, since he had little practical experience in the work force, his activities on behalf of the Arkansas Housing Development Corporation. His slogan was "Character, Competence, and Concern."

The platform he spoke about in his announcement actually evolved during the campaign. It was May, about two weeks before the primary, before Clinton started issuing position papers, most of them prepared by Steve Smith, who did all of the candidate's research on an as-needs basis.

"I would spend a week, probably over a hundred hours, reading and analyzing documents and data related to a particular campaign issue," Smith later said. "In briefing him on my conclusions, I found that he absorbed it all at first pass, remembered every statistic, and drew conclusions that I had missed. I also found myself able to anticipate his responses to what was important and why it mattered, making the job of speech writing a breeze, even if the set texts seemed weak by comparison with the speeches he was able to deliver without notes at any civic club or coffee shop in the realm. I came to respect his principles, never questioning his motives or integrity on matters relating to the *res publica*."[16]

The planks that emerged over the course of the two-month campaign included Clinton's support of compensation for victims of crime, mandatory sentences for convicted felons, fair utility rates, improved antitrust laws, and privacy rights. During the tenure of Jim Guy Tucker, who actually had been very supportive of the public's right to know how government functions, the legislature had amended the state's Freedom of Information Act to create an Information Practices Board under the guise of protecting the privacy of individuals against the "improper" use or collection of information obtained by government agencies. But as a result of well-placed opposition from journalists to what they perceived to be an information clearinghouse, no funds were appropriated for its staffing and operation.

Clinton pledged to seek financing for the board, and he studiously avoided taking head-on stands when questioned about the state's "sunshine" laws.

"The first time we met," said John R. Starr, who as chief of The Associated Press's Little Rock bureau had been involved in passage of the state's 1967 Freedom of Information Act, "Clinton was attorney general and trying to set up a state information agency that was trying to f____ up the FOI. I thought he was looking for a power base and a way to call attention to himself. It did not work."[17]

Journalists who had been around the legislature longer than Clinton managed to frustrate the new attorney general's efforts, after which he avoided the issue until, as governor, language establishing the still unfunded board was removed from the law. Although his lengthy tenure as governor eventually would give him the political strength to gut the Freedom of Information Act, after that first run-in with journalists, Clinton made a bigger effort to portray himself as a champion of open records and open meetings. "He made friends, he was the darling of the media," Starr said. "He became everybody's darling."[18]

Clinton won the primary with 55.6 percent of the vote, thus

avoiding a runoff, prompting Jernigan, in second place with 24 percent of the vote, to quip that he never again would run against someone with three home towns. Clinton credited his organization in the Third District, the site of his first campaign, in whose counties his share of the vote ranged from 65 to a staggering 91 percent. Pointing out in his victory speech that he had received contributions from one thousand individual sources, Clinton boasted that his supporters "really believe I really cared about the job, that I was able to perform well in all areas the attorney general must deal with."[19]

With his election assured—there was no Republican opposition in the general election, and no one mounted a write-in campaign— Clinton gave short shrift to his teaching duties, claiming he needed the time to prepare for his new office in January. Instead, Hillary treated the two of them to a week's vacation in Spain, after which they joined Jimmy Carter's presidential campaign, she as a field organizer in Indiana and he as campaign coordinator in Arkansas.

Ten days before the announcement of his appointment, Clinton had turned down the Texas coordinator's post, saying his obligations lay elsewhere, but he had actively campaigned for the Arkansas post, flying twice to Carter headquarters in Atlanta to make his case. Most of his public appearances through election day were on behalf of Carter, who went on to become the first Democrat since 1964 to carry Arkansas in a presidential race.

Clinton owes his first meeting with Jimmy Carter to the childhood friend who went on to become President Clinton's chief of staff, Mack McLarty. Early in his two-year campaign for president, Carter came to Arkansas for a series of speeches. He and McLarty, who at the time was chairman of the Democratic party of Arkansas, had "hit it off pretty well," McLarty recalled.[20] Their friendship was solidified when, in riding from Little Rock to Pine Bluff for an appearance at a prayer breakfast, Carter left the speech he had prepared for a later appearance at Fayetteville in McLarty's car. McLarty had the speech flown to Carter.

Somehow Clinton, who was teaching law in Fayetteville at the time, failed to connect with Carter during his brief visit to that city, so when McLarty spoke with Clinton by telephone upon Carter's return to Little Rock, Clinton was delighted to learn that McLarty had set up a meeting between them. He and Hillary boarded a small commuter airplane the same evening and flew to Little Rock. Upon their arrival, McLarty telephoned Carter's aide, Frank Moore.

"Governor Carter has already gone to bed," Moore told him.

"Frank, they're *here*. What are we going to do?"

"Well, let me call him. It's not *that* late."

Whereupon Moore "got Carter out of bed—it was 10 o'clock at night—and Clinton and Hillary went by and visited Jimmy Carter," McLarty said with a grin.[21]

In between speeches in Carter's behalf in late 1976, the attorney general-elect assembled what he had pledged during his primary campaign would be "the best people to serve in each and every capacity," people who, as it turned out, would form the nucleus of a new statewide political machine that would become the most productive and successful organization of its type since the heyday of Orval E. Faubus.

Clinton took the oath of office on January 11, 1977. Rather than permit him to assume the role before that time—Tucker, newly elected to Congress, had resigned on January 4 to assume his duties in Washington—Governor Pryor had repaid one of his own political debts by appointing an interim attorney general. His choice was William R. Wilson, who recently was appointed by Clinton as a federal judge in the Eastern District of Arkansas.

As coordinator of federal patronage in Arkansas for the new president, Clinton began exploring the limits of his influence with the Carter administration within days of taking over the attorney general's office by touting his old friend, James B. Blair, a Fayetteville lawyer, to chair the Federal Home Loan Bank Board.

Blair, who had managed the unsuccessful 1974 reelection campaign of Clinton's mentor, Senator J. William Fulbright, was a mainstay of the Arkansas Democratic party, holding the prestigious title of general legal counsel as well as a position on the state Executive Committee. He also served on the state Board of Higher Education. In the ensuing years, as chief counsel to the Tyson poultry empire, Blair would forge many financially productive connections for Clinton.

Clinton was inundated with potential candidates for the dozen or so possible federal job openings in Arkansas, and he was not shy about sharing his philosophy with Jimmy Carter, fellow Democrats, or the Arkansas reporters: "Entirely too many of these jobs have been made nonpolitical when they are not," he declared. "We've gone entirely too far in insulating some of these jobs that are policy-making instead of administrative."[22] He believed the administration should have its own people in place, even if that meant creating vacancies through the transfer of Republican appointees who had been in positions of authority throughout the Nixon and Ford administrations and considered themselves to be careerists protected by civil service.

Attorney General Bill Clinton has been described as "fearless, if not reckless" in his assaults on the Arkansas establishment. In fact, he was torn by doubt on numerous occasions. He was so intent on building a dynamic career that he was forever testing the limits of political propriety by floating trial balloons. When a balloon failed to gain altitude, such as his tentative call for decriminalizing marijuana, that was the end of it. Clinton was never reckless. Even his forays into battle with the utility companies were carefully selected and orchestrated. If Clinton could wrangle with the big boys semisuccessfully, if he could prove his mettle and his staying power, eventually they would court him. With a little give and take, both could flourish. Which is precisely what happened.

If Clinton had learned anything from his predecessor, it was that his political capital could grow if it was attached to a popular issue. As prosecuting attorney for Pulaski and Perry counties, a district that included Little Rock, Jim Guy Tucker's *métier* had been activism in consumer affairs. He had taken full advantage of the public's growing concern in this area, fueled at the national level by Ralph Nader. Moreover, his office's proximity to the Central Arkansas news media, whose newspapers and television network affiliates blanketed the state, had given him sufficient name recognition to win the Democratic nomination for attorney general handily in 1972. Tucker's continued ministrations as a public-interest advocate, which included taking on the state's public utilities and their unrelenting pursuit of ever higher rate increases, virtually assured his election to Congress in 1976, where he might have served indefinitely had he not been impatient.

Clinton kicked off his stewardship in the attorney general's office with an energy package aimed at holding down utility costs and conserving resources, propositions which held particular allure to the voters of a rural state who, after decades of cheap energy, were still smarting from the hefty price increases following the Arab oil embargo of 1973. He proposed requiring utility companies to submit environmental impact statements on major construction projects so that the state regulatory body, the Public Service Commission, could determine whether the facilities were being constructed at the lowest possible cost; directing state agencies to conduct energy audits of their facilities to determine what cost-savings measures could be taken; and authorizing the PSC to impose mandatory conservation requirements on utilities and to require utilities to promote and invest in residential insulation programs.

A final element of the package provided Clinton with his first excuse to travel to Washington at taxpayer expense, ostensibly to enlist the aid of Arkansas's congressional delegation: Clinton already had a first draft of legislation creating a Utility Facilities Finance Authority, but revisions in the Internal Revenue Service Code were needed to allow states to issue tax-exempt revenue bonds with which to finance such construction projects. To lend credibility to the three-day junket, and to solidify their support, he took several of his legislative sponsors with him—but Hillary went, too. The primary purpose of the trip was to join the Carters at a state dinner honoring Canadian Premier Pierre Trudeau. Clinton spent much of the dinner networking and table-hopping.

Clinton hopped from issue to issue with similar aplomb: utility rate cases, prison affairs, federal construction projects, antitrust cases. Attorneys general who did not want to die in or retire from that office could not content themselves with promulgating legislative reforms; only bills bearing the stamp of gubernatorial approval generated significant and steady headlines. Thus, following his predecessor's lead, Clinton began establishing himself as a consumer advocate, intervening, virtually on a weekly basis, in an endless string of requests for

utility rate increases both great and small—Arkansas Power and Light's
$56.4 million petition, Arkansas-Missouri Power's $2.9 million
request—and attempts by several telephone companies to increase the
cost of a public telephone call from a dime to a quarter.

No single utility provider covered the entire state, so it was just as
important to take on Arkansas-Missouri Power, which served several
counties in rural northeast and southeast Arkansas, or General Telephone with its paltry forty-nine exchanges as it was to take on such
bigger as Arkansas Power and Light and Southwestern Bell Telephone.
Local newspapers and grass-roots movements such as Arkansas Community Organizations for Reform Now (which evolved into the
national Association of Community Organizations for Reform Now,
or ACORN) rallied around such causes, giving Clinton more publicity without any prodding from his growing network of grass-roots
supporters.

Clinton augmented his anti-utility work, for which he was only
the head of an able staff of bright, young litigators, with media events
heretofore only used by the governor. A typical example was his visit
in April 1977 to a tiny wood-frame shack inhabited by Bertha Louise
Knuckols. Knuckols, a fifty-three-year-old divorcee who was crippled by rheumatoid arthritis and totally dependent on welfare, led
Clinton and a group of reporters and photographers on a tour of the
crumbling structure, proudly pointing to the workmen who were
improving her thirty-year-old house by laying a new roof and instal-
ling insulation, new windows, and wood siding as part of a model
home weatherization project whose federal funds were almost exhausted.

"Well, praise the Lord!" the stout woman declared, throwing her
arms into the air, when Clinton and his entourage arrived. "I've been
looking forward to meeting you. I'm a little excited." Clasping her
hand, Clinton gently asked how she was doing. "I'm just beautiful
today!" she gurgled. "You *are* beautiful today," he agreed with an
admiring smile.[23]

He was there, Clinton said, because he was on his way the next
morning to Washington to speak with John O'Leary, director of the
Federal Energy Administration, about the fine program in which she

was participating and the urgent need to replenish the weatherization program's depleted coffers. (Years later, Clinton would appoint O'Leary's widow, Hazel, to be his secretary of energy.) He wanted the Carter administration to use the program, administered by the Economic Opportunity Agency (EOA) of Pulaski County, as the model for a national program in hopes that every low- and moderate-income family could have an adequately insulated home by the end of Carter's first term. Knuckols was a believer. Because of the low-interest loan from the Farmers Home Administration and free labor provided by EOA, she was looking forward to the first winter in several years during which the inadequate heat from a floor stove and her oven did not keep her confined to her bed, nursing her aching joints, until after noon. The disabled welfare recipient was grateful to Clinton for that, and to Mr. Carter, and God bless them both for her salvation.

Energy conservation was a frequent theme during the first of Clinton's two years as attorney general. He made numerous speeches on the subject, joking that while he was not qualified to instruct program workers on the problems of the poor—the outdoor privy of his early childhood years had not yet been invented—"I did use to care an awful lot about the problems of poor people when the attorney general of Arkansas made $6,000 a year."[24] Fortunately, his bride was augmenting his $26,500-a-year salary through her work at the Rose Law Firm, raking in enough as an associate to buy the first house they owned together, a $35,000, one-story brick house in Little Rock's upscale Heights neighborhood.

Clinton's goal was to hit the front pages and the evening news with at least one good initiative a week, and to enhance that coverage with minor efforts on a near-daily basis. This he did in spades, sometimes by issuing legal opinions, then the primary function of the state's chief counsel, and occasionally by filing suit or attempting intervention in other lawsuits.

Citing President Carter's desire to eliminate more than $5 billion for water projects in nineteen states, including Arkansas, Clinton joined the Environmental Defense Fund in petitioning the 8th U.S. Circuit Court of Appeals to halt the unpopular channelization of the Cache River by the U.S. Army Corps of Engineers. And he brought litigation against General Motors, claiming the manufacturer had violated the state Consumer Protection Act by equipping Oldsmobile Delta 88s with Chevrolet engines. He also traveled numerous times to Washington to testify before congressional committees on a wide range of issues, including compensation for victims of violent crimes, utility regulation and financing, and energy conservation, and to participate in White House briefings.

When a federal grand jury brought criminal indictments against three dairy firms and two of their officials for bid-rigging and price-fixing in their sales to government agencies, school districts, and other institutions in Arkansas, he quickly filed a class-action civil lawsuit under the terms of the Sherman Antitrust Act.

All this and more occurred during his first six months in office. Political observers wondered when he found time to sleep. The answer was that he often did not sleep more than three or four hours a night— he tried to be on the jogging track by 6:30 or 7:00 each morning to run his three miles of laps. He thrived on the pace, the high profile his many and varied works generated, and expected no less of his staff. Joe Purvis, one of Clinton's friends from the sandbox days at Miss Mary Purkins's School for Little Folk at Hope, later wrote that as an assistant attorney general under Clinton, he often worked seventy hours a week on criminal appeals. The workload, he recalled, was grueling, often leaving the staff exhausted, but Clinton flourished.

"If you aren't having fun," Purvis recalls Clinton counseling him on one of their many late evenings at the office, "it's time to lay this down and move on to something else. When it becomes hard work instead of fun, it's time to do something else."[25] For Clinton, it was not merely fun, it was exhilarating, even though he was already planning to move on. After five months in office, he conceded that rather than seek a second two-year term, he probably would run for governor or the United States Senate in 1978, and why not? He had the state's most influential molders of public opinion, including the entire editorial board of the *Arkansas Gazette* and *Arkansas Democrat* columnist Bob Lancaster, then the leading political commentator in the press (the Clintons rarely missed a Lancaster New Year's Eve party), and they had declared him to be a star on the rise.

Clinton had been in office scarcely two months when he was named one of three Outstanding Young Men of the Year by the Arkansas Jaycees. The judges were three men who would play key roles in Clinton's political success: wealthy Little Rock banker William Bowen, a future chief of staff to Governor Clinton; childhood friend Mack McLarty; and lawyer David L. Hale, later to play a key role in the Whitewater/Madison Guaranty scandal.

The awards ceremony was held at one of several all-white Central Arkansas country clubs that would provide Clinton with all the privileges of membership until 1992, when frequenting such bastions of white supremacy would become politically incorrect for the future president of the United States.

Former Governor Orval E. Faubus fueled Clinton's prospects by declaring in August 1977, "I'll tell you the man you better keep your eye on mighty close if he decides to run—Bill Clinton," adding that the thirty-one-year-old attorney general had matured quickly and demonstrated responsibility in public office.[26]

Arkansas's seven state officials do not run as a slate; each seeks nomination and election independently, although nomination on the Democratic ticket is tantamount to election. While some competition exists among the lesser offices of lieutenant governor, attorney general, secretary of state, auditor, treasurer, and the outmoded position of commissioner of state lands, it is unusual for those holding these offices to effect anything more than a lateral transfer in Arkansas politics. Historically, each finds a niche and retires from it or dies while occupying it.

But in the 1970s the face of the Democratic party in Arkansas was changing. Those who had made a career in statewide offices were aging, the attorney general's office was becoming a stepping stone for ambitious young politicos, and the attributes voters were seeking in elected officials were changing. Baby boomers were steadily infiltrating the county courthouses, the legislature, and the state's constitutional offices. Governor David Pryor, a former congressman who already had his eye on the U.S. Senate because of the rumored retirement of ailing eighty-one-year-old John L. McClellan, recognized that Clinton would be his likely successor and included the dynamic young attorney general in many of his administration strategies.

The state, long under a federal court order to institute and maintain constitutional standards for incarceration, had, as now, a chronic problem with prison overcrowding. Wanting to avoid the cost and controversy of a special legislative session—Arkansas's bicameral General Assembly is only required to meet for a minimum of sixty days every other year—Pryor enlisted the state correction commissioner and Clinton to devise a three-part plan for alleviating overcrowding. By so doing, he both forged an alliance with a potential challenger and bestowed his blessings upon Clinton's next political move, which, he now could be assured, would follow Pryor's own plans for advancement.

10

PRETTY FACES

IN ARKANSAS, the decade of the 1970s—the Era of Pretty Faces—was an era of marked political change as elder statesmen were compelled to step aside for a contingent of youthful, articulate, energetic office seekers.

Beginning with the politically unknown Dale Bumpers, who displaced the ill, drink-ravaged Winthrop Rockefeller in the governor's office in 1970 at age forty-four and went on in 1974 to unseat the revered Senator J. William Fulbright, each election year brought another pretty face or two into the ranks of Democratic officeholders: Jim Guy Tucker, attorney general in 1972 at age twenty-eight and then congressman; David Pryor, a former congressman who after a brief hiatus came back as governor in 1974 at age thirty-nine and United States senator four years later; Bill Clinton, attorney general at age thirty in 1976; Paul Riviere, successful at age thirty-one in 1978 in his first run for office, secretary of state, despite little work and few party credentials; and Steve Clark, Clinton's successor as attorney general in 1978 at age thirty-one.

Fortunately, there was a place for every one of them, and virtually no competition. Only one rising politician caused anyone any disquiet: Bill Clinton. He was far and away the most successful of any officeholder in amassing statewide exposure.

As one pundit noted in the summer of 1977, Clinton was "young, looks good on television, and can be rousing on the stump."[1] The only thing that might encumber a hasty climb up the political ladder by Clinton would be "convincing voters that he's not overzealously ambitious—that he's not trying to rise too high, too fast. That problem could be less of a problem if he were completing two terms as attorney general instead of just one."

Traditionally, Arkansas's seven constitutional officers are sworn to office on the second Tuesday of January following the November general election. Until 1986, those officials—governor, lieutenant governor, attorney general, secretary of state, auditor, treasurer, and commissioner of state lands—were elected to two-year terms. The brevity of these terms had two impacts on career politicians: It kept them more attuned to the wishes of the people, and it forced them to begin their reelection campaigns in fairly short order after the swearing-in ceremony.

Another tradition of more recent vintage in Arkansas politics is that high-ranking Democratic officeholders serve two terms before moving up the ladder or to Washington. (There have been only four Republicans elected to state office, two governors and two lieutenant governors, since Reconstruction, although Arkansas's longtime auditor became a Republican in 1993.) Bill Clinton broke with that tradition.

Clinton's political aspirations were the worst-kept secret in the state. Thus it came as no surprise when, scarcely five months into his first two-year term as attorney general, speculation about his next race hit the headlines. The first trial balloon came from a high school student at the American Legion's annual Girls State camp who put the question to Clinton, and the dashing young Democrat allowed as to how he had not made up his mind between the governorship and the United States Senate. That was not altogether true.

Timing and circumstance are key elements in any campaign, and Clinton was well aware that, in accord with the state's traditions, Governor Pryor would probably not seek a third term. Given his love of legislating—Pryor had served three terms in the state House of Representatives and three terms in the U.S. Congress before his ill-timed bid to unseat the aging but still formidable Senator John L. McClellan in 1972 had thrown a detour into his career path—Pryor had his eye on another Senate race. McClellan's term was up in 1978, and it was generally agreed that the eighty-one-year-old solon, still mentally alert but in declining health, could not withstand another strong challenge if he were bullheaded enough to seek a seventh term.

History is not alone in suggesting that Clinton could have gone from the attorney general's office to Congress had he been so inclined. He had his choice of districts—in Arkansas, it is generally accepted that residence is a matter of intent, and you don't have to live in the congressional district to which you're elected. Moreover, two members of Congress, former Attorney General Jim Guy Tucker and Ray Thornton, nephew of the financially and politically powerful founder of Stephens Incorporated, also were giving serious consideration to running for the Senate. Any doubts were cast aside in late November when McClellan died, requiring the gubernatorial selection of Kaneaster Hodges, who agreed not to run for the office in 1978.

The resulting crowded field of political heavyweights in the Senate race had nothing to do with Clinton's decision to seek the governorship. Being one of 435 congressmen held absolutely no appeal for him at the moment. He was thirty-one years old, there was plenty of time in which to establish his political credentials as a presidential candidate, and there might never be a better opportunity for attaining high visibility than in 1978.

While his seemingly tireless staff kept the utility interventions and the consumer lawsuits going, Clinton pursued a seemingly tireless schedule of public and private appearances calculated to enhance his viability and expand his growing network of contacts—testifying before congressional committees, breaking bread with the Carters at the White House, and glad-handing his way into a National Association of Attorneys General committee chairmanship.

Hillary also benefited from Clinton's reputation as a comer. Although her credentials and her abilities would become better known and highly respected as she pursued her own interests, her legal profile owed its initial glow to Clinton's political promise. In fairly short order, the Rose Law Firm, one of the state's most prestigious, invited her to serve a brief tenure as an associate in anticipation of a partnership, and the Carter administration named her to the board of the Legal Services Corporation, whose chairmanship she assumed almost immediately. She also became a member of and immediately chaired the board of the Arkansas Advocates for Children and Families, which she helped found in 1977.

Just as a congressional race was never a serious consideration with Clinton, he was never seriously considered for the chairmanship of the Democratic National Committee. His reason for planting both stories—to collect laurels and promote his populist image without patting himself on the back—provoked editorial speculation in the winter of 1977. When a Memphis newspaper reported in November that he had decided to run for governor, Clinton let it be known that he was postponing any decision until a poll could be taken.[2]

About the time the alleged poll should have been completed, Clinton let it slip that he was thinking about establishing a United States Senate campaign committee. The purpose of the disclosure was twofold: it stepped up the level of contributions he had been receiving for several months, and it opened negotiations with potential competitors and their sugar daddies.

The only option which Clinton eschewed was reelection as attorney general. Opportunities for advancement were few and far between, given the Arkansas voters' habit of reelecting incumbents. The governor's office was the exception; throughout the twentieth century, only Faubus and Clinton would serve more than two terms in office. Moreover, Clinton realized that the odds were against him being able to mount a presidential campaign from Congress within the near future. Political etiquette demanded that he stand aside for more established Democratic leaders in the Senate race, and he had no desire to enter the House of Representatives where making a name for himself would be time-consuming and laborious. Besides, he reasoned, Jimmy Carter had proved that the governor's office was a viable stepping-stone to the Oval Office.

All things considered, there was nowhere except the statehouse for Clinton to go in 1978.

"The scenario is set," the *Arkansas Democrat*'s A. L. May wrote in its January 8, 1978, issue. "In the next few weeks, Governor David Pryor will announce for the Senate, followed by state Attorney General Bill Clinton's announcement for the governorship. There is nothing startling in that—these moves have been expected all along, disturbed only by the respective flirtations by Pryor with a third term as governor and by Clinton with the Senate race."[3]

The filing period for the 1978 primaries was in May, but Pryor was hesitant to come out too early, May opined, lest he become a lame-duck governor. "Never much of a master over the legislature," May wrote, "Pryor's clout would be diminished further when the boys in the statehouse know for sure that he won't be around much longer. . . . Both Clinton and Pryor will make formidable candidates and will be the front-runners in their respective races."[4]

In the race for governor, May declared, Clinton would be "super tough" to beat, although "some would say that he will be unbeatable."[5]

Many were rumored and declared as gubernatorial candidates by the time Clinton made it official, but the principal challenger was Joe D. Woodward, a Columbia County lawyer and former political operative during the Bumpers administration. There was simply no one else of any stature on the horizon, and beyond his home county and Democratic party regulars, Woodward was virtually unknown. Clinton was, as A.L. May aptly stated, seemingly omnipresent; his name recognition was well above 50 percent, he had the press at his disposal, his campaign manager, former state Representative Rudy Moore, Jr., was in place, and his headquarters was open and active a full two months before the Clinton candidacy became official.

While few realized the actual scope of his appeal, or the degree of political savvy at work, hindsight would reveal it to be one of the best political organizations ever assembled in Arkansas, not only for its effectiveness down to the precinct level, but for its stunning efficiency. The minds behind Clinton were creative, too.

The campaign apparatus found numerous ways to circumvent the state's campaign practices laws legally. One example was the production of an eight-page "Attorney General's Report" in January 1978. Ten thousand copies were printed at a reported cost of just over $1,000 for distribution to public officials "and others."[6]

The text, prepared in newspaper tabloid format with dynamic headlines and augmented by five photographs of Clinton and two political cartoons, described in glowing terms the activities and accomplishments of his first year in office.

Initially, Clinton had hoped to finance this "report" with public funds, and had it not been for an inquisitive journalist that could have been accomplished. However, when word circulated that the report was being compiled, a reporter discovered an obscure 1911 state law that called for the attorney general to put out a report on his office's activities, but the report was to be produced biannually, in odd-numbered years, and had to deal only with certain specific data. The original manuscript did not meet these criteria; rather, it reported on only one year, was scheduled to appear in an even-numbered year, and covered more than called for by the old law—not to mention the fact that the photographs and cartoons lent a political overtone to the entire project. Ultimately, Clinton financed it with campaign contributions.

Former campaign manager Steve Smith, by then the attorney general's administrative assistant, claimed that the report was a campaign document "only as much as any record of his office" would be. Among the instrument's headlines: "Consumer Recoveries Highest in History," "Record Number of Opinions Issued by Division," "25-Cent Pay Phone Charge Contested," "Aid Sought for Victims of Crime," "Clinton Leads Panel on Aged," and "Litigation Protects Interests of State."

From then until his gubernatorial announcement in March, Clinton generated headlines on a near-daily basis—not a difficult accomplishment, given the size and dedication of his administrative *cum* campaign staff and a fiercely competitive Capitol press corps whose numbers included full-time representatives of two wire services, three statewide network television affiliates, several radio stations, and a handful of newspapers, including the morning *Arkansas Gazette* and the afternoon *Arkansas Democrat*.

At that point, the Capitol press corps had been in a state of transition for a couple of years, and it was a motley collection of aging curmudgeons, middle-aged news hounds, and hungry newcomers. Given the media's preoccupation with politics and government in those post-Watergate days, access was the life's blood of any reporter worth his salt. And no one was more accessible than Bill Clinton, who found plenty of opportunities for private chats with reporters and made sure his schedule was well circulated among them.

Thus the media were there when he proselytized on behalf of a new constitution, to be drawn in 1979 by elected delegates to a state convention at which he hoped four-year terms for constitutional officers would become a reality, and, to labor's chagrin, for the retention of the right-to-work laws. They were there when he surveyed more than seven hundred public schools, hospitals, and nursing homes to determine what damage, if any, they had sustained because of alleged price fixing among milk companies in Central Arkansas. They were there when he finally kept an almost two-year-old campaign promise and inaugurated a new antitrust division to pursue violations and advise businesses that might unknowingly violate the law, and when he announced an effort to develop a system to investigate complaints of police brutality. And they were there when he brought litigation against fifteen big out-of-state manufacturers of fine paper products alleging conspiracy to fix the prices of these products.

The press was there, too, albeit on the wrong side of the closed door, when Clinton dipped into his war chest to wine and dine and woo the most influential members of the Arkansas legislature in an effort to allay their concerns about his youth and inexperience, and to let them know that he valued whatever advice they would make to a Clinton gubernatorial administration and was willing to work to their "mutual" satisfaction.[7]

Early on, gubernatorial hopeful Randall Mathis, a former Clark County judge, had chastised the news media for having created what he called the myth of Clinton's invincibility as a candidate, and while it may have been sour grapes, it was true. No news stories of the period explained why Bill Clinton was a force to be reckoned with, or how he had come to be one; they merely anointed him as a nearly unstoppable political phenomenon. Where exploration and analysis should have existed, there were only adjectives—"young," "energetic," "handsome," "articulate"—which nonetheless conveyed the crux of his appeal. People said he reminded them of John F. Kennedy.

The first public opinion survey of the election year, conducted several weeks before Clinton's entry by the state's leading pollster, Jim Ranchino, gave the attorney general 57 percent of the vote against three declared Democratic candidates, none of whom polled a percentage above a single digit.[8]

In his report on the survey, the *Arkansas Democrat's* Jerry Dean explained that "one reason Clinton will be difficult to overtake, even given the determination and perseverance of a [Randall] Mathis, is that the attorney general knows an opportune political issue when he sees one. Clinton has used his 15 months in office to hype the consumer protection division with such projects as the recovery of thousands of dollars for Arkansas motorists who bought 'Oldsrolets'—the Oldsmobiles with Chevy engines in them—from GMC, and he has appeared personally and regularly before the state Public Service Commission interceding on behalf of rate-payers in utility rate cases."[9]

For his gubernatorial announcement, Clinton abandoned the cold, marble walls and the atrocious acoustics of the state Capitol rotunda for a more picturesque setting that would better accommodate a larger contingent of journalists and 250 cheering supporters: the front lawn of the Old State House.[10]

His breath frosty against the chill of a March morning, Clinton asserted the need for more jobs, better incomes, better schools, economic expansion, and that mainstay of all Arkansas gubernatorial campaigns, a decent road program. Lest any special-interest group feel left out of a Clinton administration, he stressed the importance of preserving the family farm and promoting the sale of Arkansas products abroad. Arkansas deserved leadership that would encourage "the best quality of life we can [give] to our senior citizens and others who are swamped by inflation and don't have enough to live on."[11]

"We need a governor who will move on the problems, make decisions, bring the finest people into government, and run an open, responsive, and balanced administration. I want to be that governor."

Over the din of morning traffic and a few low-flying airplanes—the Old State House sits between what then were the two busiest streets in downtown Little Rock—he briefly reviewed his fourteen-month record as attorney general, placing particular emphasis on the stances he had taken in the areas of utility rates and consumer protection.

He said he would make only one promise: "If you will let me be your governor, no one will love this state more, care more about our people's problems, or work harder to see that we become what we ought to be."

That he would dedicate himself to helping the people achieve excellence would be a recurring theme in subsequent campaigns; his remarks would always make some pointed reference to "vision." On this day, it surfaced when he declared: "I will try to be honest about what cannot be done, but I also will try to lift our vision toward what must be done."

His wife Hillary Rodham, his mother Virginia Dwire, and his brother Roger Clinton led the enthusiastic applause.

Among Clinton's prepared remarks was this telling statement: "I really want to be governor. A governor can do more for more people in less time than any public official in the country, with the exception of the president—if the president can get along with Congress."

Under questioning from reporters afterward, Clinton was not forthcoming with details about what he would seek to accomplish as governor. He avoided giving a direct answer—and was not encouraged to be more direct—when asked about the likelihood of tax increases on his watch. Another reporter was curious about patronage under a Clinton administration. "I have not and will not until after the election promise to hire or fire, appoint or reappoint anyone to any office in state government," he declared. He would break that promise in fairly short order, although this became apparent only during a review of the Clinton record. In those days, Clinton promised little beyond generalities, and no reporter then chronicling his administration kept a balance sheet on him. Clinton's reputation as a breaker of promises would come later.

In what was now a campaign tradition, Clinton spent the rest of the day traveling aboard a small aircraft to news conferences in other major

Arkansas media markets—this time Texarkana, El Dorado, West Memphis, and Fayetteville—at which he repeated his announcement. Only Jonesboro was bypassed, but Clinton reckoned on covering that base with the greater exposure afforded by the Memphis media.

Thanks to the advance work of his budding statewide network, he was greeted at every stop like a visiting potentate. Each time he left center stage, he would ask the nearest person, "How was it?"

"Fantastic" was the inevitable response.

Clinton's remarks offered little more than optimism and leadership, but that was enough for the adoring throngs who knew a winner when they saw one.

When the filing closed, five men were on the Democratic ballot, but that did not make it a contest.

Both Randall Mathis, forty-seven, and Joe Woodward, forty-eight, touted their experience, maturity, and ability. It did not distinguish either of them, although both attracted some financial support that was more than their individual investments in their campaigns.

Frank Lady, forty-eight, an extremely conservative former state representative from northwest Arkansas who had made a dismal third-place showing in the 1976 gubernatorial primary, played the role of spoiler, taking advantage of every opportunity to portray Clinton as "the most liberal politician ever to come out of Arkansas."[12]

Monroe Schwarzlose, a seventy-five-year-old turkey farmer from rural Cleveland County whose genius at comic relief would not be used to its best advantage for two years to come, rounded out the Democratic primary roster. There would be no Republican primary; the GOP rarely fielded more than one candidate in the governor's race. For this one, Lynn Lowe, a perennial candidate who had lost several offices, carried the GOP banner.

It was, indeed, the shortest campaign of Clinton's career, and he ran it as though it were the only game in town, even interrupting his speaking tour to make another excursion to Washington. His appearance before the National Transportation Safety Board, where he repeated an earlier call for congressional action to improve enforcement of railway safety regulations, won the United Transportation Union endorsement in Arkansas.

During his Arkansas road trips, many of which were made at public expense under the guise of official state business, the attorney general's staff kept Clinton's name before the public, intervening in several high-profile utility rate cases that neither he nor they would be around to conclude.

Clinton cleaned up on endorsements, including the coveted ones of the Arkansas Education Association and the AFL-CIO, and none of the slings and arrows tossed his way by the bombastic Mathis or the ultraconservative Frank Lady struck a responsive chord with voters. If, as Mathis insisted, Clinton had consistently used the attorney general's office to further his own ambitions,[13] Arkansans did not care. It was a case of style over substance, and Clinton's style generally was informal, ingratiating, and incredibly appealing.

For instance, when asked about his youth, Clinton adopted a pat response not unlike this one to a grizzled fellow at Heber Springs:

"How old are you?"

"Old enough." Pause. "I'm thirty-one."

"Well, you sure don't look it."

"Well, I will by the time this campaign is over."[14]

Women adored his boyishness, and men responded to his firm handshake and respectful attitude. Those escorting him through a crowd learned to wear clothes with pockets to accommodate the checks and cash pressed into his hand and to carry pen and paper with which to record names and addresses and requests for assistance or campaign material. They also learned the futility of trying to rush him from one engagement to another. When Clinton worked a crowd, he really worked it, shaking each hand and speaking to each person in turn, always on the alert for clues indicating that he and the stranger before him had a person or a place in common.

His personal, personable style of campaigning, and the news media's obvious bias in his favor, resulted in a minor phenomenon in Arkansas politics: He not only placed first in the five-man primary on May 30, but he avoided a runoff by garnering 59.6 percent of the vote, carrying all but five of the state's seventy-five counties.

Clinton was understandably jubilant at his postprimary news conference, held outside his headquarters the next day. Boasting of the mandate handed him by Arkansas voters, he said that he would begin charting the course of his gubernatorial administration immediately. What about the general election? Oh, he planned a "vigorous" campaign against Lynn Lowe, he said. He meant that he would take time out from his attorney general's duties and the campaign each week to attend to gubernatorial matters because "the people will expect me to be ready if elected."[15]

The primary had cost Clinton supporters about $400,000, about $50,000 more than projected because "we had an unusually heavy demand for campaign materials and requests for opening regional campaign headquarters."[16] Clinton said he still had about $125,000, which he planned to use for both the general election campaign and the transition from attorney general to governor. But several weeks before the general election, Clinton requested a $50,000 stipend from the governor's emergency fund to help cover costs of a transition that had yet to be sanctioned by voters. Outgoing Governor David Pryor granted him $60,000.

Clinton seemed particularly pleased that Vice President Walter Mondale had telephoned his congratulations. President Carter's call would not come until the Fourth of July.

In anticipation of an easy November victory, the Clinton team wasted little time transforming the campaign headquarters into a transition office befitting a governor-elect. From there, the election material continued to pour forth, but most of the staff's energies, and Clinton's, were directed toward assembling a gubernatorial staff.

"Way down deep in my heart, I [know I] can beat Bill Clinton and will beat him," Lowe said in one of the comparatively few news stories his campaign generated.[17] But no one, least of all the Republican party, believed him. Clinton's campaign was a coronation in the making. He truly was, as Howell Raines of the *New York Times* dubbed him, "Arkansas's 31-year-old whiz kid."[18]

A common lament in many political contests is that they degenerate into personality contests and ignore the issues. The Clinton-Lowe race, which could hardly be called a contest, was a prime example of this. Lowe had the same issues as Clinton, but Clinton had something Lowe didn't have: a charismatic personality.

Lowe did his best to interest the public in his plans for addressing the state's chronic needs—a better education system, an improved highway program, industrial expansion, job creation—but his propositions were virtually ignored. One fund-raising breakfast held in his behalf attracted only thirteen attendees, and two of them were campaign aides. Lowe said the post office had failed to deliver his invitations in time. By comparison, Clinton played to packed houses.

Actually, Lowe's ideas were not that far different from Clinton's, particularly since neither candidate was long on specifics. The difference was one of approach: Lowe talked stoically and humorlessly about living within the state's means, doing more and better work with existing resources; Clinton smiled and joked and promised the moon while insinuating that a little tax reform would do far more good than a general tax increase.

Clinton also refined a technique he had used with limited success in his first campaign: he garnered voter sympathy by accusing others of having attacked him and having misrepresented his stand on issues, a gimmick I later came to refer to as his "Poor, Poor, Pitiful Me" face. To hear Clinton tell it, he was being ripped up one side and down the other for *allegedly* holding "liberal" views on gun control, marijuana laws, and women's rights.

What he was, Clinton insisted, was neither liberal nor conservative but "progressive."[19] This offensive posturing accomplished what he had hoped, and his support for gun control, decriminalization of marijuana use and possession, and the Equal Rights Amendment never became issues.

"Every time I run," he told Howell Raines in a postprimary interview, "people run the same race against me. They say, 'This guy is being foisted on us,' like I'm a creation of the media who's been cloned somehow with an Ivy League education and long hair."[20]

"He defends his Yale diploma and Rhodes scholarship," Raines wrote. "Arkansans no longer 'want to be perceived, especially by themselves, as being backward.' He said people are proud of his education."

In the interview, Clinton erroneously implied that his wife's use of her maiden name had been made an issue in the campaign—actually, it

did not become an issue until his ill-fated 1980 reelection campaign—
and said that Arkansans had demonstrated in the primary that they
wanted Rodham as a top advisor of their next governor. He called his
having been selected as the Democratic party nominee for governor a
victory for both of them, adding that "our vote was a vindication of
what my wife and I have done and what we hope to do for the state."

At the time, of course, Hillary Rodham's name recognition was
virtually nonexistent among the public.

The *New York Times* interview apparently struck a raw nerve with
Gale Hussman Arnold, the sister of the publisher of the editorially
conservative *Arkansas Democrat* who at the time served as the newspaper's Washington correspondent. Before local newspapers picked up
the interview from the wire, she wrote that "Clinton seemed to leave
the impression in the interview that his educational background was
unique for elective office in Arkansas in recent years." She went on to
point out correctly that "the Ivy League has been well represented in
recent years among the state's officeholders. Representative Ray
Thornton also attended Yale, Representative Jim Guy Tucker attended Harvard, and Senator Kaneaster Hodges received his divinity
degree from Princeton." Senator Fulbright had, of course, attended
Oxford University as a Rhodes Scholar.[21]

In the context of the Clinton-Lowe match-up, Arnold's caustic
commentary was not altogether unwarranted. Clinton's remarks
seemed patronizing and self-serving, particularly his observation that
middle- and working-class voters who once supported single-issue
candidates had begun looking to well-educated politicians as role
models for what their own children could become.

Asked at one point whether his primary victory suggested that
Arkansas was becoming more liberal, Clinton replied: "I think it
means the state is becoming more like the rest of the country, with
both liberal and conservative ideas. I think my election [sic] shows that
the people are interested in a candidate's position on the issues and not
on labels that are sometimes used to divert the voters's interest."[22]

In Arkansas, however, labels count, and nowhere have they historically carried more weight than in gubernatorial races. As Clinton's
longtime friend Diane Blair and co-author Robert L. Savage sug-

gested in a 1988 essay, Republicans win office in Arkansas when any one of three conditions is met: When the Democratic candidate "is just clearly an unacceptable alternative"; when voters are angered by the past actions of the Democratic incumbent; and when the Republican "is a distinctly palatable candidate."[23]

None of those conditions existed in 1978. Clinton entered the primary as the preordained front-runner and, predictably, outpaced and outspent a lackluster, underfinanced field of Democratic challengers. He then took on an even more lackluster, underfinanced Republican opponent who would have paled by comparison with any of the Democratic also-rans.

In August, Clinton announced a two-month halt on campaign activity, saying he needed time to tie up loose ends in the attorney general's office and pave the way for a smooth transition. He left the belated formulation of his campaign platform to members of his administrative staff and the Platform Committee of the Democratic State Committee, and busied himself with private fund-raising endeavors and a few carefully selected public appearances. These included a vocational education conference, attended by several hundred educators, at which he pledged to consider vocational education needs in formulating his comprehensive economic development program; an assembly of the Arkansas Association of Secondary School Principals at which he pledged support for special school programs for gifted and talented students; and a speech to the annual Men's Day gathering at a Little Rock African Episcopal Methodist church at which he spoke against the "excesses" of tax reform.

At the latter engagement, Clinton made a humorous statement which some critics would later invoke, without consequence, in an attempt to show his opportunistic nature. Noting the heavy attendance of both Baptists and Methodists, Clinton quipped that although he had married a Methodist, he had not converted from the Baptist faith because "God's work is truly our own, and 46 percent of the voters in Arkansas are Baptists."[24]

The platform finally produced in late September called for defeat of a proposed constitutional amendment to exempt groceries and prescription drugs from the state's 3 percent tax; giving the legislature the authority to lift Arkansas's constitutionally imposed 10 percent interest ceiling; legislative ratification of the Equal Rights Amendment; creation of a comprehensive state water policy; expansion of rural health care; and numerous education proposals promulgated by the Arkansas Education Association. Among these were a fully funded, mandatory statewide kindergarten program; a fair dismissal law for teachers; salary increases to bring teachers within range of the regional average; a state-paid health insurance plan for all 35,000 public school employees; a collective bargaining law; and reform of the formula for distributing state aid to assure equal educational opportunity for children in poor districts.

Despite the traditional laundry lists of campaign issues, the only topic that generated much attention was Amendment 59, the constitutional proposal that would have exempted food and drugs from the sales tax. Initially, Lowe halfheartedly supported the measure as a means of helping the state's large elderly and low-income population and Clinton halfheartedly opposed it on the grounds that the loss of revenue would hurt the education and human services programs on which these two segments relied. Later, Clinton's opposition would intensify as he saw more clearly the threat to the state's tax revenues— and his escalating spending proposals.

On education matters, while Clinton repeatedly stated the need for increased funding for public schools and "substantial" raises for teachers, he criticized the conclusions found in a report on the status of public education in Arkansas.

The Alexander Report, commissioned by a state legislative committee and produced by Florida professor Kern S. Alexander, opined that "by almost any standard, the Arkansas system of education must be regarded as inadequate. Children of the state are not being offered the same opportunity to develop their individual capabilities as children in other states. Stated another way, from an educational standpoint the average child in Arkansas would be much better off attending the public schools of almost any other state in the country."[25]

"That obviously is not so," Clinton said in remarks to high school principals. He praised Arkansas's educational commitment, which at that time channeled almost 50 cents of every state tax dollar into the state's Public School Fund. He conceded that "there is a wide variety of quality education provided in the state," but he insisted that "money is not the sole determinant of quality education."[26]

Among the Alexander Report's recommendations was allocation of an additional $60 million a year for schools. "In general, I can support that," Clinton said, but "that depends on the total amount of money for state services."[27] He would have to reassess his position later when several school districts successfully litigated their claim that the formula for allocating and distributing state aid to public school districts was unconstitutional.

While Lowe trudged onward if not upward—by mid-September, Clinton had raised an additional $81,547 to Lowe's $48,512—Clinton tapped into his friendship with the Carter administration and brought James Earl "Chip" Carter III to Arkansas in October. The two men appeared together at several sites, although as one newspaper account noted, "news reporter weren't much interested" in the president's son.[28]

Clinton was more circumspect two weeks later when Eunice Shriver came to Little Rock at the behest of Hillary Rodham and Arkansas Advocates for Children and Families to address a conference on parenting education. His only meeting with the sister of perennial presidential hopeful Ted Kennedy was a private one. Shriver did choose to include a light-hearted reference to Clinton in her remarks: She noted that he had the kind of qualities that "are a recipe to run for president of the United States. Please don't have him run in 1980."[29]

The first documented reference to a broken campaign promise came two weeks before the November 7 general election when, his election assured, Clinton outlined his plan for replacing the Arkansas Industrial Development Commission, which he said was too narrow in scope, with a cabinet-level Economic Development Commission. The new agency would cost twice as much to operate, he admitted, but it would better address the state's needs for economic expansion and job creation.

In outlining his plan to the Industrial Developers of Arkansas, Clinton said he no longer saw a need to create a separate agriculture commission, a promise he had made repeatedly to groups of farmers in the spring before the preferential primary. But now, he said, he intended for agriculture, then on the decline but still one of the top industries in the state, to be represented on the new Economic Development Commission.

If Clinton figured that a change of heart at this late date could do him no harm, he figured correctly. Lowe, running well over 30 points behind in the polls, was too far behind to make major headway with this or any other issue.

That is not to say that Clinton had no uneasy moments in the final days of the campaign. For a brief time, he was extremely nervous because of a retired Air Force lieutenant colonel from Fayetteville named Billy G. Geren.

With virtually no warning, Geren called a news conference at the state Capitol on October 27 and made a most astounding accusation: The attorney general of Arkansas, he declared, was a draft-dodger who had joined in protests against the United States government's involvement in the Vietnam War.[30]

Geren told a handful of reporters that he had written to members of the Arkansas Retired Officers Group of which he was vice president that Clinton was a draft-dodger who had reneged on a commitment he had made to enter the advanced Reserve Officer Training Corps in exchange for a one-year deferment from the draft in 1969. On the basis of that agreement, Geren said, Clinton had been permitted to return to Oxford University, where he was enrolled as a Rhodes Scholar, to complete the fall semester.

The governor, Geren pointed out, is the commander-in-chief of the Arkansas National Guard, and Clinton, he suggested, was not fit to hold that title on the basis of that history.

Contacted afterward, Clinton said that the accusation was absolutely untrue and had no basis in fact because *he had never received a draft deferment.*[31]

According to Clinton, while at Oxford, he had decided to "take advantage" of the ROTC opportunity and had made the agreement in the summer of 1969. The ROTC unit was supposed to mail the agreement to Washington at the end of the year so that the deferment would start in 1970. But upon returning to Oxford, Clinton said, he decided against accepting the deferment and wrote to Colonel Eugene Holmes, the ROTC commander, saying he would prefer "to get it over with" and subject himself to the draft. He added that he had told Holmes that he would proceed with the ROTC training if that was Holmes's desire.

Further, Clinton said, a relative of his had spoken with Holmes at the time and had been told that the contract would be canceled; thus, the contract was never sent to Washington and he was not deferred. As circumstance would have it, he noted, he later drew a high lottery number and so was never called to duty.

Geren, who had been on the air force ROTC staff at Fayetteville from 1972–76, then defended his claim by saying that he had once seen the army ROTC file containing the agreement between Clinton and the ROTC commander.[32] All he knew was "what was in the file," and if he was wrong, if indeed Clinton had not received a deferment, he would apologize. In any event, he said stubbornly, Clinton was not fit to be governor and commander of the state's military reserve units because of his antiwar activities. Geren said he had recently confronted Clinton at a meeting in Fayetteville and Clinton had expressed no remorse for his role in the Vietnam protest movement.

To that claim, Clinton said that Geren had merely asked him whether he had ever participated in a war protest and he replied that he had attended two of them, one at Oxford and one in Washington.[33] Clinton said he had gone to hear the speeches and that while there he had not conducted himself in a manner of which he should be ashamed.

He said that during their encounter, Geren had not asked him about the deferment.

"It's obvious to me," Clinton said, "that he didn't know the facts and that he didn't want to know them."[34]

The one man besides Geren who did know the facts wasn't talking. Contacted by a reporter at his home in Fayetteville, Eugene Holmes, by then retired, said he could not recall Clinton's case because there had been thousands of students since then.[35] It was a response he would very much regret in later years.

The press gave Geren's story scant attention, and on November 7, Bill Clinton pulled an impressive 63.3 percent of the vote against the Republican, Lynn Lowe, and an even lesser known write-in candidate, Kenneth L. Farrell of Benton. At age thirty-two, the youngest attorney general in the nation was soon to become the nation's youngest governor.

11

WARM, WITTY, EVER MINDFUL OF NAMES

VICTORY SPEECHES ARE EXPECTED to be laced with superlatives and hyperbole, but Clinton exercised his taste for the dramatic on election night in 1978 when he emerged at 9:30 to thank scores of clamorous celebrants who had gathered in the Camelot Inn ballroom to watch the returns on television sets scattered throughout the cavernous room.

Considering the ease of his victory, and the relative uneventfulness of the campaign, the governor-elect's presentation was something of an anomaly. The story Clinton told about the campaign bore little resemblance to reality. The only interruption in Clinton's march to victory had been the Geren incident, which had excited very few journalists. And given how few stories were written about Geren's claims of draft-dodging, it's doubtful that many of those present had any inkling of what Clinton meant when he said he hoped that "we will be able to put behind us the negative things that occurred—and I can't believe that some of the things that happened to this campaign anyone could have been proud of."[1]

It had been "a long and arduous effort," Clinton said, and he was so very proud of his family and friends and supporters for having stood by him throughout the "sometimes bitter struggle" of his noble quest, but he was prouder still that "the overpowering majority of our people refused to vote their fears." Near him on the dais, Hillary Rodham and Roger Clinton looked equally proud.

"This election is fundamentally a tribute to the decency and judgment and hope of the people of Arkansas," Clinton said. "I know the problems we face in the state and nation are complex and that people feel frustrated and thwarted and are prepared to believe the worst about politicians when they hear it. And in campaigns, they hear plenty. But I still believe that, beyond those of any other state, our people are devoted to the proposition that our bright future will not be realized if we turn against ourselves."

He was less concerned with being the nation's youngest governor than with becoming the best governor, he said. "I want you all to know that I will be prepared, that I will be frugal with your tax dollars, and that I will work as hard as I can to bring the finest people into government. I will try to be worthy of the enormous trust you have placed in me this evening."

Clinton had lost only six of the state's seventy-five counties—the predominantly Republican Baxter, Boone, Crawford, Franklin, and Sebastian, and Lowe's home county of Union—but an almost 2–to–1 victory could be considered a mandate, although Clinton never won an election that he did not declare a mandate.

Despite the abundance of stories Clinton had generated over the past two years, the public was not given its first intimate glimpse of the man until the day after his victory. Some of the revelations in The Associated Press profile were downright bizarre, as reflected in the story's lead paragraphs.

"Love you," he says as he tells his wife, Hillary, goodbye on the telephone. Speaking of her sometimes as "my little wife" as in "my little wife and I went for dinner last night," he unabashedly dotes on her with something akin to reverence.

"He" is Bill Clinton, the governor-elect. There's a side or two to him that few know. He confesses he once was among those who would get into cars and go "mooning" during high school days on the streets of Hot Springs. He's an "old" saxophone player. (End)[2]

Arkansans learned that the man *Arkansas Gazette* cartoonist George Fisher portrayed as a young lad in knee pants riding a tricycle drove a car like a bat out of hell, braking suddenly, shifting lanes, and tailgating; that he avoided cigarettes but sometimes smoked a pipe or a cigar; and that he liked to grab a microphone at parties and "croon."

Further, they learned that his thirty-one-year-old "little wife," Hillary Rodham, had decided at age nine to keep her maiden name. "It depresses her when she thinks it's hurting me, but she's a lawyer, and she doesn't want to go into the courtroom as somebody's wife. If people knew how old-fashioned she is in every conceivable way, they probably wouldn't" criticize her, Clinton said.

"She's just a hard-working, no-nonsense, no-frills, intelligent girl who has done well, who doesn't see any sense to extramarital sex, who doesn't care much for drink, who's witty and sharp but without being a stick in the mud—she's just great."

The story improved the impression that voters in the hinterlands had of Hillary, at least for the first few months after the election. Afterward, when public disenchantment with their new governor had begun to set in, even the birth of their first child could not convince a majority of Arkansans that she had one old-fashioned bone in her body.

Clinton, who at the time of the interview had not begun his first term, was already talking about seeking a third term "if I'm making progress." He said he planned to take a judicious approach to governing and to try not to do everything at once.

The week after Thanksgiving, Clinton managed one more state-financed junket to Washington before the inauguration, ostensibly to confer with President Carter and the Wage and Price Council about easing anti-inflation guidelines under which salary increases for public employees were to be held at 7 percent. As a candidate, Clinton had promised the state's teachers a minimum $1,500 pay raise, and the only way he could make good on that pledge was to have them placed in a special "equity and hardship" category. This exception, Clinton said, would be "the only departure from the 7 percent limit I will make." That comment would soon prove false.[3]

During the hectic one-day visit, Clinton worked in meetings with the secretaries of energy, transportation, and health, education, and welfare. In addition to his political hobnobbing, he also firmed up his plans to open a Washington office, which he hoped legislators would finance in the name of economic development, to serve as his political base in the nation's capital.

Upon his return, the public received the first details of Clinton's plans for Arkansas, which essentially boiled down to more spending and bigger government. Among his proposals were doubling the budget of the state energy office and elevating it to cabinet status, and infusing the state's youth services programs with about $3 million in additional funds while slashing $6 million from the state's adult and elderly assistance programs.

A week after the Washington trip, he was off to Memphis for the Democrats's midterm miniconvention, where he moderated a panel discussion on national health care policy and generated some more national headlines for his mother's growing scrapbook collection.

"If there is anyone who got more out of the Democratic party's Mid-Term Conference in Memphis than Bill Clinton," wrote the *Arkansas Democrat*'s executive editor Robert S. McCord, "it has to be the guy who sold the hot dogs. Of course, for the concessionaire, the profit is immediate. For Clinton, it's off in the future. How far off and where are unknown right now, probably even to Clinton. National political affairs are to politicians what fashion shows are to models."[4]

By McCord's reckoning, Clinton was the hit of the conference, which was rife with "the kind of people Clinton needs to know if he is ever to get anywhere in national politics."[5] Every time he tried to speak with Clinton, McCord said, they were interrupted. Attractive and expensively dressed women, obvious big donors to the national party, walked up to give Clinton a hug. Delegates took his picture. He and Chip Carter made the front page of the local paper. TV camera crews interviewed him. Practically every journalist present questioned McCord about him. David Broder interviewed him for an hour. Jack Nelson of the *Los Angeles Times*, who was planning to write a story about the Democrats's new starlet, remarked that Clinton "looks more like 22."

"There's no doubt that Clinton's youthful good looks are a part of his appeal," McCord said. "But there's also his personality—warm, witty, and ever mindful of names. . . . You and Clinton might disagree totally on a subject and you'll never know it unless you listen closely to every word. Most people don't. They rely on tone of voice and facial expressions, which, from Clinton, will never be harsh or unpleasant. Therefore, liberals and conservatives alike go away from him thinking he's one bright fellow."

Gressie Carnes, well known for her lavish parties for Arkansas Democrats, gave one of her elaborate receptions in Memphis, during which Clinton stationed himself by the door and shook hands for three-and-a-half hours. "Naturally," McCord noted, "all of this exposure gave rise to a lot of talk. Was Clinton campaigning for something?" Rumors circulated that Clinton had been pegged by Ted Kennedy to be his running mate in 1980. Jody Powell, who said he had campaigned for Clinton during his congressional race in 1974, was said to have predicted that Arkansas's *Wunderkind* "could easily play a national role someday."

Clinton, who claimed to have been working his heart out on behalf of Arkansas for the past several years, took another break at Christmas. Hillary treated her husband and herself to a week's vacation in England. There was really little need to stay in Arkansas. The transition was being handled by the staffs of the attorney general and governor, and by his own admission, Clinton had shelled out $100,000 of surplus campaign money to hire consultants, budget analysts, and advisors to prepare the way for him.[6] His closest aides were putting together a pocket guide for lawmakers which would explain available sources of money, the percentages spent by agencies, the Clinton priorities, and the impact those priorities would have on existing services. There was nothing for him to do except relax and enjoy himself between then and the inauguration.

Clinton took the oath of office to become the state's fortieth governor on January 10, 1979, as a horde of politicians, invited guests, and those few members of the public who could squeeze into the crowded House of Representatives chamber looked on. Hillary Rodham held the family Bible upon which he would place his hand four more times before he became president.

After three days and nights of inaugural partying, no one was in the mood to work. The festivities began in a solemn yet celebratory fashion, with a dedication service on Sunday at the Immanuel Baptist Church where Bill Clinton worshipped, followed by an elegant reception at the Arkansas Territorial Restoration, where Arkansas's government was headquartered before statehood. On Monday night, the "Diamonds and Denim" gala, an evening of song, dance, and drama, was held at Robinson Auditorium. Roger Clinton's rock-'n'-roll band was the featured act in an all-Arkansas slate of performers, among them the Arkansas Opera Theater, the Ozark Folk Center Musicians, the Art Porter and Sons jazz ensemble, and the Arkansas Repertory Theatre. At $10 a head for admission, with all proceeds earmarked for the Arkansas Arts Council, the gala was Clinton's nod to the working folks who could not afford the costlier and more opulent inaugural ball Tuesday night, which followed an exhausting but exhilarating afternoon of events that included a symphony concert and another reception.

Viewed against the other events, Clinton's inaugural address was poorly attended. In one of the planning committee's few errors in judgment, the speech was delivered on the steps of the state Capitol overlooking an expansive lawn in order to give several thousand onlookers an artistic and unrestricted view of the state's new chief executive. Bitterly cold weather, however, kept all but a couple of hundred diehard admirers from attending, and a few of them slipped indoors before Clinton's eloquent but lengthy remarks were concluded.

In addition to the customary high-flown rhetoric about moving Arkansas toward an era of excellence, he enumerated the issues he hoped to address—education, economic development, energy production and conservation, equal opportunity, highways, public health, tax relief, services to the young and the elderly—and gave brief summations about why they were of importance to Arkansans.

Except for a few extemporaneous flourishes, he stuck to his script, much as he would do nine years later in his nominating speech for Michael Dukakis in Atlanta, although in 1979, his words and the creeping chill of a January day elicited more enthusiastic applause.

Clinton was unable to savor his new office that first day, although several times he disappeared behind a closed door with a handful of aides, advisors, and designated appointees for a more private celebration. There was much to celebrate. He and his disciples were right on schedule. At age thirty-two, he was now the youngest governor in America, surrounded by one of the youngest staffs of any chief executive in the nation. They were on their way. Nothing could stop them. They believed they were the best and brightest Arkansas had to offer, and what skills they lacked could be imported from other states. In the meantime, there were changes to make and an empire to build, but not before the last toast was drunk and the last of a seemingly endless stream of well-wishers was hugged and thanked.

The newly sworn governor was delighted by the welcome gift his predecessor, David Pryor, left for him in the private restroom of his new office. Taped to the mirror over the wash basin were two packets of headache powders and a note which read: "Good luck, Bill. I am leaving something that may come in handy. David."[7]

Indeed, it would come in handy, and much sooner than Clinton could have anticipated. Before his first week in office was over, he would rattle the chain of the most powerful member of the Arkansas legislature, thus provoking a valuable first lesson about getting along with the good ol' boys.

In the bill appropriating money to pay the salaries of members of the Senate and their staff, Senator Max Howell had included a $14,400-a-year security officer's job for an old friend and political crony, Melvin S. DeLong.

DeLong, a former lieutenant colonel in the Arkansas State Police, had been forced into retirement the year before by controversy surrounding a tape-recorded radio communication in which he referred to four black men as "niggers." The tape had been mysteriously erased—DeLong denied all knowledge of the erasure—but not in time to salvage DeLong's thirty-one-year career.

The appropriations bill, the first filing of the session, had been quickly passed by both houses and transmitted to the governor's office before the perk for DeLong became general knowledge. Various members of the House wanted the bill pulled back so that the security officer's job could be deleted, but one chamber cannot recall legislation that originates in the other one, and the Senate was not inclined to offend Howell, who was not only the most senior senator, but controlled several powerful Senate committees, including those governing Senate expenditures, operations, and committee assignments.

Clinton could not return the bill to the Senate without acting on it. He had several options: he could sign the bill as written, thus offending the black community which had given him nearly unanimous support; he could veto it, delaying the issuance of paychecks to all senators and their staff until another bill could be drawn and approved by both chambers; or he could allow the bill to become law without his signature, which he reasoned also would offend black Arkansans.

Clinton was royally miffed at the House, which had facilitated Howell's move by accepting without question an amendment creating the security officer's post. His anger over "what they did to me on DeLong"[8] may have been misdirected; each house draws its own appropriation bills for maintenance and operating expenses, and it is uncommon for lawmakers to question what comes to them from the other end of the hall. When Howell had asked a member of the House to see that the DeLong amendment was attached by the House, no questions had been asked. Ironically, the person whose aid he had enlisted, Representative William F. Foster, Sr., would become Clinton's most steadfast supporter, lead sponsor, and point man for almost every tax increase Clinton would promulgate during his twelve years in office.

For his part, DeLong, filling a temporary post as one of the legislature's many sergeants-at-arms, denied all knowledge of Howell's patronage, claiming he had not sought the post and was unsure whether he would accept it.

In his ire over being placed in a seemingly untenable situation, Clinton overlooked a fourth option. It was left to Representative Grover Richardson, one of four black members of the General Assembly, to point out that the governor had line-item veto authority and could delete the problem with a single pen stroke. Richardson's stand was courageous for a lawmaker embarking upon his second term. He noted that while he respected power, and that Howell had a lot of it, "I don't want to be afraid to do anything because of it."[9] As one Capitol observer noted, Howell was quick to let outsiders and newcomers know that he ran the Senate, which had been the truth but in 1979 was less so, and that he was the only man to see should they need or want anything.

Clinton's inexperienced young staff, it should be noted, was divided on the issue. In the end, however, they united to persuade Clinton to bargain with Howell.

In return for various political considerations and a lot of ego stroking on Clinton's part, Howell emerged from the governor's office on the final day on which action could be taken before the bill automatically became law and allowed as to how he had urged Clinton to strike the DeLong appropriation by line-item veto because he, Howell, had of late been assured that state Capitol security was not as lax as he had been given to believe the week before. He went a step further, introducing a resolution formally requesting the veto. Pursuing the matter would be "a great disservice to the state," Howell said. "There are other things far too important to divide the legislature over an issue such as this."[10]

Clinton certainly didn't want a divided legislature. Following a long-standing tradition, Clinton appeared before a joint session the week after his inauguration and outlined his legislative agenda, an ambitious program of government expansion and reform that his newfound ally, Bill Foster, called wide ranging and comprehensive. He was forty minutes late in arriving, and once there, he was in no hurry to leave.

"He went into greater detail than any governor in the ten [two-year] terms I've been here," Foster enthused after the fifty-five-minute speech. "He's got a good program. He's probably going to get 90 percent of it passed. He's a popular man."[11]

Virtually every area of public policy was covered: economic development, education, energy and environmental policy, health and human services, improvements in the infrastructure, taxation and tax incentives. Clinton threw into the pot several extremely controversial measures, too, most of which, including ratification of the Equal Rights Amendment, he doubted would pass.

"Nobody knows better than Clinton that not all this idealistic stuff is going to survive the legislative ordeal," his friend Bob Lancaster wrote in the *Arkansas Democrat*, "but he didn't hold any of it back. There'll come a time when he'll have to get practical, but that time is not yet. And Clinton had several good reasons for dumping an almost unprecedentedly ambitious program on the legislators here at the start."[12]

For starters, Lancaster opined, Clinton needed "some marginal . . . measures which he can sacrifice in the interests of compromise." He needed to show that "despite his youth and the relative brevity of his acquaintance with state political affairs, he has a firm and confident grasp of the controls of the immense and complicated state government apparatus." And he needed to show lawmakers that he was prepared and eager to "give shape and direction to the state government."

It could be said that Clinton's notion of direction resembled a weather vane in a wind storm. He had not one or two priorities but scores of them, encompassing virtually every area of public policy.

In the areas of economic development and energy, the focal point was elevating the energy office to a cabinet-level position with the attendant capability of tapping federal financial sources for study and development and experimentation. In the areas of health and human services, the emphasis was on saving money while expanding services. A rural road program was the centerpiece of his highway and transportation policy.

He proposed dozens of pieces of legislation and adopted numerous others as administration bills, and he and his staff lobbied the measures so vigorously during the initial honeymoon period that most of the statehouse scribes overlooked or did not recognize the frequency of or the degree to which he was willing to compromise on a proposal so that he might proclaim victory. Neither did they realize, at least initially, how hastily some of that legislation had been drawn—or, as more than one lawmaker would say, "thrown together."

Pat Flanagin, then serving his second term in the Arkansas House of Representatives, remembers vividly the neophyte administration's approach to education reform.

"I had spent years of research and study . . . on accountability in

education, on the notion of testing teachers for competencies, basing
higher education planning and evaluation on that, and I had about an
eleven-part program that I'd sent to [director] Don Roberts over in
Education and to the governor's office," Flanagin said.[13] One of the
key components dealt with teacher competence and accountability.

"It required the research and development of what would have been
a teacher test," something not attempted until Clinton's comeback
term of 1983–84, Flanagin said.

Shortly after Flanagin introduced the bill, he was summoned to the
governor's office.

"This looks good," Clinton told him. "This is something the public's going to go for. But it's too complicated. We can't explain that to
everybody."

"But, governor," Flanagin countered, "this is the way to do it. You
take this and you can actually measure the things that teachers do or
should do to result in learning."

"No, look," Clinton said, "we've got a different bill."

Sam I. Bratton, Jr., who as an assistant attorney general under
Clinton had been legal counsel for the Department of Education and
now served the governor as special assistant for education matters,
handed Flanagin the new proposal. It was simplicity at its finest,
roughly three or four sentences long. Essentially it required new
teachers to take the National Teachers's Examination before being
certified to teach in Arkansas.

Flanagin read the brief text and shook his head.

"You know, governor," he said, "that doesn't do anything to improve the accountability of those who teach teachers in college. It
doesn't do anything to improve the evaluation systems that are in place
in the public schools. I mean, it takes a real complex issue and deals
with it on a real simple basis."

"Yeah, but we can pass this," Clinton declared.

"Yeah, we can pass this," said Bratton, who had drafted the new
proposal.

Against his better judgment but in deference to the new governor, a
fellow Democrat, Flanagin capitulated. He was one of many.

"I saw more and more things handled that way, where the people

who'd really done the research—maybe it was committees or whatever—and found a lot of things that were the best alternatives, and his
whiz-kid staff would come in and say, 'Oh, we've got a simpler way to
do it.' . . . Off the top of their head they would overrule, usually
wrongly, hours and hours and tons and tons of research and solutions
that may have worked. And then you've got this kind of window-
dressing idea, and you can say, 'Yes, we've improved education by
passing this bill,' and everybody believes you have. And you really
haven't."[14]

Clinton's first term as governor may have been overly ambitious,
but his goal at the time was to serve three two-year terms, each one
more progressive, more reform-minded than the last, as a means of
positioning himself for a national campaign.

Clinton's political career has been compared to a roller coaster,
wending and rocking its way through dazzling peaks and heart-
stopping valleys. He would agree to this assessment.

"At the moment of my greatest achievements in the legislature," he
said after his 1980 reelection loss, "I also made the errors which later
would be responsible for my defeat."[15]

For instance, time and time again Clinton pledged to improve the
lives of those on fixed incomes, primarily the state's elderly population,
then second only to Florida. To that end, he kept a campaign promise
to remove the sales tax on prescription drugs. But he rejected an appeal
to expand the number of prescription drugs covered by federal-state
matching funds. While he would later take credit for the state's system
of rural health clinics, he initially opposed legislation establishing
sixteen regional centers because, he said, it would cost too much—
they were expected to cost $400,000 apiece. He promoted an increase
in the state's Homestead Property Exemption, providing one-time
refunds and permanent tax reductions for those sixty-five and older.
But he hit the elderly with higher gasoline taxes and exorbitant
increases in the cost of licensing their aging automobiles.

In terms of sheer numbers, Clinton's first-term legislative achievements were many, but as he has noted many times, Arkansas had
nowhere to go but up. In the most vital areas of daily life, Arkansas
ranked no better than forty-seventh, and in some areas, notably educa-

tional achievement, fiftieth among the fifty states and the District of Columbia.

Clinton had definite ideas about what was important in education. He proposed, and exacted, the largest financial commitment to public education in the state's history, including a 40.5 percent increase in public education spending, the bulk of which went into pay raises for primary and secondary school teachers. He also sought significant increases in financing for special education and kindergarten programs, and orchestrated passage of two relatively conservative reform measures, the Educational Assessment Act of 1979 and the Fair Dismissal Act of 1979.

The Educational Assessment Act established a procedure for measuring student performance in basic subjects, which the Arkansas Education Association generally favored, although the standardized tests could not be used for grade placement or promotion. AEA members were less than delighted with the Fair Dismissal Act; in the face of legislative cries of "unionism" and "tenure," Clinton quickly abandoned AEA-promulgated language prohibiting school boards from dismissing teachers for other than "just cause," and accepted a compromise whereby school boards would be prohibited from dismissing teachers for "arbitrary, capricious, or discriminatory" reasons.

Clinton's 1979 education package was tame compared to future endeavors, but the Arkansas Education Association, ecstatic over the proposed $1,200-a-year average pay raise—down from a campaign proposal of $1,500—proclaimed his plan "refreshing, well-developed," and evidence of "a clear commitment to children."[16]

Vocational-technical schools, colleges, and universities, which lacked the political clout of the Arkansas Education Association, did not fare so well: Clinton's funding recommendations were substantially below the spending levels recommended by the legislature.

Ostensibly, Clinton wanted a year to study the effectiveness of the state's vocational education; it was to this end that he named a task force, one of the first of the dozens of blue-ribbon study committees he created as governor. Another ticklish subject, school consolidation, which he alternately endorsed and rejected, also was relegated to a study commission.

Clinton's excuse for not addressing the financial demands of the state's colleges and universities was his desire to meet the Carter administration's "anti-inflation guidelines." Actually, he wanted to use the money elsewhere.

Higher education was not one of Clinton's priorities, but he was keen on establishing special programs for gifted students in public schools. His initial lack of support for vo-tech, a popular alternative to higher education for thousands of Arkansans who showed no acumen for or interest in getting a college degree, was puzzling given his insistence upon the state's urgent need for economic growth and development. For instance, he convinced the legislature to redefine the scope and mission of the highly successful Arkansas Industrial Development Department by recreating it as a division of a new Department of Economic Development.

The Arkansas Industrial Development Commission, created in 1955 at the behest of Governor Faubus, was a catalyst for economic growth for more than two decades. It had both instigated and mitigated the state's transition from a state primarily dependent on agriculture to one with a burgeoning industry. Thousands of new, if low-wage, jobs had been created. Many industries that moved to Arkansas were attracted by its right-to-work laws, which made union organization difficult. By the time Clinton took office in 1979, the real average income of Arkansas workers ranked well below regional and national averages, and it seemed hopelessly stuck in the forty-ninth position in state rankings, usually just above Mississippi.[17]

The new Economic Development Department was to be given broad authority to promote and plan economic development in the state, to coordinate vocational training programs, to promote exports of state products, and to aid small businesses and local communities.

While some lawmakers had second thoughts about Clinton's approach to economic development, few quibbled with his rationale: Arkansas was sorely in need of more jobs—not necessarily high-paying jobs—and new and expanded markets for the goods the state produced. Industrial development was deemphasized. The term "high tech" would not find its way into Clinton's vocabulary for several years. During his first term, the emphasis was on expanding small business, promoting exports, and obtaining federal funds for community development programs and small, experimental farm projects. As a sop to farmers, whose call for a separate agricultural commission he had embraced during the primary campaign but rejected before the general election, Clinton pushed through legislation to restrict foreign ownership of Arkansas farmland.

Clinton sold lawmakers on the idea of opening a state office in Washington by emphasizing its value as a congressional liaison and a fund-raising tool for state programs—which, of course, provided him several excuses for trips to Capitol Hill. The office was staffed by nine highly paid employees, only two of whom hailed from the state they were supposed to promote.

He also persuaded lawmakers to beef up the state's floundering overseas trade office in Belgium, which gave him an excuse to lead a host of aides and political cronies on trade missions to Taiwan and Japan. These junkets did bring some benefits to the state: Arkansas soybean farmers found a new market, and Clinton forged long-lasting associations with numerous Far East political leaders, industrialists, and businessmen.

At one point, Mark Johnson, director of North Little Rock's community development program, interviewed for a job in the Washington office.[18] Clinton, who had once described Johnson's father, Jim, as a disgrace to Arkansas, made the first contact, and at his request, Johnson spoke at length with Anne Bartley, director of the Washington office, and administrative assistant John Danner. Johnson, who viewed with relish Arkansas's untapped opportunities for high-technology, postindustrial development, shared his notions about Arkansas's attractive location near the geographic center of the country and the possibility of developing Little Rock into a vital regional and perhaps international port and manufacturing hub.

"That's not what we're doing," Danner said before Johnson had finished his ambitious presentation. "We're not chasing smokestacks. We want to develop small business."[19]

The Clinton administration, Danner patiently explained, wanted to help the little guy. Industrial growth was all right as far as it went, and certainly the governor was interested in exploring that area, but

Arkansas needed to get back to basics. Its largely rural population was unskilled and undereducated, and required a type of assistance and nurturing that people in more advanced states did not. Change could not come overnight. So many people relied on the service industry, agriculture, and the retail trades that it made sense to invest in honing these skills, modernizing their techniques, and teaching new skills. With the proper attention, and a steady infusion of funds from government and philanthropic grants available for the asking, the quality of life in Arkansas could be vastly improved.

As Johnson listened, it struck him that what Danner was outlining was nothing more than a rehash of the small-is-beautiful philosophy that had permeated Arkansas politics during the first half of the twentieth century. He felt patronized, and he believed that the people of Arkansas were about to be patronized, too. He did not doubt Danner's sincerity, but he questioned Danner's rather simplistic idealism.

"I call it a back-to-the-earth mentality, a naive, flower-child view of the government and the state of Arkansas," Johnson said of the approach outlined by Danner that day. "I came away thinking, 'I don't think I can work with these people.' "[20]

The results of that back-to-the-earth approach—which critics have dismissed as pure intellectual arrogance—would be a series of politically embarrassing events that, coupled with Clinton's inability to understand the wants and needs of the people, would topple the Clinton administration.

"Bill Clinton was one of the most charming, polite people you'd ever want to meet," Johnson would say later, "but the public perception of his whole [first] administration was of a bunch of thirty-year-old, bearded liberals who were going to tell these dumb Arkies how to do things."[21]

Although his staff salaries were among the highest in state government, Clinton begged the legislature not to give raises to employees outside the governor's office. He cautioned that raising salaries might violate federally imposed wage and price controls and thus jeopardize President Carter's acceptance of the entire state pay schedule. His argument made little sense, since the schedule, originally drafted to take effect at the start of the state's fiscal year, July 1, had been altered to take effect in January only as a means of bringing the salaries of the lowest paid state employees in line with the new federal minimum wage.

In his first appearance before the Arkansas legislature, Clinton said some state agencies were not as effective as they should be and some might be abolished. He said he was disturbed by "the attempts to define an agency's importance by its number of employees and the size of its building." And he said he wanted to show "how we can do much more for less than they might have expected." But personally, the governor was not inclined to try to do more with less. He emphasized the need to improve efficiency and cut the size of government, but even as he said it, he was planning significant increases in the size of the governor's staff and its operating budget. Within a week, he was sounding out lawmakers about raising his office budget by more than 30 percent, from just over $600,000 to more than $800,000, and increasing the staff by 15 percent.

Administrative aide Rudy Moore defended the increases as being consistent with those in other state department budgets, but the best explanation anyone could come up with was that Clinton "thought the office should be expanded."[22]

"Saving dollars," Moore said, "does not mean more efficiency."

Moore had reason to defend the proposal: his employment, and that of administrative assistants John Danner and Steve Smith, was partially responsible for the projected growth. In the past, governors had had only one executive assistant to whom the staff reported. While Moore was tapped as the person to whom everyone else would report, Danner and Smith handled other executive functions heretofore reserved to the governor or his chief of staff. All three carried the title of executive assistant.

Efficiency was not a trademark of Clinton's first weeks in office. In future terms, he would succeed in keeping most patronage decisions under wraps until he was ready to publicize them, but his fledgling staff made many embarrassing mistakes in the early days, particularly in the area of appointments. At least one major appointment was sent to the Senate for confirmation the day before Clinton had planned to announce it at a news conference. Around the same time, two political allies were notified of their appointments to the Public

Service Commission before several utility executives had been told of their selection. Clinton had wanted the executives informed in advance "as a professional courtesy," but also because, according to one gubernatorial aide, jobs had been promised to too many people.[23]

Jimmie Lou Fisher's appointment as scheduling secretary had already been announced when Clinton realized that his childhood chum, Patty Howe, had been overlooked, so he reneged on the appointment and left Fisher on the payroll without an immediate job assignment. Fisher's feelings were more than assuaged months later when he appointed her to fill a vacancy in the elective office of the state auditor, which gave Fisher a perfect springboard into the state treasurer's office in the next election. She still holds that position, having been reelected five times without opposition from either Democrats or Republicans.

Promising too many jobs, or promising the same job to too many people, would be a recurring problem in Clinton's administration. He simply hated disappointing anyone, and as astute as were his political instincts even then, sometimes he made impolitic promises that he had to recant.

Among the factors that contributed to Clinton's ouster after one term as governor was the poor judgment he exercised in selecting those who would define and represent his administration to the legislature and the public at large. He appeared to have hit home runs with his initial round of appointees—a black man, a white man, and a woman—which was his first stab at appointing a cabinet that mirrored the diverse constituency he served. But of these three, only one did not create problems for the governor.

Among Clinton's most controversial appointments:

—Martin Borchert, director of the Department of State Building Services, who augmented his personal income by approving contracts between his state agency and three companies he owned.

—Tommy Robinson, director of the Department of Public Safety, whose running feud with the director of the state police, Doug Harp, would be a continuing source of embarrassing headlines, rumor, and innuendo for the entire fifteen months of Robinson's tenure.

—Paul Levy, director of the new Department of Energy, whose

arrogant attitude as much as wasteful spending practices would result in creation of the *Arkansas Democrat's* Boondoggler of the Month Award, a.k.a. the Sweet William Trophy.

—Peggy O'Neal, director of the Office of State Purchasing, whose propensity for what pundit John R. Starr has called "waste, mismanagement, and lunacy"[24] made her one of the most notorious noncabinet appointees of Clinton's entire career.

—B.J. McCoy, director of the Department of Local Services, who mishandled several high-profile federal-state programs for local communities, among them an urban weatherization program and a rural job training program.

—Rose Crane, director of the Department of Natural and Cultural Heritage, a childhood friend of Clinton whose intemperate disposition and frequent absences left her small department in disarray and her staff demoralized.

—Charlie Daniels, a former union leader whom Clinton retained as director of the Department of Labor, whose three-martini lunches were paid for by the state.

—James T. Dyke, director of the new Department of Economic Development, who decorated his office with potted plants rented, not bought, at a cost of $450 a month.

—John Barker, the second of three gubernatorial press secretaries during Clinton's two-year term, whose scorn for the news media hurt Clinton when he was most sorely in need of media sympathy and support.

It's ironic that the most controversial members of the Clinton team were, for the most part, native Arkansans, because one of the most frequent criticisms leveled against his staff was that it had been "imported." Legislators found fault with virtually everything attempted by folks like Paul Levy, the energy director brought in from Massachusetts; Gail Huecker, the director of human services brought in from Kentucky; and Dr. Robert W. Young, the Health Department director who had been a pioneer in rural health care in West Virginia. "Can't he find any Arkansas people smart enough for him?"[25] barked Knox Nelson, the second most powerful man in the Arkansas Senate. It was a common gripe.

"[Bill] and Hillary had friends from around the country who joined the gubernatorial transition team and later the administration," Rudy Moore noted years later, "and Bill recruited people from other states who he thought shared his ideas and could implement them. . . . Hiring so many people from outside the state was sure to arouse provincial prejudices, and the administration was roundly criticized.[26]

"The outside recruitment may have been a political mistake," Moore said. "Some of the personalities did seem to abrade people, even within the administration. It was one of the elements that contributed to the perception that many people began to have of Bill: that of a young man who was going to impose his ideas on Arkansas people whether they were ready for them or not. The perception was a likely factor that led to his stunning defeat after only one term as governor."[27]

The governor's central staff and cabinet formed a tight group seventy-five members strong consisting primarily of assorted childhood friends, college chums, campaign workers, and former employees of the attorney general's office augmented by part-time helpers and volunteers. Twenty-three additional slots were financed with federal funds totaling about $300,000.

While some of these staffers were competent—Patty Howe, another childhood friend who was Clinton's last and best press secretary, and William D. Gaddy,[28] director of the Department of Finance and Administration, come immediately to mind—their number was few. Little wonder, then, that some visitors to the governor's office snickered when they saw the campaign poster Clinton kept there for a time. It stated: "The issue is excellence."

The administration, like state government in general, was rife with nepotism. Among the married couples were Steve Smith and press secretary Julie Baldridge, and John Danner and Nancy Pietrafesa, state liaison officer to the Ozarks Regional Commission. The daughter of Clinton's secretary was given a make-work job, and Jane Wilson, who was in charge of the political patronage list, was the daughter of M.M. Satterfield, who served without pay as a gubernatorial lobbyist in the House of Representatives. Rose Crane had a cabinet position; her brother Larry, a lawyer, was one of numerous departmental liaisons. Clinton also found slots for several members of his extensive family; his cousin, Sam Tatom, eventually obtained a cabinet position as director of the Department of Public Safety; and several other relatives were named to boards and commissions that provided status within the community and per diem expenses.

"Arkansas is still a small, rural state," noted one news account in February 1980, "but Clinton's central staff alone outnumbers its counterparts in 27 other states."[29] While President Carter was asking the nation's work force to make do with annual pay raises totaling no more than 7 percent, Clinton was handing out raises totaling 50, 65, even 85 percent to many who followed him from the attorney general's office. Steve Smith, for example, realized an immediate 85 percent increase in salary—from $17,000 to $37,450—with the transition without ever missing a day's pay. In a state as poor as Arkansas, where per-capita income was less than $7,000 and the average state salary was less than $12,000, the salaries struck the average wage earner as outlandish.

"In 1978, after 10 years of research into the subject of poverty, I wrote that the most likely opportunity many citizens of Arkansas have is the opportunity to be poor," sociologist Juanita D. Sandford wrote in 1981 after Clinton and his reformers were turned out of office. "Unfortunately the fact stands, and, if anything, there are more poor people today in the state than there were three years ago. Under federal poverty guidelines, 28 percent of the population is poor."[30]

If the first Clinton administration did not leave Arkansas richer, it certainly made the governor's staff wealthier. By the end of his first year in office, Clinton had assembled what was literally a million-dollar staff, the most costly in the state's history. They were a group of people with truly unprecedented power over state government and absolutely no idea how to use it to anyone's benefit but their own. But, by the end of their two-year fling, they had outsmarted even themselves.

As a candidate, Clinton never explained how he would fulfill many of his many campaign promises. Like many gubernatorial candidates, for example, he pledged an intensive program of highway restoration and expansion, but what precisely this meant was left in the air.

A 1978 study had determined that more than eight thousand miles of the state highway system needed upgrading to meet the needs of Arkansans.[31] Several hard winters had left Arkansas's already deteriorating highways in a horrible state of disrepair. The study had suggested no less than $330 million a year over the course of a decade. In addition to Clinton's promise to overhaul the state's transportation over several years, an immediate infusion of funds totaling millions of dollars was clearly called for to meet both state and local needs.

The commission that administered the state Highway and Transportation Department, financed *in toto* by the proceeds from diesel and motor fuel taxes, had advanced a typically extravagant revenue proposal, which would generate an estimated $105 million a year. Like governors before him, Clinton balked at this huge tax increase. His staff prepared a plan calling for an annual tax increase of $45 million a year, with costs divided among motorists, truckers, and transportation companies.

The original plan included 1-cent per-gallon increases in diesel and gasoline taxes, a new automobile registration system whose annual fees were based on a car's value instead of weight, and increased heavy-truck registration and operation fees. But Clinton did not bother to discuss his proposal with the Arkansas Highway Commission before he released it.

The Arkansas Highway Commission, as a result of a couple of scandals in the early 1950s, became an independent state agency in 1952. Under Amendment 42 to the Arkansas Constitution, Highway Commission members were to be appointed to ten-year terms by the governor, staggered at two-year intervals, and the commission in turn appointed the department director. This meant that if a governor were to leave office after the traditional four-year term, no governor could exercise undue influence over the commission.

At the time Clinton took office, Henry C. Gray, appointed highway director in 1972, had outlasted two governors and had been around longer than most of the commissioners at whose pleasure he served. Gray had thus become one of the most powerful men in Arkansas government. He was the force behind the Highway Commission, which had the final word on where and how highway funds would be spent, and lawmakers and governors sidestepped him at their peril. One could negotiate with Gray, but one could not ignore him.

In devising the administration's road package, Clinton's staff not only ignored Gray, who advised increasing the gasoline tax by several cents on the gallon, but such vested interests as the heavy-trucking industry, primarily agriculture, timber, and poultry manufacturers. As a result, Clinton reduced the level of taxes he had hoped to collect from increased truck registration fees and made up the difference by increasing the title-transfer, registration, and licensing fees imposed on automobile and pickup truck owners.

Clinton recognized that Arkansas lacked a mass transportation system and that most residents had to use cars for travel. He knew, too, that at least half of the automobiles then registered were at least five years old, and that most of these heavier, aging automobiles were owned by the elderly and others on fixed incomes who could not afford newer, lighter vehicles. Nonetheless, when faced with special interest opposition, Clinton opted for the quick win instead of battling the special interests.

As each new wave of motorists went to local revenue offices to renew car tags for another year or to obtain title to another used car, many Arkansans discovered that the cost of their "car tags" had doubled. This bad news was even more painful when it was discovered after the incredibly long wait vehicle owners had to put up with at their local revenue office.

Registering a vehicle has long been a time-consuming process in Arkansas; at that time, vehicle owners had to produce a current safety inspection certificate as well as documentation that personal property had been assessed for the current year and personal property taxes had been paid for the previous year. The revenue offices were both cramped and understaffed, with few computers, and it was not uncommon for a person to stand in line an hour or more before being served. During that aggravating wait, a driver's eye would inevitably fall upon the smiling face of Governor Bill Clinton, whose full-color photograph had been strategically hung in every revenue office in the state. By the time the motorist reached the counter at which he would fork over twice the amount he had paid the year before to operate his aging Buick or Chevy, he was fit to be tied.

Governor Clinton, of course, didn't have to stand in line to get his car tags renewed.

Shortly after taking office, Clinton had been embarrassed by a story in the *Arkansas Gazette* which revealed that he and his wife were delinquent in personal property taxes owed in Washington County, the home of the University of Arkansas. Hillary's Fiat, which had been stolen and wrecked in 1978, had not been licensed or assessed for the years 1977 and 1978.[32]

Clinton insisted that this "oversight" was neither his fault nor his responsibility; one of his employees in the attorney general's office had been told to take care of licensing the car for the boss's wife. Clinton subsequently paid the outstanding $77.82 in penalties and taxes for 1977 and 1978, and his employees in the governor's office made damned sure from then on that all personal bills were paid and all personal errands run in a timely manner.

12

THE CHILDREN'S CRUSADE

WHEN BILL CLINTON DREW the design for his administration, he broke with tradition in the area of central administration. Instead of appointing a chief of staff, he selected a triumvirate of deputies—assistant governors, some lawmakers smirked—and divided the direct administration of state government among them.

John Danner, Rudy Moore, and Steve Smith, all thirtyish, all bearded, were a political cartoonist's delight, and they immediately became the butt of jokes among good ol' boys in the legislature: "Leaders of the Children's Crusade," one lawmaker quipped; "supermen, deputy governors, and whiz kids," grumbled another. More appropriately, they were, as a former lobbyist noted, "bearded visionaries" entrusted with translating that vision into policy. The problem was that each assistant chose to translate Clinton's ideas in a different way—not surprising, considering the blurred perspective of the man whose interests they ostensibly served. That is not to say that Clinton had no plan; he wanted to change virtually everything about the state, critics have noted, with what columnist John R. Starr has called "a collection of ideas—income transfer programs—like he has now [as president] but with no agenda for when it falls into place; no plan for accomplishing anything."[1] Clinton didn't appear to have a solid philosophical base from which to launch his agenda.

"Policy-making in the Clinton administration started out with the promise . . . of being more scientific, rational, and comprehensive," Phyllis Finton Johnston, who several years later joined Clinton's central office staff, wrote in a 1982 monograph about the first Clinton administration. "In the common mold of policy-making in governments everywhere, it evolved into being incremental and more responsive to political inputs."[2]

Clinton's first term was not an unmitigated disaster. His greatest accomplishments included expanding services to the elderly (nutrition, legal assistance, transportation, home health care) and establishing community-based programs for children and families. He did not go from being the most popular politician in Arkansas to the most unpopular one overnight. The Clinton administration did not disintegrate so much as erode. While poor judgment, bad management, public relations blunders, and a pervasive arrogance all contributed to Clinton's 1980 defeat, a crucial change in Arkansas politics was the budding newspaper war in Little Rock.

In theory, when Clinton assumed the governorship in 1979, there were two statewide newspapers in Arkansas, both independent and locally owned. In fact, there was but one, the *Arkansas Gazette*, a morning newspaper with a six-figure circulation with readers in every county in the state. Despite its liberal editorial voice, an aberration in such a conservative state, the *Gazette* was the standard by which all other newspapers, whether dailies or weeklies, were judged. It had a glorious heritage, not the least of which was its integration-era Pulitzer Prize, an experienced, substantial, and long-tenured staff of reporters, and unshakable domination in all areas of the marketplace, from circulation to advertising.

By comparison, the *Arkansas Democrat*, which its former managing editor, John R. Starr, once called "the afternoon repeat of the morning mistake," was near death. With its ever-changing skeleton crew of less experienced, grossly underpaid reporters, and a meager market share in rapid decline, the newspaper was very near to closing its doors when publisher Walter E. Hussman, Jr., brought Starr on board in October of 1978.

Hussman, whose family, like the *Gazette's* Patterson family, had been in newspaper publishing for decades, had bought the *Democrat* in 1975 with an eye toward making it a competitive voice in Arkansas journalism. It took several years and millions of wasted dollars, siphoned from Hussman's smaller newspapers and his burgeoning cable television enterprise, to persuade him that the management he had in place was only hastening the *Democrat's* demise. For the newspaper to succeed, Hussman realized, he needed a competitor, not a caretaker. All those whose advice he sought, including the man Starr replaced, recommended John Robert Starr, recently retired as Little Rock bureau chief of The Associated Press and at that time pursuing graduate studies in Tennessee.

Within months of settling in, Starr had assembled a young but aggressive staff of reporters who were more than willing to go head to head with their complacent colleagues at the *Gazette*. Given Starr's keen interest in government and politics, the backbone of the Arkansas AP operation during his tenure, new emphasis was placed on these areas. News bureaus were opened throughout the state, including a new three-person bureau at the state Capitol, and his reporters were expected to be fair, accurate, and tenacious.

Neither the politicians nor the *Gazette* noted the improvements in the *Arkansas Democrat*. In the long term, this attitude was one of the reasons why the *Arkansas Gazette* died. In the short term, the Clinton administration's failure to notice the *Democrat* contributed substantially to Clinton's 1980 defeat.

"The role of the media in government and other public business is greater than the average citizen suspects and much greater than most members of the media are willing to admit," Starr has said. "Politicians are acutely aware that how they impress reporters who cover them and the editors and television anchormen who comment on their performances is more important than how they impress in public appearances, because most of what they say must be filtered through the preconceptions or misconceptions of reporters, anchormen, and editorial writers on its way to the public."[3]

Shortly after Clinton's 1978 election win, Starr "called him and told him I would make him the same offer I had made [Governors] Rockefeller, Bumpers, and Pryor: 'I'm not a working reporter, and I won't be calling you for comment. If I call, it's because I've got something you need to know or to tell you what we are working on.' I did this so he would take my calls, knowing I was not trying to embarrass him but to background him."[4]

The arrangement worked for a short period but broke down when *Democrat* reporters produced a series of stories critical of the administration. At one point, Clinton summoned Starr for a private "briefing" on one of the controversies and proceeded to chastise the editor-columnist in a most colorful manner.[5] After that, Starr placed few telephone calls to the governor's office, but he might have saved himself the effort, because Clinton aides quit relaying his messages.

That probably suited Clinton just fine at that juncture; he had been wary of Starr since the previous September, when Starr had criticized him in a column concerning a speeding incident in which Clinton had been involved. As reporters trailed the car that Clinton was driving on the way to a speaking engagement for which he was late, they clocked the state car going more than 80 miles per hour. The incident was particularly newsworthy not only because Clinton was driving, but because he had urged Arkansas motorists to abide by the 55-mile-per-hour speed limit and had ordered state troopers to give tickets to those who did not.

When reporters asked the governor about his speeding, Clinton threw a fit, insisting that the reporters were exaggerating to make him look bad.[6] Even if he had exceeded the 55-mph speed limit, he said, he was just trying to keep from disappointing people who were waiting to hear from him. Besides, he went on, he had been following his state security guard's car, and if any speeding had occurred, it was the state trooper's fault. He did not mention the fact that he had instigated the speeding incident by raving about how late they were going to be if they didn't get a move on. Larry Gentry, the trooper who led the motorcade that day, insisted later that this is what happened.[7]

The state troopers, by the way, regularly complained about how they frequently went for hours without sleep, food, or even a restroom break while chauffeuring Clinton around, but were often used as baby sitters, errand boys, and, according to several of them, go-betweens for Clinton's assignations with women.

Gentry, an Arkansas State Police officer who served on the security staff during Clinton's first term, claims no knowledge of any philandering on Clinton's part, although he acknowledged that on one occasion, Clinton asked him to obtain the telephone number of a young woman whom he noticed at a function in Hot Springs.[8]

"I knew who she was—she was a friend of my ex-wife's—so I didn't think much about it," Gentry said.

"She's good looking," Gentry quoted Clinton as saying. "Get her phone number for me."

"Later, I wondered about it, but he knew that I knew her. There were enough rumors during his first term, but I figured what he did in his private life was his business." It was not unusual, Gentry said, for Clinton to comment on a woman's attractiveness as the two made their way through a crowd or drove along city streets, but Gentry put this down to the governor's attempts to make conversation or "to be one of the boys."

"I think he was just trying to be a good old boy, trying to act like he was open and friendly and just didn't know how to do it," Gentry said. "He was awkward at small talk."

Gentry and other troopers have never forgotten the poor treatment the security staff received from both Bill and Hillary. Gentry said Bill and Hillary were both short-tempered and prone to throw objects in the troopers's direction when things were not going smoothly. He and another first-term security trooper, Roger Perry, claim that Hillary loathed the state police officers who were assigned to protect, escort, and serve the first family and often refused to let them accompany her. They describe her as "bitchy,"[9] verbally abusive, and inconsiderate, and Perry says she was downright hostile, occasionally referring to them as "pigs"[10] within their earshot. The two security veterans agree that the most unpleasant aspect of serving the Clintons—or the Rodham-Clintons, as they were described during that first term—was their condescending attitude toward employees in particular and Arkansans in general.

"They were really into themselves a lot," Gentry said. "They always held themselves to be quite a bit above the average Arkansan. I remember after the [1980] defeat, being there in the [Governor's] Mansion while they went on and on, talking about how stupid the people of Arkansas were for electing Frank White. God, they were mad. . . . It goes back to this arrogance thing."[11]

Clinton's reelection loss "was a combination of little things," Starr opines. "Appointments, Cubans, car tags, Hillary, perceived arrogance, and the alienation of the *Arkansas Democrat*. Arrogance was why he felt he *could* alienate it. What he failed to see was how much influence the *Arkansas Democrat* had gained. He alienated it—not just me, but the staff. He pushed them, which created their resolve to take off after him as individuals, too, and to be very enthusiastic when there was anything embarrassing to Bill Clinton."[12]

Had Clinton been more respectful of Starr from the start, more eager to seek his advice and more receptive to it, he might have kept to his original timetable for seeking the presidency, for Starr's ego is at least as great as Clinton's. Throughout their erratic twelve-year association, Clinton was capable of wooing Starr back to his corner even when the relationship appeared irrevocably broken. Indeed, the final break did not come until Clinton entered the national spotlight as a presidential candidate and no longer felt the need for support from a local newspaper editor and commentator who had no influence in national politics.

During Clinton's two stints as governor, 1979–80 and 1983–1992, Starr's daily opinion column accompanied the straight news coverage of statehouse reporters, and yet during that first term, the Clinton administration made very little effort to influence the tone or content of Starr's commentary. Starr's criticism was often acerbic, but it was accurate. Clinton and his staff made mistakes, mistakes that were documented in the news columns and acknowledged by the people who wrote letters to the editor. Starr reminded readers daily that Clinton and his staff were on the public payroll, that it was the public, not the politicians, who should be served by government, and that it was their tax dollars that were being wasted.

"What was mainly wrong with the Clinton administration was inattention to the mechanics of running the state by the guy at the top," Starr says, "and I think, to that extent, he was extremely lucky that it did not become corrupt, because that's usually the first step to corruption. . . . But whether you agree with their philosophies or not, in large measure he just surrounded himself with pretty idealistic people. I think they picked the wrong messiah, but he did for the most part pick the kind of people that . . . didn't steal anything. They were so busy trying to put all their wild ideas into place, they didn't have time to steal anything."[13]

Most of the "wild ideas" were generated not by Clinton, but by the three men he placed in charge of devising and implementing policy.

William Rudy Moore, Jr., a lawyer and the eldest of the triumvirate at thirty-six, was a friend of Clinton's from the Fayetteville days. A native of nearby Springdale, he held degrees from Southern Methodist University and the University of Arkansas School of Law and had spent a year at American University in Cairo on a Rotary scholarship. Once, when a reporter pointed out the similarities between him and Clinton, Moore concurred, then added: "But he's a lot smarter."[14]

Moore actually had more political experience than Clinton. While in his late twenties, he served two terms in the Arkansas House of Representatives, and was a member of the Fayetteville School Board when he joined Clinton's transition staff.

Active locally in several national Democratic senatorial campaigns, Moore and Clinton met in 1973 while both were campaigning for J. William Fulbright. They did not, however, form an alliance until late 1977, when Moore got wind that Attorney General Clinton was eyeing two possibilities for advancement: the U.S. Senate and governor. At that point, Moore wrote a letter advising Clinton that "whatever he ran for, I would be very interested in helping on a statewide basis."[15] He was named chairman of the 1978 gubernatorial campaign. (Steve Smith, who managed the 1980 campaign, claimed that Clinton "was always his own campaign manager.")[16]

Even before the November election, Moore accepted Clinton's invitation to join his gubernatorial staff. He gave up a modest law practice in northwest Arkansas to oversee the smooth transfer of power from the outgoing Pryor administration, and when Clinton was inaugurated governor in January 1979, Moore joined him as senior executive assistant in charge of legislative relations and staff operations.

Stephen Austin Smith, a native of Faubus's hometown of Huntsville, had been one of the youngest people ever elected to the Arkansas General Assembly. He was only twenty when elected, thus not old enough under the Arkansas Constitution to serve in the legislature. Fortunately, his birthday arrived before the swearing-in ceremony.

Smith had begun dabbling in politics while a student, and throughout the 1970s was active at the state and local levels. He had myriad interests, but his favorite subject was the environment, which is how he caught Clinton's attention. A teacher and a scholar, he also was a card-carrying member of the American Civil Liberties Union, which immediately set him apart from the average Arkansan.

Smith was a friend from Clinton's Fayetteville days; they shared a vision—what their elders called youthful idealism—and an interest in fomenting change from within the system. It was at Smith's behest that Clinton sought advice from Faubus when he first considered seeking the Democratic nomination for the congressional seat held by Republican John Paul Hammerschmidt.[17]

At that point, Smith was wrapping up two fairly unremarkable terms in the Arkansas House of Representatives—his liberalism persuaded him he would lose a third-term bid, so he "retired" undefeated at age twenty-five. His legislative salary helped pay for his undergraduate studies at the University of Arkansas.

Smith served as deputy campaign manager in charge of policy and research in Clinton's unsuccessful 1974 congressional campaign. He later helped manage Clinton's winning race for attorney general and was rewarded with an administrative assistant's slot. When the thirty-two-year-old Clinton moved on to the governor's office, Smith, at twenty-nine, was named one of three executive assistants. His purview included community and economic development and natural resources, an assignment that eventually would prove most troublesome, and occasionally embarrassing, to his boss. Smith was intellectually gifted and particularly effective at orchestrating media relations and campaign strategies.

John David Danner, then thirty-one, was the odd man out, entre-preneurial, genteel, and intellectual—"almost professorial," one of his early Arkansas acquaintances opined[18]—but almost an invisible man within the Clinton administration. A lawyer and management analyst and consultant originally from Evanston, Illinois, and late of San Francisco, his tie to Clinton was through Hillary, whom he had met in the Boston university community and who was a close friend of his wife, Nancy "Peach" Pietrafesa, a policy planner and administrator in the areas of energy, comprehensive cancer care, and other health-related matters.

Danner had graduated *cum laude* from Harvard, where he concur-rently acted as a consultant and operated a market research business employing about one hundred students part-time and held graduate degrees in public health, law, and education from the University of California at Berkeley.

Unlike Moore and Smith, the soft-spoken Danner appeared to have no personal agenda and kept his own counsel. His interests appeared to be more governmental than political, although associates say he was no less idealistic than Smith. The notion of making government more efficient while improving existing services "to help the little guy" appealed to him. He and Pietrafesa were the first of several husband-wife teams to join the Clinton administration, and publicly they became the first to jump ship, although in fact they were sacked—not by Clinton, but on Clinton's orders.

Danner had directed much of the transitional activity for Clinton during the campaign. In the new administration, Danner filled nu-merous roles, overseeing intergovernmental relations, administrative training, long-range management, and federal grants programs for the fledgling Clinton administration. He also served as secretary of Clinton's cabinet, a curious mixture of career politicos and hungry, piss-and-vinegar young wannabes. By shutting down his manage-ment consulting firm, Danner took a substantial pay cut—the new post paid only $37,450, extravagant by Arkansas standards—but Danner viewed the move as "a rare opportunity" to improve the quality of life for the people of Arkansas, where anyone earning more than $10,000 a year was considered upper middle class. He particularly relished the prospect of working with Clinton, whose ambitious agenda promised to launch a progressive era of economic prosperity, public service expansion, and government-wide reform. It was, he said, "an exciting time," a unique opportunity to accomplish a litany of goals in which, Danner said, he and Clinton *et al.* believed "passionately."[19]

As administrative assistant for governmental affairs, Danner was the chief planner for the administration and oversaw the operation of Clinton's Washington, D.C., office. He was not only the most unassuming member of Clinton's advisory team, he also was the least abrasive, and yet he inadvertently caused Clinton more grief with the legislature than the pompous Rudy Moore and the tactless Steve Smith combined.

It didn't take long for the free-wheeling Moore to emerge as first among equals. In his first interview as senior executive, Moore had observed that although he was charged with overseeing the staff as a whole, he considered himself, Smith, and Danner to hold approximately the same level of responsibility. The triumvirate officially lasted about a year, after which Moore became the official chief of staff, but in practice it had begun to deteriorate mere months into the two-year term.

Moore and Smith did their part to undermine the Clinton administration, not by design but through arrogance and preoccupation with their individual agendas; Danner's offense was serving his leader too well.

It is ironic that Danner, whose only discernible agenda was Bill Clinton's success in politics, was the first major casualty of the Clinton administration. When Danner left the staff in March 1980, the scuttlebutt was that Clinton was unhappy with the frequency of the Danner and Pietrafesa's out-of-state trips, a strange criticism given that Danner was given ultimate responsibility for the Washington office, and Pietrafesa's work with the Ozarks Regional Commission often took her to the other member states.

Actually, bad PR did them in. Clinton blamed Danner, and by association Pietrafesa, for the negative publicity generated by several projects with which Danner had been involved.

Strike one had been the startling disclosure in January 1980 of a confidential six-page memorandum, with appropriate attachments, written in November 1979 by Danner, and signed by Clinton, dealing with what Danner called "public information strategy." It was unmistakably aimed at enhancing Clinton's political prospects through various means, including media manipulation, constituent contacts, and multilevel networking. More damning still, it proved that a recent "retreat" organized exclusively for members of Clinton's cabinet had had much less to do with improving state government that with improving Clinton's political standing.

The recommendations set forth in the memo included some whose implementation would have constituted a blatant, indefensible breach of Arkansas's election laws. The use of state employees on state time at state expense in campaign activity was, and remains, patently illegal.

"At the Cabinet Retreat," Danner wrote, "there was virtually unanimous concern about doing a better job of informing the public of key activities and accomplishments of the administration. This memo proposes a strategy for dealing with that concern.

"As I see it, we have several goals: (1) To exert more control over our own public image through greater reliance on self-initiated public information efforts and less dependence on press-initiated coverage (control our own destiny); (2) To improve the public image and support of the administration by better packaging and disseminating information about administration efforts in terms meaningful to particular interest groups, as well as the public generally (good deeds don't speak for themselves); (3) To increase our contacts and coverage by spreading the responsibility of public communication beyond the governor to the cabinet in a coordinated way; (4) To improve the administration's responsiveness to public concerns by better eliciting their opinions, ideas and reactions on major issues."

Key to accomplishing these "high-priority" goals, Danner stated, were commitment on the part of the governor, his staff, and members of his cabinet; coordination; and follow-through. This team effort should not rely primarily on "traditional press coverage and randomly scheduled governor and-or cabinet speeches or trips," but upon five elaborate initiatives:

1. Monthly "progress reports to the people" summarizing the administration's efforts and accomplishments in specific areas of government and distributed to targeted special-interest groups such as chambers of commerce, teachers's organizations, and financial leaders.

"This would ensure that the major themes and priority concerns of the administration were regularly addressed and conveyed to selected interest groups across the state in terms they understand."

2. Regular "citizen background briefings" conducted by the governor in which Clinton would describe and explain major initiatives over the course of an hour or two in an intimate setting with key administration members in attendance to augment the governor's presentation.

These briefings would be distinguished by "personalized invitations to carefully selected private citizens and appropriate legislators, well-rehearsed presentations with supporting graphics and handouts followed by focused question-and-answer period, and prompt individualized thank-you notes and acknowledgements." Danner pointed out, quite rightly, that "most folks would be flattered to receive such an opportunity," and he added that "autographed personal or group photographs would be a good memento to include with follow-up notes."

3. Coordinated governor-cabinet road trips. "At the moment, neither your [Clinton's] nor the cabinet's travel or speech plans are coordinated to ensure we are getting maximum geographical and constituency coverage for our efforts." Danner recommended that each member of the cabinet, which consisted primarily of the executive directors of the various state departments, visit one or two new counties every month for speeches, meetings with local leaders, and press interviews, giving the administration "total coverage every quarter."

Ideally, cabinet members would make detailed reports—Danner recommended a standard trip reporting form—upon their return to the Capitol. "This would be invaluable as a political 'early warning system,' as well as for later campaign scheduling. Also, it is a good way to keep your county [campaign] coordinators involved with administration activities."

4. Regular "telephone liaison" with "major interest group spokes-

persons and relevant legislators." Danner warned that the administration's liaison staff "has been structured largely along functional-departmental lines with little instruction regarding the precise political nature of their political responsibilities."

"We have missed a very easy and politically useful opportunity—making sure that we are in regular contact with the spokespersons for particular issues, whether they be legislators, private citizens, lobbyists, or interest group leaders." Danner advised creation of "an issue-specific inventory of names" and telephone numbers to be divided among the various department heads and central staff constituting a weekly telephone bank. "A simple card file could be kept for recording issues discussed and dates of contact—for later use in campaign and-or legislative lobbying."

5. Annual "reports to the people" summarizing Clinton's "commitments and fulfillment thereof," attractively laid out without being "slick" or expensive to produce.

In his own summary, Danner suggested that the Clinton administration also hold town meetings, circuit-rider cabinet sessions, "Ask the Governor-Cabinet" programs on television and radio, conferences, and workshops. He even proposed that Clinton or his designees man booths at the various annual county fairs (prompting one wag to suggest that the booths be set up inside the livestock barns).

Clinton was livid—"apoplectic," said one observer—with anger and embarrassment at the disclosure of Danner's "Proposed Public Information Strategy," which he erroneously assumed had been leaked to the news media. In fact, an enterprising young *Arkansas Democrat* reporter, new to the state Capitol beat and anxious to make a name for himself, had happened across the memo languishing in plain view in one of several offices occupied by gubernatorial staffers and had pilfered it.

Publicly, Clinton refused to comment despite reporters' repeated requests. Privately, his remarks bordered on the profane.

Ironically, the incident was paralleled more than a dozen years later in the Clinton White House. Six months into his presidency, Clinton's administration was said to be leaking like a sieve, an early sign that, at best, all was not well between the old-timers and the newcomers among the staff, and, at worst, that someone, possibly someone on the periphery of the inner circle, already had acquired a grudge against the administration or one or more of its trusted advisors.

Gleefully dubbed "the Hallelujah memo," what fell into reporters's hands in the summer of 1993 was a five-page memorandum entitled "Hallelujah: Change Is Coming," its author unidentified, instructing administration and Democratic party loyalists in the proper "body language" and propaganda techniques to use when discussing President Clinton's economic plan, which was tied up in a House-Senate conference committee. It was distributed to top officials in federal agencies and to Democratic members of Congress in mid-July.

Point by point, the memo issued instructions on how to sell the program. Among the directives:

- "Never forget that the optimism, energy, [and] enthusiasm you project is vital. Even your most cynical critics will walk away impressed with your commitment. And that's half the battle. Your body language, attitude, and confidence will be infectious."
- "If you become a merchant of pain, you'll find that the middle class isn't buying—they already have enough, thank you."
- "While you will doubtless be pressed for details beyond these principles, there is nothing wrong with demurring for the moment on the technicalities."
- "If we keep our eyes on the prize, and constantly remind folks of the Big Picture, we will have a message strategy . . . that works."
- "No matter what form the final legislation takes, the main goals will be accomplished. These goals are historic and tragically underreported. Use the period in which the conference report is being negotiated to drive home the Big Picture goals of this plan."

At its conclusion, the memo decreed: "Now go forth and spread the good news."

Washington Republicans, as well as a large number of Democrats, thought it a hoot, even as they admonished the administration for coming painfully close to violating federal laws against lobbying and using tax dollars for partisan purposes.

There was some sniggering and eye-rolling in Arkansas, too, where concern over the first-term governor's image and eagerness to promote his "progressive" agenda had resulted in a similar *faux pas*.

Clinton's statehouse staff had not sufficiently recovered from his Danner-inspired tirade when, during a special legislative session in January 1980, several of the younger, more irreverent members of the state House of Representatives introduced a mock resolution suggesting ways in which the General Assembly could improve its public image.

After a year of dealing with what they perceived as smug, self-important young upstarts in the governor's office, many members of the Arkansas General Assembly had had their fill. In no fewer than nine WHEREASes, the mock resolution introduced by Representatives Pat Flanagin, Kent Rubens, and Joseph K. Mahony II covered in minute detail every insult, real and imagined, the lawmakers had read into the Danner directive. It also contained ten scathingly sarcastic directives setting down the precise manner in which House members were to comport themselves to their best public relations advantage (see Appendix II).

The lampoon set Clinton off again—his swearing reportedly penetrated the walls of the inner enclave and filtered into the reception area of the governor's office. Obviously, Danner's worth to the administration was already undergoing reevaluation when there occurred another Danner-inspired PR disaster—a second ill-conceived memorandum.

The second memo was a directive in which Clinton's top people were given control of all policy information emanating from their respective agencies. The scope and spin of information disseminated to the public were to be strictly screened by cabinet members through departmental clearinghouses "to ensure that all significant proposed policy statements and regulations by their agencies have been reviewed and approved by them before submission to other state departments and agencies, [the] legislature or other public bodies." There were to be no off-the-cuff comments concerning anything involving the administration or its multiple components.

Members of the legislature, accustomed to quick and uncompromised response to requests for information from the bureaucrats whose salaries they set, took this statement as a personal affront. More damning was the fact that Clinton had signed off on the policy, which stated the governor's intention that "this policy will result in an improved review of the necessity for, clarification of and appropriateness of formal state policies regarding critical public programs."

Thus Danner's tenure was drawing to a close even before powerful members of the Joint Budget Committee, the interim "advisory" body composed of senior legislators, launched a frontal assault on matters within Danner's scope of responsibility. While the legislative branch can't directly interfere in executive matters, lawmakers can make their displeasure known by withholding funds, slashing salaries, or eliminating positions outright. Thus, while the legislature's interim committees cannot directly block expenditures, state agencies traditionally respect their "advice" and honor their "recommendations."

But Danner and his staff repeatedly ignored the legislature, as was the case of a $30,000 federal grant designated for use in training department heads and upper-echelon administrators in personnel and budget management matters. Danner was harshly rebuked when lawmakers learned that more than half of the money had been spent without prior legislative knowledge. His position was not enhanced when it was learned that those bureaucrats, on state time, had been studying such topics as "How to play the budget game" and "How to tell what turns you on."[20] The sarcasm of lawmakers was unrestrained, particularly since several of them had already heard rumors that Danner was on his way out. The prospect of saying goodbye to one of Clinton's "pointy-headed liberals," particularly Danner, delighted them. Danner was too stuffy, too stiff, and too humorless for their tastes, and they could not abide his wife, who was not only non-deferential and virtually devoid of femininity but, like the governor's wife, did not use her husband's name.

Rumors of Danner's impending departure were given credence when his wife, Nancy Pietrafesa, abruptly resigned on March 20. Five days later, Danner told the *Democrat* that there was no truth to reports that he and his wife had been fired, but he confirmed that they were leaving Arkansas. He said he was resigning to become executive secretary to Shirley M. Hufstedler, head of the newly created Department of Education in Washington, an offer that had come "out of the blue," and that Pietrafesa also expected to find work in the nation's capital.

"Our leaving is at our initiative," Danner said quietly. "The governor and each of us had the understanding before we came [to Arkansas] in the first place that basically we would be making a commitment to one year in the administration."[21]

The reorganization had nothing to do with their decision, Danner insisted. "It's very tough to operate in a situation where you don't have one person acting as the conduit or the broker for the full range of activities in the governor's office."

Publicly, Clinton claimed that he had not pressured Danner to resign and was unaware of any pressure brought to bear on any member of his staff. He insisted that Danner's departure had been precipitated by "a truly tremendous job opportunity."[22] Rudy Moore claimed that anyone who suggested that Danner had been mustered out was "just wrong."[23]

Both men lied, as Moore finally admitted thirteen years later.

Danner and Pietrafesa "were bright and full of ideas, but their personalities and operating styles didn't mesh with the staff's," Moore wrote in 1992. "The situation deteriorated to the point that a group of senior staff members, whom I nicknamed 'the gang of five,' came to my house one night and said that the situation was intolerable and that I should do something about it since I had the governor's ear. I went to the mansion and told Bill and Hillary, and they recognized the depth of the problem. It was difficult because of the deep personal relationship between the two couples. Bill asked me to terminate them. It was the worst thing I ever had to do."[24]

In the end, Clinton simply could not face his longtime friends, who had left lucrative careers on the West Coast to help him realize his political aspirations. That Moore took the blame, albeit belatedly, for their departure attests to Moore's unflagging devotion and exemplifies the loyalty Clinton engenders.

Moore's contribution to the undermining of the first Clinton administration was cumulative and less public than any of the controversies involving Danner or Smith. Moore, who controlled access to

Clinton, simply treated people with less courtesy than they thought they deserved. Legislators and lobbyists were often heard to grumble that Moore seemed to think that *he* was the governor, and except for his informal attitude toward office attire—like Smith, he was fond of conducting business in T-shirt and cut-offs—Moore did little to dissuade this line of thinking.

As he became more secure in his supremacy over Danner and Smith, Moore became stingier with Clinton's time and less receptive to press inquiries. Any *Democrat* reporter who complained that the *Gazette* was being hand-fed scoops by the administration was laughed at to his or her face. He thought it hilarious when the chief of the governor's security force manhandled a *Democrat* reporter half his size and tried to snatch the reporter's notebook from his hands.[25]

At Moore's behest, legislators were left to cool their heels for hours in the reception area before leaving in disgust, not having been granted an audience with Clinton or anyone else of consequence. Eventually, some of Clinton's closest friends and advisors began complaining that the governor was "isolated" and losing touch with the people. More damaging to Clinton was that the longer this situation existed, the less they blamed Moore and the more they blamed the governor himself.

A story making the rounds in the spring of 1980 was about a fellow who, upon being urged by a friend to run for governor, replied that he didn't care to take on the burdens of state government.

"That's all right," the friend retorted. "Keep Rudy Moore, and you can pose for pictures like Clinton does while Rudy runs the state."[26]

The only scandal associated with Moore was due to a "domestic" dispute between him and his girlfriend. The two got into an alcohol-fueled argument at a local uppercrust eatery and Moore dragged her outside and pushed her, screaming, into a car before driving off. A waitress observed the incident and thought the woman had been kidnapped.[27] Police were called, and Moore kept a low profile for several days afterward. Clinton, who at that point reportedly had had several shouting matches with Hillary, thought the entire episode quite amusing.

Controversies involving Smith were more substantive. Highly disdainful of "suits," Smith antagonized both business and industry, but none so irrevocably as Arkansas's timber industry. As chairman of the Governor's Task Force on Timber Management Practices, he missed no opportunity to attack business interests.

The task force was charged with making recommendations on whether and how forestry practices should be regulated. Before the final public hearing had been held, Smith fired off a letter to the executive director of the Arkansas Forestry Association in which he criticized an unnamed "corporate citizen," later identified as the Weyerhaueser Corporation, for its forestry practices.[28]

Accusing Weyerhaueser of "public insensitivity and environmental disregard," Smith launched into a lecture about the industry's responsibility "to manage the land so as not to destroy its potential for future productivity, endanger the existence of rare or endangered species of plant or animal life (which were also created by God), or to degrade the quality of the air, soil or water to which all citizens have both societal and legal interests." Smith made it clear that the clear-cutting practices of Weyerhaueser did not represent good stewardship over God's creations.

The Arkansas Forestry Association and Weyerhaueser were not alone in their displeasure with Smith. When the final report was turned over to Clinton, several members of the task force complained that Smith had bypassed his own committee in compiling the recommendations. The full task force had never discussed the wording or the substance of the recommendations. Smith had solicited their input by mail, but the final report was in Clinton's hands before Smith's fellow members knew it had been completed.

On the heels of the timber management task force report came disclosure of Smith's decision to involve Arkansas in a study of small business in four states. The eighteen-month study produced a hundred-page report at a cost of $225,000 in federal Housing and Urban Development Department funds. The consultants who undertook the research spent a grand total of four days in Arkansas at the rate of $2,500 a day. Their conclusion: Small business leaders needed more regulation and more "advocacy" on their part by state and federal agencies.

This was not the kind of advice being sought by the Arkansas Small

Business Unity Council, which was grudgingly granted a firsthand account of the consultants's preliminary findings; council members were even more disturbed by the consultants's refusal to give them copies of the study. Their findings would go to Steve Smith, the consultants explained, because he had authorized the work.[29]

The refusal gave several members a chance to complain about government waste, which was becoming an increasingly controversial issue for the Clinton administration. Neither the consultants nor Smith soothed the small business leaders, or editorialists, when they dismissed inquiries about the exorbitant cost of the study as unimportant because "it isn't costing Arkansas anything."[30]

This *blasé* attitude toward government spending was prevalent throughout the Clinton years, and he never really understood the public's displeasure with what many editorial writers and columnists viewed as Clintonian profligacy except in terms of communication: "If I had done a better job of explaining," he would say, or "If I had been able to get my message across," or "If the people had been made to realize," the outcome might have been different.

13

SNAKEBIT IN ARKANSAS

IN THE END, it was Cubans and car tags and twelve cords of wood—not much of a legacy for a rising young star in the national Democratic party, but by the end of his first term as governor, this appeared to be the sum total of Bill Clinton's accomplishments. His political opponents in the 1980 governor's race would profit by it.

It seemed like a good idea at the time, teaching the hardcore unemployed to chop firewood that in turn would be used to heat the homes of poor, elderly people "at no cost to the state." With the aid of two federal grants—$411,000 in Comprehensive Employment and Training Act funds and another $100,000 from a dubious grant-writing operation called the Ozark Institute—at least fifty strong men would learn to harvest timber while meeting the populist agenda of the Clinton administration. The program was given a catchy acronym—SAWER, pronounced "sawyer," for Special Alternative Wood Energy Resources—and a hefty budget with which to train and equip an initial sixteen two-member teams to chop firewood for at least one thousand poor and elderly Arkansans.

There was only one problem: SAWER was not viable, and the people involved with the program, including Clinton's inner circle,

knew it. Several months into the program, those charged with implementing it at the local level were calling it a "potential embarrassment"
for the Clinton administration.[1] But despite repeated warnings that
SAWER was headed toward disaster, however, the Arkansas Department of Local Services took no steps to curtail the blatant misuse of
taxpayer funds and manpower until reporters happened onto the story
six months after it began.

SAWER was the idea of a career state employee named Tedford C.
Newman, who had spent his career in various social work and mental
health programs, notably as director of mental health for the state
hospital and a deputy director of the state Department of Human
Services in October 1979. Newman resigned from Human Services
after a reorganization resulted in a sharp decrease in his job responsibilities. He took a $3,000 cut in pay to serve as SAWER project
director for $23,000 a year, a grand sum for any state employee.

This job, and for a time Newman's career, came to an abrupt halt in
April 1980, when the *Arkansas Gazette* began reporting on SAWER
with a story headlined: "$62,000 Spent by Job Program; Only Three
Cords of Lumber Cut."

A subsequent inquiry by the *Arkansas Democrat* reported that
SAWER had produced six partially trained woodcutters who cut
twelve cords of wood for two households at a cost of $68,626.[2] Three
of the workers had been forced back on the dole because they had not
been paid for two months.

John W. "Jack" Thiele, head of the Local Services Department's
Employment Development Division, which administered CETA
grants, had pronounced the initial SAWER proposal "unworkable"
and directed his staff to keep revising Newman's proposal until it met
U.S. Department of Labor eligibility requirements.

Newman apparently ignored many of the mandated changes, because, according to CETA records, he "was still referring to the project
as a commercial wood-cutting project" and attempting to obtain tree-
cutting permits from private timber companies such as Weyerhaueser
and International Paper for several months after he had been advised
that the federal government prohibited CETA workers from felling
trees and chopping wood on private land.

Despite repeated admonitions, including the results of a feasibility study, that the project was not viable, Newman was permitted to proceed under the aegis of Clinton aide Steve Smith. Repeated revisions of the project program, which continued well into February 1980, did not improve its prospects, and those whose suggestions might have made its goals achievable were ignored.

Bill Carroll, deputy director of the Black River Area Development Council in Northeast Arkansas, the only antipoverty agency that trained SAWER workers, later told me that the cash-flow problems that resulted in delayed paychecks for those workers—he twice had to borrow from other grants to pay them—was but one of myriad problems.

"The whole system was set up wrong," he said. "It should have been set up at the local level, because we know what we need to operate a program. The budget and project narrative by Ted Newman were really inadequate for our needs."[3]

For example, he noted, his agency received $1,300 for administrative costs, all of which was earmarked for gas and oil for chain saws, but "we never got the saws, so we really didn't need the money. Anyone else would know that. Apparently Ted didn't. . . . How do they expect us to cut without equipment?"

About $27,000 worth of chain saws and other equipment was purchased by SAWER, but none of the equipment ever arrived at Black River; its use had been prohibited by the U.S. Labor Department because Newman had authorized its purchase without Labor Department approval.

After SAWER'S failure became public knowledge, the Labor Department's prohibition against work on private property was blamed by Newman and Steve Smith for the project's failure. But CETA records revealed that project administrators had known about the prohibition before grant approval was ever sought and had repeatedly warned state officials attached to SAWER that ignoring that restriction would result in the project's demise. Indeed, Smith had tried as late as March 1980 to obtain a Labor Department waiver without success.

Warnings went unheeded because the Department of Local Services, the state's liaison between federal and local governments, was enmeshed in a battle between political appointees and career bureaucrats. The department's Division of Community Services was the official administrator of the program; a second division, that of Employment Development, was responsible for disbursement and compliance. Friction between the directors and staffs of the two divisions resulted in a total breakdown of cooperation, and B.J. McCoy, executive director of the Local Services Department and the man to whom both division heads reported, did little to resolve the conflict.

Thiele, who as director of employment development served as state CETA administrator, argued strenuously throughout the project that SAWER spent too much money on administrators and equipment and too little on paying workers, and that SAWER's books were rife with bookkeeping errors. Thiele also complained about the slowness of SAWER, since after six months, only five people had been hired for training.

All of Thiele's memos and telephone calls were ignored by the Community Services Division.

SAWER was overhauled numerous times, but nothing seemed to work. In a February 29, 1980, letter to McCoy, Thiele concluded: "We feel this program is a potential embarrassment to the Department of Local Services and to the governor, due to the nearly half a million dollars invested to train 26 participants—at this point, it's questionable whether even 26 can be served." (Several days after the SAWER scandal broke, McCoy announced that Thiele was leaving state government within two weeks "by mutual agreement.")

The first headlines were hardly dry when Clinton declared that the Department of Local Services had ten days in which to "fix" what needed mending in SAWER or return any outstanding balances to the government.[4] His quick response, unusual during that first term, was easily explained: It was an election year, and the Democratic primary was six weeks away. Besides that, Clinton, like other Arkansans, had learned about the SAWER fiasco.

"I shouldn't have to resolve this,"[5] he told a reporter, but what he meant was that someone else—Steve Smith—should have protected the administration against criticism.

At that point, Clinton was not worried about his reelection chances, but he was angry at the criticism being leveled at his administration. His conversations with the reporters who saw him on a daily basis became less cordial, and more frequently their exchanges had less to do with news gathering than with Clinton venting his displeasure with the day's headlines.

Monroe Schwarzlose, a seventy-seven-year-old turkey farmer who had retired to South Arkansas's Cleveland County, was making a third bid for elective office. Inspired by the silliness of the SAWER project, he had climbed into his rattletrap of a pickup truck and driven to the state Capitol where he shuffled into the press room to announce his second gubernatorial bid.

Schwarzlose was not a serious candidate but he certainly had a good time on the chicken-and-peas circuit during the two months between the filing deadline and the Democratic primary in May. He was the hit of every program in which he participated, particularly after a state-wide television news program visited his decrepit farmhouse near Kingsland and filmed him killing a copperhead snake that had crawled out of a huge pile of wood during the interview. Schwarzlose, who had just told the interviewer that he had personally cut twice as much wood as Clinton's SAWER workers at absolutely no cost to anyone, immediately quipped that if that snake had been in Clinton's woodpile, the governor would have called in a team of supervisors to find someone who knew how to handle a stick of firewood, and that would have cost taxpayers an additional $40,000 to $60,000.

Steve Smith already had fallen from the governor's good graces because he had angered the timber interests by attacking the industry's clear-cutting and land management practices, and now, as the administration's liaison to Local Services and the SAWER project, he was blamed by Clinton for SAWER's bad press. The governor took no direct action against Smith, but he fumed and cursed and vowed that heads would roll if the matter were not soon laid to rest.

Smith packed up and moved from his second-floor office to the Capitol basement.

Local Services did not "fix" SAWER, then or later. Initially, the Division of Employment Development agreed to turn it over to the Black River Area Development Council, but higher-ups in the department, still smarting from Bill Carroll's candid remarks to the news media, overruled that decision. SAWER was handed over instead to the state Commerce Department's Forestry Commission, and for the second time in a year, Ted Newman's services were no longer needed by a state agency, though he quickly found another state program to supervise.

The Arkansas Community Clearinghouse for Ex-Offenders Placement and Training program, known by the acronym ACCEPT, would have paid Newman $14,000 a year for finding jobs for parolees had he not been fired a week after he was hired. When the *Arkansas Democrat* reported on Newman's rebound, Clinton called the ACCEPT director, Harry Vines, and ordered him to "get rid of that son of a bitch immediately."[6] Vines, who only an hour or so before had defended the hiring to a reporter, dutifully sacked Newman.

When contacted, Newman broke into tears, sobbing that he was a scapegoat, brought down by the *Arkansas Democrat's* relentless pursuit of the SAWER story, and lamenting that he would not "have the opportunity to work in state government any more."[7]

In 1986, however, Newman made the news again when it was reported that he had been working for almost two years for another state program as a social services program director. In 1986, Clinton laughed and joked with Newman at the dedication of Pinnacle House, an outpatient program for the chronically mentally ill that Newman directed. "Newman isn't a bad guy," Clinton said. "He just happened to get a bad idea at the wrong time."[8]

The SAWER saga was winding down when the Clinton administration was hit by a real crisis.

In the spring of 1980, more than 120,000 Cuban criminals, mental patients, and assorted "undesirables" were deported to the United States by Fidel Castro.

On May 7, the White House advised Clinton that Fort Chaffee, the federal installation near Fort Smith, Arkansas, which had proved its worth as an intermediary relocation camp for Vietnamese refugees in 1975, would be used as a temporary housing and processing site in resettling the Cuban refugees.

Clinton, still eager to curry favor with the Carter White House, initially welcomed the unexpected influx of foreigners. Noting that the refugees "came to this country in flight from a Communist dictatorship," he pledged to do everything within his power to facilitate their resettlement.[9]

"I know that everyone in this state sympathizes and identifies with them in their desire for freedom," Clinton declared.

Whatever sympathy Arkansans felt quickly evaporated as the refugee population at Fort Chaffee began to swell. In less than two weeks of the announced relocation, almost 19,000 dispirited men, women, and children, many of them honest refugees from communist tyranny, were living in deplorable conditions in what had quickly become the eleventh largest population center in the state. The encampment resembled a cattle barn, and tension flared. Arguments and sporadic fist fights signaled the first signs of trouble.

Local law enforcement agencies were wary of the military's willingness and ability to maintain order, and their attitude fed the disquiet growing among area residents. There were reports of a few isolated escape attempts, but large-scale panic did not erupt until the evening before the 1980 primary, when an estimated 350 refugees—predictably, the initial estimate was much larger—stormed the unmanned gates of the military installation and scattered into the countryside.

Every farm family within a fifty-mile radius kept shotguns and hunting rifles loaded, and handgun sales were brisk.

Alarm quickly turned to outrage when it became obvious that federal troops, under the command of General James E. Drummond, had done nothing to restrain the refugees. They had stood watching, their weapons idle. Drummond's explanation—that federal law did not permit the use of military force against civilians—did nothing to mollify public opinion.

Voters went to the polls the next day determined to send Bill Clinton a message. Monroe Schwarzlose, a caricature of a politician, received a stunning 31 percent of the vote. The message was not entirely lost on Clinton, who called the White House and asked for immediate intervention. Clinton then dispatched two hundred National Guardsmen to Fort Chaffee.

The situation continued to deteriorate. Refugees and area residents were upset at the sluggish pace of the federal government's relocation effort and staged what at first were peaceful demonstrations. Refugees went on hunger strikes; residents marched outside the gates. Then on June 1, nonviolent protest gave way to widespread rioting.

As outmanned state and local authorities struggled to quell the uprising, several hundred refugees stormed through the barricades and rampaged down state Highway 22 toward the hamlet of Barling. Brandishing nightsticks and rifle butts, state and local law enforcement officers beat them back, containing the mob within a few dozen yards of the town limits. Again, the federal troops stood and watched, and news accounts reported that one unidentified army major had positioned himself between the marauding refugees and the local authorities yelling repeatedly, "Don't hit them! Don't hit them!"[10]

Clinton made no effort to hide his anger from either the White House or the public. President Carter had personally assured him that the military would be ordered to contain any outbreaks of aggression, but these orders were apparently not implemented. A subsequent telephone call to Carter aide Gene Eidenberg had reassured that Carter had issued orders that the refugees be restrained. "Nobody told the general!" Clinton reportedly snapped. "You get down here. You either secure Fort Chaffee or close it, or I'll ring it with the National Guard. There'll be no bloodbath down here."[11]

"I thought I had this straightened out," a red-faced Clinton told reporters after a hastily arranged flight to Fort Smith. "It appears the military did not stick to that. It appears that I have been misled. If they would use restraining force, we would not have to use deadly force."[12]

Eidenberg arrived in Fort Smith shortly after midnight on June 2, and a still smoldering Clinton was there to greet him. Although the hour was late, Clinton's motorcade took the "scenic" route to Fort Chaffee, by way of Barling and Jenny Lind. Nothing Clinton said was as sobering as the moonlit outlines of armed citizens along their course.

Before Eidenberg's visit concluded, the governor had received yet another promise that the army would maintain order. Eidenberg, Clinton told reporters at a predawn briefing, was appalled that federal troops had ignored the president's directive that all refugees be detained on site. Clinton then conceded what many had suspected: that until the morning of June 2, "state and local law officers were the only security force standing between citizens and the refugees." That would change immediately, he said; henceforth, soldiers would be permitted to use clubs and other riot control equipment to quell any outbreaks of violence, although they would not be permitted to strike the detainees in any manner that would cause serious injury and their weapons would remain unloaded.

Area residents were not altogether happy with this new policy, but they were heartened by Clinton's declaration that Carter had agreed that no additional refugees would be sent to Fort Chaffee. Within two months, both Clinton and Carter would be branded liars, and Clinton would be concerned about his reelection chances.

Meanwhile, the Republicans prepared to nominate their own candidate for governor. Little attention had been given to the candidates in the Republican primary except to note that one was a former Democrat and the other the Republican brother of a staunch Clinton supporter.

Marshall N. Chrisman, forty-six, the owner of a sand and gravel business, was active in GOP politics and had served one term in the Arkansas House of Representatives a decade before. Reportedly, he entered the race because he was upset, even if his brother Robert was not, that his brother had been overlooked by the governor when patronage had been dispensed.

Frank D. White, a forty-six-year-old investment banker from Little Rock, was a last-minute entry, and he readily admitted that he had filed as a Republican because he believed that Clinton was unbeatable by a Democratic latecomer in a short primary season. Unlike Chrisman, White had personal wealth, Central Arkansas social standing, wealthy friends, a born politician's outgoing nature, and a connection with David Pryor. White had served a two-year term as executive director of the old Arkansas Industrial Development Commission during Pryor's tenure as governor.

Insisting that Pryor, whose Senate seat Clinton was periodically accused of coveting, was not involved in his decision to run for governor, White gave a strong clue as to why he entered the race:

"David once told me, 'It's not your friends who elect you, it's your enemies who defeat you.' "[13] He was counting a great deal on Clinton's growing number of detractors. The elderly, the unemployed, and the working poor were particularly upset over the hefty rise in car-tag fees.

White handily defeated Chrisman in the primary, but for the first couple of months of the general election campaign, White, with the possible exception of his devoted wife, Gay, was virtually the only one in Arkansas who thought he could be governor. Circumstances, White's exhaustive campaign style, and some savvy advice from an unlikely source late in the general election campaign eventually changed all that.

Clinton did very little traditional campaigning during the primary season. Special legislative sessions in early February and mid–April and the birth of Chelsea Victoria Clinton on February 27 kept him fairly close to home. (The name Chelsea came from the Judy Collins song, "Chelsea Morning," a favorite of both Bill and Hillary.)

Clinton surprised many by refusing to make political capital off the arrival of the first child to be born to a sitting governor in almost thirty years. According to insiders, Hillary Rodham absolutely forbade him to generate any publicity from Chelsea's birth. Clinton was invisible from the time Hillary entered the hospital until she and the child went home six days later. He issued no statements, made no public comments, and held no news conferences during that time, although he did meet with visiting Vice President Walter Mondale. A week after Chelsea's birth, the governor's office gave in to public pressure and issued private photographs of the first family. That was the last the public heard about Chelsea or Hillary for quite some time.

John R. Starr has remarked that Hillary was "absent without leave" throughout 1980,[14] and that is largely true, although she returned to her work at the Rose Law Firm within weeks of Chelsea's birth. Longtime friend Skip Rutherford suggests that the campaign was not a high priority with Bill, either, although he attributes that not only to the arrival of his first child but to the series of controversies that befell the governor that year.[15] Mack McLarty, who served as campaign treasurer in the 1980 campaign, agrees.[16]

McLarty's "theory" is that Clinton was feeling "very disappointed, very dismayed" that he was only halfway into his first term as governor, his programs were barely initiated, his first child had just been born, and instead of running the state and spending time with his daughter, he had to campaign.[17]

"It was a very natural human reaction, and obviously a four-year term would have made a tremendous difference, but my feeling was it was like a prize fighter who campaigned hard but didn't quite have the fire . . . in his belly," McLarty said. "He just wasn't ready emotionally."[18]

There was no lack of heat elsewhere. In addition to the smoldering Cuban crisis and periodic outbreaks of bad press emanating from the governor's inner circle, the actions of such staffers as Peggy O'Neal and B.J. McCoy were causing him chronic discomfort.

O'Neal was a carry-over from the attorney general's office, where she had been state's counsel to the state Printing Board. The Printing Board had been established many years before to handle the state's stationery purchases. O'Neal engineered its demise by drafting the legislation that abolished it and transferred its duties to the state purchasing office. Her legislation, lobbied to passage by Attorney General Clinton, also struck a 1955 law that required the state purchasing director to be at least thirty years old, thus allowing the twenty-seven-year-old O'Neal to become director of the state purchasing office.

A humorless, headstrong young woman in the mold of Hillary Rodham *circa* 1980, O'Neal's method of operation was a running joke and a constant irritant to the legislature, and she was the only two-time winner of Starr's Boondoggler Award. For no apparent reason, she changed the procedure for announcing competitive bids, decreeing that only the bidder's name (but not the amount of the bid) would be made public until a decision had been made to accept the "apparent low bid," making her vulnerable to charges of bid rigging.

O'Neal ordered pages and pages of new bid specifications for items such as toilet paper, and thought nothing of boring legislative committees for hours on end with her detailed and monotonous recitations of cost savings amounting to a few dollars per gross or hundredweight. Her temperament was so erratic and her management style so nitpicky that when she fired off a bullying office directive about stale food kept in the employee refrigerator, staffers started stocking it with prespoiled sandwiches. Such memos inevitably appeared in a political commentator's column, and occasionally Clinton, who took any criticism of his appointees as a personal attack, could not restrain his anger. At one point, he telephoned me to take issue with a column that cast O'Neal in a particularly unfavorable light and launched into a profane five-minute tirade in which he accused me of trying to undermine his administration by "coming after me with raw malice."

"I'm working my heart out, my people are working their hearts out, and this bullshit you keep writing doesn't contribute a goddamned thing to the good we're trying to do for this state," he fumed.

McCoy, another carry-over from the attorney general's staff, had weathered the SAWER controversy simply because he was what many Clinton appointees were not: low-key, soft-spoken, and agreeable. Unfortunately, he reported to Steve Smith, and it was hard to know where McCoy's agenda stopped and Smith's began.

SAWER was still fresh in the public's memory when it was learned that McCoy had given a $968,189 CETA grant to a little-known outfit called the Ozark Institute.

The Ozark Institute was a tax-exempt, not-for-profit enterprise organized in 1977 to provide research and technical advice on rural development—in other words, to teach farmers how to farm. It was a grant-writing factory run by unreconstructed flower children led by an aging hippie named Edd Jeffords. It subsisted on modest contributions and as much federal grant money as it could grab; Jeffords had once used grant funds to teach his people how to write grant applications.

Among the institute's spinoffs was a radio station, but clearly its most successful venture to date had been the application for nearly a million dollars in CETA funding to train the locals, many of whom had been living off the land all their lives, how to grow gardens. The reason McCoy had funded this dubious venture became readily apparent when it was learned that before joining the Clinton administration, Steve Smith had served on the institute's board of directors. John R. Starr tried to persuade Rudy Moore, Clinton's chief of staff, that the Ozark Institute grant was a bad decision both politically and financially, but Moore advised Starr to quit wasting his time trying to stop "a done deal." The controversy dragged on until October, when political reality[19]—Clinton's sinking standing in the polls—brought about the withdrawal of McCoy's approval of the project.

Taken individually, most of the complaints against Clinton appointees were about minor matters. But their cumulative effect was to show the young governor as an ambitious fellow with questionable judgment and scant leadership ability whose administration had become a costly playhouse for friends and hangers-on.

As the campaign progressed, however, these friends and hangers-on did what they could to help their boss. They started treating lawmakers with more courtesy, Steve Smith and Rudy Moore shaved their beards, the Afro look was out among both blacks and whites on the staff, and some of the women shed the Woodstock look in favor of softer, conservative hairstyles. Gone from the governor's waiting room were the countless cartoons and caricatures of the boss, many portraying him as a tot in a baby carriage or on a tricycle, and in their place was a handful of tasteful paintings, framed photographs, and plaques.

"I don't think it was any big thing" that resulted in Clinton's defeat, Starr said. "It was a lot of little [things], losing 3 and 4 and 5 percent of the vote on each issue. Maybe Hillary cost him 4 percent. Maybe the hard-core opposition of this newspaper cost him 5 percent. You know, he lost it in small little dribbles like that rather than for any major thing. He would have survived Cubans and car tags, for example, if this newspaper had just hammered on Frank White like the other newspaper did, except the fact was by 1980 that there were two newspaper voices that were getting attention in this state," the conservative *Democrat*, which had switched from afternoon to morning publication, and the liberal *Gazette*.[20]

In August, two months after Carter promised Clinton that no additional Cubans would be detained at Fort Chaffee, the president reneged. Clinton was told that about ten thousand refugees who had not been relocated elsewhere would be transferred to Arkansas. The governor's protests fell on deaf ears, and at one point he thought about going to Washington and telling Carter to his face that he could no longer support the president's reelection effort. Clinton did not do so, he later confided to John R. Starr, because "he didn't want to hurt Carter [and] because he was genuinely fearful of what the election of Ronald Reagan would do to the country. Short of repudiating Carter, he concluded, there was nothing he could do to protect himself from the political fallout from the influx of more Cubans."[21]

It may well be that Clinton also did not want to alienate Carter, who was nominated for a second term at the national convention in New York City in mid-August. Clinton lobbied for, and was chosen, to be one of several speakers before Carter accepted the nomination on the final night of the convention. It was to be Clinton's first national television appearance, in prime time, although only one of the three networks broadcast even a portion of his remarks. Clinton's eight-minute speech, the shortest of his career, impressed the twenty thousand or so delegates and onlookers crowded inside Madison Square Garden but did little to boost his image back home.

Around that time the Frank White campaign, which White had been running pretty much singlehandedly, caught the attention of the national Republican party. It was White's good fortune that one of the people who came to Arkansas at the behest of the Republican Governors Association to help raise money for him was Barbara Pardue, a twenty-three-year-old professional political operative who was between jobs and liked the idea of spending a few months in Arkansas because her parents had recently retired there.

"I heard that this turkey farmer, Monroe Schwarzlose, had got 31 percent of the primary vote against Bill Clinton, and that was really exciting to me," she said at the time.[22] She spent one day traveling with White throughout south Arkansas before signing on to the campaign as press secretary, strategist, media advisor, fund-raiser, and general factotum. Despite her age, she had more political experience than White, having served two years as communications director of the Mississippi Republican party before linking up with an ill-fated congressional campaign in Wisconsin.

Pardue was to Frank White what Betsey Wright later would be to Bill Clinton, although Pardue was much more pragmatic and less emotionally attached to the boss. She did not see White as some sort of political messiah. She saw a rather boisterous, self-confident, self-made bear of a man who, as legend has it, had talked himself into running for governor while holding forth over a backgammon game at the country club one day.

"I never really understood why" White wanted to run for governor, she said bluntly thirteen years later. "Frank had a healthy ego, as any politician has. I think that he saw, as a business person, opportunities being missed or things being done that he thought were kind of dumb. He'd probably been bitching and moaning along those lines, and so when someone said, 'Why don't *you* run for governor?' he did. I think he saw it as a challenge."[23]

One of the first things Pardue did for White was to persuade him to abandon his "typical Jaycees uniform"[24] of tan blazer, navy slacks, and white short-sleeve shirt in favor of the executive look.

"If you want to be governor," she often admonished the tall, silver-haired White, "you have to look like a governor."

"Most people . . . think it was a normal campaign," Pardue said years later. "It wasn't. It was really put together at the last minute, maybe ninety days before the election."[25]

Pardue claims that she knew White could be elected from the moment she met him. It was not merely his outgoing personality, which was so gregarious that it bordered on obnoxious, it was his clear understanding of Clinton's weaknesses.

"All Frank could talk about was Cubans and car tags," she said. "He knew what the issues were. He did not know how potent those issues were, but he had those issues down."

Nonetheless, White made sparing use of those issues; they figured in his remarks to civic clubs, business groups, and political rallies, but the references were mostly throw-away lines, reminders to the audience about the uncaring, uninformed Clinton administration. White focused on the need for jobs, renewed emphasis on industrial development, and his success at business. He made some specific promises that found immediate favor with the public, among them pledges to reduce the vehicle licensing fees and to close the Washington office. He spoke without a prepared text or even notes.

"We never had a prepared speech except for the inaugural," Pardue said. "He gave pretty much the same speech everywhere he went."

White was not shy about seeking contributions. He had absolutely no reservations about calling even virtual strangers "out of the blue" and leaning on them for $100, $500, or $1,000, and Pardue can't remember anyone denying him. "He was shameless," she said with a grin. "He was the single biggest fund-raiser of the campaign."

If Pardue had any doubts about White's ability to attract volunteers as well as contributors, that was dispelled at the formal opening of his campaign headquarters.

"It was wall-to-wall people, at least six hundred of them, cheering and applauding for this guy running against the chairman of the Democratic Governors Association, Mr. Rising Star of the Democratic party. I'm telling you, Frank *knew* some people! It was the most amazing thing I'd ever seen."

When Pardue took over the duties of press secretary, the campaign gained a professional aura—and a momentum—that had been lacking. Despite the candidate's dedication and the backing of some particularly well-heeled Republicans, the news media were giving short shrift to the White campaign, so Pardue began making the rounds of news outlets. Before the big money started coming in, the Republican Governors Association paid for some of the campaign materials and surveys.

The first poll, conducted in mid-August by Lance Torrance, was not impressive on its face. "He had no name I.D.," Pardue said. "Maybe 20 percent." On the other hand, Clinton had similarly low name recognition, and Pardue believes this was due to Clinton's uncharacteristically low-key campaign.

"I never saw much campaign presence by Clinton, which was good, because we weren't forced to respond all the time. Frank White was able to control the agenda, and it wasn't until three weeks before the election that Bill Clinton took notice of that fact."

Many Clinton supporters, however, say that circumstances largely beyond his control undermined Clinton's reelection. "Every time you turned around, there was another disaster," recalled Patty Howe Criner, who served a brief stint near the end of his first term as Clinton's press secretary. "Chickens were dying, cows were starving; [there was] a terrible drought, Cuban refugees, and then the car tag issue."[26]

Rudy Moore placed more blame on Clinton's inattention to the campaign and the resulting disarray in which the campaign found itself.

"Perhaps because he and nearly all the rest of us had presumed an easy reelection," Moore said, "he had people running the campaign who had no experience running a state campaign. There was bickering, organizational work wasn't being done, decisions weren't being made, and most important, the charges made by his opponent weren't being answered. Bill never demanded of that campaign what he demanded before and what he has demanded since."[27]

September's disaster was an unfortunate and unpredictable accident near the town of Damascus in north-central Arkansas, a region that had been studded with a parallelogram of Titan II missile silos since the early 1960s. These silos had existed for so many years that no one thought very much about them. They were well-camouflaged, low-maintenance facilities, and after the initial publicity surrounding their construction, they had lain quietly in their silos until that day in September 1980 when one of them blew up.

A maintenance worker was working underground one September morning when he dropped a wrench, setting off an explosion that blew a warhead into a neighboring field. The worker died, and twenty-one of his colleagues were injured. Panic swept the countryside, whose residents not only feared exposure to radiation but began viewing the silos as land mines waiting to be detonated.

Tightlipped state and federal officials did an abominable job of responding to the accident and calming the public's fears. For several days, the warhead, which no one would confirm was a warhead, was left untended in the field where it had landed. Vice President Walter Mondale, detouring his campaign to Hot Springs, would say only that he could "neither confirm nor deny the existence of a nuclear weapon" at Damascus.[28]

Clinton finally conceded that the incident was frustrating for both him and Arkansans in general, who had peppered his office and state agencies with telephone calls, letters, and personal visits to demand action, answers, and reassurances that Clinton could not give them.

"It sure seems like we're snakebit in Arkansas this year," he said afterward. "I think I share the average citizen's frustration with the federal government on many occasions. I *do* feel those frustrations."[29]

It was the voice of money though that finally drew Clinton's attention to the fact that he was in trouble. In mid–October, when the last preelection campaign finance reports were filed with the secretary of state and made public, Clinton was stunned to learn that White had raised almost $400,000—only about $15,000 less than Clinton had raised. This was followed immediately by a Clinton poll showing that White was only fifteen points behind and coming on strong. The two were virtually tied among white male voters.

By then, White had established himself as a mature, common sense-type Everyman who could run state government like a business.

"Cubans, car tags, Clinton's out-of-state interests, the lack of leadership, the arrogance, his constant posturing to be a national leader—these were the issues," Pardue said. "Hillary was only a peripheral issue."[30]

Some members of Clinton's staff later conceded that the overall tone of the administration had played a significant role in his defeat.

"We really hurt Bill," one aide later would reflect. "But we were all so young, so idealistic, and so caught up in all that power that we thought we could change the world. We got carried away."

Democrats still look upon White's 1980 win as a fluke. That is not entirely true. Among White's modest campaign staff—only five or six were paid employees—were some very knowledgeable people, each of whom brought different skills to the campaign. For instance, Pardue knew the media, Paula Unruh knew people with money, and Len Blaylock, a mainstay in the Arkansas Republican party for several decades, knew the county Republican leaders.

Although "morality issues" were never raised in the 1980 campaign, White's candidacy held particular appeal for what Pardue calls "the church groups," nonfundamentalist conservative, middle-class, predominantly white, moralistic organizations such as FLAG—Family, Life, America, God—whose subscribers knew Frank and Gay White and their children as a solid, church-going family. The family had known adversity. The children were Frank's by a previous marriage; their mother, an alcoholic, had relinquished custody several years before, and Gay White was an enthusiastic, loving, and much loved stepmother whose Christian faith was rooted in traditional virtues.

Unlike rarely-seen Hillary Rodham, whose public face was unsmiling and unadorned, the red-haired, red-lipped Gay White accompanied her husband virtually everywhere he went, the children's schedules permitting, shaking hands and cracking jokes and generally charming people from all walks of life. Her idea of public speaking was witnessing for Christ in Bible discussions, but on several occasions she overcame her nervousness and spoke in Frank's behalf. A petite young woman several years younger than her husband who sometimes overcompensated for her shyness by adopting his boisterous style, Gay was the traditional middle-class housewife: she did volunteer work, ran carpools, and baked cookies. She won her husband numerous votes.

While White and his supporters reject the notion that he rode into office on the coat-tails of Ronald Reagan, some like Pardue readily concede that White benefited from the religious right. The Whites, Pardue points out, were "serious, conservative Christians," longtime members of Little Rock's Fellowship Bible Church, and their wide circle of friends shared their convictions.

"Frank can slap backs with the best of them, and he's a likeable fellow," said Skip Rutherford. "He basically not only had the anti-Clinton vote but was able to generate a lot of positive votes on his own. He was a businessman, and people thought that this guy related to them."[31]

White ran a good campaign once he was in a position financially to buy advertising. His use of footage from the Cuban riots at Fort Chaffee was devastatingly effective, although that, too, was used sparingly because, as Pardue noted, for people living outside northwest Arkansas, "their imaginations were more vivid than the reality." It is doubtful that most Arkansans ever saw these commercials, but through word of mouth, the images of knife-wielding foreigners confronted by National Guardsmen in full riot gear drove home White's message: Bill Clinton had let Jimmy Carter run roughshod over him and the citizens of Arkansas as surely as the Cubans had run roughshod over the citizens of Barling and Jenny Lind.

Bill Clinton made little effort to use his incumbency during the campaign. By the time he decided that his campaign was in trouble, White had the momentum. Some Democrats were supporting White openly, and in the final days, several of the major utility companies repaid Clinton's anti-utility stance by throwing their support behind his opponent.

Mack McLarty has confirmed that Clinton first sensed defeat about three weeks before the November election.

"Clinton talked to me, and he said, 'Mack, this is not going good. I think we'll hold on to win, but it is *not* going good.' And Hillary was quite concerned, also. You could see the tide shifting."[32]

Clinton's optimism was weakening day by day, however, as the campaign's continued tracking forecast a close race. The closing days brought frantic, frenetic activity. The state troopers assigned to the governor's security rushed him from town to town; each stop was divided into public appearances and private conferences with a select handful of local operatives whom Clinton hoped could turn the tide.

"What can we do?" Clinton asked his supporters, some of whom were there not to salvage his candidacy but to vent their displeasure at having been ignored or treated poorly by members of his staff. These grievances invariably put him on the defensive as he struggled mightily to explain what a tough thing it was to be governor in turbulent times. The excuses, all of them involving circumstances beyond Clinton's control, found their way into his speeches.

Clinton always opened each speech with a few jokes, usually directed at himself. For instance, when talking to senior citizens, he might quip that his age was no longer a handicap because after more than a year in office, he knew what it was to be thirty-three and feel sixty. After a few such ice breakers, Clinton would launch into the litany of burdens that had been visited upon the state during his watch.

"We've had three hard winters," he would say, "the worst farm crisis in my memory, tornadoes, a grueling summer that further damaged our roads, the resurgence of the Ku Klux Klan, an independent truckers's strike that could have erupted into violence, the Cubans at

Fort Chaffee, the missile explosion at Damascus, depression in the automobile and housing industries, inflation, recession.

"I've learned I'm not as smart as I thought I was. These two years have been a humbling experience. This state has seen worse times and will see better times. What is needed is responsible leadership— leadership that appeals to people's common sense and not nonsense and to their hopes instead of their fears."[33]

He would implore his audiences to "ignore those who would attempt to capitalize on your frustrations and who would hold out false hopes for easy solutions to complex problems."[34] They would respond with cheers and applause, and he would leave the podium with his self-confidence, and that of his local operatives, renewed. That warm glow would last about as long as it took to step into the crowd, where inevitably someone, and usually several someones, would approach him and ask why in tarnation the fee for renewing a car's license plate had jumped from $19.25 to $30.25 a year.

Clinton would listen pensively, nodding occasionally, and then try to explain how important it was to expand the state's highway program and repair the damage of those three hard winters. Occasionally, if the complainant persisted, Clinton would seem to grasp why this was such a tenacious issue.

At Osceola, in the heart of Democrat country, Clinton met Carl Barbee, a seventy-one-year-old retired farmer, who explained why a more than 50 percent increase in his license fee was such a hardship.

"I get $258 a month in Social Security," Barbee said. "That's what I have to live on. Out of that, I pay $51 a month for rent. After I pay my food and my utilities, there ain't a lot left." He went on to say that he had several medical problems that he could not afford to have treated.

Clinton's response was to hail one of the campaign workers accompanying him that day and direct him to take Barbee's name and address so that the governor's office could see if Barbee could get some more government aid to assist with his medical bills. The fact that $30.25 was a big lump for Barbee to pay out of one month's expendable income went right over Clinton's head.

"Hillary keeps telling me I don't understand the modern world," he mused during one two-day swing through south Arkansas. "I really should have been governor in the 1930s, when I could have stayed in the office doing all this good work and then could have gone out to see the people and talk about it. . . . I am an old-fashioned politician. Oh, I can work myself up and give an effective, hard-hitting, punctuating speech, like at the Democratic National Convention, but I really like to go out and talk to the people and answer their questions."[35]

Clinton was not, however, a man to stay in the office and do all the good work about which he spoke so wistfully. Sitting behind his desk at the state Capitol, signing letters and sorting papers, he often looked preoccupied, harried, or even constrained. Take him away from those mundane activities and give him an audience of two or two hundred, and he became invigorated. Being with people, particularly people who thought he was a star, energized him much in the same way as the rattle of dice energizes a gambler.

What he had to do in these final days, Clinton told me, was shore up the segment of his support that had become tenuous and "unpack problems from the bottom, turn them over, and turn them around."[36]

Somehow he failed in that mission.

"About a week out, you could see it was going to be a real tight race, so on election night, I went in to see Clinton and spent most of the night with him," McLarty recalled.[37]

It was a death watch. "Here was this young . . . star governor, and you could see the returns coming in and [that] he wasn't going to win," McLarty said.

"NBC declared him the winner, which was even more painful. Ted Kennedy called him to congratulate him. . . . It became apparent about 11:30 that we'd lost, and he turned to me and said, 'Mack, what do you think I ought to say?' I said, 'Governor, I think you need to be magnanimous about it and not be bitter. I know it's a terrible disappointment . . . but there'll be another day, although I don't think you need to get into all of that. It just needs to be very gracious and genuine.' And he said, 'Well, I agree.' "

McLarty recalled riding with Clinton, just the two of them and the state trooper who was playing chauffeur that night, to the Camelot Inn, where hundreds of faithful supporters had gathered to celebrate a victory that would not happen. The five-minute ride was unusually quiet, and as Clinton looked solemnly out the window, his fist pressed against his lips, McLarty saw the glimmer of a tear drop on his cheek.

"It was a very painful time, but he gave a good talk that night, handled it very gracefully and graciously."

The final tally was close: Out of more than 838,000 votes cast, White had edged out Clinton with 51.9 percent of the vote.

In the wake of public outrage over Clinton's policies, several of his allies in the Arkansas legislature also went down to defeat, among them a ten-year House veteran, Bill Stancil, who represented the district in which the Cuban refugees were being housed. A dozen or so law-makers who campaigned for reelection on the strength of their opposition to Clinton's increased license fees won handily. Several winners, among them Rep. J.W. "Bill" Ramsey, complained that Clinton had attempted to line up opposition because of those records. Clinton denied this.

"My assessment of that first term as governor is that the state had been used to Dale Bumpers and David Pryor, who spent a lot of time individually working with people one-on-one. . . . It was a big change going from Pryor to Clinton in style," Skip Rutherford said. The Clinton administration, he suggested, began with the attitude that "we're going to change things, we're going to have a bold agenda, we're going to really take on the environment, we're going to do a bunch of stuff here, we're going to move this thing," but amid all that ambition, "the personal style of Arkansas politics got lost in the big picture."[38]

"People felt alienated and people felt hurt and people felt that they were not given good treatment when they called the governor's office, when they came by," Rutherford explained. "Clinton came in, and I think there was a learning curve for the governor to get used to Arkansas governing and Arkansas to get used to this new governor.

"I think what happened in 1980 was, there was a large protest vote. I don't even believe that there was a desire to beat Clinton. I think most people wanted to send him a message. They tried to do that with Monroe Schwarzlose when he got 31 percent of the vote . . . [but] I don't think he got it. No, I *do* think he got it. I think he didn't know what to do about it at that point. I think there was not time to reverse the trend."

The loss, the second of his career but by far the more sobering, taught Clinton some valuable lessons. Pride had prevented him from responding directly to White's criticisms, which only echoed the public's grievances. He had attempted to blame everyone for his administration's shortcomings except himself.

"That defeat taught him how to fight back," Rutherford said. "He never again allowed a charge to go unanswered. He never again was uncertain about his defense. He was much more thorough from that point on—which served him very well in 1992."

14

THE ROAD BACK

THE MORNING AFTER the defeat, Bill Clinton held his first farewell to the troops, as several hundred of his faithful followers assembled on the back lawn of the Governor's Mansion to share their pain. Clinton would stage several such farewells during the two months remaining in his term, but this was to be the most poignant.

"Here are all the beautiful people," one observer commented as friends, relatives, political supporters, and appointees traded hugs and wiped away tears as they awaited the first family's appearance on the elevated porch that overlooked the well-manicured grounds.[1] From the sad and drawn faces made blotchy by weeping to those frozen in brave smiles, the men and women seemed to have one thing in common: They all looked a little shell-shocked.

Clinton, looking tired and wan, stepped outside to valiant cheers and wild applause. He smiled his down-turned smile, nodded his head knowingly, gratefully, and appeared to blink back tears. Hillary Rodham, looking solemn and composed, stood rigidly a couple of steps behind him.

Clinton presented himself as a sad optimist. He was not only a practitioner but a student of politics, he said, and as such he would be

257

analyzing his mistakes and learning from them. In the meantime, his supporters could feel good about the dreams they had shared and the efforts they had made to enhance the quality of life in Arkansas.

"We'll be back!" his half-brother, Roger, turned out in full rock-'n'-roll regalia, declared to no one in particular, punching the air with his fist. "We'll be back!"

It took some time for Clinton to come to terms with voter rejection. In one of his first postelection interviews, he was still trying to accept his defeat without blaming himself for his failure. His fault, he suggested, was that he had not adequately explained his intentions.

"I simply didn't communicate to the people that I genuinely cared about them," he lamented. "I think maybe I gave the appearance of trying to do too many things and not involving the people as I should."[2]

Clinton spent the closing weeks of his reign both in the Governor's Mansion, where he fretted over and meticulously dissected his loss, and making farewell appearances before select audiences. He briefly thought of calling another special legislative session to lower the car-tag fees but was advised against such a self-serving gesture. As the final controversies of his administration played out, chief among them the revelation that Department of Labor Director Charlie Daniels had been charging his three-martini lunches to the state, Clinton remained disengaged from his gubernatorial responsibilities. The mood among those in the governor's office was part gloom, part bewilderment, and, particularly where the press was concerned, part hostility, and no one in authority tried to remedy it.

Some friends reported that the governor was despondent and distracted—"He never thought that he was going to lose," one colleague insists[3]—but the distraction was nothing new.

"As I look back," Rudy Moore wrote in 1992, "it is more evident that Bill Clinton was not the same person psychologically in 1980 that he had been before or that he has been since. It must have been something personal, perhaps in his relationship with Hillary, but he was ambivalent and preoccupied. Those fantastic political insights had abandoned him. His reelection campaign reflected it."[4]

"This is purely conjecture, but nobody else has come up with a better one," said John R. Starr, with whom Clinton later briefly discussed his infidelity. "I have concluded that he fell in love with somebody, it was relatively brief, and because he referred to it in the singular when he offered to tell me about 'it,' I don't think there was more than one. There's another reason why I don't think there was more than one: I don't think if there had been wholesale infidelity that Hillary would have put up with it."[5]

Other people around the couple recognized a glaring change in Bill and Hillary's relationship in 1980. One state trooper who often chauffeured them recalled that the extraordinary warmth and delight in one another they shared during the first half of the two-year term waned in the second half, apparently after the birth of their daughter.[6]

"I remember him and Hillary sitting in the back seat [of the state car], eating fried chicken and throwing the trash in the floor—me and the other trooper were both starving to death—and they sat back there eating and laughing and smooching like newlyweds."

As time went on, mansion employees observed such incidents, and Hillary, several troopers have since observed, appeared to become, as one noted, "very unhappy with the world as a whole."[7] Concurrently, rumors were circulating that Clinton was playing around, although most employees assigned to the governor's detail insist that they never saw evidence of this. Many reporters were skittish about following up on those rumors, and those who did dropped their inquiries once it was determined that none of the alleged incidents had a direct bearing upon Clinton's performance as governor since there was no evidence that he was conducting liaisons on state property or using state employees to facilitate the alleged encounters.[8]

Some of the rumors emanated from the administration. At least one cabinet member who left before Clinton's term was up was particularly keen about dropping off-the-record tidbits about the governor's alleged peccadilloes, but his remarks were always long on titillation and short on substance. "You're a reporter," he would retort when asked for details that would assist in confirming or debunking his allegations. "You dig it out."

Several women who occasionally covered Clinton for local television stations boasted privately of having had sexual encounters with Clinton. One of them, Gennifer Flowers, would later reveal her allegations during the 1992 presidential campaign.

Deborah Mathis, another woman broadcaster who was later named as a Clinton paramour in a lawsuit filed by a state employee who had lost his job for alleged abuse of state property, categorically denied ever having had such a relationship with Clinton when confronted by John R. Starr several years later.[9]

Despite claims by some former members of the governor's security force that Hillary Rodham had an affair with her longtime friend and colleague, the late Vincent Foster, such allegations did not surface at any time during Clinton's governorship. The whispering campaign took a more scurrilous tack, claiming that she and an ardent feminist on Clinton's first-term staff were lovers. The allegations were never substantiated. Most likely they were the product of some good ol' boy's fantasy. In later years, she and Foster would be linked by cocktail chatter, but the veracity of these stories apparently was never seriously examined even after the Clintons's move to the White House and Foster's inexplicable suicide.

Whatever the case, many close friends say that Clinton was depressed after his defeat. Rudy Moore, however, rejects claims that Clinton was devastated by his loss.

"I was with Bill and Hillary every day from the November defeat until he left office in January, and I know firsthand that he accepted the vote of the people, he sought to analyze the reasons for the defeat, and he started planning his comeback."[10]

Another longtime friend, Skip Rutherford, agrees with Moore.

"The rebounding started the day after the election," he said in an interview. "It was not 'Well, I don't know what I want to do.' I mean, it was a stunning loss and a very big disappointment, but it never, it did not cause him to lose focus. He kept his eye on the prize, even in defeat, even when others thought he was through."[11]

What kept Clinton going, Rutherford said, was that "he was not through with being governor, his agenda was not completed, and he wasn't ready to give it up. I think that was the focus: that he was going to come back."

Mack McLarty believes that Clinton was far more distressed, although he plays down the extent of Clinton's depression.

"Despair is too strong a word," McLarty insisted in an interview. "He was kind of blue. . . . He had a lot of mixed feelings. He was looking forward to not working quite as hard and to spending time with Chelsea. It was kind of [like] 'What is my new life going to be like?' But most of it was less than positive. He was pretty understandably blue."[12]

Skip Rutherford calls the 1980 defeat the pivotal point in Bill Clinton's career.

"In retrospect, in terms of the long-term of his career, [that defeat] probably taught him more about politics on the national level than anything," Rutherford said. "He was much more thorough in his preparation, much more thorough in his defense, much more thorough on issues."[13]

Clinton's name was bandied about as a candidate for the chairmanship of the Democratic National Committee, but even though Clinton encouraged the speculation, he had no intention of committing himself to anything that would prevent him from regaining the governor's office in 1982.

"John Y. Brown [then governor of Kentucky] called him and offered him the presidency of the University of Louisville, and he had a lot of offers like that," McLarty said. "Brown talked to him several times . . . There were about ten offers like that—chairman of the national party was discussed with him, or at least a role in it; Louisville; a couple of offers from New York. He had a number of good offers of that nature, [including] law firms in Washington."[14]

"We had breakfast a couple of times at the mansion that last couple of months and it was—well, I think his word was truncate," McLarty recalled. " 'This loss has truncated my endeavor.' "

It had, indeed. Clinton's original plan had been to serve three two-year terms as governor and then run for David Pryor's Senate seat, a platform from which he hoped to mount a presidential campaign. Now he was faced not only with revamping the plan but reestablishing his electability.

In the end, Clinton accepted an offer to affiliate with the prestigious

Wright, Lindsey, and Jennings Law Firm, which was pleased to list him on the letterhead as "of counsel" while he regrouped and mended his political fences. When asked by reporters about his duties at the law firm, Clinton said he was involved in some antitrust litigation but did not elaborate. However, it was general knowledge that most of his time was spent trying to revive his political career.

At Hillary's urging, he enlisted the aid of Betsey Wright, who was then working in Washington as executive director of the National Women's Education Fund. She relinquished her job, and in a sense her life, to move to Arkansas and spearhead Clinton's comeback. She set up operations at the Wright Law Firm, to whose principal namesake she bore no relation. Her first task was to put Clinton's political records in order.

"She brought an order to the system that had not been there before," McLarty says, computerizing the information on Clinton's index cards, such as the names and addresses of donors and other useful contacts, and files for ready access during the next campaign.[15] While she was thus occupied, Clinton, operating from a cubicle, handled a few legal briefs between political strategy sessions, road trips, and fence-mending sessions.

"You know, when he got beat, of course he talked to everybody," said Sheffield Nelson, a 1990 reelection opponent who then was president and chief executive officer of Arkla, Inc.[16]

"During the two years he was out of office, gosh, I talked to him several times, as did most other people who talk to people who want to run in politics. I was committed to help Frank White, and did help Frank, when Clinton ran against him after Frank had been in the first time, and Bill knew it. I told him. . . . But, you know, I was head of the state's largest natural gas utility."

McLarty says that despite having known one another since kindergarten, he and Clinton did not become close friends until that reconstruction period, during which they met on a monthly basis to plan the comeback and to discuss plans for retiring Clinton's growing campaign debt.

One of the criticisms leveled against Clinton by Frank White and subsequent challengers was that Clinton lacked business sense because he had never had to meet a payroll or live on a budget in his life.

"Is there any record anywhere of him ever having drawn a salary from any source except a governmental agency?" Orval Faubus was still asking several years after his own ill-fated comeback effort against Clinton in 1986.[17]

By and large, the criticism was valid. Until Clinton assumed the presidency, his wife was the chief bread winner. While he was governor, the personal expenses that were not covered by Hillary's share of profits from her partnership with the Rose Law Firm or by Bill's $35,000-a-year salary were covered by the tax-financed gubernatorial public relations fund, the Governor's Mansion maintenance and operation fund, and numerous other state sources. Even the Clintons's bed linen was charged to credit cards, whose bills were paid out of mansion M&O funds.

A former neighbor of the Clintons's, Julia Hughes Jones, who had just launched her political career, remembers a conversation she had with Clinton when he was planning his first bid for governor.

"I was saying, 'Are you sure you're going to get enough money?' because it takes a lot of money, and he said, 'Hillary and I know that if there's something we really want that the money will come. We just don't worry about things like that.' Now that's probably paraphrasing, but it's pretty close to accurate, because I've tried to adopt that philosophy and it just doesn't always work," Jones recalled, then added with a laugh, "But it evidently worked for them."[18]

As governor, Clinton seldom carried cash. Aides would lend him a few dollars when necessary to make the token first donation to a charitable fund-raising effort, for instance, and he had only to mention his hunger or his thirst for the need to be met at someone else's expense. He walked into a South Arkansas clothing store once while campaigning and emerged minutes later with a promise from the proprietor to alter and send to him, free of charge, a size 42-long sport coat he had admired.[19]

On at least one occasion, Clinton's credit card was rejected by a clerk because it was "maxed out."[20] Clinton had no discernible acumen for or awareness of money matters, so McLarty's revelations about

Clinton's determination to keep spending money his campaign did not have are not surprising.

"We had about $50,000 in deficit and . . . Bill and Hillary wanted to keep on having these thank-you parties," McLarty said. "Of course, that didn't help them, to keep on spending money which was needed [to pay bills from the campaign]. I mean, it was understandable why they wanted to do it, but we didn't have any money to spend. And, of course, you know how it is: All your wonderful friends and supporters that just loved you the day before weren't there the day after. That's the way political life sometimes works."[21]

In the end, McLarty says, "I just personally called fifty people and got a thousand dollars apiece. . . . and we just raised it and paid off the debt and got it evened up."

"Margaret [Whillock] and I still laugh about that. Here we were just pulling teeth trying to get the money raised and it was still going out the door."

General disenchantment with the way Bill Clinton had done business had contributed mightily to his defeat, but there were indications before Frank White took office that White's way would not be much better. Determined to rise above politics, he vowed to "get the best people to help me run state government regardless of whether they are Republicans or Democrats or independents."[22] Although as governor he would be the *ex officio* head of the Republican party, White made it clear he would not actively try to establish a strong two-party system within the state. "He's a more nonpartisan type," Barbara Pardue said of White, a longtime Democrat until he switched parties in 1980. White passed over Republicans for key appointments and awarded them to Democrats.

While White stumbled through his two years as governor, courting Democratic support through patronage and consultation to the near-exclusion of Republicans, Clinton and Wright repaired his damaged political network. In the summer of 1981, he began touring the state, speaking with anyone who would listen about what he had attempted to do as governor, where he had gone wrong, and what he needed to do to retrieve his political career. He seemed to be more comfortable with critiques that found his leadership lacking, and he gave assurances that he would do better if given a second chance.

Clinton's efforts to revive his political career were not confined to normal working hours at his law office. Indeed, his lusty singing with the choir while strategically ensconced behind the preacher during televised Sunday services at Immanuel Baptist Church, particularly during his two-year hiatus from public office in the early 1980s, was pointedly noted by critics throughout his Arkansas political career. He also was spotted several times at Little Rock supermarkets, asking strangers and acquaintances alike about what had gone wrong with his governorship, and probing for advice on what he could have done— and again might try to do—to be a better governor.

That autumn, Clinton commissioned a statewide poll that persuaded him that a comeback was feasible. Elated, he started volunteering to reporters his opinions about where White was going wrong. Among those summoned to the Wright law firm for a private audience with the former governor were editorial writers and opinion columnists with whom, for a change, he spent more time listening than preaching.

Asked point-blank about his political plans, Clinton demurred.

"It's too early to even talk about it," he insisted. "I'm practicing law and having a good time with my family and friends."[23]

Nonetheless, Clinton's speeches were becoming more caustic. Short of calling Governor White a crook, he claimed that White had amassed a campaign war chest of $500,000 during his nine months in office by less than ethical means. That charge worked only so long as Clinton's own fund-raising efforts were not disclosed in the financial reports of his own campaign.

"I'm not kidding," Clinton told a Democratic Women's Club on one occasion. "He's got half a million dollars because the people who wanted decisions from the governor's office paid for them."[24]

"Bill Clinton was *the* dirty campaigner," newsman John R. Starr noted years later. "That's another parallel between the governor's campaigns and the presidential campaign. He kept hollering about Frank's dirty campaigning, and he was running the dirtiest campaign of all."[25]

If anyone doubted that Clinton was poised to make his comeback, they were convinced otherwise by the series of television and radio commercials launched in February 1982. In what Starr has described as "eating humble pie," the commercials featured Clinton not only soberly admitting the mistakes of his first administration, but apologizing for them. The television spot was the stronger because Arkansans could see the humility in his facial expressions and his body language. This one-on-one approach was so successful that he used it again in 1992 during the New Hampshire primary season.

While governor, White repeated many of Clinton's mistakes, among them ignoring his chief opponent's charges.

"This type of smear campaign is a disgrace to the office of governor," he said indignantly, "and as a former governor his conduct is a disgrace to the office, [but] I'm not going to discredit the office by engaging in this type of gutter politics."[26]

As Clinton regained ground with the special interests, White seemed to lose it. The trucking industry, the poultry industry, the teachers, the utilities, and any number of other formidable lobbies, some of which had benefited from White's patronage, began distancing themselves or becoming visibly critical of his administration.

Among the questions Clinton had put to the people whose advice he sought before launching his campaign, or who answered his polls, was what he could do to ameliorate the public's negative memories of his previous term. One of the most prevalent responses was that Hillary needed to take his name. In early 1982, she did so, changing the name on her law firm's stationery and her business listing in the telephone book to Hillary Rodham Clinton, although she continued to vote under her maiden name and to pay taxes as Hillary Rodham. A series of private receptions was held by supporters whose guests were invited to "meet Mr. and Mrs. Clinton." Reporters noticed during the growing number of public sightings of the Clintons that his thick, curly hair was now close-cropped and her eyeglasses were gone and she was actually wearing makeup.

There were other signs that Clinton was gearing up for another campaign, chief among them a new conservative tone to his growing number of public appearances and the frequency with which he compared his gubernatorial actions to those of the Republican incumbent.

Among the actions for which Clinton had been criticized as governor was his record of commutations. With the stroke of a pen, he had shortened the prison sentences of dozens of criminals, including thirty-eight people who had been convicted of first-degree murder. Frank White made news in early 1982 by commuting the sentence of a convicted murderer, whose life term already had been reduced eight years before by Governor Dale Bumpers. Former Congressman Jim Guy Tucker, attempting a comeback of his own by seeking the 1982 Democrat nomination for governor, was trying to make political hay out of it by accusing both White and Clinton of being soft on crime.

In a speech to a political gathering at Cave City, Clinton denounced the practice of commuting sentences, claiming that he had signed commutation orders under duress after the state parole board had pointed out that the state's penitentiaries were faced with serious overcrowding in violation of the federal court order under which the system had operated for almost a dozen years. He didn't like commuting those terms, Clinton said; in fact, he didn't even think it was right for him to have done so. He offered no explanation, and no one asked, why he had allowed white-collar criminals to complete their terms while setting free murderers and rapists.

Clinton certainly was so thorough in preparing for his rematch with White that even before he filed, he was the recognized front-runner in a field of five. Jim Guy Tucker, thirty-eight, the handsome, dynamic former congressman whose rapid rise had been stalled by a decision to run for the U.S. Senate after only one term in the House, was deemed by the pundits to be Clinton's strongest competitor. Rounding out the primary roster were Joe Purcell, fifty-eight, a well-liked but decidedly lackluster former lieutenant governor and former attorney general; Kim Hendren, forty-four, an extremely conservative state senator from northwest Arkansas; and Monroe Schwarzlose, by then seventy-nine years old.

White again faced Marshall Chrisman, and an unexpected newcomer, Connie Voll, a thirty-six-year-old nutritionist and management consultant who, after becoming the first woman to seek the Arkansas Republican gubernatorial nomination, returned to obscurity after her defeat.

White's renomination was no contest. Clinton's was a spirited effort full of posturing, pot shots, and a return to old-time politicking.

Clinton was not the only Democrat who attempted to reinvent himself. Tucker, a polished, heretofore liberal young urbanite who had spent his three-year hiatus from politics paying off debts from his Senate race and building a personal fortune, suddenly appeared in campaign ads as a shotgun-toting, camouflage-clad outdoorsman.

Purcell had been a fixture in Arkansas politics in the late 1960s and early 1970s, and in his heyday had proved to be a conscientious, high-minded public servant. He was well liked and respected by those who knew him. Unfortunately, he had the charisma of a pet rock. Too high-minded to campaign *against* any of his fellow contenders, he took a benign, grandfatherly approach to campaigning, wanting, he said, "to set an example for bright young people that politics can be clean, hoping this type of campaign will influence them and be an incentive for them to enter politics."[27] He had not a harsh word to say about his opponents, and very little of substance to say about any other facet of the campaign.

Hendren offered plenty of substance, but unfortunately it was extremely conservative, and Arkansas Democrats do not as a rule nominate conservative politicians. He also had the least name recognition of the lot and spent an undue amount of time on the campaign trail spelling his last name for people.

Schwarzlose, by then visibly aged and muddled, had lost his comic appeal.

The only real excitement in the primary campaign was provided by Clinton and Tucker, ideological twins who still shared a constituency but were bent on broadening their appeal whatever the cost. Clinton was infuriated when Tucker won the Arkansas Education Association endorsement by calling for an extravagant pay increase. While Clinton was reluctant to take a position on future tax increases, he excoriated Tucker for opposing any tax increase while making numerous and potentially costly campaign promises. The two men were constantly at one another's throat, each promising the moon to every special-interest group in the state while chastising the other for having done so, prompting one prominent Democrat to declare in disgust, "I just don't think I can vote for either one. I've never seen such childishness in my life."[28]

At one point, the chairman of the state Democratic party observed that if Clinton and Tucker did not call a halt to their pissing match, Joe Purcell might walk away with the nomination, which he almost did.

Tucker was running a strong second to Clinton a week before the primary when his campaign collapsed. The organization was out of money, out of good will, and out of ideas. Claiming that voters were tired of the "charges, counter-charges, and personal attacks," Tucker announced that he was going to clean up his act, stop griping about "what someone's done wrong," and start discussing the pocketbook issues about which voters were concerned.[29] It was too little too late. He dropped from a ten-point lead over the unassuming Purcell to a third-place finish seven points behind him.

Professional pollsters continued predicting a Clinton-Tucker runoff through election day, but an unscientific clip-and-mail ballot published on the op-ed page of the *Arkansas Democrat* accurately predicted Clinton-Purcell, although in this poll Purcell edged Clinton by 4 percent.

When the votes were counted, Clinton garnered an impressive but inconclusive 41.7 percent of primary vote, and for the first time he was forced into a run-off against an unexpected competitor.

Clinton, primed to blaze away at Tucker, found himself without a target. Purcell was so inoffensive and likeable that no one had dared criticize him during the primary, and Clinton felt helpless to do so in the runoff. He halfheartedly called upon Purcell to debate him, but Purcell, who had few plans and fewer arguments, was not naive enough to accept Clinton's challenge.

Thus the Clinton campaign turned to the only weapon in its arsenal that might harm Purcell without damaging Clinton: rumor-mongering. The campaign began circulating rumors that Purcell, a slightly built man with a slow and deliberate style, was in failing health, was living off surreptitious snorts of oxygen, and had at one point collapsed. Purcell was neither as young nor as robust as Clinton, and he did have a few medical problems, but he was in relatively good health. The rumors were investigated by the news media, but the resulting denials from the Purcell camp did not dispel public concern.

It was a base and desperate tactic on Clinton's part, because Purcell had neither the message, the appeal, nor the money to pose a serious threat to his nomination. Clinton carried sixty-seven of the state's seventy-five counties and took 53.6 percent of the vote in the runoff.

In keeping with tradition, he embarked upon a day-long whistle-stop tour of seven Arkansas cities, his most ambitious postelection thank-you schedule to date. During his airborne moments, he passed the time catnapping, working a crossword puzzle, poring over a folder full of information about the election returns, and boring the reporters who accompanied him with an exhaustive postelection analysis.[30]

Clinton took a brief respite from public campaigning—he continued to hold private confabs with select groups—before resuming his efforts in late June. While he had given assurances to former critics that the general election campaign would be run on a higher plane than in the past, this promise proved ephemeral when Clinton promptly vowed to take Frank White's record on utility issues and shove it down his throat.

White's righteous indignation over this remark did not prevent him from using similar hardball tactics with Clinton's record, so for almost two solid months the two men argued publicly about which one of them was less sympathetic to utilities.

White seemed to gain the upper hand when he pointed out that two of Clinton's strongest supporters, Mack McLarty and Richard Herget, were members of utility boards of directors, but then the *Arkansas Gazette*, with a little nudge from the Clinton camp, reported that White had sent three prospective appointees to the state's utility-regulating Public Service Commission to confer with the vice president of Arkansas Power and Light Company. The advantage shifted again when the *Arkansas Democrat* learned that Clinton had done a similar thing while governor; the only difference was that he had discussed a potential appointee with utility officials rather than send the appointee himself to do the talking.

Both White and Clinton had difficulty forgoing negative campaigning in favor of substantive issues. White was still relying on attacks he had used against Clinton during their first campaign, although he had to drop references to all the "foreigners" Clinton had brought into state government after it was revealed that his own campaign had used Texas actors in a series of commercials that featured what appeared to be Arkansas voters singing White's praises. White continued to belittle Clinton's business experience, claiming that the former governor had never "run anything in his life except an antiwar demonstration."[31] To their great embarrassment many years later, some editorial writers, believing Clinton's previous denial of any antiwar activity, defended Clinton against this "erroneous" charge.

As his campaign progressed, it became evident that White was avoiding any confrontation with the Clinton camp. He declined Clinton's debate challenge on the ground that he had nothing to gain from the exposure, and he let it be known that he would not share a stage with the man he had unseated two years before. Clinton took advantage of that.

"I wasn't too surprised when Frank White refused to debate me," he would tell audiences, "and when he refused to share a podium with me at a recent international marketing meeting, I thought he was being a little childish. But when Frank recently forced my wife to reschedule an appearance before some architects because he didn't want to be there at the same time, I began to worry. If Frank's smart enough not to speak at the same time as Hillary, he might not be smart enough to be governor."[32]

When a reporter relayed Clinton's remarks to Hillary, who was not only active in the campaign but had a public appearance schedule almost as full as her husband's, she laughed and quipped: "Frank White would probably try to avoid being in the same room as Chelsea. Chelsea could debate him and win."[33] Chelsea was five months shy of her third birthday at the time.

Just as White had been virtually alone in believing that he could win in 1980, he was virtually alone in believing he could not lose in 1982. The polls told a different story. One survey gave Clinton a 54-to-28 lead. Another called it at 48-38. Rick Eddings, a political consultant who conducted a third poll in late September, took the results of his survey of 1,400 registered voters and made an outright prediction that election results would split 52–48 in favor of Clinton. He did not miss it by much. Clinton received roughly 54.7 percent of the general election vote.

Betsey Wright, the chief architect of Clinton's comeback, later claimed that his reelection "was a passionate mission" for his supporters, which she noted was "a very solid constituency."[34]

An analysis of election returns and voting patterns revealed that black voters had given Clinton the winning edge. They had turned out in record numbers, in many instances ignoring the other races on the ballot and only voting for governor. The conventional wisdom was that "street money" distributed to local black leaders had produced the turnout. This change was not investigated by reporters, and the allegation was never formally advanced by White; it was simply taken for granted that in some communities, particularly in the Delta, black votes were for sale and had been bought. Certainly, Democrat supporters chauffeured many poor and elderly voters, blacks and whites, to the polls, as they did in every election.

Analyzing White's reelection defeat more than a decade later, Barbara Pardue noted that when he took office in January 1981, "the economy was in the toilet, and it got flushed at the end of 1981. That," she insisted, "set a foundation for defeat. A lot of us knew that summer [of 1982], when unemployment hit 10 percent nationwide and as much as 20 percent in some Arkansas counties, that that was it" for White's reelection chances.[35]

The candidate, however, was not without fault.

"Bill Clinton had spent two years putting his coalition back together, wooing the special-interest groups, and there were things that Frank did on his own" to damage his popularity, Pardue said.

During White's watch, the Arkansas General Assembly had approved a bill mandating that the Bible-based "creation science" be taught alongside the "theory" of evolution in public schools, and White had signed it into law. That was error enough because the state received unwanted and embarrassing national publicity, not only when the bill was passed but during the subsequent nine-day federal court trial (known as "Scopes II") which declared the bill unconstitutional. White compounded the error by admitting later that he had signed the bill without reading it.

The *Arkansas Gazette*, still the most powerful editorial voice in the state, had begun portraying White as a buffoon in its commentaries, photographs, and cartoons. Once he effectively admitted that Scopes II might have been avoided had he been aware of its precise contents, the public began to accept the *Gazette* image of him.

White inadvertently reinforced his bumbling image with his frequent malapropisms and sometimes simplistic, sometimes nonsensical explanations for why he had done certain things as governor. At one point, he was asked why he had vetoed a bill to legalize for-profit bingo. His response was "because it's illegal." Technically, he was correct—the Arkansas Constitution forbids lotteries, and for-profit bingo falls into that category—but instead of explaining that the bill probably would not have withstood a court challenge, he had given the most abbreviated answer possible. As a result, he looked like a fool.

"Frank changed a little bit while governor," Pardue said. "He had this sort of invincible, 'people love me' attitude that had not been there before."[36]

As Pardue bluntly observed, White "could not be characterized as a leader." The governor's office commanded respect, and White was so outgoing and friendly that strangers were drawn to him, but Clinton's appeal was entirely different. In any public setting, White always dove straight into a crowd, shaking hands and slapping backs as he made his way through it. Clinton dove only when people were seated, as at a banquet table during the traditional catfish fries and barbecues along the campaign circuit; in other settings, people came to him, crowding around him and reaching through openings in the huddles surrounding him to touch his hand or his arm or his coat.

Clinton's long-awaited return to the Capitol for his inauguration on January 11, 1983, was a veritable lovefest attended by several thousand Arkansans, many of them children. Live television coverage was provided, and there were long delays because of the crowds. Carolyn Long, who co-anchored the local ABC affiliate's live coverage of the event, noted the number of children in the audience and observed that it was as though parents had thought the inaugural an important historic event which their children ought to see.

"I've been around forty-five years," observed one aged politico, "and I've never seen such a crowd. Faubus came close, but this is the biggest."[37]

"Today is Easter," one lawmaker quipped. "He has risen."[38]

The disciples with whom his first administration was so closely associated were not resurrected along with Clinton, however. His chief aide, Rudy Moore, was rebuilding his law practice. Steve Smith, who had left the first Clinton administration to join Jim McDougal in partnership at the Bank of Kingston, had found banking not to his liking and had returned to academia at the University of Arkansas. No one seemed to know where John Danner had landed.

Publicly, lawmakers praised Clinton's new-found maturity, and they expressed optimism that his leadership would be dynamic and eventful. Privately, they took a wait-and-see attitude. They had been swept up in Clinton's messianic appeal once before, and their loyalty had almost cost them reelection, as it had several of their former colleagues.

A week later, lawmakers got their first glimpse of the Clinton agenda. In a fifty-five-minute address, he outlined a legislative program that included a modest tax increase and a variety of statutory proposals, separated into "reform" and "housekeeping" categories, that paled by comparison with his 1980 package with the exception of one issue: education. Education, he said, was the key to Arkansas's economic revival and must become a priority.

"We must dedicate more of our limited resources to paying teachers better; expanding educational opportunities in poor and small school districts; improving and diversifying vocational and high technology programs; and perhaps most important, strengthening basic education. Without competence in basic skills, our people cannot move on to more advanced achievement."

Clinton would later declare that defeat had taught him "that if you do a lot of things, and you talk about a lot of different things while you're doing it, the perception may be that you haven't done anything."[39]

Hillary Clinton was responsible for her husband's decision to emphasize education reform above all other matters in his second term. The couple and their advisors had spent untold hours examining the mistakes of his first term, and her primary observation was that Clinton had had too many priorities. He had tried to do so much so quickly that there was no reform with which he had been identified. She pointed out that when people thought of his first term, Cubans and car tags came to mind. Hillary also had a long-standing interest in children's issues and a long-held belief that education was the key to a child's future success; and she had some strong ideas about what education should entail. Her credentials, established through her efforts on behalf of children and families, were substantial enough to withstand criticism should her role in her husband's education reform movement be questioned, and she herself had a great deal to gain from being associated with a "warm" issue.

However, education was a tailor-made issue for Clinton for another reason.

Education reform was emerging as the predominant issue among state chief executives, particularly in the South, where Governors William Winter of Mississippi, Lamar Alexander of Tennessee, and Richard Riley of South Carolina had sponsored comprehensive education reform packages. Surveys indicated that the public was growing more supportive of higher taxes for education. The needs of children struck a responsive emotional chord even with the childless. Standardized tests administered to about 51,000 primary school students in April 1980 as a result of Clinton's Educational Assessment Act of 1979 had revealed serious deficiencies in basic skills. Third- and fourth-graders tested in the forty-fourth national percentile, sixth-graders at the forty-seventh, and eighth-graders at the thirty-eighth. Additionally, a 1982 study had revealed that only forty-two of the 265 school districts whose enrollment was under one thousand students and only eight of the 105 districts with more than one thousand students were accredited by the North Central Association.

The problems were obvious, and attacking them required a systematic, long-term approach whose development and implementation would justify keeping the leader of the movement in office for several years, particularly if voters could be persuaded to amend the Arkansas Constitution to expand the terms of the governor and other constitutional officers from two to four years with no term limits.

The first phase of the Clinton education package combined enhanced benefits for working and retired teachers, school consolidation proposals, and curriculum reform. Clinton borrowed liberally from the programs of Winter and Alexander, although the more radical components, notably creation of a class of "master teachers" whose exceptional abilities would be rewarded with increasing pay, were successfully blocked by the Arkansas Education Association.

Hillary's assessment was right on target, as the administration's success in the area of education during the 1983 regular and special legislative sessions attests.

As initially proposed, the Quality Education Act of 1983 did not establish minimum educational standards for public school students, but did authorize the state Board of Education to formulate them. That caused great concern among educators, lawmakers, and community leaders who believed that they ought to be included in the process of creating standards. The proposal was amended to authorize the state board of education to appoint members of an Education Standards Committee with the exception of the committee's chairman, who was to be appointed by the governor. Bill Clinton promptly named Hillary Rodham Clinton to the position. In turn, the Board of Education produced a slate of appointees who were deeply involved in education matters and generally supportive of the Clinton administration.

"Here in a small state, where everybody knows everybody, and somebody's kin to somebody that [Clinton] gave a job to or appointed, you can come up with a good handful of prominent people in any legislative district to be these thoughtless puppets, unthinking puppets," Representative Pat Flanagin contended. "I exaggerate that, but [Clinton] had those people, and sometimes he'd sell them on a package, a bag of goods like the education reform package, and then anything, any bill, tied with that label on it, no matter whether it was good, bad, had been studied, had not been studied."[40]

Flanagin claimed that the Clinton administration had drawn up most of the particulars of the education reform package before the fifteen-member committee headed by Hillary Clinton ever held a meeting. John R. Starr confirmed this.

Starr, whose relationship with Clinton fluctuated sometimes on a daily basis, had developed a deep respect and affection for Hillary Clinton during the previous year.

"I met Hillary in 1982 at a roast Tommy Robinson gave for me," Starr recalled. "She had a lot of influence in the way I treated Bill in the campaign. I talked to Hillary about fifteen minutes, and I don't remember what she said, [but] that influenced me. I was so impressed and decided that any man who could marry her can't be all bad, and that's when I reassessed Clinton."[41]

Starr, who had taught at the University of Arkansas at Little Rock and was married to a public schoolteacher, shared Hillary's interest in improving education and took a keen interest in the Education Standards Committee.

"That has to be one of the most successful committees ever put together, because as far as I know, the ideas that Hillary went in with were the ideas that were finally adopted," Starr said. "There weren't any major changes in it that she recognized as the needs before the committee held its first meeting." Starr conceded that the committee's series of statewide meetings at which members of the public naively advanced their recommendations was a well-organized dog-and-pony show. The plan, which came off without a hitch, was to go into all seventy-five counties and let teachers, administrators, and parents "know you wanted to know what they thought, and then after you'd done all that, you'd produced what you intended to produce all along."

It was, Starr said, "a very good PR effort, but that's how you generate support—making people think they've had input."

Flanagin found the charade reprehensible, although he did not publicly criticize it at the time, but he was impressed by the skill with which Clinton manipulated public opinion.

"As far as being able to sell an idea, being able to pass a bill, pass a package, to be a political leader," he said, "nobody can keep up with him."[42]

"The overall [education reform] movement was a good idea,"

Flanagin said, "but nobody wanted us [in the legislature] to look at the individual pieces and say, 'Is this really good or not?' I mean, it was like [being told to] 'Buy the whole deal because this is what Hillary came up with. Don't question any part of it. There may be some parts that need to be corrected, but if you starting chipping away, you'll mess up the whole thing, so just take the whole package and don't question it.' "

A restoration of good will between Clinton and old-timers in the legislature accounted for some of their willingness to do his bidding. There were two immediate changes in Clinton's second terms as governor: the position of chief of staff was abolished and replaced by that of executive secretary, and lawmakers were never turned away when they presented themselves, unannounced, to the governor's receptionists. They might have to wait awhile, which was a sore spot initially, but they eventually got to see the governor.

Maurice Smith, a Northeast Arkansas farmer, banker, and former highway commissioner, was given the ambiguous but all-important title of executive secretary. Smith, whose political contacts, particularly monied interests, were extensive, had served as the comeback campaign's finance chairman. He was well liked by lawmakers, who knew that he knew where the skeletons were buried but were confident that he had no interest in disinterring them.

A third change became evident as the new legislative session unfolded. Clinton did not designate any floor leaders to handle his legislation in the House and the Senate. He shared the power, distributing his proposals among Democrats and Republicans, veterans and newcomers. Lawmakers who had served during his previous term also observed that the "strong-arm" tactics he and his staff had previously employed were no longer in evidence.

"He's just got a different attitude," Representative Ed Thicksten said of the governor.[43]

"I'm trying to use my office in a more cooperative way rather than in a strong-armed way," Clinton said in a 1983 interview. "I wouldn't say I'm less aggressive, but I think I'll be more effective in the long run."[44]

He later conceded that his style during the first administration had left many with the impression that "I was going to do what I thought was right no matter what anybody else thought," and that he had made a concerted effort to change that. "I'm going to try to be fair to everybody so that they feel they are not shut out from access to this office."[45]

Clinton's strength as a political operative blossomed during that session. He stayed in his office no more than absolutely necessary, taking to the halls to lobby publicly for his legislative package. He also enlisted the aid of people living outside Little Rock. For instance, when his utility legislation met with predictable resistance, he sent out twenty thousand "Dear Friend" letters, primarily to former campaign workers, asking them to call or write their legislators to support his proposals. The gesture did not salvage the entire package, but it made his supporters feel important and involved and an integral part of the political career they had worked so hard to resurrect.

"Most of his advocacy legislation, excepting the utility matters, has been well received," veteran Senator Ben Allen observed midway through the session. "His appointments have been good, his actions excellent, and he's just working like a dog on this budget. He's done a good job."[46]

15

THE EDUCATION GOVERNOR

FOLLOWING A SPEECH by the governor of Arkansas to a convention
of funeral directors from three states meeting in Little Rock in late
June of 1983, a woman in the audience from Louisiana stood up and
demanded the group's attention.[1]

"I would like to say that this young governor—and, sir, I am a
minister and I do have a gift of discernment—I see you leading this
great country of America as our president."

"Don't say that," Bill Clinton blurted, his face growing red. "That's
bad luck. That's bad luck."

"Oh, no," the woman continued. "No, it's not bad luck. We need
such a man that thinks like you think." She looked around at her
colleagues. "I've been hearing and reading about this Arkansas new
governor. I think we need to take note of this young man. We're going
to see more of this young man. This young man is going to be your
president, the president of the United States."

However heartening the woman's comments, spoken with the enthusiasm and conviction of a proselyte, it was not the type of thing
Clinton wanted to hear in a public forum at that time. He had been
back in office six months, hardly enough time to have proved himself

to Arkansans, many of whom still resented his "national ambitions." Now was not the time to rekindle that controversy.

"I think I have to do a better job than I did when I was here before in keeping in touch with my friends and supporters, who put me here," Clinton had observed shortly after again taking office, "but I have to do a better job of trying to inform the people as a whole about what I'm trying to do and give them an opportunity to have some contact with me."[2]

From that point on, the public had frequent contact with the governor. At least one or two days a week, he was on the road, making speeches, generating goodwill and contributions for another reelection campaign still more than a year away. He preferred the dais to the desk anyway, so this commitment to stay in touch and in tune with the people was not a difficult one to keep. In between speeches, his staff continued to churn out those "Dear Friend" letters.

"These things may look like campaign activities," his new press secretary, Joan Roberts, said, "but they're not. He feels a responsibility to keep in touch. He feels he failed to do that in the first term."[3]

While Clinton did not forgo all out-of-state travel during this period, he directed most of his energy toward laying the foundation for education reform in Arkansas.

As he had expected, the state's high court finally decreed in June that the formula for distributing state aid to schools was unconstitutional because it was determined primarily by the tax base of each district, which resulted in wealthier districts receiving more state aid per student than poorer districts.

The state was mandated to "equalize educational opportunities" by redrawing the distribution formula. Further complicating the matter was a second court decree in a separate case which mandated a three-year statewide reappraisal of all property to bring tax assessments in line with the Arkansas Constitution. In effect, the state was faced with equalizing its distribution of the (tax) wealth while the amount of that wealth was still being determined.

Faced with a court decree to equalize distribution of state aid to school districts, he had decided to address that matter in the autumn in conjunction with the recommendations by the Education Standards

Committee. The issue was given added momentum by the publication of *A Nation at Risk*, in which a federally sponsored commission declared that America's standing as a world leader was threatened by a "rising tide of mediocrity" in the nation's schools.

More had been done for teachers than for education during Clinton's first legislative session. Through increases in taxes on cigarettes and alcohol, teachers had received a modest pay raise, about $750 a year. Retirement benefits were beefed up and a law enabled teachers to retire at full pension regardless of age after thirty years in the profession.

The Arkansas Education Association, despite representing fewer than half of the state's public school teachers, was then, and is now, the most forceful voice of education in Arkansas, and its leadership was not at all happy that Clinton declined during the 1983 legislative session to call for a general sales tax increase. The governor countered that there was nothing to be gained by throwing good money after bad. He reasoned that people would be willing to pay more if they were convinced that doing so would result in improvements. The administration's strategy was to build grass-roots support for education reform as a way of selling the public on a general tax increase.

It worked beautifully. While Hillary's committee went through the pretence of listening to the people, the governor met almost every day with insiders who could help him achieve his education reforms. Typically, he would invite a group of legislators, educators, business, or civic leaders, or newspaper editors and reporters to the mansion for breakfast or lunch, at which time he would lead a discussion about what was wrong in education and appear to seek their advice about what ought to be done to solve the problems.[4] A meeting with the governor in this relaxed, informal setting was not commonplace for most of the attendees, however *blasé* their attitude about it, and they were pleased to have a hand in designing the strategy for solving such a weighty problem. Two conclusions invariably were reached in these exchanges: The problems could not be solved without money, but the public would not be willing to provide the money without a reasonable guarantee of improved performance and teacher accountability.

Clinton's speeches began focusing on these two points, and while public audiences proved receptive, he was determined to move as slowly as circumstances would permit. Consensus building was paramount, because he planned to enact the state's largest tax increase in twenty-five years.

His new staff was no less committed to the administration's success than his previous staff had been, but the approach was entirely different. Arrogance had undermined Clinton once before and it must not be permitted to do so again. Public opinion was of the utmost importance to this new crew, and his staff did everything possible to influence public opinion. A few mistakes were made in the process, but with experience, most of these mistakes were quickly corrected.

There was a timetable for every step of the reform movement; thus it was understandable that Clinton's people became alarmed when the *Arkansas Gazette* reported in July 1983 that Clinton was telling friends that he intended to seek a general sales tax increase. A Clinton spokesman moved quickly to deny the story—too quickly, given the fact that Clinton had plenty of friends who missed few chances to flaunt their inside knowledge by leaking Clinton's plans. Realizing that the details of his tax plan were no longer private—he had made the mistake of telling a gathering of 150 friends that he planned a thirty-minute television program to explain why a 1-cent increase in the state's sales tax was needed—Clinton had no choice but to admit during a news conference later that day that the story was "substantially accurate."[5]

Among the promises Clinton made during the 1982 campaign was that without a dramatic upturn in the economy, he would not promote or support a general tax increase. He began fudging on the promise during his fourth month back in office and broke it altogether in October 1983.

The lawsuit that called for equalization of state school findings gave Clinton the excuse to call for a tax increase. The lawsuit was to be decided by the Arkansas Supreme Court.

Clinton argued that the tax increase was not his idea but was being "forced" on him by the court's decision in the school formula case. When public reaction proved skeptical, he went back to his original strategy, emphasizing that he would not seek a tax increase unless the legislature also approved a solid education reform package.

"I will not call a special session just to raise taxes," he insisted.[6]

Formal and informal public opinion surveys bolstered his resolve by clearly revealing the public's opposition to being asked to finance any educational program that did not emphasize excellence in such basic skills as reading, writing, and arithmetic. It irked Clinton no end when the Arkansas Education Association said that funneling more than half of any tax increase should go to raising teachers's salaries because any mention of raising teachers's salaries invariably was met by very strong, very vocal public opposition. Polls showed that the public thought that teachers, whose average pay was low compared to other states but was still 50 percent above the average Arkansan's wage, were paid very well for a nine-month work year.

The preliminary report of the Education Standards Committee was released in September on the heels of a Gallup Poll that revealed the general public's commitment to improving education. Unlike her husband, who often lamented the "hard decisions" that leadership foisted upon him, Hillary Clinton believed that controversial issues were more likely to be satisfactorily resolved by placing more emphasis on public involvement than on leadership, and that was the tack she took in presenting the report.

"To achieve and maintain a standard of consistent high quality in our schools will not be easy, it will be difficult," she said. "All our proposals will demand hard work and self-sacrifice of everyone in-volved, from school board presidents and superintendents to students and parents."[7]

Among the proposals which issued from the committee were smaller teacher-student ratios, a longer school year, mandatory school attendance for children ages six through sixteen, mandatory kinder-garten, a new foreign language requirement, tougher math, social studies, and science curricula, and tighter restrictions on the em-ployment of noncertified teachers. The committee also proposed minimum competency tests for students at the third-, sixth-, and eighth-grade levels, with retention and remedial help for any student who failed.

The eighth-grade test would be tied to a school district's overall performance, and any school which after two years of testing could not achieve an 85 percent pass rate would lose its accreditation.

Some of these proposals could be implemented administratively. Others would require legislative action.

Hillary Rodham Clinton's numerous public appearances and television and radio interviews provided the vast majority of Arkansans with their first personal glimpse of her. Many people were pleasantly surprised by the passion and humor and intelligence she revealed. Her remarks were liberally sprinkled with references to "my husband" and "our daughter," and she spoke with conviction about society's responsibility toward its children. "We Arkansans," she would say in her nasal Midwestern twang, "have to quit making excuses and accept instead the challenge of excellence."[8] Following Hillary's first appearance before a legislative committee, one House member quipped, "It looks like we've elected the wrong Clinton."[9]

Within a matter of weeks, her efforts were repaid as years of ill will were washed away, and she became a full partner in her husband's political career.

As Hillary's stock rose with the legislature, Betsey Wright's dropped. Clinton had rewarded her exceptional campaign effort by making her his "office manager" in charge of the day-to-day operations—the chief-of-staff title eventually was resurrected—but she was no more inclined to accept the political constraints of that role than Clinton was to constrain her. Heretofore, Hillary had been cast in the role of wild-eyed, man-eating resident feminist. As she softened that image, Wright, who had absolutely no feel for diplomacy, looked all the more like a brassy, bullying, male-bashing hellion. Adjectives that previously had been used to describe Hillary—cold, calculating, stern—were transferred to Betsey Wright, who always seemed to be looking to the next campaign.

Some of the resentment toward Wright stemmed from the intense fund-raising effort she orchestrated on behalf of the education reform movement. The administration raised about $130,000 from private sources to finance a series of paid political announcement, brochures, phone banks, and a letter-writing campaign encouraging community leaders and Clinton supporters to pressure legislators to raise taxes for education. Lawmakers resented being pressured by anyone, particularly voting constituents, and they would remember Wright's involvement in the effort for a long time.

"They may call her chief of staff or administrative assistant, but what she is is Clinton's political director," one lawmaker grumbled. "From what I've seen, she's not emphasizing what will do the state some good, she's emphasizing what will do Bill Clinton some good."[10]

It was to be a recurring complaint.

Two weeks after Hillary's report was made public, Clinton unveiled his plans in an address televised statewide. He was in top form, detailing an ambitious program to which, he said, he was completely and stubbornly committed. The only thing that mattered to him, he said, was bringing Arkansas's public schools into the 1980s, and if that entailed doing battle with the General Assembly and special interests in a series of special legislative sessions, he was up for the fight. He expected one, too; in addition to a 1-cent increase in the state's 3 percent sales tax, he proposed ending a number of tax exemptions and increasing the corporate income tax and the severance tax on natural gas, paid when the natural gas leaves the ground.

Both Clintons received valuable editorial support in the effort to overhaul education, not the least of which was that provided in frequent doses in the daily opinion column scripted by the *Democrat's* John R. Starr, who played a major role in convincing Clinton to include some type of teacher accountability in his plan. Teacher testing proved to be the most controversial part of the plan, and the one by which the plan was sold to the public. Virtually everyone liked the idea of testing the basic skills of teachers except the Arkansas Education Association, which found the concept insulting. There was no unanimity among teachers, some of whom were more than willing to take an arithmetic or English test if that were what was needed to convince the legislature to make a serious commitment to improving education.

By the time Clinton convened the October special session, the public generally supported increased taxes as long as they were coupled with teacher accountability. Among those opposed to a tax increase at all costs was a coalition of consumer and labor organizations which had tried for several years to persuade the General Assembly to exempt groceries and utility bills from the state sales tax. (The coalition reversed itself late in the session in return for Clinton's promise to offer an amendment granting an income tax rebate for a portion of the sales tax paid by certain low-income households on groceries. He kept his word insofar as submitting the amendment was concerned, but he did not fight to pass it, and it failed.)

The reforms Clinton outlined in a televised address on the session's first day would cost about $179.4 million. The accompanying tax package was designed to raise an additional $180.2 million. He made it clear that he was willing to put his political career on the line for the tax increases.

"This is the most important thing I've ever tried to do," he declared. "It's more important to me personally that whatever political conse- quences will come of it."

He vowed to stand firm against all comers. It was the type of promise most frequently broken by Clinton, and he would break it again before the session's end.

The warm relationship Clinton had enjoyed with the Arkansas Education Association cooled considerably when he refused to back away from teacher testing—"No test, no tax," he repeatedly assured the public—and the organization lost considerable standing with the public by rejecting the entire education reform package over that issue. Clinton branded the AEA's lobbying efforts as an "appalling" attempt at sabotage.[11]

The threat of forced consolidation for any school district whose students failed over a period of several years to achieve a good pass rate in testing riled many lawmakers from rural areas with a number of small school districts, many of which did not meet existing standards, and the likelihood that they could attain the proposed requirements within the suggested three-year period was slim. Many lawmakers properly pointed out in their objections that local identity was a cherished concept in smaller communities, one often drawn from and reflected in their support of their churches, and their schools.

Lobbyists for big business, including public utilities, united to quash his designs on tax exemptions, corporate income taxes, and severance taxes.

It was not an easy session for anyone involved. Lawmakers were asked to approve several laws designed to rework the formula for distributing state aid and overhauling public education. By the end of the session's second week, the governor's package already was leaking like a sieve, and in the weeks ahead the governor would buckle under pressure to throw out one by one proposed mandates concerning a lengthier school year, statewide kindergarten programs, and school attendance.

What was left of the program did not begin falling into place until the fourth week of the special legislative session, when Clinton pulled out all the stops. With the help of his legislative lobbyists and select legislative leaders, in a single day he pushed his teacher testing and sales tax bills from four separate committees, got them called up for votes in both the House and the Senate, passed the teacher testing bill in both chambers, and won Senate approval of the sales tax.

In the last ten days of the session, including the final weekend, the governor maintained an exhausting twenty-hour-a-day schedule of late-night telephone calls to and one-on-one meetings with strategists and recalcitrant lawmakers in an effort to consummate passage of the sales tax proposal and resurrect other tax proposals that had been rejected. Some legislators complained that Clinton had struck more deals than he could possibly honor in two more terms as governor.

Bobby Roberts, a librarian, archivist, and historian who served as one of the governor's legislative liaisons in at least a half-dozen legislative sessions, described Clinton's concept of lawmaking as "an intellectual game board on which all the players should be willing to sacrifice a few pieces so that they could advance their own positions."[12]

"His objective," Roberts claimed, "was not to give up anything that would ultimately cause him to lose either his political or policy goals. The game had serious consequences for both his own ambitions and for the people of Arkansas. He was always acutely aware of both."[13]

During the special education session, Clinton brought in reinforcements from the state's institutions of higher learning, people like former Congressman Ray Thornton, who at the time was president of Arkansas State University at Jonesboro, and Lou Holtz, then the popular football coach of the University of Arkansas Razorbacks. He roamed the halls of the Capitol, peeking into committee rooms and huddling with lawmakers who had accepted temporarily the roles of floor leaders and legislative whips. During one frantic period of gubernatorial lobbying, when the antics of the fractious House of Representatives threatened to sabotage the sales tax bill, Clinton forgot himself completely as he stood at the doorway to the chamber, waving his arms and shouting for his legislative troubleshooters to "go run up and down the aisles" to make sure that proponents remained in their seats and did not take a walk during crucial votes.[14]

At one point when he was bouncing around like a tennis ball in play, I asked him how things were going.

"I love it!" he said with a wide grin before grabbing the arm of a passing legislator.

Clinton thrived in such tumultuous, stress-driven situations, and abandoning that personal approach was, according to longtime advisor Skip Rutherford, one of the most difficult adjustments Clinton had to make once he moved into the White House.

"I've watched Bill Clinton in Washington and have talked a lot to Mack [McLarty] about his style—for example, during the budget votes. . . . Clinton is not in the halls buttonholing legislators like he did in Little Rock, [but] that's only because the presidential office is not in the same building," Rutherford said. "He sure spends a lot of time on the phone, and people come to the White House. He still spends a lot of personal time."[15]

The session lasted a grueling six weeks. As usual, there was a great disparity between the legislation Clinton proposed and the legislation finally adopted, but the governor had learned the value of compromise. He stubbornly tackled the more troublesome issues first, which might have been a good strategy had the resulting political and legislative skirmishes not left everyone exhausted. Clinton biographers Charles F. Allen and Jonathan Portis described the 1983 education reform movement as "the single most dramatic cause" of Clinton's political career in Arkansas,[16] and certainly it was that. But inattention and fatigue, and Clinton's newfound affinity for compromise coupled with his intense desire to win, whatever the cost, worked to undercut the reform effort so that ultimately it was much less than Clinton had hoped or promised, although enough was accomplished to permit him to claim a "historic victory."

It was historic primarily in the sense that the 1-cent sales tax increase was the largest general tax increase in the state's history. It constituted a 33 percent increase in the 3-cent tax that had been in place since 1957.

Clinton had asked for more money than he had expected to get, and he got far less than he had reckoned on. In the end, the only tax increase that passed was the 1-cent sales tax increase, which was quite regressive in that its greatest impact was felt by the people who could least afford it, those with low incomes. Business and utility interests emerged unscathed as severance tax increases were rejected and exemptions left intact by the lawmakers who relied so heavily on the generosity of these special interests.

The amount raised by the sales tax increase was only about half of the revenues Clinton had sought. It was not nearly enough to finance the anticipated reforms. The First Extraordinary Session of the 74th General Assembly ended amid concern over a projected $16 million revenue shortfall by the end of the fiscal year in June 1984.

"I'm afraid this session is going to go down in history as the special session for the special interests and the wealthy people," lamented Representative Bill Foster, Clinton's point man on the sales tax proposal.[17]

For his part, Clinton said lawmakers should be proud of the work they had done "to ensure a better future for the young people of this state and the rest of us, too."[18]

"We fought the good fight," he added, and he advised the public that this was only the beginning of the work that must be done.

Despite Clinton's presession sales pitch that all of the proceeds from the sales tax increase would go to primary and secondary education, higher education made off with about a third of it. In addition, some voters were permanently angered when, at the end of the biennial budget period in mid–1985, all proceeds from the tax increase reverted to the general fund, only slightly more than half of which was allocated to education. Clinton had left the impression that the additional 1 cent in sales tax, if not the existing 3 cents, would be forever exclusively committed to education.

Nonetheless, many Arkansans were confident that in return for higher taxes, they had been given something of value in the areas of teacher competency and quality education.

The Arkansas Education Association would be a long time forgiving Clinton for making the state's teachers prove they could read, write, and solve simple arithmetic problems. When he showed up at the organization's annual meeting in November 1983 to give the keynote address, which he had been invited to do months before, the estimated eight hundred delegates greeted him with silence. The delegates had been coached by their leaders to stand when he entered the auditorium "out of respect for the office," but to hold their applause and make no vocal response to his presence or his words. That included addressing him as he walked by, cheering, booing, jeering, and whispering. They also were instructed to remain seated upon the conclusion of his remarks so that he could not "walk around shaking hands." The AEA members did as they had been instructed.[19]

Clinton had been forewarned about the frosty reception, so he wasted no time on preliminaries or warm-up jokes. Instead, he arrived fairly promptly, walked immediately to the stage, gave his remarks, which included a defense of teacher testing and an unemotional plea for teachers not to let this matter interfere with their commitment to quality education, and then he left.

Kai Erickson, the AEA's executive secretary, insisted that the leadership's instructions had been issued to save Clinton public embarrassment.

"We felt that some of the teachers feel so strongly about [teacher testing] that they might have done some things that could have detracted from the decorum," he said.[20]

Clinton's standing with the Arkansas Education Association was at an all-time low, but he was not concerned about it then. Polls indicated that with the public at large, he had regained much of the ground lost in his first term. He reasoned that he would not need the teachers organization again for some time to come and might be able to forgo its support altogether, given the public's disgust with the organization's self-serving attitude.

The truth about teacher testing that emerged many months later, after the first round of tests had been administered, was that the test could be passed by virtually anyone with an eighth-grade education, including those with the Arkansas equivalent of an eighth-grade education. The tragedy of it was that about 3.5 percent of those then teaching school could not pass it even after several attempts and were forced to take remedial courses or change professions. The test results, therefore, proved little except that a handful of teachers had been poorly educated or were not capable of learning. The rest were at least as competent to stand at the front of the classroom as the average Arkansan. These facts about testing didn't affect Bill Clinton's standing at the polls.

The Education Standards Committee presented its final report to the state Education Department in December so that the state board could begin implementing those standards that the legislature had authorized it to oversee. The governor and his wife celebrated their victory with a series of holiday parties and receptions, but they understood that the Arkansas Education Association would become a formidable foe. If teachers were going to be used as a scapegoat by which Clinton pursued his education agenda, AEA leaders concluded, the least they could do was to disrupt that agenda as much as possible.

The AEA, led by president Peggy Nabors and executive secretary Kai Erickson, made its move in January, at the first postsession meeting of the Joint Interim Committee on Education, but Hillary Clinton was there to rebut every objection and defend every aspect of her committee's work. For once, lawmakers were willing to pass the buck, finally resolving that the Board of Education should make the final decision on education studies. At the end of February, the board adopted the Education Standards Committee's report, mandating that new and higher teaching and curriculum standards for school accreditation would be phased in and take full effect on June 1, 1987.

"It's a great, great day for Arkansas," Clinton declared.[21]

Clinton was so popular at this juncture that his 1984 reelection campaign was able to take a back seat to his campaigning on behalf of four-year terms for the state's seven constitutional offices, which consisted of the governor, lieutenant governor, attorney general, secretary of state, auditor, treasurer, and land commissioner. County officials, a predominantly Democratic group, were enlisted in the cause on the basis of Clinton's promise that a successful effort would be followed by an attempt to expand county terms from two to four years. Campaign finance disclosure laws in Arkansas did not at that time apply to ballot issues, but it has been estimated that almost $100,000 was raised and spent by Democrats to promote the four-year term amendment to the state's constitution.

The primary argument on behalf of four-year terms was that it would reduce the amount of time and money invested in campaigning. As Clinton noted, a person elected governor in November had only about two months in which to familiarize himself with how the state operated and compile a legislative program before being sworn in at the start of the regular biennial legislative session. Since sessions typically lasted from two to three months, that gave a new governor only a couple of months's grace before having to start preparing for the next spring's primary. A two-year term, Clinton said, meant six months of governing and eighteen months of running for reelection.

Many old-time politicos opposed the four-year term, but little attention was paid to their objections. Only one person, Orval E. Faubus, had been elected governor for more than two terms since the turn of the century, and it had to be conceded by most opponents that despite the integration crisis, Faubus had done more good than harm to the state.

"When [Faubus] moved into a third term—and I helped him get there—I'm not at all sure that we did Arkansas a favor," said Jim Johnson. "It happened that he was benevolent and he loved us, but it's a dangerous situation under the 1874 Constitution to ever give anybody in the governor's office a third term."[22]

With a third term, Johnson pointed out, came control through the appointment process of the constitutionally autonomous Highway and Game and Fish commissions and "all the boards and commissions that govern the very lives and fortunes of the bankers and the insurance people and the security people," giving birth to a virtually impenetrable political machine. A chief executive less benevolent and less greedy than Faubus, whose segregationist stance was abandoned in his third two-year term, would be in a position "to literally walk off with the state of Arkansas, dome and all," Johnson cautioned. Virtually everyone with a hand in state government, from the chairman of the most powerful commission to the lowliest state employee, and even the other independently elected constitutional officers, would be beholden to the governor.

Aside from a few editorialists and opinion columnists, voters ignored such warnings, even when it was pointed out that Clinton planned to use a four-year term to make a midterm run for the presidency, which he hoped to do in 1988. Only a handful of Arkansas governors ever attempted to break with tradition by seeking more than two terms. The last had been Republican Winthrop Rockefeller in 1970, who lost to a little-known Democrat newcomer, Dale Bumpers. Bumpers served his two terms and then moved on to the United States Senate. Clinton's third-term bid did not disturb the general public because his first two terms had not been served consecutively.

For the first time in many years, the 1984 election season in Arkansas was dominated by campaigns other than those for governor. Frank White decided to postpone a comeback for two years, and Clinton drew a decidedly bland slate of primary opponents, including an eighty-one-year-old Monroe Schwarzlose. Clinton breezed through the primary with 64.4 percent of the vote.

As governor, Clinton continued to maintain a fairly high profile that summer, although the headlines were routine and rather mundane. Clinton would breeze to victory in November, defeating the Republic nominee, Jonesboro contractor Woody Freeman, by a 63–37 margin. The fact that Clinton did not go out of his way to create news, even insofar as the presidential campaign was concerned, escaped notice until early in August, shortly before he was to leave for the Democratic National Convention in San Francisco, when all hell broke loose on the home front.

Long before he reached his majority, it was evident to the law enforcement and nightclub communities in his hometown of Hot Springs that Roger Clinton was in danger of becoming a serious problem. He had been in and out of trouble throughout his teen years; nothing serious, just minor scrapes that suggested a chronic inclination toward errant behavior.

There is little doubt that environment played a big role in the development of Roger's personality and deportment. For much of his life, he lived with a drunk who beat his mother and bullied his half-brother. As a result, both mother and brother became extremely protective and indulgent toward the youngest member of the family, who grew to maturity with a scrambled sense of propriety and a mercurial temperament. What could be characterized as typical adolescent rebelliousness in a teenager grew into a major case of arrested development by the time Bill Clinton became governor.

Roger was incredibly proud of his big brother Bill, but he lived in the shadow of Bill's accomplishments. Their interests and their talents were very different, but it was readily apparent early in Roger's life which one of them was destined for traditional greatness. Roger's need to feel worthy of esteem and important in his own right was exacerbated by Bill's virtually unbroken string of accomplishments. He found his identity in music, not the stuffy, ballroom-jazz variety favored by his brother but frenetic, rock-'n'-roll without the trimmings.

Roger's first brush with notoriety as the governor's brother—not his first offense, but the first to draw statewide attention—came during Clinton's first year in office, when Roger was arrested for ignoring two traffic violations—like Bill, he had a tendency toward speeding—and an arrest warrant for failure to appear in court on one of the offenses. He called his big brother from the Little Rock jail, and in turn the governor called the chief of police and got him released without bond into the custody of their cousin, Sam Tatom, chairman of the state Crime Commission.[23]

The governor defended his action, saying that it was prompted by Roger's obvious hysteria. Roger, he declared, had been "terrorized" by his brief incarceration in a holding cell of the city jail, and his prompt release into a relative's custody was no more than police officials would do for anyone who had someone to vouch for him.[24]

Hoping to give Roger some sense of responsibility and involvement in the administration, Clinton already had appointed him to the

Crime Commission's Juvenile Advisory Board, a twenty-five-member panel set up to oversee federal guidelines for awarding federal grants to state and local juvenile programs. The experiment did not work, and Roger eventually was kicked off the board by cousin Sam for failure to attend meetings.

Further escapades that transpired after his brother lost the 1980 reelection bid escaped public attention in part because the media ignored them. Virtually no one noticed when in March 1982, just before Bill Clinton officially launched his comeback campaign, Roger was arrested for driving while intoxicated and possession of narcotics paraphernalia. After more than a year of dillydallying with the case, the sheriff's office and the prosecutor succumbed to political pressure and agreed to drop the charges.[25] The preferential treatment continued once Bill regained the governor's office. Generally, however, Roger's exploits—drinking, fighting, getting thrown out of bars for obnoxious behavior—were tame enough for law enforcement officials to justify looking the other way.

That changed in the spring of 1984, when Roger's lifestyle took a serious downward turn and federal authorities got involved. Carousing and hell-raising and too much leniency on the part of his family, local law enforcement, and the community gave way to too much booze and dabbling in drugs. In late July, a federal grand jury indicted the twenty-six-year-old Roger Cassidy Clinton, charging him with five counts of distributing cocaine and one count of conspiracy to distribute cocaine.[26]

Bill Clinton had been living in dread of that possibility for several weeks. He had known for some time that Roger had a substance abuse problem, but other than offering the occasional piece of brotherly advice, he had looked the other way until early July when it became apparent that Roger was in very serious trouble.

Colonel Tommy Goodwin, head of the state police, went to Clinton's office to break the news, and the veteran law enforcement officer said years later that it was one of the hardest things he ever had to do.[27] Goodwin explained that for several months, his brother had been the subject of an investigation into suspected drug trafficking in Arkansas and "would probably be arrested within a short period of time." The case was about to be presented to a federal grand jury, and Goodwin had no doubt that the evidence was solid.

"It shook him," Goodwin said of the governor's reaction. "The best I can recall, the answer he gave me was something to the effect of 'You don't have any choice. Just go ahead and handle it like you would any other case.' "[28] The governor asked only that he be notified as soon as possible should an indictment be returned.

Even if Clinton had wanted to interfere in the case, Goodwin said, it would not have been possible because the case "was already handled." It was in the federal prosecutor's hands at that point.

Once the indictments came down, the governor had only a couple of hours in which to prepare himself for one of the hardest public appearances of his career. Goodwin came to his office on the second floor of the state Capitol to advise him that Roger Clinton was about to be arrested on six drug-related charges, each carrying a maximum penalty of fifteen years in prison and a $25,000 fine. The United States attorney's office in Fort Smith was ready to make its announcement; Asa Hutchinson, the Republican appointee in charge of that office, was awaiting word that the governor had been notified.

Clinton was visibly shaken when he emerged from his office for an afternoon news conference in which he read a brief statement.

"This is a time of great pain and sadness for me and my family," Clinton recited solemnly. "My brother has apparently become involved with drugs, a curse which has reached epidemic proportions and has plagued the lives of millions of families in our nation, including many in our state. I ask for the prayers of our people at this difficult time for my brother, for my family, and for me. I love my brother very much and will try to be of comfort to him, but I want his case to be handled as any other similar case would be. Because this matter is now in court, I will have no further comment."[29]

Then, ignoring questions, he turned his back on reporters and cameras and marched resolutely back to his private office.

Twelve days later, during a ten-minute hearing before United States District Judge Oren Harris, a former Democrat congressman, Roger pleaded not guilty to all charges and was released on a $5,000 bond.[30] He was represented in the case by William R. Wilson, who nine years later would be named to the federal bench by President Clinton, and by Steve Engstrom, who in December 1993 would assist Betsey Wright in drafting a statement in which a state trooper sought to retract statements he had made about a bribe the president allegedly offered him to quell controversy involving charges of Clinton's womanizing while governor.

A jury trial was scheduled for November 9. One of the alleged co-conspirators, Russell Ray Crump, had decided to turn state's evidence. In a full statement to the FBI, he said his involvement with drug trafficking had begun two years before through his association with one of Roger's former girlfriends, Lana Crews, a drama student in New York who later shared an apartment with Maurice Rodriguez, the other alleged co-conspirator in the case against Roger Clinton. In September 1981, Crump claimed, he, Rodriguez, and Roger's former girlfriend had attended a party at the Little Rock home of Jodie Mahony where Roger had spent time in an upstairs bedroom "weighing out some cocaine on a tri-beam scale."[31] Crump indicated that several cocaine deals were discussed at the residence between September 1983 and February 1984.

The revelation caused a minor stir among the Arkansas political and law enforcement communities. Jodie was the son of state Representative Joseph K. Mahony II of El Dorado; the house belonged to Jodie's mother, Assistant United States Attorney Sherry Bartley, who apparently was out-of-town at the time.

Crump said Roger made at least one trip to New York City, where he obtained an unspecified quantity of cocaine that he brought back to Arkansas for his personal use and to sell. He also claimed that Roger was still $6,000 in debt to Rodriguez for cocaine Rodriguez had advanced him.

Three days after his brother's election to a third gubernatorial term, Roger arrived at the federal courthouse with a broad grin on his face and his somber-faced mother Virginia and her husband Dick Kelley in tow.

"I feel fine," he told reporters as he jauntily approached the courthouse entrance. "I don't think I'd like to comment now, but I feel fine."[32]

He was there to change his plea, which, it was learned, had been in the works from almost the moment of his arrest. It appeared that the lawyers and the family had decided to ride out the storm until after the election on the theory that a guilty plea could affect the outcome. Bill was out of town and did not attend the proceedings.

Roger, who according to United States Attorney Asa Hutchinson was "one tentacle of cocaine distribution in Arkansas," had decided to cooperate with authorities, who said they had "plenty of video" of his drug transactions with undercover narcotics agents. He pleaded guilty to one count of distributing cocaine and to the conspiracy count. Sentencing was postponed until January while authorities prepared a presentence report on his background. During the court appearance, he appeared restless and bored, occasionally sighing impatiently and studying the ceiling.

Back in Arkansas, Clinton steadfastly refused to discuss his brother's situation. When asked whether Roger would attend the upcoming inaugural ball, Clinton said, "Sure. I want my brother to be there at my inauguration. I have no apologies to make for that. He has not sought, nor has he received, any special treatment from the law, and he will not be excluded from my family on a very important day to all of us."[33]

Roger Clinton's arrest had shocked many Arkansans, but it was not an issue in the campaign. It seems unlikely that voters would have penalized Bill Clinton had more details been forthcoming before the election, particularly given the dearth of viable campaign opposition. Besides, the governor had not been implicated in any way. Just because there had been gossip and snide remarks in some circles about Bill Clinton's chronic runny nose, that did not mean that he was a coke head, too. In casual conversation, reporters who for several years had been hearing stories, totally unsubstantiated, about the governor's alleged drug use decided that inadvertently, Roger Clinton's drug use must have provided the basis for the scurrilous rumors about his big brother; perhaps, they reasoned, when people relayed the gossip, they had simply identified the wrong Clinton. Roger was a known hell-raiser. Bill was very "straight" in demeanor and dress. There was a ten-year difference in their ages and a world of difference in their interests. It seemed preposterous that the governor could have any association with Roger's lifestyle. They didn't even move in the same circles.

As time and continued investigation of drug trafficking in Arkansas would prove, of course, Roger and Bill did have several friends in common—not among the jiving, jamming rock music set but among the urbane, beautiful people who wore thousand-dollar suits, sipped fine wine at private fund-raising *soirées*, and contributed big bucks to political candidates, including Bill Clinton.

16

FINISHING THE JOB

BILL AND HILLARY CLINTON, who were again the target of rumors about discord in their marriage, were there for Roger when he appeared in court for sentencing on January 28, 1985. There was no love lost between Hillary and Roger, or between Hillary and Virginia, but when Bill decided to accompany his family, Hillary felt she should be there, too. The strain under which the family labored was most apparent in Virginia Kelley, whose dark glasses could not mask her misery.

Roger, who had smiled bravely at reporters on his way into court, was more somber during this fateful appearance before the bar. Occasionally he rubbed his hands together and sighed heavily, but there was no sign of the boredom and impatience he had displayed in his first court appearance. Virginia, sitting between her two sons, an arm around each of them, frequently stroked or patted Roger's shoulder. The courtroom was packed with friends, reporters, and other onlookers.

His lawyers requested probation, or at least incarceration in a federal facility that provided intense drug abuse treatment and rehabilitation. Roger's therapist at a private hospital he recently had entered testified

301

that Roger had a heavy physical dependency on cocaine that was
"getting close to lethal [daily] dosage".[1]

"It's a miracle that he survived," the therapist said.

Roger admitted that he had been using drugs since high school.

Spokesmen for the family claimed that Roger's mother and brother
had had no idea that he had even tried drugs, let alone that he had
become addicted to cocaine, snorting it as many as sixteen times a day.

Judge Oren Harris, well known for his poor hearing, failing eye-
sight, and a propensity for nodding off during prolonged testimony,
was exceptionally alert that day. When he learned that Roger had
continued using cocaine after his arrest, he said he could not in good
conscience impose probation.

"If I do not do my duty in this case," he intoned, "I would be
responsible for other cases like it. I would be letting it be known that
people could commit these crimes and only receive a pat on the back.
Others would try to do it."[2]

Roger was sentenced to two years in a federal penitentiary on the
conspiracy charge. A three-year sentence on the distribution charge
was suspended. Authorities permitted him to meet privately with his
family for ninety minutes before federal marshals took him away.
Russell Crump received a year in prison; Manuel Rodriguez, the
source for Roger's drug trafficking, received three years.[3]

"I accept the judge's sentence with respect," Bill Clinton said sadly
outside the courtroom. "Now it is the duty of my family and I to do
what we can to help Roger free himself from his drug dependency. I
feel more deeply committed that ever before to do everything I can to
fight illegal drugs in our state, and I hope that in the future my efforts
can help spare some other families from the personal tragedy and pain
this drug use has brought to my family."[4]

It was a trying time for the family. The regular biennial session of the
Arkansas legislature was just hitting its stride, and the governor had his
hands full with the legislative program his staff had designed.

"Except on teacher testing," John R. Starr observed in *Yellow Dogs
and Dark Horses*, "Clinton was not very firmly in control of the 1985
Legislature. He allowed Senator Max Howell to force reorganization
of the Claims Commission because Howell did not like the way the

commission had handled a case taken before it by the Howell law firm, and he barely blocked a move to immobilize the Public Service Commission by making the PSC staff independent of the commissioners. He got his signals crossed and wound up vetoing a gasoline tax increase he had indicated he would support, irritating his friends in the House and Senate, who wanted him to take some of the heat, if any, from the increase. . . . While the AEA was diverted by the testing fight, Representative Tim Hutchinson of Bentonville sneaked through a bill to legalize home schools.[5] Although the bill had inadequate safeguards for children whose parents exercised the option to teach them at home, Clinton signed it. People who had worked overtime to help Clinton build and preserve his education program thought it ironic that in a year in which higher standards for public schools were preserved, he signed a bill that set no standards for home schools."[6]

Clinton continued to put in long, hectic hours at the Capitol each day and to work late into the night, still relying on those fabled midnight telephone calls to persuade lawmakers to do his bidding, but it was obvious to those who knew him well that he was restless, his attention often wandered, and his temperament was going haywire.

Other biographers have claimed that Clinton's self-confidence snapped as a result of Roger's problems and, by quoting friends who said he "hit a low in his mood swing and became self-destructive,"[7] hint that he was unfaithful to his wife during this time. Whether his depression was that severe is arguable and there is no evidence that he was fooling around, but it was clear that Clinton did not have a firm grip on his office or the legislature for the first several months of his third term.

Tension on the home front may have accounted for Clinton's lack of attentiveness. It was not general knowledge at the time, but during this period the McDougal-Clinton business partnership was not thriving. Despite outward appearances—Jim and Susan McDougal lived well among the *nouveau riche* in trendy West Little Rock, tooling around town in his Bentley or her Jaguar, enjoying the celebrity bestowed on them by Susan's winsome television commercials on behalf of a new real estate venture, Maple Creek Farms—Madison Guaranty and its various offshoots were stumbling. Thrift regulators were breathing down McDougal's neck for his management practices at Madison Guaranty, practices that would force McDougal out of the thrift's management in 1986.

Clinton's relations with the legislature, like his dealings with the news media, were inconstant, and the longer he was in office, the more erratic those relations became. Some of this was due to the length of his tenure as governor. The longer he stayed, the more power he accrued, and the less hope veteran lawmakers had of working with a rookie governor over whom they could wield the upper hand.

At various times, lawmakers toiled loyally for Clinton, only to turn on him at the first sign of some real or imagined slight: patronage not dispensed, a reception not attended, a bill not enthusiastically handled by his liaisons. During the 1985 legislative session, resentment over Clinton's growing power and lessening dependence on the barons of the legislature blossomed and lawmakers sought to put him in his place in sometimes petty ways. Each time Clinton caved on an issue, they redoubled their attacks. As a result, during the 1980s the balance of the Arkansas government slowly tilted toward the legislative branch.

For instance, for more than twenty years the Arkansas House of Representatives had given preferential treatment to administration bills. The governor could not directly introduce legislation, but he could sanction its introduction, and bills bearing his stamp of approval were always considered before any others. This role gave the governor and his floor leaders leverage other legislators did not have. Early in the 1985 session, the House changed the rule, ostensibly because voters had just approved the amendment extending the governor's term from two to four years beginning in 1986.

"We thought we needed to do this to strengthen our procedures, to put legislators on an equal footing with the governor,"[8] explained Representative Joseph K. Mahony II, a key player in the move, whose relationship with the governor had been strained ever since Roger had implicated Mahony's son in drug-related activity.

Mahony was not the only one whose relations with Clinton were strained. Around the same time, northeast Arkansas legislators were blasting the governor about his next appointment to the Arkansas Highway Commission.

Billy Blythe, age 4.
Arkansas Democrat-Gazette

Young Billy Blythe donned his favorite clothes—cowboy boots, neckerchief, and hat—for a ride on a pony in this undated photograph, taken near his childhood home of Hope, Arkansas. *Reuters/Bettmann*

Billy Clinton, his mother Virginia, and his half-brother Roger in a 1959 family portrait minus the man of the house, Roger M. Clinton. *Reuters/Bettmann*

As a chubby teenager, Bill Clinton found a means of "channeling my sensitivity"—playing tenor saxophone. *AP/Wide World Photos*

Attorney General Bill Clinton. *AP/Wide World Photos*

Bill Clinton's momentous meeting with President John F. Kennedy in August, 1963 fueled the 16-year-old's desire to enter politics. *Reuters/Bettmann*

When Senator George McGovern, pictured center, was campaigning for the Democratic presidential nomination, he made a whistlestop in Little Rock in June, 1972, and was met at Adams Field by his Arkansas field representative, Bill Clinton, and Joe Purcell, chairman of the Democratic party in Arkansas. *AP/Wide World Photos*

James B. McDougal, who in 1978 persuaded Bill Clinton and Hillary Rodham to go into business with him and his wife Susan in a land development deal known as Whitewater Estates. *Arkansas Democrat-Gazette*

Whitewater Estates, 230 scenic and unsalable acres along the White River in Madison County. *Arkansas Democrat-Gazette*

The Arkansas Governor's Mansion, home to the state's chief executives since 1950 and one of numerous perquisites that cost taxpayers more then $800,000 a year toward the end of Clinton's 12th and final year as governor. *Arkansas Democrat-Gazette*

Arkansas Chief Justice Carleton Harris administered the oath of office to Bill Clinton, the 40th governor of Arkansas, whose wife, Hillary Rodham, held the Bible on which he placed his left hand. *Reuters/Bettmann*

The author, foreground, accompanies Peggy O'Neal and her boss on a tour of the state purchasing office on 1979. During his first term, Clinton made numerous walk-through tours of state offices, usually accompanied by members of the press. *Arkansas Democrat-Gazette*

John R. Starr, managing editor of the *Arkansas Democrat*, whom Clinton blamed for his re-election defeat in 1980. *Author's Collection*

Arkansas' first family shortly after Chelsea Victoria Clinton's birth in February, 1980. *Reuters/Bettmann*

Betsey Wright, who masterminded Bill Clinton's 1982 comeback. *Arkansas Democrat-Gazette*

Attorney General Steve Clark and the governor were still on friendly terms in 1982. Eight years later, scandal would force Clark out of the Democratic primary for governor against Clinton, out of office, and out of politics. *Arkansas Democrat-Gazette*

Roger Clinton and Virginia Kelley, trailed by her husband Dick, following Roger's testimony in connection with cocaine trafficking in Arkansas in 1985.
Hot Springs Sentinel-Record

Political differences were forgotten long enough for former Governors Orval E. Faubus, David Pryor, and Frank White to pose with the guest of honor at the 1984 Governor's Ball. *Arkansas Democrat-Gazette*

Congressman Tommy Robinson, left, and Sheffield Nelson, the two former Democrats who squared off in the 1990 Republican gubernatorial primary. *Arkansas Democrat-Gazette*

Dan Lasater, the Arkansas bond daddy who helped Roger Clinton pay off an $8,000 cocaine debt and was later convicted on federal drug charges. *Arkansas Democrat-Gazette*

Gennifer Flowers told reporters at a New York news conference that she and presidential candidate Bill Clinton had been lovers for 12 years. *Reuters/Bettmann*

Bill Clinton did not let the impending announcement of his presidential candidacy interfere with his morning jog. *Arkansas Democrat-Gazette*

William Jefferson Clinton, flanked by daughter Chelsea and wife Hillary, shortly after the oath to become the 42nd president of the United States. *Reuters/Bettmann*

It was one of the tougher decisions of Clinton's career as governor: David Solomon had completed his ten-year term on the powerful commission, and Clinton had to fill the vacancy by choosing between a close friend who had requested the appointment and a man to whom he had promised it.

Maurice Smith had been a key player in the Clinton organization since his part in the governorship race in 1982. During that campaign, he served as finance chairman and raised more than $1 million, at the time a record in an Arkansas governor's race. He had arranged a $50,000 loan for Clinton through the Bank of Cherry Valley, in which he was the majority stockholder, to help pay off Clinton's 1984 reelection campaign debt. A grizzled, gravel-voiced farmer, banker, and businessman, the unprepossessing Smith had already served one ten-year term on the Highway Commission, a semi-autonomous board that paid its members no salary and a tiny per diem expense, but whose members were rewarded with innumerable perquisites and formidable political influence deriving from their control of highway construction contracts in a rural state that never seemed to have enough good roads.

Smith's wealthy friend were numerous, so his selection as finance chair in the 1982 campaign—and all subsequent Clinton reelection campaigns—was one of the smartest decisions Clinton made. From a political standpoint, the smartest move had been hiring Betsey Wright to mastermind his comeback. Wright never asked for anything in return for her dedication and exhaustive work in Clinton's behalf, but Smith, one of a series of father figures in Clinton's life, was a product of the political patronage system. His first political job had been as an aide to Senator J. William Fulbright in 1942.

Not satisfied serving as the governor's executive secretary, probably the most important position in the Clinton administration, Smith wanted a less stressful job that would give him more time to accumulate wealth. Moreover, a job with the governor's staff carried less job security and less prestige than a gubernatorial appointment to a commission. If Clinton would name him to the Highway Commission, Smith reasoned, the interests of both men would be better served.

Clinton would have been more than happy to place a political strongman like Smith on the Highway Commission. Unfortunately, he was under extreme pressure from northeast Arkansas supporters to make good on a promise, dating back to the 1982 campaign, to appoint a longtime supporter named Dalton Farmer.

When the Arkansas Highway Commission was reorganized in 1952, the commission's rules stated that each of the five commissioners had to live in a different congressional district. After the 1960 census, Arkansas's congressional representation was cut from six to four, so governors could not follow this rule strictly. However, tradition and political considerations dictate that each of the four districts be represented by at least one member.

The First Congressional District had been without representation for several years when Clinton promised a commission appointment in return for support in the district's most populous county, Craighead. Supporters had waited patiently for two years. Their choice, the man to whom Clinton had promised the seat, was Dalton Farmer, a wealthy but unpretentious landowner from Jonesboro, a faithful contributor who had worked for Clinton since the 1976 attorney general's race. He had been promised the next Highway Commission appointment on at least five occasions by Clinton, and his friends knew he had invested many hours in preparing for the role. Never one to speak in his own behalf, Farmer had plenty of well-placed friends to do it for him. When, shortly after his third inauguration, it appeared likely that Clinton would renege on the commitment, those friends complained to a few select political reporters.

"For four years, there has been the understanding that what we were hoping for as a possible reward for our efforts was consideration for our man, Dalton Farmer, for possible appointment to the Highway Commission," state Senator Jerry Bookout of Jonesboro told me in late January 1985. "We never made a *deal*, but between friends, there are some things that are just understood."

Both Bookout and another friend, Dan L. Pierce, Clinton's 1984 campaign coordinator in Craighead County, missed no opportunity to say that Clinton was a man of honor who, despite loyalty to Maurice Smith, would do the right thing, but their optimism was laced with dire predictions of serious harm being done to Clinton's "credibility" if he capitulated to Smith. Farmer's supporters kept their semiprivate crusade going for about a week before issuing an ultimatum the weekend of January 26–27 when, privately, they told Clinton in no uncertain terms that he would lose Craighead County and much of northeast Arkansas for all time if he did not quickly appoint Farmer to the commission and publicly reaffirm his loyalty to his supporters in the region.

After an exhaustive round of telephone calls, during which Clinton reportedly bit his nails until his fingers bled, it became clearer that nothing could be done to placate his supporters in northeast Arkansas but to appoint Farmer to the post. Further visits with legislators just returned from their districts and a weekend break from the legislative session just begun finally persuaded Clinton that he had no choice but to appoint Farmer.

On Tuesday, January 29, Clinton called a news conference at which he announced Dalton Farmer's appointment to a ten-year term on the Arkansas Highway Commission, "thereby honoring a long-standing commitment to Northeast Arkansas, Craighead County, and Mr. Farmer,"[9] a commitment he admitted dated back to 1982.

"I want to emphasize," added a somber Clinton, "that this appointment is being made with the agreement of my executive secretary, Maurice Smith, who agreed to be considered for the position only after many legislators, road builders, and others concerned about our highway system strongly urged him to do so. When Mr. Smith realized that there was in fact a prior commitment, he agreed that I had to keep it."

Farmer, who said he had been told of Clinton's decision only the night before, was administered the oath of office on the spot.

From his Cross County home, where he was said to be nursing a mild case of the flu, Smith was gracious in defeat. He verified that he had asked Clinton to disregard his request for the appointment after he learned of Clinton's long-standing commitment to Farmer. However, Smith claimed he hadn't known about that commitment until two days before Clinton nominated Farmer, highly unlikely given that it was a hot topic of political gossip for a week and that Smith had been in Clinton's inner circle since the 1982 campaign.

"I know it was a tough decision," said Smith, who shortly thereafter would leave Clinton's staff, resulting in Betsey Wright's unfortunate elevation to chief of staff. "At the time I said I wanted it, I didn't even know he'd made that commitment to Craighead County."[10]

A few months after Smith's departure, Clinton repaid his loyalty by appointing him to a ten-year term on the University of Arkansas Board of Trustees. Unlike the constitutionally autonomous Highway Commission, a University of Arkansas board seat carried more prestige than power, but it gave Smith a berth until something better came along, which it did three years later. In December 1987, Henry C. Gray retired after fourteen years as executive director of the Arkansas Highway and Transportation Department, and with Clinton's blessing, Smith became Gray's successor. Smith retired in October 1993, at age seventy-two.

The resolution pleased Craighead County, but it "disappointed" the fledgling Rainbow Coalition of Arkansas, whose leadership promptly was promised by Clinton that the next vacancy would be filled by a black person.

Clinton, whose indecisiveness and lack of candor were by now taken for granted, revealed another foible during the 1985 legislative session: an unwillingness to accept responsibility for actions that would meet with public disapproval.

The Highway Commission had introduced legislation to increase the state's tax on gasoline and diesel fuel by a staggering 5 cents a gallon. Clinton, who had felt the full impact of the public's wrath over raising road taxes in 1980, tried in vain to persuade Highway Director Henry Gray to back off, but all Gray was willing to do was accept a 4-cent increase on gasoline and 2 cents on diesel. Clinton didn't mind the tax increase, he just did not want to be held responsible for it. He told highway officials that they would be on their own on this one.

While Clinton hemmed and hawed for the public's benefit, insisting that highway officials were being "greedy" by seeking far more money than was needed to finance an adequate highway construction and maintenance program, Gray and members of his Highway Commission lined up their votes. That was not a difficult thing to do given that the commission controlled not only the highway fund but also how and where it would be spent. Lawmakers who hoped to gain any

highway patronage for their district knew that they could not block
the Highway Commission's proposals, although it was understood that
they would have to go through the motions of protesting vehemently
the "strong-arm" tactics of Gray and the Highway Commission.

The strategy was simple: if the legislature adopted the tax legislation, Clinton would veto it, and then the legislature could override the
veto. This way it would look as though Clinton had fought for the
people and was unable to stop the powerful commissioners. After
Clinton's veto was overridden, the governor was gracious in "defeat."
He said he was more than willing to let the legislature take credit for
higher fuel prices.

"I won't be at the ribbon cuttings, they will," he said. "It'll be their
[road] program."[11]

The media were easily fooled, particularly when on the day of the
override vote, Clinton's legislative liaisons made a big production of
their efforts to torpedo the vote. Members of the House helped the
liaisons out by loudly invoking a House rule that limited the number of
gubernatorial lobbyists in the chamber and had them thrown out. By
the time journalists were persuaded by a few legitimate legislative
opponents of the tax that it had been a sham, the public's attention had
shifted to other things.

"I can't believe you bought it," one lawmaker said to me sometime
after I had written glowingly about Clinton's "tough" decision to veto
the tax bill. "I thought you of all people would realize what was going
on."

Arkansas Gazette columnist Ernest Dumas may not have been aware
of Clinton's strategy, but his analysis of the outcome was right on
target.

"No matter what office he seeks next year," Dumas wrote, "he is apt
to face a campaign that he has been responsible for more new taxes
than any previous governor. The veto of a tax that was popular in the
legislature will help blunt that kind of attack and make Clinton appear
to be anti-tax."[12]

Meanwhile, lurid headlines about Roger Clinton's drug activities
continued throughout the legislative session. While he had been
awaiting sentencing on federal drug charges, a federal grand jury

returned additional indictments in the government's ongoing investigation of drug trafficking in Arkansas. One of those indictments named Sam Anderson, Jr., a twenty-eight-year-old Hot Springs lawyer. Anderson was charged with two cocaine distribution counts and two conspiracy counts in connection with his dealings with Roger.

The indictment revealed that Roger had spent the winter of 1983–84 shuttling between Little Rock and New York, buying large quantities of cocaine for thousands of dollars and distributing them in Arkansas.

More information about the degree to which Roger had been involved in illegal activity came to light once Anderson came to trial in February. The governor's brother revealed during sometimes emotional testimony that he had been a cocaine user for at least five years, and a serious trafficker for at least two years, moving through airports with laughable ease with thousands of dollars's worth of high-grade cocaine tucked inside his clothing. His growing drug dependency had created a demand for more and more money with which to buy bigger quantities for his own use, and he had fallen so far behind in payments to his suppliers that they had cut him off, compelling him to look elsewhere for sources. At one point, he said, he believed himself and his family to be in mortal danger because someone stole from his convertible a stash of cocaine he was supposed to sell to Anderson.

"Maurice was in a panic when he found out [about the theft]," Roger testified. "He was receiving pressure [from suppliers in his native Colombia] and he made me feel that pressure."[13]

Maurice Rodriguez testified that he began extending credit to Roger "after I learned who his brother was."[14]

In desperation, Roger said, he turned to Dan Lasater, the wealthy owner of a Little Rock bond house who owned several racehorses stabled at Hot Springs's Oaklawn Park, where Roger had found work as a stable hand. He told Lasater that he was in deep trouble over debts to drug dealers and needed about $8,000 to clear the slate. Lasater, a longtime friend and supporter of Bill Clinton, immediately wrote Roger a check for $8,000. (Lasater would be indicted in October 1986 for conspiring to deliver cocaine. Roger Clinton, who would testify before the grand jury investigating Lasater's drug activities, would be mentioned only as an unindicted co-conspirator. "We're still very, very close," Roger told the *Arkansas Democrat* in January 1987, "and I spent the last three days with him before he went" to prison.)

Evidence presented during the trial, including tape recordings, revealed that Roger had been approached about using his influence with the governor to lift a ban on construction in Hot Springs in return for a share of any profits from new buildings. Despite the extent of his drug dependency, Roger apparently did not take the bait.

Anderson's trial sent rumbles through the Little Rock country club set and the legislature, as testimony revealed more well-known names: the daughter of a state senator, the owner of a thriving pool and spa business, the wife of a prominent dentist, a member of a noted southwest Arkansas family with extensive timber industry holdings. What most troubled the jet setters, however, was the involvement of Dan Lasater, whose subsequent indictment and trial would provide plenty of campaign ammunition for former Governor Frank White during the 1986 gubernatorial campaign.

"I guess I'm going to do Roger's time for him," Anderson groused after his conviction on three counts of drug trafficking.[15] He was sentenced to three years in the federal penitentiary and fined $6,000. The judge in both the Clinton and Anderson trials, former Democratic Congressman Oren Harris, had indicated that he would consider reducing Roger's sentence upon his completion of a drug treatment program at the Fort Worth penitentiary in October.

Roger's scandal, however, did not influence Bill Clinton's decision to seek a fourth term. He had to seek a fourth term, the first four-year term in the state's history, if he hoped to mount a campaign for the presidency in 1988. There was no evidence that Bill Clinton had been aware of his brother's drug habits or that he had interceded in any way in the investigation and prosecution of the case. Clinton's professed oblivion to his beloved half-brother's problem might have seemed less plausible had the public known that by mid–1984, Roger spent virtually every waking hour getting high or trying to get high, but videotaped evidence of that had been suppressed by the court. No one was inclined to try to hold the governor responsible for his brother's problems, particularly since the governor had insisted that Roger receive no special treatment. Opinion writers and news editors did not believe that Clinton's personal problems were a political issue, and the public generally concurred.

The only issue with which Clinton's initial reelection planning was concerned was teacher testing, which was scheduled to begin in March 1985. The controversy had drawn national attention to Arkansas's "education governor," who had been denounced by the National Education Association. The louder teachers protested about being used as a political football, the higher Clinton's standing in the polls. That caused Arkansas's senior senator, Dale Bumpers, some concern because rumors had been emanating from the Clinton camp for several months that Clinton planned to challenge him for the Senate seat in 1986. Such a race was never seriously considered by Clinton, but he let Bumpers fret until the morning of the Clinton reelection announcement.

Clinton did not seem overly concerned when speculation about his national ambitions accompanied his election to the chairmanship of the Southern Growth Policies Board in June—in an interview with an Atlanta newspaper reporter, he had conceded that "it would be fun" to run for president and that he had long considered the possibility—but he did move the date of his reelection announcement forward by several months.

"I cannot ask you to stay the course if I am willing to spend the rest of this term as governor running for some other office instead of trying to push Arkansas forward," Clinton said at his July 23 news conference. "To put it simply, I want to stay home to finish the job."

Associates believe he announced a full eight months before the filing period opened in part because he wanted to discourage opposition, which his announcement effectively did. Attorney General Steve Clark and Sheffield Nelson, the wealthy former *protégé* of utilities magnate Witt Stephens, both of whom had been making noises for quite some time about making the race for the Democratic nomination, opted out rather quickly after Clinton's decision was made public. One school of thought is that Nelson was given further incentive by a promise from Clinton to appoint him chairman of the prestigious Arkansas Industrial Development Commission, but Nelson denied this.

"I tried to get some other people to run against Clinton," said former Governor Orval E. Faubus, who mounted his third and last unsuccessful comeback effort in 1986. "I had lost faith in his ability as governor, and I got a lot of encouragement from rank-and-file [Democrats]. I had listened to all these discontented people who were afraid to speak out that I thought might vote for me in the privacy of the voting booths."[16]

Faubus said he entered the race because it became evident that Clinton "was going to get by without opposition, which would have made him even stronger as a political figure."[17]

"I considered the chances 90 percent against any possibility of success for myself, but I thought, well, you know, 'Go back to American history. Jackson took a chance and Columbus took a chance and Washington took a chance, so don't be a coward. Just go ahead and get in and see what you can do.' But I couldn't get financed. All those big shots that used to help finance me were in his corner tight as they could be."[18]

Faubus denied that he entered the race to punish Clinton for old grievances, among them his dismissal in 1983 as state director of veterans's affairs. Frank White had appointed Faubus to the post during his term as governor.

"He had a right to choose his own personnel," Faubus said of Clinton. "I wouldn't say I hold anything against him."[19]

According to Faubus, a past master at campaign strategy from the incumbent's position, "an early announcement is generally regarded as a power play to put pressure on prospective opponents and raise money."[20]

However, Clinton's national ambitious also played a part in his early entry to the 1986 campaign. Shortly after the announcement, he departed for the National Governors Association, where, as expected, he was elected to the vice chairmanship, which put him in line to chair the influential group and establish a national presence in 1987. It was a sweet achievement for Clinton, whose defeat in 1980 had cost him the chance to chair the Democratic Governors Association. Following his comeback, he had had to proceed slowly on his climb back to the top of the national political ladder lest he offend the folks back home. Having been reelected twice, he was feeling more confident about pursuing a leadership role among his fellow governors.

Clinton improved his reputation at the National Governors Association meeting in Boise, Idaho. At that convention, a fund-raising letter signed by President Ronald Reagan for the Republican Governors Association was released. The letter, designed to help generate support for GOP gubernatorial candidates by raising $5 million in contributions, claimed that the "lopsided Democratic majority in our statehouses"—at the time, thirty-four Democrats compared to sixteen Republicans—"is the most dangerous threat facing the conservative agenda."[21]

"During the past four years," the letter stated, "as our administration cut your federal taxes by 25 percent, many Democratic governors turned right around and increased state sales taxes and income taxes, wiping out the tax cut given to you by our administration. In contrast, our Republican governors have fought to hold the line on taxes and spending."[22]

Some Republican governors, of course, were as guilty as the Democrats in raising taxes, and Governor Richard Thornburgh of Pennsylvania, the Republican Governors Association chair, did not help matters any when he said the letter was "just politics."[23]

The controversy threatened to split the bipartisan National Governors Association unless someone acted to mediate the problem. Clinton quickly volunteered. He had a vested interest in that he was in line to be elected vice chairman, and his fellow Democrats were threatening to block Republican Lamar Alexander's election as chairman. Clinton did not want or need to be elected chairman if it meant enraging Republicans with whom he could form useful alliances.

After a couple of days of private negotiating which culminated in a sometimes heated three-hour debate between Democratic and Republican "negotiators," the controversy was resolved. Clinton modestly declined to accept all the credit, but he did not miss any opportunity to talk about his prominent role in the negotiations either.

He was one of about forty governors who attended the Boise conference, but he was one of only a handful whose comments were heard
each night on the evening news or quoted each day in the nation's
largest newspapers. National political reporters clustered around him
and the Arkansas reporters who had been dispatched to cover his
activities were frequently asked by colleagues to arrange introductions
to Clinton.

"Why are you so interested in Clinton?" I asked a colleague who
persistently asked me to arrange an interview for him with Clinton.

"Well, isn't he going to run for president someday?" the reporter
responded.

The trip to Boise was one of many for Clinton. He sought reelection in 1986 under the guise of wanting to "stay home and finish the
job," but he rarely stayed home for more than a few weeks at a time.
His trips outside the state increased dramatically after Boise. He was
often in demand as a speaker, and few invitations were declined. As a
result, he was often out of town and out of touch while controversy
raged at home. A case in point was the public furor that erupted shortly
after his return from Boise over a negotiated settlement in the "Grand
Gulf" controversy. While his beleaguered office staff was struggling to
handle hundreds of calls from irate utility customers, Clinton was
leading a thirteen-member delegation on a "trade mission" to the Far
East.

As a controversy, Grand Gulf—or Grand Gulp, as some wags
dubbed it—was more than a year in the making, although the actual
case was roughly eight years old when the Federal Energy Regulatory
Commission "resolved" the matter and sparked the controversy.

After years of administrative and legal maneuvering on the part of
the state, beginning when Clinton was attorney general, the FERC
ruled that Arkansas Power and Light Company should shoulder 36
percent of the 90 percent share its parent company, Middle South
Utilities, owned in a nuclear power plant being built near Port Gibson,
Mississippi, even though AP&L said that it did not need any of the
power that would be generated by the plant.

Arkansas Power and Light executives offered to pay 17 percent of
Grand Gulf's cost, but Clinton and Attorney General Steve Clark

rejected the offer. Moreover, the Clinton-appointed members of the Arkansas Public Service Commission let it be known that they were not inclined to permit AP&L to pass *any* of the costs onto its customers. AP&L countered by suing in federal court, charging that the state utility commission was trying to force it into bankruptcy and subsequent seizure by the state. AP&L was in an excellent position to prove its claim. Documents obtained from the Public Service Commission under the Arkansas Freedom of Information Act revealed that as early as March 12, 1984, the Public Service Commission's chief attorney had speculated about AP&L's financial problems and about how, in the event of the utility's bankruptcy, the state could "pick up AP&L at a bargain price and could presumably make a profit running the company."[24]

At that point, Clinton and Clark decided that the state might want to reopen negotiations. Arkansas Power and Light was amenable.

The terms of the settlement were hammered out behind closed doors by Attorney General Steve Clark, representatives of Arkansas Power and Light Company, big industrial power users, the governor's office, and the Public Service Commission. When it was all over, the principals had agreed that the utility's residential and small-business users would be assessed 80 percent of AP&L's cost share and AP&L would absorb the rest.

Clinton had no defense for the heavy increase that consumers and small businesses took in the settlement except to say that "it was the best deal Arkansas could get under the circumstances."[25] Estimates of the resulting increase in electricity rates ranged from 10 to 122 percent.

The explanation of how and why AP&L customers got stuck with 80 percent of the bill was complex, even convoluted, and thus not easily understood. Ratepayers did not care about understanding it anyway. All they cared about was that their monthly electricity bills would increase due to causes they could not control.

Clinton used his campaign fund to pay for a series of radio advertisements in which he bragged about having fought for eight years to keep Arkansans from paying any portion of the Grand Gulf power plant and blamed the federal government for the utility bill increase.

"The federal government has ruled that we in Arkansas have to pay for a large part of the Grand Gulf plant in Mississippi," Clinton said in the advertisements. "The federal courts have demanded that our rates be raised to pay for grand Gulf."[26]

The Clinton campaign also paid for thousands of letters of explanation that were sent to voters under Clinton's signature.

Betsey Wright assigned several members of the governor's staff to handle the scores of telephone calls received each day from irate ratepayers who believed the settlement was a sell-out, which, in effect, it was, since the state's wealthiest industries did not have to pay for Grand Gulf.

Shortly after Grand Gulf, Wright had a new telephone system installed in the governor's offices, one in which all incoming calls went through a distant central switchboard, because, she said, she couldn't stand to hear telephones ring.[27]

Grand Gulf did not hurt Clinton's fund-raising abilities. In November, what was apparently the largest fund-raising gala in Arkansas's history was held. At $500 a head, the event raised more than a half-million dollars, and unlike most of the galas, a majority of the ticket holders actually attended.

"Everybody who is anybody was there, except for the utility people," a lobbyist in attendance said afterward. "Clinton's not accepting any money from the utilities."[28] It would never do for Clinton to accept utility money for the 1986 campaign; he and the utilities, particularly Arkansas Power and Light, were supposed to be mad at each other.

For their part, utility executives were happy to save the cost of the tickets.

Frank White said he was giving serious consideration to attempting a comeback as a result of the Grand Gulf controversy. He talked a great deal about reopening the settlement and said that if he could not get Arkansas ratepayers a better deal, he would not hesitate to promote legislation to revoke Arkansas Power and Light's franchise.

Despite widespread anger over the inevitability of rising electricity costs, Grand Gulf was an impossible campaign issue, since few people understood the case well enough to explain its intricacies. Reporters, even those well versed in utility matters, complained that whenever they relayed a new development in the case, they had to spend three-fourths of the story explaining what Grand Gulf was. Still, White believed he had a good, emotional issue with which the public could identify. He changed his mind very quickly, however, once he stumbled upon an even more inflammatory issue: Dan Lasater.

White, who after his defeat had joined Stephens, Inc., then touted as the largest investment house off Wall Street, was tipped by local financiers to the Clinton administration's ties to Lasater and Company, the bond-dealing firm headed by Dan Lasater, who was under investigation for alleged cocaine trafficking and was likely to be indicted.

Under Arkansas's open-records law, it did not require much snooping on White's part to discover that Lasater and Company had done a great deal of business with the state. White claimed that the Clinton administration had favored Lasater's company with state bond business only because Lasater was a political supporter who had contributed heavily to previous Clinton campaigns. He bolstered his claim by pointing out that the Rose Law Firm, whose partners included Hillary Rodham Clinton, had received a large portion of the legal business connected with state bonds during Clinton's tenure as governor.

One of White's greatest strengths as a politician was that he knew a good issue when he saw one. One of his greatest weaknesses was his seeming inability to think before speaking. Once he got wound up, he was prone to exaggerate the issue and his knowledge of it. Such was the case with the Lasater–Clinton connection. In an interview in 1986, White claimed that Hillary's share of the Rose Law Firm profits from doing business with the state amounted to a cool half-million dollars.[29]

As it turned out, records on file with the state revealed that Rose Law Firm had received only about $155,000. The Clintons claimed, and it was logical to assume, that as one of many partners, Hillary's share of that $155,000 had been very small.

One can imagine what White could have done had he been aware of the extent of Hillary Clinton's involvement in Dan Lasater's business affairs. That information did not come to light until February 1994, just before the federal grand jury issued subpoenas to six White House aides and four current or former Treasury Department officials in the Clinton administration, which turned the controversy dubbed White-watergate into a full-blown scandal.

In examining the Clinton-Lasater relationship in early 1994, the *Chicago Tribune* discovered records of a little known lawsuit filed against Lasater in 1985 by former Illinois Governor Dan Walker on behalf of First American Savings and Loan Association, an Oak Brook, Illinois, thrift Walker headed.

The lawsuit alleged that Lasater and Company had cost First American at least $361,572 as a result of Treasury bond futures trades that had not been approved by First American. The action accused the Arkansas firm of committing mail, wire, and securities fraud by using First American funds for the unauthorized T-bond futures trades.

Before the case went to court, First American was seized by federal regulators. Walker eventually was convicted of bank fraud and perjury in connection with $1.4 million in federally insured deposits he had loaned to himself, but in the meantime regulators pursued First American's $3.3 million lawsuit against Lasater in an effort to recoup some of the failed savings and loan's losses.

The law firm to which the Federal Savings and Loan Insurance Corporation turned in pursuit of the lawsuit was Rose Law Firm. The case was assigned to two partners who often worked in tandem, Vincent Foster and Hillary Rodham Clinton. In 1987 Hillary negotiated a confidential settlement in the case in which Lasater, one-time contributor to her husband's political campaigns and former employer of her brother-in-law, Roger Clinton, paid the government $300,000 in return for dismissal of the $3.3 million lawsuit.

Clinton also turned the tables on White by claiming that White had favored Stephens, Inc. with the state's bond business during his two years as governor. Then Clinton pointed out that Stephens, Inc. had received a respectable amount of the state's bond business while he was governor and White was an executive with the firm.

The 1986 governor's race may have been the most negative campaign in the state's history. Both parties held primaries, but they were mere formalities. Everyone concerned knew who the nominees would be.

On the Republican ticket with White were Maurice "Footsie" Britt, retired director of the Small Business Administration in Arkansas and a World War II Medal of Honor winner who had served two terms as lieutenant governor under Winthrop Rockefeller; T. Wayne Lanier, a northwest Arkansas dentist and former chairman of the Arkansas Educational Television Commission; and Bobby K. Hayes, a flooring manufacturer who had once run for the United States Senate.

In the Democrat primary with Clinton were Orval Faubus and W. Dean Goldsby, the former executive director of the scandal-ridden Equal Opportunity Agency of Pulaski County.

The EOA controversy proved to critics that the Clinton administration in its second and third terms had been just as lax and wasteful as in its first term. In October 1985 reporters learned that the Economic Opportunity Agency of Pulaski County had misspent thousands of tax dollars.

Initially, it appeared that the EOA's problem was mere poor administration. The agency, one of nineteen tax-supported community action agencies in Arkansas, had received a federal grant of $104,992 to help the needy pay utility bills. At the end of the two-month program, it was learned, $9,922 of the money had been spent on administrative costs, but no payments had been made to the needy.[30] W. Dean Goldsby, the agency's executive director since 1971, pleaded a cash-flow problem.

Clinton was occasionally accused of pandering to the black community while governor, but perhaps his greatest sin in this regard was that he and his staff looked the other way while black leaders enriched themselves at the expense of the poor. No one challenged Goldsby's claim about a cash-flow problem in an agency that had received hundreds of thousands of dollars of state and federal grants to operate poverty programs in predominantly black neighborhoods.

When Goldsby promised to make good on the utility payments within two weeks, state officials said that would be fine. When Goldsby missed the new deadline and claimed that the EOA had never received the $104,992, the Clinton administration said nothing, but when reporters learned that the EOA was about to receive another grant of $609,009, the administration was forced into action.

Some action was necessary, because it was clear that the state could do absolutely nothing to stop the new grant because it had been approved before the current controversy had come to light. About the only thing the Clinton administration could do was hard-nose Goldsby and the EOA board of directors to account for the utility money, which it did by threatening legal action unless an accounting was quickly made.[31]

The EOA board, composed of both white and black community leaders who feared being held liable in any legal action, gave in first. When members ordered Goldsby to fire four of his top aides, he threatened to resign. They called his bluff. Goldsby was furious. He had run the antipoverty agency as his personal fief for more than fourteen years, always stonewalling state officials who questioned his methods of operation and often going over their heads to the governors for whom they worked to silence them. He didn't want things to change.

Black activists rallied to his defense, claiming that "the white male power structure" had defamed Goldsby in an attempt to impede economic progress in the black community.

"This is clearly just an attack on black males," declared Thelma Andrews, president of 100 Black Women, Inc., disregarding the fact that black males were in the majority on the EOA board. "We've seen it before and we'll see it again. Every time a black organization or individual rises above the economic burden placed on them by the white male power structure, then it's time to dismantle his base. This is nothing but black male castration."[32]

For his part, Goldsby admitted misspending about $125,000 in federal grant money, but he insisted that his action had been a mistake of the head and not of the heart.

The FBI and the Private Industry Council, another federal grant oversight committee, were not so sure. The FBI wanted to know what happened to the $125,000. The council wanted to know whether almost $1.5 million in Job Training Partnership Act funds it had granted the agency the year before had been properly spent.

Black members of the Arkansas legislature, which had been frustrated many times in the past in its attempts to scrutinize the EOA's spending practices, added their voices to the black community's protests of the alleged conspiracy against Goldsby, who was forced to resign. Meanwhile, reporters uncovered more evidence of the EOA's mismanagement and mishandling of tax money under Goldsby and more evidence of the Clinton administration's blindness to the transgressions. These included:

• The great Furnace Project, for which the Human Services Department handed over $15,000 to EOA to develop and market energy-saving devices. State auditors had declared the project a washout because no devices were either developed or marketed.
• The great Ninth Street Project, for which the Human Services Department had shelled out $57,500 so the EOA could purchase 51 percent of Gem Theater, Inc., and renovate Gem's only asset, a dilapidated movie theater in Little Rock. A private, not-for-profit offshoot of the EOA called the Economic Development Committee, Inc., already owned 50 percent of Gem Theater, Inc., at the time the EOA sought money with which to buy 51 percent.
• The great KEYCON Project, for which the state had awarded an initial $160,000 grant to allow the EOA to purchase a majority interest in KEYEOA Electronics, a for-profit corporation that sought to develop and market a computerized antitheft device for automobiles. A subsequent $37,000 grant allowed the EOA, through the Economic Development Committee, Inc., to purchase additional stock in KEYEOA Electronics. During these ventures, Goldsby was both president and chairman of the board of KEYEOA Electronics and director of the Economic Development Committee.

The Clinton administration had known about these boondoggles, but Goldsby and the EOA had continued to waste taxpayer funds until the news media began scrutinizing the utility grant money. In late October, it was reported that the EOA was $427,000 in debt, had $1,000 in cash on hand, and needed a state bailout to meet its $60,000 payroll.

When all Goldsby's efforts to bring pressure from black activists to bear upon the Clinton administration failed, he struck back by filing for the Democratic nomination for governor to compete against a sitting governor who owed much of his success to the black vote and a former governor who was the state's most notorious segregationist.

17

WHEELING AND DEALING

AS HE HAD IN 1980, Frank White officially entered the 1986 governor's race by paying his filing fee right before the filing period expired. His campaign fund was virtually nonexistent, and only the remnants of a political organization survived, but he still had a politician's ego. White wanted very much to defeat Clinton a second time if for no other reason than to prove his first victory had not been a fluke. Much like Clinton after their first match-up, White had never stopped running for the office.

"It'll be a tough primary," he said, "because you've got two guys in there"—Britt and Lanier—"who have been working for a long time. It will take $600,000 to $700,000 to run a halfway decent race, but in 1980 a lot of the TV [advertising] was to build my name recognition. My TV ads will be more to get my issues across."[1]

Britt and Lanier had been campaigning a full two months before White entered the race. Lanier, whose political involvement heretofore had been to give money to candidates, was an unknown factor. Britt was perceived by pundits to be a sentimental favorite who could win the nomination if White stayed out, and force a runoff if White jumped in.

The polls suggested something very different. Before the primary season had run its course, a survey conducted by David Martin of Area Marketing Research which presumed Clinton and White to be the nominees of their respective parties produced results that Martin said later were virtually the same as the actual results of the November general election.

"In the absence of a positive alternative, people made up their minds very, very early in the campaign," he said.[2]

Britt's reputation was impressive and impeccable. A member of the Arkansas Sports Hall of Fame, the former Razorback's football career had been cut short by World War II. He had lost an arm at Anzio and had become the first man to win the nation's three highest combat awards in one war. He had served four unblemished years as Winthrop Rockefeller's lieutenant governor before retiring undefeated from elective politics, and that was his biggest problem: He had been too long out of Republican politics in a one-party state. His stunning third-place finish behind Lanier was for him a bitter defeat, but Republicans were philosophical about their rejection of him: By and large, they liked Footsie better, but they had felt compelled to support the man they thought had the best chance of defeating Bill Clinton, and that man was Frank White, who won the nomination without a runoff.

The other old salt in the gubernatorial sweepstakes, Orval Faubus, was not even regarded as a novelty. Despite his claim that his candidacy received a great deal of encouragement from rank-and-file Democrats, many of his friends, less ego-driven and more attuned to political realities, told him not to run.

"Many believed that Faubus was put into the primary to give the Stephens brothers two shots at unseating Clinton," says John R. Starr. "The Stephenses got a double benefit from a Faubus candidacy: If the old war horse couldn't beat Clinton, he could at least soften the governor up for White."[3]

The Stephenses, brothers Witt and Jack, had long held sway over Arkansas politics, although Witt was by far the more influential. It was he who built the financial empire into which he invited his younger brother, Jack.

Wilton R. "Witt" Stephens, then pushing eighty, was a yellow-dog Democrat, a grade-school drop-out, and a money-making genius. He had parlayed a talent for selling—belt buckles, Bibles, and costume jewelry in the hard-scrabble days of his youth—and an affinity for hard work into a multibillion-dollar oil, natural gas, and investments empire. He gave a little bit of money to Democratic candidates, raised a whole lot of money for them, and specialized in wooing and winning politicians to his corner by advising them in their usually lucrative investments.

Jackson T. "Jack" Stephens, sixteen years Witt's junior, was Witt's first *protégé*. He owed a fine education—he was former President Jimmy Carter's roommate at the United States Naval Academy—and his first break in business to Witt, and had proved himself more than worthy of Witt's confidence by adding considerably to the family fortune. He had become a Republican late in life through his friendship with Frank White and his marriage to a much younger woman whose social climbing included hosting parties, receptions, and fund-raisers for wealthy Republicans. Jack and his wife Mary Anne were behind several fund-raisers for White, but Clinton still managed to raise $4 for every $1 raised by White.

Witt Stephens had forged a political alliance with Faubus as early as 1954, and the Faubus-Stephens alliance would add considerably to the fortunes of both. Shortly after Faubus became governor in 1955, Stephens bought Arkansas-Louisiana Gas, a company that became Arkla, Inc., and Faubus persuaded the Public Service Commission to permit Arkla to charge the same price for gas from its own fields as it paid for gas from other producers. Witt Stephens backed Faubus in every subsequent campaign, although by 1986 Faubus's health and political influence were in rapid decline, making him no match for the younger Clinton. For his part, Jack Stephens was no help at all, as he had squandered his energy and a considerable amount of influence early in the year by flirting with a senatorial campaign against Dale Bumpers.

Once Clinton and White had disposed of their weak competitors, the mud-slinging began in earnest. Pundits quickly dubbed their third match-up "Rocky III." Clinton had three things going for him that

White did not: the support of the *Arkansas Gazette*, which invariably supported Democrats; the support of the *Arkansas Democrat*'s outspoken managing editor, John Starr, who was wary of White's pledge to "revisit" the new education standards and possibly delay their implementation until the economy improved; and Betsey Wright.

All White had in his corner was a two-fisted, hard-drinking, tough-talking political strategist who cut his eye teeth in the tumultuous atmosphere of Louisiana politics. Darrell Glascock had burst onto the Arkansas scene only two years before and had become something of a minor legend by masterminding the successful congressional campaign of the most volatile, most controversial politician in Arkansas, Pulaski County Sheriff Tommy F. Robinson.

Glascock always played to win, but he came to the White campaign after a bittersweet loss in which he had brought a little-known state senator to within four percentage points of defeating Representative Bill Alexander in the First District Democrat primary. Glascock did not intend to lose again. He signed on to the White campaign about a week after the primary.

"I think the style is what the candidate allows it to be," White replied when asked how he expected his campaign to be influenced by Glascock's rough-and-tumble style. "In all my campaigns, I've always had the final right of refusal."[4]

If White retained that right in the 1986 campaign, he failed to exercise it. When he failed to spark interest in three of his four predetermined campaign issues—creating jobs, reopening the Grand Gulf settlement, and easing up on education standards—he turned to the fourth one, the Clinton administration's relationship with Dan Lasater.

Midway through the general election campaign, Glascock enlisted the aid of former television newsman John Hudgens, who during the 1992 presidential campaign would claim that he had knowledge in 1986 of the affair Clinton allegedly was carrying on with Gennifer Flowers. If Hudgens made any reference to the alleged affair in his dealings with the news media during the White campaign, no one published the information.

Clinton, who never once fell behind White in the polls, used some interesting gambits to bolster his support. For instance, he suggested in interviews and in appearances at political rallies that this would be his last campaign for governor.

"I just can't conceive of any circumstances where I'll run again," he explained later, adding with a grin, "I didn't mean it to sound ominous. I meant it to sound nice. Twelve years is a long time to serve."[5]

He gave assurances that he had no intention of seeking another office in 1988, which would mark the halfway point of his first four-year term.

Clinton also permitted his political appointees to distribute campaign material in state offices, a violation of state campaign ethics laws. Clinton's campaign committee hosted a party for his fortieth birthday in August to which anyone willing to contribute at least $10 toward the campaign was welcome. Disgruntled state employees leaked the information that hundreds of invitations to the event had been distributed by supervisors within the offices of the Arkansas Departments of Health, Pollution Control and Ecology, and Finance and Administration.[6] Included with the invitations were order forms for birthday souvenirs such as buttons ($25), T-shirts ($50), and posters ($100).

"I don't think of it in terms of influencing my employees one way or the other," said Phyllis Garnett, director of Pollution Control and Ecology, when asked about her involvement in distributing campaign materials to state employees during office hours. "I simply said, 'This is available if you want it.' "[6]

There were no reports that supporters of Frank White were extended the same courtesy.

White tried to interest the local prosecutor in investigating the matter, but the prosecutor, a loyal Democrat named Chris Piazza, declined. Piazza conceded that the Arkansas Political Practices Act might have been violated, but he insisted that "justice would not be served by prosecuting these state employees and subjecting them to criminal liability." He assured the media that Betsey Wright had taken full responsibility for the infraction and would see that it never happened again. Which it did not, until two months later, in October, when it was reported that the state spent about $1,100 to mail twelve thousand copies of a four-page brochure, printed up by the National

Governors Association, which featured Clinton's comments about the problems facing the nation. Clinton's staff insisted that the mailing had nothing to do with the campaign.

While White was trying futilely to persuade Piazza to investigate Clinton, the governor was at one of his favorite luxury retreats, the exclusive enclave of South Carolina's Hilton Head Island, assuming the chairmanship of the National Governors Association. While awaiting his turn at the helm, he had been one of two co-chairs overseeing the formulation of Chairman Lamar Alexander's five-year plan for re-forming America's public schools, the issue that Clinton, who was then chairing the Education Commission of the States, had hoped to make his own. Since education was clearly identified with Alexander, Clinton sought to expand the issue's scope by also calling for reforms in welfare, public health, job creation, and economic enhancement.

Clinton surprised many by agreeing to debate White in a live, statewide television broadcast in mid-September, because incumbents rarely have anything to gain from some such an exchange. Both men were in top form for the occasion. About a dozen issues were discussed during the one-hour event, and while the studio audience had been instructed not to applaud, no one said anything about laughing. Some people, White and Clinton supporters alike, left the television that evening with tears in their eyes.

The following concerning court-ordered consolidation of three public school districts in Pulaski County was typical of the evening's repartee.

White: I went to Washington and fought forced [school] consolida-tion. I couldn't even find you. You didn't even ask the attorney general. You didn't want to say, "Steve, what do you think?" You didn't once say you opposed forced consolidation in Pulaski County schools.

Clinton: That's not true.

White: Well, it is, too.

Clinton: That's not true. I asked Steve Clark to go on that trip.

White: (interrupting) I asked Steve Clark to go.

Clinton: You ask him if I asked him.

White: Well, why don't you ask him?

Clinton: (Start of response inaudible due to audience laughter)—
White, you're crazy!

White: You call him and ask him who asked him!

Despite moderator Joe Quinn's best efforts, most of the "debate" was in this vein. White, never a match for Clinton's glib tongue, nonetheless succeeded in bringing out the worst in him. Clinton seemed incapable of keeping his remarks on a high plane when pitted against White. Nonetheless, Clinton emerged the clear winner when he foiled White's attempt to challenge him to take a drug test. At the time, Nancy Reagan's "Just say no" antidrug campaign was moving into high gear, and given Roger Clinton's previous cocaine addiction and widespread but unconfirmed rumors that Bill Clinton dabbled in illicit drugs, White thought his challenge would meet with resistance. Clinton turned the tables by announcing that he and his campaign manager, Betsey Wright, had voluntarily submitted themselves to drug tests and would make the results public.

The day after the debate, Roger Clinton, who had won parole in April, appeared before a federal grand jury in Little Rock to testify about his relationship with Dan Lasater, whose chauffeur had been indicted the week before on drug trafficking charges, and White renewed his attack on that front. Once again, he spoke out before he had his facts straight.

Calling Lasater Clinton's "biggest financial backer,"[7] White claimed that Lasater and Company had underwritten $649 million worth of Arkansas Development Finance Authority bonds.

"I think Dan Lasater had a very tight hold over the governor's office and is benefiting from it," he said.

Wooten Epes, the Clinton appointee in charge of ADFA, jumped to the governor's defense, countering that Lasater had underwritten only a portion of fourteen bond issues totaling $637.5 million.

"What [White] didn't say was that Stephens, Inc. has made more money from underwriting in the same time period," Epes added.

Campaign finance records indicated that Lasater was by no means Clinton's biggest financial backer, although he and some of his associates and employees had made a number of contributions to Clinton campaigns over the years. Clinton admitted that Lasater was "a substantial contributor and supporter" and had hosted perhaps one fund-raiser for him several years before.

The media's interest in the Lasater connection infuriated Hillary Clinton, who at one point interrupted her husband during an impromptu news conference to declare that "there have been no charges filed. The grand jury's still convened."[7] When a reporter reminded her that one person, Lasater's chauffeur, *had* been indicted, she shut up, but when the news conference was over, she marched over to reporters and demanded to know whether they intended to cross-examine other Democrats whose campaigns had benefited from Lasater's generosity. Then she launched into a lecture about the impropriety of publicizing active grand jury investigations.[8]

A week before the election, the grand jury returned federal indictments against Dan Lasater, former state Senator George Locke, and a number of Lasater's current and former colleagues. Roger, who again had cooperated, was named as the unindicted co-conspirator of a former division manager in the Education Department who was charged with conspiring to possess cocaine for distribution.

While seeking the governor's reaction to the indictments, a reporter asked Bill Clinton if he had ever used cocaine.

"No," Clinton replied. "I'm not sure I would know what it looks like if I saw it."[9]

The long-silent Lasater, stung by White's allegations, gave one more favor to the Clinton campaign three days before the November election: He revealed that Frank White had not only accepted a contribution from him in 1980 but claimed that White had solicited another contribution only two weeks before the indictment came down. Lasater produced the "dear supporter" form letter and the envelope in which he claimed to have received it.

White garnered most of the editorial criticism for his "dirty campaigning" in the 1986 campaign, but two veteran Clinton watchers took issue with postelection claims that Clinton had kept to a high standard of conduct.

"If Bill Clinton could be considered to have been on the high road, it would have to be in southeast Arkansas where everything is flat and a banked highway is known as Mount 65," Starr quipped.[10]

"Bill Clinton was Slick Willie more than ever in this campaign," the *Arkansas Gazette*'s John Brummett opined. "He took great advantage of the perceived meanness of Frank White. He would read a poll saying, 'These people are tired of negative campaigns,' and he was right there saying, 'I'm taking the high road. I think people are tired of this.' "[11]

Clinton was swept back into office with 63.9 percent of the vote.

"This election was a clear, unambiguous, and almost stunning mandate, but not for me," declared Clinton, who was not above hyperbolizing at such times. "It is a mandate for better schools, more jobs, and a better future for our state."[12]

In the afterglow of victory, Clinton joked with reporters that he was unsure what to do next because "there's never been a time in my career that I wasn't running for something."[13] No one within earshot believed a word of it. The four-year term had been tailor-made for a Clinton presidential bid.

Despite a late night, Clinton was up early Wednesday morning for an interview with NBC's "Today" show. The local news media were afforded only a photo opportunity. Two days later, Clinton appeared before a legislative committee bemoaning the hard work that lay ahead in the face of declining revenues and more demands for spending.

Within a week of his victory, *Newsweek* was touting Clinton as a potential presidential candidate in 1988. The report brought knowing smiles to the lips of his vast and still-growing campaign network, which even then was doing prep work for such a campaign.

Clinton truly had his work cut out for him in 1987. During the previous year, he had had to order cuts in state spending five times and a sixth cut seemed inevitable. A depressed economy coupled with the administration's profligacy meant not only that there were few funds available for new programs, but that revenues would keep falling. To complicate matters, the state's juvenile justice system had been declared unconstitutional, a wealth of delinquency and child neglect and abuse cases were going unheard or being dismissed, and the only immediate solution was to expand the court system, which, of course, required money.

Clinton was aware, too, that veteran lawmakers already were grumbling about the new political leverage the governor had over them now that he would not have to run for reelection in 1988 and he knew that some of them would be gunning for him come January and the regular session.

Despite the state's chronic fiscal woes and depressing revenue forecasts, Clinton had insisted throughout the campaign that no general tax increase would be necessary. On at least two occasions, he told audiences that he would not support any proposal for a general tax increase.[14]

Among the first statements Clinton made following his fourth swearing-in ceremony as governor was that the state's dire financial condition demanded additional revenues, which more than likely would require some increase in taxes. He assured lawmakers, however, that he was prepared "to stand up with you. . . . If you support a way out of the problems, I'll be glad to tell the world you did it."[15]

Stunned lawmakers, most of whom, unlike Clinton, would face reelection in two years, left the chamber less than pleased with what one wag called Clinton's pledge to fight to the last drop of their blood. Even his observation that this might be his "last trip to the lectern under these circumstances" did not cheer them.

Even people who would defend Clinton had difficulty at times explaining why a man who posed as the champion of the people persisted in promoting the enactment of legislation that hurt ordinary citizens and benefited special interests.

Clinton preferred raising taxes to cutting existing tax loopholes. In 1985 alone, studies showed, the state lost more than $300 million in revenues as a result of sales and use tax exemptions enjoyed by everyone from the Boy Scouts to Timex, and untold millions more in tax exemptions could not be identified. Instead of looking to these existing but untapped revenue sources, Clinton opted to increase existing taxes and fees, which usually were offset by the creation of still more tax exemptions.

The legislative session of 1987 was no exception. Contained within the 214-page outline of the legislative program Clinton presented to lawmakers a $200 million tax package—including new taxes on interstate telephone calls, cigarettes, advertising, catalog sales, and cable television service.

Prohibited by the Arkansas Constitution from deficit spending, Clinton devised a scheme whereby the state could raise a great deal of money in a short period of time. Included in it was a proposal to suspend the 2 percent "handling fee" retailers were permitted to take off the top of their gross sales tax collections in return for remitting the taxes well ahead of the quarterly deadline.

There was method to his madness in suspending the fee. The state's coffers were being depleted by sluggish tax collections and increased spending mandates. A great deal of money was needed if the Clinton administration was to keep all public schools functioning until the end of the school year in early June and avoid a deficit when the fiscal year ended on June 30. The governor proposed suspending the 2 percent retailers's fee through June 30, raising about $2.7 million of the anticipated $38 million shortfall. Another provision called for suspending state contributions to the Public Employees's Retirement Fund for two years.

Both proposals were met by intense opposition from special-interest groups, but Clinton, who was out of state, ostensibly on National Governors Association business, prevailed by interrupting his trip to Texas and Iowa to return home for some frantic late-night lobbying. Clinton's inattention resulted in some costly bungling, however. The retailers's fee proposal was enacted without the necessary emergency clause, which meant it could not take effect for ninety days after the legislature's adjournment; Clinton's efforts to reinstate the emergency clause only delayed the proposal further. The retirement proposal failed to win the necessary concurrence of the retirement system's trustees. Clinton had neglected to include the trustees in his planning and had not bothered to enlist their support beforehand.

Two chronic complaints legislators had about Clinton were that he could not be trusted to keep his word and that he was never prepared for legislative sessions.

One excellent example occurred during the week before he began his fourth term as governor, a period in which implementation of Clinton's 1983 education reforms would make the greatest demands on the state treasury. Following a lengthy discussion with the governor, Representative Lloyd George, who had been around long enough to know better, confidently advised the powerful Legislative Council that Clinton had endorsed the Public School Subcommittee's recommendation to budget $100 million more for the Public School Fund than Clinton had initially proposed. Before the council meeting had adjourned, Clinton called a news conference to deny that he had endorsed anything of the kind.

Two weeks into the session, George became concerned about Clinton's failure to address the shortfall in education funding. He managed to stymie House consideration of other appropriation bills until the Public School Fund appropriation bill had been acted upon. This gave him time to draft an amendment by which full funding would be restored to the Public School Fund. He had the amendment in hand several days later and was waiting for the House to convene for the day when Clinton slipped into the Joint Budget Committee meeting and proposed his own amendment for restoring the funds. The Clinton amendment was only $4 million shy of full funding, but it included more money for teachers's salaries.

"The only reason he brought it up was to get ahead of me," George fumed, "and I resent it."[16]

Clinton managed to get his amendment out of committee, but the House, apprised of the governor's latest attempt at oneupsmanship, ignored the amendment later that day and adopted George's proposal instead.

Such tactics were commonplace. Lawmakers who served with him say Clinton could not help himself, that his competitiveness got the best of him even in the worst of situations.

The "education governor" sent mixed signals about education throughout the 1987 session, one day calling for fully funding the new standards, the next day recommending additional cuts in existing programs. By the end of January, the Public School Fund's appropriation for the remainder of the fiscal year had been slashed by a remarkable $75 million and some districts doubted that they would receive enough of the promised state aid to complete the school year. Any district that failed to keep its schools open through the end of the term also would fail to meet the new school standards. It was a frustrating time for both educators and legislators.

On numerous occasions, Clinton convened special legislative sessions, always announced several weeks in advance, only to keep lawmakers waiting for three or four days before his formal proposals began trickling in. Regular sessions always began with a detailed outline of what he intended to propose, but sometimes the sixty-day session would be more than half over before the most significant pieces of legislation were introduced. Clinton's tardiness often resulted in costly delays as the legislation was drawn and amended and redrawn to make it politically palatable to lawmakers.

The 1987 session was no different. The administration had been so caught up in addressing the current round of financial problems that the governor's proposals for the next two fiscal years beginning July were not introduced until late February. Part of that was due to Clinton's chronic absences, prompted this time by his chairmanship of the National Governors Association.

"I'm starting to get concerned," one of the governor's best allies, Senator Allen Gordon, complained in mid-February. "We're halfway through the session and only 10 percent of the work is done."[17]

It surprised no one that forty days into the session some of Clinton's bill had not been drafted, and others were still without legislative sponsors. Each day seemed to bring a new round of criticism from lawmakers who were upset because the governor's proposals were late in coming, or came to them poorly drafted and requiring extensive rewrites, and because Clinton was often out of town when he should have been in the office. Because of his frequent and lengthy absences, Clinton spent much valuable lobbying time persuading friendly lawmakers to postpone action on the few pieces of legislation he had produced. Many times, they were unable to do so.

In February alone, for example, in addition to speeches in Texas and Iowa, Clinton made two trips to Washington. Aides requested, then demanded, that the press not trumpet Clinton's departures. The media were not sympathetic, particularly when the governor's office gave them no advance warning so that they could make plans to accompany him or arrange for correspondent coverage.

Representatives of two of the state's largest media outlets, news director Bob Steel of KARK-TV and news director Neal Gladner of the Arkansas Radio Network, took their complaints directly to Clinton, who in their presence ordered Betsey Wright to quit obstructing news coverage.

Immediately after the meeting, Wright and the two men exchanged words outside the governor's office.

In an attempt to explain or defend her previous actions, Wright reminded Steel that one of the reporters who had inquired about Clinton's recent travel plans had had his telephone call returned.

"Yes, but you didn't give him the information he wanted," Steel replied.

"From now on then, I just won't return his phone calls," Wright retorted.[18]

A month later, the Clinton administration's relationship with the state's news media hit an all-time low. The legislative session, which had been scheduled to adjourn March 12, was already in the second week of a fifteen-day extension because lawmakers had approved less than one-third of the administration's $140 million "revenue enhancement" package for the next two years, and Clinton was becoming alarmed at the legislature's continued resistance. He was already at loggerheads with numerous special interests—the AFL-CIO over proposed changes in workers's compensation laws, the Arkansas Education Association over teacher testing, retailers over the 2 percent collection fee—and the last thing he wanted or needed was a fight with the news media, but in the end he made what he called "the hard decision" to battle the press in return for a tax increase.

The linchpin of Clinton's tax package was an overhaul of the state's income tax code to bring it into close conformity with the federal tax code, which he hoped would generate $36.8 million a year in new revenue from middle- and upper-class Arkansans. When lawmakers balked on the grounds that his proposal would drastically increase the tax burden on middle- and low-income Arkansans, he threw his support to a revised version of the proposal introduced as House Bill 2003. HB 2003 cut new revenue projects by more than $15 million, but it offered something to lawmakers that Clinton's proposal did not—political palatability. Since, by that point, Clinton had decided to cut this tax increase request by about $80 million, and lawmakers were growing more tired and more irritable as the session dragged on, he was anxious to pass something, anything, that would salvage his program.

But HB 2003 contained what was to journalists a serious flaw: It sealed all tax records maintained by the state.

Income tax records have never been public under Arkansas law, but records of other taxes and fees collected by the state—severance taxes, motor fuels taxes, excise taxes, and the like—were at that time available to any citizen who requested them. Co-sponsors Richard Barclay and Lonnie Clark, two House members from northwest Arkansas who in private life were accountants representing a number of corporate interests, included a provision in their tax bill that would close everything.

Clinton had given his word before the start of the 1987 session that with two previously agreed upon exceptions—personnel evaluation records and the working papers of legislative auditors—he would not support any proposal that interfered with public access to information. When HB 2003 was introduced and the closure provision discovered, Clinton denounced the "sleazy" closure provision and reassured journalists that he would "take care of it."[19] Less than a week after that reassurance was given to representatives of the Society of Professional Journalists, the Arkansas Press Women's Association, and the Arkansas Press Association, Clinton's legislative lobbyists were turned out in force to promote passage of HB 2003 with the closure provision intact.

"We should know better by now," fumed Carol Griffee, a seasoned Arkansas newspaper journalist who at the time was regional director of the Society of Professional Journalists's Freedom of Information Committee. "I wonder how many times it takes betrayal by the governor for the press to get the message that he's anti-open government."[20]

In his years in government, Clinton had earned a well-deserved reputation for paying lip service to open government. On the advice of his chief counsel, several boards and commissions, among them the Board of Education and the Public Service Commission, had attempted to ignore open-meetings, open-records provisions of the

Arkansas Freedom of Information Act. Other boards and commissions had begun following their lead after Clinton dismissed a state attorney general's opinion as "one man's opinion." Before that time, the legal interpretations of state laws by the attorney general were treated by state officials as the final word in any dispute. Once the governor, himself a former attorney general, downplayed their significance, opinions with which state officials took issue were no longer given much weight by those officials, forcing members of the public to seek satisfaction through costly, time-consuming litigation or abandon their efforts to force compliance with state laws.

Journalists were still smarting from having agreed to negotiate with the administration over access to personnel evaluation records—education leaders had insisted that if teachers were to be tested and their classroom performance evaluated under the terms of Clinton's 1983 education reform package, those results ought at least to remain confidential—when Clinton broke his promise to take care of the objectionable language in HB 2003. His relationship with several journalists was irrevocably broken when he delivered what one called "a sucker punch" by doublecrossing them.

Not content to sit back and let Clinton "take care" of the matter on his own, the journalists sought to help things along by taking their concerns to sympathetic legislators. It worked. During a Monday morning meeting, Senator B.D. "Doug" Brandon of Little Rock convinced the Senate Revenue and Taxation Committee to strike the offensive language. Journalists were still grinning when the Senate convened later that day. They sobered up rather quickly when a couple of them overheard Clinton's legislative liaisons instructing senators to strike the Brandon amendment.[21] A majority of the Senate was happy to comply.

In defense of his unexpected reversal, Clinton told angry journalists that the passage of HB 2003 had been jeopardized by the Brandon amendment because both houses must concur in any amendments to a bill and time was running out on the session. He was fearful of delay because, he said, the state needed the revenue from the income tax bill. He disregarded journalists's protestations that their friends in the Senate and in the House could expedite the process by suspending the rule and that Clinton could expedite the amended bill if he would stand up for it.

The provision that removed public access to all tax records maintained by the state was far worse than it appeared at first glance. Not only did it make it illegal for state tax officials to release any type of tax information to anyone, including members of the legislature, it also made it illegal for anyone, including legislators, to *request* any type of tax information from state tax officials. A simple request was punishable by a maximum $1,000 fine and a year in jail, as was failure to report such requests to the proper authorities. Clinton ignored all the protests from the press.

Several days passed before Clinton's real motive became clear. Senator Knox Nelson, undoubtedly by then the most powerful member of the Arkansas General Assembly, had been causing Clinton grief for most of the session, in part because he wanted concessions that Clinton had not granted, and in part because he could do so and get away with it. Nelson then chaired or co-chaired the most powerful committees in the Senate, and those he did not chair he controlled through weaker members. He could block legislation, even kill it, seemingly at will, and of late he had been successfully engineering some costly assaults on Clinton's revenue bills.

As the 1987 session neared the end of its third month, it became evident to Clinton that he badly needed Nelson in his corner if any remnant of his program were to survive. Nelson wanted tax records closed; he owned an oil company that received thousands of dollars each year in "shrinkage" allowances. By law, distributors were permitted to keep 3 percent of motor tax revenues collected as compensation for estimated losses due to fuel evaporation. Nelson claimed, rather nonsensically, that this information could be used by his competitors to determine his profits, thereby putting him at a competitive disadvantage. He was still angry at journalists for disclosing the year before that his oil company had been doing a great deal of business with state government. He was willing to seal tax records to hide the information about the shrinkage allowance and to punish journalists for prying into his business affairs.

Clinton had another reason for mending the rift with Nelson: So much damage had been done to his tax package that despite his campaign pledge, he had decided to seek a quarter-cent increase in the state sales tax, which would raise about $44.5 million in the first year.

The legislature, sensing Clinton's weakened position, had begun attacking virtually every remaining proposal in his tax package. Not content merely to kill some of the legislation, lawmakers were stripping provisions from the bills and then killing them. Some of this Clinton brought on himself. While committees were testing the waters for signs of blood, Clinton had made few of his customary appearances in the halls of the Capitol to fight for any of the legislation. He had been content to sit back and accuse the legislature of standing in the way of progress, and his legislative sponsors were tired of fighting without the governor's help.

"He's running out of friends," a lawmaker conceded. "I don't know if he's just so consumed by running for president that he's lost his enthusiasm or if he's just used and abused people to the point that he's lost his ability to influence."[22]

Following a stormy exchange with journalists over his "sucker punch," Clinton tendered a peace offering: If they would just have patience and trust him, he said, he would see that the Brandon amendment to reopen tax records was placed on another bill. He kept that promise, and the amendment was duly attached to a bill that would exempt food stamps from the state sales tax. Nelson immediately tried to kill the food stamp bill by amending other pieces of legislation. There ensued an almost laughable cat-and-mouse game wherein journalist-lobbyists were kept running from one committee to another trying to keep up with Nelson's amendments. In the end, it was no contest. Nelson won.

Clinton finally was panicked when a House committee endorsed a bill to postpone implementing the new education standards for two years. On a Friday late in March, Clinton confirmed the rumors about another broken promise that had been circulating for days.

"I have been very concerned for the last week about the possibility that we might have to leave here without having funded the school standards and opening the door to some sort of weakening of our commitment," he told reporters in unveiling his "quarter-of-a-cent solution."[23]

Delaying the standards was not only, in Clinton's words, "a disastrous blow to our efforts to make Arkansas competitive in education," it was a disastrous blow for the Education Governor. Clinton sought to transfer the blame, and the heat, to the legislature in a taped radio spot that ran frequently throughout an entire weekend.

"I haven't been able to persuade the legislature to adopt my whole program," he said, "and now the [school] standards are in trouble." He asked Arkansans to help him preserve their children's future by embracing the proposed tax increase and urging their legislators to vote for it. The legislators, however, received more calls from people opposed to the tax increase than from people who wanted their taxes raised.

Clinton did not explain, and was not asked to explain, how allowing colleges and universities and vocational-education programs to share in the tax increase would contribute toward implementing higher standards of education in grades kindergarten through twelve.

At times, Clinton appeared totally lacking in diplomatic skills. This was one of those times. Having taped his radio message, Clinton did not spend the weekend lobbying lawmakers on behalf of the tax increase, he spent it in California, hobnobbing with the Hollywood crowd as the guest of television producer Norman Lear, one of his chief West Coast fund-raisers. Lawmakers were infuriated.

After a weekend of applying political pressure *in absentia* Clinton prepared to sell his proposal before a joint session of the legislature on Monday morning. When the sergeant-at-arms announced that he was waiting to enter the House chamber, Democrat Representative Tom Collier yelled, "Katie, bar the door!"

Clinton's reception was a cool one. When he commented that he felt like General U.S. Grant at Vicksburg, who may have been a no-account drunk but had stayed to get the job done, one lawmaker turned to his colleagues and pointed out that Grant had been not only a Yankee and a Republican but that he also had destroyed the South.[24]

"He'd have done better to compare himself to Stonewall Jackson," quipped a House employee standing nearby.

"I honestly don't think there's a single person in this chamber that will ever lose his or her seat for doing what had to be done in this difficult time," Clinton told members of the House and the Senate.

They didn't buy it. On the last day of the fifth longest regular legislative session in the state's history, the sales tax increase was defeated.

Journalists were not the only special-interest group with which Clinton broke faith in that session. As recompense for the encouragement the Rainbow Coalition had given W. Dean Goldsby's 1986 primary challenge, Clinton had promised the coalition's leaders that the next appointment to the Arkansas Highway Commission would go to a black person, but when the time came, he named a white man, L.W. "Bill" Clark, who for several years had faithfully served as his chief legislative liaison to the House of Representatives.

Through a twist of fate, Clinton was given a second chance two months after the Clark appointment when Dalton Farmer unexpectedly resigned, citing the need to pay more attention to his real estate investments.

Clinton awarded Farmer's seat to a black man, Rodney Slater, another faithful Clinton gubernatorial and campaign aide who hailed from southeast Arkansas. During the announcement of Slater's appointment, it was revealed that he had accepted a fortuitous offer to serve as director of governmental relations for Arkansas State University in Jonesboro. ASU's chief lobbyist, Don Tilton, was on hand for the joint announcement. With a lazy smile, Tilton told reporters that when ASU heard that Slater would be leaving the governor's staff to accept the highway appointment, officials immediately expressed an interest in hiring him. Wasn't that a happy coincidence? Certainly it was a fast one. Farmer had made his decision known only Friday. The formal resignation letter had reached Clinton's desk Monday morning. Slater's appointment was announced that afternoon.

"It proves one thing," a legislator quipped the next day. "Clinton can move fast [to fill vacancies] when he needs to."[25]

(Farmer dropped out of politics and was not heard from until ten months later when he committed suicide outside a Fulton, Mississippi, convenience store. He was fifty-two.)

Clinton emerged from the 1987 regular session with only about $54 million in new taxes, which was not enough to offset the projected shortfall. He put his staff to work on devising other tax-raising measures in anticipation of calling a special session in June and he hit the road again. Unfortunately, during one of his out-of-state trips, his second in command, Lieutenant Governor Winston Bryant, also was out of state, making the president *pro tempore* of the Senate, an irreverent, unpredictable legislative heavyweight named Nick Wilson, acting governor.

Wilson had caused Clinton almost as much grief as had Nelson, the only difference being that Wilson's colleagues were a little less indulgent of his whims than they were those of the more powerful Nelson. Before Clinton left town, he said he hoped Wilson would act responsibly in using his authority as acting governor.

"I hope Nick will come to the Capitol long enough to have his picture made sitting at my desk, then go home," Clinton said perhaps only half in jest.[26]

No such luck. Wilson's stock among lawmakers rose considerably when his first action was to order the governor's chief of staff, Betsey Wright, transferred to the Arkansas Transportation Commission, whose funding had been discontinued in the recent legislative session. Clinton quickly brought her back on staff upon his return, and while he was not pleased at this public embarrassment, he was philosophical about it, pointing out that this "was not the worst thing that could have happened" on Wilson's watch.[27]

Nonetheless, in the months ahead, while Clinton was making speeches to Democrats in New Hampshire and South Carolina and assorted other venues preparatory to launching his anticipated presidential bid, he always tried to make certain that the lieutenant governor had no concurrent travel plans. And except for one lapse in the spring of 1988, there were no slip-ups.

18

NO WAY TO RUN

THE ONLY COMPLAINT New Hampshire Democrats had about the thirty-two-minute speech presented to them at the end of April 1987 by the governor of Arkansas was that it was too long, although the new party chairman there observed that Bill Clinton had not been quite so warmly received as had Gary Hart several months before.

Hart, the dynamic, handsome former senator from Colorado, was by then the acknowledged front-runner for the Democratic presidential nomination. Clinton had not yet declared his intention to run, but an unofficial exploratory committee had been at work for several months, and Arkansas Democratic leaders were doing everything to advance the cause. For his part, Clinton claimed his mail was running 3-to-1 in favor of a presidential bid. Forgotten was his 1986 campaign promise that if reelected, he would serve out his term. Senator David Pryor lauded him as a potential candidate, and the Arkansas Democratic State Committee adopted a resolution urging him to run. At various times, members of the General Assembly put their support in writing, although the running joke among Clinton's legislative critics was that he was being encouraged to run because people wanted to get him permanently out of the state.

The applause from Clinton's enthusiastic reception in New Hampshire was still ringing in his ears when Hart was forced to withdraw as a presidential candidate after the press focused on his alleged affair with Donna Rice.

Unsubstantiated and unreported rumors about his own extramarital forays had dogged Clinton for years. Friends were fearful that unless he was ready to confront the issue publicly, his every private move would be stalked by the national news media, which was certain to be tipped to the rumors once he became a candidate. Some were uncertain he could withstand such scrutiny. Others were convinced he could not.

In any event, Clinton could not give his full attention to setting up a campaign. The state's funding crisis had continued unabated, and he had a special legislative session with which to contend, one during which he had to find a way for yet another near-immediate infusion of funds.

To meet long-range fiscal demands, Clinton came up with four proposals worth about $21 million in additional revenue, although only $7 million was to come from new taxes. In an effort to stave off a crisis at the end of the fiscal year, only four weeks away, he advanced a rather creative financial scheme that would result in a one-time revenue windfall. Critics described it as "cooking the books," but Clinton was quite pleased with the proposal, which called for accelerating sales tax collections, changing the priority rankings of some programs, allowing some end-of-year fund balances to be carried over into the next fiscal year, and shifting to the state's construction fund the debt owed to county jails for housing state prisoners for whom there was no room in the state's chronically overcrowded penitentiaries. He anticipated a $10 million windfall from enactment of these proposals.

It was a good session for tax proponents, a bad one for taxpayers, who would be paying higher personal property and franchise taxes about which they still had no right to know. An attempt to rescind the closure of all tax records except those pertaining to income had succeeded in the House of Representatives, but only one-third of the Senate had supported it. Clinton remained on the media's bad side because, despite his having made a personal appeal to legislators on behalf of the effort during the special session, journalists still blamed him for having broken his word to them and for having worked against their efforts to remove the closure language in the spring.

Having successfully pushed the governor around in the spring, the legislature was much more receptive to other proposals advanced in the special session. Except for the opening of tax records, he got virtually everything for which he asked.

"I'm voting for this bill because I don't want the governor calling me at 10:30 tonight," quipped Representative Richard Barclay after changing one nay vote on an administration bill to an aye.[1]

Clinton kept the public guessing about his campaign plans for a couple of months while Hart dropped out, jumped back in, then dropped out for good, but for all the encouragement he was receiving, some advisors suggested that he might want to sit this one out. John R. Starr had been a frequent critic of Clinton, but he had never had any reason to question Clinton's marital fidelity and saw no reason why the rumors should interfere with a Clinton candidacy. He changed his mind when Clinton confided that at least once he had been unfaithful to Hillary.

Nonetheless, Starr never learned the source of a rumor that Clinton bowed out because the *Democrat* was planning to run a front-page, Gary Hart-type *exposé* on him on the day he was scheduled to announce his plans. There was no truth to this, although a reporter for the *Arkansas Gazette* did call Starr to check it out. Starr, who usually had the details of any story critical of Clinton long before it made it into print, had no details about Clinton's infidelity. When Clinton had offered to provide them, Starr had refused to hear them.

"I didn't want to know," Starr said. "I'm just not nosy about other people's private affairs."[2]

Apparently the infidelity question was heavy on Clinton's mind. He had spoken at length with Gary Hart about the scrutiny being given to Hart's private life and the ensuing character questions. Max Brantley, an *Arkansas Gazette* editor and close friend whose wife had been Hillary's college roommate, later recalled sitting with Clinton at a softball game and listening while Clinton puzzled aloud: "Is there a point ever in a person's life, a political person's life, when the things you've done in the past are forgotten? There's nobody in the world who hasn't done things they weren't embarrassed about. Aren't you ever forgiven? Aren't they ever allowed to be in the past?"[3]

Loyalists insist that Clinton told the truth when he took himself out of the running: that his family must come first.

News of his withdrawal came in a brief prepared statement released to the press the day before his scheduled news conference. Apparently at the eleventh hour, his handlers had thought better of bringing reporters in from all over the country for an announcement that Clinton wouldn't enter the presidential race.

At the news conference, attended by about four hundred supporters and more than fifty journalists, Clinton appeared to be fairly at ease with his decision, and he became emotional only once, when he looked over the crowd and into his mother's eyes and, with tears welling in his eyes and his voice thick with passion, said that he had promised himself "a long, long time ago . . . if I was ever lucky enough to have a kid, my child would never grow up not knowing who her father was."[4]

"Our daughter is seven," he explained. "She is the most important person in the world to us, and our most important responsibility. In order to wage a winning campaign, both Hillary and I would have to leave her for long periods of time. That would not be good for her or for us."

"My head said go," Clinton said, "and my heart said, 'It isn't right for you now.' Deep down inside, I knew that it was not the right time for me."

Hillary, who had been insisting that she was ready for a presidential campaign, did an about-face at the news conference, claiming that she had not wanted to embark upon another campaign at this time. Others suspected, but only her closest friends knew for sure, that what she did not want was to face any public airing of the rumors about her husband's infidelity.

When asked privately the day before the news conference how she really felt about sitting this one out, Hillary told a friend, "I'm delighted. I'm real proud of him. Every bit of his political ability, instinct, and understanding said he could be successful, but he personally couldn't get his heart in it. We've been in fifteen contested races in thirteen years. When we got a four-year term, we thought we were looking forward for the first time to something like a normal life. He could never say, 'This is what I as a normal person want to do.' "[5]

Roger Clinton said he had mixed feelings about his half-brother's decision because "he would make a great president."[6] Asked whether his cocaine conviction would have had a negative effect on such a campaign, Roger said he did not believe so.

"I think it would have been a positive," he said. "It would have worked in our favor, as it did in the statewide campaign for governor, [because] people seem to rally behind you because they realize it is a problem, and it's a good feeling to know when somebody is really doing their best to overcome a problem."[7]

Roger, again pursuing a song-writing and singing career, boasted of having been drug-free for three years.

This was not the last the public would hear of Roger, or of Hillary, although she assumed a less prominent role in her husband's career. Instead, she pursued her own interests on behalf of children's issues and immersed herself in Rose Law Firm business. That business occasionally took her before state regulatory agencies whose administrators and regulatory boards had been appointed by her husband, but as the spouse of a constitutional officer, she was not required by state ethics laws to disclose any potential conflicts of interest. Her professional activities went practically unnoticed by the news media and, with the exception of her husband's ill-fated 1980 gubernatorial campaign, were never an issue in Arkansas politics.

"She worked almost full time for the state from '83 on to '87 on the side of the education program," Starr said. "Then in '87 she began to withdraw. And, of course, this was when Clinton's state administration began to fall apart.[8]

"I've always thought that there were three women who held him together during his reincarnation: [press secretary] Joan Roberts, now Joan Watkins, who always told him the truth and who told him the things he didn't want to hear; and Betsey Wright, who kept him getting up every morning and going to work and kept his attention focused on the day-to-day job of running state government because she was the chief of staff and that was in fact her job; and Hillary, who was, you know—when the wife elects to be an advisor, she's certainly the closest advisor that you can possibly have, because if you stay out to midnight making speeches, you're still side-by-side with her for the next eight hours."

But, as Starr pointed out, Joan Roberts left Clinton's staff after the 1986 campaign, and in 1987, with the education reform program in place, Hillary spent full time practicing law. Betsey Wright would leave sometime later under less than pleasant circumstances that she has never publicly discussed.

"Then," Starr opined, "[Clinton] was reduced to getting advice from people like Bruce Lindsey and Skip Rutherford and Bill Bowen and others who I would think had his interests less at heart than the three women I mentioned previously, any one of whom—well, I don't know about Hillary, but the other two would have died for him, as you well know. They were very, very strongly pro-Clinton."[9]

Starr suspects that the Gary Hart controversy prompted Clinton to drop out of the presidential campaign, and that around the same time he confessed his previous infidelity to his wife. If so, that might help explain her disappearance from the Arkansas political scene and the Clinton administration for the next couple of years.

Hillary was not, however, absent. Behind the scenes, she remained a dominant force in education for many months. United States District Judge Henry Woods appointed her chief counsel to a special citizens's committee charged with devising a settlement plan in the ongoing court battle over school desegregation in Pulaski County.

In 1982, the Little Rock School District had brought a lawsuit against two other school districts, North Little Rock and Pulaski County Special, in an attempt to force consolidation of the three into a single district as a means of achieving racial balance. Little Rock was then about 70 percent black, its financial base was eroding, the quality of education was in decline, and voters had steadfastly refused to grant millage increases to a district whose crime statistics were on the increase and whose student test scores were on the decline.

The lawsuit dragged on through court-appointed mediators and compliance monitors, teacher strikes, failed school property tax elections, new pupil assignment plans, growing racial unrest in the schools, decisions, appeals, and rehearings. Consolidation was ordered and then overturned. The lawyers were getting richer, the three districts were getting poorer, and public sentiment was running so loudly and strongly against Judge Henry Woods that some people began fearing for his life. Woods found the situation untenable. Nothing he did seemed to please anyone, least of all the appellate court. Woods felt like the most hated man in Arkansas, and for a time he was as far as central Arkansas residents were concerned.

"In a backhanded way," John R. Starr wrote on February 19, 1987, "Woods conceded victory to those who had abused him when he notified Pulaski County Special School District officials in a written memorandum that he would reject their pupil assignment plan because it had 'the violent opposition of a large segment of the patrons in the district.'

"Judges worthy of the name," Starr continued, "do not condition their decisions on public outcry, and Woods tried to deny that he had done so, but he exposed himself when he complained, 'My office has been flooded with mail and telephone calls in opposition to the proposed plan.' "

Finally, Woods threw up his hands and appointed a citizens' committee in an effort to resolve the matter. The committee consisted of Kenneth "Pat" Wilson, a Jacksonville banker, representing Pulaski County; Walter Smiley, president of Systematics, Inc., representing Little Rock; and Bob Russell, a North Little Rock business and civic leader.

"I worked closely with Hillary on the ironing out of what they call the school settlement," Starr said. "Judge Woods appointed her as the lawyer for this three-man committee that he put together. . . . Those three guys were as useless as tits on a boar, but Hillary kept them together. They were to promote voluntary consolidation. That didn't work, but then comes the settlement, which would take the state out of it, and Hillary really got busy then."[10]

Starr was one of a number of people with whom Hillary Clinton, and members of the committee, conferred in an effort to arrive at a settlement that would be palatable to patrons of the three districts and the community's leaders.

"I had very little contact with Hillary until Henry Woods made her counsel for the committee to straighten out the Little Rock school situation. . . . Hillary Clinton worked out that settlement," Starr said. "One thing [about] Hillary: When things changed, got altered, Hillary would call back and ask, 'Is this OK with you?' Bill Clinton did not do that. Hillary kept you up to date on the changing environment of whatever she was working on."[11]

She was, he insisted, "the prime mover and shaker in reaching that settlement, I'm sure. It seemed to me like when I talked to her and she came up with an idea and said, 'I'm going to go run this by them,' usually it was adopted."

Faced with serving out the four-year term, Clinton returned to business as usual: conducting a little state business here and there between out-of-state trips. The state business included another legislative session, this one in October, to resolve legal problems with the state's method of taxing large trucks arising from a United States Supreme Court decision in a Pennsylvania case. The session was unavoidable, but lawmakers were more than a little upset when Clinton went to Europe without issuing the formal proclamation necessary for lawmakers to reconvene as the General Assembly. Clinton returned home in time to issue the call one day before the session was due to start, but the matter was taken care of in such haste that lawmakers were not officially notified. Fortunately, they showed up anyway, receiving their copy of the proclamation when they walked into their respective chambers. As usual, there were numerous complaints about Clinton's haphazard approach to legislative sessions.

Clinton was outside the state almost as much as he was at home during 1987. The *Arkansas Democrat* reported that as of October 25, 1987, he had been gone from Arkansas on fifty of the ninety-six days since he had taken himself out of the presidential sweeps in July and he was vowing to make at least two annual trips to Europe and Asia in pursuit of foreign trade for the remainder of his term.

In one fourteen-week period, he took sixteen out-of-state trips, including one eight-day vacation in Hawaii. Cartoons such as the one depicting him as a wandering minstrel singing "On the Road Again" were common.

Legislative fatigue was his excuse for postponing a third special session until after the Christmas–New Year holidays, but his travel schedule had just as much to do with his decision.

The subject of drug use reared its head again in November following Supreme Court nominee Douglas H. Ginsburg's admission during Senate confirmation hearings that he had smoked marijuana. Reporters suddenly became interested in Clinton's drug history, if any.

"I'm still thinking through which personal questions a public figure should and shouldn't answer," Clinton said. "Even presidential candidates and Supreme Court justices should have some dividing line between public life and private past."[12]

He conceded that he probably would seek the presidency in 1992 if the Republicans should maintain their hold on the White House in the 1988 election. But right now, he said, his primary concern was tackling and solving the state's problems. He contended that the state had come a long way under his leadership but still had a long way to go. An Opinion Research Associates survey of 422 business executives, released in January 1988 by *Arkansas Business*, indicated that these business leaders gave the governor an overall grade between B– and C+ in education and a C in economic development. They suggested that, based on their hiring experiences, 37 percent of the current crop of high school graduates were no better prepared than they had been five years before, and 15 percent thought they were not as well prepared as they had been when Clinton began promoting higher educational standards in 1983.

One of the major obstacles to economic development in Arkansas, according to 67 percent of those surveyed, was the state's public schools. Once more, the Education Governor fumed over public criticism and complained that he had worked his heart out to move Arkansas forward despite the efforts of some special interests to thwart him at every turn because of their own selfish interests.

Clinton actually had two interchangeable phrases to describe how hard he worked for Arkansas. In public, he was apt to say, "I've been working my heart out." In private, it was his ass that he had been working off. If nothing else, he was usually careful not to offend

Southern Baptist sensibilities. When he was not, journalists usually cleaned up his language for him.

Clinton's language needed a lot of cleaning up during the January 1988 special session, convened to draft a new law governing ethics in government.

A year before, at the request of the legislature, Clinton had appointed a nineteen-member commission that had spent six months drafting a new code of ethics for public officials and a new lobbyist disclosure law. The result was an impressive, exhaustive piece of work when it hit Clinton's desk. By the time the legislature convened in special session on the morning of Tuesday, January 26, major portions of it already were history. Clinton's staff had trimmed, excised, and reworked entire sections in an attempt to strike a balance between what would pass legislative muster and what would satisfy the public.

The legislature did not want new ethics laws. Lawmakers had requested an opportunity to draft one because they wanted to forestall a citizens's petition drive to place on the general election ballot an ethics proposal in which they had had no say.

The document was distributed on Tuesday morning. Several hours later, Clinton hosted a luncheon for about thirty influential legislators at which he opened negotiations.

Creation of a permanent ethics commission was the biggest bone of contention. Lawmakers did not want one, but in the alternative, they were willing to consider creating one if commissioners were selected by congressional district, if Democrats and Republicans were represented on the panel, if state employees who lobbied the legislature also were required to report related expenditures, and if the spouses and children of public officials were excused from reporting gifts they received from lobbyists and special-interest groups.

With some exceptions, legislators and lobbyists were united in the assault on ethics reform, but most of the damage was done by a mere handful of members of the House and the Senate, which altogether attached forty-nine amendments to the ethics bill. Representative Joseph K. Mahony II, whose son had been subjected to some public embarrassment by his association with Roger Clinton, attacked the proposal with a scalpel. In the upper chamber, Senators Nick Wilson, Morril Harriman, and Wayne Dowd attacked it with a hatchet. In a late-night meeting with three prominent lobbyists, they concocted an alternative bill that was an ethics bill in name only. Asked by a reporter whether he intended to "eviscerate" the ethics legislation, Wilson smiled and said, "I don't like to use that word."[13] By the end of the two-week session, the death of the ethics legislation at the hands of the House, with Clinton's blessings, was nothing less than a mercy killing.

The effort to reform state ethics laws was doomed from the start. Veteran Senator Ben Allen, who happened to favor disclosure laws, revealed that before the session ever convened, a majority of the thirty-five-member Senate got together and decided they would block or gut any proposal brought before them. Several lawmakers hinted that they had been "advised" by senior senators to go along with the plan lest they find their own legislation blocked or gutted.

Lawmakers and lobbyists had valid political and professional reasons for opposing the proposed reforms in the state's disclosure laws, but their motivation was entirely personal. They went into the session suspicious of Clinton's motives, believing he was trying to advance his own political agenda at their expense. They were given to believe that he had been pressured into this reform by newspaper columnists and editorial writers, and they were hostile to their colleagues who would support the governor's "legislative bashing" in what was for many of them, but not Clinton, an election year. It was as good a time as any to teach their ambitious governor a lesson.

Except for the fact that he appeared to have lost all influence with the Arkansas Senate and a fair percentage of the House, Clinton was held virtually blameless by the public, which believed that the legislature was out of control and accountable to no one. Thus Clinton's pledge to put a comprehensive ethics bill before the voters in the form of an initiated act met with instant and widespread approval. The resulting document was far from comprehensive; local and county officials were not included, and it contained no disclosure requirements for the state's seven constitutional officers, among them the governor, or their spouses. Nonetheless, voters approved it in November.

In late 1993 and early 1994, as the Whitewater–Madison controversy began enveloping the Clinton White House, some journalists attempted to credit Hillary's former law partner, Webb Hubbell, with gutting the initiated proposal that became the state's Standards of Conduct and Disclosure Act for Lobbyists and State Officials. Some of the people who helped draft the initiated act, placed on the 1988 general election by virtue of a petition drive led by Clinton, say this is untrue.

"We really screwed it up," state Senator Jay Bradford conceded in a 1994 interview, "but we were doing our best to enact a good ethics law."[14]

Bradford, one of several lawmakers who worked with members of Clinton's staff and special-interest groups ranging from the American Association of Retired Persons to the League of Women Voters to draft the proposal that became law, said that Hubbell was not even a member of that group. Hubbell's involvement was as a member of an earlier blue-ribbon panel appointed by Clinton to draft the proposal which was reworked and gutted by the Arkansas Senate and then rejected by the House at Clinton's behest during a special legislative session in February 1988.

"It was the sausage factor," Bradford said with a grin, recalling the work that went into the Standards of Conduct and Disclosure Act for Lobbyists and State Officials. "We grabbed ethics laws from all around the country and threw them all together."

The result was a less than comprehensive law that applied only to lobbyists and public officials at the state level. No provisions were made for disclosure by associates or spouses of lobbyists and state officials, which meant that Hillary Clinton continued to practice law before state agencies under Clinton's control without having to make formal public disclosure of her activities.

Actually, the person who had the most influence over the language of the ethics law was activist Scott Trotter, director of a citizen's group called Lobby Watch. Trotter had worked in the first Clinton administration (in the Energy Department) but had left to dabble in the practice of law while pursuing his real love, consumer advocacy. As such, he became a chronic thorn in Clinton's side, speaking out against proposed utility rate increases and taking the side of the working stiff in consumer issues. Trotter rallied public support for "ethics legislation," and Clinton settled on the final draft of the 1988 proposal only after Trotter had signed off on it.

Clinton was in great demand as a speaker throughout most of 1988, so as usual, he spent an inordinate amount of time on the road. As a result, sometimes his best-laid plans went awry. Such was the case in April, when he left the state without checking first with Lieutenant Governor Winston Bryant, who also had travel plans. As president *pro tempore* of the Senate, Nick Wilson again became acting governor. "That son of a bitch," as Clinton was wont to call Wilson on the numerous occasions Wilson made mischief for him, promptly filled a vacancy on the Arkansas State University board of trustees that Clintonites in northeast Arkansas had been trying to get Clinton to fill for months. (A frequent complaint about Clinton was that he often left vacancies unfilled for months on end.)

Wilson had no reason to stop with the Arkansas State University appointment. He had friends, too, and there were plenty of vacancies on boards and commissions, so he made additional appointments, and there was nothing Clinton could do about it under the Arkansas Constitution. Clinton's anger over losing the ASU appointment was coupled with acute embarrassment when it was learned that both he and Wilson had filled a vacancy on the state Health Services Commission.

Clinton had made his appointment before leaving town, but he had neglected to inform the secretary of state of his action. When Wilson checked with the secretary of state to see which boards and commissions had outstanding vacancies, the Health Services Commission seat was still on the list. Wilson not only made his own appointment, he made sure that the new commissioner was sworn in promptly. Unaware of the conflict, Clinton's appointee was sworn in four days later.

Clinton gave his staff hell, although he had no one to blame but himself. He had not been out of state on state business, he had been completing plans for joining five of his fellow governors in endorsing the presidential candidacy of Massachusetts Governor Michael Dukakis.

Clinton had privately committed to the Dukakis campaign several months before but had not made a public commitment for what he later said were personal reasons.

"I went through the traumatic decision not to run myself—and I was gone for six or seven months doing that [running]. You know, you have an inevitable sort of letdown after that," Clinton said. "I knew then that what I had to do was to really throw myself into this job, focus on both the short-term objectives that I had [as governor] and . . . that I did not need any distractions."[15]

He knew, he confided to a reporter, that "there would be no limit, [that] if I got involved, I wouldn't be *able* to limit it. I'd be out there campaigning a lot, wondering—well, wondering, 'If I'm doing this, why didn't I run myself?' And I'd wind up with the worst of both worlds—I'd be gone all the time, yet it's not on my issues."[16]

That frustration, he said, was more than he had wanted to deal with for many months after taking himself out of the running. "I thought," he said, "I owed it to my job and to the people here and to my own peace of mind to try to stay out of it as long as I could."[17]

Clinton said he believed that other candidates rather appreciated his neutrality during the early months of the Dukakis campaign because a governor "is really sort of the titular head of the [state] party. With a lot of people who ask them to do something, they think they have to do it whether they agree with it or not."[18]

"When I go somewhere for Dukakis now, no one thinks, 'Clinton is doing that for himself because he came out early for Dukakis, [and] he's going to get something out of this.' Nobody will think that. I'll be far more effective helping the ticket in the general election because I wasn't . . . in the pecking order."[19]

Clinton did, of course, get something out of it—far more than he intended. Some people will never be convinced, particularly since for at least a brief period of time Clinton believed it, too, that Dukakis did not have a hand in what they insist was a calculated attempt to sabotage Clinton's political future.

Clinton campaigned hard for Dukakis in 1988 both before and after his embarrassing performance at the Democratic party's national nominating convention that summer. On several occasions, he was called on to respond to or intercede in Jesse Jackson's attempts to undermine Dukakis. He got caught using state resources to advance the Dukakis campaign: During business hours, he and members of his staff made numerous, costly out-of-state campaign and fund-raising calls from telephones in the governor's office. Clinton refused to provide reporters with proof that he had reimbursed the state, claiming the records were part of his "working papers" and as such were not subject to disclosure under Arkansas's Freedom of Information Act.

Clinton believed he deserved to play a major role at the convention, and Dukakis agreed, offering Clinton the plum assignment of making the nominating speech.

Confident of his ability as a public speaker and eager for the national exposure, Clinton readily accepted Dukakis's offer. It never occurred to him that anything might go wrong. With his keen memory and flair for speaking extemporaneously, Clinton was certain he could handle any potential problem.

Clinton's activity on behalf of the Dukakis campaign garnered a fair number of headlines, particularly since he was considered an excellent presidential prospect, and some insiders thought Clinton might be offered a position in President Dukakis's cabinet, most likely as secretary of education. Although no one who knew him well believed for a minute that Clinton would abandon what he called "the second best job in politics" to be another president's subordinate, reporters and opinion writers duly reported on the speculation and quoted other education leaders, such as Mary Hatwood Futrell, National Education Association president, who was personally fond of Clinton. She said that Clinton "certainly fits some of the requirements"[20] of a good secretary of education. Members of the Arkansas Education Association were less diplomatic.

"I don't think the son of a bitch should be appointed at all," AEA President Ed Bullington declared. "You can't trust him."[21]

"Look at his record in Arkansas," one teacher said. "It's not an admirable or enviable record. We have steadily declined—in salary, in working conditions, and, significantly, in morale. I don't think the record is there."[22]

Clinton promptly blew a fuse, this time in public.

"I don't think I want a cabinet position," he told a group of
reporters, "but I'm sick of this criticism. I'm sick of it for two reasons.
It ignores all the progress we've made in this state. They continue . . .
to get away with the claim that I play politics because of the teacher
test, as though it was fine to leave 2,800 illiterate teachers in the
classroom. I don't think they ought to be able to say that without ever
being challenged.

"Look at what I've tried to do," he said, his voice rising steadily. "If
my budget recommendations for education had been adopted in 1983
and 1987, teacher pay would have been over $2,000 higher than it is
now. I tried to raise more money.

"In 1983 I insisted that we spend 70 percent of state and local money
on teacher salaries. That was the first time ever to put a requirement on
local money. It took me one extra week of the special session to win
that fight, and I was virtually alone because the AEA was bent out of
shape over the test. They offered absolutely no help."[23]

He went on in that vein for several minutes, and every minute he
grew more agitated, citing the AEA's shortcomings and his numerous
accomplishments in education.

"They seem to be fixated on badmouthing everything and never
admitting any good," he said. "To try to put it all on me is just not
fair. I just wish they would take some pride and some joy in what's
happening."

Shortly before the Democratic National Convention in July, Clinton was persuaded by the Arkansas Bankers Association to convene a
fourth special legislative session; they were concerned that a federal
court ruling from Mississippi would adversely affect state-chartered
banks. As a result of that ruling, the federal comptroller of the currency
was expected to permit federally chartered banks to authorize expanded branch banking. Clinton's intent was to bring the legislature to
Little Rock for only three days, the minimum needed to enact a piece
of legislation, to legalize cross-county branch banking by state-
chartered banks so that state banks would not be placed at a competitive disadvantage.

The session lasted five days, but except for a minor ruckus created by
the news media when the House voted to ban all members of the news

media from the House chamber, the week went fairly smoothly. Clinton did not have to postpone his planned arrival in Atlanta.

Compared to his activities at the 1980 and 1984 Democratic conventions, Clinton maintained a low profile in Atlanta prior to the evening of his address. He spent a great deal of his time ensconced in his rooms at the Embassy Suites, working late into the night on the text of his speech. He emerged occasionally to grant an interview or to appear briefly at a reception, but for the most part he stayed in seclusion. At one point, he told a reporter that he was working on his thirteenth draft. The day of the speech, he faithfully reworked it to incorporate a few changes suggested by Dukakis and his advisors. The additions lengthened the text, but Clinton told friends that Dukakis wanted him to give the entire speech.

Clinton, who did not normally speak from a prepared text, preferring notecards on which he had scribbled his key points in his virtually indecipherable handwriting, wanted to give a brilliant, carefully paced speech that would build to a crescendo and maximize the rousing ovation that always accompanies the placement of a front-runner's name in nomination for the presidency.

He later claimed that he had meticulously timed each draft of the speech to last no longer than fifteen minutes. That's difficult to accept, given the nature of his remarks. The speech easily could have been read in fifteen minutes—a reporter read it later in sixteen minutes—but never *presented* in that length of time, even with no allowance for applause.

One Clinton biographer, Robert E. Levin, contended that "at the last minute, Dukakis's political advisors insisted that Clinton use the written text they had prepared for him,"[24] and that his unfamiliarity with the text and the use of TelePrompTers impaired his performance. Clinton made no such claims. In any event, he was familiar with TelePrompTers. This was his third speech to a national nominating convention. He knew the drill.

Arkansas reporters were handed copies of his speech an hour or so before he gave it so that they could get a head start on their news stories. We gave little thought to its length. We knew Clinton was a dynamic speaker with a good feel for cadence and the type of dramatic inflections that could energize the most lethargic crowd. We shared his confidence about his upcoming performance.

Shortly before he went backstage at the Omni convention center, Clinton grinned in anticipation, turned to me in the lobby, and asked, "What do you think?"

"Looks good to me," I replied. I had scanned the text and marked the catchphrases that seemed likeliest to arouse the audience. Obviously Clinton's question had been rhetorical. The speech had already been heard by the people whose opinion mattered to him, and they loved it.

The audience did not. As Clinton trundled into his speech, people in the Arkansas delegates's section, located at the back of the auditorium in front of the speaker's podium, began exchanging puzzled looks. The auditorium lights were up, the stage was brightly lit, but the crowd in the front rows showed no signs of settling down to listen. From their less than desirable vantage point, the Arkansans could see Dukakis's floor leaders walking among the delegates nearest the proscenium, and they assumed that the floor leaders were trying to calm the rowdy crowd. It seemed, however, that the noise level increased in the sections at which the floor leaders paused.

"Duke! Duke! Duke!"

"We want Mike!"

The chanting, sporadic at first, spread across the front lines of the convention floor, until Clinton was forced to interrupt his remarks and ask for quiet. I walked down to the front, where I observed two Dukakis whips, identifiable by the vests they wore, leading the chants of the Pennsylvania delegation.

"Duke! Duke! Duke!"

"We want Mike!"

In his obvious struggle to take command of the situation, Clinton's voice began to crack and take on a tinny, desperate quality. The raucous swell continued to build, and again he implored the crowd to listen, but each mention of Dukakis's name brought another clamorous round of chanting that the national television audience could not hear. All they saw was the anxiety and uncertainty on Clinton's face as he droned on and on. Finally, ABC and NBC cameras cut away from Clinton.

Those in charge of the proceedings began signaling for Clinton to wrap up the speech. Clinton kept talking. The TelePrompTer began flashing, "Your time is up," until finally someone shut it down. Clinton kept talking. For thirty-three minutes, his face growing redder by the minute, Clinton kept talking. His biggest ovation came when he said, "And in conclusion. . . ."

On the platform, Hillary Clinton radiated intense interest and pride, but she said later that she had never felt so helpless, knowing that Dukakis had wanted her husband to give the entire speech and that the entire speech was what her husband would give.[25]

State Auditor Julia Hughes Jones, who as a state official had won a superdelegate's spot to the convention, recalled returning that night to the hotel where the Arkansas delegation was housed and seeing a somber group of Clinton's supporters in the atrium bar.

"That night Virginia Kelley was obviously distraught. Betsey [Wright] and Hillary were even more so. Virginia asked what we thought, if he had ruined himself, and I said, 'Heavens, no!' I said, 'I'm really angry about this, because I think he got set up.' . . . I said, 'It's the first time I've ever seen Bill Clinton put aside his own political future for that of someone else's, and because of that I gained a lot more respect for him.' "[26]

Jones said she knew that Clinton "was doing what he was told to do."

"Dukakis liked the speech," she said. "They'd gone over it beforehand, and he didn't want [Clinton] to change a word of it. . . . I know this for a fact, because that's what Betsey told me. And it's been those many years ago, but I'll never forget that, because Dukakis wanted the whole speech given. . . . [Clinton] knew when he'd lost his audience, but he kept going because Dukakis said to, and it was his nomination. And Clinton was flattered that he was making the nomination for Dukakis, so he did as he was told, and got hung out to dry over it."

Jones believed that "probably Dukakis considered Bill Clinton a political threat" and did not want to be pressured into choosing Clinton as his running mate.

"There were other people in line to be a running mate, but Clinton and Dukakis went back a along way, so I believe that Dukakis wanted to eliminate Clinton as a potential running mate," she said.

That opinion is shared by many Arkansans who were there that evening and saw firsthand how the Dukakis floor leaders kept the demonstrations going.

"Nothing to worry about," a Clinton aide said the next morning. "It'll all blow over and be forgotten by tomorrow."[27]

Publicly, Clinton dismissed the entire episode as "just a comedy of errors."[28] "I blew it," he said. "What can I tell you?" Privately, Dukakis was the son of a bitch of the week.

Initially, the jibes from pundits and comedians, most notably Johnny Carson, infuriated Clinton, but a group of Hollywood Razorbacks— transplanted Arkansans who had found wealth and fame on the West Coast—rallied to save his national reputation. Carson agreed to invite Clinton to appear on "The Tonight Show," which he did eight days after the Atlanta debacle. Clinton turned on the charm, made himself the butt of jokes, and displayed a good-natured pragmatism. He had the studio audience and the host in the palm of his hand even before he took out his saxophone and joined Doc Severinsen and the band for what he quipped would be "a short number."

He and the Hollywood Razorbacks—Harry Thomason, Linda Bloodworth-Thomason, Gil Gerard, Mary Steenburgen, and others—had reason to celebrate his performance, which they did late into the night.

"On the mellow notes of his saxophone," John R. Starr wrote, "Bill 'The Phoenix' Clinton rose from the political ashes on national television Thursday night."[29]

The only negative consequences of that convention trip came a couple of weeks after his appearance, when it was learned that state funds had been used to pay the travel expenses of lawyer Bruce Lindsey, a longtime friend who had traveled extensively with the governor during his 1987 flirtation with the presidency.

His moment in the spotlight over, Clinton returned to Arkansas to lay the groundwork for his 1990 reelection campaign, and a subsequent 1992 bid for the presidency, which he continued to discuss with close friends and advisors around the country as polls showed Dukakis losing ground. He began work on his 1989 legislative package, which he promised would consist of "significant reforms and investments in some of our state's most important programs and institutions."[30]

"If we want to enhance our state's prosperity in the next century, we must lay the groundwork now."

The governor tried to keep his plans for hefty increases in taxes secret until after his staff had prepared a big public relations campaign, but leaks in late August revealed that Clinton would be angling for $160 million to $200 million in additional revenue in 1989.

The proposals Clinton outlined in a report that he begged lawmakers to keep private were the most ambitious tax-and-spend program of his career.

In the area of education, he wanted to raise teachers's salaries an average of $4,000 over a two-year period; implement a "report card" system for rating schools and teachers; raise the salaries of college and university faculty members and subject them to peer review; significantly increase funding for adult literacy programs; increase scholarship and financial aid programs; and create a prepayment program for college tuition through establishment of what Clinton called "an education IRA" and issuance of education savings bonds.

Under the heading of public health and welfare were included an expanded immunization program; establishment of a revolving grant and loan fund for day-care providers; increased child-care and preschool subsidies; increased child-care income tax credit; extended Medicaid coverage for pregnant women living below the poverty level; and increased welfare benefits.

His economic development plank included plans for increasing the funding of the state's European and Asian trade offices; new minority business development grants; and revision of state laws to make it more difficult to initiate hostile takeovers against Arkansas corporations.

In the area of tax reform, Clinton proposed granting tax credits on grocery purchases to low-income Arkansans; raising the minimum amount one had to earn before paying income tax; eliminating the personal property tax on household goods; and adopting a property tax "circuit breaker" to limit the amount of property tax imposed on low-income home owners whose property increased in value.

There were equally detailed proposals for prison expansion, substance abuse programs, elderly support services, and indigent health care.

In his brainstorming sessions with lawmakers, the governor assured them that he did not want to be "bound by omission."[31] If they had any other proposals, he was willing to consider them.

By the autumn of 1988, Clinton had already raised taxes more than any governor in Arkansas history. During the year he first became governor, 1979, the state's revenues were $777 million. During the 1988–89 fiscal year, revenues were projected to exceed $1.66 billion, yet the governor wanted an additional $200 million revenue increase. Critics wondered what he could do with $200 million that could not be done with a billion.

"Let me cite you some figures on the 'tax burden' being borne by Arkansans in the eighth year of the reign of Billion-Dollar Bill Clinton," John R. Starr wrote on September 10, 1988. "The figures compare Arkansas's tax effort, calculated on a percentage of per capita income, to the effort in the other forty-nine states.

"In property taxes, Arkansas is 45th. In state, city, and county taxes paid as a percentage of per capita income, Arkansas is 44th among the fifty states. In state taxes alone, Arkansas is 35th. In corporate income taxes, Arkansas is 21st. In sales taxes, Arkansas is 13th. . . . If the state ranks 44th in all taxes, it should rank no worse than 44th in any of the service categories. Instead, it ranks no better than 44th. In fact, in almost every category of services supported by taxes, Arkansas is 49th or 50th."

Most of the polls, save one extremely limited, unscientific survey by the Clinton-friendly *Arkansas Gazette* and one commissioned by the Clinton-friendly citizens's group called A-Plus Arkansas, screamed that Arkansans were in no mood to pay a penny more than they were contributing toward the state's nearly $3.5 billion two-year budget. Legislators didn't need a pollster to tell them that; their constituents were performing the service for free.

Unlike the 1983 education reform movement, for which Clinton had carefully built momentum at the grass-roots level by dispatching his wife and a blue-ribbon committee to all seventy-five counties to make the case for a 33 percent increase in the state gross receipts and sales tax, the single largest revenue source in government, the 1989 package had no such support. Telephone calls and letters to lawmakers and newspapers and radio talk show hosts were almost unanimously opposed to new taxes for education.

The state's median income was still near the bottom, with a full 20 percent of the population living below the national poverty line, yet the state was financing the governor and his family to the tune of almost $800,000 a year. Why, he spent in excess of $1,000 a week on food alone. And what about all those tax exemptions that had been granted through the years to businesses and industries and assorted special interests? A full $318 million was being lost to the state coffers each year as a result of exemptions, and that was just the amount that could be identified. In the past ten years, eight of them under a Clinton administration, the personal income of Arkansans had indeed increased 81.9 percent, but state spending had increased a stunning 111 percent. Taxpayers were convinced that any new money would be wasted or, worse, redirected, as it had been by Clinton following the 1983 tax increase, to purposes hidden and undeclared.

Many lawmakers were tired of Clinton's lies and fudges.

"We don't trust him," said a veteran Democrat in the House of Representatives. "He's shelf-worn. He's lied to us too often. We're tired of it and [of] him."[32]

Indeed, when Clinton conceded that he had not ruled out a fifth-term bid in 1990, some lawmakers, particularly House members who faced reelection every two years, were determined to give Clinton the most cantankerous legislative session of his career in hopes of discouraging him from running in 1990.

Clinton pulled out all the stops in promoting his multimillion-dollar package, christened "Moving Arkansas Forward Into the 21th Century," expending more than $2,000 on the reception and more than $16,000 in state funds on a slick booklet of "executive recommendations" that summarized a program of expansion, enhancement, and reform even more ambitious than the ill-fated catch-all agenda of his first term. Education, taxation, the environment, social and health programs, juvenile justice and economic development—nothing seemed to be omitted.

He gave radio audiences a pep talk about the program on the first Saturday night in October 1988. Then on Sunday morning, he summoned several hundred state employee "volunteers," state officials, and assorted lobbyists to the biggest Clinton dog-and-pony show of them all, with exhibits and assorted "informational" fliers, at a local hotel ballroom, where reporters were regaled by Clinton allies for an hour or so with recitations about Clinton's vision for the future before the governor finally took the stage. For fifty-seven exhausting minutes— the ballroom was too crowded for sitting, even if chairs had been available—Clinton acted as the head cheerleader at his own rally.

"It's a little like going to heaven," Senator Stanley Russ quipped when asked to assess early legislative reaction to Clinton's ambitious proposals. "Everybody wants to go to heaven, but nobody wants to die."

The governor had no details about how he planned to finance his program, and only seven minutes of his speech were devoted to his plans for reducing the tax burden on low-income families. He spent far longer exhorting the cabinet heads, state employees, members of boards and commissions, legislators, and lobbyists in the audience to take his ambitious program, study it, and then sell it to the people.

"When you walk out of here," he said, "don't tell [Arkansans] it's my program. Tell them it's yours."

Critics observed that it was little wonder that Clinton wanted no credit for what was at that point a $198.8 million package—it would grow to $211.5 million by the start of the legislative session in January—because its passage, if such was possible, would include the largest tax increase in the state's history.

19

MORTGAGING THE PROMISED LAND

CLINTON VOWED to "stump the state" for the next three months in an effort to rouse grass-roots support for his package, whose adoption was to provide the impetus for his 1990 reelection campaign. Mostly what he did was leave Arkansas and stump other states on behalf of the faltering Dukakis campaign. Those members of his Arkansas political network who were not doing likewise were busy getting the governor's 1990 campaign fund-raising ball going.

Clinton did make a few forays into the chicken-and-peas circuit, speaking primarily to hand-picked, sympathetic audiences, but generally he concentrated on wheeling and dealing, bartering with a few key lawmakers whose proposals did not yet have his support and the concomitant stamp of approval that permits legislation to be introduced as an administration bill.

"He heard only what he wanted to hear,"[1] said John R. Starr, who wrote at that time: "One would think that, given the almost unanimous antitax expressions from members of the legislature, Clinton would embark on a quixotic quest if he asks the 1989 legislature for more than a token increase in taxes. Unfortunately, that is not the way it works. Despite their antitax sentiment, legislators will come to Little

Rock nursing personal greeds. A governor who knows how to satiate those greeds, often by bargaining away the public interest, could pass a bill outlawing the Pledge of Allegiance through the General Assembly at its current stage of corruption."[2]

Generally, lawmakers liked his spending proposals. It was the tax proposals they hated. There was no sentiment among their constituents for any kind of tax increase, they kept insisting. As if to confirm that, when Arkansas voters went to the polls in November to reject Michael Dukakis, they also firmly rejected a proposed constitutional amendment that would have made it easier for the legislature to raise income and gasoline taxes and harder to raise the sales tax. Under the Arkansas Constitution, only a simple majority is needed to raise the sales tax; the other taxes require support of a three-fourths majority in both houses. At that time, only fourteen states taxed their citizens at a higher rate than Arkansas, and only three states imposed higher motor fuels taxes.

The Highway Commission intended to seek a 7-cent-per-gallon increase in the state gasoline tax. The cornerstone of the governor's package was another 1-cent increase in the state gross receipts and sales tax, which had been increased from 3 to 4 cents per dollar in 1983. Clinton sought to mitigate this big increase with a two-pronged "tax reform" proposal: In return for a flat 7 percent tax rate on incomes of $100,000 or more, an estimated 264,000 low-income Arkansans would be removed from the state income tax rolls. The bill was entrusted to Representative David Matthews, a dynamic young fire-and-brimstone stump speaker who had become a true believer while Clinton's student at the University of Arkansas Law School in the early 1970s, and who could be trusted to use every ounce of his ability to persuade his colleagues to pass the unpopular bill.

Former utility magnate and political fund-raiser *extraordinaire* Sheffield Nelson was the first to remind voters why they had made a mistake in giving the governor a four-year term without limitation or threat of recall. By not having to run in 1988, Nelson said, Clinton had "a cavalier attitude toward taxation" that resulted in "constant politicking" toward his aim of higher office.[3]

"You've got a governor whose No. 1 goal is to stay elected, and everything else falls into second or third place," said Nelson, who was preparing to run against Clinton in 1990.[4]

Clinton's inability to feel the pain higher taxes caused might have been due in part to his lack of appreciation for how most Arkansans lived. As governor, all the perks of his office were exempt from federal taxation. In fiscal year 1988 alone, taxpayers spent $783,116.33 a year to support the Clintons. That included a twelve-person security staff, food, utilities, maintenance and operation of the Governor's Mansion—which included the purchase of everything from begonias for the grounds to linen for the beds—and transportation. It did not include his $35,000-a-year salary and the public relations fund on which there were no spending restrictions. In addition, for each year he served as governor, Clinton received three years of credit toward his state pension. That and the two-for-one credit he received for his two years as attorney general constituted thirty-eight years of retirement credit for the forty-six-year-old Clinton when he resigned the governorship to become president.

Anything Clinton wanted or needed that the state or his supporters did not or could not give him, Hillary Clinton provided. With her six-figure income from Rose Law Firm, the dividends generated by most of her investments, and the income tax deductions she parlayed out of donating to charity everything from evening dresses to shower curtains to socks, she could have provided a comfortable living for the family even without the tax-free perks of Clinton's office.

In 1989 alone, the Clintons claimed charitable and religious contributions of $12,626, which included two pieces of the governor's underwear valued at $1 each.

This extravagance caused Republican Tim Hutchinson and Democrat Pat Flanagin to introduce a bill in the Arkansas House known as the Austerity in State Government Act. It sought to require all government agencies, including the governor's office, to reduce the size of their supervisory, managerial, and administrative personnel by 10 percent over a two-year period. The bill actually passed the House before Clinton's legislative whips killed it in the Senate.

Clinton never seemed to understand why his frequent calls for "sacrifice" from taxpayers inspired such resentment among Arkansans.

Despite all the antitaxation, antispending signals that had been sent his way prior to the 1989 session, he made no effort to reduce any state agency's spending or his own. Asked whether he intended to tighten his belt and reduce the amount spent on the care and feeding of the first family, Clinton said he did not. Asked whether he would reduce his request for a $400,000 increase in his office's $2.1 million annual budget, he said he would not.

The acknowledged resentment of legislators was exacerbated by a blatant attempt by the governor's office to pressure them. In violation of his own directive to state agencies the year before in which he had forbidden employees to use state letterhead stationery for personal correspondence or to lobby lawmakers, Clinton used his official gubernatorial stationery to contact the directors of state agencies to urge them to lobby lawmakers to vote for his tax package. In the letter, he bragged about his accomplishments as governor and asked recipients to send the postcards he had included to their representatives and senators.[5]

The postcards, unstamped, bore this message: "Dear Senator [or Representative]: I'm willing to pitch in another penny for good schools and tomorrow's jobs. Please vote for the sales tax increase and the other revenue measures Governor Clinton has proposed to move the state forward."

Clinton's letter to the agency directors contained a clip-and-mail form by which the directors could notify his office of their specific response to his directive. There were four responses from which to choose: "1. I have sent the postcards to my legislators; 2. I will telephone my legislators to ask them to support your program; 3. Please send me more postcards to give my friends so they can contact their legislators; 4. Enclosed is a contribution of $_____ to help you recruit others who are willing to work for Arkansas's future." Also included was a sheet of information about what Clinton was intending to do to "move Arkansas forward into the 21st Century."

Legislators thought such tactics were not only insulting, but interfered in their duties. Besides, they knew, as did their constituents, that current revenues were not only meeting but exceeding the projections of state fiscal experts.

There was no pressing need for many of Clinton's proposals, which seemed to be window dressing to obscure Clinton's effort to raise the pay of public school teachers, upon whose support he relied heavily in any campaign. Lawmakers who were aware of the state budget process and carefully read the reports argued that the governor had substantially underestimated projected revenue growth in preparing his package. They knew as well as Clinton that nothing boosts a governor's standing in the polls like an unexpected revenue surplus, particularly one that can be credited to austerity and frugality in government.

At the outset, Clinton knew the chances that a major tax increase would be passed were slim, but the governor also knew which legislators could be bought, and which could have their resolve weakened with a quiet—and private—conversation about the need to promote "the greater good." Clinton's parliamentary strategy was simple, too, and one he'd employed many times: He maneuvered to obtain commitments to new projects while delaying the legislation needed to finance them, thus allowing him to use the new projects as justification for raising the money with new taxes.

In an attempt to humanize his tax proposals, Clinton staged a news conference at which he trotted out seven Arkansans who claimed that the state would benefit by the Clinton proposals. One of the personal testimonials came from G.M. "Buddy" Nichols, the manager of the Nekoosa Paper Mill at Ashdown, who said that his company would be hard pressed to find top-quality employees in the future if Arkansas did not improve its school system by raising taxes.

It was left to opinion writers to point out that Nekoosa would not be paying any of those higher taxes until it used up a $12 million tax write-off granted Nekoosa by a law promoted and enacted by Clinton.

While Clinton lobbied for his tax package, he railed against some of the less popular legislative initiatives, among them a $4 million-a-year tax break for the extremely profitable Oaklawn Park horse racing track, then signed them into law because of deals he had struck.

"He's giving away the state treasury to save his political face," Democratic Representative Bob Teague grumbled after the House did a flip-flop and passed Clinton's income tax bill. "No price is too high for him to extract from the pockets of the taxpayers to further his political career. God help us if he ever got a hold of the national treasury."[6]

Clinton owed some of what little success he had in the legislative sessions of 1989 to the state's gaming interests, among whose lobbyists were Joe Bell and Herschel Friday. Until his death in a plane crach in March 1994, Friday was recognized as the most effective lobbyist in Arkansas. Arkansas allows only two forms of gambling—horse racing and dog racing. The state-sanctioned Oaklawn Park at Hot Springs and Southland Greyhound Park at West Memphis were fairly good money makers for local governments and for the state, but they were excellent money makers for the owners, who spent little in upkeep. As a result, despite reaping $1.8 million in net profit in 1988, Oaklawn was beginning to look a little shabby in comparison with its nearest competitor (Louisiana Downs, located near the Arkansas-Louisiana border in Bossier City, Louisiana), and owner Charles Cella decided that he needed the state's help to rectify that situation. He did not present his proposals to the legislature on that basis, of course. Cella claimed the money was needed to beef up purses. He proposed adding Sunday to the slate of weekday racing during Oaklawn's limited season, selling mixed drinks at the general concession stands, simulcast betting on races at other tracks when the horses were not running at Oaklawn, and cutting the state's share of pari-mutuel taxes by more than half, which constituted a $4 million tax break.

Clinton, who had vowed the year before to stand firm against Oaklawn's demands, capitulated early in the 1989 session. He had no choice. Two of the most effective lobbyists in the state, Joe Bell and Herschel Friday, represented Oaklawn, and what the Friday firm wanted, the legislature usually gave. Clinton had hoped to use the Oaklawn tax break as a carrot, but it did not work. The legislation was rushed through during the first month of the session, and a gubernatorial veto would not be conducive to passage of the Clinton tax package. In exchange for the promise of legislative support for the major components of that package, Clinton signed the Oaklawn tax break.

Most of Clinton's toughest financial battles were fought in the House of Representatives; most of his victories were the result of steadfast support in the Senate, many of whose members were more entrenched, hence more influential, because unlike representatives, they served four-year terms. A bill that appeared dead or at least mortally wounded after it left the House was often revived and given new life by the upper chamber as a result of the Senate's stubborn refusal to capitulate to those heathens in the House.

On that basis, Clinton was accustomed to winning; thus he was outraged when, twice within a two-week period, the Senate refused to approve his tax proposals. When his legislative liaisons emerged from the governor's office the Tuesday after the second vote, they looked shell-shocked. The governor had, in the words of one, "reamed [them] out"[7] for having failed to secure the necessary votes before allowing the second ballot.

"I just can't *believe* the Senate would just walk away and turn their backs on giving a tax break to 165,000 low-income Arkansans," Clinton fumed. "The Senate has *always* been willing to do what's right."[8] But, he hastened to add, he still believed that ultimately the Senate would come around.

He was wrong. The Senate held fast in rejecting Clinton's bill.

"Nobody's afraid of him anymore," one legislator opined. "Politically, he's dead as a carp."[9]

Even the Arkansas Highway and Transportation Department's $100 million revenue grab had been rejected, marking the first time the independent agency had walked away from a session empty-handed.

As if the furor over increased taxes wasn't enough to tip the scales of public opinion against Clinton, that same legislative session had seen the expansion of school-based health clinics, the linchpin in Dr. Joycelyn Elders's crusade to make birth control devices and abortion counseling a permanent fixture of the state's public schools.

Elders, who had been director of the Arkansas Department of Health since 1987, unveiled her proposal on the sixteenth anniversary of *Roe v. Wade*, the Supreme Court's decision that permanently legalized abortion. The state already operated about a dozen such clinics. Surprisingly, the measure to expand the size and scope of the birth control program did not meet with immediate public disapproval. It passed the Senate with relatively little fuss before anti-abortion forces were able to organize the opposition. By the time it reached the House committee, groups such as FLAG—Family, Life, America, God—had generated substantial opposition to a provision that permitted the clinics to distribute birth control information and contraceptives.

The health clinic proposal had been billed as a public health measure to improve the lives of young people from disadvantaged homes who usually didn't receive proper nutrition and did not regularly see a physician. Opponents saw the clinics as little more than a tax-supported abortion referral service for children. Those who failed initially to make the connection between "health services" and sex education did so promptly when Elders used her position to launch a crusade against teenage pregnancy, which she said was an epidemic in Arkansas. Young people were going to be promiscuous, she insisted, and it was the public's responsibility to make sure that children did not continue giving birth to children.

Eventually, she would have her way, although these clinics would not reverse or even check rising teenage pregnancy rates.

What was billed as the second education reform during the tenure of the "Education Governor" dealt with many bills that didn't have very much to do with education. Among these proposals were bills to permit police to take into custody any school-age youth found to be off school premises, to arrest and charge with a misdemeanor any parent or guardian whose school-age charge had an "excessive" number of unexcused absences, to bring misdemeanor charges of neglect of duty against any county prosecutor who failed "to timely pursue" these truancy cases, and to subject parents and guardians to fines for not attending conferences with school officials.

Another education issue was the controversial matter of settling the state's court-ordered obligation in the seven-year-old school desegregation lawsuit.

Central Arkansas has had more than its share of litigation in the name of desegregation ever since 1957, when Governor Orval Faubus activated the Arkansas National Guard to block the entry of nine black students to Little Rock's all-white Central High School. (Faubus still contends the troops were there to preserve the peace and to protect the black students from harm.) Indeed, the litigation which kept Central

Arkansas's three school districts—Little Rock, North Little Rock, and
Pulaski County Special—under federal court supervision for more
than a decade ultimately resulted from the Supreme Court *Brown v.
Board of Education* decision, which was handed down in 1954.

As the legislature prepared to wrap up business, the three school
districts and the state of Arkansas negotiated a settlement in the
desegregation lawsuit with the aid of Hillary Clinton and her three-
man committee. The terms called for an admission by the state that
through its past education policies, it had contributed to the districts'
segregation problems; payments of costs could go as high as $131
million. In return, the state did not have to pay anything if further
desegregation efforts failed.

Lawmakers who represented voters outside of central Arkansas were
fit to be tied. For many years they had been frustrated by the central
Arkansas school districts's demands on state aid to public schools.
Despite several attempts at equity, larger, wealthier districts got a
disproportionately large share of the state school aid. The three districts within Pulaski County were among the largest and wealthiest in
the state, and now the children in other school districts would be
penalized for central Arkansas's mistakes.

Nineteen senators promptly introduced a bill to levy a 5 percent
surtax on state income taxes paid by residents of central Arkansas's
Pulaski County. The proposal was patently unconstitutional, and predictably it failed, but it sent the message intended by rural lawmakers.

It also gave Clinton the excuse he needed for the biggest defeat he
had as governor: Now Clinton could say, and he lost no time in saying,
that his sales tax proposal had not passed because he had never really
pushed for its passage. He had held off, waiting for all parties to agree
upon a settlement in the desegregation case. He now contended that
the impending settlement "was the precondition for me even thinking
about considering raising major revenues."[10]

"I have no problem with the fact that we haven't dealt with revenues
in this session," he said in March as the 77th General Assembly drew to
a close. "That was my position all along."[11]

After nearly two months of late-night telephone calls and interrup-
tions to his regular schedule so he could rush from one committee

hearing to another, from the legislative chamber in the south wing of the Capitol to the one in the north wing, after hours of cajoling and bartering and counting votes, Clinton could still say with a straight face, "I think [implementing] a big revenue increase is the last thing, not the first thing, we should do."[12]

Now the only way Clinton could show he still was an effective governor was by getting the desegregation settlement passed. Most legislators didn't know that passage of this bill was important because they were unaware that federal overseers had already begun researching precedents that would allow the court to seize state funds to pay for the settlement. The importance of this bill also escaped Clinton, who had to be reminded the night before the session ended that the settlement bill, which had passed the Senate, was languishing, seemingly forgotten, on the House calendar.

Lobbyist Joe Bell credits Representative Wanda Northcutt, a Democrat from the rural town of Stuttgart, with sparking the effort to get the bill passed the night before the session was supposed to end.

"I had dinner with Wanda Northcutt down at the Flaming Arrow [a private club popular with legislators and lobbyists] and she said to me, 'Do you know what's fixing to happen tomorrow?' and I said, 'What?' She said, 'The legislature is fixing to adjourn and the school desegregation bill has not been lobbied, it hasn't been worked, it hasn't been prepared, it's just sitting there [on the calendar], and we're fixing to adjourn without it passing.' "[13]

Bell, whose law firm, Friday, Eldredge, and Clark, was representing schools involved in the lawsuit, asked Northcutt what she wanted him to do about it.

"You call Herschel [Friday], and I'll call Clinton," she replied. "Let's try to have a meeting in the morning."

"So I called Friday," Bell said, and he said, 'Do you think we can pass it?' I said, 'I don't know. We can't unless we get it churning, because tomorrow's the last day.' "

Among those at the early morning meeting besides Bell and Northcutt were the school districts' attorneys; Skip Rutherford, then a member of the Little Rock School Board; assorted members of the

Central Arkansas business community; and, from Clinton's staff, Craig Smith.[14]

"We decided then that we would get a phone call thing going, to call different people, you know bankers, school superintendents, whoever might be interested in getting the thing passed at that point so they would call *their* people Friday afternoon," Bell said. "I was just sitting there listening and thinking, damn, this is a whole lot to be done in two or three hours."

When the meeting broke, Bell and a few others went to the Capitol to begin lobbying for the bill. House members were incredulous. "You mean, you're going to try to pass that thing?" "Yeah," Bell would reply. "We've got to pass it. If we don't, lord, we're going to be in a mess. It'll be worse than Kansas City," where court-ordered taxation in a similar desegregation case was, in Bell's words, bleeding the public dry.

School proponents bivouacked in the speaker's office located just off the House floor and started counting their votes. The first attempt to pass the bill was not promising; the House was 2–1 against the settlement.

"Clinton really started to get with it at that time," Bell said. "He was in there [in the speaker's office]. He was calling people off the floor and talking and arguing how important it was and all that. We had another vote just before lunch, and I think we went up . . . but we hadn't made much progress.

"That afternoon, after lunch, some of these calls that were being generated that morning started having their effect and people started paying attention to us at that point. But at the same time, the opposition started figuring out that this thing was going to have to pass" and started "pitching fits about it."[15]

The opponents, Bell said, had a legitimate complaint: They were being asked to approve a settlement that they had not seen, whose cost to the state was unknown—the best estimates ranged from $87 million to $118 million over a ten-year period—and which had not been accepted by the federal court. They did not understand the settlement and they insisted that someone explain it to them. Bell and his group agreed that the House should resolve itself into a committee-of-the-whole so that a member of the public could be invited to address the

House and answer questions about the settlement. Herschel Friday made the presentation.

"He stayed up there [at the podium] for forty-five minutes and fielded questions, made statements," Joe Bell said. "I remember his pitch was that it would be a real setback for the state if it didn't pass because of all the educational handicaps that would occur" if the lawsuit were not resolved.[16]

"During this whole period Clinton—well, most of us just sat down and let him have it, that's all," Bell said with a laugh. "He and Craig Smith were pushing and shoving and grabbing and twisting arms, making deals. A lot of people were bargaining with them. . . . But what kind of got it all going was all these people calling in from out in the state: Wal-Mart and Cooper Communities and Tyson. Bob Lamb and the state Chamber [of Commerce] was cranking stuff out."

The Arkansas Education Association, the Association of School Superintendents, the Arkansas Bar Association, the Association of Prosecuting Attorneys, the Arkansas State Chamber of Commerce, state senators, cabinet members, civil rights activists, preachers, and assorted others converged upon the north wing of the state Capitol's second floor, calling lawmakers out of the chamber and asking them to vote for settlement. By one yes vote, each holdout was told, the House could put an end, once and for all, to the litigation. Do nothing and the litigation would continue, at even greater expense to the taxpayers. House members who had left for the day, or who had not bothered to show up, were exhorted to vote *in absentia* by pairing their votes, which they faxed to the Capitol, with lawmakers still on the premises.

After hours of intense pressure, emotions were running high.

"Don't you *ever* ask me for another vote!" Republican Jerry King screamed at an Arkansas Education Association lobbyist at one point. "Don't you *ever!*"[17]

Several of the governor's appointees were "escorted" from the House floor and booted out of the House lounge at the behest of angry lawmakers and had to confine their lobbying to the hallways and the speaker's office, from which the House was helpless to evict them.

"I remember sitting back there in that speaker's office," Bell said.

"You could sense when Clinton . . . smelled a win. You could see him getting animated. He was blowing and going."[18]

It took five votes, four of them within a five-hour period, on the final day of the session, March 17, but the House finally capitulated and gave the settlement bill fifty-four votes, three more than members had been told were needed for passage. When the bill passed, outside the House chamber, whites hugged blacks, grown men wept, and lobbyists and reporters slapped one another on the back.

"Arkansas has finally made a national statement for desegregation, and it was courageous," Skip Rutherford declared, "1957 is now behind us. The best is yet to be."[19]

But it wasn't. Neither Clinton nor the legislature had time to recover when they learned that much of their work had been for naught.[20] The General Assembly had violated a key provision of the state constitution that required a three-fourths vote in each house to ratify passage of the state's biennial General Appropriations Bill, which authorizes payment of all judicial, legislative, and executive salaries. The bill had passed each house with fewer votes than required, indicating that once the new biennium began on July 1, no one paid by the state could legally receive a paycheck, including those legislators who had voted to increase their monthly expense accounts.

A further reading of the constitution revealed that not only were the salaries of elected officials in jeopardy, the appropriations of all state agencies were, too. Another constitutional provision required passage of the General Appropriations Bill before enactment of any other type of appropriation bill. That meant that the entire state government would be shut down on July 1 unless the legislature could ratify the appropriations bill.

Initially, Clinton and lawmakers ignored the situation, insisting that salaries and operating budgets could not be stopped because another constitutional provision mandates payment of the state's "just debts." Only the state's attorney general, Steve Clark, agreed that there was cause for concern. A special legislative session was on Clinton's April agenda, but the governor said it would be strictly a one-issue session in response to a recent state Supreme Court decision that struck down the use of special masters in juvenile cases. (Many of the "reforms" attributed to the Clinton administration, among them the overhaul of the statewide property taxation system, the method of distributing state aid to public schools, reforming the social services system's treatment of child abuse and neglect cases, and reforming the juvenile justice system, were the result of litigation brought and won against the state.) He said he saw no need to revisit the General Appropriations Bill unless "somebody sues us and forces us to have a special session"[21] to address it.

"I hate to spend the money for it otherwise," he added.

Clinton was beginning to have second thoughts about the April session, however, and suggested that there might be an administrative solution to the problem. In truth, as he eventually admitted, he was reluctant to reconvene the legislature because he dreaded what lawmakers might do to the hard-won desegregation settlement. The Senate might very well behave itself, he said, "but if the House wanted to go back and revote every bill individually, you might not only have a problem [with the school settlement bill], you might have a problem with others."[22]

That was, indeed, a big gamble for a governor who at the time had worn out his welcome with the House and had seriously tested the patience of the Senate. Clinton's clout with the legislature was waning, and he knew it. State government at that time had an annual budget approaching $2 billion. Reopening the budget process could prove disastrous.

He canceled plans for an April legislative session, but the reprieve lasted only two months. That's how long it took for a lawsuit to be filed and the courts to rule that all appropriations bills, well over three hundred of them, acted upon by the 77th General Assembly were null and void as a result of the insufficient number of votes cast in each house for the General Appropriations Bill.

As far as Clinton critics were concerned, insult was added to injury when legislative sources finally conceded shortly after the court-ordered invalidation that leaders in both the House and the Senate had realized while the General Assembly was still in session that they had acted improperly but failed to mention it publicly because they hoped that no one would notice. Two months later, Clinton confessed that he had, indeed, known of the problem at the time and had decided to ignore it, which he did until forced by the courts to convene a special legislative session, at the cost of more than $40,000 a day, to rectify the situation. His excuse for having knowingly signed a bill that he knew to be constitutionally invalid was that "a governor has never challenged a legislative ruling . . . once they [lawmakers] rule, that is something that all of the rest of us usually accept."[23]

Had Clinton spoken out during the regular session, the legislature would not have had the opportunity to reconsider the school desegregation settlement, which it did during the special session at the end of June. The session was not merely fractious, it was angry.

After more than a week of wrangling, all of the questionable appropriation bills had been properly enacted save one: the desegregation settlement.

Those who were there will never forget the last day of the First Extraordinary Session of 1989, the day the Senate went crazy and the House went home.

For many years the Arkansas Senate has forced the end of a legislative session. When senators have had enough, they simply adjourn, leaving the House to rush through a final few hours before following suit, for one chamber cannot accomplish a great deal without the other. Relations between representatives and senators usually remain cordial, but between the two chambers there exists a great deal of animosity, deeply rooted in the arrogance associated with "the upper chamber."

On that steamy Friday in June 1989, however, after many hours of heated debate over the course of the four-day session, the House had resisted several efforts to readopt the school desegregation settlement. The Senate had not yet voted on a much-needed worker's compensation bill and was prepared to hold it hostage until the House capitulated on the desegregation settlement—or so a majority of the House members believed. Clinton was frantic. He had been working the House most of the day, pacing and huddling just outside the House chamber, chewing his ravaged fingernails, praying that the Senate gambit, knowledge of which his liaisons had disseminated to the lower chamber, would work. Then Nap Murphy lost his key.

Except for a two-year hiatus, Napoleon Bonaparte Murphy has been a fixture in the Arkansas House since 1959. A short, red-faced man with the studied delivery style of someone several drinks past inebriation, the southeast Arkansas legislator's sole claim to fame was his custom of dressing up like Colonel Sanders on the last day of every legislative session. (When the legislature's enactment of the controversial creation-science law in 1981 brought television news crews from around the world to the Capitol to get footage of lawmakers in action on the final day of the session, several of his colleagues physically hustled Murphy off the floor so the world could not bear witness to another "dumb Arky" acting like a fool.)

Murphy, whose confusion is well known, was as harried and care-worn as the rest of his colleagues on the last day of the special session, and it seemed a big joke, not altogether unwelcome, when, during the crucial last vote on the desegregation bill, he started hollering that the key which activated his electronic voting button was missing.[24]

Electronic voting is an efficient process. Once time has expired, there is no reversing the procedure that automatically tallies the votes. Murphy's raucous protestations could not alter the fact that he had not cast his ballot. He was advised to place a note in the House journal attesting to his intention to vote for the bill had he been able to do so. Unfortunately, the bill had received only fifty-two official votes out of a possible hundred, and via a parliamentary procedure known as "sounding the ballot," in which the roll is called to ascertain that all who voted electronically are present and accounted for, two of the fifty-two were ruled invalid. Admitting defeat—nerves were simply too frayed to try again, and proponents were now resigned to the need for a second special session at which they would try again—the House began wrapping up its business. As a matter of routine, it sent the failed settlement bill to the Senate, where it had originated, along with a copy of Murphy's affidavit. Then, with a final crack of the gavel, House Speaker B.G. Hendrix adjourned the assembly, and House members began filing out of the Capitol, worn out but somewhat pleased that, for once, they had completed their business before their colleagues in the upper chamber.

A half-hour later, the Senate leadership took a look at the situation.

The House was adjourned. The Senate was now in possession of the bill. What to do? Finish the business and go home. So they did. Without ceremony or debate, the Senate decided that Murphy had intended to vote for the bill and so he should be permitted to do so. Declaring that the bill had passed the House by fifty-one votes, the Senate proceeded to "pass" the school desegregation settlement bill.[25]

Clinton wasted no time in signing the bill, again with the full knowledge that it had been improperly approved. His excuse? A governor does not question a legislative ruling.

House members were livid. How dare Clinton sign a piece of legislation that had been rejected by the House of Representatives? Not only had Clinton shown a lack of leadership during the special session, but he had shown himself a coward. After eight-and-a-half years in office, longer than any chief executive since Faubus, he was taking his marching orders from the Arkansas Senate.

It appeared that a legislative session that had begun with a lawsuit would conclude with another. Nothing had been resolved. If the federal judge in the school desegregation case wanted, he could drain the state treasury, unless another legislative attempt could be made to approve the settlement. But the legislature could not be convened without the authorization of the governor.

While the state stewed, Clinton commenced a two-week "working" vacation in Europe (for which he subsequently billed the state $2,970 in executive-class plane travel, and several thousand dollars for lodging in hotel suites that ranged from $275 to $524 a night). He was somewhere in Germany when word reached him that Winston Bryant, the quiet, unobtrusive lieutenant governor, was giving serious consideration to convening the session himself.

Bryant already had begun polling lawmakers to determine whether such a session would be productive. In the meantime, he arranged a meeting with all the attorneys in the case to see whether together they could stave off the wrath of the federal court if they promised to resolve the stalemate by the end of August.

The attorneys thought they could do so, and that, coupled with a long-distance appeal from Clinton, persuaded Bryant not to convene the legislature.

On July 25, the lawmakers were back in session, and Clinton was back at his desk trying to find a way for the Second Extraordinary Session of the 77th General Assembly to circumvent the Arkansas Constitution in adopting the desegregation settlement. The fact was that even if Nap Murphy's vote had been valid, the House vote on the settlement bill was unconstitutional because it was *an appropriation bill* that required a three-fourths vote in each of the two chambers if it was to pass. Murphy's vote would have given the bill only a simple majority.

But there might be a way to get the bill passed without a three-fourths vote. Bill Clinton's legal advisors proposed that the settlement be introduced as a fund transfer from the Education Department budget to the authorities overseeing the desegregation case, which would require only a simple majority. While there were no funds in the education budget earmarked for such use, that could be resolved by retooling the budget. The proposal contained a dubious provision tying the transfer to the proceeds of the 1-cent sales tax increase enacted in 1983.

No one recalls who devised the winning strategy—it has been credited to Representative Joseph K. Mahony II, the wealthy, tobacco-chewing, country lawyer who by then had made peace with Clinton—but it was a brilliant stroke that Clinton almost bungled. In addition to the fund transfer authorization bill, which the administration hoped to pass by a simple majority, a second bill was introduced as insurance in the event the first bill was declared unconstitutional. Mahony introduced a bill to appropriate funds for the desegregation settlement. As an appropriation bill, it would require three-fourths vote to pass. But Mahony's bill would take effect only if the transfer bill were struck down by a court.

The legislature's business was concluded in the record time of three days, the minimum time required to send a piece of legislation through both houses and their committees. Clinton and his troubleshooters again pushed themselves to exhaustion, working late into the evening on both Tuesday and Wednesday, the governor on the telephone while his hardest-drinking aides hit the local watering holes frequented by lawmakers. At his behest, a contingent of lawyers, lobbyists, educators, and political appointees spent Wednesday working the halls.

It took several votes, one or two of them presided over by a highly agitated Bill Clinton, before exasperated lawmakers advised him that his presence was not helping matters any, but on the third day, the House not only yielded, it capitulated, giving the transfer bill an astonishing seventy-seven votes.

When it came, the vote was not altogether unexpected, given the strong-arm tactics used to persuade House members. The cavernous House of Representatives had begun undergoing an extensive, million-dollar renovation before the session, and members had no-where to meet but a cramped second-floor meeting room that once had been the state Supreme Court's hearing room. With its old-fashioned, fixed-place wooden seats and expansive wooden railing, there was barely enough room for the one hundred legislators and the staff needed to oversee and record the proceedings. News outlets were restricted in the number of reporters and camera operators they could send in, and no television lights were allowed because of the heat generated by the press of bodies and the summer sun pouring through the floor-to-ceiling windows.

"People were still raising hell about the desegregation case . . . and when the sun would get right in the south side, it would get hot, and they'd come boiling out of there whenever there was a recess," Joe Bell recalled with a laugh. Determined to oblige the governor with a three-day session, House Speaker B.G. Hendrix finally told Craig Smith during one such recess: "The next time we get 'em in here, we're going to lock this door, and we're not going to unlock it till we pass this bill. And they got them in there and really locked the door—and passed it."[26]

Clinton almost lost the final vote before it was taken, however. Edging toward acquiescence, the House delivered seventy-three votes on the transfer bill and sixty-six on Mahony's backup proposal. Made heady by the scent of victory, Clinton convened his legislative allies.

"This is incredible!" he enthused. "Seventy-three votes! *Seventy-three votes*! We can get two more! I know we can get two more!"[27]

If seventy-five lawmakers could be persuaded to endorse a fund transfer, he reasoned, surely he could persuade them to endorse an outright appropriation. What the team really needed to do now,

Clinton advised, was secure the additional votes—surely two people could be found who wanted *something*—and amend the Mahony bill so that it would no longer take effect only in the event of a successful legal challenge of the transfer bill. Then all he had to do was sign the Mahony bill instead of the fund transfer bill.

"Forget it," Representative Owen Miller, one of several who had agreed to change their nays to yeas, told a Clinton operative. "I didn't sign on to no appropriation bill."[28]

It took Clinton about five minutes to scrap this plan and go with the original one. He got his seventy-five votes and two extra ones.

"A tremendous victory," the governor said, shaking his head in wonder. "I'm real proud."[29]

It must be noted that approving the settlement did not end the litigation. The three districts remain under the watchful eye of the United States District Court for the Eastern District of Arkansas, and the Little Rock district, which initiated the lawsuit as a means of forcing consolidation of the three districts into one, only to be found more lacking in commitment to desegregation than either of its targets, remains under the court's direct supervision.

After the vote, a satirical letter began making the rounds, an adaptation of a letter which, in varying forms, had been around ever since President Harry S. Truman's day.

"Dear Friend," it stated. "I have the distinguished honor of being on a committee to place a statue of Governor Bill Clinton in the Hall of Fame at Washington, D.C.

"The committee was in a quandary as to where the statue should be placed. The committee felt it was not wise to place it beside the statue of George Washington, who never told a lie, nor beside the statue of Franklin D. Roosevelt, who never told the truth, since Bill Clinton could never tell the difference.

"The committee finally decided to place the statue beside the statue of Christopher Columbus, the greatest Democrat of all. He left not knowing where he was going, and upon arriving, he did not know where he was. He returned not knowing where he had been, and he did it all on borrowed money.

"Over 5,000 years ago, Moses said to the children of Israel, 'Pick up your shovels, mount your asses, and I will lead you to the Promised Land.'

"Nearly 5,000 years later, Franklin D. Roosevelt said, 'Lay down your shovels, sit on your asses, and light up a Camel, *this* is the Promised Land.'

"Today Bill Clinton is stealing your shovels, kicking your asses, raising the price of your Camels, and mortgaging the Promised Land."

20

SOUTHERN STRATEGY

BILL CLINTON'S FIFTH TERM as governor was predicated on a lie—
that he would serve four years as governor if reelected—but political
expediency demanded the lie if he was to seek the presidency in 1992.
He needed the credibility, the visibility, and the financial security that
holding an elective office, even that of governor of a small, Southern
state, would bring to such a campaign.

If he regretted the subterfuge, he gave no sign of it. Ever the
pragmatist, Clinton later observed that Arkansans, who had ejected
him from the governor's office ten years before, in part because of his
"national ambitions," probably would not have elected him to another
term had he revealed his true plans.

Some of his strongest supporters had encouraged him to forgo a
statewide campaign in 1990 and "recharge his batteries" for a run at
the presidency in 1992. It also was suggested that he pursue the
supporting slot on the 1992 Democratic ticket as a means of building
name recognition for an all-out campaign in 1996.

Both Bill and Hillary have denied it, but before the 1990 campaign, the couple seriously considered the possibility of Hillary running for governor. It was a frequent topic of discussion among

political junkies over coffee at the state Capitol and drinks at the local watering holes.

"I once asked Hillary—we were talking as friends—and I asked her, 'What do you want to do? What do *you* want to do?' And her answer was 'Run something,' " John R. Starr recalled.[1]

"Bill Clinton and I did an awful lot of talking before he ran for reelection in 1990," Starr continued, "and I told him I didn't think he ought to run because he hadn't done the job and that all he was looking for was the glory; he wanted to go out and make speeches. He agreed that he hadn't done the job.

"We talked a great deal during that period of time about the possibility of him retiring and Hillary running for governor, and on more than one occasion he said that that would definitely be the route they would take if they thought Hillary could win, and apparently they polled some to see whether Hillary could. . . . If he was going to run for president, he should have done what Jimmy Carter did and gone ahead and faded out of the governor's office and spent the next two years putting his presidential campaign together rather than trying to half-ass run the state and run for president at the same time. He would have still had the bully pulpit. I mean, [if] his wife's the governor of Arkansas."

Neither Clinton nor Starr lacked faith in Hillary Clinton's leadership capability. Clinton "never expressed anything but a great deal of confidence in her abilities," said Starr, who disagreed with many who believed her to be the brains behind Clinton.

"No, he's very clever. He's smart enough to get by. No, I don't think he would have to depend on her brains. I think she's been the balls behind Bill Clinton quite often. . . . During the period when Joan Roberts and Hillary and Betsey Wright were running the show, I was in close contact with them, and I know that on several occasions they persuaded him to do right while he would be wanting to do right, but he didn't want to offend anybody politically, and they would say no, do this because it is right. . . . And as long as they were telling him what to do, he did right. And it was [when Roberts and Wright left his employ] that he was just totally worthless. You couldn't make any kind of a deal with him."[2]

Starr could not recall whether the Clintons decided Hillary could not win or whether she decided that that was not what she wanted to do, but after months of considering the options, Clinton told Starr that he had decided to seek a fifth term. Starr did not encourage him.

"You live in the Governor's Mansion," Starr remembered telling Clinton. "There's no more glory in that. You set the education program up and going. There's no more glory in that. There's really no more fields for you to conquer, and if you don't want to do the job, if you don't want to really put your nose to the grindstone and be the governor of Arkansas for the next four years, then get out of the way [for] somebody who wants to be the governor and move the state forward."[3]

Clinton assured Starr that this was truly what he wanted to do, that this time, he really wanted to be the governor.

"I said, 'Bill, this doesn't mean that you just give up running around the country making speeches. You've got to give up running off in Arkansas and making speeches if they detract from what you need to do to get Arkansas put together the way you and I know it can be put together.' . . . 'Yes, sir,' he said, 'that's all I want to do.' 'Don't want to run for president. Still too young. I'm not ready to run for president.' And he convinced me that he wouldn't."

Among those poised to run for governor a full year before the primary season opened were Congressman Tommy Robinson, former utilities chieftain Sheffield Nelson, Attorney General Steve Clark, and Tom McRae, former director of the Winthrop Rockefeller Foundation. By the time Clinton announced his candidacy, there had been some remarkable changes in this lineup. Clark was out, former Congressman Jim Guy Tucker was in. Robinson and Nelson were still in, but now they were Republicans.

McRae's Democratic candidacy was the only constant among Clinton's would-be challengers. McRae, a gangly, affable, intellectual sort who was most uncomfortable pretending to be a back-slapping politician, was a curiosity. Politically naive despite a brief stint as an aide in the early 1970s to Governor Dale Bumpers, he entered the race because he sincerely believed that the old ways, Clinton's ways, were not working and that the state needed to go in a different direction. He was, he said, a "fresh alternative."[4]

In his own way, Steve Clark was far more successful than Clinton in that he had never lost a campaign. Clinton's successor in the attorney general's office, Clark was a handsome, square-jawed dynamo of a consumer advocate in the grand tradition of Bill Clinton and his predecessor, Jim Guy Tucker.

Clark had been waiting patiently for eleven years for Clinton to move on so that he could move up, and he had grown extremely tired of doing so. If he was not more popular than Clinton at the time he announced his long-awaited candidacy, he was, at least, Clinton's strongest challenger and likely to overtake him in a run-off.

Sheffield Nelson was a former *protégé* of king-maker Witt Stephens, whose tutelage had propelled him into the presidency and chairmanship of Arkla, Inc., and amassed for him a sizeable fortune. Nelson had had his eye on the governorship for years and had nearly run in 1986. He and Stephens had broken off their relationship years before, reportedly because Nelson had refused to take direction from his mentor in several questionable natural gas investment deals. After leaving Arkla an incredibly wealthy man at age forty-three, Nelson had practiced a little corporate law, had pulled a stint as the Clinton-appointed chairman of the Arkansas Industrial Development Commission, and had served as chairman of the Democratic party, for which he had led a hugely successful fund-raising effort when the party was near bankruptcy.

Thanks to Tommy Robinson, Nelson missed becoming the first prominent Arkansas Democrat to switch parties by a couple of weeks, but political junkies were delighted because it was common knowledge that Witt and Jack Stephens would move heaven and earth to keep Nelson from being elected to any office. The only thing that kept Robinson from being a wholly owned subsidiary of the Stephenses was his inherent inability to be loyal to anyone. Robinson was fond of saying, "You can rent me, but you can't buy me," and that was largely true.

At one time, Robinson was the single most popular politician in Arkansas, outstripping even Bill Clinton in the polls. He first came to the general public's attention in 1979, when Clinton hired him away from the Jacksonville Police Department, where he was a very controversial chief of police, and named him to what would prove to be a very controversial stint as director of the state Public Safety Department. In his fifteen months as a cabinet member during the first Clinton administration, Robinson had done battle with virtually every supervisor under his command, and with Clinton, too. He had resigned, much to Clinton's relief, to launch his campaign for sheriff of Pulaski County. There ensued one of the most colorful careers any local Arkansas official has ever enjoyed.

Robinson was a flashy, outspoken, fast-talking, mean-spirited, and incredibly charismatic politician who fomented discord and controversy wherever he went. He was a first-class gossip—many of the rumors about Clinton's alleged philandering during his first term were circulated, if not promulgated, by Robinson—and he loved nothing better than generating outrageous headlines. He served two turbulent terms as Pulaski County sheriff during which he became something of a folk hero throughout the state. Among his more colorful deeds was chaining a group of prisoners, who were being held in his jail because of prison overcrowding, to the chain-link fence surrounding one of the state penitentiaries. On another occasion, he arrested the county judge and the county comptroller during a budget dispute. Crime took a steep nose dive when he posted signs in convenience stores warning would-be robbers that deputies armed with shotguns might be standing guard out of sight.

Robinson was involved in several sensational murder investigations in which he was accused of manipulating evidence and eliciting confessions by force, but his grass-roots appeal remained intact. He was elected to Congress from Arkansas's Second District in 1984.

Swagger and *braggadocio* were Robinson's most prominent attributes, and they were the key to his widespread popularity. He had a knack for saying things in public that most folks only thought. One editorial cartoonist[5] launched a long-running series of cartoon strips featuring Robinson as "Captain Hotdog," and the legend grew. Several polls in the early 1980s showed him with a higher name recognition than any public figure in Arkansas, including Clinton.

During his first term in Congress, Robinson, who had campaigned as "an independent voice for Arkansas," quickly enlisted in the ranks of the Democratic party. He was named freshman whip, responsible for rounding up party-line votes for the Democratic leadership. Robinson's affinity for the liberal leaders of his party lasted about as long as it took for Robinson to find his way around the halls of Congress. In short order, he had voted against increased funding for the Democrat-controlled House committees, and he not only voted for the MX missile, but he abandoned his assignment as freshman whip to handle the MX floor fight for its chief proponent, Les Aspin of Wisconsin. He eventually dropped all pretense of liberalism and became one of the more vocal Southern Boll Weevils of his freshman class.

In July 1989, Arkansans were stunned when President George Bush called a news conference to announce Robinson's switch to the Republican party. It was not the switch that surprised, but the fact that Bush would make such a production of it. Arkansans were growing tired of Robinson's loud mouth and erratic temperament, and the conventional wisdom was that Robinson had left the Democratic party before it kicked him out. The leadership of the Republican party of Arkansas, which learned of the switch only a short time before the president's news conference, was divided into two camps: those who could live with it, and those who thought it a disastrous turn of events. None of them seemed particularly happy about Robinson's conversion.

Robinson's 1990 campaign for governor was part of what has been called the Republican party's "Southern strategy." More specifically, it became part of Republican operative Lee Atwater's Southern strategy after Robinson approached him about switching, and it might have worked in Arkansas but for three unforeseen occurrences: Sheffield Nelson entered the race as a Republican, which forced a primary; Atwater collapsed in February with the heretofore undiagnosed brain cancer that later would kill him; and the Clinton network orchestrated a magnificent cross-over vote among liberal Democrats that delivered the primary vote to Nelson.

Atwater was to George Bush what James Carville was to Bill

Clinton: a folksy, fast-talking, down-and-dirty, take-no-prisoners political phenomenon who played to win. Atwater rose to prominence
by masterminding Vice President Bush's campaign against Michael
Dukakis, and from the time of Bush's election until Atwater fell ill in
early 1990, he had one objective in mind: to secure Bush's reelection.

Rex Nelson left the *Arkansas Democrat* in the autumn of 1989 to join
Robinson's staff.[6]

"It was the thrill of the hunt, a chance to be on the inside," Nelson
said with a grin. "Tommy had told me off the record that he was going
to run for governor."[7]

Shortly after Atwater was named chairman of the Republican National Committee, Nelson attended one meeting with him at his office
in the Republican National Committee headquarters on Capitol Hill.
Robinson was not present, but several other Republican operatives
were.

"I want you to realize one thing at the outset," Atwater told Nelson.
"My ultimate goal as chairman is getting the president reelected in
1992. Don't take this wrong. Taken alone, I don't give a damn who the
governor of Arkansas is. We know how to beat a liberal from the
Northeast. We proved that with Dukakis. I ain't worried about Mario
Cuomo. Bill Clinton *does* worry me."

Atwater suspected that it might be considerably more difficult to
defeat a moderate Southern Democrat, or at least a Democrat from the
South who could be portrayed as a moderate. Atwater had some issues
that he thought could be used against Clinton, issues with which they
could not just "tar" Clinton but "tar him up and down" so that he
would be unelectable in the 1992 presidential race, and Atwater
thought Robinson could be an effective messenger. Certainly, Clinton's tax-and-spend record as governor was excellent fodder, but
Nelson said that Atwater had much more volatile information in his
Clinton file.

"There was an excellent chance that womanizing would have been
used if Atwater had lived," Nelson said in an interview in late 1993.
"He did not like Bill Clinton. I'm not saying Bill Clinton would have
lost, but if Atwater had lived, it would have been a much, much
different race in 1992. Lee Atwater was everything that George Bush

was not. He was a street fighter who loved politics. George Bush was a blueblood; politics was kind of beneath him."

Atwater apparently had no illusions about himself or his appeal to Bush. All that talk during the 1988 campaign about Bush's affection for country music and pork rinds was pure fabrication, he told Nelson.

"What you have to realize," Atwater said, "is that George Bush is doing what he considers to be public service, but he does not like politics that much. He puts up with people like me because to get where he wants to be, he needs a turd who's not afraid to get dirty."

Atwater made it clear that he was not afraid to get dirty.

"If we win this thing, great," Nelson recalled Atwater saying. "If we lose, we will have seriously reduced Bill Clinton's appeal."

"Atwater had told us that 'When you get in that race, you've got everything I've got, you've got every resource you need,' " Nelson said. "Of course, everything fell part in early 1990. Atwater collapsed, and we lost our national foundation."

Robinson agreed that the 1992 campaign would have been different had Atwater lived, but he claimed in a 1994 interview that getting down and dirty was not in Atwater's plans for the Robinson campaign.

"Lee and I had an understanding," Robinson said. "He wouldn't do a personal thing against you. He'd do a Willie Horton, but he would not stoop to delving into one's personal life. We never talked about that. . . . I never observed him even hinting that you'd hit a guy below the belt. He was a Southern boy and there are certain rules in the South you just don't violate. Everything else was fair game."[8]

That hardly squares with Robinson's description of Atwater as someone who would "cut you off at the knees and watch you bleed to death," someone who "was not really concerned about who he took down."

Robinson conceded that Atwater was "very instrumental" in persuading the Arkansas congressman to switch to the Republican party and that he encouraged him to run for governor.

"Certainly, he had his own motivations. His first priority was getting Bush reelected, and he knew that Clinton would be the only one that had any chance, notwithstanding all the garbage he would have to carry into the [presidential] campaign, of slicking his way into office."

Robinson said the he and Atwater "had basically the same type of personality: sort of a take no prisoners, praise the lord, and pass the bullets [outlook]. He and I met when I was the Conservative Democratic Forum whip, and he and I sort of hit it off."

Atwater's concern about a Clinton presidential bid in 1992 prompted his offer of assistance to the Robinson gubernatorial campaign of 1990, "but at arm's length, where no one could catch him," Robinson said with a laugh. "He offered a lot of good political advice, and there was a lot of trying to twist a few arms, trying to get certain people to tell Sheffield Nelson to take a hike. [Atwater] foresaw what was going to happen: The biggest obstacle was that Clinton would get all the damned liberals to cross over and vote in the Republican primary. [Atwater] could see the handwriting on the wall. And that's what happened, and now Bill Clinton is president."

J. J. Vigneault also insisted that Atwater gave no thought to waging an assault on Clinton's personal life. Vigneault, a native Arkansan, was then the Southern deputy political director of the RNC. "There was never any mention of women or any of that sort of stuff," he said in a 1994 interview. What was talked about at some length was the taxes Clinton had raised or tried to raise at every opportunity, the lack of economic growth and job creation in Arkansas, the power that had accrued to Clinton in his years as governor, and the need for change.

Atwater had "a couple of programs he was real interested in implementing," Vigneault said. "One was he wanted to go into the South among conservative Democrats and election officials and get them to switch parties. Phil Gramm was the first, and then it started to pick up momentum. The next guy was Fox McKeithen, the secretary of state of Louisiana."9

During the spring and summer of 1989, Atwater hit a string of Southern cities to meet with party leaders with whom he discussed strategy, fund-raising, and the recruitment of Democrats. In May, he visited Little Rock, where he met privately, but unsuccessfully, with several disgruntled Democratic office-holders. A few weeks later, while he was in Nashville, he summoned Vigneault to his hotel room.

"I think we got something big here," he confided to Vigneault. "I got a call from John Paul Hammerschmidt today. Tommy Robinson came up to him on the floor of the House and was wanting to talk about switching parties. Look into it and tell me what you find out."[10]

Vigneault dutifully returned to Little Rock, where Mary Anne Stephens, with whom he had worked closely in the 1988 Bush campaign, confirmed that Robinson was serious about making the switch.

The two flew to Washington the next day.

"That afternoon," Vigneault recalled, "there was a meeting in Lee's office at the RNC with Lee, Tommy, Charlotte Jones, John Paul Hammerschmidt, Mary Anne, myself, and I believe Mary Matalin was there."

After the requisite pleasantries, the group settled around a table and Atwater got down to business.

"I understand you're interested in finally leaving that bunch," he said to Robinson.[11]

The resulting torrent of complaints from Robinson boiled down to one thing. He'd had enough of the Democratic party.

"What are you gonna do about it?" Atwater responded.

"Well, I'm here. What can you offer me?"

"Well, you can be a member of a party that's got a leader like George Bush instead of folks like Ted Kennedy, Jesse Jackson, and Michael Dukakis."

Robinson laughed, Vigneault said, "and told some Tommy stories about Dukakis." After the digression, Atwater smiled and got back to the point.

"What are your plans, Congressman?"

"Hey, Atwater, nobody calls me 'Congressman.' I'm Tommy."

"All right, Tommy, what are your plans?"

Robinson replied that he was "ready to switch under certain conditions."

"I want it to be a big deal when I switch, because I'm going to run for governor."

"That's good," Atwater said and explained that one of his goals was to make the Republican party the predominant party in the South.

"We think we've got that except for one or two states. Arkansas is the worst state in the South for us."

Atwater said he believed that Bill Clinton was the reason the GOP had had such a tough time making inroads in Arkansas. "He has a stranglehold on that state. He's made all the appointments all these years. I really believe that if we don't face Clinton now, we're gonna face him later. I don't know that Clinton will ever be on top of the ticket, but there's a good chance he's gonna be the vice presidential nominee next time."

"No, he wants to be president," someone said, and everyone laughed except Atwater.

"Bill Clinton's a good politician. I'd just as soon head him off right now instead of the president having to face him in 1992, or whoever in 1996."

"Well, if I switch, what will be done for me?" Robinson asked.

"What do you want done?"

Robinson reiterated his desire for "a big deal" to be made out of his announcement. Maybe the president could hold a news conference. Vigneault said that Atwater immediately picked up the telephone and placed a call to Chief of Staff John Sununu. He told Sununu that he needed to talk to him about a very important matter.

"I'm going over now to see [Sununu] and we'll see if we can't get the president to do this," Atwater announced after hanging up the phone.

"I don't think Tommy was prepared for that quick a deal," Vigneault said. Robinson did not physically blanch, but he hastened to sweeten the bargain.

"If I run," he said to Atwater, "will you help me beat Clinton?"

"Tommy, I will make it one of my top priorities."

"No, no. I want this to be your number one priority."

"Tommy, you will be my top priority."

"Now," Vigneault said, "if you knew Lee, you'd know that he meant it at the time. He might have told two or three other congressmen the same thing, but it wasn't that he was lying, it was just typical Lee, saying at the time that he meant it, and he *did* mean it at the time."

The meeting broke up. Atwater left to see Sununu, the congressmen peeled off one by one to return to the House, and the others sat around discussing the Robinson coup. That evening, Atwater told Robinson, "The president would be more than honored to have a news conference at the White House announcing your switch to the Republican party."[12]

As the time approached, Vigneault was assigned to coordinate activities in Arkansas, but he was admonished to say nothing to anyone. Ken Coon, head of the Arkansas Republican party, was instructed to assemble party leaders at the GOP headquarters "for a highly confidential meeting" on the morning of the big announcement, but he was not told the reason for it. To impress upon Coon the importance of the meeting, Vigneault did tell him that Atwater had requested it. Atwater, Vigneault said, planned to call headquarters and speak to the group over a speaker phone.

"It was a pretty small crowd, which tells me that Ken was unable to gather a crowd or people didn't care," Vigneault said.

Shortly before the news conference, which was broadcast live on television, Vigneault told the few gathered what was happening.

"Bob Leslie was upset about it. He was the national committeeman and had been working to get Sheffield Nelson to switch, and he was very, very upset. [State Representatives] Jim Keet and Ron Fuller were kind of surrounding him, trying to calm Bob down and not being very successful.

"Lee called about that time—the speaker phone wasn't working— and Leslie talked to him, and he had some pretty negative things to say about Tommy. Lee said, 'Bob, this is the president of the United States, the leader of the party, and he wants to get as many members of Congress to switch as he can. He needs the votes. He needs to build the party in Arkansas.' "

A more intimate knowledge of Republican politics in Arkansas would have told Atwater that Robinson's switch would not necessarily advance the GOP cause in Arkansas. In fact, the recruitment of Robinson caused a serious split in the precarious foundation of the Republican party of Arkansas.

The Tommy Robinson-Sheffield Nelson contest was a match made in hell. Both promised to "take the high road," but it surprised no one when neither did. The major issues between them emanated from Stephens, Inc.; Robinson was inextricably tied, politically and financially, to Jack and Mary Anne Stephens, and Nelson was neck-deep in what became known as the Arkla-Arkoma controversy.

Nelson, who had grown up in poverty in East Arkansas, had parlayed a keen business sense and Witt Stephens's affection for him into a personal fortune as president and chief executive officer of Arkansas-Louisiana Gas Company, later Arkla, Inc., the largest natural gas provider in the state. In 1982, while still head of Arkla, Nelson had entered into a contract with a gas drilling and production firm, Arkoma, Inc. Under terms of the agreement, Arkoma was granted leases on natural gas fields whose development costs would be shared by Arkla, and Arkoma was guaranteed a generous price from Arkla for its product. Arkoma, which paid $15 million for the leases, was owned by Jerry Jones, a longtime friend of Nelson's and a lifelong friend of Robinson's. Jones made millions on the deal when the price of natural gas plummeted and Arkla, locked in to exorbitant prices under terms of the contract, was forced to buy its way out of the deal for $146 million. (Jones later used part of his fortune to purchase the Dallas Cowboys.)

Reportedly, the Arkla-Arkoma deal contributed heavily to the split between Nelson and Witt Stephens, who was not accustomed to losing money.

Jones found himself caught in the middle of the Nelson-Robinson campaign because he had helped to bankroll Robinson's political career, and Robinson had returned the favor by giving Jones's twenty-three-year-old daughter, Charlotte, a $63,000-a-year job as a congressional aide. (Shortly after Robinson raised the Arkla-Arkoma deal as a campaign issue, Charlotte Jones quit because of the increasing tension in the friendship between her father and Robinson.)

Stephens, Inc. also was in the middle of the campaign, not by circumstance but by choice. Witt and Jack Stephens had an abiding hatred of Sheffield Nelson, and while Witt did not like Robinson, Jack Stephens and his wife Mary Anne were among Robinson's most ardent supporters. Mary Anne Stephens co-chaired his gubernatorial campaign, and Jack offered the use of their mansion in Florida for Robinson's strategy sessions.

As the Arkla-Arkoma controversy was taking root, Clinton convened another special session in October, but education would have no significant role in his agenda. A year before, he had tried to persuade the legislature to enact a major general tax increase on the grounds that education reform could not continue with it, and he had lost. A month before, he had insisted that an infusion of $100 million was vital to the state's progress. When he announced plans for the October session, however, the priority was not education but the war on drugs.

"Announced and unannounced candidates for governor have rushed to promise no new taxes," Starr wrote in a column chastising Clinton for having "abandoned his bid for meaningful improvements in education."

"Clinton," Starr declared, "will be forced into the same posture if he runs."

While legislative committees prepared a package of antidrug legislation, Clinton flew to Washington, where he did a little networking and gave a few interviews. Although Clinton had convened the session, the session was almost a week old before the governor got around to introducing his own proposals.

"We are leaderless and floating out here," one of his staunchest legislative supporters grumbled.[13]

The Clinton package included relatively modest but controversial tax proposals totaling $20 million from increases in the "sin taxes" on cigarettes and alcohol and a flat rate of 7 percent on the incomes of taxpayers making more than $100,000 a year. He needed that amount, he claimed, so that all of an anticipated $50 million in surplus funds could be dedicated to education. (Because of the Arkansas Constitution's requirement that regular legislative sessions be held only once every two years, the state's budget cycle consists of two fiscal years. In drawing up the state's budget every two years, lawmakers must rely on revenue projections forecast by a panel of fiscal experts. It's an inexact science, and sometimes revenue shortfalls threaten to occur. Because the Arkansas Constitution also requires a balanced budget, sometimes budgeted expenditures must be cut in midyear. As a general rule, revenue surpluses often follow tax increases in Arkansas.)

By enlisting in President George Bush's war on drugs, Clinton again was met with questions about his own drug history. Asked whether he had ever used illicit drugs, Clinton responded: "I've made it clear that in Arkansas ever since I have been an adult, I haven't."[14]

Reporters did not pursue the subject, so critics took his response to mean that he had used drugs in his youth and that since becoming an adult, he had confined any drug activity to places outside Arkansas.

Under Arkansas law, the governor must outline his agenda in the proclamation required to convene a special session of the legislature. Lawmakers cannot expand upon this agenda—introduce any piece of legislation that is not germane to the items in the proclamation, referred to as "the call"—until they have concluded the governor's business. In a last-minute addition to the call, Clinton took the opportunity to launch another assault on the state's Freedom of Information Act. It did not take much encouragement from him for the legislature to approve a provision closing virtually all records of the Arkansas Industrial Development Commission expenditures on the grounds that public disclosure might put industrial prospects at a competitive disadvantage.

Clinton was spurred to action when the *Arkansas Democrat* learned before the commission was ready to announce the deal that a Japanese firm, Tokusen USA, was going to locate a production plant in Conway, a college town in a predominantly white county just a few miles northwest of Little Rock. In the course of gathering information about Tokusen, reporters asked AIDC officials whether any other Arkansas sites had been considered. David Harrington, the AIDC director, refused to release the information, claiming an exception to the state's open-records laws that did not exist. He stalled the request long enough for Clinton to resolve the matter by closing the records, but not long enough for word to surface that Harrington and Clinton wanted the records closed to conceal the AIDC's role in helping Tokusen find a plant site in a predominantly white community. The Japanese, sources insisted, did not want to hire black workers, and AIDC records would prove that the Clinton administration had acquiesced to that demand.

The allegation created a breach in relations between Clinton and black lawmakers, but the legislation was enacted before anyone could force the AIDC to prove or disprove the charge.

Clinton dropped all pretense of respect for the state's "sunshine" laws during the session when, in violation of the Freedom of Information Act, he ordered a reporter's eviction from a legislative committee meeting at which he implored lawmakers to salvage his tax package.

Once again lobbyists were enlisted to help save Clinton's face during a legislative session. Heavyweights such as Joe Bell, who was representing the Soft Drink Bottlers Association, and Bob Lamb of the Arkansas State Chamber of Commerce agreed to help him pass a 2 percent surtax on the incomes of all Arkansans to finance his war on drugs, which essentially entailed hiring a state "drug czar," if the governor would abandon proposed increases in cigarette and alcohol taxes, and stop the rise in income taxes of an estimated 5,900 Arkansans who earned above $100,000 a year, withdraw his support for a special "soda pop" tax, and forget about taking a larger share of the collection fee that retailers kept for collecting and remitting sales taxes. He also bowed to pressure from veteran lawmakers who wanted a share of the $50 million surplus, which he had earmarked for education, to be diverted to the Human Services Department.

"Big business is running Arkansas," his legislative critics charged before they delivered the fatal blow to Clinton's retooled revenue package. Despite the best efforts of Clinton, who made an impassioned plea to the House of Representatives, and his gang of legislative liaisons and lobbyists, the House defeated the 2 percent income surcharge four times on the last day of the two-week session.

"Clinton was so poorly prepared for this special session that he wound up fighting for a tax proposal that was not his own and one that, in fact, wasn't even mentioned until lawmakers had been in town a week," Starr pointed out.[15]

One editorial cartoon in the usually laudatory *Arkansas Gazette* depicted the governor as a deer tied to the hood of a pickup truck beside a legislator dressed as a hunter who boasted, "Got him!"

Clinton's compulsion to win at any cost, whether compromise or forfeiture, ran rampant during this session primarily because Betsey Wright, his chief of staff, was not around to keep him on track. Tension between them had been building for several months, and shortly before the session began, she left for good.

Wright, dubbed the Iron Maiden of the Clinton administration, had never been popular with most members of the General Assembly. The good ole boys saw her as a heavyhanded, pushy broad who was altogether too self-important, and in truth she was totally without diplomatic skills. She was prone to wild mood swings exacerbated by lack of sleep from an exhausting, self-imposed work schedule that frequently found her at the office or at her home computer in the wee hours of the morning and on weekends. She probably slept less than Clinton, who could manage on three or four hours of sleep augmented by the occasional catnap. Wright did not catnap. Neither did she take vacations.

A longtime Clinton supporter who now serves as an advisor to the Clinton White House said that Wright, whom he counts as a close friend, was obsessive about her work and her role in Clinton's political career.

"She throws herself into it so deep and becomes so involved in it that it just dominates her," he confided after insisting that his name not be used. "She really alienated everyone around her" in the governor's office, and later in the presidential campaign, which did not hire her or invite her aboard until she resigned a fellowship at Harvard and returned to Little Rock of her own volition to handle "bimbo eruptions." When James Carville and his War Room colleagues realized that she was not going to be excluded from the campaign, they reluctantly made a place for her.

"Betsey's world is Betsey, Bill, and Hillary," the anonymous Clinton supporter said. "She will always be a player, but she has trouble playing in moderation. She is so protective of Bill Clinton, so loyal to him, that sometimes she is not rational."

There were conflicting stories about what provoked her abrupt departure from Clinton's staff—rumors that she and Clinton had quarreled, that she and Hillary had quarreled, that she had given

Clinton an ultimatum of some sort and that he had called her bluff. Clinton claimed she was on vacation, but he was vague about when and whether she would be returning to work.

"I've not asked for her resignation and I hope she won't quit," Clinton said.[16] Wright could not be located.

It was common knowledge that Wright was intimately involved in strategy and fund-raising for the 1990 campaign, the one that would position him to run for president in 1992. She had worked arduously on the education summit held in September 1989 at the request of President Bush, who had asked the National Governors Association to help him develop a national education policy. Clinton and Republican Carroll A. Campbell, Jr., of South Carolina led the governors efforts on the project.

For a time, Clinton and his staff kept up the pretense that Wright would be coming back. On November 14, Clinton claimed that she was still on the payroll and "everything is fine." On November 17, her resignation was announced by Clinton's office.

"My great respect for her as a professional and my affection for her as a very dear, very close friend prevent me from prolonging the strain on both of us any longer by asking her to reconsider," Clinton said in the news release.

"Bill Clinton is the best thing Arkansas has going for it," Wright said in the same news release. "Whatever he chooses to do in the future, he'll have my full support and any contribution I can make. He's just the best there is."

The news release said that Wright wanted to "pursue other career options" and that Clinton had accepted her resignation reluctantly. He said she would not be in charge of any campaign he might enter "only because she's tired of campaigns and doesn't want to run them anymore."

Given Wright's enthusiastic declaration during a radio interview[17] in September that she was getting ready for Clinton's next campaign, reporters were puzzled about the claim that she was tired of campaigning.

Wright made herself available to reporters who called her home, but she had little to add. She gave them a somewhat rambling account of how Clinton had wanted to "restructure" her job, and try as they might, she and he had been unable to "find a way for [her] to stay" under that restructuring. Everything she said suggested that she would have remained on staff had Clinton invited her to do so.

What the reporters did not know was that several days before her resignation was announced, Wright had telephoned at least two Clinton advisors in whom she often confided, Skip Rutherford and John R. Starr. Both men said she was crying profusely and that she rambled incoherently about having severed her ties with Clinton but failed to make clear the circumstances.[18]

Clinton and Wright publicly reconciled at a December 1989 banquet at which Wright was recognized as one of twelve women who had made outstanding contributions to politics in Arkansas. Clinton was on hand to present her award. The breach was completely healed for a time after he named her executive director of the state Democratic party, a decision that would cause both Wright and the party a great deal of heartbreak.

In mid-January, Clinton told reporters he would decide by the end of the month whether to seek a fifth term, but the announcement was not made until March 1. While his favorability ratings remained high, polls indicated that the electorate was growing tired of his tenure. He had been governor for ten of the past twelve years. A telephone survey conducted in mid-February by Opinion Research Associates indicated that fully 50 percent of the voters believed he had served long enough.

Once again, however, fate gave Clinton a much needed boost.

Steve Clark, Arkansas's attorney general since 1979, was the most formidable Democratic challenger Clinton ever encountered, and Clark might well have beaten Clinton in the 1990 Democratic primary had he not grown overly anxious and greedy while waiting for Clinton to move on. Shortly before entering the 1990 gubernatorial campaign, Clark decided to build some momentum by implicating a popular lobbyist in an alleged bribery attempt.

Earl Jones, Jr. (no relation to Jerry Jones) had had a brief and unremarkable career as a legislator which served him well when he decided to become a lobbyist. In late 1989, Jones was hired by the Pride House Care Corporation.

The Arkansas Development Finance Authority, created during Clinton's tenure ostensibly to issue bonds to provide financing for low-interest mortgages, gave a great deal of business to the state's bond dealers, who profited from commissions they received from commissioners. Among these dealers were Stephens, Inc. and Dan Lasater's firm of Lasater and Company.

In December 1989, the ADFA board was prepared to approve an $81 million bond issue so that Texan Bruce Whitehead's Pride House Care Corporation could buy seventeen nursing homes and lease fifteen others from Beverly Enterprises. Stephens, Inc., which owned almost 10 percent of Beverly's stock, stood to gain a sizeable fee for representing Beverly in the proposed bond deal.

The bonds would have been secured only by the interest Pride House would have owned in the nursing homes. Financial experts claimed that the nursing homes were not worth anywhere near $81 million, that there was no way they could generate enough income to pay loan interest, and that the uncollateralized bonds would be a poor investment risk.

Whitehead stood to make an immediate $1.95 million profit off the deal, and another of his companies was looking at a potential profit of $2.5 million a year for running the nursing homes.

Journalistic scrutiny and editorial criticism persuaded Clinton that the deal should not go through as intended, and ADFA president Bob Nash, a former Clinton aide, prevailed upon the ADFA board first to postpone action, then to reject the bid. Beverly was invited to submit a new proposal.

In surprise testimony before an ADFA board meeting, Steve Clark launched into a tirade about the "arrogance of wealth and the arrogance of power" exhibited by the Clinton administration and representatives of Stephens, Inc. in dealings involving the proposed bond issue, and he charged that he had been the target of an attempted bribe by an unnamed representative of Beverly and Stephens, Inc.

Clark said that several days before the hearing, he had been offered $100,000 for his gubernatorial campaign if he would remain neutral on the Pride House-Beverly bond deal. Clark's testimony, and his pledge to turn the matter over to the prosecuting attorney's office, compelled

Clinton to kill the second bond proposal, but not before denouncing Clark for having withheld "a criminal accusation for several days so it could be made in front of the TV cameras."[19]

Earl Jones, Jr., was thrown into a panic, although it has not been determined whether he honestly feared that Clark would eventually name him or whether his bosses at Stephens, Inc. pressured him into going public. Many politicians felt that Clark was set up by people with a vested interest in taking him out of the governor's race.

Jones quickly said that he was the unnamed representative about whom Clark spoke, but he insisted that Clark had misunderstood his intentions and that he had not attempted to bribe the state's attorney general.

In a private interview in December 1989, a visibly shaken Jones told me that he had probably been hired to lobby on behalf of the bond issue because he was perceived as "being stout" with people like Bill Clinton and Steve Clark, and that he had, indeed, offered to *help* Clark raise $100,000 or more toward his campaign against Clinton.[20] He said that he and Clark had discussed the bond issue on at least two occasions during which they also discussed Jones's offer to raise money for the gubernatorial campaign. However, Jones insisted, no connection between the two topics was ever made by Jones or Clark during these conversations, and he just could not understand why Clark would say otherwise. Sure, Jones admitted, he had written a note to Clark that mentioned both the bond deal and the $100,000 war chest Jones hoped to raise, and yes, he *had* scrawled across the bottom of the note the instruction that Clark destroy the note after having read it, but that was "just a joke."

Other lobbyists rallied to the defense of Jones, who was later cleared of any wrongdoing. Money for Clark's anticipated campaign against Clinton began to dry up, and Clintonites moved Clark to the top of the enemies's list.

Clark was a candidate for governor for only nineteen days. Shortly after his announcement, the press reported that Clark had been using state credit cards to cover thousands of dollars in personal expenses that consisted primarily of lavish meals washed down with expensive booze with "phantom" guests at some of the state's most expensive restaurants. Dozens of Arkansans who had never dined with Clark, or who had never discussed the state business he claimed was the purpose of luncheon and dinner meetings, had their names listed on meal receipts. (Clark was convicted on November 1, 1990, of theft by deception for fraudulently charging food and entertainment on his state-issued credit card and fined $10,000. He resigned as attorney general four days later. The conviction was affirmed on appeal in 1992.)

The Beverly-Pride House bond deal made headlines again after Bill Clinton became president when it was learned that William H. Kennedy III, who at Hillary's behest had been named associate White House counsel in February 1993, had had a pretty heavy hand in the Pride House deal as well as in several more lucrative business transactions on behalf of Beverly Enterprises while a partner at Rose Law Firm.

The attorney of record for Beverly in the Pride House project was former Rose Law Firm partner C.J. "Joe" Giroir, Jr., but Bill Kennedy was the lawyer behind the Pride House proposal and three others which, had all gone well, would have been worth an estimated $300 million to Beverly Enterprises.

Roy P. Drew, a Little Rock investments analyst who tried to sound the alarm about the Pride House deal in 1989, claims that Giroir "was just a front man"[21] for Rose Law Firm.

"Had we known [in 1989] that Rose Law Firm was acting as Beverly's lawyer, that would have been big news, that would have been the smoking gun," Drew said.[22]

According to court documents, Bill Kennedy represented Beverly Enterprises in a plan to purchase groups of nursing homes in Arkansas, Iowa, South Dakota, and Nebraska in 1989, but one of the transactions fell through: the Pride House proposal in Arkansas. The law firm's involvement in this venture was not disclosed for several years, and only then as the result of litigation involving the Iowa transaction.

In 1989, Stephen, Inc., the Little Rock-based investment giant whose associates had contributed thousands of dollars to Clinton campaigns, owned almost 10 percent of Beverly Enterprises. Beverly's business dealings with Stephens had made it the largest owner of nursing homes in the nation, but Beverly was on the brink of bank-ruptcy because of a debt load created by fast expansion and heavy cuts in Medicaid and other medical payments by the Reagan administration. Its debts were estimated at $850 million, calling for a hefty infusion of funds.

Beverly Enterprises became involved in several money-making sales transactions it proposed to finance through the issuance of tax-exempt bonds. Ensuing legal problems with the Iowa transaction shed the first light on the ill-fated Arkansas venture.

While the ADFA negotiations were under way, Texas businessman Bruce Whitehead floated a similar proposal in Iowa. Through his Ventana Investments, Whitehead sought to buy forty-five Iowa nursing homes. When he went before the Iowa Finance Authority to obtain help with financing his purchase, he said he needed $86 million in bonds to avoid closing the facilities and evicting about three thousand elderly clients. The finance authority agreed to issue the tax-exempt bonds.

In closing the deal, Beverly transferred ownership of the nursing homes to Ventana Investments for $57 million. Whitehead promptly "sold" the facilities to another entity he controlled, a not-for-profit organization known as Mercy Health Initiatives, for $63.5 million.

"Whitehead made an instant profit of $6.5 million," the *Sunday Times* of London reported in 1994, "with a further guaranteed annual income of $2.3 million for another of his companies to run the homes. He also received four homes worth $1.8 million in his personal ownership and a contract for $5 million for his construction company."[23]

Legal and financial experts have estimated that Rose Law Firm netted up to $500,000 on the transaction, resulting in hefty bonuses for the law firm's partners, including Hillary Clinton.

The connection between Rose Law Firm and the Beverly-Pride House deal in Arkansas might never have been known had not tax assessors for several Iowa school districts balked at the loss of tax revenue as a result of Mercy Health Initiative's not-for-profit, hence tax-exempt, status. The assessors sued to overturn that status and won.

The decision handed down by Union County District Court Judge Gene Needles held that the debt structure created for the Beverly-

Mercy Health deal was "unconscionable," that the transaction generated excessive profits of more than $30 million for properties worth no more than $47 million, and that Ventana Investments's shell corporation, Mercy Health, "serves no legitimate purpose and was used primarily to obtain tax-exempt financing, shield the parties . . . from liabilities and obligations as owners, and to evade the payment of property taxes."[24]

His ruling was affirmed by the Iowa Supreme Court in May 1993.

As a result of the heavy debt assumed by Mercy Health and its loss of tax-exempt status, the *Sunday Times* reported, the cost of care at some of the Iowa nursing homes rose as much as 14 percent, a bitter irony considering First Lady Hillary Clinton's attacks on health care "profiteers" as she sought to redesign the nation's health care system.[25]

Roy Drew was an expert witness for the tax assessors in the Iowa case, and among the documents he provided me as proof that Bill Kennedy, not Joe Giroir, was the author of the Beverly-Pride House proposal was a copy of a letter dated May 9, 1989, and written by Bill Kennedy on Rose Law Firm stationery to Bruce Whitehead.

The letter references "Beverly Enterprises—sales of facilities in Iowa and Arkansas."

"Dear Bruce," the letter begins, "At the request of Jim Pietrzac, I am enclosing a clean and red-lined draft of the purchase and sales agreement relating to the above referenced transaction. The marked draft of the agreement indicates changes to the previous draft dated April 17, 1989. Please be advised that I am awaiting information and instructions from the appropriate Beverly personnel regarding the financial statement warranties and representatives of the Beverly companies set forth herein, and this draft is thus incomplete in that respect. The enclosed draft, as to paragraph references and the like, is still in rough form. Moreover, this draft was red-lined in haste and thus, despite this firm's best efforts, there may have been changes made but have been missed in the red-lining. Please review the draft accordingly. In addition, this draft has not been seen by anyone at Beverly or BIP [Beverly Investment Properties] and is thus subject to their review and comment. Please do not hesitate to advise if I may be of assistance. All best wishes. Sincerely yours, William H. Kennedy III." It was signed, "Bill."

"If Rose Law Firm had been known to be involved then," Roy Drew told me in a March 1994 interview, "it would have been real hard for [Bill] Clinton to have gotten reelected governor."[26] As it turned out, Steve Clark's grandstanding not only killed the Arkansas deal, it also diverted the media's attention. It's doubtful that Clark was aware of Rose Law Firm's involvement; otherwise, he would have used that instead of the alleged bribe to further his gubernatorial campaign.

With his most formidable Democratic challenger out of the race, it would seem that Clinton would be anxious to announce his reelection plans, particularly after former Congressman Jim Guy Tucker entered the race. But Clinton continued to dawdle. Clinton's standing in the polls had been consistently low for many months and the governor was told by many advisors not to run again because many Arkansans thought it was time for change.

State Senator Lu Hardin, who was prepared to make the race if his former law professor did not, said that as early as November or December of 1989, Clinton had "expressed that the possibility existed that he would not seek reelection."[27]

"I can remember calling Clinton before Christmas to see how he was leaning, and I visited with him a couple of times and got no indication," Hardin said. "Now I respected that. It's a very difficult decision. . . . He just said there were a lot of personal and professional . . . considerations that were to go into this decision."

Hardin said he had no desire to oppose Clinton for the nomination. Friendship was part of it, but there was a practical reason, too.

"Not only was Governor Clinton well funded, but he had at that time one of the best statewide-county organizations this state has seen. While I did not personally see Faubus's or know about Faubus's, I'm sure it equaled Faubus's. The loyalty of those county coordinators was strong. He had an excellent statewide organization. It was very strong.

"Now having said that, he was also going in with a little higher negative than most incumbent governors," Hardin explained. "Many project as high as 38 percent. You'll hear as low as 33 percent, but some were projecting a negative of 38 percent. Now, by that I mean that any reasonable candidate would have gotten, a viable candidate, would have gotten 38 percent of the vote and only needed to pick up 12 percent plus 1 to win the election. So there was at least a degree of vulnerability."

Hardin, who had been trying to line up seed money for a campaign that might not happen, went to see Clinton the evening before the governor's March 1 news conference. Clinton told him that he still had not reached a decision and did not know whether he would be announcing his reelection bid or his retirement the next day.

"If I don't run, you don't need to let speculation develop," Clinton told Hardin. "If I don't run, you need to announce so that you will be a part of the story."[28] He advised Hardin to schedule a news conference an hour after his own news conference.

"Me telling you to hold this press conference does not mean that I'm not running," Clinton cautioned. "I have not made that decision. I'm leaning a certain direction, but I have not made a decision. It's just that you don't have anything to lose. If I run, you'll get your reelection announcement on statewide television, and what state senator ever does that?"

Clinton would be shameless in his appeals to the electorate throughout the campaign, but for sheer drama, nothing could top his March 1 reelection announcement, during which he played his audience, composed primarily of longtime employees, supporters, and contributors, like an amen corner on salvation Sunday.

As he read through an uncharacteristically downbeat but predictably self-aggrandizing speech, his voice weary and his face drawn, an estimated seven hundred onlookers, many whose attendance had been personally solicited by their leader or his employees within the past three days, were still not sure about his intentions. Why would the governor summon them from all parts of the state, compatriots throughout various phases of his political career, if his intention were merely to seek reelection?

Was he or wasn't he going to run again? Neither Hillary Clinton nor his mother, Virginia Kelley, said they had any inside information about his decision. Virginia Kelley confided to me that she had attended a party for Chelsea's tenth birthday the night before and had left the Governor's Mansion "more confused than ever"[29] about her son's plans. She suggested that only Hillary had known in advance.

John R. Starr recalled a telephone conversation he had with Clinton soon after the announcement in which Clinton admitted that he had summoned his closest friends and strongest supporters to the news conference because he intended to leave office when his term expired the following January. Clinton confided that midway through his remarks, he changed his mind.

There was a decidedly funereal tone to the event as Clinton addressed the anxious audience, crowded around the well of the cavernous statehouse rotunda after cold, rainy weather drove the news conference indoors, and alternately credited himself with dragging a backwater state kicking and screaming into the twentieth century and lamenting the personal toll that this feat had extracted. Clinton did not appear to be a happy man; rather, he looked resigned to his fate.

"I think it is no surprise to any of you that the decision that I am here to announce today has not been a particularly easy one for me to reach—difficult for reasons that relate to my family and my friends and the future of this state to which I have given my best for many years," Clinton said.

That was an unexpected note, not for the words but for the somber mood enveloping them. Then he eased into a litany of his accomplishments as governor, his legacy, really, although he carefully omitted reference to his disastrous first term.

"When I took office in 1983, we were in deep trouble—economically, educationally, psychologically—and I set about then working with you to try to rebuild our state so that all of our people could live up to their God-given potential. And in these last seven years and two months, the record we have made together is truly remarkable. By any measure, our schools are much better, our economy is much stronger, we've begun to tackle our serious drug problems and our other social problems. We've begun to face up to our environmental responsibilities of the future. We have begun to have a different view of ourselves and our future, and all over the country, people have begun to look at us in a different way.

"All this I have been privileged to do not alone, but with you. It has been the most wonderful, rewarding experience of my life."

Those lucky enough to be standing near the podium, where the acoustics were marginally better than anywhere else in the circular expanse of the second-floor lobby, had heard similar words before, most recently in 1987, after Clinton, on the eve of a highly touted, much anticipated news conference, had ditched plans to run for the Democratic presidential nomination.

As Clinton plodded through his remarks—one of the three local network affiliates lost interest after nine minutes and returned to "The Oprah Winfrey Show"—Hillary's mouth tightened. Reporters moved closer to the front, and those at the rear stood on tiptoe, as though the added height would improve their hearing.

"There are many whom I treasure who have urged me to run again, who say that it is the thing to do for the state and who are obviously worried about at least one of the alternatives. There are others who say with a great deal of conviction that ten years is a long time. And I can see that there is an argument for that proposition. . . . And then there is the whole question of the personal toll which is taken on every family, on every life in the public. The things which make it so wonderful also make it quite difficult from time to time. Ambition always takes its price sooner or later.

"And I see so many of you who have been my friends for all these years nodding your heads. And so I have listened carefully to my friends and counselors around the country, but mostly here at home. Some who say, 'Leave while you're on top, walk away from a nasty political campaign,' say that 'the legacy of your administration will be secured by the decisions the voters will make in this election.' I have listened to others who say, 'My God, you're only forty-three years old; surely you're good for one more term.' "

Then, he noted, there were his opponents—"people who have already filed for the office who are older than me"—who declared that he was "washed up" and had served as governor long enough.

It was an extremely tense moment as Clinton spoke of his wife and his daughter and the time he had spent in prayer trying to decide what was best for them, for himself, and for Arkansans. Clinton sounded like a man who was ready to walk away from politics, and that confused those who knew him well, because Bill Clinton was not one to walk away from a political challenge. Surely he was not writing his own epitaph in reminding onlookers how much he had sacrificed for them. There were tears in their eyes, and in his.

"In spite of all the talk of who is and who is not ambitious," Clinton continued, his voice hovering amid the higher registers, as though it pained him to state the obvious, "I am the only person in this decade who has wanted only to be governor of Arkansas, who has never longed for the opportunity to run for any other job. When I had the chance to run for one other in 1987, I decided to stay here with you and finish this term because I believe in you and what we can make for you and your children and your grandchildren and our future together. . . . I confess to you that one of the reasons I have been reluctant to face this day," he continued, his voice choking on each word of the metaphor, "is that the fire of an election no longer burns in me."

His eyes scanned the anguished faces in the crowd, some of whom would quip later, not altogether in jest, that Clinton, unaided by notes, did not make up his mind whether to run until midway through the seventeen-minute speech. Some pundits, none in whom Clinton confided as much as editor Starr, suggested that the long faces on his oldest friends and supporters turned the tide and that, when confronted by their imploring looks, Clinton capitulated. According to Starr, this is precisely what happened.

It was a fine piece of handiwork. Only a handful of stoics— reporters, mostly—failed to join the jubilant demonstration that erupted when Clinton finally made it clear that rather than forgoing another campaign, he was once again sacrificing his own best interests at the altar of public service.

"I believe in what you and I and we can do together," Clinton said. "And so I am here to say this: In spite of all my reservations about the personal considerations, I believe that more than any other person who could serve as governor, I could do the best job."

In a subsequent column, Starr declared the performance "99 and 44–100ths percent pure pap, but it was great theater."[30]

"Critics may think his modesty has no bounds," Starr cracked, "but his words delighted the pack of people he has named to positions of prestige and profit." While not all present and accounted for, that pack already numbered in the hundreds—aside from the numerous political appointees in cabinet and subcabinet positions, at least 80 percent of the members of Arkansas's numerous boards and commissions and supporters nominated to numerous special task forces and advisory councils.

Near the end of his remarks, Clinton conceded that arrogance of power is always a problem for a longtime incumbent, but "we are bending over backwards to be as humble as we can in this campaign."

"I plead with you: Go home and lift up the spirits of the people where you live. Tell them to vote for themselves and their children and the future of the state. Ask them to give me four more years. It will be the best years I ever gave, the four best years the state ever got. . . ."

As applause rumbled through the Capitol, he and Hillary, now smiling radiantly, embraced and exchanged a few quiet words before disappearing in a sea of well-wishers.

"When he said the fire no longer burned in his belly—he never would have said that if he hadn't planned to quit," Sheffield Nelson later insisted. "But when he got down to the point of talking about the 'dark cloud' hanging over Arkansas in Tommy Robinson, I think that's when he made up his mind that he would run. I . . . don't think Tommy stimulated his running. I do think Tommy gave him the avenue he needed to get back on track to actually make the race in 1990 by talking about the dark cloud hanging over the state."[31]

"He was up there talking and thinking about how wonderful he was and how everybody looked up to him and how everybody loved him where he was, and he couldn't let go," opined Representative Pat Flanagin. "I think he was a little fearful of his chances. . . . People were ready for some changes. A lot of those promises Clinton had made about education reform and about other things, they were grandiose, and there were a lot of Clinton promises that were never delivered upon and had come due and past due."[32]

Clinton's horoscope for that day, compliments of Jeane Dixon: "Think twice before changing jobs."

21

PROMISE BROKEN,
PROMISE SEEN

BILL CLINTON LISTENED earnestly, nodding slightly as the reporter-panelist Craig Cannon posed the much anticipated question, his lips curled like a happy-face smile turned upside-down. Without missing a beat, Clinton looked straight into the camera that was broadcasting the debate live throughout Arkansas and asserted that he absolutely, positively would complete his term as governor if the people would reelect him.

There was no mistaking the question or the answer. The interviewer, perhaps familiar with Clinton's talent for obfuscation, placed a question that even Clinton could not avoid.

"Will you guarantee to us," Cannon intoned, "that if reelected, there is absolutely, positively no way that you'll run for any other political office and that you'll serve out your term in full?"

"You bet!" Clinton said. "I told you when I announced for governor I intended to run, and that's what I'm gonna do. I'm gonna serve four years. I made that decision when I decided to run. I'm being considered as a candidate for governor. That's the job I want. That's the job I'll do for the next four years."[1]

Sheffield Nelson tried throughout the 1990 general election campaign to tell voters otherwise.

"After his abortive run for president in 1988, I knew that Bill Clinton no longer had Arkansas at the top of his agenda but instead was pushing his own personal political agenda," Nelson said in a 1993 interview. "That is what really [prompted] my determination to take him on in 1990. You may remember, I promised the people that he would run for president if he were reelected and that he would raise taxes. He promised he wouldn't do either . . . but he did both."[2]

Some of the most astute minds in Arkansas politics, among them Skip Rutherford, now a consultant to the Democratic National Committee, believe Nelson owed his nomination to the Clinton organization, which orchestrated the impressive cross-over vote that occurred in the Republican primary. Given the choice between facing Tommy Robinson, who might or might not have any dirt on Clinton but who Clinton knew would not hesitate to play hardball, and Sheffield Nelson, who was not perceived to be a formidable opponent, the obvious choice was Nelson.

"Lee Atwater was very much involved in the Tommy Robinson 1990 gubernatorial race," Rutherford said. "Atwater knew Bill Clinton was going to be a factor in 1992, and he wanted to defeat him or to bruise him in 1990, and what better person to defeat or bruise than Tommy Robinson?"[3]

Thanks to the Clinton campaign's efforts, Rutherford said, liberal Democrats turned out in droves to vote for Nelson in the May primary, which they could do because Arkansas, an "open primary" state, allowed registered voters to vote in the other party's primary; it cost Robinson the nomination.

J.J. Vigneault, whom Atwater had assigned to the Robinson campaign, agreed that "Tommy won the most traditional Republican strongholds, but he just got killed in Pulaski County."[4]

"We had a good strategy, we had a good team, we didn't lack for money," Vigneault said. "Tommy was a good money raiser. Resources win elections, and we had the resources. I think there were two things that happened: Clinton's cross-over rally was the main factor, but Tommy had rubbed so many people the wrong way. I think those two combined drew so many people out that never would have voted in a Republican primary, before or since, particularly in Pulaski County, that that was the determining factor. . . . Tommy just got killed in Pulaski County."

In the end, the cross-over vote negated Robinson's appeal among conservative, rural Democrats, and Republicans who did not like Robinson; they voted for Nelson. As Rex Nelson pointed out, there were "a lot of competing interests"[5] in the Tommy Robinson-Sheffield Nelson campaign. Republicans were convinced that Clinton would run for president in 1992, and they wanted to back a potential winner in the primary. Robinson was seen as a winner, but many Republicans could not bring themselves to vote for him. The GOP was bitterly divided. The Stephens brothers, notwithstanding Jack's support for Robinson, were anxious to defeat Nelson.

With Atwater incapacitated, Robinson's campaign stumbled. Much of it was his own doing.

"Tommy has good qualities and bad qualities," Vigneault said. "One of the bad qualities was that he could not keep his mouth shut. The campaign got totally out of hand. I remember at a reception at [Ron] Fuller's, a television reporter asked if it was true that the Republican party in Washington was behind him, and Tommy made that famous statement, 'President Bush knows what I'm doing, and Lee Atwater and George Bush are 100 percent for me in the Republican party.' That was true, but he didn't need to get out and say it."

From that point on, Robinson began to lose ground in the polls. Two weeks before the primary, Nelson had a 2-point lead. He finally beat Robinson by a 58–42 margin.

The Democrat primary was rather dull except for two unexpected events.

Shortly before the filing period closed, Jim Guy Tucker mysteriously changed his mind and filed instead for lieutenant governor. Tucker declined to be interviewed for this book, but the conventional wisdom was and remains that he and Clinton "came to an understanding" about the governorship: If Tucker would run instead for the lieutenant governor's seat, which he had an outstanding chance of winning even without Clinton's help, he stood to become governor if

Clinton won the presidency in 1992. (The incumbent lieutenant governor, Winston Bryant, decided to run for the now vacant attorney general's position, which he won easily.)

The second event occurred when Hillary Clinton blasted Tom McRae at a news conference he held at the Capitol a week before the election. McRae was complaining that Clinton had refused to debate him when, according to Hillary, she just happened to come along to overhear his remarks.[6] McRae became flustered when she contradicted him. He became dumbstruck when she pulled out and began reading from a four-page statement prepared from old reports of the Winthrop Rockefeller Foundation in which McRae, during his fourteen years as the think tank's director, had praised Clinton on some of the same issues about which he had been criticizing him in the campaign. The entire exchange was captured by television cameras and was given prominent play in all the media.

McRae later said his name recognition "more than doubled in the next three days"[7] as a result of Hillary's grandstanding. He garnered more than 40 percent of the vote, but Clinton took the nomination with the smallest percentage of votes he had ever received in a primary, 54.8 percent.

There were actually six names on the Democrat primary ballot that year, but the largely frivolous candidacies of Jerry Tolliver, Joe Holmes, Otis Oliver Woodrow Wilson, and Cyrus Young were ignored by the media and the voters.

It should surprise no one that during the 1990 campaign, Clinton sought and received help from his occasional adversary, the *Arkansas Democrat*'s John R. Starr, who spoke candidly after the election about "the deal that we cut."[8]

"I had told Sheffield at the start of the campaign that if he came up with an education program, I would support him, and I told Clinton that if Sheffield came up with an education program, I would support Sheffield," Starr said. "Clinton said that Sheffield was more likely to come up with an agenda that would dismantle what had already been done, and that in fact was what happened. But I put off everything until this education debate, which I think was the first week in October."

Several months before the November election, Starr had gotten Nelson and Clinton to agree to a public debate on education, which Starr believed to be the most important issue of the campaign.

"I'd told Sheffield all along—this [debate] was scheduled for two, three months—I'd told him all along, 'This is your last chance. Either you come up with a good education program that night or I'm going to be for Bill Clinton.' . . . He said he was going to, and then he claimed he had, but Sheffield didn't even know how to spell education, much less have a program. He didn't know the difference in education and training.

"Anyway, Sheffield was a bust on the debate, just an absolute bust, and so I told Bill the next day, 'OK, I'm going to be for you and I'm going to write favorably about you, but I don't want to endorse you, and I'm not going to endorse you unless you get into trouble. If you get into trouble, then I will endorse you.' "

At the time, Starr said, neither he nor Clinton anticipated any trouble. Then on the Sunday morning before the Tuesday election, Starr got an early morning telephone call from Clinton.[9]

"I'm in trouble," he said.

"There's no way you can be in trouble," Starr replied.

"Yeah, the raise-and-spend commercials have got me dropping like a rock. I'm below 50 percent and headed down. We gotta do something to reverse it."

That weekend, Sheffield Nelson had played his ace. It was masterful: A commercial reminding voters how many times Bill Clinton had raised taxes during his tenure and overlaid with Clinton's own voice repeating the words "raise" and "spend."

Nelson recalled the waiting game his campaign played before the commercials started running. Timing was the key.

"That Wednesday, prior to the election the following Tuesday, [the Clinton campaign] ran what they considered to be their last poll that showed Clinton at 56–57 percent," Nelson said. "They decided they wouldn't need any more polling; it had stayed pretty static. I started 'raise-and-spend' Friday afternoon late."[10]

On Saturday, Clinton's pollster, Dick Morris, persuaded the governor to run one more poll. He sensed strong public reaction to the "raise-and-spend" commercial, and since the campaign had the money to spare, he thought it advisable to make a more scientific check on how the commercial was playing.

"They got their results back late Saturday night," Nelson said, "and my understanding is that [Morris] had to call Clinton and get him out of bed at midnight Saturday night, which would have been early Sunday morning, to tell him that we had knocked him to 44 [percent] in the polls and he was in deep trouble, that the chances of coming back were slim, that they had to come out with something that was dynamite."

Clinton did two things. He hastily taped a new commercial in which he claimed that Nelson had taken the words from a speech he had made to the legislature and used them out of context and that Nelson was the true raise-and-spend candidate. He also placed the call to Starr.

In the face of Clinton's entreaties, Starr fulfilled what he described as his part of the bargain.

"I came down to the office, pulled out the column I already had in the paper for Monday, and I wrote a column endorsing him, and then wrote another for Tuesday," Starr said.[11]

"Now what I said was, 'If you believe the most important thing in Arkansas is the education program, then Bill Clinton's the only choice.' I didn't say, 'I love Bill Clinton,' I didn't say, 'Bill Clinton's a great man.' He said later he thought that was better than if I'd said, 'He's a great man, I love him, vote for him,' because that way I'm saying to people who also like me might be on the fence, 'Look, I really looked at this thing, and if you want the education program to continue, then you've got to endorse Bill Clinton.' So I kept my part of the bargain and he began almost immediately to break his."

Clinton won reelection with 59 percent of the vote.

Relations between Starr and Clinton, who had always seemed to overcome any breaches of faith and differences of opinions, became frosty in January 1991, when Clinton kicked off his fifth term as governor by proposing the most regressive tax package of his career.

"A half-cent increase in the sales tax and a sales tax on used cars were the two major planks in it," Starr said. "I went to Honduras about the time the legislature started, but Clinton had done an awful lot of work preselling the tax program. Always previously, with anything that was likely to be that controversial, he would sign a bunch of people onto it beforehand, including me. Now, believe it or not, these were not cabals. We didn't all get together and decide. The Clintons were dealing with me individually and with Skip Rutherford individually, probably with Mack McLarty individually, with some of the movers and shakers individually."

Starr left the country with the understanding that Clinton would propose a 1-cent increase in the state sales tax with groceries exempted, which would raise an estimated $150 million. That was $100 million less than Clinton had suggested in initial conversations with his advisors, who had persuaded him to lower his sights if he wanted to avoid leaving the 1991 session emptyhanded.

"That is a pretty progressive tax program," Starr said, "and it was the last opportunity we'll ever have to take sales tax off food in Arkansas."

By the time Starr returned from Honduras, Clinton had cut the sales-tax request in half, abandoned the exemption for groceries, and endorsed a proposal to impose the sales tax on the resale of used cars, which had never been taxed. Altogether, Clinton had raised taxes by another $155 million.

"There was a hook in that tax on used cars," Starr said. "It gave buyers of new cars a break. Up until that time, buyers of new cars had paid full tax on the total purchase price of the vehicle and got no credit for the trade-in. Under the new law, a guy trades in a $20,000 car to buy a $30,000 car, he only pays $10,000 tax. So this was double regressive. It hit the little guy who was buying used cars and gave the guy who was buying the $50,000 Mercedes a break, and the guy who was buying a $50,000 Mercedes *every* year a *big* break.

"I raised hell about that, and Clinton said, 'Well, I talked to the people of the legislature and they're not willing to go along with the other.' I said, 'You know, you can fight them for it. We all agreed this was right.' He said everybody else had agreed to go that way. So he went ahead and went that way."

Starr conceded that he "wound up supporting that because it was the only tax proposal in town, and the teachers had taken a licking all

the way through the [education reform] program, which never provided any additional money for teachers and provided a lot of additional work for them."

"But the day after the tax passed in the legislature, then I began to
whip up on him some because of the regressiveness of the tax, and the
weak-willed way in which he had agreed to abandon what we had all
worked so hard to put together prior to the session.

"And shortly after that it became obvious—the legislature goes
home, and it quickly becomes obvious that he's lost all interest in
Arkansas altogether and is not going to fulfill his part of the promise to
stay here and build the state. I apologize for being provincial, but I
never thought I'd have any influence over anything past the borders of
this state, and I thought it was very important that we get done the job
that we had started with the education program."

Clinton and Starr had few contacts between then and June, when
Clinton telephoned him and accused him and other *Arkansas Democrat*
commentators and cartoonists of treating him unfairly.

"Son, you might get better treatment if you would tell me you plan
to keep your word about serving out your term as governor," Starr
said.[12]

"One reason I might run for president is that I would get away from
that load of bullshit that y'all dump on me in the *Democrat* every
morning," Clinton retorted.

"I told him . . . before he formally announced that he had lied to
me," Starr recalled. Clinton's unapologetic response was that "it was
important for the country that he run" for president. The few conversations they had after the announcement were "extremely busi-
nesslike."

"There was no friendly exchange after that," Starr said, and no need
for friendly exchanges, since Starr's journalistic approval and support
were no longer required. For the next thirteen months, Clinton would
be playing to a national audience that would neither follow nor care
what any Arkansas pundit thought about him or his ideas.

There also were no more friendly exchanges with *Arkansas Gazette*
columnists or editorial writers after October 18, 1991, when Gannett
abruptly announced that the *Gazette*, then the oldest newspaper west

of the Mississippi, had become a financial liability in a statewide market that could no longer support two competing newspapers and that publication would cease immediately. Employees would get severance pay, but they would not be permitted to complete work on the next day's editions. The Little Rock newspaper war was over. Within days, the *Gazette*'s assets—its buildings, presses, furnishings, and archives—were sold to the *Arkansas Democrat*, whose publisher, Walter E. Hussman, Jr., promptly renamed his newspaper the *Arkansas Democrat-Gazette*. It was a bitter blow to *Gazette* veterans, but although Bill Clinton also mourned its passing, he no longer needed to curry favor with the Arkansas news media.

Several former *Gazette* staffers did join his campaign, however, among them Capitol reporter Maxine Parker, who served as his campaign press secretary in Arkansas and later became press secretary to Clinton's successor as governor, Jim Guy Tucker. Ironically, Hussman had no immediate use for the building that had housed the *Gazette*'s news, advertising, and circulation departments, so he was amenable when the Clinton campaign, now burgeoning with staff and the growing press demands placed on a front-runner's presidential campaign, sought a short-term lease on the building. Thus the site of the newspaper that had championed Clinton's "national ambitions" since his arrival on the Arkansas political scene became the national headquarters for that much anticipated presidential campaign.

Despite several lingering controversies that surfaced periodically during the 1991 legislative session, the session was a remarkably successful one for Clinton. The lobbyists who had overwhelmed him in years past had begun getting with the program, and those who protested—most notably J. Bill Becker of the Arkansas AFL-CIO and Brownie Ledbetter of the Fairness Council, the umbrella for more than a dozen "citizens's" lobbies—did so more out of habit than out of any expectation of victory. The legislature, which had undergone a rather dramatic overhaul of its membership and its method of doing business as a result of the new ethics legislation and attrition, was well aware and very respectful of the power possessed by a governor embarking upon his fifth term. Lawmakers were delighted when Clinton still seemed inclined to compromise, because they realized that he could have had virtually anything he wanted had he only pressured them for it. This new and improved relationship meant that when lawmakers moved to increase their own pensions by 50 percent, Clinton did not resist.

Low- and middle-income Arkansans were hit hard in the 1992 session. The sales tax increased to 4.5 percent and was applied for the first time on used car sales, and gasoline and diesel fuel taxes were increased. A study released in April by a group called Citizens for Tax Justice revealed that Arkansas was taxing its poor at a rate 1.7 times higher than its wealthiest residents and that the percentage of income an Arkansan paid in taxes dropped across the board as income increased.

There were only a few jarring notes in the 1991 debate, the shrillest one sounded by Dr. Joycelyn Elders, director of the state Health Department. Once again, prolife advocates were complaining about school-based health clinics, but this time they were well organized. The letters and telephone calls and demonstrations they orchestrated kept the state Health Department's proposed $200 million biennial budget tied up in committee for days as lawmakers debated whether to continue the clinics's financing. Elders responded by denouncing "the religious, non-Christian Religious Right" and advised them to "get over their love affair with the fetus." It took a written apology from Elders to break the bottleneck.

Concurrently, some of Elders's opponents in the legislature questioned the manner in which she and another cabinet member, Dr. Terry Yamauchi, director of the Human Services Department, were paid. It was revealed that the six-figure salaries of the two for their work as department heads were being split between the budgets of the agencies they headed and the University of Arkansas for Medical Sciences, on whose faculty they served.

Public criticism of Elders and Yamauchi also escalated during this period because of policies that a growing number of people believed were detrimental to the health and welfare of the state's children. Problems in Yamauchi's department had been highlighted by two sensational child abuse cases in 1990, one resulting in a child's death and another in the loss of a child's leg. The latter was by far the more poignant because the victim was still alive to bear witness.

Daniel Toric was a sweet-faced child with a temperament to match. He usually had a toothy grin and a cheerful wave for the people who crowded around him. The microphones and tape recorders and brilliant lights did not faze him. From the first time Daniel Toric solemnly wiggled his tiny fingers toward the curious sea of observers that had gathered at the Pulaski County Courthouse and the first flicker of a smile creased his face, Daniel was a media star.

Daniel was only seven years old when he became front-page news. He handled the spotlight with considerable aplomb for a child who had survived so much trauma. His sparkling eyes cast no shadows. He seemed like an average, albeit unusually quiet little boy both awed and delighted at being the center of attention.

In September 1990, Daniel Toric had arrived at a local hospital near death, weighing only thirty-two pounds, his body ravaged by bruises, burns, and gangrene. Doctors said his head had become "mushy [and] soft, consistent with prolonged beatings."[13] He had two healed broken ribs, was suffering from chronic malnutrition, and the flesh was peeling from his gangrenous left leg, which his foster brother had forcibly plunged into a bucket of scalding water. The leg had to be amputated below the knee. For three years, Daniel had been entrusted to the care of a foster family who tortured him.

"Our investigation revealed he was regularly beaten and abused by several people living in that house," said Detective Lieutenant Richard Fulks of the Little Rock Police Department. "He was treated like an animal. He was forced to sleep under the bed, and food was routinely held from him, causing him to sneak food from the kitchen during the night. When he was caught sneaking food, he was beaten."[14]

Just as scandalous was the revelation that employees of the Arkansas Department of Human Services had been aware that Daniel had lived in the foster home since being abandoned at age three by his natural mother but claimed to have been unaware of his plight because they did not have enough caseworkers in the field to monitor "voluntary" placement cases such as Daniel's.

Daniel's foster mother, Frances Maudine Watson, and two of her children, Alglister Cunningham, nineteen, and Rita Watson, twenty-one, were arrested and eventually served prison time on child abuse charges. Watson's two teenage children were turned over to juvenile authorities.

The Daniel Toric case brought much needed scrutiny to the Department of Human Services, whose employees had been overworked and underpaid, and in many instances poorly trained, for years. But changes were extremely slow in coming.

In November 1990, the director of the department's Children and Family Services Division, Richard Dietz, said that several proposals for closer monitoring of children in foster care were under consideration, but that reform would be costly.

"At a bare minimum," he said, "we would need at least one hundred new field staff," a cost of $3 million. "We're talking about a lot of money, and we understand that, but at the same time, we have to provide the services."[15]

The proposal under primary consideration would require the department to seek a court order outlining its obligation to monitor each voluntary placement, Dietz said. He added that the department had 328 case workers but needed 699. Realizing the state's limitations, the department had asked for only 161 additional case workers over the next two years.

The Department of Human Services, then the largest department in state government, was also one of the most inefficient. With almost eight thousand employees and thirteen administrative subdivisions covering everything from drug abuse, children, and the aged, to disabilities and volunteerism, the department was unwieldy, poorly managed, and chronically inattentive to the needs of its hundreds of thousands of clients. Its problems were constantly revisited during legislative sessions, and while the Clinton administration and the legislature remained sympathetic, there never seemed to be enough money left over from the millions of dollars in tax revenue raised each session to pay for the new programs that seemed necessary. The department had undergone one reorganization during Clinton's tenure, in 1985, that had proved disastrous. Clients and sympathetic taxpayers were constantly calling for meaningful reform.

The stories about the Daniel Toric case and several fatal examples of the department's negligence that came to light brought some political pressure to bear on Bill Clinton. So did the subsequent threat of litigation lodged by Central Arkansas Legal Services and the National Center for Youth Law, a child advocacy organization based in San Francisco. An investigation by the Center for Youth Law concluded that Arkansas's youth services system was actually jeopardizing the lives of children in its care. Not only did the system violate the statutory and constitutional rights of children, the center contended, but the alleged violations had occurred for so long that they were endemic to the institution.

At the time, the Clinton administration claimed to be studying the problem with an eye toward correcting the department's deficiencies in the 1991 legislative session. In furtherance of that endeavor, the governor enlisted my aid because of several columns I had written indicting the state's child welfare system.

"We've come up with a gangbusters legislative program" in the area of human services, Clinton told me in December 1990. "We've been able to come to consensus on everything except child abuse and neglect."[16]

The problem, he said, left him "with a heavy heart," and he was frustrated that after several weeks of brainstorming, his administration still lacked a firm strategy "to try to make something good happen."

He said he wanted the state's commitment "to be more than money. I'm looking for any model for how to address this problem. I honestly don't believe most people want to get to the point that they beat their children. The predictable thing for us to do is treat this problem the way we treat the prison problem: to say that this is a terrible problem and we're going to hire more people to take care of it and hope to goodness they can keep some children alive."

Clinton asked me to describe the problem to *Arkansas Democrat* readers and solicit their advice and ideas for overhauling the state's child welfare system. Response was overwhelming. Letters came from throughout the state, from housewives, blue-collar workers, educators, retirees, lawyers, social workers, teachers, medical professionals, and ministers. People who had been victimized by the system, abusers and abused, shared the problems and deficiencies they had encountered in the state program and made thoughtful, knowledgeable suggestions about needed reforms. Their complaints and recommendations were delineated in a report presented to Clinton early in the 1991 session.

In March, Clinton announced that he planned to use money from his emergency fund to hire a consultant to help state officials receive federal grants for child welfare services. He said he also planned to put together a team of national experts to review and make recommendations for improving the existing child welfare system. In the meantime, he pointed out, he had persuaded the legislature to increase the budget of the Children and Family Services Division by 22 percent in fiscal 1992—about $2 million, most of which was to be used to hire more case workers and aides. (By the time Clinton announced his candidacy for president seven months later, only thirteen of the twenty-one new aides and nineteen of the forty-four new case workers had been hired and no substantive changes had been made in administrative procedures.)

Considering the enormity of the problem and the number of studies, both professional and informal, that had been conducted, child abuse activists were stunned that Clinton's response to the problem was to commission yet another study. In July 1991, Central Arkansas Legal Services and the National Center for Youth Law sued the state. Clinton's response was that it would do no good to throw good money after bad.

"I did not say we should not spend more money," Clinton hastened to tell me. "What I said was money alone will not solve the problems. . . . A lot of the allegations [in the lawsuit] are not money problems, they are management and operations problems. What I tried to stress is that if we don't solve the non-money problems, we will just be adding money to a system that's not working."[17]

In August, as Clinton was busy at the National Governors Association conference, more trouble for the state's beleaguered public health and welfare systems was brewing.

In the wake of the lawsuit against the Human Services Department's Division of Children and Family Services, a second lawsuit was filed against the department's Division of Youth Services. This one was brought by the parents of two teenage residents of the Pine Bluff Youth Services Center who charged that violence was rampant at the center. The lawsuit resulted in a court order imposing greater security at the facility. In the aftermath, one of the youths alleged that drug use was widespread at the facility. Yamauchi said he was not trying to hide the problems but that they were not that much different from those in other states.

As Bill Clinton celebrated his forty-fifth birthday in Seattle reacting to the news that Mikhail Gorbachev had been ousted as head of the Soviet Union, Acting Governor Tucker summoned Yamauchi to his office at the state Capitol for the first of several meetings on the latest round of crises in DHS. Tucker said he wanted to discuss "a number of issues"[18] involving the department, not the least of which were the administration, or lack thereof, of the Pine Bluff Youth Services Center, plans for closing the Alexander Youth Services Center, an advisory committee's recommendation that DHS temporarily be relieved of its license for placing children in foster care and for adoption, and alleged failings of the child welfare system.

"I'm very disturbed at some of the things that happened, but rather than try to get into details, just let me say that I think there will be some announcements within the week," Tucker told reporters.[19] Clinton, he said, would be briefed on the details of his meetings with Yamauchi. "You can expect that it will be something that is coordinated and Governor Clinton is fully advised of and in favor of."

In dealing with children, "the tradition for the entire department is to respond to crisis and nothing more,"[20] grumbled Ami Rossi, executive director of Arkansas Advocates for Children and Families. Well aware of the Clinton administration's *modus operandi*, she predicted "a flurry of activity that looks like they are going to do something and then that will die down."

Tucker began to prepare for a special legislative session that he would postpone as long as possible to avoid any conflict or adverse publicity for Clinton following what Tucker believed to be Clinton's imminent presidential campaign.

"I will be the acting governor if I have to, and I am assuming that I will have to assume that duty," Tucker told reporters.[21]

When Clinton returned to work on August 26, Yamauchi announced numerous administrative changes in the state's child welfare system and proposals for more that would require legislative support. Through a spokesman, Clinton commended Yamauchi's "good first steps" but noted that "more may need to be done."[22] He conceded that many of Yamauchi's proposals had been proposed the year before, when child advocacy groups asked the administration "to raise more money than we could possibly raise in the last [legislative] session."

During the presidential campaign, Clinton's Arkansas critics often referred to the two DHS lawsuits as examples of his poor leadership. They pointed out that the reforms resulting from these lawsuits were merely two in a decade-long string of litigation-driven reforms in state government. Prison conditions, child welfare, juvenile justice, statewide redistricting, environmental pollution, and the state's role in school desegregation were but a few of the issues addressed by the legislature as a direct result of class-action lawsuits. The cost to the state's treasury as a result of these lawsuits has never been determined, but $1 billion would be a modest estimate.

The national press showed little interest in the Clinton administration's deficiencies, numerous examples of which could have been found in both the pro-Clinton *Arkansas Gazette* and the anti-Clinton *Arkansas Democrat* had out-of-state reporters bothered to look. Two recent examples were the cases of Fahmy Malak and Wayne Dumond.

Fahmy Malak had survived twelve tumultuous years as the state's medical examiner. Given the favored treatment extended to Malak by Clinton over the years, many Arkansans are still amazed that he was overlooked when President Clinton began inviting Arkansas supporters into his administration. But observers of Arkansas politics knew Malak could not have survived Senate confirmation hearings. That Malak survived in Arkansas is a testament to Clinton's power.

Malak was not only an unorthodox state medical examiner, he was by most accounts unqualified for the job. He repeatedly lied about his credentials, misconstrued his findings, and misrepresented autopsy procedures. In the lab, he misplaced bodies and destroyed evidence. On the witness stand, he was a prosecutor's dream, and if his deductions and conjectures and professional opinions did not fit the design, he merely dug deeper into his memory bank, or introduced heretofore overlooked variables, or located misplaced evidence to prove the point.

Malak caused the Clinton administration more embarrassment and more grief than anyone else, yet he managed to hang onto his job. Arkansans were thus quite surprised when Malak finally resigned under pressure from Clinton in the summer of 1991 rather than undergo a long overdue review of his job performance. Surprise turned to astonishment a few weeks later, when it was learned that Joycelyn Elders had created a job for him at the Health Department as coordinator of the state's AIDS education program. The job paid about one-fourth less than that of medical examiner, but the mere fact that anyone would want to hire him was amazing. Why was the Clinton administration so reluctant to fire Malak and be done with him?

The popular theory was that Malak "had something on Clinton" that made the governor loath to fire him. That is mere conjecture, but more than likely based on two medical controversies involving Clinton's mother in the early 1980s.

The first case involved the 1978 death of twenty-two-year-old Laura Lee Slayton, who died ten days after undergoing abdominal surgery at what was then Ouachita Memorial Hospital. Alleging negligence, Slayton's family sued the surgeon, Dr. John H. Brunner, in 1980, but the suit was later dismissed by Circuit Judge Henry M. Britt, who in 1968 had assisted Raymond Clinton in his efforts to help his brother's stepson avoid the draft.[23]

On appeal, the state Supreme Court ruled that Britt had erred by disallowing testimony by an expert witness. The witness, Dr. Robert King, an Oklahoma anesthesiologist, testified that Brunner and the nurse anesthetist in the case, Virginia Dwire, had not adequately monitored Slayton before transferring her to recovery after surgery and that they had not taken the proper steps when her breathing and heart stopped almost immediately after the surgery. Litigation was reinstituted in March 1983, and Virginia Dwire, by then Virginia Kelley, was added as a defendant in the alleged wrongful death of Slayton.[24]

In an out-of-court settlement in the Slayton case that summer, Brunner was dropped as a defendant and Virginia Dwire Kelley agreed to pay Slayton's survivors $90,000.[25]

The second case involved the June 1981 death of seventeen-year-old Susie Deer during surgery at Ouachita Memorial Hospital. Hospital records stated that Deer died after her heart stopped while the nurse anesthetist, Virginia Dwire, was attempting to move a breathing tube from Deer's nose to her mouth during the surgery.[26]

Deer had been injured when someone threw a rock at the moving car in which she was riding. Before the surgery to repair her broken jaw, nose, and sinus cavity, doctors told her family that the prognosis was good. Deer reportedly was sitting up in bed and talking before the surgery.[27]

One of the surgeons present, Dr. William Schuelte, later said that Dwire had tried "at least two times, maybe more"[28] to place the breathing tube into Deer's lungs. He said another surgeon told Dwire to force air into Deer's lungs because she was showing signs of having too little oxygen. By the time the tube was successfully inserted, Deer's heart had stopped.

An autopsy was performed by Dr. Fahmy Malak, who had been appointed state medical examiner during Clinton's first term as governor. At the time of the autopsy, Clinton was out of office but Governor White allowed Malak to retain his job. Malak's report stated that Deer died of "blunt trauma"[29] to the head. It did not mention the problems with the breathing tube and it did not address the question of why Deer's heart stopped.

Three out-of-state medical examiners who reviewed the report agreed that brain damage could have occurred if the rock that struck Deer had "jiggled" the brain and banged it against the inside of Deer's skull. Schuelte said that brain damage had not been suspected or diagnosed before Deer's death.

Schuelte later told the *Arkansas Gazette* that Deer's death became the last straw for some doctors who already were uncomfortable working with Kelley and that the doctors pressured the hospital to stop using Kelley's services as a nurse anesthetist.[30]

In September 1981, the hospital hired Dr. Robert Humphries to take over anesthesiology services. (Kelley later filed a $3 million federal antitrust lawsuit against the hospital and Humphries's firm, Ouachita Anesthesia Services, claiming that the two had conspired to monopolize anesthesia work in Hot Springs and to deprive her of her $80,000 job. The case was settled out of court in 1984. The terms were not disclosed. Virginia Kelley did not renew her nurse anesthetist's license and retired.) That same month, Billy Ray Washington, the man who threw the rock that injured Deer, pleaded no contest to a charge of negligent homicide and was sentenced to six months in jail.[31]

Several weeks later, Washington's attorney, J. Sky Tapp, filed a motion to withdraw the plea. He said in his motion that "this matter involves a death which conceivably was not caused by the defendant's negligence and caused by other intervening circumstances."[32]

Tapp then issued subpoenas for the doctors, nurses, police, and others involved in the Deer case but did not pursue discovery, and Washington again pleaded no contest and served his six months.

Tapp later told the *Arkansas Gazette* that all subpoenaed parties indicated that they would not be readily cooperative, and because Washington did not have the kind of money it would have taken to compel them to provide information or to hire an outside medical examiner, the matter was dropped. Tapp conceded that his law practice was only three years old at the time and that he believed pursuing the matter could cause him "a lot of problems" given the powerful people involved.[33]

These matters were resurrected June 1992 by NBC's "Dateline" in a lead story about Fahmy Malak's controversial twelve years as state medical examiner. In that broadcast, Jesse Chandler, identified as a former top aide to Malak and the investigator in charge of the Susie Deer case, claimed that Malak had mounted "a cover-up to protect Clinton's mother." The director of the state Crime Laboratory Board claimed that Chandler's only involvement with the Deer case was to pick up Deer's body and take it to the morgue. These matters were not pursued beyond that "Dateline" report and an accompanying story in the *New Republic*.

The ongoing controversy surrounding Wayne Dumond has spawned one true crime book, *Unequal Justice: Wayne Dumond, Bill Clinton, and the Politics of Rape in Arkansas*, in which author Guy Reel delineated the travesties of "a judicial system gone terribly wrong."[34] There were two victims of crime in the Dumond case: the 1984 abduction and rape of Bill Clinton's seventeen-year-old cousin, and the subsequent beating, sodomization, and castration of her alleged assailant, Wayne Dumond, a decorated Vietnam War veteran and the unemployed father of three.

Dumond maintained that his arrest was a case of mistaken identity, and testimony indicates that it was, but he was found guilty in 1985 and sentenced to twenty years on the kidnapping charge and life in prison for rape. Despite evidence of prosecutorial error and local prejudice on the part of law enforcement officials and numerous appeals by his attorney, John Wesley Hall, Jr., in an attempt to reopen the case and admit new genetic evidence that Hall said would prove Dumond's innocence, he remained behind bars. In the meantime, Hall petitioned the state Board of Pardons and Paroles to modify Dumond's sentence.

In June 1990, after Dumond had served four years and ten months in state prison, the Parole Board recommended that Clinton commute the life term to time served and release Dumond immediately. The board expressed numerous concerns in arriving at the decision, among them the failure of Dumond's original attorney, Larry Horton, to seek a change of venue, Horton's subsequent acquisition of literary rights to the case, and Dumond's castration. Mike Gaines, the Parole Board chairman, said he was troubled, too, by the life sentence, which was much longer than had been imposed on convicted rapists in St. Francis County.

Dumond's guilt or innocence was not a factor in his decision, Gaines said. "I didn't even get that far in it," he added. "I simply came to the conclusion that whether he's guilty or not, he did not get the kind of justice that he should have."[35]

. Clinton, then seeking his fifth term as governor, rejected the recommendation.

"It seems to me very inappropriate to take action on this case while Mr. Dumond had an appeal pending in federal court," Clinton said through a spokesman, adding that it would set "a very questionable precedent."[36] His office noted the receipt of about four hundred commutation requests a year and pointed out that Clinton had granted only five since resuming the governorship in 1983.

"I expected more out of Bill Clinton than this crap," Hall fumed. "The case before the Eighth Circuit [Court of Appeals] is an entirely independent issue," that of whether to order a new trial at which genetic evidence supporting Dumond's innocence could be admitted.[37] Hall expressed disbelief that Clinton would reject the board's recommendation out of hand. "What if the appeals court says he's entitled to relief? Does that mean that Wayne Dumond spends another year in jail because Bill Clinton doesn't have the guts to do what's right? . . . He used to be attorney general. Where's his mind? Wayne Dumond isn't the only man without balls."

A widely held belief was that Dumond was a victim of politics at both the local and state levels. The rape victim was not only Clinton's cousin, but her father was the county coroner and her mother had been appointed by Clinton to the Governor's Mansion Commission.

Several weeks after having recommended commutation of Dumond's sentence, the Parole Board, in an unprecedented action, asked the governor to return its letter of recommendation for Dumond's immediate release. Gaines hand-delivered it to Clinton's office the same day. He defended the board's reversal by saying that the family of the victim had not been given an opportunity to be heard. Actually, the family of the victim had been discouraged by its lawyer from attending.[38] The girl, then a student at the University of Arkansas at Fayetteville, had voiced her opposition to leniency in a letter to the board.

Hall kept pursuing leniency, and the stalemate continued until shortly after Clinton announced his bid for the presidency. While Clinton was campaigning at a health clinic in Houston, Texas, a woman quietly stepped in front of him and asked why he had refused to commute Wayne Dumond's sentence. The woman, Debbie Riddle, a friend of Dumond's wife, Dusty, announced for the benefit of reporters that Wayne Dumond already had served more time in prison than others convicted of rape.[39]

"That's not true," Clinton declared as local reporters gawked. He countered that the average person convicted of first-degree rape in Arkansas serves much longer than Dumond had at that point served.

"Just because I'm in national politics doesn't mean I'm going to let *exposés* govern what I think is right or wrong," he snapped before aides stepped between him and Riddle. Riddle told the handful of reporters who would listen that she intended to make the Dumond case a thorn in Clinton's side, but little came of it. Three months later, Dusty Dumond, long since relocated to Houston, where she worked as a legal assistant, tried to organize a protest outside a Clinton fundraiser at the posh Wyndham Warwick Hotel. Only about a dozen people joined her, but their signs and chants quickly attracted Clinton's attention. Taking a break from the fund-raising, Clinton said he found it "amazing that someone would make a claim that it is inherently unfair for someone convicted of intentional first-degree rape to serve seven years or more in the penitentiary."[40] Later, he was confronted by Dusty Dumond outside the hotel, where she extracted from him a promise that he would have the case reviewed again.

In April 1992, Acting Governor Jim Guy Tucker commuted the life-plus-twenty-years sentence of Wayne Dumond to 39.5 years in prison, making him eligible for parole in 1995.

Tucker graciously gave Clinton some credit. Tucker's spokesman, Neil Turner, claimed that Clinton asked Tucker to review the clemency application "to remove any doubts about his objectivity."[41]

22

TAKING CARE OF BUSINESS

SCARCELY NINE MONTHS into his fifth gubernatorial term, Clinton officially broke his promise not to seek another office, a promise he had made in full knowledge that it would never be kept. But, as Clinton had advised intimates, he had to tell the lie or he might not have been reelected, and he needed that reelection to enhance his viability as a presidential candidate.[1]

Clinton's rationale for breaking faith with the people would be that he had not broken faith at all: The people *wanted* him to seek the presidency. It would bring honor and glory to their humble little state, and besides, this was his destiny. He was meant to be president of the United States. This is what he had worked his entire adult life to attain. He had given his people so much that the least they could do was give him up, let him go, release him from his vow.

In effect, he rationalized later, he had meant it when he said it, but the situation had changed. When he announced his candidacy for president, the prospective field was bleak. George Bush was still doing well in the polls, soaring not quite as high so he had at the height and in the immediate aftermath of the conflict in the Persian Gulf, but well enough to promulgate a formidable reelection effort—

and no one among the Democratic party's roster had the charisma or the politics to take him on. The Democrats needed a moderate, and as a founder member and former chair of the Democratic Leadership Council, Clinton was the natural choice. He was the only viable Democrat "name" he knew who could or even would want to hold his liberal propensities in check long enough to secure the nomination.

Before handing over the chairmanship of the Democratic Leadership Council in March 1990, United States Senator Sam Nunn of Georgia quipped that Bill Clinton was "the very first person in the political history of the United States to be identified as a 'bright, young, rising star' in three different decades."[2]

Part of the credit for that goes to the DLC, which gave Clinton's political career a much needed boost after his disastrous performance at the 1988 Democrat National Convention. Unnoticed by many pundits during the 1992 campaign was the contribution to Clinton's candidacy made by the DLC.

The council was formed within weeks after Walter Mondale's stunning 1984 loss to President Ronald Reagan by a group of Southern and Western Democrats who had long realized that their party was seriously out of step with the concerns of many longtime Democrats and were determined to do something about it.

"We would like to be a positive and constructive force in moving the DNC back to what we might call mainstream America," said Arkansas Senator David Pryor, one of its founder members.[3] Pryor said publicly what many rank-and-file Democrats had been saying among themselves for years—that the structure and the leadership of the national party was hopelessly mired in an elitist, liberal agenda that shut out moderate and conservative Democrats.

"The DNC is a large, cumbersome, insensitive bureaucracy," Pryor declared. "None of the people working down there are elected officials who are close enough to the people."[4]

One of the chief complaints of the founders was that the national party had splintered into a number of special-interest groups whose individual agendas were undermining the party's collective strength. The DLC, Pryor said, would provide an "independent voice" for those Democrats whose views were not adequately represented by the national committee.

Almost from the council's inception, it was evident that the disenfranchised Democrats in question were largely middle- and upper-class white males, hence the derisive nickname, "the Southern white boys club," bestowed upon it by more cynical partisans. Despite protesting the emphasis placed on that voting segment, DLC spokesman could not avoid the obvious: Since the death of Franklin Delano Roosevelt, the Democratic party had attracted more than 50 percent of the white male vote in only one national election, that of Lyndon B. Johnson in 1964. The DLC meant to reverse that trend, although that was not the only part of its agenda.

Thanks to the rapidly growing Sunbelt states and the increasingly virulent factional warfare in the Democratic party, the major philosophical identifiers (conservative versus liberal) had displaced partisan identifiers (Republican versus Democrat) in the South. Jimmy Carter had proved the South's value as a voting bloc in the 1976 election, and Ronald Reagan's campaign had capitalized on that knowledge in 1980. The lesson apparently had been lost on Mondale. Southern Democrats, who dominated the DLC, wanted to play a larger role in future presidential elections and believed their alliance could force the point, which, indeed, it did, resulting in establishment of the twenty-state regional presidential primary known as Super Tuesday in 1988. Fourteen of those states, which represented 207 electoral votes, or 76 percent of what a candidate needs to be elected president, were in or bordered the South.

In addition to seeking a larger role in the presidential nominating process, many of the DLC's most industrious proponents were men who wanted to be on the ticket, among them Bruce Babbitt of Arizona, Charles Robb of Virginia, Richard Gephardt of Missouri, and Bill Clinton of Arkansas.

Arkansas's governor, who was giving serious consideration to a presidential bid in 1988, played a key role in the council's endeavors, stumping the South in an effort to promote the Super Tuesday regional primary and, somewhat ironically, to downplay the party's reliance on liberal special-interest groups on which he personally relied. However, as he assumed a larger role in the organization, he began trying to alter the public's perception of it as a conservative white caucus, recruiting black members and espousing a more populist set of issues, among them poverty, illiteracy, drug abuse, teenage pregnancy, and the "family-values" issues with which the Republicans were more closely identified.

If the Democratic Leadership Council was discouraged by the results of Super Tuesday, which produced only one Southern Democratic candidate, Senator Al Gore, Jr., of Tennessee, Clinton was not.

"The only ones who might be defensive are those who thought Super Tuesday would dictate a Southern nominee," Clinton said in 1988. "I never thought that would happen. The two things I did hope would happen . . . have occurred. First, the South has received numerous visits from all of the candidates. Secondly, the looming presence of a broad regional primary has had an effect on what the candidates are saying. Knowing that a large, regional primary was coming up, they were not as inclined to make promises to narrow special-interest groups in Iowa and New Hampshire."[5]

The main objective of the Democratic Leadership Council, of course, was to regain the White House, something the DLC was ill-equipped to influence as long as it was at odds with the leadership of the Democratic National Committee. From the very beginning, the DLC had distanced itself from the central party structure, setting up its own staff and soliciting its own contributions. Clinton was heavily involved in expanding the DLC's base of support, which at some point, he believed, had to include the Democratic National Committee if the fortunes of the party were to be reversed. The Democratic Leadership Council had not been considered a major influence in the 1988 primaries, but Michael Dukakis's defeat in the election appeared to validate the DLC's assertion that the Democrats must become more centrist if they were to win the presidency. Clinton, whom Al From, the DLC's executive director, had called "as articulate a spokesman for the DLC as there is,"[6] was tapped for the chairmanship almost a year before the decision became official.

"You can't talk about moving into the mainstream in the abstract," Clinton said upon offering his services to his fellow DLC executive committee members. "You have to have some ideas that appeal to the mainstream."[7]

To appeal to the mainstream, however, one had to look beyond the Beltway, so in addition to fund-raising, Clinton's chief contribution to the DLC was expanding its membership base, as well as his own political network, by bringing more state legislators and governors into the fold, "grass-roots people throughout the country who are actually doing things."[8] Shifting the focus of debate from national policy to state and local issues was his major objective, Clinton said, because these were the issues about which the average American was most concerned. "I think it will be very helpful to me," Clinton told one reporter, hastening to explain, "It will give me access to people and ideas, good ideas."[9]

The roster of participants for the New Orleans conference, a lavish affair staged at the luxurious Fairmont Hotel in March 1990, had a decidedly liberal tilt, prompting Clinton to declare the meeting a rousing success before it commenced. Among the speakers were Democratic National Committee Chairman Ron Brown, Jesse Jackson, Senator Daniel Patrick Moynihan, House Majority leader Richard Gephardt, and Senator Lloyd Bentsen. The DLC also could boast of more than 170 corporate sponsors.

"I think it's fair to say the battle's over and we won," Clinton declared.[10]

In subsequent interviews, Clinton repeatedly rejected any suggestion that he was using the Democratic Leadership Council as a launching pad for a 1992 presidential campaign.

"I expect to get as much good, if not more good, out of this in terms of developing positions on important issues that could be implemented in Arkansas as any of these other groups I've been involved with over the years," he said.[11]

Lest anyone else misinterpret his motives for courting the chairmanship, in his acceptance speech Clinton urged his fellow Democrats to end "this obsession with the presidency."[12]

"The real tragedy is [that] most people go about their business every day and we don't ever cross their minds because they don't now what we stand for, they don't know who we are, they don't know what we're trying to do," he said. "And so help me, I believe that that is what we ought to spend the rest of 1990 working on, and we should forget about who is going to run for president and whether that person can win in 1992."

Senator John Breaux of Louisiana, Clinton's choice to head the "mainstream movement" to establish state DLC chapters, called him "a national leader."[13]

"I can mention Bill Clinton's name in Ohio or Florida or Washington State and they know who I'm talking about," he said.

"Bright, energetic, dynamic,"[14] Sam Nunn enthused.

"The four hundred council members sat hushed in the Fairmont Hotel ballroom as Clinton spoke," wrote the *Arkansas Democrat*'s Joan Duffy, who covered the New Orleans meeting. "Then many knocked over chairs as they leaped to their feet in applause when he finished."[15]

Following his 1990 victory in the Arkansas gubernatorial race, Clinton spent a good deal of time organizing state chapters of the Democratic Leadership Council, not for himself, he insisted, but for the good of the party.

"I am far more interested in building a movement than helping myself," he said.[16]

Al From agreed, saying, "We hope to build a network of people who might not have been involved in Democratic [presidential] primaries, an alternative infrastructure for the candidate or candidates delivering the message we hope the Democrats will emphasize in 1992."[17]

If, as one unnamed "major" DLC supporter told the *Washington Post*'s David Broder, the organization's goal was "to create the potential of a national organization that might offset the advantage in money and publicity a Mario Cuomo would have the day he announced his candidacy," it had chosen wisely in Bill Clinton.[18]

The DLC leadership's protestations aside, Clinton's potential as a candidate was fully appreciated by the organization's membership. As Arkansas labor leader J. Bill Becker remarked, "The establishment [organizations] are smart. They know whose bandwagon to get on and who to accommodate."[19]

Having secured his governor's seat, Clinton spent the spring and summer of 1991 building a national DLC network, fostering new chapters in Kentucky, the Carolinas, Alabama, Mississippi, and Texas. His aim was to have twenty such chapters in place by the organization's May convention in Cleveland and an additional twenty by year's end. As the convention date approached, he crisscrossed the western half of the nation, addressing groups in Salem, Oregon; Cheyenne, Wyoming; Los Angeles, California; and Denver, Colorado. *Newsweek* suggested that his traveling and money-raising activities were "drawing him closer to a decision to run"[20] for president. *Entertainment Tonight* featured him with actor-director Sidney Poitier in a clip from the Los Angeles appearance.

But he continued to disavow any interest in a 1992 presidential bid, telling reporters that his name kept resurfacing because he had "been around a long time" and because "there's nobody out there running."[21]

"Once there are four or five people running, the ones that aren't running won't be mentioned anymore," he said. "As long as nobody runs, everybody can be on the list. And it's kind of nice. It makes my mother happy to read my name in the paper."

Clinton's stock with mainstream Democrats rose considerably when he not only neglected to invite Jesse Jackson to address the Cleveland convention in May 1991 but refused to be bullied into doing so. (Jackson returned the favor by not inviting Clinton to join other prospective Democrat presidential candidates in addressing the Rainbow Coalition's national meeting in Washington a month later.)

Al From had been rather impolitic, claiming that neither Jackson nor George McGovern would be asked to address the Democratic Leadership Council convention because they represented the "old-style politics" that the DLC was trying to supplant.[22] Jackson reacted predictably, denouncing the "Southern White Boys Club" and "Democrats for the leisure class" and firing off letters to the DLC leadership, including Clinton, demanding to know whether he had been banned from the convention because they shared From's opinion.[23]

Clinton denied that Jackson had been barred from the conference for any reason whatsoever. It was true, he said, that Jackson had not been invited to speak, "but he made a major speech at the last convention. I think he made the longest speech of the convention. Half of it was rather critical of the DLC, but we wanted to hear his message and invited him."[24]

After the New Orleans convention in 1990, Clinton said, delegates had been asked what could be done to improve the convention. "They said make fewer speeches, have them shorter, have more panels, more discussion groups, and give the delegates themselves more time to debate the issues," he said. "There's no deliberate attempt to snub [Jackson] by not extending an invitation to speak."[25]

Jackson took a few public swings at the DLC, but Clinton would not be swayed. He had had to contend with Jackson's antics on too many occasions, most notably during the Dukakis campaign, and he was determined not to be upstaged or intimidated by Jackson's self-serving demagoguery. It was time to show Jackson who was in charge. The most Jackson would get from the chairman of the Democratic Leadership Council was a personal invitation to attend the convention.

"You missed my point," Jackson responded. "The issue is whether staff members speak on behalf of, and in the interests of, your organization when they launch a personal, provocative, and unprovoked attack against fellow Democrats."[26]

Clinton responded with yet another invitation to Jackson to attend, but not address, the convention. As Jackson stepped up his offense, Clinton became less agreeable.

"I don't want to get into labeling or name-calling," he said, but "we've heard his views. He's been criticizing us for years."[27]

Five days before the Cleveland convention, former Massachusetts Senator Paul Tsongas became the first Democrat officially to announce his presidential candidacy. His timing could not have been worse. Pundits had already decided that the three-day conference at Cleveland would be something akin to a nominating convention, with Bill Clinton as the Democratic Leadership Council's favorite son.

"I think there are a lot of people who would like to see the Cleveland convention as the start of the 'Bill Clinton for president' campaign," said Democrat political consultant Mike McCurry.[28]

Throughout the convention, whose eight hundred participants included no fewer than fifty Arkansas delegates consisting of corporate lobbyists, political advisors, legislators, party leaders, and gubernatorial staff members, Clinton was badgered about his political plans. He was adamant: "I'm not running."[29]

But he was being encouraged at every turn. Despite appearances by Tsongas and potential candidates such as Doug Wilder, Sam Nunn, Richard Gephardt, Al Gore, and Jay Rockefeller, Clinton was the undisputed star, beginning with a dynamic twenty-two-minute key-note address that energized the assembly and elicited widespread encouragement that he seek the party's nomination. Calling on all the expertise he had acquired as a stump speaker in a state that still prefers the fish fry to the cocktail party, the Arkansas governor was in turn pragmatic and dramatic. For once, his voice was rested, untouched by the chronic hoarseness that dogged him throughout every heavy speaking schedule, and it was able to ebb and soar.

At the convention, the preliminaries dispensed with, Clinton appealed to the assembly to dispel the common perception that the Democratic party was married to the notion of making the working middle class carry a disproportionate share of the national tax burden, that it was soft on defending the nation's interests abroad, and that profligacy with hard-earned tax dollars drove its agenda.

"We've got to turn these perceptions around or we won't continue as a national party," he declared. "But that is not the most important issue.[30]

"The most important thing," he said, his voice rising, "is that this United States of America needs at least one political party that's not afraid to tell the people the truth and address the real needs of human beings. We're not here to save the Democratic party, we're here to save the United States of America. . . . For more than a decade, we have lived in a fantasy world in which it was bad form and terrible politics to admit that we had problems of this magnitude. . . . The Republican burden is their record of denial, evasion, and neglect. But our burden is to give the people a new choice rooted in old values. . . . We've got to have a message that touches everybody, that makes sense to everybody, that goes beyond the state orthodoxies of 'left' and 'right.' "

The thunderous standing ovation that met the close of his remarks was not a mere courtesy. Many of the delegates came away persuaded that they had the right message and the right messenger. Clinton's disastrous speech nominating Michael Dukakis was all but forgotten. Clinton had given the entire address without a prepared text. Consultant Bob Beckel deemed his keynote "the best Democratic speech I've heard in the last ten years," and he included in that assessment Mario Cuomo's electrifying speech to the 1984 nominating convention at San Francisco.[31] Writing in the *Washington Post*, David Broder and Dan Balz observed that "despite a reputation as a long-winded bore that dates to his interminable nominating speech for Michael Dukakis at the 1988 convention, Clinton has dazzled DLC delegates at the last two gatherings in New Orleans and Cleveland."[32]

"Swayed by the praise—and perhaps by seeing the indifferent reaction to other potential challengers—Clinton has let some elasticity into his reelection campaign promise to serve out his current term as governor."[33]

"It's all very flattering," Clinton said of the many enthusiastic observations by fellow politicians and pundits that he spoke and acted like presidential material. "It means, I think, that they agree with what I said."[34] As for his political plans, he said, "I'd do it only if I thought the people at home were supportive and really wanted me to" run for president.[35]

The national policy platform unveiled by Clinton and adopted by the Democratic Leadership Council in Cleveland was touted as a near-perfect blueprint for the right Democrat candidate in 1992, centrist at its core but embracing the more attractive components of liberal (the Brady Bill, mandating a five-day waiting period for guns) and conservative (a free-trade agreement with Mexico) agendas. The convention delegates endorsed lower taxes on the middle class, a renewed commitment to a strong defense, and more fiscal accountability in the national government.

The platform also affirmed the Democratic party's "historic commitment to secure civil, equal, and human rights"; advocated the creation of a "permanent war powers delegation" of congressional leaders to be consulted before any deployment of United States troops abroad; supported the "right of reproductive freedom for all women regardless of socioeconomic status or age"; and advocated many of the so-called reforms in education championed by Clinton in Arkansas.

To some degree, an offhand remark made by Clinton following a Little Rock speech to the Governor's Quality Management Conference characterized his subsequent approach to the 1992 campaign.

"If we can elect a smart, good person [as] president," he said, "or just nominate someone who will say these things and run on the program I tried to outline [at the convention], I think it will change the country's view of the Democratic party."[36]

When his time came, Clinton was more than happy to accommodate as many special-interest groups as possible by "say[ing] these things" which he believed would result in the first Democrat presidency in a dozen years.

Not everyone was happy with the platform advanced at Clinton's behest by the Democratic Leadership Council, although most of the criticism came from those who knew him best.

"I'm very concerned about some of the positions the governor has taken,"[37] said state Representative Bill Walker of the Arkansas General Assembly's Black Caucus, whose members were horrified that the DLC would reject mainstream Democrat support for racial hiring quotas.

Brownie Ledbetter, director of an umbrella organization for numerous populist citizens's groups called the Arkansas Fairness Council, accused the DLC of "playing off racism" and likened the statement on quotas to the "smoke and mirrors" used by Republican opponents of civil rights legislation.[38]

"I certainly hope that the national Democrats won't pay any attention to what they did over there," said J. Bill Becker, president of the Arkansas AFL-CIO, whose primary concern was that the DLC had made "a terrible mistake" by endorsing a free-trade agreement with Mexico. However, he added his voice to that of blacks who joined Jesse Jackson in decrying the racial quota issue, calling it a "red herring," since civil rights legislation pending in Congress did not address the matter except to state that it was not a quota bill.[39]

"There's a reason for making that a major issue when that wasn't one," observed state Representative Irma Hunter Brown, chairman of the Black Caucus. "I just wonder what that reason might be."[40]

There was a general sense, of course, that racial hiring quotas had been made an issue in an effort to pander to the white American majority just as the free-trade agreement had been a sop to conservatives who abhorred the increasing flow of illegal immigrants from Mexico. Clinton had, in fact, been buttonholed by a group of about thirty black delegates in Cleveland who demanded to know whether the Democratic Leadership Council was indeed abandoning minority voters in its attempts to appeal to middle-class, meaning primarily white, voters.

"Give us time," Clinton told the contentious group. "We're sort of making it up as we go along."[41] He assured the delegates, many of whom had only recently joined the DLC, that the organization had no intention of abandoning the Democrats's historic commitment to civil rights and affirmative action. In time, he said, as the DLC developed a larger, grass-roots base of support, the concerns expressed by the black delegates would be heard.

In response to criticism at home from two of his traditional but sometimes skittish constituencies, blacks and organized labor, Clinton insisted that there was nothing "elitist or discriminatory about the program we adopted. I believe that if people will look at what we had to say, it will receive broad support."[42]

Betsey Wright, with whom Clinton had mended a schism by appointing her chair of the Democratic party of Arkansas, leaped to his defense.

"No one who claims that the meeting that adopted those resolutions is conservative or mimicking the Republican party has read the resolutions," she said. "No Republican party would adopt this platform."[43]

"If they're for black people," retorted Jesse Turner, the black co-chairman of Arkansas's Jefferson County Republican Committee, "Bill and Betsey should have led the fight for a civil rights bill with some teeth in it."[44] He aptly pointed out that Arkansas lacked a comprehensive civil rights law and added that "the Democratic party of Arkansas is the reason that we don't."

Clinton could handle criticism from black politicians, even Republican ones, with a good deal more aplomb than he could from white politicians of equal or greater standing. Criticism from Mario Cuomo, the brusque governor of New York, never failed to irritate him. He was particularly stung when Cuomo commented that Clinton and other members of the Democratic Leadership Council sounded like Republicans, "but they wear a jackass instead of an elephant."[45]

Washington reporters were only slightly less skeptical than Arkansas reporters about Clinton's campaign plans. Had the national media kept up with his activities as closely as had the hometown media, they might have realized just how determined Clinton was to expand his reach before officially entering the race. For example, in the fifty-two-day period following the 1991 legislative session, the governor of Arkansas was in his home state only fourteen days. Most of the travel expenses were paid by the Democratic Leadership Council, but the state always picked up the tab for the troopers who accompanied Clinton everywhere he went. Although the troopers had much more modest accommodations on these excursions, some Arkansans were still upset that several thousand of their tax dollars went to "protect" Clinton at out-of-state functions staffed by other law enforcement officials.

In his June 1, 1991, column, the *Arkansas Democrat*'s John R. Starr pointed out that the state was still owed $2,629 "for air fare alone" in connection with several of Clinton's "vanity-fanning trips . . . to other states."

"Clinton's press secretary says that the organizations that sponsored Clinton's trips will eventually reimburse him for them and when that happens, Clinton will reimburse the state. Sure, he will. But what he should do is to pay those expenses either out of his own pocket or out of a campaign fund and then get himself reimbursed . . . There is no reason why Arkansas taxpayers should make loans to the Clinton for President campaign."

Arkansans also picked up the $7,264 tab for five thousand booklets giving the details of what the 1991 General Assembly accomplished.[46] Several hundred copies went to Arkansas media outlets, legislators, state agencies, and local government officials, but most were distributed among delegates to the Democratic Leadership Council convention and to prospective supporters in other states.

Preparing the way for his candidacy was not without its missteps. In June, the festering resentment of mainstream Democrats in New Hampshire toward the Democratic Leadership Council erupted when the state's Democratic party Executive Committee refused to sanction the new DLC chapter because its name was "deceptively" similar to the party name.

"We're not McDonald's," New Hampshire Democratic party Chairman Chris Spirou groused. "We don't grant franchises."[47] By not sanctioning the DLC, he said, the party also was not sanctioning the "bashing" of Democrats by Democrats. Lest anyone misunderstand that statement, Spirou added that Democrat-bashing was just what the DLC had been doing.

Betsey Wright tried to dismiss it as "an inside family feud,"[48] and Clinton maintained that "it doesn't have anything to do with me,"[49] but he was concerned that the fallout might carry into the February primary, the first in the nation. He spent many hours on the telephone, gathering intelligence about the controversy and discussing ways in which to neutralize it. The one thing he could not do was distance himself from it. He was the chairman. He intended to be a candidate. The next best thing, then, was to surround himself with a few well-chosen signatories when he traveled to Concord in August to dedicate the chapter.

Among those selected were four members of the United States House of Representatives whose value was succinctly explained by the *Arkansas Gazette's* Washington correspondent, Jeffrey Stinson: Mike Espy of Mississippi, "who is black and whose active DLC membership symbolizes that the group isn't hostile to minorities despite coming out against racial hiring quotas"; Jill Long of Indiana, "who holds Vice President Dan Quayle's old seat in Congress and who represents how Democrats can win traditional Republican seats"; Stephen Solarz of New York, "who led the charge earlier this year to use military force in the Persian Gulf and who demonstrates that Democrats aren't all afraid to go to war if necessary"; and Dick Swett of New Hampshire, "who became the New Hampshire Democrats's leading office holder last year when he beat a sitting Republican to get to Congress."[50]

Joe Grandmaison, a former state party chairman, called it a "win-win" situation for Clinton, because the appearance of these four members of Congress would hold strong appeal for rank-and-file Democrats and would signal that Clinton "might have something going for him."[51]

What was ostensibly an obligatory visit to dedicate a new Democratic Leadership Council chapter was really an opportunity for Clinton to convey his empathy for the "pain" New Hampshire residents were suffering as a result of the recessionary tailspin into which the state had fallen after a decade of unprecedented economic growth.

"He has a message to carry, and it's an important message of revitalizing the economy, of family values, a strong defense, and of restoring a balance between foreign policy and taking care of domestic problems," said George Bruno, another former party chairman. "These are the things people want to hear."[52]

Again, Clinton did not disappoint. The DLC "issues forum" attracted the state's best known Democrats and a healthy contingent of Washington media, which duly reported the emphasis placed on domestic issues and Clinton's moderately successful efforts to assuage the feelings of Spirou and other DLC detractors. After a surprisingly brief private meeting—about ten minutes—Clinton and Spirou appeared together at a news conference to tell reporters that all was well.[53] However, when asked whether the state party would relent and sanction the DLC chapter—which had agreed to incorporate using only its initials so as not to infringe upon the party's name—Spirou tersely replied, "No."

"We are too small of a state and too small of a party to have auxiliary Democratic organizations, whether to the right or the left or wherever they want to take it," Spirou said.

The "grass-roots" emphasis of the Democratic Leadership Council's agenda did not mean that chapters, including the fledgling chapter in the DLC chairman's home state, would necessarily flourish. As head of the state Democratic party, Betsey Wright restricted membership to elected officials, although she promised that regular citizens eventually would be welcomed as associate members. Wright explained that membership to the DLC had to be limited because elected officials needed a private forum for discussing and developing issues.

"It is the big void nationally in the Democratic party," she said.[54]

Inclusion was, and remains, the big void in Arkansas's Democratic party, which had been under the command of the same handful of elected officials for more than a decade—for more than two decades, if the still formidable influence of such national leaders as David Pryor and Dale Bumpers were taken into account. Among the lieutenants and foot soldiers, there were some Bumpers people and some Pryor people, but virtually all of them were first and foremost Clinton people. Even many of them realized that stagnation had settled in, but under the aegis of Clinton's hand-picked overseers, "grass-roots" partisans were helpless to do anything about it. By 1991, party leadership was an exclusive club with a jealously guarded inner circle that kept the party functioning for the sole purpose of electing Bill Clinton president. A year into that presidency, one prospective congressional candidate who had been elected to state and local offices for nearly twenty years complained that he had to start from scratch to organize a campaign in many of his district's counties because the Democratic party's grass-roots committee structure had fallen into such disarray.

"With Clinton in the White House," the politician lamented, "everyone's at loose ends. No one knows what to do to even begin rebuilding, [because] they served his interests for so long."

If Orval E. Faubus popularized the axiom, "Just because I said it doesn't make it so," Clinton epitomized it. He was already putting together his campaign staff in August 1991 when, while attending the National Governors Association convention in Seattle, Washington, badgered at every turn by reporters about his political plans, he revealed that following the conference, after a few days of down time in the Pacific Northwest, he would embark upon a three-week road trip through Arkansas to put the question to the people who had reelected him the year before. His decision would be guided by their comments.

"I am inclined to run," he told a group of reporters he was treating to a midconference breakfast in Seattle, "but I've not made a decision on it because I still have some things to work out at home."[55] He alluded to "preconditions" that meant nothing to the non-Arkansans in the room, but which reporters from the *Arkansas Democrat* and *Arkansas Gazette* knew to be that 1990 reelection promise. Practically speaking, of course, those conditions meant nothing to Clinton, either; the day before he left for Seattle, he had announced both his resignation as chair of the Democratic Leadership Council and the formation of a presidential exploratory committee, and weeks before he had obtained a commitment from Mark Gearan, then executive director of the Democratic Governors Association, to work at the top level in organizing his presidential campaign. Others had been hard at work for months.

Was there actually a moment in which Clinton formally made the decision to seek the nomination in 1992? Some of those closest to him doubt it. Running for president, they say, was a foregone conclusion in their dealings with Clinton, and the timing would never be better. He would have a high-profile berth to which to return, since his governorship would have two more years to run, and a higher name recognition and stronger national political network should he lose, which was certainly possible against a reasonably popular first-term president.

Arkansas Democrat Skip Rutherford believed from the start that Clinton actually could defeat George Bush regardless of the circumstances. Rutherford, a boyish-looking man in his midforties who began working for the Democratic party as a teenager, was a former aide to Arkansas Senator David Pryor who succeeded years ago in wedding his love for politics to his career in public relations. Rutherford met Bill Clinton in 1974. They were introduced by Rutherford's fraternity brother, Steve Smith, during the Clinton-Hammerschmidt campaign. "You better watch this guy. He might win the race," Smith told Rutherford.[56] Rutherford doubted that and told Smith as much, but he was impressed with the effort Clinton was making and agreeably offered what advice he could. Beginning with Clinton's campaign for Arkansas attorney general in 1976, he began advising Clinton in earnest, always as a volunteer when needed. Rutherford's first loyalty has always been to David Pryor.

Through the years, Rutherford became one of Clinton's most trusted advisors, as well as an enthusiastic supporter, the recipient of

many midnight telephone calls and one of the first volunteer operatives to whom Clinton turned whenever crises arose and monumental
decisions had to be made.

Rutherford, who was by then working for Arkla, Inc., where he
served as vice president, chief political liaison, and best friend to Arkla
President Thomas F. "Mack" McLarty III, was one of the first to
notice Clinton's impending presidential campaign.

"It was in the summer of 1991 when I was sitting at the ball park of
the Hillcrest Softball League, sitting by Hillary Rodham Clinton, in
the stands, where she often frequented the games," Rutherford later
recalled. "And sitting in the stands, she said to me, 'You know, I think
that we can win in 1992.' "[57]

"You think that George Bush can be beat?" Rutherford asked.

"What the Democrats need is a message and a messenger," Hillary
responded. "That's what the Democrats need."

Rutherford places that brief exchange in April 1991, toward the end
of the three-month season of the softball team, the Molar Rollers, on
which his daughter Martha Luin and the Clintons's daughter Chelsea
played. He remembers wondering as he returned home that evening,
"Now, if she's telling *me* that, you know she's telling the governor
that." Among his circle of friends, when conversation turned, as it
often did, to politics, Rutherford privately recalled Hillary Clinton's
observation and opined that Bill Clinton might just have a big decision
to make soon.

He became more convinced of that one Saturday in early summer
when his morning jog was unceremoniously interrupted by Clinton
staffer Craig Smith. Rutherford still blanches at the memory of Smith's
car pulling up beside him. "I was running, sweating . . . smelled
terrible, looked terrible, hadn't brushed my teeth—had gotten up and
just hit the street."

"I've been driving all over this neighborhood looking for you!"
Smith declared.

"For what?"

"Get in!" Smith barked.

"For what?"

"You've got to go to the Mansion!"

Rutherford demurred. He was not going to the Governor's Mansion in his current condition.

"Bill won't care," Smith insisted. "Get in."

"I don't care if Bill won't care, *I* care!"

"Get in. This is important. He's only got an hour."

Continuing to protest, Rutherford climbed into the car for the ten-minute ride to the Governor's Mansion. When they arrived, Bill and Hillary and Bruce Lindsey were assembled in the kitchen, drinking coffee and discussing the topic so urgent that Rutherford could not take a quick shower or change his jogging clothes: Running for president.

Rutherford's most vivid memory is the game of cat and mouse he played with the assembly. "I talked over counters, because I smelled and I didn't want to get close to anybody . . . When they'd leave the coffee pot, I'd run over there and get some, then run back over to my little perch." No one else paid it much attention. They had moved from a general discussion of the 1992 presidential campaign to Clinton's possible role in it. Paramount was "Should he run?"

"Everybody started talking theories," Rutherford recalls, "the same theories that you might imagine: 'Well, if you run and lose, does it help you for 1996? If you run and lose, what does it do about your reelection as governor?' All the political issues that you might imagine were contemplated, the whole gamut. 'Can George Bush be beat?' He was at 90 percent in the polls at this point," shortly after America's victory in the Gulf War.

Clinton's inner circle talked about how Clinton would do against likely Democrat challengers. Could he run well enough against the likes of, for instance, Mario Cuomo to snag the nomination, and should Cuomo win, would he likely be offered, and should he accept, a vice-presidential slot?

After examining all of the various scenarios but one, Bruce Lindsey looked up at Bill Clinton and said: "Governor, what if we win?"

"Then," Hillary Clinton interjected, "we serve."

No definitive decision was reached that day—at least, while Rutherford was listening—but Rutherford left the meeting "99 percent convinced" that Clinton was going to run for president.

For Rutherford and a handful of other loyalists, Clinton's mid-August announcement that he was forming an exploratory committee was anticlimactic, but it played hell with the schedules of journalists who had decided to skip the National Governors Association meeting in Seattle. The last-minute rush to secure an airline ticket and a hotel room, as well as the convoluted route into the downtown area that freeway construction forced them to take once their airplanes had landed, left many reporters out of sorts before the convention began.

Theoretically, Clinton was attending the conference in his capacity as vice chair of the National Governors Association Task Force on Health Care, to which he had turned his attention after the education reform became old news.

Clinton skipped most of the convention sessions on his schedule, although once or twice he made it as far as the meeting room door before diving back into a sea of lights, cameras, and tape recorders, and he was chronically late for the few sessions at which he had to make a presentation.

Clinton arrived in Seattle two days early and immediately held the first of several dozen private meetings, some preplanned, others hastily arranged, in his two-room hotel suite. Clinton had a late night followed by an early morning, as evidenced by the dark circles under his eyes at the traditional opening news conference and photo opportunity on Saturday. He spent the remainder of the day and late into the evening discussing his presidential plans with and seeking advice from as many governors as he could corner, and still managed to jog four miles through the deserted streets of Seattle before climbing into a limousine at a quarter to 7:00 Sunday morning for a short commute to the studios of the local ABC affiliate for an appearance on "This Week With David Brinkley."

I and another bleary-eyed reporter from Arkansas dutifully climbed in with him to see for ourselves what we just as easily could have viewed on the television sets in our hotel rooms. Our presence was a stroke of luck for Clinton, who upon his arrival at the television studios was handed over to an inexperienced makeup artist. At his most rested, Clinton's features tend to become distorted under studio lights without proper makeup; his chronically red nose appears even more bulbous, his eyes sink, and his eyebrows all but disappear. Once settled in an adjoining anteroom, from which we could view both the monitor and the man, Maxine Parker and I gasped in horror at how ghastly Clinton looked. The production assistant who had groomed him for this momentous national link-up with Brinkley and two other early presidential hopefuls, former Massachusetts Senator Paul Tsongas and Virginia Governor L. Douglas Wilder, had used an excessive amount of eyebrow pencil, giving Clinton thick false brows.

Arkansas pride sent us scurrying into the studio to point out how garish Clinton looked. A tissue was found, and the folks back home were saved having their governor embarrass them on national television.

Parker and I took a separate car back to the hotel—the governor had yet another private meeting—and during the ride, a local admirer who had coordinated this most recent series of television appearances eagerly asked for our assessment of Clinton's remarks.

"Oh, I'm not allowed to give an opinion," Parker replied.

"Well," I responded, "I can truthfully say that Clinton was the only one who didn't have an accent."

Clinton was the only potential presidential candidate attending the conference, and he quickly found that national reporters were more interested in whether he would run than in anything he had to say about health care.

Clinton was willing to provide a brief stand-up interview outside the men's room or a quick sound bite on his way from one committee to another, but the requests for lengthy interviews were too numerous to accommodate, so his staff suggested a breakfast session, which was as intimate as a White House news conference. The meeting room was far too big for the small gathering, and the reporters, few of whom knew him or one another very well, spread themselves sparsely around the banquet tables. Sitting uncomfortably in front of them upon a low-slung aluminum folding chair, folding and refolding his long legs, and nursing the ever present coffee cup, Clinton fielded a variety of mundane questions about education, health care, the economy, and international trade, but none of that was at the front of anyone's mind. Each inquiry and each response always doubled back to the same topic.

Except for the Arkansas reporters, this was the first glimpse the press had of a Clinton platform in the making.

How did he assess the current popularity of President George Bush? Notwithstanding the recession, Clinton noted, a near-united Congress and widespread public support for American involvement in the Gulf War had maintained Bush's high standing in the polls, and that was "probably currently not an encouragement"[58] to any potential challenger.

"The American people made a kind of personal commitment to [Bush] during that war which I think is strong, and when they talk and think about it, they say, 'Well, I obviously like the aftermath [of U.S. involvement in the Gulf],' so there is a kind of disconnect there between what people are really worried about—the economy—and how they view the president.

"I think his position is further reinforced by the fact that for the last eleven years, Presidents Reagan and Bush have worked very hard and very skillfully to sort of disempower the presidency on the domestic front. They shoved responsibility for economic development, education, and social policy back to the states, local governments, and private sectors."

This argument, a particular favorite of Clinton throughout his governorship, was fueled by frustration. He could never come to grips with the notion that Washington should demand that states pay for new social programs and yet not provide any money to the states with which to pay for these programs. Every year, the number of mandates Washington imposed on the states increased. Clinton viewed these unfunded mandates as putting the states "under the federal gun," and to his way of thinking, Washington should "put its money where its mouth is" or else some state treasuries were going to go broke. The argument was familiar to Arkansans, who heard it virtually every time the Department of Human Services or the State Hospital for the mentally ill came under bureaucratic or legal fire for falling below standards.

Clinton, ever the student of politics, revealed to reporters another potential stumbling block to any Bush challenger. "If you read history," he mused, "I don't know that ever in the history of the country people have denied election or reelection to a war winner. I don't know that they have. I was thinking about it the other day: Grant got two terms . . . Eisenhower got two terms . . . I think people gave Roosevelt more credit for the war than anything else."

If he actually entered the race, he said, it would be to give the people the debate they wanted and did not witness in the previous campaign between George Bush and Michael Dukakis. Government must change to serve the people better, the "customer," he said, invoking a favorite analogy of his 1990 reelection campaign, and it was the obligation of those seeking the presidency not to repeat ideological debates, but to call for programs that would actually work.

"I think, really, people desperately wanted a debate in 1988 about the future of the country and instead they got a sort of rehash of the same old liberal-conservative divide," Clinton opined, adding that what was really needed to make America globally competitive was to "basically redefine the relationship of citizens for each other and the government."

Democrats in 1992 should approach the campaign, he added, by first deciding what they believe, "however radical," and then stick to that agenda and that message even if it meant putting themselves at risk in the primaries.

If he should become a candidate, Clinton said, "my view would be that I should say what I believe and stick with it and let the chips fall where they may."

"I believe the Democratic party has to be tomorrow's party . . . We have to stake out a claim for the future. I think we have to emphasize some things that the Democrats have not normally emphasized in the past. First of all, we have to show that we're serious about economic recovery and expansion . . . [and] we have to be for social programs that help middle-class people as well as poor people."

If Clinton hoped to alleviate the press's demands on his time, he was disappointed by world news. Monday morning, his forty-fifth birthday, dawned to the news that Mikhail Gorbachev had been ousted in a coup as president of the Soviet Union, and reporters begged Clinton to comment on Gorbachev's fall. As the press reminded Clinton about his lack of foreign policy experience, Clinton said that he had made a "recent visit to Moscow,"[59] which in fact had lasted for only a few hours. He was careful not to criticize or "second-guess" President Bush's cautious approach to the situation. "I think the president has taken the only position he can right now to say that he's very concerned, that we have been supportive of the move toward political and economic freedom, and national independence within the Soviet Union," he said.

"I'd do what he's apparently trying to do . . . [I would] send a clear, early signal that I was very concerned about it and that I wanted to know [the coup leaders's] intentions on the major issues: Have they changed their intentions toward Eastern Europe? Have they changed their intentions on the START [arms control] treaty? Have they changed their intentions on how to treat people in the republics that are independent? Have they change their intentions on how to deal with [Russian President Boris] Yeltsin and the movement toward democracy inside Russia? Have they changed their intentions on economic issues?"

Pundits, among them Thomas Mann of the Brookings Institution and Stuart Rothenberg, publisher of *The Political Report*, suggested that the uprising against Gorbachev—which was crushed after three days—would harm a Clinton candidacy because it underscored the Arkansas governor's lack of experience in foreign policy. But Mann added that while none of the Democrats rumored to be considering a presidential campaign was particularly strong on foreign policy experience, among them Iowa Senator Tom Harkin, "all it takes is an economic downturn next year and they will suddenly look competitive."[60]

In an interview with the *Arkansas Democrat*, John C. White, a former chair of the Democratic National Committee, said that while Clinton was certainly the most articulate and intelligent of all the potential Democratic candidates, "the truth of the matter, at this point, is that most Democrats and most people in this country don't know him. It's not in the people's guts that 'Bill Clinton is the guy I want to be president.'"[61]

A frequent question asked of Clinton during his four days in Seattle concerned his ability to raise money for a nationwide campaign. He invariably said that money would not be a major factor in his decision, noting that "I've never lost a race because of lack of money. I doubt it would be a factor."[62]

But money was clearly on his mind; accompanying him on the trip was Bruce Lindsey, treasurer of the exploratory committee, whose portable phone and heavy briefcase never left his side. Lindsey had almost as many private meetings as did Clinton at which he lined up fund-raising projects and contribution pledges. Accompanying Lindsey was his wife, Bev, a former Clinton deputy press secretary and veteran political organizer who also had done advance work for several Democratic presidential campaigns. For a woman on vacation, which she claimed to be, she put in an inordinate amount of time huddling with Gearan and various staff of both the Democratic and National Governors Associations.

Clinton's entourage at the convention, including not the customary one but two state troopers, numbered fourteen, more than at any national conference Governor Clinton had attended. But from Clinton's standpoint, every one of the fourteen was a vital member of the team. So, too, were the dozen or so lobbyists and "invited guests" who flew from Little Rock to Seattle to assist Clinton's precampaign efforts.

On the final day of the session, Clinton said that while none of the governors he talked to discouraged his presidential bid, a few of the newcomers and a few who he said might be on the ballot themselves in 1992 "were slightly more reserved in the sense that they want me to come to their states, meet their supporters, meet their friends, and make a joint decision."[63] Even one Republican governor, whom he declined to name, had been encouraging.

Apparently the Republican in question was not South Carolina's Carroll A. Campbell, Jr., with whom Clinton had established a warm relationship even before they co-chaired the historic Education Summit called by President Bush in 1989.

"I think Bill has done a good job as governor," Campbell told a reporter. "Of the Democratic candidates out there, I think he's one of the best. But because the presidency requires both domestic and international experience, I think Bill might well take another look at whether that's the path he wants to go on."[64]

In Arkansas, Clinton's presidential candidacy was a foregone conclusion. Lieutenant Governor Jim Guy Tucker was preparing to be acting governor. He was, he said, "operating on the assumption" that Clinton would seek the presidency in 1992, and found it "prudent" to be ready to step in at any time.[65]

"I have to assume that in the absence of a national emergency that he will become a candidate," Tucker said. "If that turns out not to be the case, that will be hunky-dory with me and I will be delighted to spend the year the way I thought I should spend it." By way of preparation, Tucker already had begun holding briefings on the day-to-day operations of state government and beefing up his minimal lieutenant governor's staff with wealthy volunteers. Also, much to the surprise of Clinton's staff, members of the governor's security detachment, drawn from the ranks of the Arkansas State Police, had begun squiring Tucker to and from work and speaking engagements in one of the Lincoln Continentals assigned to the governor's office.

Some constituents had begun to notice Clinton's more frequent absences and to acknowledge that soon he would be spending more time out-of-state than at home. Clinton critic John R. Starr, who had taken to calling Clinton "Governor Gulliver" in his daily column, summarized the rising hostility to Clinton by quoting one reader's reaction to Clinton's Seattle appearance on the David Brinkley show. During the interview, Clinton had advised President Bush to spend less time on foreign affairs and turn his attention toward home. "Clinton is telling Bush to come home," the reader observed. "We in Arkansas might tell Clinton the same thing."[66]

Although Clinton would not resign his governorship until well after he was elected, for all practical purposes Tucker was Arkansas's chief executive for most of Clinton's four-year term. Clinton's fifth term was less than a year old when he announced his bid for the presidency, and when he resigned, the term was eleven days shy of the halfway mark.

Following the conference, the Clintons took a five-day vacation in Canada where they learned that Tennessee Senator Al Gore, who campaigned as a Southern moderate in the 1988 Democrat presidential race, had decided not to seek the nomination in 1992.

"I know from having run before that you have to put your whole heart and soul and all your time and all your attention into a presidential campaign," Gore said in a prepared statement. "If this decision had been based on politics alone, I would be announcing my candidacy for the White House right now. Indeed, I would have done so already. But this is about more than politics."[67] Despite a "yearning" to be president, he deemed his family, which was still coming to grips with his young son's near-fatal traffic accident in 1989, more important than his political ambitions.

In his own statement, released by his Little Rock press office, Clinton empathized with the "difficult" decision Gore had reached but conceded that his withdrawal "will increase the pressure [for Clinton] to run."[68]

As, indeed, it did. He spent much of his short vacation on the telephone, keeping abreast of reaction to Gore's announcement and, despite those unresolved "preconditions," directing the opening of his exploratory committee's headquarters, the site of his 1990 gubernatorial campaign operation. His advisors urged him to enter the race in short order to tie up the money—which Robert A. Farmer, treasurer of the Democratic National Committee and top fundraiser for the 1988 Dukakis campaign, already was helping Clinton to raise—and the support that otherwise might go to someone like Cuomo. They also believed that Gore's withdrawal left the South wide open for Clinton. If there was a deal between Clinton and his future vice-presidential running mate at that point, which seems unlikely, those in the Clinton camp seemed unaware of it. "I guess I'm a little surprised by the timing," said Bruce Lindsey back in Little Rock. "It seems like less than a week ago he [Gore] sent a letter to supporters asking them to hold on."[69]

In Washington, Bob Squier, the consultant and strategist who played a major role in Jimmy Carter's winning 1976 campaign and occasionally advised Clinton, was ecstatic: "I would say that two things happened today: Gorbachev and Clinton were liberated."[70] He predicted that Gore's withdrawal would "kick-start Clinton's campaign . . . I can't think of anything that would stop him from running now."

David Sawyer, a New York political consultant, was one of many who declared Clinton the new front-runner based on the fact that there now appeared to be no competition for "the ideological base" that Clinton and Gore shared.[71]

"What you have to understand is [that] there's no serious candidate out there yet," said Tom Mann. "Clinton is the closest thing to a serious candidate. He could earn the nomination by default."[72]

Given that Gore had been the last remaining Democratic candidate with substantial foreign policy experience, because of his membership on the Senate Armed Services Committee, pundits did not see Clinton's lack of foreign policy skills as a problem unique to Clinton. As Mann pointed out, "They all have a foreign policy weakness. There's no one out there [among Democratic hopefuls] with foreign policy experience."[73]

Visiting in Little Rock, Republican National Committee chair Clayton Yeutter was unimpressed by the increased rumblings of a Clinton candidacy. He predicted that Clinton's apparent move from the liberal to the moderate wing of the Democratic party would hurt him among partisans.

"The typical reaction of the Democratic electorate is to pick a nominee that is to the left end of the political spectrum," Yeutter said. "I doubt that will change in 1992."[74] Yeutter also presciently observed that George Bush "is rated as performing better at this stage of his presidency than any other president in memory. If he simply continues to do that from now until November of 1992, he doesn't have to have any kind of clever campaign strategy." At that point, insiders say only one person was trying to warn the Bush camp to take Clinton seriously: John Sununu, the cerebral wiseacre who as governor of New Hampshire had come to know Clinton extremely well and thought him "bright and tough."

Despite the flurry of activity that had surrounded his brief stay in the Pacific Northwest, Clinton returned to Little Rock looking fit and rested. He allowed that he had spent some time in "serious" discussion about the potential campaign with Hillary and Chelsea, and that both "made it very clear to me that if I want to do it that they're more than ready to get after it."[75] As his former chief of staff Betsey Wright had observed a few days earlier, Chelsea's youth had been a deciding factor in his decision not to run for president in 1988. But now Chelsea was eleven and old enough to deal with the stress, and the frequent separations, of a national presidential campaign.

Clinton was not prepared, however, to reveal details about those or any other discussions he may have had during the hiatus. He angrily refused to answer questions about Bob Farmer's rumored imminent departure from the Democratic National Committee to lead a Clinton fund-raising effort, and he continued to insist that any decision would have to wait until the end of September, at which point he would have concluded an exhaustive survey of Arkansas voters whom he had promised he would not seek the presidency in 1992.

"It is true to say that I'm as happy and well satisfied with my work here, my job here, and my life here [in Arkansas] as I have ever been in my entire adult life," he told reporters upon his return to the state. "If I do it [run for president], it will be largely because I really do believe we have to have a serious debate on these domestic issues."

That seemed to many an incongruous statement, given his long-held desire to seek the presidency. As he would admit only four days later, "Four years ago, I wanted to do this so bad I could spit, but I had to admit I wasn't ready."[76] No one who met with him behind closed doors doubted that he was ready now.

In Seattle, Clinton had declared that he would spend at least three weeks sampling constituent opinion before reaching a decision, but the much heralded road trip on which he embarked only days after returning to Arkansas actually lasted only three days.

He appeared in a mere handful of locations around the state, meeting with small groups whose members's names had been hand-picked from his vast computer bank of financial and political stalwarts. All sessions were closed to the news media—"call it Bill Clinton's mystery tour," a reporter wrote at the time[77]—and his itinerary was a closely guarded secret, but under persistent questioning by reporters, Clinton finally conceded that at no time during those intimate sessions had he asked anyone in the assemblies to release him from his promise not to run for higher office. Rather, these voters had discussed issues and strategy, and had basked in the excitement of an impending presidential campaign that could, for the first time, put a native son in the White House.

"Based on what I heard," noted Woody Bassett, a Fayetteville lawyer and longtime friend of the Clintons who attended one of the gatherings, "most people feel it would be good for Arkansas."[78]

A local reporter who managed to gain admittance to a meeting in the back room of a restaurant in Conway, a college town in north-central Arkansas, said the group of business and community leaders and former campaign aides was almost unanimous in encouraging the governor to seek the Democratic nomination for the presidency.

State Senator Stanley Russ of Conway joked that "we had caucuses at our table and we decided that since criminals don't have to serve their full term, he ought to be excused from serving his full term."[79]

In Russellville, the director of the local Chamber of Commerce said that during the session to which she was invited, she told the governor: "I feel that if you had asked me to the prom and then got a better deal, I wouldn't be too happy, but I know that things change."[80]

For his part, Clinton observed at one stop that "a change in circumstances is not enough to break a commitment. Last year, when I was running for governor and told the people what I honestly believe, I couldn't imagine anything like this occurring,"[81] an apparent reference to the dearth of well-known Democratic challengers.

"Most people, in the end, say that 'if you believe what you're doing is best for us and you, we're with you,'" Clinton said after the second of three days spent sampling opinion.[82]

Once again, state resources helped pay for a Clinton political endeavor. He traveled in a state car and was accompanied on each of his precampaign stops by two state employees. Spokesmen assured the public that the exploratory committee would reimburse the state.

Midway through Clinton's road show, Bob Farmer announced his resignation as treasurer of the Democratic National Committee.

"If Bill Clinton decides to run for president, the resources will be there for him,"[83] Farmer told reporters in Washington before boarding a flight to Little Rock, where he met with members of the local news media.

"Bill Clinton has a great deal more national exposure and experience than Michael Dukakis did at this same time four years ago," Farmer said. "Bill is a national governor in the sense he has spoken out on the issues in many forums across the country and has spoken out effectively. He is esteemed by his colleagues and his opinion is respected."

Farmer speculated that Clinton, who had to date raised only about $10,000, would need at least $10 million, and possibly $15 million, for the 1992 primaries. Pledges had begun trickling in weeks before, with the bulk of them coming from California, New York, Washington, D.C., Arkansas, and, to a lesser degree, Minnesota and South Carolina. While acknowledging that the governor of a small, struggling, Southern state might have more trouble than others raising campaign funds, Farmer expressed confidence in Clinton's fund-raising abilities, particularly among moderates. "To the extent that his message resonates with the people," Farmer added, "it will be very helpful."[84]

Clinton, hesitant to expose his hand too soon, was adamant that Farmer's addition to his exploratory committee was not a guarantee that Clinton would run for the presidency. Farmer understood, he said, that he might yet back out.

"What I don't want to see you do," Farmer reportedly told Clinton, "is work through this decision and then find yourself crippled because you haven't set up the financial infrastructure it takes to raise the funds you have to raise to escape obscurity."[85] In the end, Clinton said Farmer reminded him, "they can't vote for you if they don't know you."[86]

It was important, Farmer opined, that Arkansans provide the seed money, but some local Clinton political observers noted that most major donors had contributed heavily to the 1990 gubernatorial campaign and any remaining funds might be needed for Senator Dale Bumpers's reelection campaign. Clinton was unfazed. After all, he had never lost an election because he lacked money.

If Clinton's desire to meet with Arkansans throughout the state was sincere, it was overpowered by the need to raise his name recognition and campaign pledges beyond the borders of Arkansas. His road trip was interrupted after a few days, and ultimately scrapped, as the result of an invitation to appear at the Tri-State Democratic Unity dinner in Sioux City, Iowa, on September 6. Also invited to speak were former Massachusetts Senator Paul Tsongas, the only announced Democratic

candidate, and Iowa's favorite son, Senator Tom Harkin. The event
would attract political reporters from throughout the nation, according to Tina Hall, the Woodbury County Democratic party chair, and
would give each of the prospective contenders the first chance to "give
their message to the world." Democrats from Iowa, South Dakota, and
Nebraska would be in attendance, so Harkin's presence would not
necessarily diminish the value of Clinton's appearance. From there,
Clinton planned an appearance at a party fundraiser in Carbondale,
Illinois, where he hoped to meet with members of the reconstituted
Daley organization, among them a bright young fellow named George
Stephanopoulos who came highly recommended by Midwestern
Democrats.

In Texarkana, during one of his final road stops in Arkansas before
his Iowa trip, Clinton met with two hundred loyal followers at a
reception at the King's Row Inn restaurant.

After voicing his heartfelt gratitude and humility, Clinton advised
those who thought he had nothing to lose by entering the presidential
sweepstakes that such a campaign was not without risk.[87] Few presidential candidates who had won their party's nomination but had lost
the general election had ever gone on to the White House, he said. He
could cite only three exceptions: Richard Nixon, Grover Cleveland,
and William Henry Harrison. This might be his only shot. He warned
that with his candidacy would come "painful" criticism of the state,
whose lot he said was improving but still had "a ways to go." He
wondered aloud whether his 1990 promise to serve a full four years as
governor, from which he had not yet asked to be released, should be an
obstacle to making a run for the White House.

"I think it bothers you more than it bothers the people," a man in
the audience responded.

"It would be good for the world!" gushed a woman before observing that "smart people change their minds; fools never do."

"It will be a hard fight, but you can win the battle!" a third person
declared, not knowing how prophetic his words would be.

A flurry of activity swept the governor's office as preparations for the
announcement began. Mike Gauldin, the press secretary, and his staff
worked almost around the clock to respond to press inquiries. It

seemed as though every major news agency in the world, a few of which no one had ever heard, wanted an hour of Clinton's time.

There were fundraisers to coordinate, hotel and transportation arrangements to make for visiting dignitaries, telegrams to be elicited from dignitaries who could not be present. Although Hollywood television producer Harry Thomason was responsible for staging the event, most of the details were handled out of the governor's office in direct violation of state campaign ethics laws. Thomason oversaw some of that activity, too.

Gauldin took Thomason's orders in stride, but his work load had increased to the point that he was a bit perturbed when Jesse Jackson demanded a meeting with Clinton two days before his presidential announcement.

Although originally a journalist by trade, Gauldin, a tall, lanky, rather stoic country boy in his midthirties from southwest Arkansas, had given up a slow-moving but promising career in editorial cartooning to enter the field of public relations at the University of Arkansas at Fayetteville, which led to the press secretary's job in 1986. It was a position for which he was ideally suited despite having produced some of the most scathing editorial criticism to which Clinton had ever been submitted on the editorial pages of a newspaper. Even-tempered and quietly authoritative, he knew Arkansas and he knew Clinton, and unlike most of his predecessors in the press secretary's office—and, indeed, unlike most Clintonites—he was able to keep his personal feelings and opinions in check.

Gauldin did not always agree with Clinton, although only those closest to him had any inkling when such disagreements occurred. Whenever the pressure became too much, and his ever present cigarettes and coffee were not enough to sustain him, Gauldin would steal away to Fayetteville to clear his mind and recharge his batteries. A few hours in the mountains and a few beers with old friends and he was right as rain, back at his desk and up to his elbows in the engine room of the Clinton publicity machine. Gauldin had not aspired to the press secretary's job but had taken it when offered because, frankly, the money was good, he had a wife and children to feed, and the experience would look good on a resume. When the time came, it took him awhile to get around to submitting a resume to the Clinton transition team for a post in Washington. After he did, he was named public affairs director of the Energy Department, his reward for a job well done.

Gauldin was more irritated than angered by Jackson's demand for a private audience with Clinton. He well knew that relations between the two men had been strained for many months, a result of words exchanged over Jackson's perceived snub by the Democratic Leadership Council.

This meeting, one of a series Jackson was holding with prospective Democratic presidential candidates, could be an important one for Clinton since Clinton was halfway expecting Jackson to enter the race. For Gauldin's part, he had, as Southerners say, more than he could say grace over with the impending announcement and didn't need what he derisively referred to as a Jackson dog-and-pony show added to it.

Clinton was eager to meet with the once and possibly future presidential candidate. He hoped to iron out their differences and possibly plant the seeds of a new alliance. That possibility looked dubious at best for a few hours before the meeting. Word reached Clinton that Jackson, during a side trip to attend a rally in support of workers seeking to unionize a Crittenden County textile plant, had been asked whether he would be amenable to being vice president on a Clinton-Jackson ticket. Jackson responded by declaring that any such link-up should rightfully place Clinton in the Number 2 position. "After all, I have run before, I know the country better, and I've gotten the most votes, and that's the key to winning," he had declared.[88]

Whatever the tone of their private ninety-five-minute meeting, when Jackson emerged from the Governor's Mansion to address local and national reporters, he was conciliatory.

"I believe we have more common ground than dividing ground," Jackson said crisply. "It is resolved because it is behind us."[89] Of the substance of their conversation, Clinton would say only that they had discussed the need for the Democratic presidential candidates "to spend their time focusing on an agenda for the country and the real problems of real people."[90] But Clinton did endorse Jackson's call for statehood for the District of Columbia.

Clinton conducted little state business and made no more news until Thursday, October 3, 1991, the day of the long-awaited presidential announcement. He stayed in seclusion, working with advisors on his remarks when not glued to the telephone. He received an abundance of calls from well-wishers, and he placed a few, notably a last-minute call to State Treasurer Jimmie Lou Fisher, whom he asked to introduce him at the announcement. None of the state's more prominent politicians, including any member of the state's congressional delegation, was willing to make that introduction.

"Today's the day," John R. Starr wrote in his October 3 column. "Billy the Eternal Wunderkind Clinton is going to tell us whether he has decided to anoint himself as a Democratic candidate for president of these United States. . . . If he does, he will be breaking a solemn promise he made to the people of Arkansas while he was beseeching them last year to elect him to a fifth term as governor. . . . Political scoundrels always find a way."

Starr also pointed out that Clinton would be reneging on a pledge, made in early 1990, that he would stay in Little Rock and see that the latest round of education reforms was implemented.

"He told me in a voice so sincere that I had to believe him that not only would he prowl the country in search of admirers, he also would give up fanning his vanity by declining to accept every speech invitation he might get in Arkansas," Starr wrote. "He said that for the first time in his gubernatorial tenure, he would stay home and mind the store.

"Further, I had a promise from Hillary that if her husband were reelected, she would resume the active involvement in state government that made Clinton a decent governor from 1983 to 1987.

"Now both of them are running for president, blinded by the stars in their eyes to the needs of Arkansas."

A press packet distributed on the eve of the announcement portrayed the Arkansas governor as an education reformer, a coalition builder, and a determined leader. Included were an assortment of old speeches—but not the notorious monologue he had delivered in nominating Michael Dukakis at the Democratic Convention three years before—and a list of his accomplishments, many of which detailed the education reform program he had launched in 1983.

Clinton made his first public appearance shortly after 8:00 Thursday morning, jogging for the cameras past the Old State House on a three-mile run following a workout at the nearby YMCA. He waved away reporters, saying he had no idea "how many more mornings I'll have like this" and "wanted to spend this one like I normally do."[91]

In anticipation of a large turnout for the open-air event, projected to reach five thousand (though only 3,500 people showed up), city officials closed three downtown streets. The traditional American red, white, and blue bunting went up at the headquarters of Clinton's exploratory committee. The lush, well-manicured grounds of the 149-year-old Old State House looked like a construction site as workers prepared platforms to hold the large crowd. Each airplane that landed at the Little Rock Regional Airport seemed to be packed with reporters and camera crews, and city officials rubbed their hands in anticipation of all the money the press would spend. Robert "Say" McIntosh, who had been trying for several years to interest the media in his tales about Clinton's alleged illegitimate black son, prepared to pepper the downtown area with a new supply of anti-Clinton fliers. The *Arkansas Democrat* prepared a five-thousand-copy run for a special four-page "extra" to be hawked during and after the event for 50 cents apiece. A group of Republicans known as ARIAS (Alliance for Rebirth of an Independent American Spirit) took out half-page newspaper advertisements poking fun at a nonexistent "Arkansas Miracle," a takeoff on the short-lived Massachusetts Miracle, and sardonically beseeching Clinton not to "do to America what you've done for Arkansas."

Clinton's announcement was made for television from its inception. The Old State House, an impressive Antebellum structure whose Doric pillars had been the backdrop for numerous important announcements of import, had been selected for its historic significance, its telegenic qualities, and the large open space, which could accommodate a dais, VIP seating, viewing stands, and camera scaffolding as well as standing room for several thousand people. It was a near-perfect setting, allowing controlled access for observers while permitting a huge contingent of state and local law enforcement officers to segregate those involved in anti-Clinton protest activities. Protesters were prevented from bringing their signs onto the Old State House grounds within range of television cameras in the name of public safety, so they kept to the sidewalk outside the compound.

The ceremony began with a half-hour's entertainment by a variety of acts, among them the Hope High School band. This was followed by a half-hour's worth of warm-up speeches that were remarkably uninspired, such as the salutatory remarks of Jimmie Lou Fisher, who minutes before making her presentation turned to state Auditor Julia Hughes Jones and, according to Jones, asked whether Jones had any suggestions about what to say.[92]

Then Bill Clinton gave a thirty-two-minute speech he had been wanting to make all his life. He pledged himself to a presidency that would "restore the American dream" and "fight for the forgotten middle class" through more and better taxpayer-supported programs. And he promised his presidency would ensure universal access to higher education, universal health care, universal literacy, and "opportunity for all."

The presidential platform revealed that day relied heavily on national domestic issues such as the economy, education, health care, and the environment, coupled with a liberal dose of popular buzzwords: "middle class" appeared thirteen times, "responsibility" twelve times, and "opportunity" ten times. As one reporter noted, the speech "was more or less a slowed-down summary of the speeches he had been giving around the country since March."[93]

To local journalists, Clinton was running a liberal platform couched in terms calculated to appeal to middle-class voters who worked overtime to support their children and their parents in the face of a failing health care system, crime-infested neighborhoods, a stumbling economy, and a crumbling education system. National pundits, on the other hand, would pronounce it to be a quite moderate platform.

"Today we stand on the threshold of a new era," Clinton declared. "I believe we need a new kind of leadership, leadership not mired in the past, leadership not tied to the old ideologies, but proven leadership, capable of reinventing government to help solve those real problems real people face. . . . This is not a campaign for the presidency, it is a campaign for the future, for the forgotten, hard-working, middle-class people of America who deserve a government that fights for them."

As most of the throng broke into cheers and applause, the loud-speakers burst forth with the spirited, earshattering strains of Fleet-wood Mac's "Don't Stop Thinking About Tomorrow." He and Hillary grinned, waved, clapped, and embraced one another and their daughter, Chelsea, whose tight smile and tear-filled eyes revealed her mixed feelings about this momentous event. "I hope it won't change things," she shyly told the *Arkansas Democrat* afterward.

About half the crowd stayed with Clinton; the other half began leaving in droves during the last ten minutes of his remarks as watches heralded the end of their lunch hour.

"Clinton, the man of the people," one onlooker said wryly, gesturing toward the press platform that obscured Clinton from much of the crowd. "Tell me this ain't going to be no media campaign."[94]

That is, of course, precisely what it was, and many of the faithful in the crowd, people who were on a first-name basis with Clinton, people who could count on having their telephone calls put through to or at least returned by him, had their last personal contact with him on that fateful day.

23

VIETNAM REVISITED

CLIFF JACKSON'S INITIAL CLAIM to fame outside Arkansas came from his involvement in ARIAS, a home-grown political group that pooled its resources to warn New Hampshire voters in early 1992 against casting their lot with "a pig in a poke."

Clinton paid the group's limited activities little attention other than denouncing it as a Republican front, which it essentially was.

ARIAS—initially said to stand for Alliance for a Republican-Independent Agenda and Spirit and later an acronym for Alliance for Rebirth of an Independent American Spirit—was the brainchild of Jackson and Everett Ham, Jr., a former aide to the Republican Governor Winthrop Rockefeller. Jackson and Ham tapped selected anti-Clinton forces for money to mount a modest assault on the New Hampshire electorate through radio and newspaper advertisements before the February 18 primary. The ads cautioned voters that Bill Clinton was no friend to the middle class, having raised taxes more than any governor in Arkansas history, and advised them that he was not a man of his word, having broken his 1990 promise to complete his four-year term as governor. There were reminders of Clinton's tape-recorded conversations with a sometimes lounge singer, Gennifer

Flowers, who claimed to be his former lover. The tapes included his indiscreet observation that New York Governor Mario Cuomo acted like a *Mafioso.*

Jackson, a former state Republican party official whose hoped-for political career had gone nowhere, was the spokesman for ARIAS. Among its handful of contributors were a Teamsters local that had endorsed Republican Sheffield Nelson in Clinton's last gubernatorial campaign, and another former Rockefeller aide, Marshall Martin.

ARIAS first surfaced in Arkansas in January 1991 when a member, John Penn, tacked a document called "the preamble of the thesis of ARIAS" to doors at the state Capitol and several other public office buildings. John Penn, who claimed to be descended from William Penn, would say only that he represented "a grass-roots movement to awaken our people and get them more concerned about their roles in politics."[1] The preamble consisted of twelve goals, among them "to reinvigorate through a fundamental restructuring and redefining the Republican ideals, which have become static and doctrinaire, with an infusion of compassionate populism" and "to reverse and counter the obsolete and irrelevant and destructive Democratic tax-and-spend mentality, which taxes our dreams along with our pocketbooks." Soon after, Jackson came forward to identify ARIAS as a nonpartisan organization bent on developing "a strong political presence in Arkansas within this decade, a movement which will play an effective role in developing and proposing new ideas and more practical solutions"[2] for old problems.

Jackson said ARIAS was not affiliated with the Republican party but included "grass-roots Republicans as well as reform-minded Democrats and independents" anxious to build "pragmatic winning coalitions." Beyond distributing a few newsletters, however, the group was not heard from again until October 3, the day Clinton announced his candidacy for president. In a newspaper advertisement, ARIAS disparaged Clinton's twelve years as governor, noting twelve statistical rankings in which Arkansas was at or near the bottom—teacher pay, percentage of population living in poverty and median household income, and so on—and admonished: "Please, Gov. Clinton, don't do to America what you've done for Arkansas." The ad wished him good luck "in peddling 'The Arkansas Miracle.' "

ARIAS was an obscure political group formed to oppose Clinton's candidacy and cause him grief at every turn, which it did with limited success, during the months before the opening of the 1992 primary season. The group financed a series of radio spots in New Hampshire telling voters about the broken promise to serve out his full four years as governor and advising them that this self-proclaimed moderate and friend of the working class had a well-earned reputation in Arkansas as a liberal tax-and-spender, having raised and spent more than $1.5 billion in taxes whose burden fell heaviest upon low- and middle-income households.

Clinton wasted little time in countering the ARIAS campaign. He called its members "gutless" and "sneaky" and "a front for the Republican party." When the ads continued to run, he tried intimidation: The Clinton campaign's legal counsel, David M. Ifshin of the Washington, D.C., law firm of Ross & Hardies, sent letters to media outlets in New Hampshire, advising them that they were under no obligation to broadcast the anti-Clinton spots and that by doing so, they might be obligated to provide equal time to the campaign under Federal Communications Commission regulations.

How much the ARIAS assault contributed to Clinton's second-place showing behind Paul Tsongas in New Hampshire is open to debate, because Clinton had to contend with two matters he repeatedly had been warned would surface should he ever run for president: allegations of draft-dodging and womanizing. It is a matter of record, however, that he spent an inordinate amount of time defending his gubernatorial record to New Hampshire voters.

Clinton's record was the primary subject of the ARIAS campaign, which all but disappeared after the New Hampshire primary February 18, but Jackson, who had been working on his own behind the scenes, continued his efforts to make Clinton's draft history an issue. He said he knew that history well, because his tenure as a Fulbright Scholar at Oxford University had overlapped Clinton's term as a Rhodes Scholar. They had been on friendly terms during that period.

Jackson, who would provide a great deal of negative, but largely accurate, information about Clinton's years at Oxford actually was a party to but not the purveyor of the first piece of evidence that Clinton had actively avoided being drafted. That evidence came from the camp of third-party presidential candidate H. Ross Perot.[3] Leslie Campbell, a dean at Auburn University who only a week before had resigned his post with a Democratic county committee in Alabama to work for the Texas billionaire's campaign, released a letter, dated May 8, 1969, in which Jackson expressed hope that he would not face military service in light of the fact that other Rhodes and Fulbright scholarship recipients "are being regularly drafted out of Oxford. Bill Clinton, friend and Rhodes from Hot Springs, Arkansas, received his induction notice last week."

The revelation, made just days before the crucial New York primary, appeared damning.

Clinton had never denied receiving an induction notice, but pundits immediately chastised him for not volunteering the information in previous statements about his draft status during the Vietnam War. The Clinton campaign provided conflicting rebuttals to the document.

Clinton advisor Paul Begala contended that when Clinton received the notice, he placed a telephone call to local draft board officials and was advised that the notice had been issued by mistake.[4] The official statement released simultaneously by the campaign did not allude to any mistake but said he had been granted a "routine" waiver.[5]

"Governor Clinton recalls receiving an induction notice while at Oxford in April 1969," the campaign said in a prepared statement. "The notice was sent by surface mail"—which then could take up to three weeks, and sometimes as many as four, to reach its destination—"and arrived after the induction date. Governor Clinton immediately sought guidance from his local draft board about the induction date that had passed. He asked whether he could finish his current term at Oxford. As was routine procedure, the request was granted and his induction was postponed. Governor Clinton completed the spring term and returned to the United States in late June or early July."

The statement maintained that Clinton then signed up for the Reserve Officers's Training Corps program at the University of Arkansas at Fayetteville, but changed his mind, resulting in loss of deferment, so that from August 7 to October 30, 1969, he again was subject to being drafted. (It was later learned that August 7 was the date on which Clinton's student deferment was reinstated; October 30 was the date on which it was withdrawn by his local draft board after having been notified of Clinton's plans to return to Oxford by his Uncle Raymond. At that point, the lottery system had been announced and President Nixon had pledged that graduate students would be permitted to finish the school year before being drafted. Clinton's number, 311, which represented all draft-age American males born on August 19, was never called. It was high enough that those who drew it were given to believe they never would be called.)

The letter raised new questions about the way in which Clinton had dealt with the draft. Two days after the letter's release, Clinton broached the subject for the first time in the presidential campaign. He said he had never mentioned the induction notice because he had not considered it important.[6]

Clinton's explanation matched the one issued by his campaign. He said that while a student, he had been informed by local draft board officials that he could finish the 1968–69 term at University College and that they granted him an automatic extension when he contacted them in April 1969. "It was literally so routine at the time that when I called, they just acted like it was not at all unusual. They just said, 'We'll give you an extension. This is what we do. But you'll have to come home this summer and make arrangements.' "

Clinton said he had not intended to deceive anyone. "I would gladly have told you this if it had even occurred to me that this was relevant." Nonetheless, he continued to assert that he had received no special treatment or consideration.

Robert Corrado, a member of the Hot Springs draft board in 1969, said he could not recall Clinton having received an induction notice, "but, in all probability, it happened."[7] He agreed that it was not unusual for the board to grant an induction postponement to a student already enrolled in classes.

Opal Ellis, who at the time was executive secretary of the draft board, emphatically denied having sent an induction notice to Clinton.[8] She boasted of having reviewed a 1969 draft registry, provided by a *Wall Street Journal* reporter, that contained no reference to a draft notice for Clinton, but the declaration carried little weight because, according to the Selective Service System, the registry was merely a classification summary, and while it would indicate a person's draft status on a given date, it would not reflect when or whether a draft notice had been issued.

The plot thickened after the *Los Angeles Times* contacted retired Lieutenant Commander Clinton D. Jones, who was administrator of the ROTC program at the University of Arkansas and interviewed Clinton in the summer of 1969 when Clinton applied for admission. Jones revealed that Clinton, who said he was planning to attend the University of Arkansas School of Law, had not mentioned having received a draft notice. Had he done so, Jones said, he would have urged rejection of Clinton's ROTC application.

"If he had a valid letter of induction, no, we wouldn't have taken him," Jones said. "This is a man who didn't walk in and say, 'Hey, I want to get out of the draft.' This was a man of high character and high qualifications, the type you want in your program. I accepted his word, and the word of the man in the [state] draft headquarters in Little Rock, that he was classified I-A and was going to be drafted and couldn't go back to England."[9]

George Stephanopoulos, Clinton's deputy campaign manager, insisted that Clinton "did not conceal anything"[10] from ROTC officials, who he said were in constant contact with the local draft board and should have been well advised of all changes in Clinton's draft status.

Clinton then offered a second explanation claiming his faulty memory prevented him from giving an accurate history of his draft evasion. "Whatever the facts were, the draft board and the ROTC were in contact," he said. "So I think, at my age"—he was twenty-two at the time of the draft notice—"not being a legal expert on either one, I was entitled to assume that whatever the facts were, they'd shared all the information between each other, because they were certainly in touch. So that's not my problem. I didn't *not* disclose anything."[11]

The Arkansas journalists who advised the national media about Clinton's life were little help. Reporters who had covered his political career in Arkansas had always given short shrift to any rumors about Clinton's antiwar sympathies, and the one person to whom he is known to have confided, John R. Starr, who retired in 1992 as managing editor of the *Arkansas Democrat-Gazette*, was told a lie.[12] Clinton "confided" to Starr that he had once observed an antiwar demonstration in Washington while he was a student at Georgetown but had not taken part in the protest. That was the gist of his experience with antiwar activity, Clinton declared.

The issue actually became an issue only once before Clinton became a presidential candidate. In 1978, a retired air force officer, Billy G. Geren, called a news conference at which he branded Clinton, then the attorney general and a Democrat gubernatorial candidate, a "draft-dodger."[13] Clinton's response then was that he had made an agreement in the summer of 1969 to join the ROTC program at the University of Arkansas, which would have netted him a student deferment during the 1970 semester. However, Clinton said at the time, he resumed his studies at Oxford instead and, relinquishing the promise of deferment, had made himself eligible for the draft. Because of a high lottery number, he was never called.

The ROTC commander with whom he had struck the agreement, Colonel Eugene J. Holmes, did not contradict the popular young politician in 1978, and the draft issue generally was ignored thereafter in the Arkansas press.

The question appeared to be laid to rest when Clinton, worn down by repeated inquiries from the press and the growing concerns of his wife and other close advisors, finally gave what appeared to be the definitive explanation of the events of 1969. He said he had intentionally relinquished his deferment because he had had second thoughts about the morality of joining the ROTC to avoid being drafted.

As Clinton campaigned feverishly in New York, whose primary was scheduled for April 7, the first angry rumblings were being heard from Vietnam veterans, many of whom were as disgusted with his apparent lack of candor as by his calculated attempts to manipulate the system and avoid wartime service.

Clinton promised to "root through" his files for material that could help him clarify the series of events in 1969. If he did so, his findings were never released, and the controversy lost steam for several months.

After the Republican Convention in Houston, Texas, Clinton's Arkansas detractors, frustrated that George Bush's campaign still lacked momentum and unaware of how many attempts had been made to persuade the campaign to attack Clinton's most vulnerable points, most notably his propensity for circumventing or misrepresenting the truth, began discussing ways to jump start the Bush attack.

Jackson, again working with the *Los Angeles Times*, pointed *Times* reporters toward retired Lieutenant Commander Trice Ellis, Jr., who confirmed that in 1968, Clinton had been offered a Navy Reserve assignment.[14] The offer came after Clinton's well-connected uncle, Raymond Clinton, contacted Ellis, then the commanding officer of the Hot Springs Naval Reserve.

Trice Ellis insisted that Clinton had not received special treatment by being offered a billet. Raymond Clinton had been an acquaintance who had inquired about the availability of an enlistment slot based on his nephew's expressed desire to join the navy. Ellis said he instructed one of his men to call the 8th Naval Station in New Orleans to see whether a slot was available. When one opened up, Ellis said, he personally telephoned his stepmother, Opal Ellis, to find out whether the navy could admit Bill Clinton and was told it could.

Ellis said that when he relayed that information to Raymond Clinton a week to ten days later, he was advised that the young man would not be taking the assignment. He was given no explanation and did not seek one.

Jackson, who had contacted most of the people still alive who were associated with Clinton's attempt to evade the draft, even admitting his own efforts to assist Clinton in avoiding military service, claimed that Clinton also attempted to enlist in the National Guard and the Army Reserve, both of whose quotas were filled.[15] He identified other well-connected Arkansas politicos, among them Raymond Clinton's lawyer, former Judge Henry M. Britt, and Lee Williams, an aide to Bill's former boss, Senator J. William Fulbright, who had interceded in his behalf at various times. Britt lobbied for the Naval Reserve billet. On July 16, 1969, Williams contacted Colonel Eugene J. Holmes at the University of Arkansas about enrolling Clinton in the ROTC program there.

Jackson, under the auspices of ARIAS, continued throughout the summer to discredit Clinton's candidacy. At one point, he wrote a letter, published in the *Arkansas Democrat-Gazette*, berating Clinton for not admitting his draft history: "You, Bill, and even the Republican party fail to comprehend the significance of the draft story. It is not about your draft-dodging, even though you did. More precisely, it is about how you maneuvered to void a draft notice already issued to you and to avoid reporting on your scheduled induction date. On a higher level, however, the story is more universal than mere draft-dodging. It is about trust and betrayal of trust; it is about deceit and manipulation and exploitation of people for your personal benefit; it is about binding legal commitments and your cavalier disregard and breach of them. It is about duty and honor and pride and commitment and integrity—or, more precisely, the absence of such."[16]

Jackson's letter to Clinton was followed within days by his release of selected excerpts from other personal correspondence from 1969 that expressed Clinton's concerns about being drafted. In a letter to a friend dated July 11, 1969, Jackson wrote that his friend from Hot Springs "is feverishly trying to find a way to avoid entering the Army as a drafted private. At the moment, though he is still pursuing several leads, all avenues seemed closed to him."[17]

"The Army Reserve and National Guard units are seemingly completely full, and there is a law prohibiting a draftee from enlisting in one of these anyway. The director of the state Selective Service is willing to ignore this law, but there simply are no vacancies. I have had several of my friends in influential positions trying to pull strings on Bill's behalf, but we don't have any results yet. I have also arranged for Bill to be admitted to the U of A law school at Fayetteville, where there is a ROTC unit which is affiliated with the law school. But Bill is too late to enter this year's unit and would have to wait until next April. Possibly Colonel Holmes, the commander, will grant Bill a special ROTC 'deferment,' which would commit him to the program next April, but the draft board would have to approve such an arrangement. They have already refused to permit him to teach, join the Peace Corps or VISTA, etc. So Bill has only until July 28 to find some alternative military service."

Among the "influential friends" Jackson called was Van Rush, who in 1969 was executive director of the Republican party of Arkansas, In an interview in September 1992, Rush corroborated Jackson's assertions, recalling that Jackson asked him in the summer of 1969 to arrange a meeting between now-deceased Willard A. "Lefty" Hawkins, then head of the Selective Service System in Arkansas, and a couple of Jackson's friends who were having draft problems.[18] Rush said Clinton was one of the young men in question, but he could not recall the other man's name. His only other recollection was that he called Hawkins and relayed Jackson's request. According to retired Selective Service officials, Hawkins had the power to cancel induction notices and did so many times.

Once again, Clinton's response was to claim a bad memory. He said he simply could not recall such a meeting ever having taken place. Clinton eventually conceded that he was "actively working to find an alternative to induction, another service alternative," but he insisted that this was by no means evidence that he had actively tried to avoid serving in the military. "Whatever the rules were, I followed them," he said.[19]

Perhaps because Jackson had decided to give information exclusively to the *Los Angeles Times*, the story, and ultimately ARIAS, lost steam. Although the organization was given a much appreciated boost in the autumn by renewed interest in the Clinton draft controversy, that, too, floundered when George Bush declined to get directly involved.

The effort involved veteran Arkansas politician Jim Johnson. Throughout the summer of 1992, Johnson, who after losing several races as a Democrat switched to the Republican party, became increasingly troubled by the lack of direction and momentum in the Bush campaign. Having observed Clinton's rise over twenty years, Johnson knew that Clinton would win the presidential contest unless more damaging information surfaced. He resolved to do what he could to stop Clinton.[20]

In the summer of 1992, Johnson called Jim Lindsey, a football hero with the Arkansas Razorbacks and a Minnesota Vikings football star who subsequently had a lucrative career in real estate. Lindsey had once sought the Democratic nomination for governor, losing to the incumbent, David Pryor, but in recent years had drifted toward Republicanism.

"There has got to be some way to bring that draft issue back to the public consciousness," Johnson told Lindsey. "This Colonel Holmes has got to have some more papers in his files, some way to get this letter back before the public for consideration in the general election."[21]

Lindsey agreed, and he was in a position to find out. He and Holmes, who had retired in 1971 after thirty-one years of army service, were members of the same church in Fayetteville, a church pastored by a former general in the Chaplain's Corps. Lindsey persuaded the pastor to accompany him to Holmes's bedside—he had been ailing for some time—to discuss the matter. Holmes said he no longer had access to any correspondence or support documents involving Clinton's case, so they persuaded him to draft and sign an affidavit, later released by Holmes's daughter, to restoke interest in Clinton's draft record.

"Once this affidavit was in final form, it was read to me, and I thought, 'Man, that'll kill corn knee high,' " Johnson later recalled.[22]

The plan was to have Clinton's former nemesis, retiring Republican Representative John Paul Hammerschmidt, convey the document to George Bush in time for the president's speech to the National Guard Association, felt to be a most appropriate setting for casting aspersions on Clinton's patriotism and sense of duty. Hammerschmidt, a close friend of Bush since their freshman year in the U.S. House of Representatives in 1966, agreed, but shortly before the appointed date, even before the affidavit arrived at his Washington office by express mail, Hammerschmidt was out of the country, off to China on one of his frequent junkets.

"The timing was perfect, and John Paul was going to get it in his [Bush's] hands personally," Johnson recalled with a wry laugh, "and John Paul decides to go to China, to get one more free trip out of the damned thing."[23]

Johnson turned then to one of his oldest friends, Wesley Pruden, managing editor of the *Washington Times*, who in turn contacted *his*

old friend, John Sununu, Bush's former chief of staff.[24] Sununu re-
trieved the affidavit from Hammerschmidt's office. Upon reading it,
he or someone else involved in the Bush campaign sent word to
Johnson and Lindsey that the information it contained "ought to be
broken in Fayetteville" rather than at the National Guard Association
convention.

"I think it was stupid," Johnson said later, "but it was a policy
decision. Bush never called Clinton anything except [he said] that he
wanted everyone to know that he wasn't questioning his [Clinton's]
patriotism. Shit. He had no patriotism. And this just demonstrated that
he didn't."

Nonetheless, at the behest of Bush's advisors, the affidavit, dated
September 7, 1992, and labeled "Memorandum for Record," was
released from Fayetteville on September 16. It recounted Holmes's
memories of his dealings with Bill Clinton in 1969 and decried the
notion "that a man who was not merely unwilling to serve his country,
but actually protested against its military, should ever be in the position
of commander-in-chief of our armed forces." (Letter appears in full in
Appendix III.)

Clinton was not immediately available for comment; he was attending one of his nine Hollywood fundraisers, this one presided over by
Barbra Streisand, the evening Holmes's affidavit was released. While
Holmes has steadfastly refused to elaborate on his September 1992
statement, his daughter, Linda Burnett, later branded as false Clinton's
claim that he had advised Holmes in September or October of 1969
that he would not be participating in the ROTC program at the
University of Arkansas.[25] She said that according to her father, the
December 3, 1969, letter was the first knowledge Holmes had of
Clinton's true intentions. Holmes's continued reticence leaves open to
speculation why, in 1978, Holmes insisted that he did not remember
the Clinton case specifically but that he recalled thinking that Clinton
would have made a fine officer and that Clinton's account of what
happened was probably true.

The day after Holmes's affidavit was made public, while campaigning in California and Colorado, Clinton was flooded with questions
about Holmes's statement which he studiously ignored. On the tarmac

in Denver, he literally turned his back on members of the national press traveling with his entourage and sauntered over to a group of local reporters who, predictably, did not ask about the draft. Afterward, at a Denver hotel, he was asked whether he would take a question from reporters. "No, no questions," he snapped.[26]

The day after that, the campaign finally acknowledged that in 1969, Clinton had "discussed options"[27] to the draft with members of Fulbright's staff while he was seeking an ROTC slot at the University of Arkansas but declared that he had not sought assistance in avoiding military service. Later in the day, while campaigning in Albuquerque, New Mexico, Clinton made this comment: "I think I should just let the facts speak for themselves."[28]

The facts, heretofore clouded by misstatements and convolutions, about his draft history appeared to be catching up with Clinton, and with the release of the Holmes affidavit, it became painfully obvious that Clinton had, indeed, evaded the draft. If, as he claimed, he had been reclassified by his local draft board as fit and available for military service in the summer on 1969, he had not attempted before December 3, 1969, to advise the source of his current student deferment that he would not be enrolling in the University of Arkansas ROTC program.

In fact, Clinton had never directly contacted his local draft board about his change of plans; the letter that was dated September 12, 1969, had never been mailed. He knew in early October that there were no plans to draft graduate students before the end of the 1970–71 school year. He had returned to Oxford, where on December 1 he learned that his birth date had drawn Number 311 in the lottery. On December 2, he had submitted his application to Yale Law School. He had not written to Holmes until December 3.

Troubling questions about Clinton's draft record remained to be answered: Who canceled the April 1969 draft notice? Were there actually two draft notices, and if so, who canceled the second one, purported to have been issued in July 1969? Why had Clinton's preinduction physical been delayed for more than ten months? Why was Clinton classified I-A for seventeen months without being called to duty?

After months of silence, J. William Fulbright himself finally leaped to Clinton's defense. Fulbright, to whom President Clinton would present the first Presidential Medal of Freedom of his administration, dismissed Holmes's affidavit as a smokescreen engineered by the Bush organization after Republicans found their campaign arsenal bare. "The president has nothing else to talk about,"[29] he grumbled. (Actually, the president, much to the chagrin of his Arkansas supporters, was doing very little talking about this subject at all. That was left to Vice President Dan Quayle and presidential press secretary Marlin Fitzwater.)

Fulbright's former press secretary, Hoyt Purvis, then observed that it was improbable that Fulbright helped Clinton avoid the draft, given that Fulbright was in no position to influence a local draft board.[30] Fulbright was a Democrat in a Republican administration, a vocal critic of Richard M. Nixon and the war in Southeast Asia, Purvis reminded reporters, and even if he thought that intercession on behalf of a constituent was appropriate, such an effort would not have been productive. "The claims made by the former ROTC official belie common sense and the reality of the times," Purvis said.

Jackson, as happened periodically throughout the campaign, clammed up for a time, refusing to confirm or deny that a meeting had taken place between Colonel Holmes and Clinton. When less than a month before the general election, the state of Arkansas suddenly billed Jackson and Everett Ham for back taxes—a "coincidence,"[31] said the Clinton appointee responsible—Jackson was ready to talk about the draft again, but as Jackson had nothing new to add, the draft issue quietly died, with remaining questions left unanswered.

Sheffield Nelson, the Democratic fundraiser who became a Republican to take on Clinton in the 1990 gubernatorial election, opined that Bush's was "the worst run campaign I've ever seen in my life."[32]

"I gave them my entire [Clinton] file," he said. "I sent a box of stuff up there. You know where it stopped? It stopped at Charlie Black. Black couldn't get their interest, couldn't get them interested. They didn't do a thing of a defensive nature. They waited too late until Bill had established in the minds of the electorate who Bill Clinton was. Bush and them should have taken the initiative and told them about

Bill Clinton early on. I mean, the minute Bill Clinton was the Democratic nominee, they should have started in on the things he had done here. They didn't do that."

Numerous Arkansas Republicans and a substantial number of Arkansas Democrats tried to persuade the Bush campaign to take command of the campaign by defining both the opposition and the issues, and there was much evidence that low-echelon campaign operatives did the same, but all to no avail. Several Arkansans who had videotapes of Clinton's 1990 pledge to Arkansans that he would serve out his four-year term if reelected mailed those tapes to Bush's central campaign staff with entreaties to use it in a nationally televised campaign advertisement. Others sent chapter and verse of broken promises and failed programs that likewise went ignored, perhaps because Bush was campaigning in the shadow of his own broken promise of "Read my lips: No new taxes."

"I'll tell you what I told a bunch of them at the highest level" of the Bush campaign, Nelson said. "I said, 'Let me tell you something. Clinton has an unbelievable ability to land on his feet, and if you ever give him a chance, he will come back. He's just like a rattlesnake. If you have a chance to cut his head off, you better do it or you're going to live to regret the day you didn't,' "[33]

ARIAS tried one last gambit before the November 3 election. The FBI was formally asked to investigate the possibility that Clinton had committed treason when he organized demonstrations against the war in 1969. "This is an issue that doesn't resonate with Americans," said a Clinton campaign spokesman. "It's pathetic."[34] No investigation was undertaken.

Jackson offers no explanation of why he retained so much material dating back more than twenty years, or why so much of it appears to be the original correspondence, but it is conceivable that the ambitious young Republican recognized in Clinton an equally ambitious young Democrat with whom he might face off for elective office and banked the material until it would prove useful. Politics in Arkansas is a way of life for many involved, and career-planning starts early. Jackson, a lawyer, entertained notions of climbing the political ladder as a Young Republican, and while his ambitions were never realized and he claims no political affiliation today, he has resurfaced periodically as a voice for the GOP.

The origin of his animosity toward Clinton is open to conjecture. The Clinton campaign repeatedly claimed that Jackson was never more than a "friendly acquaintance" of Clinton, although the letters produced by Jackson indicate that they spent many hours in reflective conversation during their time at Oxford. Jackson, who himself received a medical deferment from the Vietnam-era draft from what he termed "a friendly doctor," claims that he came to feel used by Clinton in Clinton's quest to avoid military service.[35]

Neither does Jackson shed much light on why Clinton, to whom "political viability" was so important as far back 1969, would record for posterity his loathing of the military and his attempts to avoid military service during wartime.

Jim Johnson, however, has a theory.

"In analyzing that statement [by Clinton in his original letter to Holmes], I am convinced that Clinton had determined that at some later date in history, those activists were going to become the heroes on the political scene, as those activists that were in the integration forefront became the heroes at a later date,"[36] Johnson said shortly after Clinton's inauguration. "I think he was so genuinely convinced that he sought to capitalize on that by writing this in-depth dissertation to Colonel Holmes. If you'll carefully read that, you'll find that he's setting the stage for a future political pay-off, because it's too well handled for a young man. He's looking down the road at a political career. He admits that in this letter, but even so, when you're dealing from that position of intellectual arrogance that they go through, and that period in his scholarship—it's pretty heady wine to be among the best of the best intellectually, and they often don't reckon with these little things that affect the common herd."

24

HILLARY'S CONTRIBUTION

DURING THE NEWS conference at which her husband explained why he would not be seeking the presidency in 1988, a reporter asked Hillary Clinton whether she still harbored ambitions to be the nation's first lady, to which she responded that she had never aspired to be first lady.

It was a fitting response from the woman who always waved away any suggestion that she run for elective office, the woman who once told a friend that what she really wanted to do with her life was "to run something."[1] It was no slip of the tongue when First Lady Hillary Clinton told reporters during her husband's first year in the White House that after she had solved the nation's health care problems, her next objective would be to tackle the deficit.

"I really want to make a contribution," she once told writer Roxanne Roberts. "That's what I've always wanted to do."[2]

Certainly, Hillary never aspired to be a traditional first lady. She made that clear during the 1992 campaign, frequently telling interviewers that she planned to play an active and significant role in a Clinton presidency as problem-solver and all-around advisor. In a relationship such as she enjoys with Clinton, being first lady is the next best thing to being president.

For her purposes, it actually might be better. She can pick and choose the issues on which to work. Throughout most of Clinton's governorship, she was extremely active but selective, serving on corporate boards of directors, among them Wal-Mart, TCBY Enterprises, and Winrock International, and chairing numerous not-for-profit organizations such as the Children's Defense Fund, the Legal Services Corporation, and the New World Foundation, a New York-based philanthropy that described itself as "a people-to-people partnership for social change."

Hillary's affiliation with the New World Foundation attracted modest scrutiny during the 1992 campaign. During her chairmanship, the foundation awarded at least one $15,000 to Grassroots International, which in turn contributed money to the Union of Palestinian Working Women's Committees and the Union of Palestinian Medical Relief Committees. Both organizations were affiliated with the Palestinian Liberation Organization, which had not then renounced terrorism or recognized Israel's right to exist.

Other grants awarded on Hillary Clinton's watch went to the Committees in Solidarity with the People of El Salvador (CISPES) and the National Lawyers Guild. These grants were reported in conservative publications, but ignored by most news organizations. Hillary's ideas about children's rights *vis-à-vis* parental rights, gleaned from essays she had written while a law professor at the University of Arkansas and as a member of the Children's Defense Fund board, were somewhat more controversial.

Basically, she espoused the belief that children should have the same procedural rights as adults in matters of law, and she argued for reversal of the legal presumption that all minors are incompetent to make or assist in making decisions affecting their lives.

"The basic rationale for depriving people of rights in a dependency relationship," she wrote in a 1973 essay, "is that certain individuals are incapable or undeserving of the right to take care of themselves and consequently need social institutions specifically designed to safeguard their position. . . . It is presumed that under the circumstances society is doing what is best for the individuals. Along with the family, past and present examples of such arrangements included marriage, slavery, and the Indian reservation system."[3]

That the wife of the Democratic nominee for president would equate marriage with slavery elicited indignation from conservative pundits and the Bush campaign, who were also outraged by the suggestion that children should have control of their own destiny in matters of health, education, and general well-being.

"Decisions about motherhood and abortion, schooling, cosmetic surgery, treatment of venereal disease, or employment, and others where the decision or lack of one will significantly affect the child's future should not be made unilaterally by parents," she had written in 1979.[4]

Interestingly, although these controversial legal articles were reported by both conservative and liberal journalists, no one bothered to report one of the most glaring inconsistencies between Hillary's theories about children and how she behaved as a mother: She forbade her daughter Chelsea to pierce her ears before her thirteenth birthday. Bill sided with his wife in the matter.

Several people who have known the couple for years believe Bill and Hillary were ideally matched because they both wanted the same thing, but for different reasons—for him, it's glory; for her, it's power. It would seem significant, therefore, that Bill Clinton's best-known reform as governor of Arkansas, transforming the state's public schools, was Hillary Clinton's idea. She crafted all the planks in the education platform, and he promoted it. That is not to say she did not influence other parts of the Clinton administration.

"If you think about it," John R. Starr once said, "most of the people in his first [gubernatorial] administration were Hillary's friends."[5] That may be overstating the case, but the fact is that many of the people who were brought to Arkansas and given positions of influence in the first Clinton administration had stronger ties to Hillary than to Bill, and throughout his time as governor, a large number of the political appointments he made—to boards and commissions, to fill vacancies among the state's judiciary, to special advisory committees—were friends and colleagues of his wife. The same held true during his first year as president, when Hillary not only recommended certain people for specific jobs but took an active role in interviewing potential appointees recommended by others. The Clintons have always been a team, independent but joined by a mutual purpose.

Several of the men who worked security detail at the Governor's Mansion during the Clinton occupancy were highly amused by the homey, intimate portrait of the couple drawn by Harry Thomason in the film unveiled at Madison Square Garden on the evening that Clinton accepted his party's nomination for president. The couple these state troopers knew went separate ways, pursued individual interests, and were rarely at home at the same time unless they were entertaining. The sight of Hillary in blue jeans, snuggling with Bill in a hammock, struck them as nothing short of bizarre. However, they were not taking into consideration the fact that Hillary never hesitated to reinvent herself, or at least her public person, wherever necessary to achieve power. The girlish headbands and the wifely, pie-eyed gazes that followed criticism that she was becoming too intrusive in the presidential campaign attest to that.

"Nobody who had worked with Bill and Hillary as they persuaded, bullied, cajoled, and threatened the state's public schools onto a higher plateau could ever doubt the amount of brain power, willpower, strategizing, and sheer nonstop stamina these two will put into a worthy endeavor," observed longtime friend Diane Blair.[6]

Capturing the White House, Bill and Hillary agreed early in their relationship, was a most worthy goal, which is one reason they never considered severing their union even at its lowest points. One of those low points came in the first months of the 1992 presidential campaign.

Details about Clinton's womanizing which surfaced during the presidential campaign and during his first year in the White House were new. The allegations were not.

Outrageous rumors of his extramarital predilections had circulated for years but were fueled in the mid–1980s by the often titillating pronouncements contained in handbills produced by a local trouble-maker and small-time restaurateur named Robert "Say" McIntosh.

McIntosh's first claim to fame was as Little Rock's benevolent, hard-working "Black Santa." Using his own money, initially generated by the sale of his locally famous sweet potato pies and his barbecue and the modest profits from a janitorial service, he bought and donated countless gifts to needy youngsters in the poorer sections of Little Rock. McIntosh's good deeds came to the attention of the news media and a group of local business leaders who came to be known as his "white angels," and a star was born.

But over the years, the media hype or McIntosh's own megalomania seemed to transform him into a media terror. His manner of airing his grievances became bizarre. At various times, he upended the desk at which the local prosecuting attorney sat,[7] and he physically assaulted the *Arkansas Democrat's* John R. Starr.[8] He went from dumping garbage on the steps at City Hall[9] to attaching himself to a cross opposite the state Capitol.[10] With greater frequency, his good deeds were overshadowed by his violent outbursts and vitriol until finally some members of the local press imposed a "black-out" on his activities, which included distribution of handbills containing scurrilous allegations about the sex lives of public figures. Sometimes he reworked old rumors, changing only some of the names of the principals.

A case in point was his claim that Clinton had fathered a black woman's illegitimate child, an allegation picked up during the presidential campaign and published in the *Globe*, a supermarket tabloid.

In its many incarnations in McIntosh's handbills, only the photograph of the child in question remained the same. The name of the mother changed constantly. At various times, two different television reporters were identified as the child's mother. On another occasion, the mother was identified as a local prostitute. Neither the Clinton administration nor the local news media paid any attention to McIntosh's charges. On the few occasions a journalist condescended to question McIntosh about his sources, he refused to answer or suggested that he would provide more information for a price. Since a number of prominent people were known to have "contributed" money to him on many occasions, his allegations were considered by many to be retaliation against those who refused to pay to keep their names out of his offensive handbills, although he also used the fliers to air real or imagined grievances against other public figures, including journalists.

Given his lack of credibility, McIntosh was not in a position to harm anyone's reputation. The same could not be said for Larry Nichols, whose allegations of sexual promiscuity were raised in several lawsuits he filed against Clinton over a period of several years.

Although by no means the only source, Nichols was a primary source of the allegations of womanizing raised against Clinton during the 1992 presidential campaign.

Nichols had been marketing director of Clinton's Arkansas Development Finance Corporation for only five months when he was forced by ADFA president Wooten Epes to resign in September 1988. Acting on a tip, a local wire service reporter had reviewed Nichols's ADFA telephone log and discovered 142 long-distance calls made to American-based *Contra* leaders active in the move to oust Nicaragua's ruling Sandinista government.[11]

ADFA was created by the legislature in May 1985 to issue bonds for financing low-interest home mortgages, housing developments, industrial enterprises, educational facilities, health care facilities, and capital improvements. Nichols claimed that he had made the telephone calls in an attempt to reach conservative congressmen with whom he hoped to discuss legislation pertaining to mortgage revenue bonds. He insisted that Epes had authorized the telephone calls to Adolfo Calero, his brother Mario, and other Nicaraguan resistance leaders. He denied allegations by other ADFA employees that he had directed them to handle *Contra*-related material on state time.

Epes, then accompanying Clinton on a trade mission to the Far East, denied having authorized the calls. Upon his return a few days later, Clinton publicly called for an investigation of the matter, saying he doubted very much Nichols's explanation.[12] Nichols, contending that he had been "forced out," immediately resigned.

"I guess my knowing the *Contras* poses a problem for Bill Clinton because of his position with Dukakis,"[13] Nichols said, referring to Clinton's position as one of twelve co-chairs of the Massachusetts's governor's presidential campaign.

"I resigned at the specific request of the director to keep from getting fired and to spare my family further embarrassment," Nichols said. "If justice does prevail, the record will eventually show that Larry Nichols was forced out of his job for doing his job."

What the record immediately showed was that Nichols had billed 642 unauthorized telephone calls to the state: forty-eight personal calls, 202 calls to *contra* leaders, and 392 calls to Darrell Glascock.

Glascock, a former administrative assistant to Congressman Tommy Robinson, was then doing public relations work for the Caleros's fund-raising efforts on behalf of the Nicaraguan revolutionary movement and had produced a pro-*Contra* film to assist in that endeavor. Nichols and Glascock both contended that they had discussed mortgage revenue bonds in their numerous conversations.[14]

Nichols disappeared from the public eye after that, although he resurfaced briefly a year later as an organizer of a fund-raising event on behalf of Sheffield Nelson's Republican campaign for governor. He was not heard from again for another eleven months, just before Nelson and Clinton squared off in the 1990 general election.

In September 1990, Nichols sued Clinton, Epes, and ADFA for more than $3 million in damages, claiming they had lied about the facts surrounding his resignation and slandered him in the process.

In the lawsuit, which he filed without a lawyer in Pulaski County Circuit Court, Nichols said that he had been fired because he had knowledge that Clinton had made trips, financed with ADFA funds, "for improper purposes." He claimed that Clinton and Epes tried to discredit him because of his knowledge of Clinton's sexual improprieties perpetrated at state expense.

Nichols gave some of the names of Clinton's alleged paramours—a local television journalist, a Clinton staff member, a lounge singer, a former Miss America, and a former Miss Arkansas—and claimed that state funds had been used to wine and dine them and that state troopers had been used to escort the governor on his dates.

The general public was not apprised of these particulars by the news media. Although both daily newspapers ran short, ambiguous stories about the lawsuit having been filed, only one local news outlet, all-talk radio station KBIS-AM, gave any specifics. The commentator who discussed the allegations in some detail was promptly contacted by a lawyer for lounge singer Gennifer Flowers and threatened with a lawsuit for having mentioned her name in connection with the lawsuit. Journalists later claimed that all five women named in Nichols's lawsuit had denied having had affairs with Clinton.

Clinton labeled the allegations "an entire fabrication"[15] and suggested that the lawsuit might be politically motivated. His suggestion was given some credence, but not in the manner he had intended, by a series of judicial irregularities that accompanied the lawsuit's trek through the courts.

Nichols's lawsuit, filed in September 1990, was dismissed in November 1990, but Nichols did not learn of this until July 1991, when he read about it in the newspaper, more than seven months after expiration of the deadline for appealing dismissal.

Nichols's lawsuit had been assigned first to Circuit Judge David Bogard, whose judicial career had begun with an appointment from Clinton as Pulaski County chancellor in 1981. Bogard, who was seeking reelection, claimed he lacked time to preside over the case, so it was transferred to Circuit Judge John Plegge, whose judicial career had begun with an appointment from Clinton as a Little Rock traffic judge in 1985.

Minutes before an October hearing on a defense motion to quash subpoenas issued by Nichols, Nichols petitioned Plegge to remove himself from the case to avoid a conflict of interest. Then Nichols excused himself, telling a court official that he had to pick up someone at the airport. While he was gone, Plegge sealed the file of the civil lawsuit, saying that allegations contained therein could cause "irreparable damage between now and November 6," the date of the 1990 general election in which Clinton was seeking a fifth term. Plegge then quashed the subpoenas and withdrew from the case.

Angered by Judge Plegge's action, Nichols promptly filed a similar lawsuit in federal court in which he claimed he was a scapegoat in "the largest scandal ever perpetrated on the taxpayers of the state of Arkansas." The specifics of the alleged scandal were not reported by the news media.

Nothing more was forthcoming until July 1991, when Nichols read that his state lawsuit had been dismissed with prejudice, hence could not be refiled, thirteen days after the November 1990 election by yet a third jurist, Circuit Judge Perry V. Whitmore. None of the parties in the lawsuit had been notified of Whitmore's action, and Whitmore had retired in December.

The *Arkansas Democrat* then sued to unseal the lawsuit, and Nichols asked Circuit Judge Chris Piazza to permit him to file a long overdue appeal.

"My life has been devastated by the Clinton machine and I deserve my only chance to prove it,"[16] Nichols said. The Pulaski County circuit clerk refused to accept Nichols's filing until advised to do so by Piazza, and Piazza set a hearing for September. In the meantime, he ordered the case file reopened. Local newspapers erroneously reported that most of the information contained in the file already had been made public.

Robert "Say" McIntosh also filed a lawsuit against Clinton that summer. He claimed that the governor had reneged on a promise to pay him $25,000 "to stem a wave of negative publicity about [Clinton's] extramarital affairs" during the 1990 gubernatorial campaign.[17] He further claimed that Clinton had promised to secure financing from Yarnell Ice Cream Company of Arkansas for distribution of McIntosh's sweet potato pie mix and to order the release of McIntosh's son, Tommy, who was serving a fifty-year prison term for cocaine possession and distribution.

Clinton's press secretary, Mike Gauldin, tried to explain the genesis of McIntosh's charges.

In 1990, Gauldin said, "Say had come to us and told us that Sheffield Nelson had tried to pay him to circulate a flier pretty much like the one he's doing now and he [said he] wouldn't do it. We got another call from the Nelson campaign saying that a fellow named Larry Nichols was going to hold a news conference on the Capitol steps" to publicize the alleged affairs.[18]

Gauldin admitted that he had called McIntosh "since he had told us about the connection between Nelson and Nichols in the first place and told him to go" to the Nichols news conference.

"If Sheffield was going to try to hurt a lot of innocent people," Gauldin said, "I wanted somebody there who could point to the connection between Nichols and Nelson."

The claim that McIntosh had been promised a fee for his services was denied.

"Nothing that he says that I promised to do is true," Clinton said, although he conceded that he talked "in passing" with a Yarnell official about marketing the pie mix.[19]

After Clinton displayed no interest in settling the lawsuit, McIntosh distributed twenty thousand handbills relating to one of the governor's alleged affairs. McIntosh made it clear that he was interested in thwarting Clinton's plan to enter the 1992 presidential campaign.

In August 1991, in an ineffective attempt at damage control before Clinton's announcement of his presidential campaign, Gauldin told reporters that Nichols had approached him two days before the November 1990 election with an offer to settle the lawsuit for "$150,000 and a house."[20] The offer had been rejected.

Nichols admitted that he had contacted Gauldin about a possible settlement because he was in serious financial trouble and was about to lose his house to foreclosure, but he said Gauldin had tried to "bait" him into discrediting himself.[21]

Piazza subsequently gave Nichols thirty days in which to file his appeal, and Nichols again went underground.

When Clinton announced in October 1991 that he was a presidential candidate, the tabloids began to look around for scandalous information about the governor of Arkansas. The ground proved fertile beyond any Clinton critic's expectations, and the fledgling central staff of the Clinton campaign was ill prepared to respond. Heretofore, Clinton had been the subject of many *risque* jokes, rumors, and innuendos, but no one had ever come forward to lend credence to the stories. Now journalists could cite two public records—lawsuits filed in state and federal courts, alleging sexual improprieties, abuse of power, and questionable political activity.

In November, the governor's office was confronted with the first in what proved to be a rash of sex-related controversies. Connie Hamzy, a thirty-six-year-old self-professed "groupie" whose sexual expertise had been immortalized years before in Grand Funk's paean to rock-'n'-roll superstardom, "We're an American Band," advised Clinton's staff that she had "told all" to *Penthouse* for its upcoming January issue, among which was an anecdote about her encounter with the governor of Arkansas in 1984.

Actually, there wasn't much to tell as far as Clinton was concerned. Hamzy claimed only that Clinton had groped her during a 1984 encounter and that he had suggested they get together at some future date that never materialized.[22]

According to Hamzy, a Clinton aide had approached her in 1984 as she sat beside the swimming pool at a local hotel, where Clinton had made a speech, and told her that the governor wanted to meet her. During that encounter, she claimed, Clinton had hustled her into a nearby storage closet where they had fondled one another and kissed before Clinton had reluctantly broken away to go to his next engagement.

Warned about the upcoming article, the Clinton campaign produced sworn affidavits from several of Clinton's aides and supporters who were present when he was introduced to Hamzy. All of them denied Hamzy's account and insisted there had been nothing improper about the encounter.[23]

In a 1994 interview, Hamzy said she warned Clinton's staff that *Penthouse* would carry a story in which she recounted the 1984 incident "because I try to play fair, and I was under pressure by different people" to retract that part of the *Penthouse* interview.[23]

"I thought they had a right to know what was coming out. I mean, it's the truth. I didn't expect them to call me a liar. . . . I might be a groupie and a whore, but I'm not a liar."

The "Sweet, Sweet Connie" episode was mild compared to what followed. In January the *Star* tabloid led one issue with allegations about Clinton's extramarital affairs. Based on the Nichols and McIntosh lawsuits, the story named names.

Although both suits were nearly two years old, the Clinton campaign was caught completely off guard by the allegations. The best it could muster was a hasty denunciation by spokeswoman Dee Dee

Myers, a non-Arkansan who apparently had not been briefed about this potential mine field.

"What the *Star* is doing is rehashing charges that were raised and disproved," Myers said. "This is the lowest form of sleazy tabloid journalism."[25]

Campaigning in New Hampshire, Clinton arrived at Nashua ready to discuss his health care agenda. Reporters were singularly uninterested. They wanted a reaction to the *Star*'s story.

"It's a totally bogus lawsuit," Clinton insisted. "The guy was fired for making illegal phone calls on private property and then tried to bribe me, and I just wouldn't do it."[26]

The Nichols story, he said, was "rehashed lies."

"It's made news now here because it's not old news, but it is old news at home. It was thoroughly investigated. It's not true."

Reporters took him at his word.

That evening, Clinton appeared live on WMUR-TV's 6:00 p.m. newscast to respond to the allegations, which had been aired by the Manchester television station and had been picked up by several New Hampshire newspapers.

"I think voters always try to make judgments about a person's character and fitness to serve," he said. "The question is whether it's relevant and whether it's true. In this particular case, the charges are untrue and have been thoroughly investigated, are old news at home, and the person who made them has been discredited."[27]

Asked whether he had ever had an extramarital affair, Clinton replied, "If I had, I wouldn't tell you."

Back in Arkansas, reporter Bill Simmons of The Associated Press was asked about the local media's handling of the Nichols story.

"We've interviewed most of the persons named in his allegations and we gave checked records pertaining to the allegations," Simmons said. "So far, we have found nothing to substantiate the allegations and know of no one who corroborates them."[28]

Gennifer Flowers soon changed all that. In a subsequent issue of the *Star*, prereleased to the mainstream press a week before it hit the newsstands, she rescinded her previous denial of an intimate relationship with Clinton and boasted of having been his mistress for a dozen years.

Of the numerous women mentioned throughout his years in public life as having had illicit relationships with Clinton, no woman before Gennifer Flowers ever deigned to lend credence to the rumors, and she did so in return for money from a supermarket tabloid, the *Star*. There are three possible explanations for the lack of corroboration by other alleged Clinton paramours: The women are extremely loyal, they are extremely intimidated, or the stories about them aren't true. Later in the campaign, during the Democratic National Convention in New York City, a second woman would step forward to claim a brief affair with Clinton. Sally Miller Perdue, Miss Arkansas of 1958 and a Republican loser in the 1984 Pine Bluff, Arkansas, mayoral race, chose as her forum the popular national television program hosted by Sally Jessy Raphael. Perdue, then fifty-five, claimed that she and Clinton, twelve years her junior, had had sexual relations several times during a three-and-a-half to four-month period in late 1983. She said that only four other people had known about the affair. One of those, Anna Lessenby, appeared with Perdue on the Raphael show but conceded that she had never seen Perdue and Clinton together. No one else stepped forward to validate Perdue's claims, and the Clinton campaign refused to comment. Raphael's New York affiliate, WNBC-TV, refused to carry the broadcast in deference to convention delegates.

In its attempt to discredit Flowers, the Clinton campaign claimed she had concocted the affair after having been offered a six-figure enticement from the tabloid. While Flowers was paid for her story, just as she was paid for a subsequent feature story and nude layout in *Penthouse*, she was paid for details of an affair about which she had been boasting for free to friends and associates for several years. One person in whom she had confided passed along some of those details in off-the-record conversations with me a couple of years before Clinton was a presidential contender. Some of the more intimate anecdotes relayed to me surfaced later in the tape recordings Flowers made of her telephone conversations with Clinton.

Few who knew her well during this period were given to believe that Flowers's relationship with Clinton had been anything more than a couple of one-night stands. She had a reputation for one-night stands, and one of her favorite stories was how she duped another well-known Arkansas politician when, as they sat drinking with some acquaintances at a Little Rock bar, he boldly offered her $1,000 to spend the night with him and she dared him to lay his money on the table. When he did so, she recalled with a laugh, she simply gathered up the money and walked out of the bar—alone. Many who know her are convinced that she fabricated the "love affair" with Clinton to increase the marketability of her story and herself.

Eura Gean Flowers had been trying to find the right market for her talents for more than twenty years. After graduating from Brinkley High School in 1968, she tried college and found it boring. She worked as a dental assistant and found it unglamorous. She tried singing and found it less than profitable. For a time, she worked as a reporter for KARK-TV, the NBC affiliate in Little Rock, where, she says, she met the handsome young attorney general of Arkansas, Bill Clinton, who chased her relentlessly until she succumbed to his charms.

There ensued, according to Flowers, a torrid love affair that lasted from 1977 to 1989.

That's not exactly the slant she put on their relationship to those in whom she initially confided. Lauren Kirk, a former roommate, later told *Penthouse* that Flowers "pumped up her affair with Clinton to make it look long and passionate, but . . . that doesn't alter the fact [that] she did have an affair with Clinton. She just can't accept the fact that he came, wiped himself off, zipped up, and left."[29]

In that same interview, Kirk described Flowers as "a frustrated actress who can't do it onstage, so she does it in real life."

Another former acquaintance agreed, saying that Flowers often gave conflicting accounts of her liaisons with men, many of whom she boasted paid dearly for the privilege of spending time with her.[30]

It is a fact that her acquaintanceship with Clinton led to the state job from which she was fired when she failed to show up for work after her appearance at a New York news conference in which she publicized the *Star's* follow-up story, a partial transcript of the Clinton-Flowers tapes. By the same token, it could be said that Larry Nichols's acquaintanceship with Betsey Wright led to the state job from which *he* was fired in 1988. Nichols was acquainted with Wright, and when he contacted her about obtaining a state job, she referred him to someone who gave him one.[31] A referral from the governor's office in Arkansas is no guarantee of employment, but it is known to give an applicant an edge not enjoyed by people who come in off the street. The same is true of referrals from legislators and other elected officials.

Left virtually to their own devices by a largely imported campaign staff still not equipped to handle controversies from Arkansas, Bill and Hillary Clinton spent what was for them an inordinate amount of time responding to the Gennifer Flowers scandal during the weeks before the New Hampshire primary. The only public relations achievement attributable during that period to the campaign staff was Larry Nichols's sudden decision to withdraw his lawsuit. At that point, however, no one was really interested.

In a signed, one-page statement issued by Clinton's Little Rock campaign staff, Nichols declared, "The feud is over."[32]

In the wake of the *Star* story about his lawsuit, Nichols claimed, he had been approached by several women seeking money to say that they had had an affair with Clinton and a London newspaper had offered him $500,000 for a story.

"It is time to call the fight I have with Bill Clinton over," Nichols stated. "I want to tell everybody what I did to try to destroy Governor Clinton. I set out to destroy him for what I believed happened to me. I believe I was wrongfully fired from my job. Nobody has wanted to listen to me. All I wanted was a fair and honest hearing about what really happened. I want my family to know that I didn't do the things I've been accused of. . . . [N]o one can make an ass out of himself better than I can, so I've got to be the one that corrects it and stops it."

He blamed the news media for having "made a circus out of this thing" and said it had gone too far. He stopped short of admitting that the allegations he had raised were false.

"I apologize to the women who I named in the suit. I brought them into the public's eye and I shouldn't have done that. The least significant parts of my case were those concerning the rumors."

When contacted by reporters, Nichols was vague about whether that meant his allegations were false. "I'm going to leave that a mystery," he said.[33]

Nichols, who a year before had been pleading with the governor's office to settle the lawsuit out of court for $150,000, claimed he had received nothing of value from the Clinton campaign in return for his statement or for the affidavit he had signed previously in which he withdrew his allegations about an affair between Clinton and a member of the governor's staff.

"I respect Larry Nichols for having the courage to come forward to set the record straight," Clinton said in a prepared statement released along with the Nichols statement. "It takes a strong man to admit he's wrong."[34]

The truce lasted until May, when Nichols filed another lawsuit in which he sought to oust Clinton from the governorship on the grounds that he had state property and state employees to conduct illicit meetings with women. Given Nichols's track record, no one was buying this one. For his part, Robert "Say" McIntosh continued to pass out handbills on the Little Rock streets.

During this period and for many weeks thereafter, Clinton's best asset was not his charm or his message or his incredibly extensive and well-organized political network but his partner on the road to the White House, Hillary Rodham Clinton. Just as she had done in preparation for the 1982 comeback, she had recreated herself into a softer, more attractive, more personable image. With the help of hairdressers, wardrobe advisors, and makeup artists, the degree of glamour she brought to the campaign stunned those who had known her in Arkansas, and yet she spoke with the self-confidence and forcefulness of a full partner in the campaign. Not yet exposed to the criticism that would compel her to take a subordinate role in the campaign, she maintained an exhaustive schedule of personal appearances in which she persuasively articulated the Clinton agenda. The public adored her.

"If I get elected president," her husband told writer Gail Sheehy, "it will be an unprecedented partnership, far more than Franklin Roosevelt and Eleanor. They were two great people, but on different tracks. If I get elected, we'll do things together like we always have."[35]

The allusion to FDR and the woman he wronged was perhaps an unfortunate one, given the similarities of the Clinton union, but this was a different era, and Hillary Clinton was not a reluctant recruit to her husband's quest for greatness. Without her concentration, her strength, and her determination, that quest might have been lost on any number of occasions.

Throughout the campaign, Bill's first and best advisor was neither James Carville nor George Stephanopoulos, but Hillary. Months before Betsey Wright ever inserted herself into the campaign, Hillary was in command of the damage control required by those first and potentially most damaging bimbo eruptions. Displeased with the tentative manner in which the campaign staff had handled the earliest controversies, and infuriated by Bill's apparent lack of concern when the first Gennifer Flowers story broke, she took charge.

Hillary made the decision to confront the Gennifer Flowers scandal head-on, but she rejected a recommendation that Clinton appear on *Nightline*. Ted Koppel, who occasionally relaxed his interviewing format to permit VIPs to sit beside him on-camera, never relaxed his blunt, tenacious method of interviewing. Hillary, suspecting that Clinton would have difficulty putting a positive spin on the womanizing issue under Koppel's peerless cross-examination, wanted none of that.

Fortunately, Clinton enjoyed considerable support from others among the major media, including Don Hewitt of *60 Minutes*. With that knowledge, Hillary, Carville, and the other spin doctors saw a chance to seize control of the controversy. They offered *60 Minutes* an exclusive interview with the Clintons, and the producers quickly agreed to broadcast the interview in an unprecedented fifteen-minute "special edition" of *60 Minutes* following the 1992 Super Bowl.

The Clintons's appearance was meticulously planned and carefully orchestrated to present the candidate in the best possible light. Industry sources later claimed that interviewer Steve Kroft was given the precise wording of his questions about allegations of Clinton's infidelity and was ordered not to stray from the agreed-upon text.

"Before the interview," Hillary Clinton biographer Judith Warner contended, "the campaign had decided that Bill Clinton's only hope of not falling into an endless quagmire of questions about the history of his marriage was to refuse to speak specifically about any single alleged affair. But the governor was not a very wily interviewee."[36]

Nothing could be farther from the truth, as anyone who knows Clinton well or has spent any time interviewing him will attest. Time and time again, Kroft's questions, one-shot interrogatories with no specific follow-up on the answers given, allowed Clinton to avoid a direct and specific response. Consider the following exchange concerning Gennifer Flowers's allegations.

Kroft: She is alleging and has described in some detail in a supermarket tabloid what she calls a twelve-year affair with you.

Clinton: *That* allegation is false.

By that statement, Clinton did not deny having had an affair with Flowers, he merely denied having had an affair of twelve years's duration.

Kroft: I am assuming from your answer that you're categorically denying that you ever had an affair with Gennifer Flowers.

Clinton: I've said that before, and so has she.

Again, Clinton did not answer the question, he merely stated that he had denied it previously.

The next day, a lot of Arkansans had a good laugh over how well Clinton had avoided giving direct answers to Kroft's questions.

The public's response was overwhelmingly favorable, although a few skeptics and one country music singer were less than pleased with Hillary's declaration that she was "not sitting there because I'm some little woman standing by my man like Tammy Wynette. I'm sitting here because I love him and I respect him and I honor what he's been through and what we've been through together, and you know, if that's not enough for the people, then heck, don't vote for him."

The *60 Minutes* segment did much to strengthen the public's perception of the Clintons as a devoted couple who had fought mightily to preserve their marriage in the face of some tough, if ill-defined, problems. Hillary had evoked sympathy and understanding with her dignified display of righteous indignation in telling Kroft: "There isn't a person watching this who would feel comfortable sitting on this couch detailing everything that ever went on in their life or their marriage, and I think it's real dangerous in this country if we don't have a zone of privacy for everybody."

Those who were there said that throughout the ninety-minute

taping, the tension was so thick that it was not even broken when a row of heavy lights came crashing down, narrowly missing Hillary's head and sending her rushing into Bill's arms. As the interview concluded, his relief was so great that Carville reportedly broke down and cried.[37]

It was generally agreed among campaign insiders that although Hillary had tended to dominate the proceedings, the interview had been a great success for both Clintons. She had kept the interview on track during those moments that Clinton was inclined to wander, she broke in whenever he threatened to stray from the script, and the two of them had given witness to their affection for one another and their dedication to the marriage. As Kroft later noted, "Hillary is tougher and more disciplined than Bill is, and she's analytical. Among his faults, he has a tendency not to think of the consequences of things he says. I think she knows."[38]

The Clintons's feeling of triumph was short-lived. When a new week of campaigning began the day after the *60 Minutes* segment aired, the Clintons were stunned to learn that Gennifer Flowers had tape recordings of her conversations with Bill Clinton. Once again separated by their campaign schedules, the couple conferred long distance. Bill was defensive, suggesting hopefully that no one would believe a woman who obviously had been paid to say these outrageous things. Hillary was disgusted. She heatedly pointed out that many would be left to wonder why he had even wasted time talking to such a disreputable person.[39]

Later that day, while campaigning in South Dakota, Hillary learned that the story of the Gennifer tapes had led all three network evening newscasts. It was the final straw.[40] Henceforth, she and Clinton would not sit back and be victimized by assaults on his character. They would take the offensive, placing the blame on the media, the Republicans, whoever and whatever was available to be blamed. She wanted no more surprises, and she wanted a prepackaged strategy ready and waiting for every conceivable eventuality.

There were a few more surprises in store, although a number of potentially damaging stories went overlooked or undeveloped by most reporters in the early stages of the 1992 campaign, and by the time the national press became interested in them, many of Clinton's most

credible detractors, disgusted with the press's lack of interest in anything critical of the Democratic front-runner, had stopped granting
interviews.

Among the stories largely ignored by the bulk of the national media
was a March 1992 *New York Times* account of Clinton's involvement in
an Arkansas land development deal on which he said he lost $68,900.
The *Times* story pointed out that a principal in the land deal, Jim
McDougal, also was a principal in a state-regulated thrift, Madison
Guaranty Savings and Loan Association, that eventually went bankrupt.

Some members of the national press jumped to Clinton's defense
against such revelations. A case in point was an April 1992 story in the
Minneapolis-St. Paul Star-Tribune by Tom Hamburger, a former *Arkansas Gazette* reporter and longtime acquaintance and admirer of
Clinton who attempted to debunk several potentially controversial
matters that were first published in the *Times*.

Hamburger wrote that the *Times* had "planted the suggestion that
Clinton may have been associated with the [Madison Guaranty] S&L
scandal."

"Even if the association did prove true," he opined, "its significance
would pale in comparison to those linking members of the Bush
family to S&L mismanagement and corruption."

He defended Hillary Clinton's association with the Rose Law Firm
and stated that any state business the firm had received as a result of her
association "accounts for a tiny part of its revenues."

Hamburger further defended the Clintons and another Rose law
partner, Webb Hubbell, against any implications that as a member of
the Clinton-appointed committee that "refined" the proposed state
ethics law, which eventually was submitted to and approved by voters
as an initiated act, Hubbell had purposely deleted the original conflict-
of-interest clause so that Hillary would not have to divulge the names
of clients she represented before state agencies.

Had that provision been included, Arkansans would have learned a
great deal more about the obvious conflicts of interest inherent in
Hillary's roster of clients, and perhaps more light would have been shed

on the couple's involvement with Madison Guaranty Savings and Loan and Whitewater Development Company.

The Clintons's political and business dealings with Jim and Susan McDougal were not unknown in Arkansas, but the extent of those dealings was never seriously explored. McDougal had served as an aide to Clinton during his first term. And he had entered the thrift business in partnership with several prominent Democrats, among them another former Clinton aide, Steve Smith. Susan McDougal's brother, Bill Henley, served in the Arkansas Senate in the 1980s. The Whitewater venture had been reported as early as 1979.

Pam Strickland, an *Arkansas Democrat-Gazette* columnist and a former reporter, recalled that she first saw the words "Whitewater Development Company" on a 1986 financial disclosure statement filed by the Clinton reelection campaign.

"What I remember is a press aide saying it was 'a bad investment they're trying to get out of,'" she wrote in a 1994 column. "I found only a couple of 1979 clips in the morgue file and went on to other things."[41]

Paul Barton, who also covered the 1986 gubernatorial campaign, suggested that he and his colleagues had been too distracted by other events to pay close attention to Whitewater.[42] More accurate was his idea that the reporters assigned to cover state government at that time "were all youthful and naive," too inexperienced to pick up the thread and follow it. Most of those involved in substantive coverage—the print reporters—were hard working and enthusiastic, but they also were relatively new to their respective assignments. There was a near-constant turnover on the state Capitol beat in those days, and the emphasis was on daily campaign coverage, not investigative stories or news analysis.

As it was, these matters were ignored until the 1992 presidential campaign, when the *New York Times* questioned the relationship between the Clintons and the McDougals, their involvement in a speculative 1978 land development deal, and their affiliation with a state-regulated savings and loan association that went bankrupt in 1987.

What later would be christened Whitewatergate was a story as complex as the convoluted Grand Gulf saga. Among Clinton's challengers for the nomination, only Edmund G. "Jerry" Brown, Jr., tried to cultivate it as an issue in the campaign. But Brown's charges were submerged in the fallout from the Gennifer Flowers tapes, the debates, and the draft issue.

The now-infamous Gennifer Flowers tapes, select portions of which were being reprinted and broadcast nationwide, took a toll on the Clintons, who were becoming short-tempered and impatient with each other and those around them, and on the candidate's standing in the polls in those all-important early primary states. In New Hampshire alone, Clinton lost his early lead over Paul Tsongas, dropping twelve points after Gennifer Flowers made her revelations.

Hillary's steadfast defense of her husband and their marriage helped slow the womanizing stories, but the harm these stories caused Clinton was reversed in large part by the efforts of the Arkansas Travelers, groups of Arkansans who visited key primary states on behalf of Clinton's candidacy to offer personal testimony about his trustworthiness, his achievements, and his character. Their numbers included retirees, students, lobbyists, legislators, homemakers, political appointees, business and community leaders, teachers, and assorted other professionals.

There were only two requirements for becoming an Arkansas Traveler: availability and money. Being intimately acquainted with the candidate was not a prerequisite, but it helped, particularly when called upon by a local organization to defend the beleaguered candidate. Generally, if one could pay his or her own way to, say, New Hampshire, and also absorb the cost of food and lodging, any Arkansas volunteer was welcome to come along for the ride. Once assembled, however, the volunteers undertook a rigorous schedule of door-to-door, one-on-one proselytizing from early morning to late at night. They were expected to follow orders, their every move was dictated by key campaign volunteers, and slackers were neither appreciated nor tolerated. The Arkansas Travelers worked faithfully throughout the campaign, but nowhere was their presence more keenly felt, or more seriously needed, than in New Hampshire, whose important first primary of the season came shortly after the Gennifer Flowers revelations.

"I'd do just about anything for Bill Clinton, but I wouldn't share a hotel room for him," one Arkansan quipped after enduring several days of trooping through the February snow. "They told me when I got there that I was going to share a room with this other guy, and I told them that I was paying for it, so I was going to sleep where I wanted to."

Some of the Arkansas Travelers were also FOBs—Friends of Bill. They were an equally diverse group of Clintonites who bore little relation to those idealistic young collegians who had initiated "The Conversation" twenty-five years before at Oxford, although some pundits erroneously made that connection. The FOBs took orders from no one, although they were occasionally called upon to advise the campaign or to host another fundraiser. It was very easy to be a Friend of Bill. If you had money or could find money and were loyal to the cause, you qualified as an FOB, although some people such as David Leopoulos and Carolyn Staley qualified by virtue of long-standing friendship.

Oxford classmates such as Strobe Talbott and Robert Reich qualified for FOB membership, but so did a large percentage of the beautiful people in Hollywood and virtually anyone invited to a Pamela Harriman party within the last ten years. MCA Chairman Lew Wasserman, Creative Artists Agency's Michael Ovitz, Time Warner's Bob Pittman, former banking executive Susan Ness, and investment bankers Stan Shuman and Roy Furman raised enough money for the campaign to become FOBs. By virtue of their glowing insights and authoritatively laudatory pontifications, Newsweek's Eleanor Clift and Joe Klein were dubbed honorary FOBs by Arkansas pundits.

On the Republican side, Bush's chief handlers believed that Clinton had so many warts that the voters would pick up on them without being told about Clinton's problems and ultimately would reject him. But those who knew him knew otherwise.

"You're talking about somebody who has trained himself for this [1992 campaign], someone for whom this was the long-range goal," Starr said. "I mean, he really probably started thinking about the time he was sixteen years old he might be elected president someday, which is not an unusual belief for somebody who's sixteen, but most of us outgrow that by the time we're twenty-one, and he didn't."[43]

"He apparently spent most of his life—and Hillary is much better at this than he is—buttering up people, making friends with people across this country, so that when Tom Harkin, who had never been anywhere except from Iowa to Washington, and Bob Kerrey, who had never been anywhere except from Nebraska to Washington, start looking for support countrywide, they find out that Bill Clinton knows every political leader in every state, and almost every Democratic governor is already on his side, and the Democratic senators.

"Listen, don't underestimate the power of the Democratic Leadership Council, OK? Because here are a lot of conservative Democrats, or at least not wet-noodle liberal Democrats, who have put together a pretty good power base, and he helped them put it together, and he didn't just reap the benefit of somebody else's labor. They had put together this base, and they had done a pretty good job of selling the people of America on this idea that we didn't need Republicans to run the country, what we needed was a new kind of Democrat.

"And I think that was where his great success was," Starr said. "He convinced everybody he was a new kind of Democrat. He wasn't, of course, but he convinced everybody that he was.

25

WHITEWATER, WOMEN, AND THE WHITE HOUSE

PERSONALLY AND POLITICALLY, Bill Clinton's first thirteen months as president were as tumultuous as the thirteen months he spent campaigning, except that revelations about his draft-dodging and his experiments with marijuana while a student were replaced with revelations about his and his wife's political and financial dealings while he was governor. Allegations of extramarital affairs arose during both periods. These postelection controversies quickly acquired a catchy nickname: Whitewatergate, the catch-all reference for matters involving two ill-fated Arkansas enterprises, the Whitewater Development Company and Madison Guaranty Savings and Loan Association, and Troopergate.

It is undeniable that most of the news media had given short shrift to the draft-dodging and the dope-smoking episodes. Clinton's assertion that he had tried to smoke marijuana on several occasions while a student but "didn't inhale" was so lame that it could not be taken seriously. The Vietnam War had been so unpopular that only the most diehard veteran could complain about Clinton's maneuverings. And the campaign-era allegations of womanizing were discredited before they could take root in the mainstream press because the main purveyor of the accusation had chosen to sell her story to a super-market tabloid.

All in all, the American public was not impressed by such revelations; character was not an issue in the 1992 campaign.

It is interesting that the types of scandals with which Bill Clinton was associated first as a candidate and later as president had been examined by the Arkansas news media years before they developed as national news stories. However, no in-depth coverage was ever given to allegations of womanizing, drug use, draft-dodging, or conflict of interest. Whether for lack of information or lack of interest—both seem applicable—few news outlets invested much energy in exploring or gave much play to the allegations. Even Clinton's harshest critics among the media failed to pursue the allegations beyond the obligatory inquiry, and often no story was produced. For all the journalistic ranting against the Clinton administration, the news media were not persistent in their pursuit of stories about the Whitewater Development Company or Madison Guaranty, and Hillary Clinton's business and professional pursuits received virtually no attention at all from the media.

Hillary may have been bored by the teas-and-cookies role assigned by the public to the state's first ladies, but it served her personal interests well. She was able to ply her lawyer's trade and manage the couple's investment portfolio without public scrutiny of any sort. Indeed, no one was more surprised than the Arkansas news media when revelations about Hillary's involvement in Whitewater–Madison began surfacing in late 1993. Clinton's foibles were well known and even accepted in his home state; Hillary's were not.

The Clinton White House has received numerous kudos for its ability to stage-manage the news in the face of some embarrassing missteps, but on those rare occasions that its occupants's actions were called into question, the Clinton statehouse was no less effective. For a variety a reasons, some potentially embarrassing disclosures were never made by the Arkansas news media because their substance was never explored.

The dynamic nature of the news does not lend itself to extended inquiry by small news organizations, a description applicable to Arkansas's major media outlets; many stories that might have ripened into full-blown scandals over time were long forgotten by the time they bore fruit.

The Clintons's involvement with James and Susan McDougal in the Whitewater Development Company was publicized during the first Clinton administration, and then it was forgotten, only to reappear as mere background information as the McDougals's ventures began failing several years later.

McDougal, who had met Clinton while both were working for J. William Fulbright, had wanted a career in politics, but despite his fascination with and enthusiasm for the subject, he lacked the temperament and the charisma necessary to become a successful politician. McDougal worked for several successful politicians, among them the late U.S. Senator John L. McClellan and then-Governor Bill Clinton, but with the exception of his seven-year stint as an aide to Fulbright, he never held any of his patronage positions for more than a few months because of his volatile temper, his inattentiveness, and the wild mood swings that eventually were diagnosed as manic depression.

Between government jobs, which were few and far between, McDougal generated campaign funds for his patrons and looked for ways in which to make money for himself and his friends. Essentially, he was a speculator. One of his earliest ventures involved farming mussel shells from Arkansas's White River and exporting them to Japan for use in culturing pearls.

Whitewater Development Company was one in a series of unsuccessful money-making gambits McDougal played during the 1970s. In 1978, he and his bride Susan Henley McDougal persuaded Bill Clinton and Hillary Rodham to join them in developing an overgrown 230-acre tract along the White River in Northwest Arkansas's Madison County.

In defending his Whitewater role years later, President Clinton would plead ignorance of the investment's details, and that seems likely. By all accounts, including McDougal's, the major players in this partnership were Jim McDougal and Hillary Rodham. But they did rely heavily upon Bill Clinton's prestige as attorney general and the likelihood that he would be elected governor later that year, to tap financial sources to buy the property in August 1978.

None of those involved had a great deal of personal wealth on which to draw. Hillary's law practice was supplementing Bill's modest annual state salary by about $40,000 a year, but they were making monthly mortgage payments on a home. She also had begun dabbling in the stock market.

Purchase of the White River property was entirely financed with borrowed money. The down payment was made with a $20,000 unsecured loan to Hillary from Union Bank of Little Rock, whose board of directors included one of Clinton's chief fundraisers, Walter A. "Wally" DeRoeck. Additionally, a mortgage loan of $182,611.20 was provided by Citizens Bank and Trust of Flippin, whose board also included several Clinton supporters.

Among the bankers who approved loans for the enterprise was Marlin D. Jackson, who later served as state bank commissioner under Clinton. In a 1993 interview with the *Washington Post*, Jackson noted that Arkansas banks often granted unsecured loans to politicians. It was, he said, "just a slight accommodation for people of prominence in state government. The notion is you somehow ingratiate yourself slightly by doing this."[1]

McDougal ingratiated himself to Clinton well enough to secure a position on the new governor's staff in January 1980, although he later claimed that such a position had not been discussed until long after they entered into partnership. Officially, McDougal was a member of the "issues staff," and he served as gubernatorial liaison to the state Highway and Transportation Department, the Economic Development Department, the state Securities Commission, and the state Bank Commission. He also coordinated activities of the Governor's Task Force on Investments and Capital Expenditures.

McDougal's qualifications for these responsibilities were set out in the resume he was required to file with the governor's office: In addition to various political jobs, he cited self-employment as an export broker from March 1964 to March 1968 and the presidency, from May 1976 to January 1979, of Great Southern Land Company, "engaged in buying and selling of unimproved land. During this period, applicant served as officer of various other small family-owned companies which dealt in land investment."

During his eleven months in the governor's office, during which he seemed to excel at joining lawmakers and lobbyists in closing down Little Rock bars, McDougal continued to oversee the development of what was known as Whitewater Estates, although very little development transpired. It was, in fact, public disclosure of that activity that resulted in his abrupt resignation from Clinton's staff. Although at the time he insisted that his job on the governor's staff was temporary, other personnel notes provided by Clinton's office indicated that McDougal had been in line to become the governor's alternate representative on the Ozarks Regional Commission.

Little was heard of McDougal until the following October when, a couple of weeks before Clinton's defeat in the 1980 general election, administrative assistant Steve Smith announced that he would be leaving the staff to assume the presidency of a small bank in his home county of Madison in northwest Arkansas. Smith said that he and six other investors, among them former Congressman Jim Guy Tucker and former Clinton aide Jim McDougal, had an option to buy the bank, an opportunity too good to resist.

Smith's banking career was short-lived; he eventually left the presidency of the Bank of Kingston and joined the communications faculty of the University of Arkansas, where he remains. McDougal continued to wheel and deal, and although he and Susan continued to live the good life, their endeavors continued to lose money. The Clintons wrote off as much of their losses as possible, and perhaps more than they were entitled to write off. Once in the White House, the Clintons would claim to have lost $68,900 on their Whitewater investment. The few financial and tax records available to the public before a special counsel was appointed by Attorney General Janet Reno in January 1994 to investigate Whitewater-Madison and related issues indicated to independent tax experts consulted by *Time* in February 1994 that the Clintons may have deducted too much interest on several years' worth of income tax returns and paid an insufficient amount of tax in those years.

During Clinton's unexpected two-year hiatus from the governor's office, McDougal and Hillary Rodham Clinton, as she became known during that period, actively pursued their business partnership. Any reservations she may have had about the public's lack of interest in buying lots in Whitewater Estates may have been alleviated when McDougal's small financial empire appeared to flourish. In 1982, using borrowed money, he sold his interest in the Bank of Kingston and bought controlling interest in a small two-branch thrift, Woodruff County Savings and Loan Association, which he renamed Madison Guaranty. Although he had no training in the savings and loan industry, he became the thrift's president and chairman of the board.

If there was any suspicion among Capitol watchers less familiar with the nature of the Clinton-McDougal relationship that their friendship was less than warm, that was dispelled in February 1983 when the newly reelected governor announced that McDougal would serve as one of his liaisons to the Senate during the 1983 legislative session. Six months later, McDougal applied for, and received, permission from state regulators to open a Little Rock branch of Madison Guaranty. The *Arkansas Gazette* reported that the branch would have the limited purpose of providing mortgage financing for "a booming Madison Guaranty real estate venture—Maple Creek Farms,"[2] a 1,300-acre development of Madison Guaranty's subsidiary, Madison Financial Corporation.

Of course, neither Maple Creek nor Whitewater was booming, and state regulators were seeing troublesome signs in McDougal's management style: The Bank of Kingston seemed to be making an alarming number of risky loans without proper surety, which concerned state bank officials, but no action was taken. About six months after McDougal applied for permission to open a third Madison Guaranty branch in Little Rock, federal regulators began questioning the thrift's loan policies.

In early 1984, the Federal Home Loan Bank Board concluded that investments made by Madison Guaranty through a real estate subsidiary, Madison Financial Corporation, were double the amount allowable under Arkansas law.

It seems unlikely that Hillary Clinton was unaware of the dubious nature of McDougal's investment practices until 1988, when she asked

Jim and Susan McDougal to give her power of attorney over the Whitewater venture. In a state as small as Arkansas, there are few secrets in government between patrons and their appointees, and Clinton had replaced almost all of Frank White appointees upon regaining the governorship in 1982. Even without benefit of the grapevine, Hillary had more than an inkling of McDougal's problems with Madison Guaranty: In 1985, she represented the faltering thrift before the Arkansas Securities Commission.

Shortly after purchasing the Bank of Kingston, McDougal had been served with a cease-and-desist order by regulators who wanted the bank's management to halt unsafe and unsound practices. In August 1983, Madison Guaranty had $10 million in assets. In June 1986, when the thrift's assets had ballooned to $123 million, although regulators held that the so-called profits were hefty losses and it was technically bankrupt, McDougal was forced to resign.

Bill Clinton suffered his own losses during this period, and it was McDougal who came to the rescue. According to McDougal, he was in the Little Rock office of Madison Guaranty in early 1985 when Clinton dropped by while on his daily jog up Main Street and spent the bulk of their visit complaining that he and Hillary were having difficulty making ends meet. At this time, Clinton was drawing $35,000 a year as governor, Hillary was pulling down six figures in salary and commissions from her law firm, and all their living expenses were being paid by the state. As a result of that conversation, McDougal said, he awarded a $2,000-a-month retainer to Rose Law Firm to represent Madison Guaranty. Reportedly, one of the lawyers who later helped prepare a plan for state regulators to keep Madison Guaranty open in the wake of staggering losses was Hillary Rodham Clinton.

Shortly after Clinton's visit, McDougal also hosted a fund-raiser at which about $30,000 was raised to help Clinton retire a $50,000 debt owed to Clinton Executive Secretary Maurice Smith's Bank of Cherry Valley for the 1984 gubernatorial campaign.

Most of this activity, however, went unreported in Arkansas. Throughout Clinton's tenure as governor, the major sources of news in Arkansas were the two statewide daily newspapers because they contained more information than any statewide television newscast, which had only thirty minutes in which to cram news highlights, human-interest stories, weather, and sports. During that time, the *Arkansas Democrat* and the *Arkansas Gazette* were engaged in a bitter competition to dominate the market, and the ongoing struggle to present the most news and information in the best possible manner to the largest number of readers made the two print operations less than vigilant over potential or developing controversies. Both newspapers prided themselves on their coverage of politics and government, but there was a certain selectivity in what they chose to cover. Part of this was of necessity; part of it was overinvolvement with their news subjects.

In the wake of Whitewatergate and Troopergate, Arkansas has been exposed to the world as a politically incestuous state whose domination by the Democratic party has kept the same people in positions of statewide power and influence through several generations in a manner not unlike that exhibited in the large cities of more populous states. As in any other locale, there are several tiers of power and influence, among them select members of the journalism establishment, and any politician worth his salt cultivates those molders of public opinion. During the halcyon days of the Clinton administration, with the war between the *Arkansas Gazette* and the *Arkansas Democrat*, that was very easy to do.

The relations between the Clinton administration and the press were informal. Editors and reporters were on a first-name basis with Bill Clinton, his political appointees and operatives, and his staff. Some members of the press counted themselves among the Clintons's circle of close friends; they played golf or tennis together, sat side-by-side as their children played softball, and swapped party or dinner invitations. The editor in charge of state political coverage for the *Arkansas Gazette* was married to Hillary Clinton's former college roommate. Some journalists, both newspaper and television, had campaigned for Bill Clinton in his congressional race; some eventually went to work for him, in the attorney general's office, in the governor's office, in the presidential campaign. Because relations were cordial, and in some cases quite warm, and because Clinton was very accomplished in the art of personal persuasion, he had great success at putting out brush fires.

When Jim McDougal was indicted by a federal grand jury in 1989, after Madison Guaranty had been seized by the federal government, his involvement with many of the state's most prominent politicians was but a footnote in the resulting stories. It should be noted that none of these politicians was implicated in any wrongdoing, and none of the allegations concerned Whitewater Development Company, but they did involve Madison Guaranty Savings and Loan Association, the presidency of which McDougal said he had relinquished in 1984 to concentrate on one of the thrift's several subsidiaries, Madison Financial Corporation.

The government claimed that McDougal formed Master Developers Corporation to buy property from Madison Financial, and that Madison Guaranty had provided the loan money for a land development venture dubbed Castle Grande Estates.

According to the federal indictment, McDougal had used Master Developers and Madison Financial to facilitate two bogus land sales to the detriment of Madison Guaranty, which was declared insolvent in 1989.

The transactions, one in 1985 and another in 1986, allegedly were designed to skirt thrift regulations and enrich McDougal with phony commissions. The indictment alleged that the sales involved the filing of false financial statements, misapplication of almost $1 million in two loans, deceiving thrift regulators, and conspiracy. McDougal was exonerated of all charges, including bank fraud and conspiracy, in June 1990.

One result of the Clinton administration's machinations was that the attention of the *Gazette* and the *Democrat* could be easily diverted. Because of the liberalism of the *Gazette*, Clinton enjoyed more political and personal support from its staff. The more conservative *Arkansas Democrat* was a tougher proposition, more likely to find fault with the administration in its news and editorial pages, but Clinton had several not-so-secret weapons to combat that: the women in his life.

Reporters came and went, but John R. Starr, the outspoken, hands-on managing editor of the *Democrat*, was a constant throughout most of Clinton's career in Arkansas. Because of the volatile nature of their relationship—Starr was intent on being an active participant in the formulation of state policy, and Clinton had plenty of other advisors and policy-makers to appease—Clinton often dispatched his closest female advisors to placate Starr. If Clinton and Starr had one thing in common, it was a weakness for and appreciation of strong-willed, outspoken, independent women, given that both men had been reared in strong matriarchal households.

During Clinton's first term, press secretary Julie Baldridge had played the peace maker. During Clinton's comeback campaign and thereafter until 1989, Betsey Wright often filled the role, augmented at various times by press secretary Joan Roberts or even Hillary Clinton. The scenarios usually followed the same form: Starr would become agitated at the breaking of some real or imagined Clinton promise and persistently excoriate the governor in print; Julie or Joan or Betsey or Hillary would call Starr and engage him in a surreptitious scheme to make Bill Clinton "do right"; and Starr would be mollified and editorially supportive until the next falling out.

"She played him like a drum,"[3] Bobby Roberts said of his ex-wife, who was Clinton's press secretary from 1983 until mid–1986. Roberts frequently lobbied the Arkansas legislature on Clinton's behalf and then served as a Clinton appointee to the state Board of Correction. He later recalled that on numerous occasions, usually during the daily strategy meetings Clinton held with key advisors during legislative sessions, he witnessed Clinton giving Joan Roberts marching orders to placate Starr.

Starr apparently did not realize the calculation that went into the "friendship" he enjoyed with Clinton's distaff operatives, who sometimes called upon him for editorial support under the pretense of forcing the governor to do his bidding. Many times, those contacts were instigated by Clinton because he knew that Julie or Joan or Betsey or Hillary would find a sympathetic ear. Once these people left public life or left Arkansas, they apparently saw no further need to pursue their "friendships" with Starr, for the contacts ceased with their departure.

In some instances, notably those dealing with character issues, the Clinton White House has had less success than the Clinton statehouse in its attempt to repress or manipulate coverage. Betsey Wright, the former Clinton aide turned lobbyist for the Wexler Group, botched an unnecessary attempt to deflate the "bimbo eruption" known as Troopergate—unnecessary, because polls indicated that the public had long since had its fill of muckrakers unduly fascinated by Bill Clinton's sexual exploits. Had Wright stayed out of it, the public might never have known that the president himself intervened to try and silence the allegations that as governor he had used members of his Arkansas State Police security detail to procure for him the sexual favors of numerous women.

Midway through Clinton's first year as president, both the *American Spectator* and the *Los Angeles Times* launched inquiries into allegations that state troopers assigned to the governor's security force had, in effect, pimped for him and carried him to and from various sexual encounters. Initially, four former members of Clinton's security staff claimed to have firsthand knowledge of these events, but as publication dates neared, two of the troopers, including Danny Ferguson, declined to be identified. Roger Perry and Larry Patterson held firm, and in December the *American Spectator* broke the story. It didn't provide very many names or dates, but its yarns were nonetheless titillating, filled with firsthand accounts of domestic disharmony between Bill and Hillary Clinton and intimate details of Clinton's philandering in the Governor's Mansion, in state police cars, on the grounds of his daughter's school, and in various locales around the state. One of the troopers even claimed that Hillary and her former law partner, Vince Foster, the deputy White House counsel whose July 20, 1992, shooting death was declared a suicide, had been lovers. Hillary and Foster *were* seen together without their spouses at a number of Little Rock social events during her husband's tenure as governor, which may have accounted for the occasional snide remark about their relationship by the Clintons's detractors, but no corroborating evidence of a love affair has surfaced.

Clinton spin doctors made a valiant effort to discredit Perry and Patterson, including releasing details about their alleged complicity in a 1990 automobile accident that occurred after the two men had been drinking. All the troopers were trying to do, White House aides insisted, was sell a book.

Because their chief spokesman and intermediary with the media was Cliff Jackson, who had caused Clinton so much grief during the presidential campaign, the claims of Perry and Patterson might have carried less weight had Wright not volunteered to help and flown from Washington, D.C., to Arkansas to persuade Ferguson to denounce their allegations and to withdraw his claim that Clinton had promised him a cushy federal job if he would kill the Troopergate story. Then it was learned that Clinton had contacted Arkansas troopers in an effort to learn firsthand what was going on. The calls were viewed by many as a blatant attempt at intimidation on Clinton's part, particularly once the media learned that Buddy Young, who as the former chief of governor's security under Clinton had disputed the claims of Perry and Patterson, was ensconced in a $92,000-a-year job with the Federal Emergency Management Agency, compliments of the Clinton White House.

Were the claims by Perry and Patterson true? Members of the Arkansas State Police are divided on that question. "Patterson has never lied to me; Perry has," one trooper will say. "I've never known Perry to lie," another will counter, "but I can't say the same about Patterson." As Troopergate wound down, public opinion surveys indicated that the public remained unimpressed by tales of Clinton's philandering—at least, unimpressed insofar as believing that these stories would affect Clinton's ability or job performance as president.

Whitewatergate was another matter, raising questions in the public's mind that remain unanswered at this writing because the matter was turned over to a special counsel in January 1994 amid growing bipartisan demands in Congress for an independent investigation. Ostensibly, a special counsel was sought to determine whether any money was transferred illegally between Madison Guaranty and Whitewater Development Company and what involvement, if any, the Clintons as investors or Bill Clinton as governor had in these matters. The controversy seemed to be constantly taking new twists.

The Clinton White House and Attorney General Janet Reno steadfastly resisted calls for an independent investigation as long as congressional Republicans were the primary agitators, but they acquiesced after several Senate Democrats joined the chorus.

Special Counsel Robert B. Fiske, Jr., did not come on board in time to prevent the Whitewatergate scandal from taking a bizarre turn: Based on interviews with some of the technicians who were dispatched to the Virginia national park in which Vince Foster's body had been found in July 1993, the *New York Post* fueled speculation in January 1994 that Foster's death had not been a suicide.[4] When emergency medical technicians and U.S. Park Service police arrived, several of them claimed, the antique handgun that apparently had fired the fatal shot into Foster's brain was still clutched in his hand, and his body was stretched out on a slight incline as though he were asleep, two of several elements about the scene that suggested he might have been killed elsewhere. This speculation coupled with the refusal of authorities and Foster's family to disclose the case file, including the autopsy results, rekindled supposition about the true nature of the tragedy.

For months, those who knew Foster or who were touched by his sudden and violent death had been mystified by a note he had left behind at his office. The note, handwritten and torn into twenty-eight pieces, twenty-seven of which reportedly had been recovered from his briefcase, seemed to depict Foster's despair, disillusionment, and bitterness with life in Washington. In the wake of the first *Post* story and the appointment of a special counsel, more revelations were forthcoming. It began to appear that Foster's death was somehow related to Whitewatergate. Some of the papers appropriated from Foster's office and withheld from investigators for many months by White House Chief Counsel Bernard Nussbaum, the longtime friend of Hillary Clinton to whom Foster reported, were identified as Whitewater Development Company documents.

On the heels of these disclosures came word that Jim McDougal's ill-fated financial ventures were not the only ones in which both Foster and Hillary Clinton had been involved. The name of Dan Lasater, the former Little Rock bond daddy who had once given Roger Clinton a job at his Florida horse farm and a $8,000 check with which to pay off a 1984 drug debt, resurfaced.

In February 1994, the acting chairman of the Federal Deposit Insurance Corporation ordered investigators to reopen their inquiry into two cases involving Hillary Clinton and her former law firm to determine whether there had been any conflicts of interest or "other improprieties" in the cases. The initial investigation had indicated that there had been no improprieties, findings that sent up a howl among Republicans on the Senate Banking Committee. They howled even louder a couple of weeks later when it was learned that Deputy Treasury Secretary Robert C. Altman, acting head of the Resolution Trust Corporation, whose own investigation of Madison Guaranty was under way, had briefed Bernard Nussbaum, Deputy Chief of Staff Harold M. Ickes, and Hillary's chief of staff, Margaret A. Williams, on the RTC inquiry.

Acting head of the FDIC, Andrew Hove, Jr., had no choice but to order his investigators to reopen their inquiry into two Arkansas cases.

One case involved Hillary Clinton's representation of Madison Guaranty before state regulators in 1985 and the law firm's subsequent representation of the FDIC in a lawsuit against Madison Guaranty and Frost and Company, the Little Rock accounting firm whose audit had been offered, but never used, to reorganize Madison and keep it solvent. Webb Hubbell, the number three person in the Clinton Justice Department, had been the lead attorney for Rose Law Firm in the case against Madison and Frost.

The other case concerned Lasater, his long-defunct Little Rock investment company, and First American Savings and Loan Association of Oak Brook, Illinois.

Hillary Clinton was among the Rose Law Firm attorneys who had represented First American on behalf of the now-defunct Federal Savings and Loan Insurance Corporation in a 1985 case against Lasater and Company, which had been accused of mishandling money from First American. The lawsuit had sought $3.3 million from Lasater and Company, but Hillary later signed off on an amended complaint that reduced the $3.3 million to $1.3 million. The case was eventually resolved out of court for a mere $200,000, which Lasater paid over to First American in return for dismissal of the lawsuit. According to court records, that incredibly low settlement was negotiated by Hillary Clinton and her best friend and colleague, Vince Foster.

Thus it was that as the Clintons entered the second year of what wags have dubbed their co-presidency, their public images had somehow reversed. Over time, it was her credibility more than his that had been called into question—a sobering turn of events given that throughout most of his career, she had been his greatest asset, his steady hand, the one constant in a roller-coaster ride to the most powerful elective office in the world.

By the end of their first year in the White House, Bill and Hillary Clinton stood at the top of the nation's "most admired" lists, a predictable slot for a new president and his first lady. What will be their standings at the end of their first term is anyone's guess—but the smart money is always on the Clintons.

Appendix I

LETTER FROM BILL CLINTON TO COLONEL HOLMES, DECEMBER 3, 1969

I am sorry to be so long in writing. I know I promised to let you hear from me at least once a month, and from now on you will, but I have had to have some time to think about this first letter. Almost daily since my return to England I have thought about writing, about what I want to and ought to say.

First, I want to thank you, not just for saving me from the draft, but for being so kind and decent to me last summer, when I was as low as I have ever been. One thing which made the bond we struck in good faith somewhat palatable to me was my high regard for you personally. In retrospect, it seems that the admiration might not have been mutual had you known a little more about me, about my political beliefs and activities. At least you might have thought me more fit for the draft than for ROTC.

Let me try to explain. As you know, I worked for two years in a very minor position on the Senate Foreign Relations Committee. I did it for the experience and the salary but also for the opportunity, however small, of working every day against a war I opposed and despised with a depth of feeling I had reserved solely for racism in America before

Vietnam. I did not take the matter lightly but studied it carefully, and there was a time when not many people had more information about Vietnam at hand than I did.

I have written and spoken and marched against the war. One of the national organizers of the Vietnam Moratorium is a close friend of mine. After I left Arkansas last summer, I went to Washington to work in the national headquarters of the Moratorium, then to England to organize the Americans for the demonstrations Oct. 15 and Nov. 16.

Interlocked with the war is the draft issue, which I did not begin to consider separately until early 1968. For a law seminar at Georgetown I wrote a paper on the legal arguments for and against allowing, within the Selective Service System, the classification of selective conscientious objection, for those opposed to participation in a particular war, not simply to "participation in war in any form."

From my work I came to believe that the draft system itself is illegitimate. No government really rooted in limited, parliamentary democracy should have the power to make its citizens fight and kill and die in a war they may oppose, a war which even possibly may be wrong, a war which, in any case, does not involve immediately the peace and freedom of the nation.

The draft was justified in World War II because the life of the people collectively was at stake. Individuals had to fight, if the nation was to survive, for the lives of their countrymen and their way of life. Vietnam is no such case. Nor was Korea an example where, in my opinion, certain military action was justified but the draft was not, for the reasons stated above.

Because of my opposition to the draft and the war, I am in great sympathy with those who are not willing to fight, kill, and maybe die for their country (i.e., the particular policy of a particular government) right or wrong. Two of my friends at Oxford are conscientious objectors. I wrote a letter of recommendation for one of them to his Mississippi draft board, a letter which I am more proud of than anything else I wrote at Oxford last year. One of my roommates is a draft resister who is possibly under indictment and may never be able to go home again. He is one of the bravest, best men I know. That he is considered a criminal is an obscenity.

The decision not to be a resister and the related subsequent decisions were the most difficult of my life. I decided to accept the draft in spite of my beliefs for one reason: to maintain my political viability within the system. For years I have worked to prepare myself for a political life characterized by both practical and political ability and concern for rapid social progress. It is a life I still feel compelled to try to lead. I do not think our system of government is by definition corrupt, however dangerous and inadequate it has been in recent years. (The society may be corrupt, but that is not the same thing, and if that is true we are all finished anyway.)

When the draft came, despite political convictions, I was having a hard time facing the prospect of fighting a war I had been fighting against, and that is why I contacted you. ROTC was the one way left in which I could possibly, but not positively, avoid both Vietnam and resistance. Going on with my education, even coming back to England, played no part in my decision to join ROTC. I am back here, and would have been at Arkansas Law School because there is nothing else I can do. In fact, I would like to have been able to take a year out perhaps to teach at a small college or work in some community action project and in the process to decide whether to attend law school or graduate school and how to begin putting what I have learned to use.

But the particulars of my personal life are not nearly as important to me as the principles involved. After I signed the ROTC letter of intent I began to wonder whether the compromise I had made with myself was not more objectionable than the draft would have been, because I had no interest in the ROTC program in itself and all I seemed to have done was to protect myself from physical harm. Also, I began to think I had deceived you, not by lies because there were none, but by failing to tell you all the things I'm writing now. I doubt that I had the mental coherence to articulate them then.

At that time, after we had made our agreement and you had sent my I-D deferment to my draft board, the anguish and loss of my self-regard and self-confidence really set in. I hardly slept for weeks and kept going by eating compulsively and reading until exhaustion brought sleep. Finally, on Sept. 12, I stayed up all night writing a letter to the chairman of my draft board, saying basically what is in the preceding paragraph, thanking him for trying to help in a case where he really couldn't, and stating that I couldn't do the ROTC after all and would he please draft me as soon as possible.

I never mailed the letter, but I did carry it on me every day until I got on the plane to return to England. I didn't mail the letter because I didn't see, in the end, how my going in the army and maybe going to Vietnam would achieve anything except a feeling that I had punished myself and gotten what I deserved. So I came back to England to try to make something of this second year of my Rhodes scholarship.

And that is where I am now, writing to you because you have been good to me and have a right to know what I think and feel. I am writing too in the hope that my telling this one story will help you to understand more clearly how so many fine people have come to find themselves still loving their country but loathing the military, to which you and other good men have devoted years, lifetimes, of the best service you could give. To many of us, it is no longer clear what is service and what is disservice, or if it is clear, the conclusion is likely to be illegal.

Forgive the length of this letter. There was much to say. There is still a lot to be said, but it can wait. Please say hello to Col. Jones for me.

Merry Christmas.

Appendix II

MOCK RESOLUTION, ARKANSAS GENERAL ASSEMBLY, JANUARY 1980

"WHEREAS, a special memorandum has been drafted and distributed to the Governor's elite guard outlining 'a Proposed Public Information Strategy' for the Chief Executive's Office; and

"WHEREAS, such memorandum, exposed by Arkansas's largest newspaper, outlines specific strategy which the Governor and his staff should employ in further strengthening the Governor's power, including how legislators should be treated; and

"WHEREAS, such memo insults the intelligence of most legislators, public officials, and the entire citizenry; and

"WHEREAS, such memo clearly threatens the delicate balance of powers by plotting a dangerous usurpation of power for the Executive Branch of State Government; and

"WHEREAS, it is now apparent that the Governor pushed through the 1979 Regular Session of the General Assembly legislation increasing the license fees for motor vehicles in order to free up other revenues to help offset the expense involved in paying the salaries of the 'Think Tank' which prepared the Governor's Public Information Strategy Schedule; and

"WHEREAS, the Think Tank Plan seeks to 'control the Governor's destiny' by increasing 'contacts and coverage'; and

"WHEREAS, the Think Tank's plan for the Governor includes 'well rehearsed presentations' to 'hand selected audiences' at 'elegant' dinner parties at the [Governor's] Mansion where 'carefully selected private citizens and APPROPRIATE [note: the capitalized letters were underscored twice] legislators apparently will be wined and dined at taxpayers's expense; and

"WHEREAS, the plan proposes a 'Governor's Booth at county and state fairs' and suggests questions which staff members should ask when phoning local government leaders on WATS line calls from the Governor's office, such as 'Hi [blank], what's on your mind? Any suggestions on how we can deal with [blank]?'; and

"WHEREAS, the Legislature must remain ever vigilant to prevent the constant attempts to broaden the powers of the Executive Branch, especially in light of the young Governor's attempts to manipulate the news media, his own lower echelon staff public officials, private individuals, an APPROPRIATE [note: no underscoring] legislators,

"NOW, THEREFORE BE IT RESOLVED BY THE HOUSE OF REPRESENTATIVES OF THE FIRST EXTRAORDINARY SESSION OF THE SEVENTY-SECOND GENERAL ASSEMBLY OF THE STATE OF ARKANSAS (provided the Supreme Court rules this a legal resolution)

"That the following Public Image Strategy Schedule be adopted for members of the Arkansas House of Representatives to counter the Governor's elaborate plan in order that the proper balance of power contained in the precious separation of powers of our State Constitution be preserved and the rights of our citizens maintained as well:

"(1) That the House Information Office use only photos of our most handsome members in ALL press releases regardless of news content. The intent is to create the public illusion that House members are every bit as young and cute as the Governor.

"(2) That the House leadership counter the Governor's attempt to sway influential businessmen and APPROPRIATE legislators by hosting dinner parties of their own, perhaps at Representative Bill Thompson's apartment with the most influential guest being served dinner in Mr. Thompson's recliner.

"(3) That dinner party guests be given autographed pictures of Representative Bill Stancil and other influential House leaders to counter the Governor's plan to dole out autographed photos of himself.

"(4) That House members read from a standard form in making calls to the Governor's office. This would assure uniformity and enhance our chances that all 100 House members might someday become APPROPRIATE in the eyes of the Governor, and be invited to dinner at the Mansion. The standard form to read from in making calls should include the following: 'Hi. This is Representative [blank] calling from my home in [blank] and ask if you have [blank] more racing passes to send to my cousin, who is a big ERA supporter down in [blank] County.'

"(5) That each House member be required to set up his or her own booth at the local county fair, perhaps even volunteering for the water dunk in order to divert attention from the Governor's booth and the fancy machine that autographs his black-and-white photos.

"(6) That the Speaker of the House judge all booths and the top three finalists receive invitations to appear at the State Fair in Little Rock in October. In case a finalist is unable to attend, an alternate shall be appointed by the Speaker with the concurrence of two-thirds of a quorum meeting in a Special Session to be called by the Supreme Court.

"(7) That the House speaker schedule at least one toga party per quarter for the House of Representatives, an their 'hand-selected' guests.

"(8) That the collected speeches of Representatives Nap Murphy and Buddy Turner be published by the House Management Committee as a form book for use by other House members.

"(9) That [one-time political boss and former Conway County sheriff] Marlin Hawkins be retained by the House to act as the House Liaison Officer on Aging to the Governor.

"(10) That in response to the Governor's voluntary payment of an amount of money equal to the fine he should have received for speeding last fall, each member of the House contribute to the State Police Retirement Fund an amount of money equal to the fine that member should have paid were it not for legislative immunity."

Appendix III

COLONEL HOLMES'S AFFIDAVIT, SEPTEMBER 7, 1992

There have been many unanswered questions as to the circumstances surrounding Bill Clinton's involvement with the ROTC department at the University of Arkansas. Prior to this time I have not felt the necessity for discussing the details. The reason I have not done so before is that my poor physical health (a consequence of participation in the Bataan Death March and the subsequent 3½ years internment in Japanese POW camps) has precluded me from getting into what I felt was unnecessary involvement. However, present polls show that there is the imminent danger to our country of a draft dodger becoming commander-in-chief of the armed forces of the United States. While it is true, as Mr. Clinton has stated, that there were many others who avoided serving their country in the Vietnam war, they are not aspiring to be president of the United States.

The tremendous implications of the possibility of his becoming commander-in-chief of the United States Armed Forces compels me now to comment on the facts concerning Mr. Clinton's evasion of the draft.

This account would not have been imperative had Bill Clinton been completely honest with the American public concerning this matter.

But as Mr. Clinton replied on a news conference this evening (Sept. 5) after being asked another particular about his dodging the draft, "Almost everyone concerned with these incidents are dead. I have no more comments to make," since I may be the only person living who can give a firsthand account of what actually transpired, I am obligated by my love for my country and my sense of duty to divulge what actually happened and make it a matter of record.

Bill Clinton came to see me at my home in 1969 to discuss his desire to enroll in the ROTC program at the University of Arkansas. We engaged in an extensive, approximately two (2) hour interview. At no time during this long conversation about his desire to join the program did he inform me of his involvement, participation and actually organizing protests against the United States involvement in South East Asia. He was shrewed [sic] enough to realize that had I been aware of his activities, he would not have been accepted into the ROTC program as a potential officer in the United States Army.

The next day I began to receive telephone calls regarding Bill Clinton's draft status. I was informed by the draft board that it was of interest to Senator Fullbright's [sic] office that Bill Clinton, a Rhodes Scholar, should be admitted to the ROTC program. I received several such calls. The general message conveyed by the draft board to me was that Senator Fullbright's [sic] office was putting pressure on them and that they needed my help. I then made the necessary arrangements to enroll Mr. Clinton into the ROTC program at the University of Arkansas.

I was not "saving" him from serving his country, as he erroneously thanked me for in his letter from England (dated Dec. 3, 1969). I was making it possible for a Rhodes Scholar to serve in the military as an officer.

In retrospect I see that Mr. Clinton had no intention of following through with his agreement to join the Army ROTC program at the University of Arkansas or to attend the University of Arkansas Law School. I had explained to him the necessity of enrolling at the University of Arkansas as a student in order to be eligible to take the ROTC program as the University. He never enrolled at the University of Arkansas, but instead enrolled at Yale after attending Oxford. I believe that he purposely deceived me, using the possibility of joining the ROTC as a ploy to work with the draft board to delay his induction and get a new draft classification.

The Dec. 3 letter written to me by Mr. Clinton, and subsequently taken from the files by Lt. Col. Clint Jones, my executive officer, was placed into the ROTC files so that a record would be available in case the applicant should again petition to enter the ROTC program. The information in that letter alone would have restricted Bill Clinton from ever qualifying to be an officer in the United States Military. Even more significant was his lack of veracity in purposefully defrauding the military by deceiving me, both in concealing his anti-military activities overseas and his counterfeit intentions for later military service. These actions cause me to question both his patriotism and his integrity.

When I consider the calibre, the bravery, and the patriotism of the fine young soldiers whose deaths I have witnessed, and others whose funerals I have attended . . . When I reflect on not only the willingness but eagerness that so many of them displayed in their earnest desire to defend and serve their country, it is untenable and incomprehensible to me that a man who was not merely unwilling to serve his country, but actually protested against its military, should ever be in the position of commander-in-chief of our armed forces.

I write this declaration not only for the living and future generations, but for those who fought and died for our country. If space and time permitted I would include the names of the ones I knew and fought with, and along with them I would mention my brother Bob, who was killed during World War II and is buried in Cambridge, England (at the age of 23, about the age Bill Clinton was when he was over in England protesting the war).

I have agonized over whether or not to submit this statement to the American people. But, I realize that even though I served my country by being in the military over 32 years, and having gone through the ordeal of months of combat under the worst of conditions followed by years of imprisonment by the Japanese, it is not enough. I'm writing these comments to let everyone know that I love my country more than I do my own personal security and well-being. I will go to my grave loving these United States of America and the liberty for which so many men have fought and died.

Because of my poor physical condition this will be my final statement. I will make no further comments to any of the media regarding this issue.

Endnotes

Chapter 1

1. Bill Clinton, *Arkansas Democrat-Gazette*, November 5, 1992.
2. Virginia Kelley, interview with John Wallworth, *Hot Springs Sentinel Record*, March 16, 1974.
3. Bill Clinton, column by Bob Lancaster, *Arkansas Democrat*, August 25, 1977.
4. Cliff Jackson, interview with author, July 12, 1993.
5. Clinton's enthusiasm for election demographics is not confined to his own campaigns. A keen student of politics, he is almost as comfortable discussing other campaigns—for instance, the Kennedy-Nixon race—as he is discussing his own.
6. Carolyn Staley, *Arkansas Gazette*, October 3, 1991.
7. Robert E. Levin, *Bill Clinton: The Inside Story* (New York, N.Y., 1992), 50–51.
8. Jim Johnson, interview with author, April 25, 1993.
9. Orval E. Faubus, interview with author, April 24, 1993.
10. Patrick Flanagin, interview with author, August 17, 1993.
11. Ibid.
12. Arkansas legislator, interview with author on condition of anonymity.
13. Faubus, interview with author.
14. John R. Starr, *Yellow Dogs and Dark Horses* (Little Rock, 1987), 171.

Chapter 2

1. Virginia Kelley, interview with Pam Strickland, *Arkansas Democrat*, June 28, 1987.
2. Compilation assisted by conventional reference material, notable among them the 1946–55 editions of the *Arkansas Almanac* (Little Rock).
3. Kelley, interview with John Wallworth, *Hot Springs Sentinel Record*, March 16, 1974.
4. Reconstruction of W.J. Blythe's accident relied on various newspaper interviews with Virginia Kelley and newspaper accounts, notable among them the *Washington Post* account of June 20, 1993.
5. Kelley, interview with Todd S. Purdom, *New York Times*, August 1992.
6. Reconstruction of W.J. Blythe's background relied upon public documents obtained from government agencies in Arkansas, Oklahoma, Missouri, and Texas; statements by his widow, Virginia, and his son, Bill, in numerous interviews; and various newspaper and magazine accounts, notable among them the *Washington Post* account of June 20, 1993.
7. Kelley, *Lear's*, September 1992.
8. Kelley, *Arkansas Democrat*, June 28, 1987.
9. Bill Clinton, *Texarkana Gazette*, June 6, 1988.
10. Clinton, *Arkansas Democrat*, August 25, 1977.
11. Kelley, interview with Phyllis D. Brandon, *Arkansas Democrat-Gazette*, October 3, 1993.
12. Kelley, interview with author, July 20, 1988.
13. Dr. Jim McKenzie, interview with *Arkansas Democrat-Gazette*, July 17, 1992.
14. Joe Purvis, *The Clintons of Arkansas*, ed. Ernest Dumas (Little Rock, 1993), 32.
15. Pod Rogers, interview with author, March 31, 1993.
16. Ibid.
17. Deposition by Virginia C. Clinton, *Virginia C. Clinton v. Roger M. Clinton*, May 15, 1962.
18. "When Owney Madden got off that train [from New York in 1935], he became a different man and a real citizen, a first-class citizen," said Arkansas State Senator Q. Byrum Hurst of Hot Springs in the eulogy he presented before about two hundred friends and admirers who attended Madden's funeral. (*Arkansas Gazette*, April 28, 1965). Hurst went on to cite Madden's numerous charitable works on behalf of organizations in his adopted hometown, among them the Boys Club, the Chamber of Commerce, the Navy League, local schools and churches, and the Civil Air Patrol.

19. Biographical sketch, The Associated Press, April 14, 1952, updated April 24, 1965.
20. Charles Samuels, "Owney Madden: Only Gangster Exiled in America," *Cavalier*, November 1961.
21. Robert E. Levin, *Bill Clinton: The Inside Story* (New York, N.Y., 1992), 11; Charles F. Allen and Jonathan Portis, *Bill Clinton: Comeback Kid* (New York, N.Y., 1992), 6.
22. Allen and Portis, *Bill Clinton: Comeback Kid*, and various newspaper and magazine accounts.
23. Deposition, *Clinton v. Clinton*, May 15, 1962.
24. Kelley, *Hot Springs Sentinel Record*, March 16, 1974.
25. Deposition, *Clinton v. Clinton*, May 15, 1962.
26. Carolyn Staley, interview with Noel Oman, *Arkansas Democrat*, October 4, 1991.
27. David Leopoulos, quoted by Robert E. Levin, *Bill Clinton: The Inside Story* (New York, N.Y., 1992), 12.
28. Deposition, *Clinton v. Clinton*, May 15, 1962.
29. Complaint in Equity, *Clinton v. Clinton*, April 14, 1962.
30. Deposition, *Clinton v. Clinton*, May 15, 1962.
31. Ibid.
32. Ibid.
33. Clinton, interview with Joe Klein, *New York*, January 20, 1992.
34. Deposition by William J. Clinton, *Clinton v. Clinton*, May 15, 1962.
35. Petition, Garland County Chancery Court, June 12, 1962.
36. Kelley, *Hot Springs Sentinel Record*, March 16, 1974.
37. Kelley, quoted by Katharine Seelye, Knight-Ridder, July 26, 1993.
38. Jim Moore with Rick Ihde, *Clinton: Young Man in a Hurry* (Fort Worth, Texas, 1992), 29.
39. Jerry Dean, *Arkansas Democrat-Gazette*, September 6, 1992.
40. *Arkansas Democrat*, October 4, 1991.
41. Clinton, interview with Bill Simmons of The Associated Press, *Arkansas Democrat*, November 8, 1978.
42. Clinton, interview with Bob Lancaster, *Arkansas Democrat*, August 25, 1977.
43. Randy Goodrum, quoted by Robert E. Levin, *Bill Clinton: The Inside Story* (New York, N.Y., 1992), 28.
44. Allen and Portis, *Bill Clinton: Comeback Kid* (New York, N.Y., 1992), 14.
45. Edith Irons, quoted by Robert E. Levin, *Bill Clinton: The Inside Story* (New York, N.Y., 1992), 36.
46. Paul Root, *The Clintons of Arkansas*, ed. Ernest Dumas (Little Rock, 1993), 114.

47. Thomas F. "Mack" McLarty III, interview with author, October 16, 1993.
48. Levin, *Bill Clinton: The Inside Story* (New York, N.Y., 1992), 34.
49. Kelley, *Arkansas Democrat*, June 28, 1987.
50. Kelley, *Hot Springs Sentinel Record*, March 16, 1974.

Chapter 3

1. Bill Clinton, interview with Bob Lancaster, *Arkansas Democrat*, August 25, 1977.
2. Virgil Spurlin, quoted by Charles F. Allen and Jonathan Portis, *Bill Clinton: Comeback Kid* (New York, N.Y., 1992), 15.
3. Clinton, *Arkansas Democrat*, August 25, 1977.
4. Tom Campbell, *The Clintons of Arkansas*, ed. Ernest Dumas (Little Rock, 1993) 50.
5. Clinton, Allen and Portis, *Bill Clinton: Comeback Kid* (New York, N.Y., 1992), 21.
6. Campbell, *The Clintons of Arkansas*, ed. Ernest Dumas (Little Rock, 1993), 51.
7. Dru Bachman Francis, Robert E. Levin, *Bill Clinton: The Inside Story* (New York, N.Y., 1992), 50.
8. Tom Caplan, Jim Moore with Rick Ihde, *Clinton: Young Man in a Hurry* (Fort Worth, Texas, 1992), 28.
9. Campbell, *The Clintons of Arkansas*, ed. Ernest Dumas (Little Rock, 1993), 42.
10. Christopher Ashby, quoted by Levin, *Bill Clinton: The Inside Story* (New York, N.Y., 1992), 40.
11. J. Bill Becker, interview with author, September 8, 1993.
12. Patrick Flanagin, interview with author, August 17, 1993.
13. Thomas F. "Mack" McLarty III, interview with author, October 16, 1993.
14. Helen Henry, *Bill Clinton: The Inside Story* (New York, N.Y., 1992), 42.
15. Ibid.
16. Campbell, *The Clintons of Arkansas*, ed. Ernest Dumas (Little Rock, 1993), 43.
17. Stephanie Weldon, *Bill Clinton: The Inside Story* (New York, N.Y., 1992), 41.
18. *Bill Clinton: The Inside Story* (New York, N.Y., 1992), 42–43.
19. Clinton, *Bill Clinton: The Inside Story* (New York, N.Y., 1992), 48.
20. Campbell, *The Clintons of Arkansas*, ed. Ernest Dumas (Little Rock, 1993), 44.

21. Campbell, *The Clintons of Arkansas*, ed. Ernest Dumas (Little Rock, 1993), 45.
22. William T. Coleman III, *The Clintons of Arkansas*, ed. Ernest Dumas (Little Rock, 1993), 57.
23. Campbell, *The Clintons of Arkansas*, ed. Ernest Dumas (Little Rock, 1993), 44.
24. Campbell, *The Clintons of Arkansas*, ed. Ernest Dumas (Little Rock, 1993), 45.
25. Ibid.
26. Ashby, *Bill Clinton: The Inside Story* (New York, N.Y., 1992), 43.
27. Clinton, *Bill Clinton: The Inside Story* (New York, N.Y., 1992), 43.
28. Ibid.
29. Ashby, *Bill Clinton: The Inside Story* (New York, N.Y., 1992), 44.
30. Ibid.
31. Ibid.
32. Clinton, *Clinton: Young Man in a Hurry* (Fort Worth, Texas, 1992), 30.
33. Ibid.
34. Allen and Portis, *Bill Clinton: Comeback Kid* (New York, N.Y., 1992), 24.
35. Ibid.
36. *Arkansas Democrat*, September 28, 1960.
37. Clinton, letter to Colonel Eugene J. Holmes, December 3, 1969.
38. Ashby, quoted by Levin, *Bill Clinton: The Inside Story* (New York, N.Y., 1992), 51.
39. Clinton, quoted by Lancaster, *Arkansas Democrat*, August 25, 1977.
40. Campbell, *The Clintons of Arkansas*, ed. Ernest Dumas (Little Rock, 1993), 48.
41. Ibid.
42. Clinton, letter to Holmes, December 3, 1969.
43. Campbell, *The Clintons of Arkansas*, ed. Ernest Dumas (Little Rock, 1993), 48.
44. Edith Irons, quoted by Levin, *Bill Clinton: The Inside Story* (New York, N.Y., 1992), 39.

Chapter 4

1. Bill Clinton, interview with Maurice Moore, *Arkansas Democrat*, April 24, 1968.
2. This anecdote has been retold by Carolyn Yeldell Staley to numerous reporters, including those for the *Arkansas Democrat* and the *Arkansas Gazette*, and was reproduced in *Bill Clinton: The Inside Story* and *Bill Clinton: Comeback Kid*.
3. Ibid.

4. Ibid.
5. Tom Campbell, *The Clintons of Arkansas*, ed. Ernest Dumas (Little Rock, 1993), 50.
6. Clinton, interview with Maurice Moore, *Arkansas Democrat*, April 24, 1968.
7. Ibid.
8. Campbell, *The Clintons of Arkansas*, ed. Ernest Dumas (Little Rock, 1993), 49.
9. Campbell, *The Clintons of Arkansas*, ed. Ernest Dumas (Little Rock, 1993), 51.
10. Tom Williamson, *The Sunday Times*, October 25, 1992.
11. Cliff Jackson, interview with author, July 12, 1993.
12. Stephen Oxman, quoted by Robert E. Levin, *Bill Clinton: The Inside Story* (New York, N.Y., 1992), 64.
13. James Crawford, *The Sunday Times*, October 25, 1992.
14. Robert B. Reich, quoted by Jim Moore with Rick Ihde, *Clinton: Young Man in a Hurry* (Fort Worth, Texas, 1992), 33.
15. Darryl Gless, *The Sunday Times*, October 25, 1992.
16. Clinton, *The Sunday Times*, October 25, 1992.
17. David Millward, *The Daily Telegraph*, January 27, 1992.
18. Ibid.
19. *The Sunday Times*, October 25, 1992.
20. Alan Bersin, *The Sunday Times*, October 25, 1992.
21. Wilf Stevenson, *The Sunday Times*, October 25, 1992.
22. Zbigniew Pelczynski, *The Sunday Times*, October 25, 1992.
23. These titles are a sampling of books "drawn" by "W.J. Clinton" from the University College Library.
24. *The Times* of London, October 24, 1992.
25. Sir Edgar Williams, *The Sunday Telegraph*, October 11, 1992.
26. Christopher Laidlaw, *The Sunday Times*, October 25, 1992.
27. Philip Hodson, *The Sunday Times*, October 25, 1992.
28. Mandy Merck, *The Independent on Sunday*, October 11, 1992.
29. Michael Shea, *The Sunday Times*, October 25, 1992.
30. Sara Maitland, *Evening Standard*, June 18, 1993.
31. Ibid.
32. Thomas F. "Mack" McLarty III, interview with author, October 16, 1993.
33. Ibid.
34. Ibid.
35. Cliff Jackson, interview with author, July 12, 1993.
36. Chris McCooey, *Daily Mail*, January 22, 1993.
37. Jackson, interview with author, July 12, 1993.

38. Ibid.
39. Ibid.
40. Williams, *The Times* of London, January 27, 1992.
41. *The Sunday Times*, October 25, 1992.
42. Jackson, interview with author, July 12, 1993.
43. Tamara Eccles-Williams, *Today*, October 29, 1992.
44. Katherine Gieve, *The Sunday Times*, October 25, 1992.
45. Jackson, interview with author, July 12, 1993.
46. David Singer, *The Sunday Times*, October 25, 1992.
47. Jackson, interview with author, July 12, 1993.
48. Ibid.
49. Clinton, letter to Cliff Jackson dated November 17, 1970, from Jackson files.
50. Jackson, interview with author, July 12, 1993.
51. Eccles-Williams, *Today*, October 29, 1992.
52. Sharon Evans, *The Sunday Times*, October 25, 1992.
53. Jackson, interview with author, July 12, 1993.
54. Ibid.
55. Ibid.
56. Ibid.

Chapter 5

1. *Arkansas Gazette*, October 28, 1978.
2. David Mixner, quoted by Robert E. Levin, *Bill Clinton: The Inside Story* (New York, N.Y., 1992), 77.
3. Francine Du Plessix Gray, "A Reporter at Large: The Moratorium and the New Mobe," *The New Yorker*, January 3, 1970.
4. Mixner, Mixner, quoted by Robert E. Levin, *Bill Clinton: The Inside Story* (New York, N.Y., 1992), 77.
5. Gray, "A Reporter at Large: The Moratorium and the New Mobe," *The New Yorker*, January 3, 1970.
6. Ibid.
7. Ibid.
8. John Bainbridge, "Our Far-Flung Correspondents: The Demo," *The New Yorker*, November 30, 1968.
9. *The Sunday Times*, October 25, 1992.
10. Cliff Jackson, interview with author, July 12, 1993.
11. Ibid.
12. Jackson, letter to friend dated November 17, 1970, from Jackson files.
13. Jackson, interview with author, July 12, 1993.

14. Eugene J. Holmes, affidavit, September 7, 1992.
15. *The Sunday Times*, October 25, 1992.
16. *The Wall Street Journal*, May 14, 1969.
17. Ibid.
18. Ibid., June 9, 1969.
19. Ibid., June 20, 1969.
20. Ibid., July 11, 1969.
21. Ibid., September 18, 1969.
22. Strobe Talbott, quoted by Levin, *Bill Clinton: The Inside Story* (New York, N.Y., 1992), 79.
23. *The Sunday Times*, October 25, 1992.
24. Ibid.
25. *Oxford Mail*, October 13, 1992.
26. Alan Bersin, *The Sunday Times*, October 25, 1992.
27. Bill Clinton, letter to Colonel Eugene J. Holmes, December 3, 1969.
28. Tom Williamson, *The Sunday Times*, October 25, 1992.
29. Richard McSorley, S.J., *Peace Eyes*, "Peace Eyes (Washington, D.C. 1978).
30. Ibid.
31. Holmes, affidavit, September 7, 1992.
32. Ibid.
33. Ibid.
34. Jim Johnson, interview with author, April 25, 1993.
35. McSorley, *Peace Eyes*, "Peace Eyes (Washington, D.C. 1978).
36. Ibid.
37. *The Sunday Times*, October 25, 1992.
38. Richard Shullau, *The Sunday Times*, October 25, 1992.
39. Charlie Daniels, *The Sunday Times*, October 25, 1992.
40. *The Sunday Times*, October 25, 1992.
41. Sarah Maitland, *Evening Standard*, June 18, 1993.
42. Wayland Dennis, *Oxford Mail*, October 13, 1992.
43. Maitland, *Evening Standard*, June 18, 1993.
44. Mixner, quoted by Levin, *Bill Clinton: The Inside Story* (New York, N.Y., 1992), 77.
45. *The Scotsman*, October 9, 1992.
46. *The Guardian*, November 5, 1992.
47. Ibid.
48. Ibid.

Chapter 6

1. Hillary Rodham Clinton, *Vanity Fair*, May 1992.
2. Bill Clinton, *Vanity Fair*, May 1992.
3. Rodham Clinton, *Family Circle*, May 18, 1993.
4. *The Washington Post*, April 2, 1993.
5. Ibid.
6. Dorothy Rodham, *Vanity Fair*, May 1992.
7. Ibid.
8. Tony Rodham, *People*, January 25, 1993.
9. *Arkansas Democrat-Gazette*, April 10, 1993.
10. Hugh Rodham, Jr., *The Washington Post*, April 2, 1993.
11. Sherry Heiden, quoted by Judith Warner, *Hillary Clinton: The Inside Story* (New York, N.Y., 1993), 18.
12. Don Jones, quoted by Warner, *Hillary Clinton: The Inside Story* (New York, N.Y., 1993), 19.
13. Jones, *People*, January 25, 1993.
14. Jones, quoted by Warner, *Hillary Clinton: The Inside Story* (New York, N.Y., 1993), 19.
15. Dorothy Rodham, *Family Circle*, May 18, 1993.
16. Warner, *Hillary Clinton: The Inside Story* (New York, N.Y., 1993), 23.
17. Dorothy Rodham, *Vanity Fair*, May 1992.
18. Kenneth Reece, quoted by Warner, *Hillary Clinton: The Inside Story* (New York, N.Y., 1993), 25.
19. Rodham Clinton, *Glamour*, August 1992.
20. Rodham Clinton, *Vanity Fair*, May 1992.
21. Warner, *Hillary Clinton: The Inside Story* (New York, N.Y., 1993), 28.
22. Jeff Shields, quoted by Warner, *Hillary Clinton: The Inside Story* (New York, N.Y., 1993), 29.
23. Alan Schechter, *People*, January 25, 1993.
24. Rodham Clinton, *Vanity Fair*, May 1992.
25. Rodham Clinton, *Vanity Fair*, May 1992.
26. Harlon Dalton, *Chicago Tribune*, May 14, 1993.
27. William T. Coleman III, *The Clintons of Arkansas*, ed. Ernest Dumas (Little Rock, 1993), 54.
28. Ibid.
29. Penn Rhodeen, *Chicago Tribune*, May 14, 1993.
30. Rodham Clinton, *Glamour*, August 1992.
31. Coleman, *The Clintons of Arkansas*, ed. Ernest Dumas (Little Rock, 1993) 50.

Chapter 7

1. Jim Johnson, interview with author, April 25, 1993.
2. Bill Clinton, quoted by David S. Broder, *Changing of the Guard* (New York, N.Y., 1980), 381.
3. Gil Troy, *See How They Ran* (New York, N.Y., 1991), 230.
4. Johnson, interview with author, April 25, 1993.
5. Troy, *See How They Ran* (New York, N.Y., 1991), 229–30.
6. Johnson, interview with author, April 25, 1993.
7. Mark Johnson, interview with author, April 22, 1993.
8. Clinton, *Arkansas Gazette*, June 11, 1972.
9. Ibid.
10. Ibid.
11. Clinton, *Arkansas Democrat*, June 27, 1972.
12. Betsey Wright, quoted by Broder, *Changing of the Guard* (New York, N.Y., 1980), 259.
13. Wright, *Arkansas Gazette*, September 15, 1985.
14. Ibid.
15. Wright, interview with Billy Burton of The Associated Press, *Arkansas Democrat*, September 22, 1985.
16. Wright, *Arkansas Gazette*, September 15, 1985.
17. Hillary Rodham Clinton, quoted by Charles F. Allen and Jonathan Portis, *Bill Clinton: Comeback Kid* (New York, N.Y., 1992) 211.
18. Virginia Kelley, quoted by Allen and Portis, *Bill Clinton: Comeback Kid* (New York, N.Y., 1992), 67.
19. Diane Blair, *The Clintons of Arkansas*, ed. Ernest Dumas (Little Rock, 1993), 63.
20. Kelley, quoted by Allen and Portis, *Bill Clinton: Comeback Kid* (New York, N.Y., 1992), 67.
21. James. L. "Skip" Rutherford, interview with author, September 15, 1993.
22. William T. Coleman III, *The Clintons of Arkansas*, ed. Ernest Dumas (Little Rock, 1993), 57.
23. Clinton, quoted by Allen and Portis, *Bill Clinton: Comeback Kid* (New York, N.Y., 1992), 38.
24. Rodham Clinton, *Arkansas Democrat*, February 11, 1979.
25. Rodham Clinton, quoted by Judith Warner, *Hillary Clinton: The Inside Story* (New York, N.Y., 1993), 71.
26. John R. Starr, interview with author, November 12, 1993.
27. Carl Whillock, *The Clintons of Arkansas*, ed. Ernest Dumas (Little Rock, 1993), 79.

Chapter 8

1. Rudy Moore, Jr., *The Clintons of Arkansas*, ed. Ernest Dumas (Little Rock, 1993), 86.
2. Lu Hardin, interview with author, September 28, 1993.
3. *The Grapevine*, September 1974.
4. Ibid.
5. Julia Hughes Jones, interview with author, September 8, 1993.
6. Bill Clinton, quoted by Charles F. Allen and Jonathan Portis, *Bill Clinton: Comeback Kid* (New York, N.Y., 1992), 41.
7. J. Bill Becker, interview with author, September 8, 1993.
8. Jim Clark, interview with author, March 31, 1993.
9. Clinton, *Arkansas Democrat*, July 24, 1974.
10. *Arkansas Democrat*, September 20, 1974.
11. News release, Arkansas Education Association, May 23, 1974.
12. *Arkansas Gazette*, June 4, 1974.
13. *Arkansas Gazette*, July 7, 1974.
14. Robert Fisher, *Arkansas Democrat*, January 13, 1974.
15. Clinton, *Arkansas Gazette*, July 25, 1974.
16. Ibid.
17. John Paul Hammerschmidt, *Arkansas Gazette*, August 6, 1974.
18. Ibid.
19. Clinton, *Arkansas Gazette*, August 8, 1974.
20. John Paul Hammerschmidt, *Arkansas Gazette*, September 8, 1974.
21. Diane Blair, *The Clintons of Arkansas*, ed. Ernest Dumas (Little Rock, 1993), 63.
22. Clinton, *Arkansas Democrat*, September 14, 1974.
23. Ibid., September 8, 1974.
24. Hammerschmidt, quoted by The Associated Press, *Arkansas Democrat*, July 17, 1974.
25. Clinton, quoted by The Associated Press, *Arkansas Democrat*, September 8, 1974.
26. Clinton, *Arkansas Gazette*, October 6, 1974.
27. David Terrell, *Arkansas Democrat*, November 3, 1974.
28. John Paul Hammerschmidt, *Arkansas Gazette*, September 8, 1974.
29. Ibid.
30. *Arkansas Gazette*, April 19, 1969.
31. Becker, interview with author, September 8, 1993.

Chapter 9

1. Woody Bassett, quoted by Judith Warner, *Hillary Clinton: The Inside Story* (New York, N.Y., 1993), 85–86.
2. Diane Blair, *The Clintons of Arkansas*, ed. Ernest Dumas (Little Rock, 1993), 63.
3. John R. Starr, interview with author, November 15, 1993.
4. Ibid.
5. Stephen A. Smith, *The Clintons of Arkansas*, ed. Ernest Dumas (Little Rock, 1993), 9.
6. Bill Clinton, text of announcement, April 17, 1976, *Arkansas Democrat-Gazette* archives.
7. J. Bill Becker, interview with author, September 8, 1993.
8. *Arkansas Gazette*, March 19, 1976.
9. Ibid.
10. Becker, interview with author, September 8, 1993.
11. Clinton, United Press International, *Arkansas Gazette*, March 23, 1976.
12. Becker, interview with author, September 8, 1993.
13. *Arkansas Gazette*, May 2, 1976.
14. *Arkansas Democrat*, May 9, 1976.
15. *Arkansas Gazette*, April 2, 1976.
16. Smith, *The Clintons of Arkansas*, ed. Ernest Dumas (Little Rock, 1993), 8.
17. Starr, interview with author, April 23, 1993.
18. Ibid.
19. *Arkansas Democrat*, May 26, 1976.
20. Thomas F. "Mack" McLarty, III, interview with author, October 16, 1993.
21. Ibid.
22. *Arkansas Gazette*, April 6, 1977.
23. *Arkansas Democrat*, April 14, 1977.
24. *Arkansas Gazette*, Clinton, March 26, 1977.
25. Joe Purvis, *The Clintons of Arkansas*, ed. Ernest Dumas (Little Rock, 1993), 33.
26. *Arkansas Gazette*, August 19, 1977.

Chapter 10

1. Bob Lancaster, *Arkansas Democrat*, July 17, 1977.
2. Bill Clinton, *Arkansas Gazette*, November 22, 1977.
3. A.L. May, *Arkansas Democrat*, January 8, 1978.
4. Ibid.
5. Ibid.

6. *Arkansas Gazette*, January 2, 1978.
7. Ibid., January 28, 1978.
8. *Arkansas Democrat*, March 5, 1978.
9. Ibid.
10. *Arkansas Democrat*, March 6, 1978.
11. Ibid.
12. Frank Lady, quoted by The Associated Press, *Arkansas Democrat*, April 30, 1978.
13. *Arkansas Gazette*, May 19, 1978; *Arkansas Gazette*, May 21, 1978; Joe Woodward also made this charge late in the primary campaign, notably on May 26, 1978, when he accused Clinton of being "an opportunist" who was running for governor only so he could use the office as a stepping stone to go up against United States Senator Dale Bumpers in 1980: See *Arkansas Democrat*, May 26, 1978.
14. *Arkansas Democrat*, May 14, 1978.
15. Clinton, *Arkansas Democrat*, June 1, 1978.
16. Ibid.
17. Lynn Lowe, *Arkansas Democrat*, July 6, 1978.
18. Howell Raines, *New York Times*, reprinted in *Arkansas Gazette*, July 9, 1978.
19. Clinton, *New York Times*, reprinted in *Arkansas Gazette*, July 9, 1978.
21. Gale Arnold, *Arkansas Democrat*, July 9, 1978.
22. Clinton, *New York Times*, reprinted in *Arkansas Gazette*, July 9, 1978.
23. Diane D. Blair and Robert L. Savage, *The South's New Politics*, ed. Robert H. Swansbrough and David M. Brodsky (Columbia, S.C., 1988), 138–39.
24. Clinton, *Arkansas Democrat*, August 21, 1978.
25. Kern Alexander and James Hale, *Educational Equity, Improving School Finance in Arkansas*, report to Advisory Committee of the Special School Formula Project of the Joint Interim Committee on Education, 1978.
26. Clinton, *Arkansas Gazette*, October 4, 1978.
27. Ibid.
28. *Arkansas Democrat*, October 13, 1978.
29. Ibid., October 24, 1978.
30. *Arkansas Gazette*, October 28, 1978.
31. Ibid.
32. Ibid.
33. Ibid.
34. Ibid.
35. Ibid.

Chapter 11

1. Bill Clinton, *Arkansas Democrat*, November 8, 1978.
2. Clinton, interview with Bill Simmons of The Associated Press, *Arkansas Democrat*, November 8, 1978.
3. Clinton, *Arkansas Gazette*, December 2, 1978.
4. Robert McCord, *Arkansas Democrat*, December 12, 1978.
5. Ibid.
6. *Arkansas Democrat*, December 29, 1978.
7. *Arkansas Gazette*, December 28, 1978.
8. Clinton, *Arkansas Gazette*, January 12, 1979.
9. Grover Richardson, *Arkansas Gazette*, January 14, 1979.
10. Max Howell, *Arkansas Democrat*, January 16, 1979.
11. William F. Foster, Sr., *Arkansas Gazette*, January 16, 1979.
12. Bob Lancaster, *Arkansas Democrat*, January 17, 1979.
13. Patrick Flanagin, interview with author, August 17, 1993.
14. Ibid.
15. Clinton, interview with Phyllis Finton Johnston, May 26, 1981.
16. Sherry Price, Arkansas Education Association president, *Arkansas Gazette*, January 16, 1979.
17. A 1981 essay by Juanita D. Sandford, assistant professor of sociology at Arkansas's Henderson State University and author of *Poverty in the Land of Opportunity* (Rose Publishing Company, Little Rock, 1978), noted that "While the per capita income has risen from $5,073 in 1977 to $6,933 today, Arkansas has dropped from 48th to 49th place in the nation, ahead of Mississippi only." *Arkansas: State of Transition* (Little Rock, 1981), 21.
18. Mark Johnson, interview with author, April 22, 1993.
19. Ibid.
20. Ibid.
21. Ibid.
22. Rudy Moore, Jr., quoted by The Associated Press, *Arkansas Democrat*, January 20, 1979.
23. Unidentified aide, quoted by The Associated Press, *Arkansas Democrat*, January 20, 1979.
24. John R. Starr, *Yellow Dogs and Dark Horses* (Little Rock, 1987), 178.
25. Moore, *The Clintons of Arkansas*, ed. Ernest Dumas (Little Rock, 1993), 88–89.
26. Ibid.
27. William D. Gaddy later declined Governor Frank White's offer to remain in the state's service, but he returned to state government when he resumed the governorship in 1983. He was director of the state Employment Security Division in early 1994, when Governor Jim Guy Tucker

requested his resignation after it was learned that ESD had given Bill Clinton's primary and general election campaign committees illegal financial breaks on delinquent employee withholding taxes.

28. *Arkansas Democrat*, February 10, 1980.
29. Sandford, 1981.
30. R.J. Hansen and Associates, Report to the Highway Needs Committee of the Arkansas Legislative Council, 1978.
31. *Arkansas Gazette*, March 22, 1979.
32. *Arkansas Gazette*, March 31, 1979.

Chapter 12

1. John R. Starr, interview with author, April 23, 1993.
2. Phyllis Finton Johnston, *Bill Clinton's Public Policy for Arkansas: 1979–1980* (Little Rock, 1982), 99.
3. Starr, *Yellow Dogs and Dark Horses* (Little Rock, 1987), 11.
4. Starr, interview with author, April 23, 1993.
5. Ibid.
6. *Arkansas Gazette*, September 24, 1979.
7. Larry Gentry, interview with author, June 30, 1993.
8. Ibid.
9. Ibid.; Roger Perry, interview with author, December 22, 1993.
10. Perry, Ibid.
11. Gentry, interview with author, June 30, 1993.
12. Starr, interview with author, April 23, 1993.
13. Starr, interview with author, November 15, 1993.
14. Rudy Moore, Jr., *Arkansas Democrat*, January 14, 1979.
15. Moore, *The Clintons of Arkansas*, ed. Ernest Dumas (Little Rock, 1993), 88.
16. Stephen A. Smith, *The Clintons of Arkansas*, ed. Ernest Dumas (Little Rock, 1993), 9.
17. Orval E. Faubus, interview with author, April 24, 1993.
18. Mark Johnson, interview with author, April 22, 1993.
19. John Danner, *Arkansas Democrat*, January 14, 1979.
20. *Arkansas Gazette*, March 21, 1980.
21. Danner, *Arkansas Democrat*, March 25, 1980.
22. Bill Clinton, *Arkansas Gazette*, March 26, 1980.
23. Moore, *Arkansas Gazette*, March 26, 1980.
24. Moore, *The Clintons of Arkansas*, ed. Ernest Dumas (Little Rock, 1993), 91.
25. *Arkansas Democrat*, February 22, 1979.
26. From a "Politics 1980" column by author, *Arkansas Democrat*, March 2, 1980.

27. *Arkansas Democrat*, March 30, 1980.
28. Ibid., March 7, 1980.
29. Ibid., April 26, 1980.
30. Ibid.

Chapter 13

1. *Arkansas Democrat*, April 14, 1980.
2. That inquiry was undertaken and reported on by the author in the April 8–15, 1980, editions of the *Arkansas Democrat*.
3. Bill Carroll, *Arkansas Democrat*, April 15, 1980.
4. Bill Clinton, *Arkansas Gazette*, April 5, 1980.
5. Ibid.
6. This quote never appeared in print. It was relayed to the author by a member of Clinton's staff.
7. The Associated Press, *Arkansas Democrat*, May 10, 1980.
8. Clinton, *Arkansas Gazette*, June 6, 1986.
9. Ibid., May 8, 1980.
10. John R. Starr, *Yellow Dogs and Dark Horses* (Little Rock, 1987), 176.
11. Ibid.
12. Ibid.
13. Frank White, *Arkansas Democrat*, April 27, 1980.
14. Starr, interview with author, April 23, 1993.
15. James L. "Skip" Rutherford, interview with author, September 15, 1993.
16. Thomas F. "Mack" McLarty III, interview with author, October 16, 1993.
17. Ibid.
18. Ibid.
19. Starr, interview with author, November 15, 1993.
20. Ibid.
21. Starr, *Yellow Dogs and Dark Horses* (Little Rock, 1987), 177.
22. Barbara Pardue, *Arkansas Democrat*, December 15, 1980.
23. Pardue, interview with author, May 13, 1993.
24. Ibid.
25. Ibid.
26. Patty Howe Criner, quoted by Charles F. Allen and Jonathan Portis, *Bill Clinton: Comeback Kid* (New York, N.Y., 1992), 67.
27. Rudy Moore, Jr., *The Clintons of Arkansas*, ed. Ernest Dumas (Little Rock, 1993), 91.
28. *Arkansas Democrat*, September 20, 1980.
29. Clinton, *Arkansas Democrat*, September 25, 1980.
30. Pardue, interview with author, May 13, 1993.

31. Rutherford, interview with author, September 15, 1993.
32. McLarty, interview with author, October 16, 1993.
33. Clinton, *Arkansas Democrat*, October 23, 1980.
34. Ibid.
35. *Arkansas Democrat*, October 23, 1980.
36. Ibid.
37. McLarty, interview with author, October 16, 1993.
38. Rutherford, interview with author, September 15, 1993.

Chapter 14

1. *Arkansas Democrat*, November 12, 1980.
2. Bill Clinton, *Arkansas Gazette*, November 11, 1980.
3. Member of the 1980 governor's security detail, interview with author on condition of anonymity, 1993.
4. Rudy Moore, Jr., *The Clintons of Arkansas*, ed. Ernest Dumas (Little Rock, 1993), 90.
5. Member of the 1980 governor's security detail, interview with author on condition of anonymity, 1993.
6. Ibid.
7. Larry Gentry, interview with author, June 30, 1993.
8. The author was among those reporters who investigated several allegations of extramarital affairs involving Clinton. None was substantiated.
9. John R. Starr told the author about his exchange with Deborah Mathis shortly after it occurred at a political event and on several subsequent occasions. She later publicly denied any intimate relationship with Clinton, in an Associated Press account dated January 28, 1992.
10. Moore, *The Clintons of Arkansas*, ed. Ernest Dumas (Little Rock, 1993), 93.
11. James L. "Skip" Rutherford, interview with author, September 15, 1993.
12. Thomas F. "Mack" McLarty III, interview with author, October 16, 1993.
13. Rutherford, interview with author, September 15, 1993.
14. McLarty, interview with author, October 16, 1993.
15. Ibid.
16. Sheffield Nelson, interview with author, September 2, 1993.
17. Orval E. Faubus, interview with author, April 24, 1993.
18. Julia Hughes Jones, interview with author, September 15, 1993.
19. The author was present and witnessed this event.
20. The clerk in question is now an employee of the *Arkansas Democrat-Gazette* and discussed this encounter on condition of anonymity.
21. McLarty, interview with author, October 16, 1993.

22. *Arkansas Democrat*, December 2, 1980.
23. Ibid.
24. Clinton, *Arkansas Gazette*, December 2, 1981.
25. Starr, interview with author, April 23, 1993.
26. Frank White, *Arkansas Democrat*, December 3, 1981.
27. Joe Purcell, *Arkansas Democrat*, April 14, 1982.
28. Unidentified Clinton supporter, *Arkansas Democrat*, April 27, 1982.
29. Jim Guy Tucker, *Arkansas Democrat*, May 18, 1982.
30. *Arkansas Democrat*, June 12, 1982.
31. White, *Arkansas Gazette*, September 16, 1983.
32. Clinton, *Arkansas Democrat*, September 5, 1982.
33. Hillary Rodham Clinton, *Arkansas Democrat*, September 5, 1982.
34. From a "Politics 1983" column by the author, *Arkansas Democrat*, May 5, 1983.
35. Barbara Pardue, interview with author, May 13, 1993.
36. Ibid.
37. From a "Politics 1983" column by author, *Arkansas Democrat*, January 12, 1983.
38. Ibid.
39. Clinton, quoted by David Osborne, *Laboratories in Democracy* (Boston, 1988), 92.
40. Patrick Flanagin, interview with author, August 17, 1993.
41. Starr, interview with author, April 23, 1993.
42. Flanagin, interview with author, August 17, 1993.
43. Ed Thicksten, *Arkansas Democrat*, February 8, 1983.
44. Clinton, *Arkansas Democrat*, February 15, 1983.
45. Clinton, interview with author, March 31, 1983.
46. Ben Allen, *Arkansas Democrat*, February 18, 1983.

Chapter 15

1. From a "Politics 1983" column by the author, *Arkansas Democrat*, June 28, 1983.
2. Ibid., April 10, 1983.
3. Ibid., May 26, 1983.
4. The author attended several such meetings as a member of the *Arkansas Democrat* editorial board.
5. From a "Politics 1983" column by the author, *Arkansas Democrat*, July 14, 1983.
6. Ibid., June 12, 1983.
7. Ibid., September 8, 1983.
8. Ibid.

9. Similar observations were made by numerous lawmakers after state Representative Lloyd R. George made the original remark during a legislative committee meeting in September 1983.
10. From a "Politics 1983" column by the author, *Arkansas Democrat*, September 27, 1983.
11. Bill Clinton, *Arkansas Democrat*, October 29, 1983.
12. Bobby Roberts, *The Clintons of Arkansas*, ed. Ernest Dumas (Little Rock, 1993), 129.
13. Ibid.
14. From a "Politics 1983" column by the author, *Arkansas Democrat*, November 4, 1983.
15. James L. "Skip" Rutherford, interview with author, September 15, 1993.
16. Charles F. Allen and Jonathan Portis, *Bill Clinton: Comeback Kid* (New York, N.Y., 1992), 86.
17. From a "Politics 1983" column by the author, *Arkansas Democrat*, November 10, 1983.
18. Clinton, to a joint session of the Arkansas legislature, November 10, 1983.
19. From a "Politics 1983" column by the author, *Arkansas Democrat*, November 22, 1983.
20. Ibid.
21. *Arkansas Democrat*, February 23, 1984.
22. Jim Johnson, interview with author, April 25, 1993.
23. *Arkansas Gazette*, September 21, 1979.
24. Ibid., September 22, 1979.
25. Ibid., August 3, 1984.
26. Ibid.
27. Tommy Goodwin, interview with author, January 10, 1994.
28. Ibid.
29. Ibid.
30. *Arkansas Democrat*, August 15, 1984.
31. *Arkansas Democrat*, November 9, 1984.
32. *Arkansas Gazette*, November 10, 1984.
33. The Associated Press, January 14, 1985.

Chapter 16

1. Karen Keller, *Arkansas Democrat*, January 29, 1985.
2. United States District Judge Oren Harris, *Arkansas Democrat*, January 29, 1985.
3. *Arkansas Democrat*, January 29, 1985.
4. Ibid.

5. Tim Hutchinson was elected to the U.S. House of Representatives in 1992.
6. John R. Starr, *Yellow Dogs and Dark Horses* (Little Rock, 1987), 197.
7. Charles F. Allen and Jonathan Portis, *Bill Clinton: Comeback Kid* (New York, N.Y., 1992) 104.
8. From a "Politics 1985" column by the author, *Arkansas Democrat*, January 22, 1985.
9. Bill Clinton news conference, January 29, 1985.
10. Maurice Smith, interview with author, January 29, 1985.
11. From a "Politics 1985" column by the author, *Arkansas Democrat*, March 24, 1985.
12. Ernest Dumas, quoted by Jim Moore with Rick Ihde, *Clinton: Young Man in a Hurry* (Fort Worth, Texas, 1992), 111.
13. *Arkansas Democrat*, February 26, 1985.
14. Ibid., February 27, 1985.
15. Ibid., March 2, 1985.
16. Orval E. Faubus, interview with author, April 24, 1993.
17. Ibid.
18. Ibid.
19. Ibid.
20. Ibid.
21. From a "Politics 1985" column by the author, *Arkansas Democrat*, August 8, 1985.
22. Ibid.
23. Ibid.
24. *Arkansas Democrat*, August 2, 1985.
25. Starr, *Yellow Dogs and Dark Horses* (Little Rock, 1987), 200.
26. From a "Politics 1985" column by the author, *Arkansas Democrat*, September 15, 1985.
27. Ibid., December 1, 1985.
28. Ibid., November 14, 1985.
29. Frank White, *Arkansas Democrat*, October 11, 1986.
30. *Arkansas Democrat*, October 2, 1985.
31. *Arkansas Democrat*, October 5, 1985.
32. Ibid., October 11, 1985.

Chapter 17

1. Frank White, March 31, 1986.
2. David Martin, "Arkansas Week," AETN Public Television, November 7, 1986.
3. John R. Starr, *Yellow Dogs and Dark Horses* (Little Rock, 1987), 199–200.

4. White, interview with author, June 10, 1986.
5. From a "Politics 1986" column by the author, *Arkansas Democrat*, August 14, 1986.
6. Ibid., August 24, 1986.
7. *Arkansas Democrat*, September 18, 1986.
8. From a "Politics 1986" column by the author, *Arkansas Democrat*, September 21, 1986.
9. *Arkansas Democrat*, October 25, 1986.
10. Starr, "Arkansas Week," AETN Public Television, November 7, 1986.
11. John Brummett, "Arkansas Week," AETN Public Television, November 7, 1986.
12. Bill Clinton, November 4, 1986.
13. Ibid.
14. The author was present on two occasions when Clinton made this pledge, once at Benton, Arkansas, and again at Lonoke, Arkansas.
15. Clinton, January 13, 1987.
16. From a "Legislative Focus" column by the author, *Arkansas Democrat*, January 30, 1987.
17. Ibid., February 10, 1987.
18. Ibid., February 12, 1987.
19. The author was among those journalists to whom Clinton gave his reassurances in a private meeting on March 20, 1987.
20. From a "Legislative Focus 1987" column by the author, *Arkansas Democrat*, March 24, 1987.
21. Carol Griffee, a free-lance journalist and the Society of Professional Journalists' Region 12 deputy director for freedom of information matters, and Bill Rutherford of the *Arkansas Gazette* witnessed these encounters between lawmakers and the governor's legislative liaisons on March 23, 1987.
22. From a "Politics 1987" column by the author, *Arkansas Democrat*, March 29, 1987.
23. From a "Legislative Focus" column by the author, *Arkansas Democrat*, March 28, 1987.
24. Ibid., March 31, 1987.
25. *Arkansas Democrat*, March 25, 1987.
26. From a "Politics 1987" column by the author, *Arkansas Democrat*, April 16, 1987.
27. Ibid.

Chapter 18

1. From a "Politics 1987" column by the author, *Arkansas Democrat*, June 3, 1987.
2. John R. Starr, interview with author, November 15, 1993.
3. Max Brantley, quoted by Judith Warner, *Hillary Clinton: The Inside Story* (New York, N.Y., 1993), 145.
4. Bill Clinton, July 15, 1987.
5. Hillary Rodham Clinton, July 14, 1987.
6. Roger Clinton, July 15, 1987.
7. Roger Clinton, the Associated Press, July 15, 1987.
8. Starr, interview with author, November 15, 1993.
9. Ibid.
10. Ibid.
11. Ibid.
12. Bill Clinton, *Arkansas Democrat*, November 11, 1987.
13. Nick Wilson, *Arkansas Democrat*, February 3, 1988.
14. Jay Bradford, interview with author, March 2, 1994.
15. From a "Politics 1988" column by the author, *Arkansas Democrat*, May 10, 1988.
16. Ibid.
17. Ibid.
18. Ibid.
19. Ibid.
20. From a "Politics 1988" column by the author, *Arkansas Democrat*, June 14, 1988.
21. Ibid.
22. Ibid.
23. Ibid., June 16, 1988.
24. Robert E. Levin, *Bill Clinton: The Inside Story* (New York, N.Y., 1992), 176.
25. Hillary Rodham Clinton, quoted by Charles F. Allen and Jonathan Portis, *Bill Clinton: Comeback Kid* (New York, N.Y., 1992), 127.
26. Julia Hughes Jones, interview with author, September 15, 1993.
27. From a "Politics 1988" column by the author, *Arkansas Democrat*, July 28, 1988.
28. Bill Clinton, interview with author, July 20, 1988.
29. Starr, *Arkansas Democrat*, July 30, 1988.
30. From a "Politics 1988" column by the author, *Arkansas Democrat*, September 11, 1988.
31. Ibid.

32. From a "Politics 1988" column by the author, *Arkansas Democrat*, September 13, 1988.

Chapter 19

1. John R. Starr, *Arkansas Democrat*, November 16, 1988.
2. Ibid.
3. From a "Legislative Focus" column by the author, *Arkansas Democrat*, January 25, 1989.
4. Ibid.
5. Ibid.
6. Ibid., February 5, 1989.
7. Comment from Clinton liaison to author, February 7, 1989.
8. From a "Legislative Focus" column by the author, *Arkansas Democrat*, February 9, 1989.
9. Ibid., February 16, 1989.
10. Ibid., March 3, 1989.
11. Ibid.
12. Ibid.
13. Joe Bell, interview with author, January 19, 1994.
14. Ibid.
15. Ibid.
16. Ibid.
17. From a "Legislative Focus" column by the author, *Arkansas Democrat*, March 19, 1989.
18. Bell, interview with author, January 19, 1994.
19. Ibid.
20. From a "Politics 1989" column by the author, *Arkansas Democrat*, March 26, 1989.
21. Bill Clinton, interview with author, April 11, 1989.
22. From a "Politics 1989" column by the author, *Arkansas Democrat*, April 16, 1989.
23. Ibid., June 29, 1989.
24. Ibid., June 25, 1989.
25. Ibid.
26. Bell, interview with author, January 19, 1994.
27. From a "Legislative Focus" column by the author and news accounts, *Arkansas Democrat*, July 28, 1989.
28. Ibid.
29. Ibid.

Chapter 20

1. John R. Starr, interview with author, November 15, 1993.
2. Ibid.
3. Ibid.
4. Tom McRae, news conference, April 11, 1990.
5. Bruce Plante, then of the *Arkansas Democrat* cartoon staff.
6. Rex Nelson, interview with author, September 16, 1993.
7. Ibid.
8. Tommy Robinson, interview with author, June 28, 1993.
9. J.J. Vigneault, interview with author, January 21, 1994.
10. Ibid.
11. Ibid.
12. Ibid.
13. Starr, *Arkansas Democrat*, October 29, 1989.
14. Bill Clinton, *Arkansas Gazette*, October 24, 1989.
15. Starr, *Arkansas Democrat*, November 5, 1989.
16. From a "Politics 1989" column by the author, *Arkansas Democrat*, October 28, 1989.
17. Betsey Wright, interview with Vince Insalaco, KARN-AM, September 23, 1989.
18. Starr and Rutherford discussed with the author their individual conversations with Wright shortly after those telephone calls occurred.
19. Clinton, *Arkansas Democrat*, December 21, 1989.
20. Earl Jones, interview with author, December 20, 1989.
21. Roy Drew, interview with author, March 12, 1994.
22. Ibid.
23. *The Sunday Times*, February 13, 1994.
24. Ibid.
25. Ibid.
26. Drew, interview with author, March 12, 1994.
27. Lu Hardin, interview with author, September 28, 1993.
28. Ibid.
29. Virginia Kelley, interview with author, March 1, 1990.
30. Starr, *Arkansas Democrat*, March 2, 1990.
31. Sheffield Nelson, interview with author, September 2, 1993.
32. Patrick Flanagin, interview with author, August 17, 1993.

Chapter 21

1. Bill Clinton, October 15, 1990.
2. Sheffield Nelson, interview with author, September 2, 1993.

3. James L. "Skip" Rutherford, interview with author, September 15, 1993.
4. J.J. Vigneault, interview with author, January 21, 1994.
5. Rex Nelson, interview with author, September 16, 1993.
6. *Arkansas Democrat*, May 17, 1990.
7. Tom McRae, quoted by Judith Warner, *Hillary Clinton: The Inside Story* (New York, N.Y., 1993), 159.
8. John R. Starr, interview with author, November 15, 1993.
9. Ibid.
10. Nelson, interview with author, September 2, 1993.
11. John R. Starr, interview with author, November 15, 1993.
12. Starr, interview with author, November 17, 1993.
13. *Arkansas Democrat*, October 12, 1990.
14. Ibid.
15. *Arkansas Gazette*, November 14, 1990.
16. From a "Politics 1990" column by author, *Arkansas Democrat*, December 16, 1990.
17. Ibid., July 12, 1991.
18. *Arkansas Democrat*, August 20, 1991.
19. Ibid.
20. Ibid., August 15, 1991.
21. Ibid., August 20, 1991.
22. Ibid., August 28, 1991.
23. *Arkansas Gazette*, May 25, 1982.
24. Ibid., March 16, 1983.
25. The Associated Press, July 30, 1983.
26. *Arkansas Gazette*, March 24, 1991.
27. Ibid.
28. Ibid.
29. Ibid.
30. *Arkansas Gazette*, March 24, 1991.
31. Ibid.
32. Ibid.
33. Ibid.
34. Guy Reel, *Unequal Justice: Wayne Dumond, Bill Clinton, and the Politics of Rape in Arkansas* (Buffalo, N.Y., 1993).
35. *Arkansas Gazette*, June 29, 1990.
36. Ibid.
37. *Arkansas Democrat*, July 1, 1990.
38. Ibid., July 27, 1990.
39. *Arkansas Gazette*, October 11, 1991.
40. *Arkansas Democrat-Gazette*, January 29, 1992.
41. Ibid., April 16, 1992.

Chapter 22

1. John R. Starr, interview with author, March 2, 1993.
2. Sam Nunn, *Arkansas Democrat*, March 25, 1990.
3. David Pryor, *Arkansas Gazette*, March 1, 1985.
4. David Pryor, *Arkansas Democrat*, March 1, 1985.
5. Bill Clinton, *Arkansas Democrat*, March 1, 1988.
6. Al From, *Arkansas Democrat*, June 23, 1989.
7. Clinton, *Arkansas Gazette*, March 15, 1990.
8. Clinton, *Arkansas Democrat*, March 23, 1990.
9. Ibid., March 15, 1990.
10. Clinton, *Arkansas Gazette*, March 24, 1990.
11. Clinton, *Arkansas Democrat*, March 23, 1990.
12. Clinton, *Arkansas Gazette*, March 25, 1990.
13. John Breaux, *Arkansas Democrat*, March 25, 1990.
14. Nunn, *Arkansas Democrat*, March 25, 1990.
15. *Arkansas Democrat*, March 25, 1990.
16. Clinton, quoted by David S. Broder, *Washington Post*, December 12, 1990.
17. From, quoted by Broder, *Washington Post*, December 12, 1990.
18. Broder, *Washington Post*, December 12, 1990.
19. J. Bill Becker, interview with author, September 8, 1993.
20. *Newsweek*, April 15, 1991.
21. Clinton, *Arkansas Gazette*, April 11, 1991.
22. *Arkansas Gazette*, April 20, 1991.
23. Ibid., April 25, 1991.
24. *Arkansas Democrat*, April 18, 1991.
25. Ibid.
26. *Arkansas Gazette*, April 25, 1991.
27. Clinton, *Arkansas Democrat*, May 6, 1991.
28. Mike McCurry, *Arkansas Gazette*, May 5, 1991.
29. Clinton, *Arkansas Gazette*, May 6, 1991.
30. Clinton, *Arkansas Democrat*, May 7, 1991.
31. Bob Beckel, *Arkansas Democrat*, May 7, 1991; *Arkansas Gazette*, May 9, 1991.
32. Broder and Dan Balz, *Washington Post*, April 12, 1991.
33. Ibid.
34. Clinton, *Arkansas Gazette*, May 9, 1991.
35. Ibid.
36. Ibid.
37. Bill Walker, *Arkansas Gazette*, May 11, 1991.
38. Ibid.

39. Ibid.

40. Ibid.

41. Clinton, *Washington Post*, May 7, 1991.

42. Clinton, *Arkansas Democrat*, May 11, 1991.

43. Betsey Wright, *Arkansas Gazette*, May 12, 1991.

44. Jesse Turner, *Arkansas Democrat*, May 14, 1991.

45. Mario Cuomo, *Arkansas Democrat*, May 14, 1991.

46. *Arkansas Democrat*, June 4, 1991.

47. Chris Spirou, *Arkansas Democrat*, June 19, 1991.

48. Wright, *Arkansas Democrat*, June 4, 1991.

49. Clinton, *Arkansas Democrat*, June 4, 1991.

50. Jeffrey Stinson, *Arkansas Gazette*, August 5, 1991.

51. Ibid.

52. Ibid.

53. *Arkansas Democrat*, August 6, 1991.

54. *Arkansas Gazette*, June 2, 1991.

55. Clinton, from author's tape recording transcript, August 17, 1991.

56. James. L. "Skip" Rutherford, interview with author, September 15, 1993.

57. Ibid.

58. Clinton, from author's tape recording transcript, August 17, 1991.

59. Clinton, *Arkansas Democrat*, August 20, 1991.

60. Thomas Mann, *Arkansas Gazette*, August 21, 1991.

61. John C. White, *Arkansas Democrat*, August 21, 1991.

62. Clinton, from author's tape recording transcript, August 19, 1991.

63. From a "Politics 1991" column by author, *Arkansas Democrat*, August 21, 1991.

64. Carroll A. Campbell, Jr., *Arkansas Gazette*, August 20, 1991.

65. Jim Guy Tucker, *Arkansas Democrat*, August 20, 1991.

66. Starr, *Arkansas Democrat*, August 22, 1991.

67. Al Gore, *Arkansas Democrat*, August 22, 1991.

68. Clinton, *Arkansas Democrat*, August 22, 1991.

69. Bruce Lindsey, *Arkansas Gazette*, August 22, 1991.

70. Bob Squier, *Arkansas Democrat*, August 22, 1991.

71. David Sawyer, *Arkansas Democrat*, August 22, 1991.

72. Thomas Mann, *Arkansas Democrat*, August 22, 1991.

73. Ibid.

74. Clayton Yeutter, *Arkansas Democrat*, August 25, 1991.

75. Clinton, *Arkansas Gazette*, August 27, 1991.

76. Ibid., August 30, 1991.

77. Mark Oswald, *Arkansas Gazette*, August 29, 1991.

78. Woody Bassett, *Arkansas Democrat*, August 30, 1991.

79. Stanley Russ, *Arkansas Democrat*, August 29, 1991.
80. Betty Lagrone, *Arkansas Gazette*, August 29, 1991.
81. Clinton, *Arkansas Democrat*, August 30, 1991.
82. Clinton, *Arkansas Gazette*, August 30, 1991.
83. Bob Farmer, *Arkansas Democrat*, August 29, 1991.
84. Ibid.
85. Clinton quoting Farmer, *Arkansas Gazette*, August 30, 1991.
86. Ibid.
87. Clinton, *Arkansas Democrat*, August 31, 1991.
88. *Arkansas Democrat*, October 2, 1991.
89. Ibid.
90. Ibid.
91. Clinton, *Arkansas Gazette*, October 4, 1991.
92. Julia Hughes Jones, interview with author, September 15, 1993.
93. Oswald, *Arkansas Gazette*, October 4, 1991.
94. *Arkansas Gazette*, October 4, 1991.

Chapter 23

1. John Penn, *Arkansas Gazette*, January 2, 1991.
2. Cliff Jackson, *Arkansas Democrat*, January 9, 1991.
3. The Associated Press, April 5, 1992.
4. Paul Begala, The Associated Press, April 4, 1992.
5. The Associated Press, April 4, 1992.
6. Bill Clinton, *Arkansas Democrat-Gazette*, April 6, 1992.
7. Robert Corrado, *Arkansas Democrat-Gazette*, April 6, 1992.
8. Opal Ellis, *Arkansas Democrat-Gazette*, April 6, 1992.
9. Clinton D. Jones, *Los Angeles Times*, April 5, 1992.
10. George Stephanopoulos, *Los Angeles Times*, April 5, 1992.
11. Clinton, *Arkansas Democrat-Gazette*, April 8, 1992.
12. John R. Starr, interview with author, November 15, 1993.
13. Billy G. Geren, *Arkansas Gazette*, October 28, 1978.
14. *Los Angeles Times*, September 2, 1992.
15. Jackson, *Arkansas Democrat-Gazette*, September 3, 1992.
16. Ibid., September 8, 1992.
17. Ibid., September 16, 1992.
18. Van Rush, *Arkansas Democrat-Gazette*, September 18, 1992.
19. Clinton, *Arkansas Democrat-Gazette*, September 17, 1992.
20. Jim Johnson, interview with author, April 25, 1993.
21. Ibid.
22. Ibid.
23. Ibid.

24. Ibid.
25. Linda Burnett, *Arkansas Democrat-Gazette*, September 19, 1992.
26. Clinton, *Arkansas Democrat-Gazette*, September 19, 1992.
27. New York Times News Service, *Arkansas Democrat-Gazette*, September 19, 1992.
28. Clinton, *Arkansas Democrat-Gazette*, September 19, 1992.
29. J. William Fulbright, *Arkansas Democrat-Gazette*, September 19, 1992.
30. Hoyt H. Purvis, *Arkansas Democrat-Gazette*, September 19, 1992.
31. *Arkansas Democrat-Gazette*, October 8, 1992.
32. Sheffield Nelson, interview with author, September 2, 1993.
33. Ibid.
34. Avis LaVelle, *Arkansas Democrat-Gazette*, October 29, 1992.
35. Jackson, interview with author, July 12, 1993.
36. Johnson, interview with author, April 25, 1993.

Chapter 24

1. John R. Starr, interview with author, November 15, 1993.
2. Hillary Rodham Clinton, *Redbook*, March 1993.
3. Hillary Rodham, "Children Under the Law," *Harvard Educational Review*, January 1974.
4. Rodham, "Children's Rights: A Legal Perspective," *Children's Rights: Contemporary Perspectives*, ed. Patricia A. Vardin and Ilene N. Brody (Teacher's College Press, 1979).
5. Starr, interview with author, April 3, 1993.
6. Diane Blair, *The Clintons of Arkansas*, ed. Ernest Dumas (Little Rock, 1993), 68.
7. *Arkansas Democrat*, October 19, 1978.
8. Ibid., October 30, 1986.
9. *Arkansas Gazette*, August 16, 1976.
10. Ibid., July 21, 1981.
11. The Associated Press, September 10, 1988.
12. Bill Clinton, *Arkansas Democrat*, September 13, 1988.
13. Larry Nichols, The Associated Press, September 17, 1988.
14. Nichols and Darrell Glascock, *Arkansas Democrat*, September 18, 1988.
15. Clinton, September 12, 1990.
16. Nichols, *Arkansas Gazette*, July 31, 1991.
17. *Arkansas Democrat*, July 23, 1991.
18. Michael G. Gauldin, *Arkansas Democrat*, July 23, 1991.
19. Clinton, *Arkansas Democrat*, July 23, 1991.
20. Gauldin, *Arkansas Gazette*, August 1, 1991.
21. Nichols, *Arkansas Gazette*, August 1, 1991.

22. Connie Hamzy, *Arkansas Democrat-Gazette*, November 27, 1991.
23. Ibid.
24. Connie Hamzy, interview with author, January 17, 1994.
25. Dee Dee Myers, *Arkansas Democrat-Gazette*, January 17, 1992.
26. Clinton, *Arkansas Democrat-Gazette*, January 18, 1992.
27. Ibid.
28. Bill Simmons, *Arkansas Democrat-Gazette*, January 18, 1992.
29. Lauren Kirk, *Penthouse*, December 1992.
30. Unidentified, *Penthouse*, December 1992.
31. Nichols, The Associated Press, September 11, 1988.
32. Nichols, *Arkansas Democrat-Gazette*, January 26, 1992.
33. Ibid.
34. Clinton, *Arkansas Democrat-Gazette*, January 18, 1992.
35. Clinton, *Vanity Fair*, May 1992.
36. Hillary Rodham Clinton, quoted by Judith Warner, *Hillary Clinton: The Inside Story* (New York, N.Y., 1993), 170.
37. Warner, *Hillary Clinton: The Inside Story* (New York, N.Y., 1993), 170.
38. Steve Kroft, *Vanity Fair*, May 1992.
39. *Vanity Fair*, May 1992.
40. Ibid.
41. Pam Strickland, *Arkansas Democrat-Gazette*, January 24, 1994.
42. Ibid.
43. Starr, interview with author, November 15, 1993.

Chapter 25

1. Marlin D. Jackson, *Washington Post*, November 28, 1993.
2. *Arkansas Gazette*, August 13, 1983.
3. Bobby Roberts, interview with author, February 8, 1994.
4. *New York Post*, January 27, 1994.

Other Sources Consulted

Arkansas: A Bicentennial History, Harry S. Ashmore (New York, 1978).
Call the Roll, Jerry E. Hinshaw (Little Rock, 1986).
The Arkansas Frontier, Boyd W. Johnson (Little Rock, 1957).
First Ladies of Arkansas: Women of Their Times, Anne McMath (Little Rock, 1989).
A Documentary History of Arkansas, ed. C. Fred Williams, S. Charles Bolton, Carl H. Moneyhon, and LeRoy T. Williams (Fayetteville, Arkansas, 1984).

Index

King, Martin Luther, Jr., 56, 58, 97
Kirk, Lauren, 508
Klein, Joe, 517
Knuckols, Bertha Louise, 164, 165
Kopold, Jan, 80, 84
Koppel, Ted, 511
Kroft, Steve, 511–513

Lady, Frank, 178–179
Laidlaw, Christopher, 62
Lamb, Bob, 404
Lancaster, Bob, 166, 198
Lanier, T. Wayne, 320, 323
Lasater, Dan
  Clinton administration ties to Lasater
    and Co., 318–319, 326, 329–330,
    408
  employment of Roger Clinton, 310–
    311
  savings and loan controversy, 531–532
Lasater and Co., 318–319, 408
Lear, Norman, 341
Ledbetter, Brownie, 427, 451
Legal Assistance Association, 106
Leopoulos, David, 29, 517
Leslie, Bob, 400
Lessenby, Anna, 507
Levin, Robert E., 33, 43, 64, 85, 360
Levy, Paul, 206, 207
Lewis, Robert E., 29
Lindsey, Bev, 465
Lindsey, Bruce, 349, 363, 459, 465, 467
Lindsey, Jim, 488–490
Locke, George, 330
Loewe, Rudi, 87
Long, Carolyn, 273
Long, Jill, 454
Lowe, Lynn, 180–181, 184–185, 188
Luin, Martha, 458

Madden, Owen Vincent "Owney," 26, 27
Madison Guaranty Savings and Loan
    Association
  McDougal's management practices,
    303–304
  news media revelations, 167, 514–515,
    519, 523–530
Mahony, Jodie, 298
Mahony, Joseph K., II, 227, 298, 304,
    353–354, 385–387

Maitland, Sara, 63, 66, 84–85
Malak, Fahmy, 434–437
Mann, Thomas, 464, 468
Maple Creek Farms, 524
Marijuana use, 519
Marijuana use admission, 80
Marks, Howard, 80
Marshall, Burke, 123
Martin, David, 324
Martin, Marshall, 480
Marty, Mary, 39
Matalin, Mary, 398
Mathis, Deborah, 260
Mathis, Randall, 175–177, 179
Matthews, David, 369
May, A.L., 173
McCarthy, Eugene, 58, 74
McClellan, John L., 50, 139, 167, 171,
    521
McCoeey, Chris, 64
McCord, Robert S., 192–193
McCoy, B.J., 207, 236, 243–245
McCurry, Mike, 448
McDougal, James B.
  Bank of Kingston, 274
  campaign for House, 134–135
  Democratic party work, 50
  Madison Guaranty management
    practices, 303–304
  Whitewater/Madison Guaranty
    scandal, 514–515, 521–527, 531
McDougal, Susan, 303–304, 515, 521,
    523, 525
McGovern, George, 107, 122, 447
McGovern campaign, 107, 109, 111–119,
    130–131, 158
McGovern-Hatfield amendment, 107
McIntosh, Robert "Say," 476, 498–500,
    503–504, 510
McIntosh, Tommy, 503
McKeithen, Fox, 397
McKenzie, Dr. Jim, 24
McLarty, Thomas F. "Mack", III
  on the 1992 primary, 43
  biographical sketch, 26
  on Clinton's 1980 defeat, 252, 254–
    255, 261–264
  on Clinton's college years, 63–64, 65,
    101
  introduction of Clinton to Carter, 139

590   INDEX